18th Nordic Conference of Computational Linguistics (NODALIDA 2011)

NEALT Proceedings Series Volume 11

Riga, Latvia
11 – 13 May 2011

Editors:

Bolette Sandford Pedersen   **Inguna Skadina**
Gunta Nespore

ISBN: 978-1-5108-3464-4

NEALT PROCEEDINGS SERIES
VOL. 11

Proceedings of the
18th Nordic Conference of Computational Linguistics
NODALIDA 2011

May 11-13, 2011
Riga, Latvia

Editors
Bolette Sandford Pedersen, Gunta Nešpore and Inguna Skadiņa

NORTHERN EUROPEAN ASSOCIATION FOR LANGUAGE TECHNOLOGY

Volume Editors
Bolette Sandford Pedersen, Gunta Nešpore and Inguna Skadiņa

Series Editor-in-Chief
Mare Koit

Series Editorial Board
Lars Ahrenberg
Koenraad De Smedt
Kristiina Jokinen
Joakim Nivre
Patrizia Paggio
Vytautas Rudžionis

Supported by
Institute of Mathematics and Computer Science, University of Latvia (ERAF project, agreement No. 2010/0206/2DP/2.1.1.2.0/10/APIA/VIAA/011)

Contents

Preface

The computational linguistics and language technology communities in the Nordic and Baltic countries have always considered the NODALIDA conference as one of the important events for meeting and interchanging new research in the field. Through the establishment of the Northern European Association of Language Technology (NEALT) in 2006, the NODALIDA conference has increased its importance and is now recognized outside the Nordic regions, as can be seen by the fact that we have received several European submissions from outside the Nordic and Baltic countries, as well as submissions from outside Europe such as the US, India, and Pakistan. We are very pleased to hereby present the Proceedings of NODALIDA 2011, the 18th Nordic Conference of Computational Linguistics, held 11-13 May 2011 in Riga, Latvia. We hope that these proceedings will serve as a useful and comprehensive repository of information, will facilitate research in language technology and will encourage the development of further language resources for the Nordic and Baltic languages!

According to the reviews provided by the review committee, a vast majority of the papers submitted for the conference this year were of very good quality. This is a positive sign of the fact that language technology in the Nordic and Baltic countries is striving. However, maintaining the tradition of the NODALIDA conference running over two days plus a workshop day, time scarcity has enforced us to accept only a limited number of papers. This means that even with an acceptance rate above 60%, several quality papers have been rejected. To sum up in figures, we received altogether 85 submissions from 20 countries in the four categories of full papers, short /demo papers, student papers, and workshops. Each submission received three reviews and borderline cases were further subjected to discussion among the Program Committee members. For the conference, we have accepted 52 papers which appear in these proceedings, as well as three workshops which will produce their own proceedings. Of the accepted papers in the main conference, 33 are long papers presented as talk or poster, 14 are short papers presented as poster or demo and five are student papers of which three are presented as talk and two as poster. It should be pointed out that most of the submissions are from the Nordic countries and only a limited number of papers are from the Baltic region. This may be because the Baltic HLT conference was held only recently. The papers selected for the conference represent a wide range of topics of research, including corpus linguistics, lexicography, morphological and syntactic processing, machine translation, speech technologies, semantics, and other areas of language technology.

We also have the pleasure of presenting three invited speakers at NODALIDA 2011, one of which is invited to present ongoing research in the host country, Latvia, and two others to present ongoing research in Sweden and Scotland, respectively. The invited talks concern central aspects of language technology such as discourse analysis, dependency parsing, and controlled natural languages. Bonnie Webber from University of Edinburgh talks about discourse structures and language technology and discusses how discourse structures can help to improve language technologies, and further, how language technologies can help to induce and model discourse structures. Joakim Nivre from Uppsala University gives a survey of recent advances in so-called bare-bones dependency parsing; focusing in particular on transition-based methods for highly efficient parsing. Guntis Bārzdiņš from University of Latvia talks about a new kind of rich controlled natural language which allows to narrow the gap with true natural language.

In addition, the conference program includes three workshops; two on the specialized topics terminology and Constraint Grammar, and one with the broader focus on visibility of language resources.

Moreover, the conference has attracted a satellite event, held before the workshops: The project-related meeting in META-NET/META-NORD which is the Nordic and Baltic branch of a Network of Excellence dedicated to building the technological foundations of a multilingual European information society. Finally, during the conference there will be the third NEALT business meeting.

The organization of a conference of this size is a joint effort between several organizational units. We would first like to thank our reviewers for their conscientious work in reviewing all the submitted contributions. We also wish to thank the Program Committee for inviting the reviewers as well as for the fruitful discussions regarding how to ensure a conference of high quality. A big thank you goes to the Local Organization Committee at the Institute of Mathematics and Computer Science of University of Latvia for their work concerning practical issues for the conference. Special thanks go to Mare Koit, Editor-in-Chief of the NEALT Publication Series at University of Tartu, for producing the electronic proceedings.

We wish you an inspiring conference!

Bolette Sandford Pedersen
Program Chair
NODALIDA 2011

Inguna Skadiņa
Local Chair
NODALIDA 2011

Committees

PROGRAM COMMITTEE
Bolette Sandford Pedersen (Program Chair), University of Copenhagen, Denmark
Kristiina Jokinen, University of Helsinki, Finland
Jussi Karlgren, Swedish Institute of Computer Science, Sweden
Ruta Marcinkeviciene, Vytautas Magnus University, Lithuania
Meelis Mihkla, Institute of the Estonian Language, Estonia
Costanza Navarretta, University of Copenhagen, Denmark
Anders Nøklestad, University of Oslo, Norway
Eirikur Rögnvaldsson, University of Iceland, Iceland

LOCAL ORGANIZATION COMMITTEE
Inguna Skadiņa (Local Chair), Institute of Mathematics and Computer Science,
    University of Latvia
Rihards Balodis, Institute of Mathematics and Computer Science, University of Latvia
Gunta Nešpore, Institute of Mathematics and Computer Science, University of Latvia
Gunta Plataiskalna, Institute of Mathematics and Computer Science, University of Latvia
Ilmārs Poikāns, Institute of Mathematics and Computer Science, University of Latvia
Baiba Saulīte, Institute of Mathematics and Computer Science, University of Latvia
Andrejs Spektors, Institute of Mathematics and Computer Science, University of Latvia

REVIEWERS
Toomas Altosaar, Helsinki University of Technology, Finland
Tanel Alumäe, Tallinn University of Technology, Estonia
Ilze Auziņa, University of Latvia, Latvia
Eckhard Bick, Syddansk Universitet, Denmark
Kristín Bjarnadóttir, Árni Magnússon Institute, Iceland
Anne Bjerre, Syddansk Universitet, Denmark
Anna Braach, University of Copenhagen, Denmark
Hanne Fersøe, University of Copenhagen, Denmark
Jody Foo, Linköping University, Sweden
Björn Gambäck, Norwegian University of Science and Technology, Norway & Swedish
Institute of Computer Science, Sweden
Tatiana Gornostay, Tilde, Latvia
Gintare Grigonyte, Vytautas Magnus University, Lithuania
Joakim Gustafson, Kungliga Tekniska Högskolan, Sweden
Kristin Hagen, University of Oslo, Norway
Daniel Hardt, Copenhagen Business School, Denmark
Sigrún Helgadóttir, Árni Magnússon Institute, Iceland
Janne Bondi Johannessen, University of Oslo, Norway
Lars G. Johnsen, University of Bergen, Norway
Heikki-Jaan Kaalep, University of Tartu, Estonia
Mari-Liis Kalvik, Institute of the Estonian Language, Estonia
Sabine Kirchmeier-Andersen, Danish Language Council, Denmark
Krista Lagus, Aalto University, Finland
Yves Lepage, Waseda University, Japan

Krister Linden, University of Helsinki, Finland
Hrafn Loftsson, Reykjavik University, Iceland
Jan Tore Lønning, University of Oslo, Norway
Bente Maegaard, University of Copenhagen, Denmark
Sanni Nimb, Danish Society for Language and Literature, Denmark
Joakim Nivre, Uppsala University, Sweden
Stephan Oepen, University of Oslo, Norway
Fredrik Olsson, Gavagai, Sweden
Patrizia Paggio, University of Copenhagen, Denmark
Hille Pajupuu, Institute of the Estonian Language, Estonia
Ari Pirkola, Tampere, Univesrity of Tampere, Finland
Gailius Raskinis, Vytautas Magnus University, Lithuania
Anders Søgaard, University of Copenhagen, Denmark
Hanne Erdman Thomsen, Copenhagen Business School, Denmark
Trond Trosterud, University of Tromsø, Norway
Oscar Täckström, Swedish Institute of Computer Science & Uppsala University, Sweden
Andrius Utka, Vytautas Magnus University, Lithuania
Martti Vainio, University of Helsinki, Finland
Erik Velldal, University of Oslo, Norway
Sumithra Velupillai, Stockholm University, Sweden
Carl Vogel, Trinity College Dublin, Ireland
Joel Wallenberg, University of Iceland, Iceland
Jürgen Wedekind, University of Copenhagen, Denmark
Matthew Whelpton, University of Iceland, Iceland
Atro Voutilainen, University of Helsinki, Finland
Mats Wirén, Stockholm University, Sweden
Roman Yangarber, University of Helsinki, Finland
Robert Östling, Stockholm University
Lilja Øvrelid, University of Oslo, Norway

Conference program

NODALIDA-2011

11 May

Satellite events

Workshops
- Workshop on Creation, Harmonization and Application of Terminology Resources
- Workshop in Constraint Grammar Applications
- Workshop on Visibility and Availability of LT resources

19.00   ***Welcome reception***

12 May

9.00–9.30   **Opening**

Mārcis Auziņš (Rector of the University of Latvia)
Janne Bondi Johannessen (President of NEALT)
Inguna Skadiņa (Chair of the Local Organizing Committee)
Bolette Sandford Pedersen (Chair of the Program Committee)

9.30–10.30   **Invited Talk** (Chair: Costanza Navarretta)

Prof. Bonnie Webber (University of Edinburgh). *Discourse Structures and Language Technologies*

10.30–11.00   *Coffee*

11.00–13.00   **3 parallel sessions: REGULAR papers**

Corpus creation, annotation and use (Chair: Eiríkur Rögnvaldsson)

11.00–11.30	Costanza Navarretta, Elisabeth Ahlsén, Jens Allwood, Kristiina Jokinen and Patrizia Paggio. *Creating Comparable Multimodal Corpora for Nordic Languages*
11.30–12.00	Rico Sennrich and Martin Volk. *Iterative, MT-based Sentence Alignment of Parallel Texts*
12.00–12.30	Estelle Delpech. *Evaluation of Terminologies Acquired from Comparable Corpora: an Application Perspective*
12.30–13.00	Janne Bondi Johannessen and Emiliano Raúl Guevara. *What Kind of Corpus is a Web Corpus?*

Text and language classification (Chair: Hanne Fersøe)

11.00–11.30	Taraka Rama and Lars Borin. *Estimating Language Relationships from a Parallel Corpus. A Study of the Europarl Corpus*
11.30–12.00	Robert Remus. *Improving Sentence-level Subjectivity Classification through Readability Measurement*
12.00-12.30	Michael Wiegand and Dietrich Klakow. *Convolution Kernels for Subjectivity Detection*

Morphology and POS tagging (Chair: Janne Bondi Johannessen)

11.00–11.30	Miikka Silfverberg and Krister Lindén. *Combining Statistical Models for POS Tagging using Finite-State Calculus*
11.30–12.00	Niels Beuck, Arne Köhn and Wolfgang Menzel. *Decision Strategies for Incremental POS Tagging*
12.00–12.30	Anssi Yli-Jyrä. *Explorations on Positionwise Flag Diacritics in Finite-State Morphology*
12.30–13.00	Heiki-Jaan Kaalep and Kadri Muischnek. *Morphological Analysis of a Non-Standard Language Variety*

13.00–14.00   Lunch

15.45–17.15   **3 parallel sessions: REGULAR papers**

Speech (Chair: Meelis Mihkla)

15.45–16.15	Sofia Strömbergsson. *Corrective Re-synthesis of Deviant Speech Using Unit Selection*
16.15–16.45	Peter Juel Henrichsen. *Fishing in a Speech Stream, Angling for a Lexicon*
16.45–17.15	Bea Valkenier, Dirkjan Krijnders, Ronald van Elburg and Tjeerd Andringa. *Psycho-Acoustically Motivated Formant Feature Extraction*

Search and information extraction (Chair: Costanza Navarretta)

15.45–16.15	Lars Borin, Markus Forsberg and Christer Ahlberger. *Semantic Search in Literature as an e-Humanities Research Tool: CONPLISIT — Consumption Patterns and Life-Style in 19th Century Swedish Literature*
16.15–16.45	Silja Huttunen, Arto Vihavainen and Roman Yangarber. *Relevance Prediction in Information Extraction Using Discourse and Lexical Features*
16.45–17.15	Gintarė Grigonytė, Erika Rimkutė, Andrius Utka and Loïc Boizou. *Experiments on Lithuanian Term Extraction*

Syntax, indexing (Chair: Jussi Karlgren)

15.45–16.15	Peter Ljunglöf. *Editing Syntax Trees on the Surface*
16.15–16.45	Anders Søgaard. *Using Graphical Models for PP Attachment*
16.45–17.15	Erik Velldal. *Random Indexing Re-Hashed*

17.15–18.15   **Invited Talk** (Chair: Inguna Skadiņa)

Prof. Guntis Bārzdiņš (University of Latvia). *When FrameNet Meets a Controlled Natural Language*

19.30   ***Conference dinner***

9.00–10.00	**Invited Talk** (Chair: Kristiina Jokinen)

Prof. Joakim Nivre (Uppsala University). *Bare-Bones Dependency Parsing — A Case for Occam's Razor?*

10.00–10.30	*Coffee*
10.30–12.00	**3 parallel sessions: REGULAR papers and STUDENT papers**

Lexicon, etymology (Chair: Bolette Sandford Pedersen)

10.30–11.00	Eckhard Bick. *A FrameNet for Danish*
11.00–11.30	Ingemar Hjälmstad, Martin Hassel and Maria Skeppstedt. *The Impact of Part-of-Speech Filtering on Generation of a Swedish-Japanese Dictionary using English as Pivot Language*
11.30–12.00	Hannes Wettig and Roman Yangarber. *Probabilistic Models for Alignment of Etymological Data*

Machine translation; classification (Chair: Andrejs Vasiļjevs)

10.30–11.00	Martin Volk and Rico Sennrich. *Disambiguation of English Contractions for Machine Translation of TV Subtitles*
11.00–11.30	Raivis Skadiņš, Tatiana Gornostay and Valters Šics. *Toponym Disambiguation in English-Lithuanian SMT System with Spatial Knowledge*
11.30–12.00	Eirini Florou and Stasinos Konstantopoulos. *A Quantitative and Qualitative Analysis of Nordic Surnames*

Student papers (Chair: Normunds Grūzītis)

10.30–11.00	Marius Olaussen. *Evaluating the Speech Quality of the Norwegian Synthetic Voice Brage*
11.00–11.30	Mojgan Seraji. *A Statistical Part-of-Speech Tagger for Persian*
11.30–12.00	Angel Genov and Georgi Iliev. *Linguistic Motivation in Automatic Sentence Alignment of Parallel Corpora: the Case of Danish-Bulgarian and English-Bulgarian*

12.00–13.00	*Lunch*

13.00–14.30   **12 Posters/demos** (Chair: Kristiina Jokinen)

Classification & summarization

Christian Smith and Arne Jönsson. *Automatic Summarization as Means of Simplifying Texts, an Evaluation for Swedish*

Per Almquist and Jussi Karlgren. *Experiments to Investigate the Utility of Nearest Neighbor Metrics Based on Linguistically Informed Features for Detecting Textual Plagiarism*

Jody Foo. *A Categorization Scheme for Analyzing Rules from a Handbook of Swedish Writing Rules*

Anju Saxena and Lars Borin. *Dialect Classification in the Himalayas: a Computational Approach*

Knowledge systems

Ann-Marie Eklund. *Query Constraining Aspects of Knowledge*

Kenneth Wilhelmsson. *Automatic Question Generation from Swedish Documents as a Tool for Information Extraction*

Corpus creation, annotation and use

Christian Hänig. *Knowledge-free Verb Detection through Sentence Sequence Alignment*

Maria Holmqvist and Lars Ahrenberg. *A Gold Standard for English-Swedish Word Alignment*

Anne-Kathrin Schumann. *Corpus-based Terminology: Detection, Description and Representation of Knowledge-rich Contexts in Russian*

Student posters

Anastasia Shimorina and Maria Grachkova. *Identification of Context Markers for Russian Nouns*

Gideon Kotzé. *Finding Statistically Motivated Features Influencing Subtree Alignment Performance*

14.30–15.30   **NEALT Business meeting**

15.30–16.00   **Closing**

16.00-16.30   *Coffee*

I Invited Papers

When FrameNet meets a Controlled Natural Language

Guntis Bārzdiņš
University of Latvia
Riga, Latvia
`guntis.barzdins@mii.lu.lv`

Abstract

There are two approaches to the natural language processing – one is going in width to cover at shallow level (parsing, syntax) the rich linguistic variety found in the natural language, while another is going in depth (semantics, discourse structure) for a monosemous subset of natural language referred to as a controlled natural language (CNL). Today we are nowhere near to bridging the gap between the two approaches. In this presentation I argue that despite elusiveness of this goal, FrameNet might provide a sufficient insight into the deeper semantic layers of the natural language to envision a new kind of a rich CNL narrowing the gap with the true natural language. A blueprint for PAO, a procedural CNL of such new kind is discussed.

1   Introduction

Despite substantial achievements in the computational linguistics, such as rather reliable POS-tagging, syntax-tree parsing, word sense disambiguation, and statistical translation, in reality computational linguistics is still no where near to really understanding the natural language. All the mentioned techniques fail in certain situations and a human verification is always needed to achieve true accuracy - this is why accuracy measures such as precision and recall are commonly used to evaluate the computation linguistics methods. Missing background knowledge is often considered as the key reason for shortcomings of the machine-based systems.

On the other hand there are controlled natural languages (CNL) - their sole purpose is to go further in language semantics understanding than we are able for unrestricted natural language (Wiener, 2010). ACE (Fuchs, 2006), HALO project (Friedland, 2004), CYC NL subsystem (Lenat, 1995) and various OWL verbalizations (Schwitter, 2008) are among the best known CNLs. Although these CNLs are rooted in natural language, due to their narrow coverage limited by the underlying logical representation, these languages still largely resemble a programming language with strict grammar and monosemous lexicon. The main advantage of CNLs so far is that CNL text can be read and understood by an untrained person, while writing a correct CNL text is quite difficult and is similar to programming, where certain syntax and semantic constraints shall be strictly followed.

In this presentation will be discussed a possibility for constructing a more natural controlled language based on the ideas of FrameNet and situation semantics in general (Frame). The proposed approach incorporates the elements of traditional logic-based CNLs, but extends them with explicit procedural constructs derived from FrameNet. Since FrameNet itself covers a large portion of natural language constructs (Johansson, 2008), such approach bears a promise for a substantially more natural controlled language. A procedural extension of ACE-OWL (Kaljurand, 2007) controlled language (named PAO) will be used to illustrate the proposed approach (Gruzitis, 2010).

2   Defining the Background Knowledge

The key difference of PAO is that it adds support for procedural background knowledge through FrameNet like constructs besides the more traditional declarative background knowledge typically expressed through OWL ontologies. Based on the available background knowledge, PAO defines a translation from the controlled language input text into a combination of OWL and SPARQL statements.

In PAO background knowledge consists of two parts — declarative OWL ontologies (Fig.1) and procedural templates (Fig.2). The purpose of ontologies is to define the concept hierarchies (OWL classes), their relationships (OWL properties) and restriction axioms (cardinality restrictions and others).

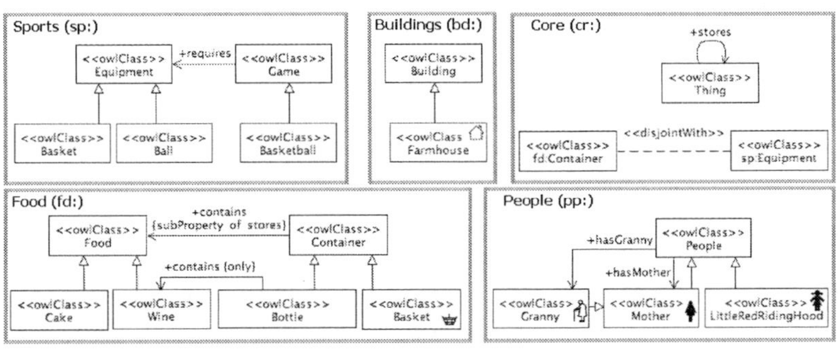

Fig 1: Declarative background knowledge ontologies

In Fig.1 OWL ontologies are visualized using UML-style OWLGrEd editor (Barzdins, 2010). Alternatively, ontologies may be defined verbally in CNL itself through ACE-OWL statements like:

Every Bottle is a Container.
Everything that contains something is a Container.
Everything that is contained by something is a Food.
If X contains Y then X stores Y.

The procedural background knowledge in Fig.2 provides a link between the action words (verbs) and their 'meaning' in SPARQL. The distinction between actions and properties is often neglected in CNLs, but in PAO they are strictly separated: in PAO action is a non-ontological SPARQL procedure, which creates/deletes OWL individuals or connects/disconnects them through the OWL properties. PAO action, unlike binary OWL properties, has no arity restriction — it can link any number of arguments as is typical for verb valencies in natural language. Syntactically a procedural template in PAO is a combination of elements inspired by FrameNet (Fillmore, 2003), Planning Domain Description Language (PDDL) (McDermott, 1998) and SPARQL. The procedural template itself corresponds to a FrameNet frame, the parameters section corresponds to FrameNet frame elements, and the lexical units section is a direct copy from FrameNet. Inclusion of precondition and effect sections in the procedural template is inspired by PDDL and has two-fold purpose: this is a compact represen-

tation of SELECT, INSERT, DELETE, MODIFY and WHERE patterns of the corresponding SPARQL statement and at the same time it preserves compatibility with PDDL for planning purposes. Elements of planning will become necessary in the final steps of PAO interpretation described later.

The ontologies and procedural templates shown in Fig.1 and Fig.2 are specifically crafted for the PAO example in the next section; for more realistic applications it would be necessary to create a much larger collection of ontologies and procedural templates covering the whole lexicon and domain-knowledge of interest.

Procedure: Residence
:parameters (?resident ?co-resident ?location)
 :precondition ()
 :effect (and(stores ?location ?resident)
        (stores ?location ?co_resident))
 :lexicalUnits (camp, inhabit, live, lodge, stay)

Procedure: Removing
 :parameters (?agent ?source ?theme)
 :precondition (stores ?source ?theme)
 :effect (and(stores ?agent ?theme)
        (not(stores ?source ?theme)))
 :lexicalUnits (confiscate, remove, take)

Procedure: Bringing
 :parameters (?agent ?goal ?theme)
 :precondition (and(stores ?agent ?theme)
        (stores ?a ?agent) (not(= ?a ?goal)))
 :effect (and(stores ?goal ?theme)
        (stores ?goal ?agent)
        (not(stores ?agent ?theme))
        (not(stores ?a ?agent)))
 :lexicalUnits (bring, carry, convey, drive)

Fig 2: Procedural templates of background knowledge

3   Example of PAO Text Processing

In PAO text has to be written in simple present tense to avoid complex event sequencing — the described events are assumed to be atomic and to occur sequentially as they are mentioned in the text. The following PAO input text will be used to illustrate the PAO processing stages:

"LittleRedRidingHood lives in a farmhouse with her mother. She takes a basket from the farmhouse and carries it to her granny."

The initial stage of PAO processing is anaphora resolution and paraphrasing of the input text into the sequence of elementary statements as shown in Fig.3.

A.   Obj4 is a LittleRedRidingHood.
B.   Obj4 **lives** in Obj8 with Obj11.
C.   Obj8 is a farmhouse.
D.   Obj4 hasMother Obj11.
E.   Obj4 **takes** Obj15 from Obj8.
F.   Obj15 is a food-basket.
G.   Obj4 **carries** Obj15 to Obj25.
H.   Obj4 hasGranny Obj25.

Fig. 3: Paraphrased PAO input text

Note that in the generated paraphrase in Fig.3 the statements A, C, D, F, and H are actually regular ACE-OWL factual statements about individuals and thus translate into regular OWL/RDF triples:

A:(<obj4> <rdf:type> <LittleRedRidingHood>)
C: (<obj8> <rdf:type> <Farmhouse>)
D: (<obj4> <hasMother> <obj11>)
   (<obj11> <rdf:type> <Mother>)
F: (<obj15> <rdf:type> <Basket>)
H: (<obj4> <hasGranny> <obj25>)
   (<obj25> <rdf:type> <Granny>)

Meanwhile the procedural statements B, E, and G do not belong to ACE-OWL and require a procedural template from the background knowledge in Fig.2 for their translation. The translation includes mapping of syntactic roles into procedural template parameters and converting the precondition and effect notation into equivalent SPARQL statements. PDDL-like planning stage is needed as well, because in the input text some obvious intermediate steps of action might often be omitted and they need to be filled-in by the planning to satisfy the procedural template preconditions — in our example for Little Red Riding Hood to be able to take a basket from the farmhouse, the basket had to be at the farmhouse in the first place.

The last analysis stage is to generate the RDF database content trace resulting from the execution of the above OWL/RDF and SPARQL translations — Fig.4 shows the resulting stepwise RDF database content trace.

	RDF content trace	Spatial visualization
A	<obj4> <type> <Little Red Riding Hood>.	Obj4 is a Little Red Riding Hood.
B	<obj4> <type> <Little Red Riding Hood>. <obj8> <stores> <obj4>. <obj8> <stores> <obj11>.	Obj4 lives in obj8 with obj11.
C	<obj4> <type> <Little Red Riding Hood>. <obj8> <stores> <obj4>. <obj8> <stores> <obj11>. <obj8> <type> <farmhouse>. <obj8> <stores> <obj15>	Obj8 is a farmhouse.
D	<obj4> <type> <Little Red Riding Hood>. <obj8> <stores> <obj4>. <obj8> <stores> <obj11>. <obj8> <type> <farmhouse>. <obj4> <hasMother> <obj11>. <obj11> <type> <mother>. <obj8> <stores> <obj15>	Obj4 hasMother Obj11. hasMother
E	<obj4> <type> <Little Red Riding Hood>. <obj8> <stores> <obj4>. <obj8> <stores> <obj11>. <obj8> <type> <farmhouse>. <obj4> <hasMother> <obj11>. <obj11> <type> <mother>. <obj4> <stores> <obj15>	Obj4 removing-takes obj15 from obj8. hasMother
F	<obj4> <type> <Little Red Riding Hood>. <obj8> <stores> <obj4>. <obj8> <stores> <obj11>. <obj8> <type> <farmhouse>. <obj4> <hasMother> <obj11>. <obj11> <type> <mother>. <obj4> <stores> <obj15> <obj15> <type> <food-basket>	Obj15 is a food-basket. hasMother
G	<obj4> <type> <Little Red Riding Hood>. <obj25> <stores> <obj4>. <obj8> <stores> <obj11>. <obj8> <type> <farmhouse>. <obj4> <hasMother> <obj11>. <obj11> <type> <mother>. <obj25> <stores> <obj15>. <obj15> <type> <food-basket>.	Obj4 carries obj15 to obj25. hasMother
H	<obj4> <type> <Little Red Riding Hood>. <obj25> <stores> <obj4>. <obj8> <stores> <obj11>. <obj8> <type> <farmhouse>. <obj4> <hasMother> <obj11>. <obj11> <type> <mother>. <obj25> <stores> <obj15>. <obj15> <type> <food-basket>. <obj4> <hasGranny> <obj25>. <obj25> <type> <granny>	Obj4 hasGranny Obj25. hasGranny hasMother

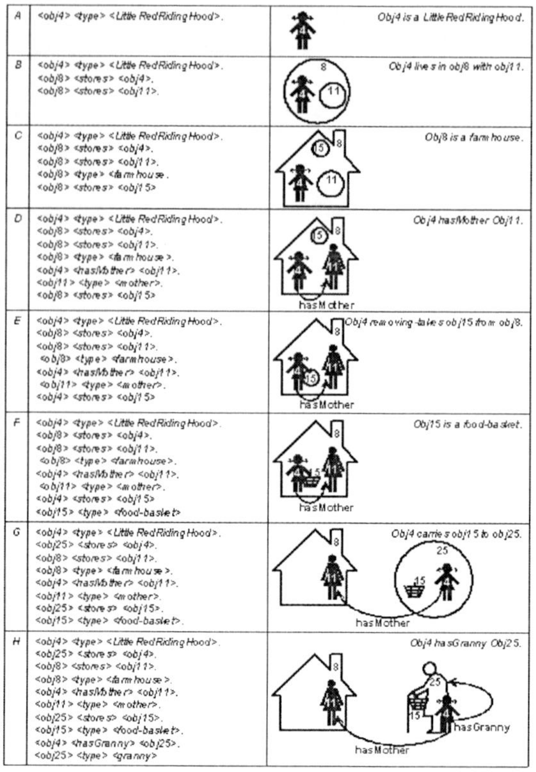

Fig. 4: RDF content trace and its spatial visualization

The generated RDF database content trace is the final result of PAO text analysis — this trace is the actual discourse conveyed by the PAO input text. In the right column of Fig.4 the discourse is optionally visualized also as a sequence of graphic scenes — similarly to text-to-scene animation approach described in (Johansson, 2005). These visualizations can be generated automatically from the graphic icons provided for OWL classes in the background knowledge (Fig.1 actually includes the necessary icons); OWL properties are visualized as labeled arrows or alternatively as graphic inclusion for spatial properties like "stores". These visual scenes highlight the similarity of PAO analysis result to the dynamic scene likely imagined by a human reader incrementally reading the same input text.

4   Query Answering in PAO

The constructed RDF database trace in Fig.4 can further be used to answer queries about the input text, for example:

1. Who delivered a basket to a granny?
2. Did LittleRedRidingHood visit her granny?

3. Where initially was the basket?
4. When did the granny got the basket?

These queries can be answered through translating them into the appropriate SPARQL queries through techniques similar to those used to translate PAO paraphrase in Fig.3 earlier. The answers produced by such SPARQL queries on the RDF trace in Fig.4 would be:

1. ?x = obj4
2. yes
3. ?x = obj8
4. ?n = H

These very technical SPARQL answers can afterwards be rendered into more verbose answers:

1. LittleRedRidingHood [delivered a basket to granny].
2. Yes [, LittleRedRidingHood visited granny].
3. [Basket initially was] in the farmhouse.
4. In step H [, when LittleRedRidingHood brought the basket to granny].

Although we have not described the question answering process here in detail, these examples provide an overview of PAO potential for factual and temporal question answering over narrative input texts.

5 Conclusion

The described PAO controlled language is only a rather simple attempt to exploit the rich declarative and procedural background knowledge in a CNL to make it more natural through the inclusion of FrameNet like procedural semantics. The added expressivity allows for rich query answering about the provided input text. We are quite pleased to to been able to include ACE-OWL as a proper subset of PAO thus achieving a complementary integration of procedural and declarative approaches.

An obvious limitation of the presented PAO language is its treatment of time only as a linear sequence of events mentioned in the input text. A richer time conceptualization would be generally needed, including hypothetical, parallel and negated events to handle texts like *"Mother told LittleRedRidingHood to go directly to the granny's house and not to engage in conversations with strangers"*.

The briefly mentioned optional visualization of PAO discourse is a promising area for further exploration — inversion of the mentioned visualization technique could potentially lead to a visual data acquisition in the form of CNL grounded in the same ontological and procedural background knowledge.

References

Lenat, D.1995. *Cyc: A Large-Scale Investment in Knowledge Infrastructure*. Communications of the ACM, 38:11, pp. 33--38

McDermott D. 1998. *PDDL — The Planning Domain Definition Language*. Technical report, Yale Center for Computational Vision and Control, http://www.cs.yale.edu/homes/dvm/

Fillmore, C.J., Johnson, C.R., Petruck, M.R.L. 2003. *Background to FrameNet*. International Journal of Lexicography, 16, pp. 235--250

Friedland, N., and Allen, P. 2004. *Project halo: Towards a digital aristotle*. In AI Magazine.

Johansson, R., Berglund, A., Danielsson, M., Nugues, P. 2005. *Automatic text-to-scene conversion in the traffic accident domain*. In: 19th International Joint Conference on Artificial Intelligence, pp. 1073--1078

Fuchs, N.E., Kaljurand, K., Schneider, G. 2006. *Atempto Controlled English Meets the Challenges of Knowledge Representation, Reasoning, Interoperability and User Interfaces*. In: 19th International FLAIRS Conference (2006)

Kaljurand, K., Fuchs, N.E. 2007. *Verbalizing OWL in Atempto Controlled English*. In: 3rd International OWLED Workshop

Schwitter, R., Kaljurand, K., Cregan, A., Dolbear, C., Hart, G. 2008. *A Comparison of three Controlled Natural Languages for OWL 1.1*. In: 4th International OWLED Workshop

Johansson, R., Nugues, P. 2008. *Comparing dependency and constituent syntax for frame-semantic analysis*. In: 6th International LREC Conference

Wyner A. et.al. 2010. *On Controlled Natural Languages: Properties and Prospects*. LNCS/LNAI5972, Springer, Heidelberg, 281-289

Gruzitis N. and Barzdins G. 2010: *Polysemy in Controlled Natural Language Texts*. In: CNL 2009 Workshop, LNCS/LNAI 5972, Springer, Heidelberg, 2010, pp. 102–120

Barzdins J., et.al. 2010. *OWLGrEd: a UML Style Graphical Editor for OWL //* Proceedings of ORES-2010, CEUR Workshop Proceedings, Vol-596

ISSN 1736-6305 Vol. 11
http://hdl.handle.net/10062/16955

Bare-Bones Dependency Parsing – A Case for Occam's Razor?

Joakim Nivre
Uppsala University
Uppsala, Sweden
`joakim.nivre@lingfil.uu.se`

Abstract

If all we want from a syntactic parser is a dependency tree, what do we gain by first computing a different representation such as a phrase structure tree? The principle of parsimony suggests that a simpler model should be preferred over a more complex model, all other things being equal, and the simplest model is arguably one that maps a sentence directly to a dependency tree – a bare-bones dependency parser. In this paper, I characterize the parsing problem faced by such a system, survey the major parsing techniques currently in use, and begin to examine whether the simpler model can in fact rival the performance of more complex systems. Although the empirical evidence is still limited, I conclude that bare-bones dependency parsers fare well in terms of parsing accuracy and often excel in terms of efficiency.

1 Introduction

The notion of dependency has come to play an increasingly central role in natural language parsing in recent years. On the one hand, lexical dependencies have been incorporated in statistical models for a variety of syntactic representations such as phrase structure trees (Collins, 1999), LFG representations (Riezler et al., 2002), and CCG derivations (Clark and Curran, 2004). On the other hand, dependency relations extracted from such representations have been exploited in many practical applications, for example, information extraction (Culotta and Sorensen, 2004), question answering (Bouma et al., 2005), and machine translation (Ding and Palmer, 2004). Given these developments, it is not surprising that there has also been a growing interest in parsing models that map sentences directly to dependency trees,

an approach that will be referred to as *bare-bones dependency parsing* to distinguish it from parsing methods where dependencies are embedded into or extracted from other types of syntactic representations.

The bare-bones model can be motivated by the principle known as Occam's razor, which says that entities should not be postulated beyond necessity. If we can show that bare-bones dependency parsers produce dependency trees with at least the same accuracy and efficiency as more complex models, then they would be preferred on grounds of simplicity. In this paper, I will begin by explaining how the parsing problem for bare-bones dependency parsers differs from the more familiar parsing problem for phrase structure parsers. I will go on to survey the main techniques that are currently in use, grouped into four broad categories: chart parsing, constraint-based parsing, transition-based parsing, and hybrid methods. Finally, I will examine a number of recent studies that compare the performance of different types of parsers and conclude that bare-bones dependency parsers fare well in terms of accuracy as well as efficiency.

2 Parsing Problem

A dependency structure for a sentence $w_1, \ldots, w_n$ is a directed graph whose nodes represent the input tokens $w_1, \ldots, w_n$ and whose arcs represent syntactic relations from head to dependent. Arcs are normally labeled with dependency types, although unlabeled dependency graphs are also used. Depending on what formal constraints are adopted, we get different classes of dependency graphs, with different expressivity and complexity. If we only require graphs to be connected and acyclic, then words can have more than one head, which is convenient for representing deep syntactic relations. If we require the graph to be a tree, then each word can have at most one head, but we can still represent extraction phenomena using non-

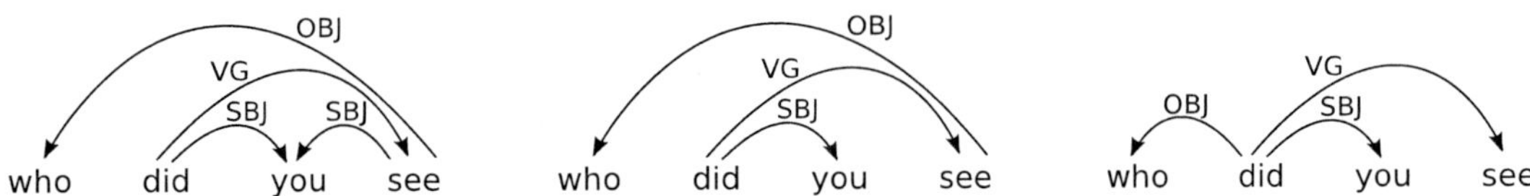

Figure 1: Dependency graphs: directed acyclic graph (left), tree (middle), projective tree (right).

projective arcs. If we require every subtree to have a contiguous yield, finally, we get the class of projective trees. The different classes are illustrated in Figure 1.

Regardless of what restrictions we put on dependency graphs, the parsing problem consists in finding the optimal set of arcs, given the nodes as input. This is different from phrase structure parsing, where only the terminal nodes are given as input and both internal nodes and edges have to be inferred during parsing. Many algorithms for dependency parsing are restricted to projective trees, which reduces the complexity of the parsing problem, but a number of systems are capable of handling non-projective trees, either by using nonstandard algorithms or through post-processing. Very few systems can deal with directed acyclic graphs. Dependency parsers are generally evaluated by measuring precision and recall on dependency relations, with or without labels. When dependency graphs are restricted to trees, precision and recall coincide and are normally referred to as the attachment score.

3 Parsing Techniques

3.1 Chart Parsing Techniques

A straightforward method for dependency parsing is to view it as a restricted form of context-free parsing and reuse chart parsing algorithms like CKY and Earley, an idea that is implicit already in Hays (1964). Thanks to the constraints on dependency trees, it is possible to reduce complexity to $O(n^3)$ for lexicalized parsing using the span-based representation proposed by Eisner (1996). Coupled with statistical models of increasing complexity, this technique has resulted in excellent parsing accuracy for projective trees, with features defined over single arcs (McDonald et al., 2005a), pairs of arcs (McDonald and Pereira, 2006; Carreras, 2007) or even triples of arcs (Koo and Collins, 2010). These models are usually referred to as first-, second- and third-order models. One limitation of this parsing approach is that it does not easily extend to non-projective trees, let alone

directed acyclic graphs. However, as shown by McDonald and Pereira (2006), it is possible to recover both non-projective arcs and multiple heads through post-processing.

3.2 Parsing as Constraint Satisfaction

A different approach is to view parsing as a constraint satisfaction problem, starting from a compact representation of all dependency graphs compatible with the input and successively eliminating invalid graphs through the propagation of grammatical constraints, as originally proposed by Maruyama (1990). By adding numerical weights to constraints and defining the score of a graph as a function of the weights of violated constraints, Menzel and Schröder (1998) turned this into an optimization problem where the goal is to find the highest-scoring dependency graph. Constraint-based parsing can easily accommodate different classes of dependency graphs and do not have the same inherent limitations on features or constraints as chart parsing, but the parsing problem is computationally intractable in general, so exact search methods cannot be used except in special cases. An interesting special case is the arc-factored model defined by McDonald et al. (2005b), where the score of a dependency tree is a sum of independent arc weights. Under these assumptions, finding the highest scoring dependency tree is equivalent to finding the maximum directed spanning tree in a complete graph containing all possible dependency arcs, a problem that can be computed in $O(n^2)$ time using algorithms from graph theory. Unfortunately, any attempt to extend the scope of weighted constraints beyond single arcs makes the parsing problem NP complete. Another variation of the constraint-based approach is the use of integer linear programming, which was pioneered by Riedel et al. (2006) and further improved by Martins et al. (2009).

3.3 Transition-Based Parsing

A third prominent method is to view parsing as deterministic search through a transition system (or state machine), guided by a statistical

Parser	Type	UAS
Yamada and Matsumoto (2003)	Trans-Local	90.3
McDonald et al. (2005a)	Chart-1st	90.9
Collins (1999)	PCFG	91.5
McDonald and Pereira (2006)	Chart-2nd	91.5
Charniak (2000)	PCFG	92.1
Koo et al. (2010)	Hybrid-Dual	92.5
Sagae and Lavie (2006)	Hybrid-MST	92.7
Zhang and Nivre (2011)	Trans-Global	92.9
Koo and Collins (2010)	Chart-3rd	93.0

Table 1: Dependency parsing for English (WSJ-PTB, Penn2Malt); unlabeled attachment scores.

Parser	Type	UAS
Collins (1999)	PCFG	82.2
McDonald et al. (2005a)	Chart-1st	83.3
Charniak (2000)	PCFG	84.3
McDonald et al. (2005b)	MST	84.4
Hall and Novák (2005)	PCFG+Post	85.0
McDonald and Pereira (2006)	Chart-2nd+Post	85.2
Nivre (2009)	Trans-Local	86.1
Zeman and Žabokrtský (2005)	Hybrid-Greedy	86.3
Koo et al. (2010)	Hybrid-Dual	87.3

Table 2: Dependency parsing for Czech (PDT); unlabeled attachment scores.

model for predicting the next transition, an idea first proposed by Yamada and Matsumoto (2003). Transition-based parsing can be very efficient, with linear running time for projective dependency trees (Nivre, 2003) and limited subsets of non-projective trees (Attardi, 2006). For arbitrary non-projective trees, the worst-case complexity is quadratic, but observed running time can still be linear with an appropriate choice of transition system Nivre (2009), and transition systems can be extended to handle directed acyclic graphs (Sagae and Tsujii, 2008). Transition-based parsers can base their decisions on very rich representations of the derivation history (including the partially built dependency graph) but may suffer from error propagation due to search errors especially if the statistical model is trained to maximize the accuracy of local transitions rather than complete transition sequences. Zhang and Clark (2008) showed how these problems can be alleviated by global optimization and beam search, and Huang and Sagae (2010) obtained further improvements through ambiguity packing.

3.4 Hybrid Methods

For parsing as for many other problems, it is often possible to improve accuracy by combining methods with different strengths. Thus, Zeman and Žabokrtský (2005) reported substantial improvements in parsing Czech by letting a number of parsers vote for the syntactic head of each word. A drawback of this simple voting scheme is that the output may not be a well-formed dependency graphs even if all the component parsers output well-formed graphs. This problem was solved by Sagae and Lavie (2006), who showed that we can use the spanning tree method of McDonald et al. (2005b) for parser combination by letting parsers vote for arcs in the complete graph and then extract the maximum spanning tree. Another hybrid

technique is parser stacking, where one parser is used to generate input features for another parser, a method that was used by Nivre and McDonald (2008) to combine chart parsing and transition-based parsing, with further improvements reported by Torres Martins et al. (2008). Finally, Koo et al. (2010) used dual decomposition to combine third-order chart parsing and arc-factored spanning tree parsing with excellent empirical results.

4 Comparative Evaluation

When Yamada and Matsumoto (2003) presented the first comparative evaluation of dependency parsing for English, using data from the WSJ section of the Penn Treebank (Marcus et al., 1993) with what has later become known as the Penn2Malt conversion to dependencies, they observed that although their own bare-bones dependency parser had the advantage of simplicity and efficiency, it was not quite as accurate as the parsers of Collins (1999) and Charniak (2000). However, as the results reported in Table 1 clearly show, there has been a tremendous development since then, and the third-order chart parser of Koo and Collins (2010) is now as accurate as any phrase structure parser. Bare-bones dependency parsers are also the most efficient parsers available, with an average parsing time per sentence of 20 msec for the parser of Zhang and Nivre (2011), for example. As shown in Table 2, a very similar development has taken place in the case of Czech dependency parsing, as evaluated on the Prague Dependency Treebank (Hajič et al., 2001).

Cer et al. (2010) evaluated a number of systems for producing Stanford typed dependencies (de Marneffe et al., 2006) and found that bare-bones dependency parsers like MaltParser (Nivre et al., 2006) and MSTParser (McDonald and Pereira, 2006) had considerably lower accuracy than the best phrase structure parsers like the Berkeley parser (Petrov et al., 2006; Petrov and Klein, 2007) and the parser of Charniak and Johnson (2005). However, the evaluation was performed after converting the parser output to so-called collapsed dependencies, a conversion process that is less accurate for dependency trees than for phrase structure trees. More importantly, the bare-bones dependency parsers were run without proper optimization, whereas most of the phrase structure parsers have been optimized for a long time not only for English but in particular for the type of Wall Street Journal text that was used in the evaluation. It is therefore likely that the evaluation results, although representative for out-of-the-box comparisons on this particular data set, do not generalize to other settings. Evidence for this conclusion comes from a similar study by Candito et al. (2010), where different types of parsers were evaluated on data from the French Treebank, and where there was practically no difference in accuracy between the best bare-bones dependency parsers (MaltParser, MSTParser) and the best phrase structure parser (Berkeley). With respect to efficiency, the transition-based Malt-Parser was found to be about ten times faster than the other two parsers.

Rimell et al. (2009) evaluated a number of statistical parsers specifically on their capacity to recover unbounded dependencies like those involved in different types of relative clauses, interrogative clauses and right node raising. The evaluation was extended to bare-bones dependency parsers in Nivre et al. (2010), and the overall results show that systems like MaltParser and MST-Parser, augmented with simple post-processing for inferring multiple heads, perform at least as well as other types of treebank parsers, although not quite as well as grammar-driven systems like those of Clark and Curran (2004) and Miyao and Tsujii (2005).

5   Conclusion

Although the available evidence is still scattered and incomplete, the empirical results so far seem to support the hypothesis that bare-bones dependency parsers can achieve the same level of accuracy as more complex systems. Since they have the advantage of simplicity and are often highly efficient, they clearly seem to merit their place in contexts where the main requirement on syntactic analysis is to produce a dependency tree. To what extent they are also adequate as theoretical models of natural language syntax in general is of course a completely different question.

References

Giuseppe Attardi. 2006. Experiments with a multilanguage non-projective dependency parser. In *Proceedings of the 10th Conference on Computational Natural Language Learning (CoNLL)*, pages 166–170.

Gosse Bouma, Jori Mur, Gertjan van Noord, Lonneke van der Plas, and Jörg Tiedemann. 2005. Question answering for dutch using dependency relations. In *Working Notes of the 6th Workshop of the Cross-Language Evaluation Forum (CLEF 2005)*.

Marie Candito, Joakim Nivre, Pascal Denis, and Enrique Henestroza Anguiano. 2010. Benchmarking of statistical dependency parsers for french. In *Coling 2010: Posters*, pages 108–116.

Xavier Carreras. 2007. Experiments with a higher-order projective dependency parser. In *Proceedings of the CoNLL Shared Task of EMNLP-CoNLL 2007*, pages 957–961.

Daniel Cer, Marie-Catherine de Marneffe, Dan Jurafsky, and Chris Manning. 2010. Parsing to stanford dependencies: Trade-offs between speed and accuracy. In *Proceedings of the Seventh conference on International Language Resources and Evaluation (LREC'10)*.

Eugene Charniak and Mark Johnson. 2005. Coarse-to-fine n-best parsing and MaxEnt discriminative reranking. In *Proceedings of the 43rd Annual Meeting of the Association for Computational Linguistics (ACL)*, pages 173–180.

Eugene Charniak. 2000. A maximum-entropy-inspired parser. In *Proceedings of the First Meeting of the North American Chapter of the Association for Computational Linguistics (NAACL)*, pages 132–139.

Stephen Clark and James R. Curran. 2004. Parsing the WSJ using CCG and log-linear models. In *Proceedings of the 42nd Annual Meeting of the Association for Computational Linguistics (ACL)*, pages 104–111.

Michael Collins. 1999. *Head-Driven Statistical Models for Natural Language Parsing*. Ph.D. thesis, University of Pennsylvania.

Aron Culotta and Jeffery Sorensen. 2004. Dependency tree kernels for relation extraction. In *Proceedings of the 42nd Annual Meeting of the Association for Computational Linguistics (ACL)*, pages 423–429.

Marie-Catherine de Marneffe, Bill MacCartney, and Christopher D. Manning. 2006. Generating typed dependency parses from phrase structure parses. In *Proceedings of the 5th International Conference on Language Resources and Evaluation (LREC)*.

Yuan Ding and Martha Palmer. 2004. Synchronous dependency insertion grammars: A grammar formalism for syntax based statistical MT. In *Proceedings of the Workshop on Recent Advances in Dependency Grammar*, pages 90–97.

Jason M. Eisner. 1996. Three new probabilistic models for dependency parsing: An exploration. In *Proceedings of the 16th International Conference on Computational Linguistics (COLING)*, pages 340–345.

Jan Hajič, Barbora Vidova Hladka, Jarmila Panevová, Eva Hajičová, Petr Sgall, and Petr Pajas. 2001. Prague Dependency Treebank 1.0. LDC, 2001T10.

Keith Hall and Vaclav Novák. 2005. Corrective modeling for non-projective dependency parsing. In *Proceedings of the 9th International Workshop on Parsing Technologies (IWPT)*, pages 42–52.

David G. Hays. 1964. Dependency theory: A formalism and some observations. *Language*, 40:511–525.

Liang Huang and Kenji Sagae. 2010. Dynamic programming for linear-time incremental parsing. In *Proceedings of the 48th Annual Meeting of the Association for Computational Linguistics (ACL)*, pages 1077–1086.

Terry Koo and Michael Collins. 2010. Efficient third-order dependency parsers. In *Proceedings of the 48th Annual Meeting of the Association for Computational Linguistics (ACL)*, pages 1–11.

Terry Koo, Alexander M. Rush, Michael Collins, Tommi Jaakkola, and David Sontag. 2010. Dual decomposition for parsing with non-projective head automata. In *Proceedings of the 2010 Conference on Empirical Methods in Natural Language Processing*, pages 1288–1298.

Mitchell P. Marcus, Beatrice Santorini, and Mary Ann Marcinkiewicz. 1993. Building a large annotated corpus of English: The Penn Treebank. *Computational Linguistics*, 19:313–330.

Andre Martins, Noah Smith, and Eric Xing. 2009. Concise integer linear programming formulations for dependency parsing. In *Proceedings of the Joint Conference of the 47th Annual Meeting of the ACL and the 4th International Joint Conference on Natural Language Processing of the AFNLP (ACL-IJCNLP)*, pages 342–350.

Hiroshi Maruyama. 1990. Structural disambiguation with constraint propagation. In *Proceedings of the 28th Meeting of the Association for Computational Linguistics (ACL)*, pages 31–38.

Ryan McDonald and Fernando Pereira. 2006. Online learning of approximate dependency parsing algorithms. In *Proceedings of the 11th Conference of the European Chapter of the Association for Computational Linguistics (EACL)*, pages 81–88.

Ryan McDonald, Koby Crammer, and Fernando Pereira. 2005a. Online large-margin training of dependency parsers. In *Proceedings of the 43rd Annual Meeting of the Association for Computational Linguistics (ACL)*, pages 91–98.

Ryan McDonald, Fernando Pereira, Kiril Ribarov, and Jan Hajič. 2005b. Non-projective dependency parsing using spanning tree algorithms. In *Proceedings of the Human Language Technology Conference and the Conference on Empirical Methods in Natural Language Processing (HLT/EMNLP)*, pages 523–530.

Wolfgang Menzel and Ingo Schröder. 1998. Decision procedures for dependency parsing using graded constraints. In *Proceedings of the Workshop on Processing of Dependency-Based Grammars (ACL-COLING)*, pages 78–87.

Yusuke Miyao and Jun'ichi Tsujii. 2005. Probabilistic disambiguation models for wide-coverage HPSG parsing. In *Proceedings of the 43rd Annual Meeting of the Association for Computational Linguistics (ACL)*, pages 83–90.

Joakim Nivre and Ryan McDonald. 2008. Integrating graph-based and transition-based dependency parsers. In *Proceedings of the 46th Annual Meeting of the Association for Computational Linguistics (ACL)*, pages 950–958.

Joakim Nivre, Johan Hall, and Jens Nilsson. 2006. Maltparser: A data-driven parser-generator for dependency parsing. In *Proceedings of the 5th International Conference on Language Resources and Evaluation (LREC)*, pages 2216–2219.

Joakim Nivre, Laura Rimell, Ryan McDonald, and Carlos Gómez Rodríguez. 2010. Evaluation of dependency parsers on unbounded dependencies. In *Proceedings of the 23rd International Conference on Computational Linguistics (Coling 2010)*, pages 833–841.

Joakim Nivre. 2003. An efficient algorithm for projective dependency parsing. In *Proceedings of the 8th International Workshop on Parsing Technologies (IWPT)*, pages 149–160.

Joakim Nivre. 2009. Non-projective dependency parsing in expected linear time. In *Proceedings of the Joint Conference of the 47th Annual Meeting of the ACL and the 4th International Joint Conference on Natural Language Processing of the AFNLP (ACL-IJCNLP)*, pages 351–359.

Slav Petrov and Dan Klein. 2007. Improved inference for unlexicalized parsing. In *Proceedings of Human Language Technologies: The Annual Conference of the North American Chapter of the Association for Computational Linguistics (NAACL HLT)*, pages 404–411.

Slav Petrov, Leon Barrett, Romain Thibaux, and Dan Klein. 2006. Learning accurate, compact, and interpretable tree annotation. In *Proceedings of the 21st International Conference on Computational Linguistics and the 44th Annual Meeting of the Association for Computational Linguistics*, pages 433–440.

Sebastian Riedel, Ruket Çakıcı, and Ivan Meza-Ruiz. 2006. Multi-lingual dependency parsing with incremental integer linear programming. In *Proceedings of the 10th Conference on Computational Natural Language Learning (CoNLL)*, pages 226–230.

Stephan Riezler, Margaret H. King, Ronald M. Kaplan, Richard Crouch, John T. Maxwell III, and Mark Johnson. 2002. Parsing the Wall Street Journal using a Lexical-Functional Grammar and discriminative estimation techniques. In *Proceedings of the 40th Annual Meeting of the Association for Computational Linguistics (ACL)*, pages 271–278.

Laura Rimell, Stephen Clark, and Mark Steedman. 2009. Unbounded dependency recovery for parser evaluation. In *Proceedings of the 2009 Conference on Empirical Methods in Natural Language Processing*, pages 813–821.

Kenji Sagae and Alon Lavie. 2006. Parser combination by reparsing. In *Proceedings of the Human Language Technology Conference of the NAACL, Companion Volume: Short Papers*, pages 129–132.

Kenji Sagae and Jun'ichi Tsujii. 2008. Shift-reduce dependency DAG parsing. In *Proceedings of the 22nd International Conference on Computational Linguistics (COLING)*, pages 753–760.

André Filipe Torres Martins, Dipanjan Das, Noah A. Smith, and Eric P. Xing. 2008. Stacking dependency parsers. In *Proceedings of the Conference on Empirical Methods in Natural Language Processing (EMNLP)*, pages 157–166.

Hiroyasu Yamada and Yuji Matsumoto. 2003. Statistical dependency analysis with support vector machines. In *Proceedings of the 8th International Workshop on Parsing Technologies (IWPT)*, pages 195–206.

Daniel Zeman and Zdeněk Žabokrtský. 2005. Improving parsing accuracy by combining diverse dependency parsers. In *Proceedings of the 9th International Workshop on Parsing Technologies (IWPT)*, pages 171–178.

Yue Zhang and Stephen Clark. 2008. A tale of two parsers: Investigating and combining graph-based and transition-based dependency parsing. In *Proceedings of the Conference on Empirical Methods in Natural Language Processing (EMNLP)*, pages 562–571.

Yue Zhang and Joakim Nivre. 2011. Transition-based parsing with rich non-local features. In *Proceedings of the 49th Annual Meeting of the Association for Computational Linguistics (ACL)*.

ISSN 1736-6305 Vol. 11
http://hdl.handle.net/10062/16955

Discourse Structures and Language Technologies

Bonnie Webber
Institute for Language, Cognition and Computation
School of Informatics, University of Edinburgh
bonnie.webber@ed.ac.uk

1   Introduction

I want to tell a story about computational approaches to discourse structure. Like all such stories, it takes some liberty with actual events and times, but I think stories put things into perspective, and make it easier to understand where we are and how we might progress.

Part 1 of the story (Section 2) is the past. Here we see early computational work on discourse structure aiming to assign a simple tree structure to a discourse. At issue was what its internal nodes corresponded to. The debate was fierce, and suggestions that other structures might be more appropriate were ignored or subjected to ridicule. The main uses of discourse structure were text generation and summarization, but mostly in small-scale experiments.

Part 2 of the story (Section 3) is the present. We now see different types of discourse structure being recognized, though perhaps not always clearly distinguished. An increasing number of credible efforts are aimed at recognizing these structures automatically, though performance on unrestricted text still resembles that of the early days of robust parsing. Generic applications are also beginning to appear, as researchers recognize the value of these structures to tasks of interest to them.

Part 3 of the story (Section 4) is the future. We now see the need for a mid-line between approaches hostage to theory and empirical approaches free of theory. An empirical approach underpinned by theory will not only motivate sensible back-off strategies in the face of unseen data, but also enable us to understand how the different discourse structures inter-relate and thereby to exploit their mutual recognition. This should allow more challenging applications, such as improving the performance of statistical machine translation (SMT) through the extended locality of discourse structures and the linguistic phenomena they correlate with.

2   Early computatational approaches to discourse structure

Early computational work generally assumed discourse structure had an underlying tree structure, similar to the parse tree of a sentence. At issue was what its internal nodes and other formal properties corresponded to. In Rhetorical Structure Theory (Mann and Thompson, 1988), used in both text generation (Scott and de Souza, 1990; Moore, 1995; O'Donnell et al., 2001) and analysis (Marcu, 1996; Marcu, 2000), an internal node corresponded to a rhetorical relation holding between the text units associated with its daughters, and *precedence* corresponded to their order in the text. In work on generating task instructions (Dale, 1992), each internal node corresponded to the next step to take to accomplish the plan associated with its parent. In (Grosz and Sidner, 1986), which I will return to in Section 4, internal nodes corresponded to speaker intentions, with *dominance* in the tree corresponding to a daughter node's intention supporting that of its parent and *precedence* corresponding to one intention needing to be accomplished before another. The internal nodes in (Moser and Moore, 1996) reflected an attempt to reconcile Grosz and Sidner's approach with that of Mann and Thompson.

Work that attempted to show that a simple linear model might be a better account for types of expository text (Sibun, 1992) was, by and large, ignored.

3   Current computatational approaches to discourse

As well as further elaboration of recursive discourse structures (Asher and Lascarides, 2003; Polanyi et al., 2004), current computational approaches have focussed on discourse structures more easily linked to data: structure associated with changes in *topic*, structure associated with the *function* of the parts of a text within a given genre, and structure associated with what one might call *higher-order* predicate-argument relations or *discourse relations*.

3.1   Topic structure

Expository text can be viewed as a linear sequence of *topically coherent* segments (sequences of sentences), where the sequence of topics is either specific to a text or conventionalized (Figure 1).

Interest in topic structure originally came from its perceived potential to improve information retrieval (Hearst, 1994; Hearst, 1997). More recent interest comes from its potential use in segmenting lectures, meetings or other speech events, making them more amenable to search (Galley et al., 2003; Malioutov and Barzilay, 2006).

Computational approaches to topic segmentation all assume that: (1) Relations hold between the topic of discourse segments and the topic of the discourse as a whole (eg, History of Vermont → Vermont). (2) The only relation holding between sister segments, if any, is sequence, though certain sequences may be more common than others (Figure 1). (3) The topic of a segment will differ from those of its adjacent sisters. (Adjacent spans that share a topic will belong to the same segment.) (4) Topic predicts lexical choice, either of all the words of a segment or just of its content words (ie, excluding "stop-words").

Making topic structure explicit (ie, topic segmentation) is based on either **semantic-relatedness**, where each segment is taken to consist of words more related to each other than to words outside the segment (Hearst, 1994; Hearst, 1997; Choi et al., 2001; Bestgen, 2006; Galley et al., 2003; Malioutov and Barzilay, 2006) or **topic models**, where each segment is taken to be produced by a distinct, compact lexical distribution (Purver et al., 2006; Eisenstein and Barzilay, 2008; Chen et al., 2009).

3.2   Function-based structure

Texts within a given genre (eg, news reports, errata, scientific papers, letters to the editor, etc.) generally share a similar structure that is independent of topic and reflects the **function** played by each of its parts. Best known is the *inverted pyramid* of news reports, consisting of a headline; a lead paragraph, conveying *who* is involved, *what* happened, *when* it happened, *where* it happened, *why* it happened, and (optionally) *how* it happened; a body that provides more detail; and a tail, containing less important information. This is why the first (ie, lead) paragraph can provide the best *extractive summary* of a news report.

In the genre of scientific papers (and, more recently, their abstracts), high-level structure comprises the following ordered sections: *Objective* (also called *Introduction, Background, Aim,* or *Hypothesis*); *Methods* (also called *Method, Study Design,* or *Methodology*); *Results* (also called *Outcomes*); *Discussion* and optionally, *Conclusions*. This does not mean that every sentence within a section realises the same function: Fine-grained functional characterizations of scientific papers (Liakata et al., 2010; Teufel, 2010) show a range of functions served by the sentences in a section.

Interest in automatic annotation of functional structure comes from its value for summarization (noted above), sentiment analysis, where words may have an objective sense in one section and a subjective sense in another (Taboada et al., 2009), and citation analysis, where a citation may mean different things in different sections (Teufel, 2010).

As with computational models of topic-based structure, computational models of function-based structure make assumptions that may or may not actually hold: (1) Relations hold between the function of a segment and that of the discourse as a whole: While relations may hold between sisters (eg, *Methods* constrain *Results*), only sequence has been used in modelling. (2) Function predicts more than lexical choice: it can predict indicative phrases such as "results show" (→ *Results*) or indicative stop-words such as "then" (→

	Wisconsin	Louisiana	Vermont
1	Etymology	Etymology	Geography
2	History	Geography	History
3	Geography	History	Demographics
4	Demographics	Demographics	Economy
5	Law and government	Economy	Transportation
6	Economy	Law and government	Media
7	Municipalities	Education	Utilities
8	Education	Sports	Law and government
9	Culture	Culture	Public Health

Figure 1: Structure of Wikipedia articles about US states, as shown in sub-headings

Method). (3) Functional segments usually appear in a specific order, so either sentence position is a feature used in modelling or sequential models are used..

While the internal structure of a functional segment has usually been ignored in high-level modeling (Chung, 2009; Lin et al., 2006; McKnight and Srinivasan, 2003; Ruch et al., 2007), (Hirohata et al., 2008) found that assuming that properties of the first sentence of a segment differ from those of the rest (as in 'BIO' approaches to Named Entity Recognition) leads to improved performance in segmentation (ie, 94.3% per sentence accuracy vs. 93.3%).

While most functional modelling has been on biomedical text, where texts with explicitly labelled sections serve as "free" training data for segmenting unlabelled texts, there has also been some work on functional segmentation of legal texts and student essays.

3.3 "Higher-order" pred-arg structure

The third type of discourse structure receiving significant attention from the computational world is what can be called *higher-order* predicate-argument structure, or structure associated with *discourse relations*. Whereas at the sentence level, pred-arg structures are usually headed by a verb (Kingsbury and Palmer, 2002) or a noun (Gerber et al., 2009), predicate-argument structures in discourse are usually headed by a discourse connective — eg, a conjunction like *because* or *but*, or a discourse adverbial like *nevertheless* or *instead*.

And just as pred-arg relations within a sentence can conveyed through adjacency (eg, English noun-noun modifiers such as *container ship crane operator courses* – courses to train operators of cranes that load/unload ships whose cargo is packed in containers), pred-arg relations in discourse can be conveyed through adjacency between clauses or sentences.

The Penn Discourse TreeBank is currently the largest resource manually annotated for discourse connectives, their arguments, and the senses they convey (Prasad et al., 2008). Related resources are also being created for Modern Standard Arabic (Al-Saif and Markert, 2010), Chinese (Xue, 2005), Czech (Mladová et al., 2008), Danish and Italian parallel treebanks (Buch-Kromann and Korzen, 2010), Dutch (van der Vliet et al., 2011), German (Stede, 2004; Stede, 2008), Hindi (Oza et al., 2009), and Turkish (Zeyrek et al., 2010).

The potential value of being able to automatically recognize these discourse relations, their arguments and their senses comes from their help in question generation (Mannem et al., 2010), extractive summarization (Louis et al., 2010) and sentiment detection (Taboada et al., 2009). So efforts are increasing to automatically recognize them (Elwell and Baldridge, 2008; Lin et al., 2010; Pitler et al., 2008; Pitler et al., 2009; Pitler and Nenkova, 2009; Prasad et al., 2010; Wellner and Pustejovsky, 2007; Wellner, 2008).

4 Future computatational approaches to discourse

This story closes with some speculations about the future. I have sketched a past in which computational approaches to discourse structure were hostage to theory and a present in which they are essentially free of theory. What we really want is an empirical approach underpinned by theory, that allows us to understand (at the very least) the ways in which the various types of discourse structures fit together. Early on, (Grosz and Sidner, 1986) attempted to meld a theory of intention-based discourse structure with a theory of attentional structure (ie, what the conversational participants were attending to), but the link between theory and data was not sufficiently robust. Later attempts to link multiple discourse structures were motivated by purely practical concerns. (Marcu, 2000) used semantic-relatedness methods from topic segmentation to decide what RST-relation to assign to adjacent non-elementary text spans because he could find no other way to do so reliably. (Schilder, 2002) just assumed that RST-relations could only be computed reliably for elementary spans (ie, single clauses or sentences), and used semantic-relatedness methods for other decisions. More recently, (Louis et al., 2010) have shown that features based on RST text structures complement those from *discourse relations* when it comes to choosing sentences for extractive summaries that are similar to those chosen manually.

While these purely practical links between discourse structures clearly lead to better performance in applications, extensive improvements can, I think, only come with a more theoretically-grounded understanding of how the different types of discourse structure fit together.

References

Amal Al-Saif and Katja Markert. 2010. The Leeds Arabic Discourse Treebank. In *Proc. of the 7th Int'l Conference on Language Resources and Evaluation*, Valletta, Malta.

Nicholas Asher and Alex Lascarides. 2003. *Logics of Conversation*. Cambridge University Press.

Yves Bestgen. 2006. Improving text segmentation using Latent Semantic Analysis: A reanalysis of Choi, Wiemer-Hastings, and Moore (2001). *Computational Linguistics*, 32(1):5–12.

Matthias Buch-Kromann and Iørn Korzen. 2010. The unified annotation of syntax and discourse in the Copenhagen Dependency Treebanks. In *Proc. 4th Linguistic Annotation Workshop*, pages 127–131, Uppsala, Sweden.

Harr Chen, S. R. K. Branavan, Regina Barzilay, and David Karger. 2009. Global models of document structure using latent permutations. In *Proc. HLT/NAACL*, pages 371–379.

Freddy Y. Y. Choi, Peter Wiemer-Hastings, and Johanna Moore. 2001. Latent Semantic Analysis for text segmentation. In *Proc. of the Conference on Empirical Methods in Natural Language Processing*, pages 109–117.

Grace Chung. 2009. Sentence retrieval for abstracts of randomized controlled trials. *BMC Medical Informatics and Decision Making*, 10(9), February.

Robert Dale. 1992. *Generating Referring Expressions*. MIT Press, Cambridge MA.

Jacob Eisenstein and Regina Barzilay. 2008. Bayesian unsupervised topic segmentation. In *Proc. of the Conference on Empirical Methods in Natural Language Processing*, pages 334–343.

Robert Elwell and Jason Baldridge. 2008. Discourse connective argument identification with connective specific rankers. In *Proc. IEEE Conference on Semantic Computing (ICSC-08)*, Santa Clara CA.

Michel Galley, Kathleen McKeown, Eric Fosler-Lussier, and Hongyan Jing. 2003. Discourse segmentation of multi-party conversation. In *Proc. 41st Annual Meeting of the ACL*, pages 562–569.

Matt Gerber, Joyce Chai, and Adam Meyers. 2009. The role of implicit argumentation in nominal srl. In *Proc. HLT/ACL*, pages 146–154, Boulder CO.

Barbara Grosz and Candy Sidner. 1986. Attention, intention, and the structure of discourse. *Computational Linguistics*, 12(3):175–204.

Marti Hearst. 1994. Multi-paragraph segmentation of expository text. In *Proc. 32nd Annual Meeting of the ACL*, pages 9–16.

Marti Hearst. 1997. TextTiling. *Computational Linguistics*, 23(1):33–64.

Kenji Hirohata, Naoki Okazaki, Sophia Ananiadou, and Mitsuru Ishizuka. 2008. Identifying sections in scientic abstracts using conditional random fields. In *Proc 3rd Int'l Joint Conference on Natural Language Processing*, pages 381–388.

Paul Kingsbury and Martha Palmer. 2002. From treebank to propbank. In *Proc. 3rd Int'l Conference on Language Resources and Evaluation*, Las Palmas.

Maria Liakata, Simone Teufel, Advaith Siddharthan, and Colin Batchelor. 2010. Corpora for the conceptualisation and zoning of scientific papers. In *Proc. 7th Conference on Language Resources and Evaluation*, Valletta, Malta.

Jimmy Lin, Damianos Karakos, Dina Demner-Fushman, and Sanjeev Khudanpur. 2006. Generative content models for structural analysis of medical abstracts. In *Proc. HLT-NAACL Workshop on BioNLP*, pages 65–72.

Ziheng Lin, Hwee Tou Ng, , and Min-Yen Kan. 2010. A PDTB-styled end-to-end discourse parser. Technical Report 1011.0835, TRB8/10, arXiv.

Annie Louis, Aravind Joshi, and Ani Nenkova. 2010. Discourse indicators for content selection in summarization. In *Proc. SIGDIAL*, pages 147–156, Tokyo.

Igor Malioutov and Regina Barzilay. 2006. Minimum cut model for spoken lecture segmentation. In *Proc. 21st International COLING Conference and 44th Annual Meeting of the ACL*.

William Mann and Sandra Thompson. 1988. Rhetorical Structure Theory: Toward a functional theory of text organization. *Text*, 8(3):243–281.

Prashanth Mannem, Rashmi Prasad, and Aravind Joshi. 2010. Question generation from paragraphs at upenn. In *Proc. 3rd Workshop on Question Generation (QG2010)*, Pittsburgh PA.

Daniel Marcu. 1996. Building up Rhetorical Structure Trees. In *Proc. AAAI*, pages 1069–1074, Portland OR.

Daniel Marcu. 2000. The rhetorical parsing of unrestricted texts. *Computational Linguistics*, 26(3):395–448.

Larry McKnight and Padmini Srinivasan. 2003. Categorization of sentence types in medical abstracts. In *Proceedings of the AMIA Annual Symposium*, pages 440–444.

Lucie Mladová, Šárka Zikánová, and Eva Hajičová. 2008. From sentence to discourse: Building an annotation scheme for discourse based on the Prague Dependency Treebank. In *Proc. 6th Int'l Conference on Language Resources and Evaluation*.

Johanna Moore. 1995. *Participating in Explanatory Dialogues*. MIT Press, Cambridge MA.

Megan Moser and Johanna Moore. 1996. Toward a synthesis of two accounts of discourse structure. *Computational Linguistics*, 22(3):409–419.

M. O'Donnell, C. Mellish, J. Oberlander, and A. Knott. 2001. Ilex: an architecture for a dynamic hypertext generation system. *Natural Language Engineering*, 7:225–250.

Umangi Oza, Rashmi Prasad, Sudheer Kolachina, Dipti Misra Sharma, and Aravind Joshi. 2009. The Hindi Discourse Relation Bank. In *Proc. 3rd ACL Language Annotation Workshop*, Singapore.

Emily Pitler and Ani Nenkova. 2009. Using syntax to disambiguate explicit discourse connectives in text. In *Proc. 47th Meeting of the ACL and 4th Int'l Joint Conference on Natural Language Processing*.

Emily Pitler, Mridhula Raghupathy, Hena Mehta, Ani Nenkova, Alan Lee, and Aravind Joshi. 2008. Easily identifiable discourse relations. In *Proceedings of COLING*, Manchester.

Emily Pitler, Annie Louis, and Ani Nenkova. 2009. Automatic sense prediction for implicit discourse relations in text. In *Proc. 47th Meeting of the ACL and 4th Int'l Joint Conference on Natural Language Processing*.

Livia Polanyi, Chris Culy, Martin van den Berg, Gian Lorenzo Thione, and David Ahn. 2004. Sentential structure and discourse parsing. In *In Proceedings of the ACL 2004 Workshop on Discourse Annotation*.

Rashmi Prasad, Nikhil Dinesh, Alan Lee, Eleni Miltsakaki, and et al. 2008. The Penn Discourse Treebank 2.0. In *Proc. of the 6th Int'l Conference on Language Resources and Evaluation*, Marrakech.

Rashmi Prasad, Aravind Joshi, and Bonnie Webber. 2010. Exploiting scope for shallow discourse parsing. In *Proc. 7th Int'l Conference on Language Resources and Evaluation*, Valletta, Malta.

Matthew Purver, Konrad Körding, Thomas Griffiths, and Joshua Tenenbaum. 2006. Unsupervised topic modelling for multi-party spoken discourse. In *Proc. 21st COLING and 44th Annual Meeting of the ACL*, pages 17–24, Sydney.

Patrick Ruch, Celia Boyer, Christine Chichester, Imad Tbahriti, Antoine Geissbühler, Paul Fabry, and et al. 2007. Using argumentation to extract key sentences from biomedical abstracts. *International Journal of Medical Informatics*, 76(2–3):195–200.

Frank Schilder. 2002. Robust discourse parsing via discourse markers, topicality and position. *Natural Language Engineering*, 8(3):235–255.

Donia Scott and Clarisse Sieckenius de Souza. 1990. Getting the message across in RST-based text generation. In Robert Dale, Chris Mellish, and Michael Zock, editors, *Current Research in Natural Language Generation*, pages 47–73. Academic Press, London, England.

Penni Sibun. 1992. Generating text without trees. *Computational Intelligence*, 8(1):102–122.

Manfred Stede. 2004. The Potsdam Commentary Corpus. In *ACL Workshop on Discourse Annotation*, Barcelona, Spain.

Manfred Stede. 2008. Disambiguating rhetorical structure. *Research on Language and Computation*, 6:311–332.

Maite Taboada, J. Brooke, and Manfred Stede. 2009. Genre-based paragraph classification for sentiment analysis. In *Proc. 10th SIGDIAL Conference on Discourse and Dialogue*, pages 62–70, London.

Simone Teufel. 2010. *The Structure of Scientific Articles*. CSLI Publications, Stanford CA.

Nynke van der Vliet, Ildikó Berzlánovich, Gosse Bouma, Markus Egg, and Gisela Redeker. 2011. Building a discourse-annotated Dutch text corpus. In *Beyond Semantics: Corpus-based Investigations of Pragmatic and Discourse Phenomena*, Gottingen.

Ben Wellner and James Pustejovsky. 2007. Automatically identifying the arguments of discourse connectives. In *Proc. Conference on Empirical Methods in Natural Language Processing*.

Ben Wellner. 2008. *Sequence Models and Ranking Methods for Discourse Parsing*. Ph.D. thesis, Brandeis University.

Nianwen Xue. 2005. Annotating discourse connectives in the Chinese Treebank. In *Proc. ACL Workshop in Frontiers in Annotation II*, Ann Arbor MI.

Deniz Zeyrek, Işın Demirşahin, Ayışığı Sevdik-Çallı, Hale Ögel Balaban, İhsan Yalçınkaya, and Ümut Deniz Turan. 2010. The annotation scheme of the Turkish Discourse Bank and an evaluation of inconsistent annotations. In *Proc. 4th Linguistic Annotation Workshop*, Uppsala, Sweden.

ISSN 1736-6305 Vol. 11
http://hdl.handle.net/10062/16955

II Regular Papers

Identification of Sense Selection in Regular Polysemy Using Shallow Features

Héctor Martínez Alonso,
Bolette Sandford Pedersen
University of Copenhagen
Copenhagen, Denmark

`alonso@hum.ku.dk`
`bsp@hum.ku.dk`

Núria Bel
Universitat Pompeu Fabra
Barcelona, Spain

`nuria.bel@upf.edu`

Abstract

The following work describes a method to automatically classify the sense selection of the complex type Location/Organization –which depends on regular polysemy– using shallow features, as well as a way to increase the volume of sense-selection gold standards by using monosemous data as filler. The classifier results show that grammatical features are the most relevant cues for the identification of sense selection in this instance of regular polysemy.

1 Introduction

In this paper we report on our experiments to automatically assess the distributional evidence that allow the recognition of sense selection for regular polysemy, focusing on the Location/Organization alternation or *dot type* (Pustejovsky, 1995). Broadly speaking, regular polysemy involves the predictable alternation between senses in a systematic way for a significant number of words, i.e. a semantic class or type (cf. section 2). The definition of dot type is further elaborated in 2.1.

The analysis of this data has been implemented by applying a decision tree classifier to the shallow features obtained from a set of occurrences of dot-type words in order to obtain their selected sense. In this aspect, our work is akin to Word Sense Disambiguation (WSD) but it includes an attempt to identify underspecified senses. The machine-learning strategy is also different from state-of-the-art WSD, as seen in sections 3 and 4.

We also propose a method to increase the volume of gold-standard training data by using monosemous words as an aid to provide distribu-

tional information of one of the possible senses in a sense alternation.

The results are expected to give pointers on how to face a general approach for the computational treatment of cases of regular polysemy described as the sense selection of dot types, along with the recognition and tagging of dot predication. The technical application of this research can be used to improve results on information retrieval, semantic role annotation, etc.

2 Regular polysemy

Regular polysemy is known by several names throughout the literature: *logical, complementary* or *systematic polysemy* or even *logical metonymy*.

The wordings are naturally different and may be slightly nuanced, as can be seen by comparing Apresjan's definition (1974, p. 18): "*For any word that has a meaning of type 'A', is true that it can be used in a meaning of type 'B' as well [...] Regular polysemy is triggered by metonymy, whereas irregular polysemy is triggered by other metaphorical processes.*"

...with Pustejovsky's definition (1995, p. 28): "*I will define logical polysemy as a complementary ambiguity where there is no change of lexical category, and the multiple senses of the word have overlapping, dependent or shared meanings.*"

From these definitions we understand regular polysemy as a phenomenon whereby a word that belongs to a semantic type can act as a member of another semantic type without incurring in metaphor, as this change of type is the result of metonymy. Some well known examples are:

a) Container for content: *He drank a whole glass.*

b) Property for subject of property: *The authorities arrived quickly.*
c) Producer for product: *I drive a Honda.*
d) Location for organization: *France elects a new president.*

This differentiates regular polysemy from what is traditionally referred as polysemy (*irregular polysemy* according to Apresjan), which is more often metaphorical in nature and is sometimes pooled together with homonymy as in the cases of "*olive pit*" vs. "*tar pit*" or "*sand bank*" vs. "*federal bank*".

2.1 Dot type

The Generative Lexicon or GL (Pustejovsky, 1995) is a theoretical framework of lexical semantics that tackles the description of the generativity of word meaning. The GL introduces a series of theoretical objects like *qualia structure*, *type coercion* and *dot type*.

The dot type is, according to the GL a type of noun that is simultaneously a member of more than one semantic class. According to Rumshisky (2007), the senses –i.e. classes or types– that a dot object presents are metonymically related to one another. This means that the relation between the semantic classes of a dot type is one of regular polysemy. Some examples of dot types are:

e) *book* : Artifact/Information
f) *construction* : Process/Result
g) *chicken*: Animal/Food
h) *country*: Location/Organization

A dot type selects one or more of its possible senses when placed in a context, as shown by the following examples from the American National Corpus or ANC (Ide and Macleod, 2001):

i) *Manuel died in exile in 1932 in England.*
j) *England was being kept busy with other concerns*
k) *England was, after all, an important wine market*

In case i), *England* selects the Location sense, whereas in case j) it selects the Organization sense. In k) however, the sense of *England* is both "*the English organizations*" and "*the English territory*". We use the name *dot predication* for the instances of a dot type that do not have one of the possible senses as most salient, as in k), which can be seen a kind of underspecification.

In spite of the GL's computational perspective, Natural Language Processing (NLP) implementations that examine the actual computational feasibility of the GL are few. Moreover,

there is no overt attempt to identify the possible three behaviors of a dot type, as the dot predication has not been computationally tackled, which is related to the lack of strategies to capture meaning underspecification.

3 State of the art

The computational study of systematic polysemy has been geared to the collapsing of senses (Vossen et al., 1999; Buitelaar, 1998; Tomuro, 2001) prior to Word Sense Disambiguation (WSD). The best performance in WSD is obtained by supervised methods that require a very large amount of annotated learning data. The other main approach is to use a lexical knowledge base such as WordNet and a Page-Rank algorithm to compute the most likely sense in the sense enumeration of the lexical knowledge base (Agirre and Soroa, 2009). WordNet does not include the Location/Organization alternation in geopolitical locations, so the task at hands falls outside the traditional scope of WSD.

The field of Named Entity Recognition (NER) shows two different approaches to regular-polysemy based sense alternations. In their account, Johannessen et al. (2005) differentiate what they call the *Form over Function* and the *Function over Form* strategy. Some NER systems assign a constant value to a word type, enforcing what Finkel et al. (2005) call *label consistency*, namely *Form over Function*. The *Function over Form* strategy, however, assigns a semantic type to the analyzed word depending on how it behaves in each context and is analogous to the work exposed in this article.

A class of nominals that shows regular polysemy and is well studied is the deverbal noun (*destruction*, *examination*), which has distinct grammatical features that can help pinpoint its reading as either process or result, as covered in theory by Grimshaw (1990) and computationally acknowledged by Peris et al. (2009).

There is also recent work in the identification of metonymy (Markert and Nissim, 2009) as well as other Generative-Lexicon based sense-disambiguation works, such as Rumshisky et al. (2007) or Pustejovsky et al. (2010). Disambiguation systems, however, are still coping with the need of a representation and recognition of underspecification (Pustejovsky, 2009).

The SIMPLE lexicon (Lenci et al., 2000) is a GL-compliant lexicon for twelve European languages. It describes its lexical items in terms of their position within a type ontology as well as a qualia structure. SIMPLE list the *Geopolitical Location* class as a class associated to a complex type *<Location,Human_Group>*, which expresses the dot-type ambiguity of words of this class. Words that are considered geopolitical locations can be proper (*Africa, Boston, China*) or common (*city, nation, state,* etc) nouns.

4 Experiment

We propose a classification experiment that identifies the senses of Location/Organization words by firstly characterizing the grammatical and lexical features of each and using the extracted features as input for a decision tree classifier. Our experiment can be regarded as a case of WSD in which all disambiguated words can have a Location sense, an Organization sense, or a mixed or underspecified sense which corresponds to the dot predication.

Let *t* be the analyzed token of a sentence – the *headword* in WSD jargon–, which belongs to the dot type Location/Organization. The goal of the task is to determine whether each *t* has the Location or Organization sense, or rather, if it exhibits a mixed or underspecified behavior, i.e. a dot predication.

The goal of the experiment is to assess the distribution of the complex type Location/Organization and its sense selection in a series of occurrences of proper names for geopolitical locations. A supervised method has been chosen, as this specific phenomenon was expected to require a smaller volume of training data than the general case of supervised WSD.

Markert and Nissim (2009) assume in their metonymy resolution account that the semantic class of the analyzed nouns was already known; claiming that standard NER can be followed by metonymy resolution. We have taken the same assumption and also chosen named entities to build our datasets following their claim that "*Named entities [...] are also very often used figuratively but not listed in dictionaries*".

After evaluating the SensEval-2007 results, Markert and Nissim (2009) acknowledge the difficulty of identifying specific cases of metonymy for Location and Organization words, and we have considered derived metonymies from a given class as symptoms ·of the class itself. For instance, if an Organization type appears very often as a subject, it is very likely to be experiencing the *org-for-members* metonymy, which we do not separate from the Organization-type behavior, but instead count the presence of

the word as subject as a potential indicator of its ORG sense.

A total of 2132 instances of Location/Organization words were obtained from the ANC from the occurrences of high-frequency (>500) nouns: Each of the instances was manually identified to obtain their selected sense: *Location, Organization* or *Dot,* henceforth LOC, ORG and DOT.

Only one annotator has tagged the data, but Market and Nissim offer a rationale for using one annotator for such coarse-grained distinctions, because they identify an inter-encoder agreement of 0.88. Noise examples (homonymies like *China* being a part of a larger named entity like *AOL China*) were discarded.

For any given instance of a proper noun X, it was seen if it could be acceptably (albeit possibly in an awkward manner) paraphrased as "*the territory of X*" (LOC) or "*the institutions of X*" (ORG). If both applied, it was considered a dot predication (DOT).

4.1 Boosting dataset

The initial distribution of senses is skewed on the side of LOC. In order to balance the Location/Organization distribution of senses, 200 occurrences of *CIA, Microsoft, NATO* and *Pentagon* (also high-frequency words in the ANC) were added because they are purely Organization words that only have Location sense if they experience the *organization-for-headquarters* metonymy, which has not been accounted for. This provides the final distribution of senses in the gold-standard data. It is expected that the Organization sense of the dot types has a similar distributional behavior to the purely Organization-typed word, which allows us to compensate the asymmetry of the data. This has created two different datasets, *Total-dots*, which only has occurrences of words belonging to dot types, and *Total-boost*, which also includes the 800 rows of Organization-type words.

4.2 Distribution of senses

The sense distribution is as follows:

	LOC	ORG	DOT	Total
Afghanistan	213	12	60	285
Africa	110	11	18	139
America	69	70	65	204
Boston	121	2	25	148
California	88	16	61	165
Canada	91	43	69	203
China	60	80	27	167
England	86	21	41	148
Europe	151	32	59	242
Germany	123	62	62	247
London	102	6	76	184
Total-dots	**1214**	**355**	**563**	**2132**
CIA	0	200	0	200
Microsoft	0	200	0	200
NATO	0	200	0	200
Pentagon	0	200	0	200
Total-boost	**1214**	**1155**	**563**	**2932**

Table 1: distribution of senses for the two datasets

As it can be seen, some lexical elements are much more often Location, which is their fundamental type, but the Organization reading is more common, for instance, for country names. It can also be seen that each lexical item has a different distribution of senses.

5 Feature space

The features have been extracted from the POS-tagged, XML version of the ANC with noun chunks, the only source of external information for feature extraction system is the WordSketch (Kilgarrif et al, 2004), which has only been used to establish the nominal word space. No other external resources like Frame-Net or WordNet have been used, following Markert and Nissim's (2009) claim that grammatical features tend to be the most discriminating features. For similar remarks, cf. Peris (2009), Rumshisky (2007).

The hypotheses that regular polysemy alternations are often determined at subphrasal level can contradict traditional WSD algorithms like Page Rank, which have a larger scope of analysis. Selection of metonymical senses falls outside of the One-sense-per-discourse approach (Gale et al., 1992), since such approach has been phrased re-

ferring to irregular polysemy like *"olive pit"* vs. *"tar pit"*.

5.1 Lexical and grammatical features

Extracted features are meant to describe the dot type Location/Organization, be it by its grammatical behavior or the lexical environmental that words of this type appear in.

So-called grammatical features describe aspects of the structure of the headword's NP, its position within the sentence, the relative presence of verbs and punctuations, and most importantly, the presence of prepositions before the headword t. Prepositions are regarded as function words and therefore considered part of the grammar.

Lexical features list the words that appear around the instances of the dot type. In order to increase the recall of the system, a set of verbs and nouns from the word sketch of the words *city*, *country* and *continent* –hypernyms for the dot types in the training data– was obtained.

A word sketch is a corpus-based automatic summary of a word's grammatical and collocational behavior obtained using the Sketch Engine tool (Kilgarrif et al, 2004). Each binary feature informs of the presence of one of the mentioned lemmas in the whole sentence. The verbs were taken from the *object_of* and *subject_of* relations, whereas the nouns were taken from the *n_modifier, modifies, posession, pp_obj_of-p* and *pp_of-p*. Only common nouns have been used. To avoid overfitting the experiment to the sample by using the lexical environment of the analyzed word themselves, the BNC (British National Corpus, distributed by Oxford University Computing Services on behalf of the BNC Consortium) was used. The usage of a lexical environment to assist the disambiguation of a dot type follows Rumshisky (2007).

country (noun)   bnc freq = 47969

object_of	4871	1.1	subject_of	4322	1.7	adj_subject_of	1046	1.9
flee	70	8.29	ratify	17	6.68	concerned	89	7.34
tour	37	7.51	afford	34	6.62	dependent	21	6.84
visit	102	7.36	border	15	6.54	willing	16	6.36
govern	47	7.22	sign	47	6.29	prepared	18	6.2
rule	47	7.21	experience	34	6.21	capable	8	5.75
leave	332	6.9	benefit	22	6.2	involved	19	5.49
divide	50	6.67	export	15	6.16	rich	10	5.39
represent	94	6.57	suffer	45	6.11	unable	10	5.09
defend	28	6.38	participate	15	6.1	poor	15	4.98

Figure 1: word sketch for "country"

5.2 List of features

Following Joanis et al. (2006), the occurrences have been characterized in order to assess the amount of semantic information that their distributional data can provide. The total size of the feature space is of 317 binary features, divided as follows:

1. NP-traits (6 features): which describe the internal structure of the NP where t appears. The features indicate the presence of an adjective in the NP, of a common noun before or after t, of a genitive mark after t, of a coordinate "*X and Y*" and the presence of an article at the beginning of the NP.
2. Position of t (2 features): t being the first or last token of the sentence.
3. Prepositions before t (57 features): each binary feature indicates whether the NP where t is included is introduced by a preposition. The list of checked prepositions it the one used by the Preposition Project (Litkowski and Hargraves, 2005).
4. Previous and next token after t's NP (4 features): each binary feature describes whether the previous or next token is either a comma or a parenthesis.
5. Verb after of before t (2 features): informs whether there is a verb immediately before t, or whether there is a modal or non-modal verb thereafter.
6. Lexical space (243 features): The nouns and verbs obtained from the hypernyms' word sketch.

5.3 Classifier runs

In order to establish a classifier, C.45 pruned decision trees from the Weka (Witten and Frank, 2005) implementation were used, as in Resnik and Bel (2009). Decision trees provide an analysis of the importance of the features for a given class, and are more adequate for sparse enviroments than other families of algorithms (Quinlan, 1993). Due to the relatively small amount of data, performance was evaluated by means of 10-fold cross-validation instead of keeping separate training and test sets.

The six classifier runs can be paired in three groups:

1. *Allthree*: 3-way identification of LOC, ORG and DOT senses from the *Total-dots* and the *Total-boost* datasets.
2. *Loc/Org*: Binary identification of LOC and ORG senses from the *Total-dots* and the *Total-boost* datasets, discarding occurrences tagged as DOT.
3. *Dot/NoDot*: Binary identification of DOT classes from the *Total-dots* and the *Total-boost* datasets, treating both cases of LOC and ORG selection as a NODOT sense.

6 Evaluation

The following section details the importance of the lexical features for the construction of the decision tree, as well as the performance measures of the classifier.

6.1 Impact of lexical features

This section details the relevance of the lexical features for the decision tree classifier, that is, how relevant the lexical environment is when choosing a possible sense. A very high prevalence of lexical features versus grammatical features would contradict the statement that grammatical features are often key to establish the sense selection of a dot type.

The following tables describe the dimensions of the resulting decision trees for the experiments. *Size of tree* indicates the number of nodes, *number of leaves* is the amount of nodes that assign a sense when reached during the decision process, and *lexical nodes* are those that correspond to one of the 243 lexical features in the feature space. Each binary feature generates two nodes when incorporated into the tree, so 15 lexical items will generate 30 lexical nodes in the decision tree.

	ALL	LOC/ORG	DOT
Size of tree	107	55	65
# leaves	54	28	33
# lexical nodes	38	16	12

Table 2: tree dimensions for Total-boost

	ALL	LOC/ORG	DOT
Size of tree	129	91	51
# leaves	65	46	26
# lexical nodes	30	18	18

Table 3: tree dimensions for Total-dot

The *Total-boost* data, although much larger than the *Total-dots* dataset, generates decision trees that have a very similar amount of lexical nodes. Lexical nodes are about a third of the total of nodes for a given tree, which always use all the grammatical features such as prepositions and the position of token *t* before anything else. Lexical nodes do not appear before the third level in the decision tree, as the first levels are occupied by grammatical features, with the exception of frequents word like *control*, *road* or *south*, which can appear at that level in the different decision trees. Figure 2 shows the first four levels of the LOC/ORG decision trees. The left branch of a given node indicates *feature=0* while right branch means *feature=1*. The nodes *p_in* and *p_from* and *p_to* represent the features that inform of the presence of the corresponding preposition before the headword. *L_paren* informs of the presence of a left parenthesis, *NP_comm* indicates if there is another common noun in the headword's NP and *control* is the lexical feature that indicates the presence of the word control in the sentence. Underlined nodes are the leaves or output of classifier.

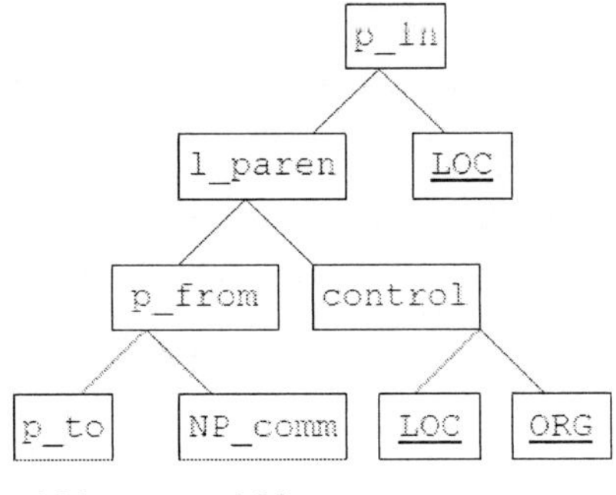

Figure 2: top levels for the LOC/ORG decision tree.

Some prepositions are very safe indicators for LOC, like *in*, *from*, *across*, *over*, while ORG is very often indicated by the relative position of a verb after *t* (and therefore a higher likelihood of being a subject) and by prepositions such as *with*, *against*, or *by*, as well as *t* being followed by a genitive mark. The contexts that select DOT are much more varied and scarce and the same time, but the prepositions *of* and *for* tend to select for dot predication.

This confirms the position that grammatical elements have more predictive power throughout the datasets than lexical elements for this sort of classification task. The DOT sense is difficult to identify but some prepositions and syntactic contexts favor its unspecified reading. Pure Location/Organization distinction is easy

due to the abundance of fixed syntactic patterns like word order and prepositional cues

6.2 Performance

On the account of sparseness, 42 of the lexical features are all-zero, but only 15 rows are all-zero and the rest have at least a feature with a value of 1. Most of the empty lexical features are common collocates for country or city but not for the named-entities which are their hyponyms, like "*country bumpkin*" or "*city dweller*".

The following tables show the performance of the classifiers in the six runs, the last column lists the Most Frequent Sense (MFS) baseline that the performance is compared against.

	Precision	Recall	F-measure	Accuracy	MFS
Allthree	0,713	0,72	0,72	72%	41%
LOC	0,77	0,8	0,79		
ORG	0,73	0,79	0,76		
DOT	0,55	0,41	0,47		
Loc/Org	0,85	0,85	0,85	85%	51%
LOC	0,86	0,86	0,86		
ORG	0,85	0,85	0,85		
Dot/NoDot	0,57	0,8	0,83	83%	81%
DOT	0,6	0,3	0,4		
NODOT	0,85	0,95	0,9		

Table 4: classifier performance for Total-boost

	Precision	Recall	F-measure	Accuracy	MFS
Allthree	0,69	0,7	0,69	70%	57%
LOC	0,78	0,85	0,81		
ORG	0,57	0,46	0,51		
DOT	0,56	0,53	0,55		
Loc/Org	0,86	0,86	0,86	86%	77%
LOC	0,89	0,94	0,91		
ORG	0,73	0,61	0,67		
Dot/NoDot	0,44	0,76	0,77	77%	74%
DOT	0,6	0,44	0,5		
NODOT	0,82	0,89	0,85		

Table 5: classifier performance for Total-dot

We can see how the *Dot-DoNot* alternation has very poor performance on the DOT class, which is the target class of the experiment. The

DOT class is fuzzier than the other two, and overlaps largely with the ORG class, as it can be seen in the cases of *Allthree* selection. The increase in accuracy in the *Dot-NoDoT* experiment for the *Total-boost* dataset with regards to *Total-dots* is not conclusive, since accuracy is only higher because there are 800 more instances of the most frequent sense, while f-measure remains largely constant for the DOT class in both datasets. The same also holds for the *Allthree* experiment.

In the LOC/ORG case, however, we can see how the *Total-boost* performs substantially better for the ORG class than the *Total-dots*, which is to be expected because it has almost as many examples of each class, while the performance for the LOC class does not become significantly hindered. This supports the usage of boosted datasets as exposed in section 4.1. Accuracy defeats both the expected MFS baseline and the usual baseline for WSD of ~60%.

7 Conclusions

It has been seen that the identification of LOC and ORG selection is feasible with good performance measures using only a set of easy-to-obtain linguistic cues and a very naive use of one external resource (WordSketch) which could anyway be replaced by other means of collocation extraction. The experiments confirm the hypothesis that grammatical features are more relevant for the identification of senses in this particular instance of regular polysemy, as lexical items are less represented in the decision trees and seldom appear before the third level of the decision tree. Sparseness means some patterns are underrepresented.

As shown by the performance of the *Total-boost* dataset over *Total-dots*, it is a good idea to increase the volume of sense-selection gold standards by using monosemous data as filler, as this allows training the system on more balanced data. This method can be used to compensate for the skewness of senses in related experiments, as well as to help create faster gold-standard data with a reduced impact on the precision of the system.

The exposed combination of feature space and classifier is suitable for the identification of Location/Organization type selection, but remains insufficient to identify dot predications, although some of them, which are introduced by certain prepositions (*of, for*) can be recognized beforehand and separated from the data in a pre- or postprocessing step.

The poor performance on the identification of dot predication requires a deeper analysis and measure of the inter-encoder agreement for this phenomenon, which is very likely to be lower than the expected value of 0.88 mentioned in section 4.

8 Further work

The research has to be expanded to comprise the whole Location/Organization dot type and not only proper nouns, that is, by including common nouns.

After fully studying the Location/Organization dot type, the other listed types (Artifact/Information, etc.) need to be studied in order to grasp the general picture of the soundness of dot type as a theoretical object that can be incorporated into NLP.

More complex, non-shallow features might be necessary for the identification of dot predications. Dependency parsing could indicate some types of dot predications, such as copredications and multiple selections. For other dot types or subtle dot predications, the usage of lexical semantic resources like WordNet might become necessary. The dot type Artifact/Information, for instance, could have a lower inter-encoder agreement than Location/Organization and possibly also a higher relevance of lexical features for the selection of senses, which would imply a smaller role for the grammatical features in the selectional behavior.

An increase in the need to deal with lexical information would also raise the number of features for the sense selection classifiers. Using the ontological types of the words in the lexical feature space instead of the words themselves would reduce the size of the lexical feature space and improve its coverage, as words like *secretary*, *chairman* and *president* would fall under the same ontological type. Ontological types could be obtained from resources like WordNet or the SIMPLE lexicon.

Acknowledgments
The research leading to these results has received funding from the European Commission's 7th Framework Program under grant agreement n° 238405 (CLARA).

References

Agirre, E. and Soroa, A. 2009, *Personalizing pagerank for word sense disambiguation*, Proceedings of the 12th Conference of the European Chapter of the Association for Computational Linguistics, Association for Computational Linguistics, pp. 33.

Apresjan, J.D. 1974, *Regular Polysemy*, Linguistics.

Buitelaar, P. 1998, Phd Thesis, *CoreLex: systematic polysemy and underspecification.*

Finkel, J.R., Grenager, T. & Manning, C. 2005, "Incorporating non-local information into information extraction systems by gibbs sampling", *Proceedings of the 43rd Annual Meeting on Association for Computational Linguistics*Association for Computational Linguistics, , pp. 363.

Gale, W.A., Church, K.W. and Yarowsky, D. 1992, One sense per discourse, Proceedings of the workshop on Speech and Natural Language,Association for Computational Linguistics, pp. 237.

Grimshaw, J.B. 1991, Argument structure, MIT press Cambridge, MA.

Ide, N. and Macleod, C. 2001, *The american national corpus: A standardized resource of american english*, Proceedings of Corpus Linguistics 2001, pp. 274.

Joanis, E., Stevenson, S. and James, D. 2006, *A general feature space for automatic verb classification*, Natural Language Engineering, vol. 14, no. 03, pp. 337-367.

Johannessen, J.B., Hagen, K., Haaland, Å., Jónsdottir, A.B., Nøklestad, A., Kokkinakis, D., Meurer, P., Bick, E. & Haltrup, D. 2005, "Named entity recognition for the mainland Scandinavian languages", *Literary and Linguistic Computing,* vol. 20, no. 1, pp. 91.

Kilgarriff, A., Rychly, P., Smrz, P. and Tugwell, D. 2004, *The sketch engine*, Proceedings of the Eleventh EURALEX International Congress, pp. 105–116.

Lapata, M. and Lascarides, A. 2003, *A probabilistic account of logical metonymy*, Computational Linguistics, vol. 29, no. 2, pp. 261-315.

Lenci, A., Bel, N., Busa, F., Calzolari, N., Gola, E., Monachini, M., Ogonowski, A., Peters, I., Peters, W. and Ruimy, N. 2000, *SIMPLE: A general framework for the development of multilingual lexicons*, International Journal of Lexicography, vol. 13, no. 4, pp. 249.

Litkowski, K.C. and Hargraves, O. 2005, *The preposition project*, Proceedings of the Second ACL-SIGSEM Workshop on the Linguistic Dimensions of Prepositions and their Use in Computational Linguistics Formalisms and Applications, pp. 171–179.

Markert, K. and Nissim, M. 2009, *Data and models for metonymy resolution*, Language Resources and Evaluation, vol. 43, no. 2, pp. 123-138.

Peris, A., Taulp, M. and Rodríguez, H. 2009, *Hacia un sistema de clasificación automática de sustantivos deverbales*, Procesamiento del Lenguaje Natural, vol. 43, pp. 23-31.

Pustejovsky, J. 1995, *The generative lexicon*: a theory of computational lexical semantics, MIT press.

Pustejovsky, J., Rumshisky, A., Plotnick, A., Jezek, E., Batiukova, O. and Quochi, V. 2010, *SemEval-2010 task 7: argument selection and coercion*, Proceedings of the 5th International Workshop on Semantic Evaluation,Association for Computational Linguistics, pp. 27.

Quinlan, J.R. 1993, *C4.5: Programs for Machine Learning*, Morgan Kaufmann.

Resnik, G. and Bel, N. 2009, *Automatic Detection of Non-deverbal Event Nouns in Spanish*, Proceedings of the 5th International Conference on Generative Approaches to the Lexicon, .

Rumshisky, A., Grinberg, V. and Pustejovsky, J. 2007, *Detecting selectional behavior of complex types in text*, Fourth International Workshop on Generative Approaches to the Lexicon, Paris, France.

Tomuro, N. 2001, *Tree-cut and a lexicon based on systematic polysemy*, Proceedings of the second meeting of the North American Chapter of the Association for Computational Linguistics on Language technologies, Association for Computational Linguistics.

Vossen, P., Peters, W. & Gonzalo, J. 1999, *Towards a universal index of meaning*, Proceedings of SIGLEX99: Standardizing Lexical Resources.

Witten, I.H. and Frank, E. 2005, *Data Mining: Practical machine learning tools and techniques*, Morgan Kaufman.

ISSN 1736-6305 Vol. 11
http://hdl.handle.net/10062/16955

Decision Strategies for Incremental POS Tagging

Niels Beuck, Arne Köhn and Wolfgang Menzel
Department Informatik, University of Hamburg
Vogt-Kölln-Straße 30, 22527 Hamburg, Germany
`{beuck, 5koehn, menzel}@informatik.uni-hamburg.de`

Abstract

In an incremental NLP pipeline every module needs to work incrementally. However, an incremental processing mode can lead to a degradation of accuracy due to the missing context to the right. We discuss three properties of incremental output that can be traded for accuracy, namely *timeliness*, *monotonicity* and *decisiveness*. The consequences of these trade-offs are evaluated systematically for the task of part-of-speech tagging.

1   Introduction

Incremental language processing does not consume input at once but in a word-by-word manner and a sequence of incomplete, but successively more complete interpretations is generated as output. Such a processing mode is especially beneficial in scenarios where language input evolves over time like in human-computer or human-robot interaction. By processing the input while it is still incomplete, a speed-up can be achieved by using production time as processing time. Another benefit is the possibility to immediately respond to partial input, e.g. by providing non-verbal feedback to the speaker. This requires the system to be able to produce a partial analysis for partial input, which, of course, needs to be available early enough. Otherwise, the receiver could as easily wait until the whole utterance is complete and the benefit of incremental processing vanishes.

In natural language the correct interpretation of a word often depends on the context to the right. Therefore, an incremental NL processor that is selecting an interpretation for a word without being aware of the right context is likely to select the wrong interpretation more often than a non-incremental processor. There are several possible strategies to deal with this problem. In the first part

of this paper we will discuss these strategies and how they can be implemented for a simple NLP task, namely part-of-speech (POS) tagging. In the second part we will present a quantitative evaluation and compare the different trade-offs made by the different strategies. To our knowledge there is no previous work evaluating these trade-offs systematically.

POS tagging is particularly attractive for an initial investigation of incremental processing behavior, as in this task the input consists of a small number of discrete tokens (in contrast to speech recognition) where each of them has to be mapped to exactly one output token (in contrast to syntactic or semantic structures which combine several input tokens). Moreover POS tagging does not depend on previous processing steps. Therefore, the results of this paper provide the basis for a broader range of investigations with more complex NLP tasks.

In Section 2 we will define the notion of incrementality used in this paper. Based on this, the challenges of disambiguation in incremental NLP and several strategies to meet them are discussed in Section 3. Section 4 describes the POS taggers used in the evaluation. The results of the evaluation are presented and discussed in Section 5. We finish with an outlook on future work in Section 6.

2   Incrementality

Incremental processing can be realized for procedures that take a sequence of input tokens and generate a sequence of output tokens[1]. The output is called the analysis of the input. Depending on the task an input token could be a word from an utterance perhaps accompanied by additional morphosyntactic information like a POS tag. Exam-

---

[1] In contrast to what Wirén (1992) defines as full incrementality, we only regard left-right-incremental processes here. This restricts the modifications of the input to simply adding new tokens at the end of the sequence.

ples for output tokens could be phrases, chunks, POS tags associated to the input words or dependencies to other words.

Incrementality is not a binary feature but comes in different grades and flavors. First of all, we have to distinguish between incremental interfaces and incremental algorithms. According to Wirén (1993) an algorithm is incremental *"if it uses information from an old analysis in computing the new analysis."* The interface is incremental, if it accepts partial input and provides partial output. On the one hand, a process could provide an incremental interface without a corresponding algorithm by applying a non-incremental algorithm on successively extended prefixes of the input sequence. On the other hand, an incremental algorithm does not automatically facilitate an incremental interface.

With respect to the kind of interface we can distinguish incremental input consumption (IIC) from incremental output production (IOP) (Kilger and Finkler, 1995). While the former is the ability to start processing on partial input, the latter is the ability to produce a sequence of partial analyses and provide them as output as soon as they become available.

A system without IIC will have to wait with the computation until the input is complete and a system without IOP will not start to generate output before the input is complete. That means, a combination of both processing modes is needed to be able to provide output while the input has not yet been completed. We shall call a system that applies both, IIC and IOP, to be input/output-incremental or IO-incremental. For a system consisting of several processing modules to be IO-incremental, each of its modules has to be IO-incremental, otherwise the final output of the system is delayed at least until the end of the input.

3 Disambiguating in incremental processing

In many applications, like POS tagging or syntactic parsing, the not yet seen input may have an influence on the analysis of the current input token. Therefore, incremental processing has only a limited access to the disambiguating context information. There are several strategies to mitigate the impact of limited context information on the output accuracy but they affect other properties of the output. In addition to accuracy we have identified

three other parameters, namely timeliness, monotonicity and decisiveness, necessary to sufficiently characterize incremental processing behavior results. Timeliness and monotonicity are features unique to incremental output while decisiveness can also be applied to non-incremental output.

Timely output is generated for every input increment before the next input token is available. **Delayed** output lags behind the input stream. The delay can be a fixed number of tokens due to a lookahead of a fixed window size, or a dynamic range as in stack based approaches.

Monotonicity is given if the output stream can only be modified by adding new information. Once committed information may not be changed later on. In contrast, **non-monotonic** input implies that previous output can be revoked or changed. By allowing non-monotonic updates intermediate output becomes unreliable to a certain degree.

Decisiveness is the property of the system to commit to one analysis at a time. In contrast to this, **inconclusive** output consists of several possible alternatives. These alternatives can be stated implicitly by leaving features of the output unspecified, by enumerating alternatives for each token or by explicitly representing alternatives for the overall output.

Delay and non-monotonicity can be interpreted as a gradual reduction of IIC and IOP respectively. A process which cannot start before the input sequence is complete behaves like a process without IIC. On the other hand, a process with extreme non-monotonic behavior cannot guarantee persistence. This leads to a high degree of unreliability that might render all intermediate partial analyses except the very last one useless to their consumer. Such a module has to be considered as not exhibiting IOP at all. Inconclusiveness is equivalent to a reduction of the informational contribution of the output. A totally inconclusive output that (explicitly or implicitly) permits all analyses contains no information at all.

In summary there is a trade-off between timeliness, monotonicity, decisiveness and accuracy. The first three properties can be exchanged against accuracy which in the ideal case converges to the accuracy of non-incremental processing. Whenever the decision on the current token depends on a not yet observed token, four options are available. Either the decision can be delayed, a range of possible variants is provided (inconclusiveness), or a possibly erroneous decision is either accepted as unavoidable (loss of accuracy) or perhaps can be corrected later on (non-monotonicity).

3.1 General strategies

Based on the trade-offs presented in the last section different strategies are possible. We will call a strategy which takes decisions without considering the right context and accepting a loss of accuracy instead of affecting one of the other three properties best-guess (BG).

A common strategy for disambiguation using delay is lookahead (LA). Here a fixed number of tokens to the right of the current token is taken into account when calculating the output. As processing cannot start before the lookahead window is filled with input, a lookahead of n tokens makes the output lag behind the input by the same amount of tokens. Additionally, this strategy can only resolve ambiguity regarding the near future. Long distance influence cannot be captured, e.g. if a later word in a sentence possibly invalidates the previously more probable interpretation like in a German sub-clause where the verb is placed last. A lookahead size of zero is equivalent to the BG strategy.

A strategy resulting in non-monotonic output is reanalysis (RA). Here previous output is recalculated if new information is available and thus earlier decisions can be changed. Ideally reanalysis does not take as long as the initial processing, as otherwise one of the advantages of incremental processing would disappear. Pruning of pending alternatives or a revision of earlier results are possible techniques. In POS tagging where processing speed is fast compared to speech rate or the processing speed of other modules this is of little concern. Reanalysis can deal with long distance influences and, therefore, is able to provide the optimal analysis of the full sentence, but partial output becomes non-monotonic and thus unreliable to a certain degree.

A general strategy to deal with ambiguity in general consists in providing several possible solutions instead of committing to a single one. In contrast to the two previously mentioned ones, the multiple alternatives (MA) strategy affects not only the partial solutions but also the form of the complete analysis. Hybrid strategies are possible like a MA strategy where the alternatives are pruned by reanalysis later on.

	Input	Output	
Best guess	A	→ A/w	
	A B	→ A/w	B/t
Look-ahead	A	→	
	A B	→ A/r	
Re-analysis	A	→ A/w	
	A B	→ A/r	B/t
Multiple alternatives	A	→ A/{w,r}	
	A B	→ A/{w,r}	B/{t}

Figure 1: Four strategies to deal with a situation where a decision between a correct tag 'r' and a wrong one 'w' has to be made for the input token 'A' but depends on a subsequent input token 'B'

An illustration of the four strategies is given in Figure 1. Each strategy has certain implications for subsequent processing modules and the behavior of the overall system. First of all, even in the absence of further requirements, delay accumulates in a pipe of modules. Non-monotonicity requires subsequent modules to be able to handle changing input, i.e. be able to perform reanalysis itself. Finally, output consisting of multiple analyses requires a consumer to be able to handle that kind of input, either by selecting one interpretation or by passing the ambiguity on along the processing chain.

3.2 Quantification of delay, non-monotonicity and inconclusiveness

The delay induced by a fixed lookahead can be quantified by the size of lookahead. Dynamic delay could be quantified by the average of the actual delays for each input token or by a recall value measuring the completeness of the output. As we only regard POS tagging strategies with a fixed delay, a predefined lookahead size is used here. The final accuracy is determined for different lookahead sizes.

The degree of non-monotonicity in a RA strategy is not as easy to define or guarantee. One could restrict the possibilities for reanalysis to a window of a certain size or constrain the kind of changes that are allowed. Another possibility consists in restricting reanalysis beforehand but to determine empirically how often a process actually does change its output. This approach was used by Baumann et al. (2009) for incremental speech recognition. Schlangen et al. (2009) applied it to incremental reference resolution where the so called edit overhead was measured. We also use this latter approach by determining the percentage of output tokens which will not be be changed in further processing steps as a stability measure. To be able to decide on an acceptable trade-off between delay, accuracy and non-monotonicity we will plot stability and accuracy for different delays.

To quantify inconclusiveness we use the number of output alternatives to be considered and measure accuracy for different numbers. This requires the number of alternatives to be configurable or to be ranked so that further alternatives can be ignored. Weights, e.g. assigned probabilities, are only used for ranking and are otherwise ignored in this measure.

3.3 Incremental POS tagging algorithms

POS tagging algorithms typically consist of two steps. First, tag probabilities are determined incrementally on a word-by-word basis. Here only local features, e.g., the trigram probability of the current word depending on the tags of the two previous words, or features of adjacent words in support vector machines (SVMs) are used. The second optional step is a global optimization. When only applying the first phase, incremental output of tags is possible in the sense of IOP and the output is monotonic. Approaches using Hidden Markov Models do not use a lookahead (n-grams only regard the tags to the left of the current word), while SVM approaches may use a lookahead by including features of the words to the right.

In the optional second phase, global optimization, either the optimal path is determined, e.g. by the Viterbi algorithm, or an algorithm like the forward backwards algorithm is used to compute probabilities. Theoretically this optimization can also be applied to every prefix analysis. In this case tags to the right can influence tags further left, resulting in a non-monotonic behavior every time a new word changes the optimal path for the previous words. Care has to be taken not to introduce errors by handling prefixes as full sentences. An example for this are end of sentence tags sometimes automatically inserted by a tagger at the end of the current tag sequence. They are likely to influence the best path and thus should not be used in prefixes.

Global optimization can be modified to provide lookahead by not including the rightmost n words of a prefix in the output, but only including them in the calculation of the best path.

Most tagging algorithms work with multiple tag hypotheses for each word internally. A MA strategy can thus be achieved by providing a ranked list of all alternative tags for each word (multi-tagging), while uni-tagging is achieved by suppressing all but the best tag.

As we have seen, tagging algorithms are able to realize all three proposed strategies directly: lookahead by feature lookahead in SVMs, reanalysis by carrying out a global optimization on prefixes and multi-tagging by considering all possible tags for each word. In the next section we will present the POS taggers used in the evaluation and discuss the strategies they are compatible with.

4 Experimental setup

4.1 POS taggers

In order to compare the different strategies of incremental processing in the task of POS tagging we will compare different taggers in different configurations. The taggers used are TnT[2] (Brants, 2000), SVMTool[3] (Giménez and Màrquez, 2004) and HunPos (Halácsy et al., 2007) modified to work incrementally[4].

TnT is a statistical POS tagger implementing the Viterbi algorithm for second order Markov models. As such it does not support incremental processing, but can be made to simulate a non-monotonic incremental mode by tagging successively extended prefixes of the input sequence, thereby providing an incremental interface.[5] To force TnT into a monotonic mode, only the tag for the new word in each prefix is added, the other tags are taken from the tagging results for the previous prefix. This mode, of course, diminishes the utility of the Viterbi algorithm. A lookahead of size n is simulated by introducing a temporal difference between the current token of the input and the output where the former is n tokens ahead of the latter. Therefore, the n rightmost tags are ignored in the

---

[2]http://www.coli.uni-saarland.de/ thorsten/tnt/

[3]http://www.lsi.upc.es/ nlp/SVMTool/

[4]http://gitorious.org/hunpos

[5]Based on our tests, we believe that TnT doesn't treat such prefixes as whole sentences, which would lead to some errors such as not assigning tags that are improbable for the last word of a sentence.

output (they belong to the lookahead), while the preceding ones are passed on.

SVMTool is a tagger generator based on support vector machines. It can be configured with arbitrary feature sets thereby supporting incremental tagging with various lookahead sizes, including no lookahead at all. Every feature set can be used with the Viterbi algorithm for global optimization. We have applied a feature window consisting of two words to the left of the current word and zero (LA0), one (LA1) or two (LA2, non-incremental) to the right of it.

HunPos is an open source statistical trigram tagger resembling the architecture of TnT. It was specifically modified by us for incremental use by removing the global optimization. In this mode, HunPos keeps a list of possible tag sequences along with their probabilities. For each word new sequences are created by appending each possible tag to all sequences. Given a sequence of tags S_{curr}, the probability of the subsequent sequence assigning tag t_i to the current word is the probability of S_{curr} times the probability of the assignment given S_{curr}. The probability of the assignment of a tag t to the ith word is the sum of all sequences that assign t to the ith word. The algorithm starts with the empty sequence that has a probability of 1. With this modification we obtain an incremental and monotonic tagger that is able to assign probabilities to tags.

As a baseline we used a simplistic tagger that uses unigrams and assigns "normal noun" to each unknown word.

4.2 Data

Evaluation is carried out on sentences from NEGRA Corpus (German), a subset of the WSJ corpus (English), and the Danish and Swedish corpora from the CoNLL-X shared task (Buchholz and Marsi, 2006).

For German and English, the taggers were trained on a subset of 15000 sentences, the evaluation was carried out on the remaining 4058 sentences. The Swedish dataset consists of 11042 sentences for training and 322 for evaluation, the Danish one consists of 5190 and 322 sentences.

To be able to estimate the reliability of the accuracy numbers in the face of the different corpora sizes, we performed a 10-fold cross-validation. Average and standard error values are given for every measure.

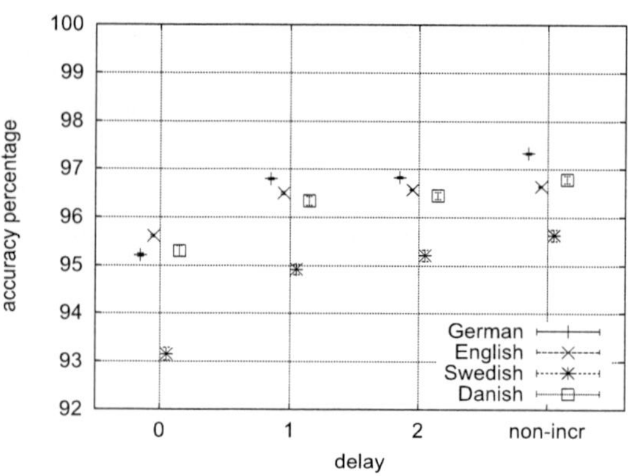

Figure 2: Tagging accuracy of SVMT for different delay sizes

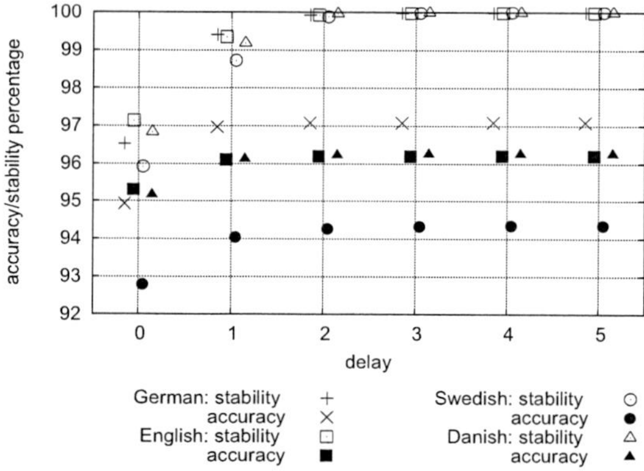

Figure 3: Tagging accuracy and stability of intermediate tags in non-monotonic tagging with TnT. On the x-axis the number of tokens since the word first appeared is given.

5   Results and discussion

Table 1 lists the tagging accuracy for the different incremental strategies. Compared to non-incremental tagging, BG incremental tagging leads to an absolute reduction of tagging accuracy by between 0.69% (HunPos, English) and 2.48% (SVMT, Swedish). Language has a higher influence than the tagger used, with the exception of Swedish, where the 3 evaluated taggers performed very differently. The impact of the incremental mode is generally highest for German and lowest for English.

This loss of accuracy is mitigated by a lookahead of 1 word to around 0.1% and nearly vanishes with a lookahead of 2 words for HunPos and TnT. For SVMT the gap of accuracy between the lookahead of 2 and the non-incremental configu-

Strategy	Tagger	LA	German $\bar{X}(SE)$	English $\bar{X}(SE)$	Swedish $\bar{X}(SE)$	Danish $\bar{X}(SE)$
NonIncr/	TnT		97.14% (0.014)	96.26% (0.004)	94.41% (0.106)	96.45% (0.099)
Reana-	SVMT		**97.33%** (0.020)	**96.64%** (0.014)	**95.63%** (0.121)	**96.79%** (0.079)
lysis	HunPos		97.10% (0.018)	96.32% (0.004)	94.76% (0.135)	96.55% (0.082)
Best	TnT		94.93% (0.024)	95.30% (0.014)	92.79% (0.090)	95.16% (0.106)
Guess	SVMT		**95.21%** (0.031)	95.61% (0.019)	93.15% (0.133)	**95.30%** (0.108)
	HunPos		95.13% (0.029)	**95.63%** (0.006)	**93.64%** (0.095)	**95.30%** (0.106)
Look-	TnT	1	96.97% (0.017)	96.10% (0.003)	94.04% (0.101)	96.12% (0.102)
ahead	TnT	2	97.08% (0.016)	96.19% (0.003)	94.26% (0.112)	96.22% (0.107)
	SVMT	1	96.80% (0.020)	96.50% (0.025)	94.92% (0.105)	96.34% (0.092)
	SVMT	2	96.83% (0.021)	**96.57%** (0.012)	**95.21%** (0.115)	96.45% (0.075)
	HunPos	1	96.99% (0.020)	96.27% (0.004)	94.67% (0.121)	96.40% (0.090)
	HunPos	2	**97.09%** (0.021)	96.32% (0.004)	94.78% (0.136)	**96.56%** (0.082)
Multi-	TnT		**98.63%** (0.018)	98.62% (0.007)	97.99% (0.064)	98.71% (0.029)
tagging	SVMT		98.51% (0.019)	98.60% (0.008)	97.60% (0.092)	98.46% (0.049)
2 tags	HunPos		98.60% (0.020)	**98.70%** (0.004)	**98.20%** (0.075)	**98.74%** (0.033)
Baseline			90.66% (0.027)	90.97% (0.011)	89.65% (0.105)	89.98% (0.184)

Table 1: Tagging accuracy on final results for different combinations of taggers, strategies and languages averages and standard errors from the cross-validation are given

tagger	German	English	Swedish	Danish
TnT	**96.53%**	97.14%	95.14%	**94.93%**
SVMT	93.12%	96.43%	**95.92%**	94.41%
HunPos	96.52%	**97.29%**	95.57%	96.11%

Table 2: Stability numbers of non-monotonic tagging, i.e., the percentage of tags that did not get changed in later output increments

ration is still about 0.5%. This can be explained by the fact that the incremental SVMT configurations used here do not include the global Viterbi optimization. Only feature lookahead is used for SVMT, while for the other two taggers the global optimization was used to implement the lookahead strategy (c.f. Section 4.1).

Alternatively non-incremental output accuracy can be preserved, if between 2.7% (English, Hun-Pos) and 6.9% (German, SVMT) of the tags can be changed within 2 words after they have first been assigned. As can be seen in Figure 3, changes are marginal after that, which is not surprising given the fact that no parser uses features with a distance of more than 2 words. While the delay is the same, reanalysis provides an advantage over lookahead because it makes a tag available immediately with only a minor loss of accuracy. Of course, the consumer of the output needs to be able to process non-monotonic output.

If the top-most two tags from incremental multi-tagging output are considered, the likelihood of the correct one being among them is higher than the accuracy in non-incremental single best mode for all considered languages, as can be seen in Table 1 and in Figure 4. Of course, multi-tagging can also be applied to the non-incremental case, where it produced a slightly better performance than in incremental multi-tagging, e.g., 0.3% for TnT in German (c.f. Figure 4).

In Table 3 the errors contributing most to the accuracy drop in best-guess incremental tagging are shown for English and German. In German a major source of the errors are determiner pronoun confusions and in English a third of all the errors (rows 1, 4 and 7 in Table 3) are wrongly assigned preposition (IN) tags. Ambiguities like these can usually be resolved given the next word and thus explain the big improvement of accuracy between a lookahead of zero and one. A noteworthy observation is the absence of confusions between nouns and proper nouns. They rank among the most common tagging errors in many languages (e.g., 18% in German with TnT for NN $\leftrightarrow$ NE

TnT German			TnT English	
PTKVZ tagged as APPR	11.8%		WDT tagged as IN	19.3%
ART tagged as PRELS	10.6%		JJ tagged as NN	12.8%
ART tagged as PDS	6.2%		VBN tagged as VBD	10.0%
APPR tagged as PTKZU	6.1%		RB tagged as IN	9.0%
VVINF tagged as VVFIN	5.3%		JJ tagged as NNP	6.3%
PRELS tagged as ART	4.9%		NNP tagged as JJ	4.6%
VVFIN tagged as VVINF	4.6%		DT tagged as IN	4.6%
PDS tagged as ART	4.0%		NN tagged as JJ	4.2%
ADJA tagged as NN	3.6%		RBR tagged as JJR	4.2%
NN tagged as ADJA	3.0%		RB tagged as JJ	4.0%
...				
VMFIN tagged as VMINF	−0.7%		DT tagged as WDT'	−1.8%
NE tagged as FM	−0.8%		VBP tagged as VB'	−2.1%
ADV tagged as PIAT	−0.8%		IN tagged as RB',	−2.9%

Table 3: Errors types contributing to the increased error rate of best-guess incremental tagging compared to non-incremental tagging, exemplary for TnT for German and English. Listed are the 10 error types which contribute most to the loss of accuracy and 3 others which even let to an improvement, ranked according to their relative share of the overall error increase.

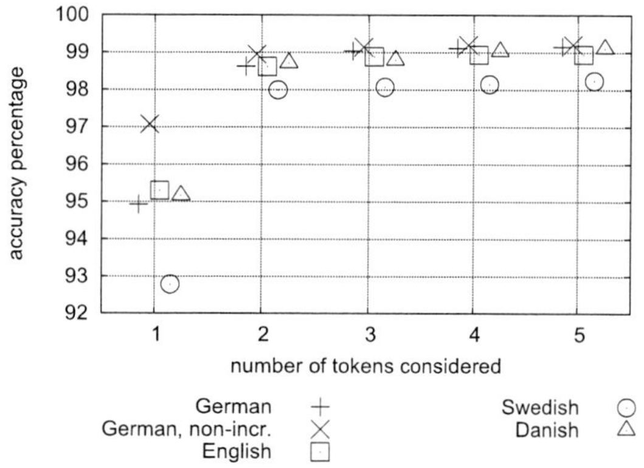

Figure 4: Tagging accuracy of incremental and non-incremental multi-tagging with TnT for different numbers of tags considered

confusion) but have little effect on further processing, as noun and proper noun behave syntactically very similar. This indicates that a BG incremental tagger produces additional errors which are rather severe and likely to have a high negative impact on performance of a consumer component (like a parser).

6 Conclusions and outlook

In this paper we have described the impact of incremental processing modes on the task of POS tagging and how accuracy can be traded against other output parameters like timeliness, mono-

tonicity and decisiveness. A summary of possible trade-offs is given in Figure 5.

It depends on the application which of these trade-offs is acceptable. For non-monotonic and inconclusive output, a consumer is needed that is able to handle such output. Even a slight delay might be unacceptable in applications where an immediate analysis of the most recent input element is needed at all times. Moreover, delay accumulates for all modules in a processing pipeline.

> The cost of incremental tagging are one of
>
> - an accuracy drop between 0.7% and 2.5% depending on the language.
>
> - a delay of 2 words (a delay of 1 already considerably reduces the accuracy drop to ca. 0.1%)
>
> - a 2.7% − 6.9% chance that the output will be changed later on
>
> - or an ambiguity factor of 2, i.e the two best tags given by the tagger need to be considered.

Figure 5: A summary of the possible trade-offs in incremental POS tagging

The three identified parameters are not specific for POS tagger output but can also be applied to other NLP tasks. Related work has been done for speech recognition (Baumann et al., 2009) and reference resolution (Schlangen et al., 2009). Both papers consider non-monotonic systems and focus on the trade-off between delay and edit overhead.

To our knowledge no comparable investigation has been carried out for syntactic parsing. Besides studying the above mentioned trade-off for the parser itself it would also be interesting to measure the impact of different kinds of incremental POS tagging on the performance of the parser. Dependency parsing lends itself particularly well to such an investigation, because by assigning attachments to input words it shares crucial similarities to POS-tagging. Parsing differs from tagging however, since it considers relations instead of atomic labels. Therefore, the output of dependency arcs needs to be either delayed at least until both ends of the dependency are known or otherwise underspecified dependency arcs need to be produced. The former strategy is applied, e.g., in MaltParser (Nivre, 2004) where words are kept on the stack until a possible attachment becomes available, adding a dynamic delay in addition to the one already caused by lookahead. The incremental variant of the WCDG parser (Foth, 2006) used in Menzel (2009) instead applies the latter approach and provides a placeholder for future input words so that partially specified dependencies can be generated. MaltParser classifies as a monotonic but delayed incremental parser, while output of WCDG is timely but non-monotonic. To deal with and compare dynamic delay and underspecified dependencies the evaluation methods presented here will have to be adapted.

Acknowledgement

This research was funded by the Deutsche Forschungsgemeinschaft (DFG) as part of the International Graduate Research Group CINACS.

References

Timo Baumann, Michaela Atterer, and David Schlangen. 2009. Assessing and improving the performance of speech recognition for incremental systems. In *NAACL '09: Proceedings of Human Language Technologies*, pages 380–388, Morristown, NJ, USA. Association for Computational Linguistics.

Thorsten Brants. 2000. Tnt - a statistical part-of-speech tagger. In *ANLC 00 Proceedings of the sixth conference on Applied natural language processing.*

Sabine Buchholz and Erwin Marsi. 2006. Conll-x shared task on multilingual dependency parsing. In *Proceedings of CoNLL-X.*

Kilian A. Foth. 2006. *Hybrid Methods of Natural Language Analysis.* Ph.D. thesis, Universität Hamburg, Fachbereich Informatik.

Jesús Giménez and Lluís Màrquez. 2004. Svmtool: A general pos tagger generator based on support vector machines. In *Proceedings of the 4th LREC.*

Péter Halácsy, András Kornai, and Csaba Oravecz. 2007. Hunpos - an open source trigram tagger. In *ACL.*

Anne Kilger and Wolfgang Finkler. 1995. Incremental generation for real-time applications. Technical report, Deutsches Forschungzentrum für Künstliche Intelligenz GmbH (DFKI).

Wolfgang Menzel, 2009. *Recent Advances in Natural Language Processing V*, chapter Towards radically incremental parsing of natural language, pages 41–56. Number 309 in Current Issues in Linguistic Theory. John Benjamin's Publisher.

Joakim Nivre. 2004. Incrementality in deterministic dependency parsing. In *Incremental Parsing: Bringing Engineering and Cognition Together, Workshop at ACL-2004, Barcelona, Spain.*

David Schlangen, Timo Baumann, and Michaela Atterer. 2009. Incremental reference resolution: the task, metrics for evaluation, and a bayesian filtering model that is sensitive to disfluencies. In *SIGDIAL '09: Proceedings of the SIGDIAL 2009 Conference*, pages 30–37, Morristown, NJ, USA. Association for Computational Linguistics.

Mats Wirén. 1992. *Studies in Incremental Natural-Language Analysis.* Ph.D. thesis, Linköping University, Department of Computer and Information Science, Linköping.

Mats Wirén. 1993. Bounded incremental parsing. In *6th Twente Workshop on Language Technology (TWLT-6).*

ISSN 1736-6305 Vol. 11
http://hdl.handle.net/10062/16955

A FrameNet for Danish

Eckhard Bick
University of Southern Denmark
eckhard.bick@mail.dk

Abstract

This paper presents work on a comprehensive FrameNet for Danish (cf. www.framenet.dk), with over 12.000 frames, and an almost complete coverage of Danish verb lemmas. We discuss design principles and frame roles as well as the distinctional use of valency, syntactic function and semantic noun classes. By converting frame distinctors into Constraint Grammar rules, we were able to build a robust frame tagger for running Danish text, using DanGram parses as input. The combined context-informed coverage of the parser-frametagger was 94.3%, with an overall F-score for frame senses of 85.12.

1   The FrameNet concept

Classification of the lexicon is central to many aspects of linguistic research, and modern computational linguistics in particular has a need for robust classification systems to support on the one hand automatic analysis, on the other hand applicational tasks such as information extraction and question answering. As the pivot of the sentence, verbs play a special, integrative role in lexical ontologies. While noun ontologies are relatively easy to build around ISA/hypernym-relations, verbs are somewhat harder to classify because structural aspects are meshed with semantics, with complex combinatorial restrictions residing in both a verb's meaning and its syntactic nature. While one of the largest ontological resources, WordNet (Fellbaum 1998), does cover verbs, but provides little structural-relational information, a number of other classification projects link verb classes to certain verbo-nominal combination patterns, providing information on the form, function and semantics of complements. For English, Levin's original verb classification (Levin 1993) has been expanded in the VerbNet project (Kipper et al. 2006) to include non-np complements and employs 23 (25) thematic roles and 94 semantic predicates. In the FrameNet project (Baker et al. 1998, Johnson & Fillmore 2000, Ruppenhofer et al. 2010), semantic frames like *Commerce* are drawn up with roles like *Buyer, Seller, Goods* and *Money,* which are then associated with verbs (or nouns

and adjectives) from corpus examples. Since the same verb may appear in more than one frame, verb sense lists are created implicitly, with no guarantee for full coverage. Conversely, the PropBank Project (Palmer et al. 2005) departs from syntactically annotated corpus data to assign both roles and argument structure to each verb consecutively. Both FrameNet and Prop-Bank provide morphosyntactic restrictions, while FrameNet also adds ontological information on slot fillers.

For Danish, the target language of our own work, some semantic verb classification has been undertaken as part of the Danish DanNet project (Pedersen et al. 2008), covering ca. 3000 verbs with 6000 senses falling into 80 top classes, e.g. BoundedEvent + Physical + Location. However, while some incorporated adverbial material and reflexivity are provided as verb sense discriminators, no frame roles or systematic selection restrictions are listed. Earlier work comprises the STO database, with almost 6000 verbal entries of which 4/5 offer syntactic, and 1/5 semantic information (Braasch & Olsen 2004), and the Odense Valency Dictionary (Schösler & Kirchmeier-Andersen 1997), that classified verbal argument semantics through the semantics of pronoun complements, covering ca. 4000 verbs.

The project described here, launched in 2006, also regards valency as a useful stepping stone towards the semantic classification of verb structures, assuming that almost all subsenses of a given verb can be distinguished, and a full thematic role frame assigned, if the form, function and (noun) semantics of complements are known. Thus, using the DanGram parser's valency dictionary (Bick 2001) as a point of departure, we manually assigned verb classes and thematic role frames to each valency "sense" of a given verb, using corpus data and dictionaries to check sense coverage, and adding sense-based subdistinctions for the broader valency senses where necessary. Syntactic functions and forms of complements were already implicit in the valency tags and could therefore be assigned semi-automatically. At the same time, our methodology of building semantic frames from "syntactic frames" considerably facilitated locating and checking corpus examples, since all syntactic complementation patterns were already available - and searchable - in corpora annotated with the DanGram parser (Bick 2001), allowing focused inspection of semantic variation.

2   The Danish FrameNet

After 4 years, our framenet (inspection demo at www.framenet.dk) has a very good coverage for the DanGram lexicon, and while further senses and patterns are being added and existing ones revised, the overall number of lexemes is now fairly stable, at 6825, with an average of 1.77 frames and 1.46 senses per lexeme. At the time of writing, this corresponds to about 11.000 valency patterns and 12.075 different verb frames, roughly twice the volume of DanNet. We use 494 different verb categories[1] (cp. Appendix 1) that are grouped using the original Levine senses and VerbNet numbering system, albeit with a modified naming system[2] and expanded subclassification system. Thus, though syntactic alternations such as diathesis or word order are not considered frame-distinctors, we do deviate from WordNet and VerbNet by making a class distinction for polarity antonyms like *increase - decrease, like - dislike,* and for the self/other distinction (*move_self, move_other*). We also try to avoid large underspecified classes (e.g. change_of_state), while at the same time keeping the classification scheme as flat as possible, in order to facilitate the use of our categories as corpus annotation tags or Constraint Grammar disambiguation tags. We have therefore introduced classes like *heat - cool, activate - deactivate* or *open - close,* reducing the larger *change_of_state* to a kind of wastebin rest category.

3   Frame role distinctors: valency, syntactic function and semantic classes

The distinctional backbone of our frame inventory are syntactic valency frames like <vt> (monotransitive), <vdt> (ditransitive), <på^vtp-ind> (prepositional ditransitive with the preposition "på" and a verb-incorporated 'ind'-adverb). Each of these valency frames is assigned at least one (or more[3]) verb senses, each with its own semantic frame. Depending, for instance, on the number of obligatory arguments, several valency or semantic frames may share the same verb sense, but two different verb senses will almost always differ in at least one syntactic or semantic aspect of their argument frame - guaranteeing that all senses can in principle be disambiguated exploiting a parser's argument tags and dependency links.

For each of our 12.000 verb sense frames, we provide a list of arguments with the following information:

1. Thematic role (Table 1)
2. Syntactic function (Table 2)
3. Morphosyntactic form (Table 4)
4. for np's, a list of typical semantic prototypes to fill the slot (Table 3)
5. An English language gloss / skeleton sentence

For about half the frames (46%), a best-guess link to a DanNet verb sense is also provided, based on semi-automatic matches on adverb incorporation and hypernym classification.

Our FrameNet uses 38 thematic roles (or case/semantic roles, Fillmore 1968), leaving out adverbial roles that never occur as valency-bound elements in a frame, but only in free adverbials (such as §COND for conditional subclauses). The 38 roles are far from evenly distributed in running text. Table 1 provides some live corpus data, showing that the top 5 roles account for 2/3 of all role taggings in running text.

	Thematic Role	in corpus
§TH	Theme	31.75%
§AG	Agent	12.25%
§ATR	Attribute	12.25%
§PAT	Patient	5.12%
§COG	Cognizer	4.69%
§SP	Speaker	4.15%
§RES	Result	3.78%
§LOC	Location	2.95%
§DES	Destination	2.86%

---

[1]   A smaller set of 200 frame senses was also established, with a hypernym-mapping from the more fine-grained set, in part to allow some generalisation when used in e.g. syntactic disambiguation rules, in part to facilitate robust cross-language comparison - and possibly transfer - of frame types.

[2]   We wanted the class names to on the one hand be real verbs, on the other to reflect hypernym meanings wherever possible. Therefore, we avoided both example-based names (common in VerbNet) and - mostly - abstrac concept names (commen in FrameNet) that are not verbs themselves.

[3]   In 780 cases multiple verb senses share the same valency frame - in other words, in 6.5% of cases, verb senses cannot be disambiguated on syntactic function and form alone, but need help from semantic (noun) classes.

§ACT	Action	2.19%
§REC	Recipient	1.75%
§BEN	Beneficiary	1.65%
§EV	Event	1.56%
§EXP	Experiencer	1.31%

Table 1: Thematic Roles

Other roles: §STI - Stimulus; §REFL - Reflexive; §DON - Donor; §PATH - Path; §ORI - Origin; §EXT - Extension, §VAL - Value; §EXT-TMP - Duration; §MES - Message, §TP - Topic; §SOA - State of Affairs; §CAU - Cause; §ROLE - Role; §INS - Instrument, §MNR - Manner; §FIN - Purpose; §COMP - Comparison; §HOL - Whole, §PART - Part; §POSS Possessor, §ASS - Asset; §CONT - Content; §COM - Co-role; §INC - Incorporated

Even in a case-poor language like Danish, we found some clear likelihood relations between thematic roles and syntactic functions (table 2). Thus, agents (§AG, §COG, §SP) are typical subject roles, while patients (§PAT), actions (§ACT) and results (§RES) are typical direct object roles, and recipients (§REC) and beneficiaries (§BEN) call for dative object function.

	Function	most likely role
@SUBJ	Subject	TH > AG > COG > SP > PAT > EV > REC > EXP
@S-SUBJ	Situative subject	TH-NIL
@F-SUBJ	Formal subject	TH-NIL
@ACC	Accusative object	TH > PAT > ACT > RES > REFL > BEN > EV
@DAT	Dative object	REC > BEN > EXP
@PIV	Prepositional obj.	TH > DES > LOC > TP > AG > RES
@...-REFL	Reflexive	REFL
@SC	Subject complem.	ATR > RES
@OC	Object complem.	RES > ATR
@SA	SC Adverbial	LOC > DES
@OA	OC Adverbial	DES > MNR > LOC
@AUX<	Argument of aux.	-

Table 2: Syntactic Functions

The prototypical frame consists of a full verb and its nominal, adverbial or subclause complements. Like most other languages, however, Danish employs also verb incorporations that are not, in the semantical sense, complements. The simplest kind are adverb incorporates, which we mark in the valency frame, but not in the argument list:

kaste op (vomit) - <vi-op>

slå fra (deactivate) - <vt-fra>

komme ind på (discuss) - <på^vt-ind>

More complicated are support verb constructions, where the semantic weight and - to a certain degree - valency reside in a nominal element, typically a noun that syntactically fills a (direct or prepositional) object slot, but semantically orchestrates the other complements. While adverb incorporates are marked as such already at the syntactic level (@MV<)[4], noun incorporates receive an ordinary syntactic tag (@ACC), but are marked with an empty §INC (incorporate) role tag at the semantic level:

holde kæft (shut up) - <vt-kæft>

have brug for (need) - <for^vtp-brug>

One could argue that the real frame arguments (like the noun expressing what is needed in *have brug for*) should be dependency-linked to the §INC noun *brug* and the frame class marked on the latter, but for consistency and processing reasons we decided to center all dependency relations on the support verb in these cases, and also mark the frame name on the verbal element of support constructions.

Pp incorporates are in principle handled in the same way, with a syntactic @PIV tag on the preposition and an §INC role tag on its argument:

træde i kraft (take effect) - <vi-i=kraft>

However, some of these incorporates, especially those containing dative case, which is otherwise extinct in Danish, can be said to be so "frozen" that a preprocessing stage can turn them into one token, assigning an adverb tag to the pp, and allowing the role-free adverb incorporation solution:

have i sinde (intend) - <vt-i=sinde>

være på færde (be going on) - <vi-på=færde>

Independently of the one- or two-token treatment, incorporated pp's are treated alike in our FrameNet dictionary, as '-prp=noun' parts in the valency frame, without a separate argument line, the annotational difference being triggered solely by preprocessing conventions.

4   Frame annotation

One would assume that using argument information from our verb frame lexicon on the one hand and a functional dependency parser on the other,

---

[4]   We are here taking into account the (syntactic) annotation performed by DanGram, the parser used as input for our frame annotation system.

it should in theory be possible to annotate running text with verb senses and frame elements, simply by checking verb-argument dependencies for function and semantic class. To prove this assumption, we implemented our annotation module in the Constraint Grammar formalism, choosing this particular approach in part because that made it easier to exploit the DanGram-parser's existing CG annotation tags, but also to allow for later fine-tuning and contextual exceptions.

As a first step, we wrote a converter program (framenet2cgrules.pl) that turned each frame into a verb sense mapping rule - a relatively simple task, since argument checking amounts to simple LINKed dependency contexts in the CG formalism:

SUBSTITUTE (V) (<fn:consist> <r:SUBJ:HOL> <r:PIV:PART/MAT> V) TARGET ("bestå" <mv> V)
(1 (*) LINK *-1 VFIN LINK c @SUBJ LINK 0 <cc>) (c @PIV LINK 0 ("af") LINK c @P< LINK 0 <cc> OR <mat>) ;

In the example rule, apart from the <fn:consist> framenet class (implicitly: sense), argument relation tags (<r:....>) are added indicating a HOL role (whole) for the subject and a PART/MAT role (part/material) for the prepositional "af"-object, IF the former is a concrete object (<cc>) and the latter a physical object (<cc> = concrete countable) or a material (<mat>). In the definition section of the grammar, such semantic noun sets are expanded to individual semantic prototype classes (table 3):

LIST <cc> = <cc.*>r <cloH.*>r <con> <fruit> <furn> <tool.*>r <V.*>r ; (subtypes, clothing, containers, fruits, furniture, tools, vehicles)
LIST <mat> = <mat> <mat-cloth> <cm-chem> <cm.*>r ; (materials, chemicals, mass nouns)

	Semantic (prototype) noun class
<H>	human (<Hprof>, <Hfam>, <Hideo> ....)
<cc>	concrete object
<act>	action
<L>	location (<Lh, Ltop, Lwater, Labs ...)
<fact>	fact
<event>	event
<A>	animal
<sem-r>	"read"-semantical
<sem-s>	"speak"-semantical
<food>	food
<cm-liq>	liquid
<mon>	money
<sit>	situation
<sem-c>	semantic concept

<cm>	substance (concrete mass noun)
<Lsurf>	surface
<V>	vehicle (<Vground>,<Vair> ...)
<conv>	convention
<HH>	group
<an>	anatomical (body part)
.....	(about 200 classes)

Table 3: Semantic prototypes

Apart from semantic classes, the frame mapping rules in step one may exploit word class or phrase type (table 4). With noun phrases being the default, special context conditions will be added for finite or non-finite clausal arguments, adverbs or pronouns.

	Form type	
np	noun phrase or noun phrase in @PIV	
refl	reflexive pronoun	
fcl	finite subclause	
icl	non-finite subclause	
advl	adverb, adverb phrase or adverbial pp	
pl	plural np	
pron	impersonal pronoun (usually 'det')	
adj	adjective	
num	numeral	
pp	prepositional phrase, not in @PIV	
lex	incorporated lexical item	

Table 4: Morphosyntactic Form

For the second step, assigning thematic roles to arguments, we needed to either perform mappings on multiple (argument) contexts, or to target arguments and unify their function with the head verb's new <r:....> tag in order to retrieve (and map) the correct thematic role from the latter. To the best of our knowledge, no current CG compiler allowed either method, so we had to make changes in the compiler code of the open source CG3 variant we were using, for the first time allowing unification between tag-internal string variables and ordinary tag and map sets.

MAP KEEPORDER (VSTR:§§1) TARGET @SUBJ (*p V LINK -1 (*) LINK *1 (<r:.*>r) LINK 0 PAS LINK 0 (<r:ACC:\(.*\)>r)) ;

The rule above is a simple example, retrieving a thematic role variable from the verb's accusative argument tag (<r:ACC.:..>) and mapping it as a VSTR expression onto the subject in case the verb is in the passive voice. Complete rules will also contain negative contexts (omitted here), for instance ruling out the presence of objects for intransitive valency frames.

While helping to distinguish between verb senses with the same syntactic argument frame, using semantic noun classes as context restrictions raises the issue of circularity in terms of corpus example extraction, and also reduces overall robustness of frame tagging, not least in the presence of metaphor. Therefore, all frame mapping rules are run twice - first with semantic noun class restrictions in place, then - if necessary - without. This way "skeletal-syntactic" (semantics-free) argument structures can still be used as a backup for frame assignment, allowing corpus-based extension of semantic noun class restrictions.

In a vertical, one-word-per-line CG notation, the frame-tagger adds <fn:sense> and <v:valency> tags on verbs, and §ROLE tags on arguments. So far, free adverbial adjuncts are not role-tagged. The example demonstrates a frame sense distinction for the Danish verb *nedsætte*. Dependency arcs are shown as #n->m ID-links.

```
Nu "nu" <atemp> ADV @ADVL> #5->6
nedsætter "nedsætte" <mv> <v:vt> <fn:establish>
    PR AKT @FS-STA #6->0
regeringen "regering" <HH> N UTR S DEF NOM
    @<SUBJ §AG #7->6
en "en" ART UTR S IDF @>N #8->9
kommission "kommission" <HH> N UTR S IDF
    NOM @<ACC §RES #9->6
der skal undersøge, hvordan ...
```

(Literally: *Now establishes government-the a commission that shall investigate how ...*)

```
I Odenses Vollsmose er det først og fremmest
    miljøets manglende anseelse,
der "der" <clb> <rel> INDP nG nN NOM
    @SUBJ> §AG #12->13
nedsætter "nedsætte" <cjt-head> <mv> <v:vt>
    <fn:decrease> V PR AKT @FS-<SUBJ #13->5
forventningerne "forventning" <f-psych> N UTR P
    DEF NOM @<ACC §PAT #14->13
og "og" <co-fin> KC @CO #15->13
øger "øge" <nosubj> <cjt> <mv> <v:vt> <fn:in-
    crease> PR AKT @FS-<SUBJ #16->13
problemerne "problem" <ac> N NEU P DEF NOM
    @<ACC §PAT #17->16
```

(Literally: *In Odense's Vollsmose is it first of all the environment's lacking standing,that decreases expectations-the and increases problems-the.)*

N=noun, V=verb, ADV=adverb, INDP=independent pronoun, ART=article, KC=coordinating conjunction, @SUBJ=subject, @ACC=accusative object, @ADVL=adverbial, @CO=coordinator, @>N prenominal, @FS=finite clause, @STA=statement,

§AG=agent, §PAT=patient, §RES=result

5 Evaluation

To evaluate the coverage and precision of our frame tagger, we annotated a 2.4 million word chunk of newspaper text from the Danish daily *Information,* building on a DanGram dependency annotation (Bick 2005) as input, and using only the rules automatically created by our FrameNet conversion program, with no manual rule changes, rule ordering or additions.

Out of 289.720 main verbs, 98.8% were assigned a frame verb sense, albeit 19.2% of assignments were default senses for the verb in question because of the lack of surface arguments to match for sense-disambiguation. 15.0% of frames were subject-less infinitive and participle constructions, but of these, two thirds (10.9%) did have other, non-subject arguments to support frame assignment. The corpus contained 4051 verb lexeme types, and the frame tagger assigned 9195 different frame types, and 5929 verb sense types. Type-wise, this amounts to 2.26 frames, and 1.46 senses per verb type (similar to the distribution in the frame lexicon itself), but token-wise ambiguity is about double that figure, as we will discuss later in this chapter.

	frame slots	expressed surface arguments with frame roles	percentage of filled slots
SUBJ	176831	90981	51.45%
ACC	92610	71336	77.03%
DAT	806	433	53.72%
PIV	22718	22542	99.23%
SC	15120	15120	100.00%
OC	432	432	100.00%
SA	6024	6024	100.00%
OA	191	191	100.00%
ADVL	92	92	100.00%

Table 5: Surface expression of arguments

Table 5 contains a break-down of surface expression percentages for individual argument types. Apart from subjects in non-finite clauses, dative objects are the least obligatory category. Predicative arguments, of verbs like *være (be)*, *blive (become)*, are 100% expressed, and prepositional arguments (PIV) have almost as high an expression rate simply because most verbs have alternative valency frames of lower order (intransitive or monotransitive accusative) that the tagger would have chosen in the absence of a PIV argument. In other words, PIV arguments are strong sense markers, and there absence will sooner lead to false-positive senses of lower valency-order than to PIV-senses without surface PIV.

On a random 5000-word chunk of the frame-annotated data, a complete error count was performed for all verbs. All in all, there were 566 main verb tags, 4 of which (0.7%) had been wrongly verb-tagged by the parser, in one case due to a spelling error. For 3 verbs (0.5%), the parser offered a wrong (same-form) lemma. Our frame tagger assigned 561 frames, missing out on 3 regular verbs, and (wrongly) tagging 2 of the false-positive verbs. Only 1 verb was not covered by the frame lexicon, suggesting a very good raw coverage (99.82%). In 15.7% of cases, the frame tagger assigned a default frame, usually a low-order valency frame without incorporates[5]. Of 562 possible frames, 478 were correctly tagged, yielding the following correctness figures:

	Recall	Precision	F-score
total	85.05%	85.20%	85,12
ignoring parse errors	85.51%	86.91%	86,20

Table 6: Recall and precision

These figures are an encouraging result, despite the "weak" (inspection-based) evaluation method. No other frame-/role-tagger could be found for Danish, but Shi & Mihalcea (2004), also using FrameNet-derived rules, report an F-score of 74.5% for English, while Gildea & Jurafsky (2002), using statistical methods, report F-scores of 80.4% and 82.1% for frame roles and abstract thematic roles, respectively. For copula and support verb constructions, not included in the earlier evaluations, Johansson & Nugues (2006) report tagging accuracies for English of 71-73%, respectively, but a comparison is hard to make, since we only looked at support constructions that our FrameNet does know, with no idea about the theoretical lexical "coverage ceiling".

A break-down of error types revealed that 39% of all false positive errors (but only 5.7% of all frames) were cases where the human "gold sense" was not on the list of possible senses in the framenet database. 11 false positives

(13.3%) were caused by errors from the parsing stage (wrong lemma, auxiliary or syntactic tag). Ignoring these errors, i.e. assuming correct parsing input, would influence precision, in particular, and raise the overall F-score by 1 percentage point. As one might expect, default mappings accounted for a higher percentage (24.7%) among error verbs than in the chunk as a whole (15.7%), and contributed to almost a third of the "frame-not-in-lexicon" cases.

Frequent verbs have a high sense ambiguity, and verbs with a high sense ambiguity were more error-prone than one-sense verbs, as can be seen from table 7. Thus, the verbs occurring in our evaluation chunk had 4.21 potential senses per verb (6.77 for the ambiguous ones), and the verbs accounting for frame tagging errors had a theoretical 10.08 senses each.

	count	theoretical sense count	senses / verb	sense count in chunk (as tagged)
framenet lexicon	6825	9933	1.46	-
verb types in chunk	243	1022	4.21	275
sense ambiguous	135	914	6.77	167
frame error verbs	40	403	10.08	51

Table 7: Sense ambiguity per verb

6 Conclusion and future work

We have reported work on a comprehensive framenet for Danish, with over 12.000 frames, and a lexeme coverage of almost 100%. After conversion of our framenet into CG rules, the combined parser-frametagger coverage was 94.3% (i.e. only 5.7% match-less default mappings), with an overall F-score for frame senses of 85.12.

Still, given the fact that almost 40% of frame tagging errors were due to missing frame senses, the current framenet should be checked against larger amounts of corpus data to identify senses not captured by our valency-based approach. In particular, noun-incorporations (e.g. *finde sted - take place*) may require further research, since the original DanGram valency lexicon only treated adverb incorporations, and all other incorporations were added in a piecemeal fashion.

On the frametagger side, our CG conversion approach should allow improvements by manually ordering or modifying frame-derived map-

---

[5] The default frame is not currently based on statistics, but decided upon when converting the framenet lexicon into a Constraing Grammar, as the first intransitive or monotransitive valency frame by order of appearance in the lexicon. Ultimately, therefore, the default choice is under the control of the lexicographer, who can change the frame order in the lexicon.

ping rules, adding more complex context conditions where necessary. Finally, to confirm our intuition as to the effectiveness of the CG conversion approach, it should be compared to a scoring method where frame conditions are matched and counted individually against the parse tree. With either method, the Danish FrameNet could be used to annotate large corpora for manual revision, ultimately allowing hybridization with a statistical frame tagger.

References

Bick, Eckhard. 2001. En Constraint Grammar Parser for Dansk. in Peter Widell & Mette Kunøe (eds.): *8. Møde om Udforskningen af Dansk Sprog,* 12.-13. oktober 2000, pp. 40-50, Århus University

Bick, Eckhard. 2005. Turning Constraint Grammar Data into Running Dependency Treebanks. In: Civit, Montserrat & Kübler, Sandra & Martí, Ma. Antònia (red.), *Proceedings of TLT 2005,* Barcelona, December 9th - 10th, 2005, pp.19-27

Baker, Collin F., Fillmore, J. Charles & John B. Lowe. 1998. The Berkeley FrameNet project. In Proceedings of the COLING-ACL, Montreal, Canada

Braasch, Anna & Sussi Olsen. 2004. STO: A Danish Lexicon Resource - Ready for Applications. In: Fourth International Conference on Language Resources and Evaluation, Proceedings, Vol. IV. Lisbon, pp. 1079-1082.

Fellbaum, Christiane (ed.). 1998. *WordNet: An Eletronic Lexical Database.* Language, Speech and Communications. MIT Press: Cambridge, Massachusetts.

Fillmore, Charles J. 1968. The case for case. In Bach and Harms (Ed.): *Universals in Linguistic Theory.* New York: Holt, Rinehart, and Winston, 1-88.

Gildea, D. and D. Jurafsky. 2002. Automatic Labeling of Semantic Roles, Computational Linguistics, 28(3) 245-288.

Johansson, Richard & Pierre Nugues. 2006. Automatic Annotation for All Semantic Layers in FrameNet. *Proceedings of EACL 2006.* Trento, Italy.

Johnson, Christopher R. & Charles J. Fillmore. 2000. The FrameNet tagset for frame-semantic and syntactic coding of predicate-argument structure. In *Proceedings of the 1st Meeting of the North American Chapter of the Association for Computational Linguistics* (ANLP-NAACL 2000), April 29-May 4, 2000, Seattle WA, pp. 56-62.

Kipper, Karin & Anna Korhonen, Neville Ryant, and Martha Palmer. 2006. Extensive Classifications of English verbs. *Proceedings of the 12th EURALEX International Congress.* Turin, Italy. September, 2006.

Levin, Beth. 1993. *English Verb Classes and Alternation, A Preliminary Investigation.* The University of Chicago Press.

Palmer, Martha, Dan Gildea, Paul Kingsbury. 2005. The Proposition Bank: An Annotated Corpus of Semantic Roles. *Computational Linguistics, 31:1.,* pp. 71-105, March, 2005.

Pedersen, B.S., S. Nimb & L. Trap-Jensen. 2008. DanNet: udvikling og anvendelse af det danske wordnet. In: *Nordiske Studier i leksikografi Vol. 9, Skrifter published by Nordisk Forening for Leksikografi, pp. 353-370*

Ruppenhofer, Josef, Michael Ellsworth, Miriam R. L. Petruck, Christopher R. Johnson, Jan Scheffczyk. 2010. *FrameNet II: Extended Theory and Practice.* (http://framenet.icsi.berkeley.edu/index.php?option=com_wrapper&Itemid=126)

Schøsler, Lene & Sabine Kirchmeier-Andersen (eds.). 1997. The Pronominal Approach Applied to Danish. Studies in Valency II. Rask Supplement Vol. 5. Odense University Press.

Shi, Lei & Rada Mihalcea. 2004. Open Text Semantic Parsing Using FrameNet and WordNet. In HLT-NAACL 2004, Demonstration Papers. pp. 19-22

Appendix 1 - verb categories

Groups	Verbal Classes (494)
Aux and simple construction verbs (30)	(1) be_copula, be_place, consist, be_name, be_part, be_like, be_attribute, be_valid, abound, lack_itr, become, (2) become_be, become_part, get_part, (3) do, work, work_as, work_for, function, do_leisure, take_action, resist, train, (5) have, have_attr, have_part, lack, contain_have (6) must, (7) can
Puttning (22)	(9) put, put_deposit, put_spatial, funnel, raise, lower, flow, pour, spread, coil, uncoil, spray, heap, cover_ize, pollute, fill, uncover_ize, cover, uncover, adorn, confine, park
Removing (16)	(10) remove, exclude, come_off, banish, empty, wipe, clean suck, steal, rid, cheat, exonerate, peel, mine, unhire, resign, renounce
Taking and Bringing (9)	(11) transfer, send, moveO, take, bring, carry, transport, (12) pull, push
Giving and Getting (20)	(13) give, sell, accrue_to, contribute, salary, future_having, supply, equip, man, burden, buy, gain, obtain, employ, get, lose, cause_gain, exchange, trade, berry
Handling (20)	(14) lean, study, get_to_know, forget, check_if, read, (15) hold, grasp, keep, handle, (16) hide, (17) throw, pelt, discard, (18) hit, beat, hit_goal, hurt, spank, bump

Manipulating Entities (79)	(19) poke, (20) touch, touch_exp, (21) cut, crush, perforate, prune, (22) combine, add, absorb, connect, integrate, associate, contrast, link_soc, register, exempt, scramble, group, bond, fasten, cling, (23) separate, divide, split, unattach, differ, (24) colouring, lighting, (25) mark, write, note, label, transcribe, imitate, (26) make, grow, breed, cultivate, create_food, prepare_food, prepare, create, create_finish, create_semantic, shape, deflect, turn_into, convert, modify, perform, rehearse, adjust, process, (27) cause, interact, implement, (28) spawn, (29) appoint, predestine, characterize, portray, name, declare, declare_oc, proclaim, assume, predict, behave, role_as, role_oc, role_sc, now, think, regard_as, remember, classify, dicide, choose
Percepting and emoting (20)	(30) see, hear, sense, undergo, notice, watch, listen, percep, stimulus_subj, (31) affect_exp, emote_obj, like, dislike, obey, disobey, emote, suffer, marvel, attract, repel
Wanting (14)	(32) wish, prefer_to, prefer_oc, long, (33) judge, accuse, praise, speak_affect, analyze, (35) hunt, capture, search, investigate, rummage
Speaking and meeting (33)	(36) socialize, socializeO, play, encounter, fight, dispute, (37) explain, quote, dedicate, inquire, interrogate, teach, tell, identify, speak_mnr, speak_tool, talk, discuss, say, suggest, hint, answer, refuse, advertise, lie, speak_emot, advise, concede, elaborate, emphasize, promise, invoke, reveal
Body (32)	(38) sound_biocom, eat, drink, booze, chew, swallow, dine, thrive, feed, digest, (40) sound_body, excrete, breathe, show_emot, gesture, body_moveO, politing, bodystate, body_moveSA, die, pain, hurt_self, change_bodystate, (41) body_care, comb, dress, undress, serve, (42) kill, kill_method, subjugate
Emanating (8)	(43) light_emission, sound_emission, make_noise, smell_emission, substance_emission, reflect, burn, emit
Changing (27)	(44) destroy, collapse, (45) break, deform, heat, cool, alter, activate, deactivate, open, close, improve, worsen, tighten, loosen, change_process, decay, increase, decrease, oscillate, double, changeS, calibrate, repair, therapy, solve, damage
Moving and Placing (35)	(46) lodge, enter, invade, usurp, permeate, (47) exist, persist, endure, depend, moveS_fluidic, moveO_fluidic, moveO_lokal, moveS_local, orient, sound_move, swarm, collect, accumulate, gather, bulge, spatial_conf, shape_change, meander, border, cross, stretch, (48) appear, show, originate, result, disappear, occur, befall, occur_dynamic, (49) body_moveSC
Mdes of Movement (19)	(50) change_body_pos, body_pos, (51) move_dir, rise, fall, leave, roll, run, vehicle, steer, dance, chase, accompany, reach, (52) avoid, (53) linger, delay, rush
Measuring (7)	(54) measure_tr, measure_itr, cost, contain_quant, fit, assess, bill
Starting, stopping and ongoing (14)	(55) start, begin, start_movement, complete_process, continue, stop, end, hinder, halt, establish, unestablish, run_obj, sustain, (57) weather
Influencing (13)	(58) urge, beg, (59) force, (60) order, demand, summon, (61) try_to, test, (62) plan, (63) enforce, (64) allow, welcome, (65) facilitate
Social interaction (24)	(66) consume, economize, (67) forbid, (68) pay, (69) refrain, (70) rely, (71) conspire, (72) help, benefit, detriment, affect, punish, (73) cooperate, participate, vicariate, (74) succeed, fail, (75) neglect, (76) limit, (77) approve, reject, (78) indicate, confirm, (79) devote
Handling conflicts (19)	(80) liberate, (82) withdraw, (83) cope, (84) discover, (85) defend_phys, defend_cog, attack, (86) correlate, relate, compensate, match, (87) focus, comprehend, (88) mind, (89) agree, (90) exceed, vanquish, exaggerate, (91) matter
Rest - ressource allocation, complex operations (23)	(92) institutionalize, (93) adopt, (94) risk, (95) surrender, (96) accustom, (97) base, deduce, (98) confront, (99) ensure, insure, (100) own, belong_to, (101) patent, (102) promote, (102) require, (104) spend_time, (105) use, serve_as, serve_to, (106) void, (107) include, involve, (108) math

ISSN 1736-6305 Vol. 11
http://hdl.handle.net/10062/16955

Extraction from Relative and Embedded Interrogative Clauses in Danish

Anne Bjerre
University of Southern Denmark
Engstien 1
DK-6000 Kolding
bjerre@sitkom.sdu.dk

Abstract

In Danish relative clauses and embedded interrogative clauses are not extraction islands. However, there is an asymmetry between the two clauses. In Danish it is possible to extract the subject out of an embedded interrogative clause. Extraction of the subject out of a relative clause, on the other hand, is not allowed. In this paper we present a formal HPSG analysis of extraction in Danish which treats the extraction out of relative and embedded interrogative clauses in a uniform manner, and the asymmetry between the clauses will be shown to follow from a more general constraint on adjuncts.

1 Introduction

Relative clauses and embedded interrogative clauses are commonly taken not to allow extraction. This has been extensively discussed under the headings of extraction islands, (Ross, 1967), subjacency and the Empty Category Principle, (Chomsky, 1973). In Danish, relative clauses and embedded interrogative clauses are not extraction islands. However, there is an asymmetry between the two clauses, as also noted by e.g. Engdahl (1984), in that it is not possible to extract the highest subject out of a relative clause, a restriction that does not apply to embedded interrogatives.

It has been suggested that there is a structural difference between relative clauses and embedded interrogative clauses that might explain the different behaviour when it comes to subject extraction, e.g. Engdahl (1984). She suggests that relative clauses are of category $\bar{S}$, whereas interrogative clauses are of type $\bar{\bar{S}}$ which has an extra XP position. This difference has the consequence that the empty category in subject position in relative clauses is not properly governed. Consequently

the Empty Category Principle rules out extractions of subjects from relative clauses.

In feature-based analyses it has been suggested that subject extraction does not involve extraction at all, e.g. Gazdar (1981) and Pollard and Sag (1994). However, in more recent feature-based analyses, e.g. Sag (1997), Bouma et al. (2000), Ginzburg and Sag (2000) and Sag (to appear), subjects are also treated as being extracted. The analyses have been influenced by discussions by e.g. Hukari and Levine (1996) concerning subject extraction, arguing that there is cross-language evidence that subjects are also extracted in the same way as complements.

In this paper we provide a feature-based analysis of extraction that treats the extraction of subjects out of embedded interrogatives and relative clauses in a uniform manner, and show that the asymmetry between the clauses follow from a more general constraint on adjuncts clauses.

In section 2 we show the relevant Danish extraction data. Then in section 3 we go on to present the analytical background that the formalization of our analysis is based on. Then our analysis is formalized in section 4. In section 5 we discuss the Complex NP Constraint, and finally we conclude in section 6.

2 The Danish data

As stated above, relative and embedded interrogative clauses are not extraction islands in Danish. In (1) we find examples of object extractions from these clauses.[1]

(1) a. Bøden fatter   jeg ikke hvem
         The fine understand I   not   whom
         der   har modtaget.
         there has received

---

[1]The examples in the present paper are from Hansen (1974), KORPUSDK and the Internet.

">

b. Betændelse kender jeg mange der
Infection   know   I   many   there
har   haft, i   en mild fom.
have had, in a   mild form

In (2) we find examples of subject extractions from embedded interrogatives.

(2)   a. Nu   har   jeg fundet det dokument,
Now have I   found the document,
som jeg i går   ikke vidste hvor
C   I   yesterday not   knew   where
var.
was

b. ?Jeg traf en fyr som jeg bare ikke
I   met a   guy C   I   just not
kan huske   hvor   der   boede.
can remember where there lived

In contrast, (3) shows that subject extraction out of relative clauses is not possible.

(3)   a. Tv-nævnet   bad   TV2 om en
The Tv committee asked TV2 for a
redegørelse i sagen,   hvilken
report   in the case, which
Pernille fik til opgave at skrive.
Pernille got to task   to write
'The Tv committee asked TV2 for a
report in the case, which Pernille got
the task of writing'

b. *Pernille bad   tv-nævnet
Pernille   asked The Tv committee
TV2 om en redegørelse i sagen,
TV2 for a report   in the case,
hvilken fik til opgave at skrive.
which   got to task   to write

c. *Pernille bad   tv-nævnet
Pernille   asked The Tv committee
TV2 om en redegørelse i sagen,
TV2 for a report   in the case,
hvilken der   fik til opgave at skrive.
which   there got to task   to write

d. Han stillede et spørgsmål, som
He   asked   a   question,   C
ministeren   ikke var forberedt på.
the minister not   was prepared for

e. *Ministeren stillede han et
The minister asked he   a
spørgsmål, som ikke var forberedt
question,   C   not was prepared

på.
for

f. *Ministeren stillede han et
The minister asked he   a
spørgsmål, som der   ikke var
question,   C   there not   was
forberedt på.
prepared for

Apart from the difference in extraction potential between subjects and objects, the insertion of expletive *der* ('there') instead of a gap in some of the clauses should be noted. As observed in Hansen (1974), *der* is inserted in local subject extractions in standard Danish, cf. (1a) and (1b). In non-local subject extractions *der* is not inserted in standard Danish, cf. (2a). In non-standard Danish *der* insertion is also found in non-local subject extractions, cf. (2b).

3   Analytical background

Before our analysis is presented we will go through the analytical background that we base our analysis on. The analysis is largely based on the feature-based account of extraction in Ginzburg and Sag (2000), cf. also Neville and Paggio (2004) for an analysis of Danish relative clause constructions. The presentation of the formal background here is by no means exhaustive, and the semantics of the analysis is left out. However, a number of important assumptions for the purpose of understanding the formalization in section 4 are explained. The grammar used is a hierarchy of typed feature structures with associated implicational constraints constraining what constitutes well-formed linguistic entities.

Within the HPSG framework, constructions involving extractions are called filler-gap constructions. Filler-gap constructions are specified for the feature SLASH, and filler-gap dependencies are established through the inheritance of SLASH specifications. A non-empty SLASH specification is introduced at the lowest level where the "gap" is introduced, then passed up through the structure, to be bound off by the filler. In (5) the specification for the SLASH feature in a filler-gap construction, like the highlighted part of (4), is illustrated.

(4)   Han var klippen *på hvilken, man stod*.
He   was the rock on which   one stood

(5)
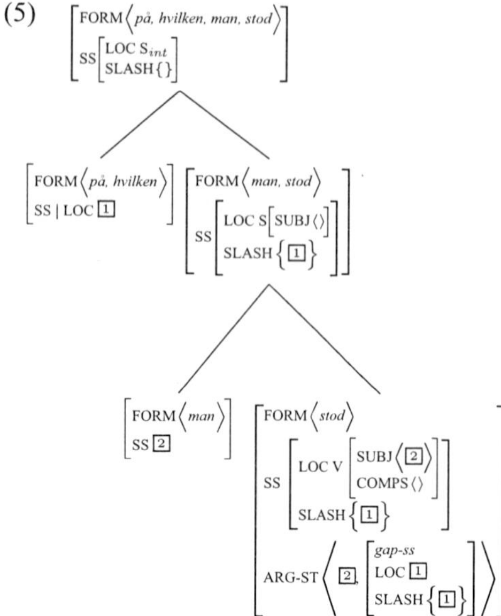

A "gap" in the structure is a feature structure of type *gap-s(yn)s(em)*. The *gap-ss* type does not have any phonological content, and it shares its syntactic and semantic content with its corresponding overt element. It is constrained by the constraint in (6).

(6) $gap\text{-}ss \Longrightarrow \begin{bmatrix} \text{LOC } \boxed{1} \\ \text{SLASH} \{\boxed{1}\} \end{bmatrix}$

The structure in (5) is constrained by a set of constraints. The non-empty SLASH feature is introduced by the Argument Realization Principle, (Ginzburg and Sag, 2000, p. 171), and the SLASH-Amalgamation Constraint, (Ginzburg and Sag, 2000, p. 169). These are shown in (7) and (8), respectively.

(7)
Argument Realization Principle:
word $\Longrightarrow$
$$\begin{bmatrix} \text{SS} \,|\, \text{LOC} \,|\, \text{CAT} \begin{bmatrix} \text{SUBJ } \boxed{A} \\ \text{SPR } \boxed{B} \\ \text{COMPS } \boxed{C} \ominus list(gap\text{-}ss) \end{bmatrix} \\ \text{ARG-ST } \boxed{A} \oplus \boxed{B} \oplus \boxed{C} \end{bmatrix}$$

(8)
SLASH-Amalgamation Constraint:
word $\Longrightarrow$
$$\begin{bmatrix} \text{SS} \,|\, \text{SLASH } \boxed{\Sigma_1} \cup ... \cup \boxed{\Sigma_n} \\ \text{ARG-ST} \left\langle \begin{bmatrix} \text{SLASH } \boxed{\Sigma_1} \end{bmatrix}, ... , \begin{bmatrix} \text{SLASH } \boxed{\Sigma_n} \end{bmatrix} \right\rangle \end{bmatrix}$$

The Argument Realization Principle may introduce a "gap" on the ARG-ST list of a word,

at the same time, removing *synsem*s that have been resolved to *gap-ss* from the COMPS list of a word. The SLASH-Amalgamation Constraint ensures that the SLASH values of the arguments of a word are inherited by the word itself. This is also known as lexicalized SLASH-amalgamation. The SLASH-Amalgamation Constraint is a default constraint. The inheritance of the SLASH value in constructions is taken care of by the Generalized Head Feature Principle, (Ginzburg and Sag, 2000, p. 33), which specifies inter alia the inheritance of the SLASH feature from the head-daughter to the mother in a construction.

Finally, various constraints are responsible for binding off the SLASH value, either constraints involving a filler daughter or constraints involving constructional gap-binding. Constraints involving a filler daughter are constraints that are subtypes of the more general constraint on *hd-fill-ph*, e.g. wh[2]-interrogative clauses. This contraint is shown in (9), cf. Ginzburg and Sag (2000, p. 174).

(9) *hd-fill-ph*:
$$\begin{bmatrix} \text{SLASH } \boxed{\Sigma_2} \end{bmatrix} \rightarrow$$
$$\begin{bmatrix} \text{LOC } \boxed{1} \end{bmatrix}, \mathbf{H} \begin{bmatrix} phrase \\ \text{HEAD } v \\ \text{SLASH} \{\boxed{1}\} \uplus \boxed{\Sigma_2} \end{bmatrix}$$

This constraint removes the *gap-ss* from the SLASH set which corresponds to the LOCAL value of the filler daughter.

Constructional gap-binding occurs in e.g. relative clauses which do not contain relative pronouns. In such cases a certain construction binds off the "gap" instead of a wh-word. Sag (1997) introduces the *non-wh-rel-cl* with the constraint shown in (10).

(10) *non-wh-rel-cl*:
$$\begin{bmatrix} \text{HEAD} \,|\, \text{MOD } \overline{\text{N}}_i \\ \text{SLASH} \{\} \end{bmatrix} \rightarrow \mathbf{H} \begin{bmatrix} \text{SLASH} \{\text{NP}_i\} \end{bmatrix}$$

The effect is to build a unary branching structure which turns a clause into a relative clause by binding off the "gap", while at the same time introducing a MOD feature and co-indexing the index on the element in the SLASH set with the index of the MOD value. In this way co-indexing between the modified noun and the "gap" is ensured. The

---

[2] We use "wh" for the Danish "hv" words.

highlighted part of (11) is an example of constructional gap-binding which is shown in (12).[3,4]

(11) Det er fordi de i naturen skal
This is because they in the nature must
kunne følge de   fisk, *som de   spiser.*
could follow those fish, C   they eat

(12)

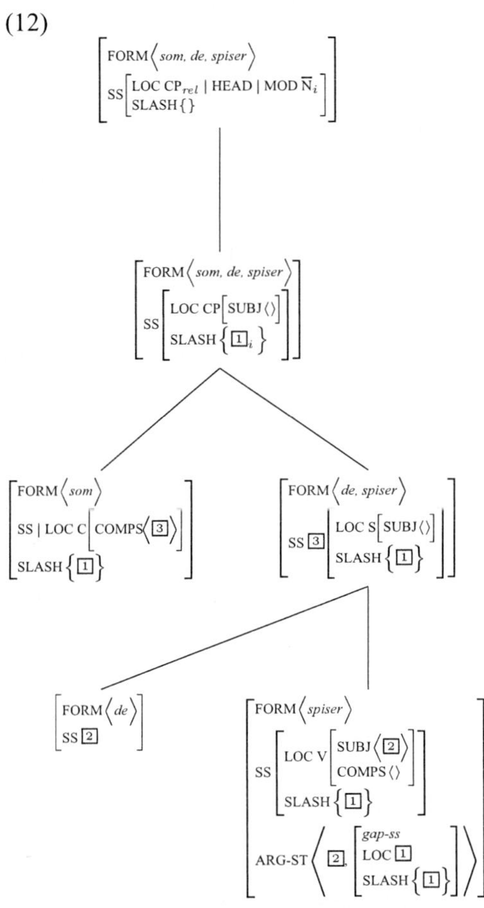

Note that because of the Generalized Head Feature Principle, the SLASH value is passed up to the clause via the complementizer which is analyzed as the head of the clause.

4 Formal analysis

In this section the proposed formal analysis of Danish extraction is presented. The analysis is a further development of the analysis presented in Bjerre (to appear).

As explained in section 3, a "gap" in the structure is a feature structure of type *gap-s(yn)s(em)* which does not have any phonological content, cf. the constraint in (6). To account for the Danish *der* insertion phenomenon in certain subject extraction contexts, we introduce another type of noncanonical *synsem* type. The extended hierarchy is shown in (13).

(13)

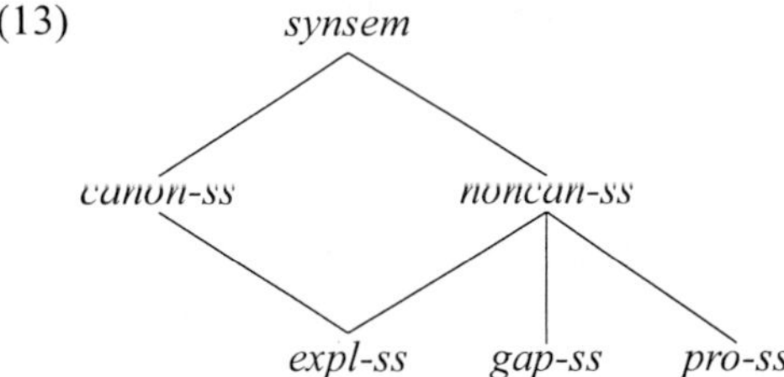

The type *expl-ss* is a synsem which has phonological content, and it is consequently a subtype of *canon-ss*. But, as the *gap-ss*, the *expl-ss* does not have any semantic content of its own. The two latter types differ in that the *gap-ss* also has no syntactic content, unlike the expletive. (14) shows the constraint for *expl-ss*.

(14) $expl\text{-}ss \Longrightarrow \left[\text{LOC} \begin{bmatrix} \text{CAT} \mid \text{HEAD } expl \\ \text{CONT } \boxed{1} \end{bmatrix} \right.$
$\left. \text{SLASH} \left\{ \left[\text{CONT } \boxed{1} \right] \right\} \right]$

In Danish, the Argument Realization Principle additionally removes *synsem*s that have been resolved to *gap-ss* from the SUBJ list of the word. However, the subject is visible as the value of the SUBJECT feature.[5] The Danish Argument Realization Principle is shown in (15).

(15)

Argument Realization Principle (Danish):
word $\Longrightarrow$

---

[3]We follow Erteschik-Shir (1984) and Vikner (1991) in treating "som" as a complementizer. This is motivated e.g. by (non-standard) examples like (1) where we have combinations of wh-pronouns and "som", and another complementizer "at" ('that'). In such cases, the wh-pronoun binds off the slash value.

(1) ?Ved du hvem som at der ellers   kommer
Know you who C   that there otherwise comes
til nytår?
to new year

[4]Another example is relative clauses without both relative pronoun and "som", as the example in (1).

(1) Der var engang en dreng, der fik en lillesøster
There was once a boy, there had a little sister
med vinger.
with wings

[5]Cf. Meurers (1999) for further arguments that we need a SUBJECT feature as part of the HEAD feature.

$$\left[\begin{array}{l} \text{SS}\,|\,\text{LOC}\,|\,\text{CAT}\left[\begin{array}{l} \text{HEAD}\,|\,\text{SUBJECT}\;\boxed{A} \\ \text{SUBJ}\;\boxed{A}\ominus list(gap\text{-}ss) \\ \text{SPR}\;\boxed{B} \\ \text{COMPS}\;\boxed{C}\ominus list(gap\text{-}ss) \end{array}\right] \\ \text{ARG-ST}\;\boxed{A}\oplus\boxed{B}\oplus\boxed{C} \end{array}\right]$$

The Argument Realization Principle gives rise to inter alia the words in (16) and (17).

(16)
$$\left[\begin{array}{l} word \\ \text{SS}\,|\,\text{LOC}\,|\,\text{CAT}\left[\begin{array}{l} \text{HEAD}\,|\,\text{SUBJECT}\;\boxed{A} \\ \text{SUBJ}\;\langle\rangle \\ \text{COMPS}\;\boxed{B} \end{array}\right] \\ \text{ARG-ST}\;\boxed{A}\big\langle gap\text{-}ss\big\rangle\oplus\boxed{B} \end{array}\right]$$

(17)
$$\left[\begin{array}{l} word \\ \text{SS}\,|\,\text{LOC}\,|\,\text{CAT}\left[\begin{array}{l} \text{HEAD}\,|\,\text{SUBJECT}\;\boxed{A} \\ \text{SUBJ}\;\boxed{A} \\ \text{COMPS}\;\boxed{B} \end{array}\right] \\ \text{ARG-ST}\;\boxed{A}\big\langle expl\text{-}ss\big\rangle\oplus\boxed{B} \end{array}\right]$$

Words with a subject which has a *gap-ss* value have an empty SUBJ list. This is in contrast to Ginzburg and Sag (2000), where a *gap-ss* remains on the SUBJ list. This is to account for the potential realization of an expletive in subject position in Danish. If the subject is resolved to an *expl-ss*, it remains on the SUBJ list to be cancelled off in the *hd-subj-ph*.

Now to the lexical inheritance of SLASH specifications. Here we have to take into account the Danish *der* insertion phenomenon. So in addition to the default SLASH-Amalgamation Constraint we need a second constraint for Danish, the *Expletive* SLASH Constraint in (18), cf. (Bjerre, to appear).

(18)
Expletive SLASH Constraint:

$$\neg\left[\begin{array}{l} word \\ \text{ARG-ST}\;\left\langle\left[\begin{array}{l} \text{L}\,|\,\text{C}\,|\,\text{H}\,|\,\text{S}\;\big\langle expl\text{-}ss_i\big\rangle \\ \text{SLASH}\;\{\boxed{1}_i\}\uplus\boxed{\Sigma_1} \end{array}\right],\dots\right\rangle \end{array}\right]$$

The constraint in (18) makes sure that *der* insertion only takes place if we have a local subject extraction. The constraint excludes words which contain an element on the ARG-ST list with an expletive subject corresponding to an element in the

SLASH set. This means that a SLASH value originating from an expletive can only be bound off locally. The *Expletive* SLASH Constraint applies in standard Danish, but as we saw in section 2, not in non-standard Danish.

Now we come to the binding off of the SLASH value. For the present purpose, extraction out of embedded interrogatives and relative, we need the types listed in (19), cf. the clause hierarchy set up in Ginzburg and Sag (2000).

(19)   a. *fin-wh-ns-int-cl*

        b. *fin-wh-ns-rel-cl*

        c. *fin-non-wh-rel-cl*

In the following we will concentrate on what constraints are involved in structures of these types, but we will not be specific about where the constraints originate from. Some of the constraints may be specific to these types, others may be inherited from more general types.

The data we need to account for with the *fin-wh-ns-int-cl* construction are (2) repeated in (20). The construction covers the highlighted parts of the examples.

(20)   a. Nu har jeg fundet det dokument,
          Now have I   found the document,

          som jeg i går   ikke vidste ***hvor***
          C I   yesterday not knew where

          var.
          was

        b. ?Jeg traf en fyr som jeg bare ikke
          I   met a guy C   I   just not

          kan huske   ***hvor der boede.***
          can remember where there lived

The constraints for the highlighted embedded wh-interrogative clauses in (20) are given in (21).

(21) *fin-wh-ns-int-cl*

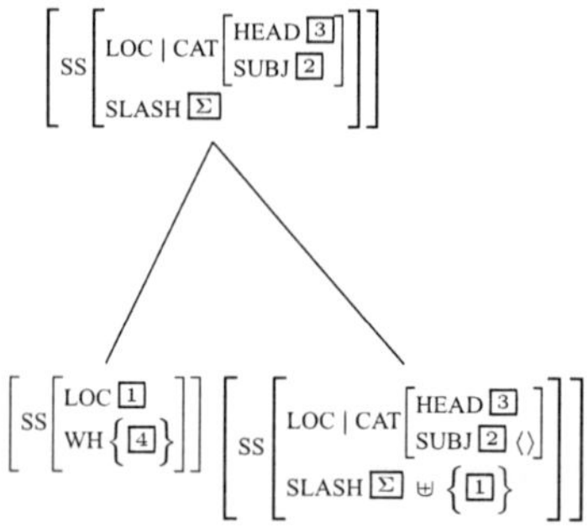

The element in the head daughter's SLASH set which corresponds to the filler daughter is bound off. The SLASH set may contain a second element, corresponding to an extracted subject. This element is not bound off, but passed on to the mother. The value of the head daughter's scshape subject list may in that case be either a *gap-ss*, as in (20a) or a *expl-ss* as in (20b). If both the SLASH-Amalgamation Constraint and the *Expletive* SLASH Constraint are applied, only the example without an expletive subject is well-formed, as an element in the SLASH set corresponding to the expletive subject will not be amalgamated by a selecting head. If only the SLASH-Amalgamation Constraint is applied both examples are well-formed, as the SLASH set corresponding to an expletive subject is not excluded by the *Expletive* SLASH Constraint. Importantly, nothing prevents a subject from being extracted.

We turn now to the relative clause examples. The data we need to account for with the *fin-wh-ns-rel-cl* construction are the examples in (3b) and (3c) repeated in (22). The construction covers the highlighted parts.

(22)   a.   *Pernille bad   tv-nævnet
              Pernille   asked The Tv committee
              TV2 om en redegørelse i   sagen,
              TV2 for a   report   in the case,
              hvilken fik   til opgave at skrive.
              which   got to task   to write

        b.   *Pernille bad   tv-nævnet
              Pernille   asked The Tv committee
              TV2 om en redegørelse i   sagen,
              TV2 for a   report   in the case,
              hvilken der   fik   til opgave at skrive.
              which   there got to task   to write

We use an extended ARG-ST list for words as in Ginzburg and Sag (2000). There it is used for certain optionally selected adjuncts. We assume that noun words may be derived from noun lexemes with an additional element on the ARG-ST list, ie. a restrictive relative clause. This means that the Argument Realization Principle will give rise to a representation as shown in (23) with a restrictive relative clause on the COMPS list.

(23)

$$\begin{bmatrix} \textit{noun} \\ \text{SS} \mid \text{LOC} \mid \text{CAT} \begin{bmatrix} \text{SPR } \boxed{A} \\ \text{COMPS } \boxed{B} \end{bmatrix} \\ \text{ARG-ST } \boxed{A} \oplus \boxed{B} \left\langle \left[\text{L} \mid \text{C} \mid \text{H} \mid \text{MOD } \overline{\text{N}} \right] \right\rangle \end{bmatrix}$$

The consequence of this analysis is that the SLASH value of a restrictive relative clause will be passed on to the head noun by the SLASH-Amalgamation Constraint.

The important constraint on finite adjunct clauses that gives rise to the asymmetry between relative clauses and embedded interrogative clauses is introduced in (24).

(24)

$$\neg \begin{bmatrix} \textit{fin-adjunct-cl} \\ \text{SS} \begin{bmatrix} \text{LOC} \mid \text{CAT} \begin{bmatrix} \text{HEAD} \mid \text{S} \left\langle \textit{noncan-ss}_i \right\rangle \\ \text{SUBJ} \left\langle \right\rangle \end{bmatrix} \\ \text{SLASH } \boxed{1} \left\{ \textit{local}_i \right\} \uplus \boxed{\Sigma} \end{bmatrix} \end{bmatrix}$$

The constraint expresses the generalization that adjunct clauses require a subject. The constraint excludes adjunct clauses which contain a non-canonical subject which has not already been bound off.

The *fin-wh-ns-rel-cl* is a subtype of *fin-adjunct-cl* and is subject to the constraint in (24). The constraints for non-subject wh-relative clauses is given in (25).

(25)   *fin-wh-ns-rel-cl*

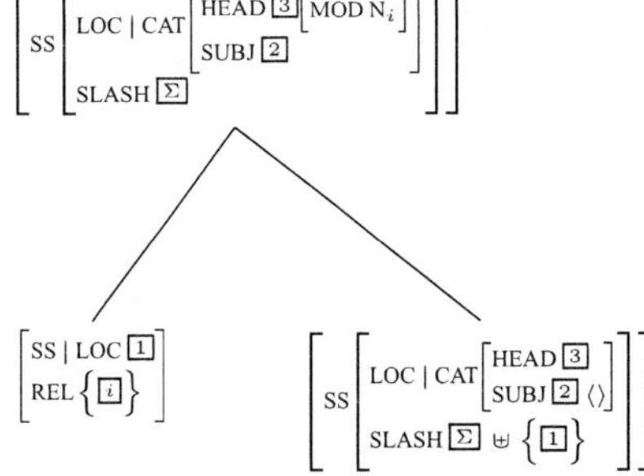

$$\begin{bmatrix} \text{SS} \begin{bmatrix} \text{LOC} \mid \text{CAT} \begin{bmatrix} \text{HEAD } \boxed{3} \left[\text{MOD } \overline{\text{N}}_i \right] \\ \text{SUBJ } \boxed{2} \end{bmatrix} \\ \text{SLASH } \boxed{\Sigma} \end{bmatrix} \end{bmatrix}$$

$$\begin{bmatrix} \text{SS} \mid \text{LOC } \boxed{1} \\ \text{REL } \left\{ \boxed{i} \right\} \end{bmatrix} \qquad \begin{bmatrix} \text{SS} \begin{bmatrix} \text{LOC} \mid \text{CAT} \begin{bmatrix} \text{HEAD } \boxed{3} \\ \text{SUBJ } \boxed{2} \left\langle \right\rangle \end{bmatrix} \\ \text{SLASH } \boxed{\Sigma} \uplus \left\{ \boxed{1} \right\} \end{bmatrix} \end{bmatrix}$$

As in (21) the element in the head daughter's SLASH set which corresponds to the filler daughter is bound off and the SLASH set may contain a second element, corresponding to an extracted subject. The value of the head daughter's scshape subject list may again be either a *gap-ss*, as in (22a) or a *expl-ss* as in (22b). This element is not bound off, but passed on to the mother. If the SLASH-Amalgamation Constraint and the *Expletive* SLASH Constraint are both applied to the examples in (22), only the example with a *gap-ss* subject will pass on the corresponding SLASH element. However, because of the constraint in (24) on adjunct clauses, the example in (22a) is ill-formed, as it contains a non-canonical subject not bound off. If only the SLASH-Amalgamation Constraint is applied, the example with a *expl-ss* subject will also pass on the corresponding SLASH element. However, again because of the additional contraint in (24) on adjunct clauses, the example in (22b) is also ill-formed. Importantly, in neither case is it allowed to extract the subject.

With respect to the *fin-non-wh-rel-cl*, it is the examples in (3e) and (3f) repeated in (26) we need to exclude. The construction covers the highlighted part of the examples.

(26)   a.   *Ministeren stillede han et
            The minister asked he   a
            spørgsmål, *som ikke var forberedt*
            question, C   not was prepared
            på.
            for

       b.   *Ministeren stillede han et
            The minister asked he   a
            spørgsmål, *som der   ikke var*
            question, C   there not was
            forberedt på.
            prepared for

The constraints on the *fin-non-wh-rel-cl* are shown in (27).

(27)   *non-wh-rel-cl*:

$$
\left[\; \text{SS}\; \left[\begin{array}{l} \text{LOC} \mid \text{CAT}\left[\begin{array}{l} \text{HEAD}\;\boxed{3}\,[\text{MOD}\;\overline{\text{N}}_i] \\ \text{SUBJ}\;\boxed{2} \end{array} \right] \\ \text{SLASH}\;\boxed{\Sigma} \end{array} \right] \right]
$$

$$
\left[\; \text{SS}\; \left[\begin{array}{l} \text{LOC} \mid \text{CAT}\left[\begin{array}{l} \text{HEAD}\;\boxed{3} \\ \text{SUBJ}\;\boxed{2}\;\langle\rangle \end{array} \right] \\ \text{SLASH}\;\boxed{\Sigma}\;\uplus\;\{\boxed{1}_i\} \end{array} \right] \right]
$$

In (27) the "object" element in the head daughter's SLASH set is bound off constructionally. Again the SLASH set may contain a second element, corresponding to an extracted subject which is passed on to the mother. Again the value of the head daughter's scshape subject list may be either a *gap-ss*, as in (26a)or a *expl-ss* as in (26b). In any case, because of the constraint on finite adjunct clauses, a SLASH element corresponding to the highest subject in the clause will not be passed on for the noun to amalgamate so that it can escape the noun phrase. Again, we see it is not allowed to extract a subject in (26a) and (26b) as predicted.

5   The Complex NP Constraint

We have already seen that Ross' Complex NP Constraint does not apply for Danish NPs with relative clauses, when we looked at object extraction from relative clauses. The constraint that finite adjunct clauses cannot contain a non-canonical subject which is not already bound off rules out subject extraction from relative clauses in an NP. Now, our analysis predicts that subject extraction out of complement clauses in NPs is allowed, and hence that the Complex NP Constraint does not apply in Danish. The examples in (28) contain subject extractions out of complement clauses in NPs.

(28)   a.   Teltet   er jeg ikke i tvivl
            The tent am I   not in doubt
            om   ville være et hit.
            whether would be   a hit

       b.   Markedet   er afventende forud for
            The market is hesitant   before
            eftermiddagens længe ventede
            the afternoon's long awaited
            amerikanske arbejdsmarkedsrapport
            American   labour market report
            for februar, som der har været
            for February, C   there have been
            spekulationer om   vil overraske
            speculations whether will surprise
            positivt.
            positively

       c.   For   så bliver der læst
            Because then is   there put
            noget   ind i mine ord, jeg
            something in to my   words, I
            ikke selv har haft intentioner om
            not self have had intentions about
            skulle være der.
            should be   there

       d.   Et samarbejde hun udtrykte et
            A cooperation she expressed a
            dybtfølt håb om   vil fortsætte.
            deepfelt hope about will continue

Our analysis thus correctly predicts that Danish does not adhere to the Complex NP constraint, cf. also Allwood (1976) and Andersson (1982) for a discussion of the Complex NP Contstraint in Swedish.

6 Conclusion and further research

The paper has shown that Danish allows extraction extensively. We have presented a formal HPSG analysis of extraction which treats the extraction out of relative and embedded interrogative clauses in a uniform manner. The apparent asymmetry wrt. extraction between the two clause types have been shown to follow from a more general constraint on adjunct clauses, i.e. Danish finite adjunct clauses require a subject. If the subject is non-canonical, it must have be bound off internally. We have presented data which show that subject extraction out of complement clauses in NPs is possible. This was shown not to contradict our analysis, rather it follows naturally as our constraint on adjunct clauses does not apply to NP complements. Finally it should be noted that the apparent lack of syntactic constraints on extraction, with varying degrees of acceptability, admittedly, suggests that further research into the pragmatics of extraction is called for in Danish, cf. Erteschik-Shir (1973) and Erteschik-Shir (1982), and for Swedish Allwood (1976) and Engdahl (1997).

References

Jens Allwood. 1976. The complex NP constraint as a non-universal rule and some semantic factors influencing the acceptability of Swedish sentences which violate the CNPC. *University of Massachusetts Occasional Papers in Linguistics II.*

Lars-Gunnar Andersson. 1982. What is Swedish an exception to? Extractions and island constraints. In Elisabeth Engdahl and Eva Ejerhed, editors, *Readings on Unbounded Dependencies in Scandinavian Languages*. Almquist & Wiksell.

Anne Bjerre. to appear. The locality of expletive *der* in Danish embedded interrogatives and relative clauses. In *Proceedings from the 24th Scandinavian Conference of Linguistics*. Joensuu, Finland.

Gosse Bouma, Rob Malouf, and Ivan Sag. 2000. Satisfying constraints on adjunction and extraction. *Natural Language and Linguistic Theory.*

Noam Chomsky. 1973. Conditions on transformations. In S. Sanderson and P. Kiparsky, editors, *A Festschrift for Morris Halle*. Holt, Rinehart and Winston.

Elisabeth Engdahl. 1984. Subject gaps. *Working Papers in Scandinavian Syntax*, 7.

Elisabeth Engdahl. 1997. Relative clause extraction in context. *Working Papers in Scandinavian Syntax*, 60:51–79.

Nomi Erteschik-Shir. 1973. *On the nature of island constraints*. Ph.D. thesis, MIT.

Nomi Erteschik-Shir. 1982. Extractability in Danish and the Pragmatic Principle of Dominance. In Elisabeth Engdahl and Eva Ejerhed, editors, *Readings on Unbounded Dependencies in Scandinavian Languages*. Almquist & Wiksell.

Nomi Erteschik-Shir. 1984. Der. *Nordic Journal of Linguistics*, 8.

Gerald Gazdar. 1981. Unbounded dependencies and coordinate structure. *Linguistic Enquiry*, 12:155–184.

Jonathan Ginzburg and Ivan Sag. 2000. *Interrogative Investigations: The Form, Meaning and Use of English Interrogatives*. Stanford: CSLI.

Erik Hansen. 1974. De nye *der*-konstruktioner. In *Festskrift til Kristian Hald*.

Thomas E. Hukari and Robert D. Levine. 1996. Phrase structure grammar: the next generation. *Journal of Linguistics*, 32:465–496.

Walt Detmar Meurers. 1999. Raising spirits (and assigning them case). *Groninger Arbeiten zur Germanistischen Linguistik*, 43:173–226.

Anne Neville and Patrizia Paggio. 2004. Developing a Danish grammar in the GRASP project: A construction-based approach to topology and extraction in Danish. *Electronic Notes in Computer Science*, 53.

Carl Pollard and Ivan A. Sag. 1994. *Head-Driven Phrase Structure Grammar*. University of Chicago Press.

John Robert Ross. 1967. *Constraints on Variables in Syntax*. Ph.D. thesis, MIT.

Ivan Sag. 1997. English relative clause constructions. *Journal of Linguistics*, 33:431–484.

Ivan Sag. to appear. English filler gap constructions. *Language*.

Sten Vikner. 1991. Relative *der* and other C^0 elements in Danish. *Lingua*, 84:109–136.

ISSN 1736-6305 Vol. 11
http://hdl.handle.net/10062/16955

The Formal Patterns of the Lithuanian Verb Forms

Loïc Boizou
Centre of Computational Linguistics (http://donelaitis.vdu.lt)
Vytautas Magnus University
Kaunas, Lithuania
`l.boizou@hmf.vdu.lt`

Abstract

This paper describes the formal structure of the Lithuanian verbs, emphasizing the difference between two kinds of formal patterns called primary and secondary. This short outline attemps to highlight some salient aspects of different descriptive levels (traditionnal model, formalized model and implemented model).

1 Introduction

In Lithuanian, morphology plays a considerable role in both domains of inflection and derivation. This property is obvious for both nouns and verbs. Although Lithuanian verbal morphology in general is quite thoroughly described, automatic processing gives some opportunities to consider the question somehow differently.

The aim of this study is to describe the formal patterns of Lithuanian verbs from the perspective of the written language. The study is restricted to the conjugated forms, putting the main emphasis on the word forms instead of lexemes. It covers only the question of analysis and interpretation : the problem of lemmatization is left beyond the scope.

This paper gives a short theoretical account of the question, it raises some problematic issues concerning the formal interpretation of verbal word forms and outlines a possible implementation of verbal formal patterns using the analyzer ALeksas.

2 Primary vs secondary verb forms

According to Stankiewicz (Stankiewicz, 1999), verbs tend to be formally simpler than nouns. Lithuanian seems to conform to this remark, as, in spite of the complexity of the Lithuanian conjugation, verbs forms follow a limited set of patterns. There are two families of patterns, the primary and

	simple	mixed	complex
present	*perk-a*	*mieg-a*	**auk-oj-a**
preterit	*pirk-o*	**mieg-oj-o**	**auk-oj-o**
infinitive	*pirk-ti*	**mieg-o-ti**	**auk-o-ti**

Table 1: Types of verbal lexemes

the secondary ones, which differ in many respects. It must be emphasized that these patterns describe verbal word forms, not verbal lexemes. Indeed, while verbal word forms are either primary or secondary, verbal lexemes may have

- only primary forms (simple verbs)

- only secondary forms (complex verbs) or

- a combination of primary and secondary forms (mixed).

These three categories, well known in the Lithuanian grammatical tradition (ex: DLKG, (Ambrazas (red.), 1996), are shown in the table 1 (primary verb forms in italics, secondary ones in bold). The given forms are the usual ones in the Lithuanian lexicographic tradition, present tense, preterit, infinitive, called by Hoskovec (Hoskovec, 2009) the lemmatic root triplet.

Furthermore, all the verb forms in the past iterative tense are secondary ones, since there are made with the suffix dav-, ex. *dainuodavome* 'we used to sing, we often sang', *šokdavo* 'used to dance, often danced'.

2.1 The primary verbs forms

The number of verbs with primary verb forms reaches few thousands item, but this list seems to be a closed set. From a lexematic perspective, these verbs often show complex models of inflexion, with vowel alteration, infixation, inflexional suffixes. In general, they offer a large panel of paradigmatic variety.

2.1.1 Formal structure

Primary forms follow quite a simple pattern[1] (with optional elements in brackets):

(ModPfx+) (Pfx+) (Refl+) Root' (+Enlargement) +Ending[2]

Each element of the structure may appear only once.

The root The root is in fact a lexically actualized root (hence the notation *Root'*), where the vocalism is fully specified. In some cases, actualized roots contain an infix *-n-*, or *-m-* in prelabial context, (*randa*[3] vs *rado*, *tampa* vs *tapo*).

All the primary verb roots are monosyllabic, with the exception of GALANDA 'to sharpen' (at least in a synchronic perspective). They match the following pattern (Ambrazas (red.), 1996), where all consonant parts are optional :

Spir + Occl + Son + V + Son + Occl + Spir

The root may be extended by optional elements, enlargements and prefixes.

Enlargements Enlargements (the term used by Hoskovec (2009) is taken from Benveniste) make up a small group of consonant suffixes appearing only after the root (this principle excluding the possibility of iteration). The list includes *-st-* (*tirpsta* 'melt'), *-d-* (*pildo* 'fill'), *-s-* (*linksi* 'to nod' from LINKSI).

Prefixes Primary verb forms may include one prefix. Proper prefixes, which are mainly of prepositional origin, belong to a narrow set : *ap(i)-*, *at(i)-*, *į-*, *iš-*, *nu-*, *pa-*, *par-*, *per-*, *pra-*, *pri-*, *su-*, *už-*. As a rule, prefixation does not modify the inflection of the base verb.

Beside the proper prefixes, some modal prefixes (in fact prefixed particles) can be added to prefixed or unprefixed verb forms : *ne-* (negation), *be-* (duration), *te-* (restriction) and the combinations *tebe-* (continuation), *nebe-* (interruption). These modal prefixes appear at the absolute beginning, before proper prefixes.

The status of the particle *ne-* is specific, since it can also be used like a proper prefix, for example

NERIMSTA 'to worry'. Besides, the related verb SUNERIMSTA deviates from the normal pattern.

Paradigms and desinences Lithuanian is characterized by the coexistence of several verbal desinential systems (for the description of the formal structure of the desinences, see (Chicouène and Skūpas, 1998) and (Hoskovec, 2009)) presented in the table 2. The form of desinences may change before the reflexive clitic.

From a lexematic point of view, the present tense (*-a*, *-ia*, *-o* or *-i*) and the preterit (*-o* or *-ė*) show a concurrence between desinential system, while other tenses and moods have a unique paradigm (future *-i'*, imperative *-i"*). All concurrent systems appear with some primary verb forms, for example:

- -a : *tinka*, *verda* (present)

- -ia : *keikia*, *taria* (present)

- -i : *nori*, *žiūri* (present)

- -o : *šaudo*, *sako* (present), *tirpo* (preterit)

- -ė : *liepė*, *valdė* (preterit)

Possible combinations of present and preterit desinential systems draw a set of eight theorically conjugation paradigms, seven being eventually used by the system (numbers indicate conjugation class and subclass in the Grammar of the contemporary Lithuanian(Ambrazas (red.), 1996)), as shown in the table 3.

The quantitative weigth of each model greatly varies from one isolated verb (I-IV) to some several hundreds (I-I, taking in account primary verbs only). Furthermore, a full description of the paradigms needs to integrate enlargements and root alterations, but given the present approach focused on the words forms and not on the lexemes, this question will not be further discussed.

The split description of the reflexive clitic In Lithuanian, the reflexive clitic (*-si*) may appear in two different positions: if the verb is prefixed (even by a modal prefix), the reflexive clitic is between the prefix(es) and the root, ex. *ne-at-si-kelė* 'did not wake up'; else, the clitic is at the end of the word (possibly with a formal alteration of the desinence), ex. *džiaugia-si* 'is/are delighted'.

Taking in account the efficiency of the implementation, the traditionnal unified description of the of the clitic was abandoned. Thus, the model includes

---

[1] The present outline is quite brief, for a more complete description, see (Hoskovec, 2009), which largely inspired this presentation.

[2] ModPfx: modal prefix, Pfx: (non modal) prefix, Refl: reflexive marker.

[3] The paper follows the notational convention of Matthews (1991): small capitals for lexemes, italic for word forms.

	a	ia	o	ė	i	i'	i"	ė'
1sg	renku	šaukiu	sakau	liepiau	žiūriu	kviesiu	×	imčiau
2sg	renki	šauki	sakai	liepei	žiūri	kviesi	lauk	imtum(ei)
3	renka	šaukia	sako	liepė	žiūri	kvies	×	imtų
1pl	renkame	šaukiame	sakome	liepėme	žiūrime	kviesime	laukime	imtumėme
2pl	renkate	šaukiate	sakote	liepėte	žiūrite	kviesite	laukite	imtumėt(e)

Remark the paradigm of the conditionnal (ė') is made of two components, a suffixal segment *-tum-* and a desinence of type ė. Nonetheless, given the lack of stability of both components, the whole structure is considered in the present model as a specific desinential system.

Table 2: Verb desinential systems

pres	preterit	
	o	ė
a	I-I	I-II
ia	I-IV	I-III
o	III-II	III-I
i	II	×

Table 3: Verbal paradigms

Before consonant	Before present (paradigm -a)	Before preterit (paradigm -o)
-in-, -en-		
-o-, -ė-, -y-	-oj-, -ėj-, -ij-	
-au-, -uo-	-auj-, -uoj-	-av-

Table 4: Compatibility of the verbal suffixes

1. a reflexive prefix (unable to take the initial position) ;

2. a set of reflexive endings;

3. a rule of incompatibility between them.

It allows to give a simpler formalization of the morphological expression of reflexivity in Lithuanian, since the split avoids to handle a single morphological unit with two different positions in the morphematic structure.

2.2 The secondary verb forms

The set of secondary verbs is an open collection, insofar as it includes verbal derivatives and borrowed verbs.

2.2.1 Formal structure

The pattern of secondary verbs is made of an arbitrarily complex morphological structure containing an actualized root, followed by a verb suffixe and a desinence. That is, suffixes may follow an already suffixed base (*mok-y-toj-auja* 'work(s) as a teacher'), a prefixed one (*nebe-žiūrės* 'won't look any more', *ne-už-ant-spauduoja* 'do(es) not stamp') or even a compound one (*šun-uodegavo* 'toadied', *su-daikta-vardėjo* 'became a noun'). It results from the derivational role of suffixes.

The set of verbal suffixes is quite restricted : *-o-, -ė-, -au-, -uo-, -av-, -i-, -y-, -in-, -en-*. There are some cases of combined suffixes : *-st-y-, -d-in-*

(both with enlargement), *-in-ė-, -tel-ė-*. Besides, Lithuanian shows several examples of formal variants (although most of them are not productive any more) with different initial segments : ex. *-dė-, -sė-, -ė-; -dy-, -sy-, -y-*. It seems to confirm the remark of Kuryłowicz (Kuryłowicz, 1936) about the trend of initial segments in complex suffixes to lose their individual function, the whole combination becoming a free variant of the second suffix used separately.

Contrary to primary verb forms, which show a great variety of paradigms, secondary forms are compatible only with the -a paradigm for the present and with the -o paradigm for the preterit (as type I-I). Given the compatibility of suffixes with endings, different groups of suffixes may be recognized (see table number 4).

The prefixes *-en-* and *-in-* may appear before all types of ending (-a, -o and consonant[4]). The suffixes *-oj-, -ėj-* and *-ij-* appear before vowels, *-o-, -ė-* and *-y-* before consonant. The suffixes *-auj-* and *-uoj-* appear only before the present and *-au-/-uo-* before consonants, while *-av-* appears only before past endings.

The remarks concerning primary verbs about modal prefixes and reflexive clitic are shared by secondary verbs.

---

[4]All tenses other than the present and the preterit, that is, future, conditional, past iterative, imperative, are made with a consonantic onset.

noun	verbal derivative
-as (auksas 'gold')	-uo-j-a (auksuoja 'to gild')
-a (auka 'sacrifice')	-o-j-a (aukoja 'to sacrifice')
-ė (dėmė 'stain')	-ė-j-a (dėmėja 'to stain')
-is (dalis 'part')	-i-j-a (dalija 'to share')

Table 5: Reactulisation of the noun desinential base

2.2.2 General features of the suffixation

The weak specification of verbal suffixes It must be emphasized that most of the Lithuanian proper suffixes and enlargements are not specific to either derivation or inflexion. That is, they are general morphological devices. In fact, many morphological markers (prefixes, suffixes, endings) are obviously multi-functional in Lithuanian.

For example, the enlargement *-st-* can be used as an inflexion marker indicating the present[5] (*dingsta* 'disappear(s)' vs *dingo* 'disappeared') or as a derivation marker indicating the repetition of the process (PJAUNA 'cut (once)' vs. PJAUSTO 'cut (repeating the process several times)').

It is possible to give a similar example with the suffix *-ė(j)-*, in (rare) derivational use, cf ČIULPĖJA 'to touch several times' vs. ČIULPA 'to touch', and in inflexional use, *kalbėjo* 'talked' vs. *kalba* 'talk(s), is/are talking'.

Desinential traces The semantic typology of the denominal verbal suffixes given in the Grammar of the Contemporary Lithuanian (Ambrazas (red.), 1996) proved to be in many respects inaccurate. Indeed, this description offers a widespread synonymy and homonymy rising doubt on the relevancy of the classification.

In fact, despite their formal identity, some morphological elements are not suffixes, but a remaining part of the desinential vocalic base of the base lexeme. Selected allomorphs depend on the paradigms of declension of the base noun, as shown in the table 5.

Desinential traces are only formal elements bereft of semantic motivation, and thus, invalidating the semantic categorization. The formal concordance between traces and suffixes must be emphasized : it accounts to a large extent for the shortcomings in the presentation of verbal suffixes in the Lithuanian tradition. The description of the

desinential traces explains some essential features of the morphological system. From a historical perspective, it must be noticed that, although such cases are not exceptional, it concerns old derivatives, remaining as a legacy. As a general feature in morphology (Kerleroux, 2005), not all the system is semantically motivated

Main semantic values The core semantic system is made of the suffixes *-in-*, *-ė-*, *-uo-*, *-au-*, *-av-* (counterpart to *-uo-* and *-au-* in the preterit), *-telė-*.

By comparing some verbs like GELTONUOJA 'to appear green', GELTONĖJA 'to become green' and GELTONINA 'to make sth green', it seems possible to state that *-uo-* is intransitive and static, *-ė-* intransitive dynamic and *-in-* transitive dynamic. That's why *-in-* (and some other related suffixes *-din-*, *-y-*, *-dy-*) is used for causative verbs, since they also involve a transitive dynamic process. Thus, *-in-* may derive verbs from nouns (RUSINA 'to russify s.o.' from RUSAS 'Russian') as well as from verbs (TALPINA 'to make sth fit into' from TELPA 'to fit into')

The suffix *-au-* expresses activity (MOKYTOJAUJA 'to work as/be a teacher (MOKYTOJAS)', UOGAUJA 'to pick berries (UOGOS)').

The suffix *-telė-* (deverbal verbal suffix) expresses a very short process (ŽVELGIA 'to look', ŽVILGTELĖJA 'to glance').

Borrowed verbs Some borrowed verbs follow the semantic system, ex. BROKERIAUJA (unconventional) 'to deal', SPORTUOJA 'to practice sport', EUROPINA 'to europeanize s.o./sth', EUROPĖJA 'to europeanize, to acquire european features', but for most of them the question of the present productivity is open.

Contemporary loanwords seem to use the suffixes *-uo-* (and its allomorphs *-uoj-* / *-au-*) or *-in-* as general integrators (Corbin, 1986) into the verb class, ex. SKENUOJA 'to scan', DEVALVUOJA 'to devaluate', SINCHRONIZUOJA 'to synchronize', GUGLINTI (unconventional) 'to use Google', TVITINTI (unconventional) 'to use Twitter'. Although in such cases the suffix seems to be unspecified regarding semantic value and transitivity, the couple FORMUOJA 'to form sth' / FORMUOJASI 'to form (intr)' is an (older) example where opposition is renewed by resort to the category of reflexivity.

---

[5]In fact, it might be better described as a co-marker, whose value results from the combination of the enlargement and the desinence.

After this brief general presentation, it must be dealt with the more practical aspects of recognition and interpretation of the verbal word forms.

3 Interpretation of the word forms

In a perspective of NLP, we consider the description of the verb structures as a way to extract or analyse some word forms in a symbolic framework.

3.1 Recognition of the verb forms

The recognition of verb forms without lexicon is not an easy task. The main problem is that primary verb forms are highly ambiguous (it is general tendency in Lithuanian, (Rimkutė and Grigonytė, 2006)). Different factors explain this situation:

- formal simplicity : nouns can be formally more complex than verbs, but they can also be as simple as primary verbs ;

- ambiguity of endings : desinences tend to be short segments often a vowel or a vowel and a consonant (although some Lithuanian desinence may be dissyllabic), leading to a widespread homonymy, increased by the high number of inflexion categories and the concurrence of multiple paradigms ;

- prosodic deficiency : the written language does not mark prosody, which conveys very useful grammatical information in the spoken language;

- extended conversion : the same root can be easily actualized according to different parts of speech : ex. *kalbos* 'languages', *kalbu* 'I speak', *kalbus* 'loquacious'.

As a consequence, analysis without dictionary frequently generates multiple interpretations. For example, formally *rauda*, *teka* and *gera* are all possible verbs (candidate verbs), but while *teka* is really a verb ('flows'), *gera* is an adjective ('good'), and *rauda* might be either a verb ('cries') or a noun ('lamentation').

It is yet possible to recognize few well marked verb forms. Thus, some prefixes are specific to the verb category : *pri-*, *nu-*, *su-*, *api-*, *ati-*. With few exceptions, words with monosyllabic roots combined with these prefixes are all verb forms. There are two systematic exceptions concerning some deverbal noun forms :

- words with the element *-t-*, which seems to be a general mark of deverbalization in Lithuanian. It appears in the infinitive forms (ex. TARTI 'to pronounce, to utter'), in the so called past passive participle (ex. LAUKTAS 'waited') and in some other deverbal nouns (TARTIS 'pronunciation', to be compared to infinitive, NAŠTA 'burden'[6])). Such derivatives may all present the given prefixes, therefore bases ended with *-t-* are ambiguous in almost all cases;

- verbal adjective derived by conversion, ex. NUMANUS, PRIVALUS.

In such cases, the recognition must rely on some unambiguous desinences.

Furthermore, the frequency of the conversion strongly limits the possibility to use marked forms to tag less marked ones. For example given a form *tebekalba*, which is obviously a verb to the 3rd person present, it does not imply that *kalba* (without the modal particle) is always a verb (*kalba* 'speaks'), since it can also be a noun (*kalba* 'language'). Nevertheless, it may be possible to recognize some verbo-nominal roots. This idea given by Patrice Pognan (oral communication) comes from the Semitic tradition and would lead to a distinction between verbo-nominal roots (SKUBA 'to hurry', SKUBA 'haste', SKUBUS 'urgent') and purely nominal ones (MEDIS 'tree', ŠUO 'dog').

It is usually easier to deal with secondary forms, since longer forms are usually more marked. Nonetheless, there are some systematic interferences which stem from noun suffixes such as *-ija* (collective suffix), *-ėjas* and *-tojas* (agent suffixes), ex. genitive masc. sg. *kėpėjo* 'backer's' vs. *girdėjo* 'heard'.

3.2 Grammatical interpretation

Once a word form is recognized as verbal the next step is to interpret its grammatical features.

As for recognition, secondary forms are easier to interpret. Given the strict limitation of paradigms, their grammatical interpretation is unambiguous. The only exception concerns the inference between the preterit forms of some derivatives in *-avo* and the past iterative tense (in *-davo*). It arises when the suffixal variant *-av-* is preceded

---

[6]The same element appears in many deverbal compound suffixes (ĮKURTUVĖS, LENKTYNĖS, SPAUSTUVĖ, KASTUVAS, JUNGTUKAS, DEGTINĖ, TEIKTINAS), but in such cases word forms are not monosyllabic any more.

by *-d*, for example pret. *maldavo* 'begged' (cf. pres. *maldauja*, past iter. *maldaudavo*) vs past iter. *maldavo* 'used to grind' (cf. pres. *mala* 'grinds').

For primary forms, problems mainly arise from the tenses using enlargement, which can be :

- future (enlargement *-s*, allomorph *-š*) : *kep-s-iu* fut. 'I will cook' (pres. *kep-u*) vs *juos-iu* pres. 'I wear a belt' (fut. *juos-ė-s-iu*)

- imperative (enlargement *-k*) : *tar-k-ime* imper. 'let's say' (pres. *tar-iame*) vs. *tik-ime* pres. 'we believe' (imper. *tik-ė-k-ime*);

- the 1st pers. of the conditional : *dirb-č-iau* cond. (pret. *dirb-au*) vs *kvieč-iau* pret. (cond. *kvies-čiau*)

The previous examples involved the category of tense and mood, but the *-i* paradigm imply a systematic ambiguity between the 2nd pers. sg. and the 3rd pers. (ex. *nori*)

From the point of view of the implementation, all these formal interferences require either a lexicon and/or the handling of multiple interpretations (possibly solvable by a following syntactic or semantic disambiguation).

4   Formal approach

The present section gives a short account of a possible formalization of the verbal lexical structure. This is a complementary approach to lexicon-based analysis, since it allows to provide interpretations for verbal word forms absent from a given lexical database, be it neologisms, rare verbs or occasionalisms.

4.1   Patterns

The verbal patterns may be expressed by regular expressions.

Conventions   Conjunction is indicated by direct concatenation (ex. $\alpha\beta$), disjunction by a vertical stroke ($\alpha|\beta$). Generic symbols are indicated by upper case letters (for morphological classes) or by Greek letters (for phonological classes, more precisely from a phonographic point of view).

Generic symbols:

X	base of arbitrary morphological complexity
A	desinences of type -a
C	desinences of the conditional
Ė	desinences of type -ė
I	desinences of type -i
I'	desinences of type -i'
I"	desinences of type -i"
'A	desinences of type -ia
O	desinences of type -o
T	A	'A	O	Ė	I
T'	sI'	kI"	C
V	T	T'

Σ	syllable
Σ^α	syllable ending in α
$\Sigma^{-\alpha}$	syllable ending by coda other than α
σ'	s	š	ž
σ	s	š
δ'	t	d	s
δ	t	d
γ	k	g

Primary verbal patterns

ΣdO|Ė	(ex. *įvykdė*)
ΣstAI'A|O|Ė	(ex. *tirpsta*)
$\Sigma^{\sigma'}$t|A|O|Ė	(ex. *klysta, laužta, pjaustė + niežti*)
Σ^σI'	(ex. *kvies*)
Σ^kI"	(ex *bėk*)
ΣV	

Remark: all the preceding patterns may be preceded by (M)(P)(si), where M is a modal prefix and P a proper prefix.

In fact, some patterns are slightly more strict than ΣV. For example, ΣsI' (implied by ΣV) should be defined as $\Sigma^{-\delta'}$sI' (and similarly $\Sigma^{-}\delta'$C and $\Sigma^{-}\gamma$kI"). It is a consequence of some morphophonological alternations ($t+s \rightarrow s$, $d+s \rightarrow s$, $s+s \rightarrow s$). But since such configurations are impossible in Lithuanian, the approximation ΣsI' is sufficient.

Secondary verbal patterns

XinA|O|T'	
XenA|O|T'	
XėjA|O	
XojA|O	
XijA|O	
XėT'	
XoT'	
XyT'	
XuoT'	
XuojA	
XaujA	
XavO	
XdavO	(past iterative tense)

4.2   The analyzer formalism

The model is implemented with ALeksas (Boizou, 2009), a morphological analyzer of the Lithuanian language, based on a structural description of the lexicon by formal patterns expressed by finite state automata. The data are given in quite a rough format, with a numerical input state, a numerical output state and a transition symbol.

```
Ex.  (1, 2, "pri").
```

However, the formalism is extended by some features which give to the description a more natural linguistic expression:

- complex symbols

- generic symbols and inheritance

- grammatical values recording

Besides, ALeksas allows recursive structures: a transition by an automaton is possible. Thus, the automaton representing the root (made of characters) is nested in the automaton of the lexical structure (made of morphological elements). The aim is to avoid the mixing of different levels of description (morphemic vs graphematic).

Complex symbols In the first example, the symbol was a simple string ("pri"), but ALeksas allows complex symbols made of a string, a set of grammatical values and a set of operations on the grammatical context (see *Value recording*).

```
Ex.  (250, 30, { "is"; TM(DSN),
CAS(NOM), GNR(M), NB(SG) ; }).
```

The three mentioned parts of symbol are separated by semi-colons (in the previous example, the last part is empty). Features encoding grammatical information are made of a name of feature and a corresponding value in brackets. The number of features bound to a symbol is free.

Generic symbols and inheritance With the aim of minimizing redundancy in automata, ALeksas allows the use of generic symbols. For example, instead of listing all the prefixes as transitions, it is possible to declare a transition by a generic symbol (written without quotes) :

```
Ex.  (1, 2, Pfx).
```

All generic symbols must be defined in the header of the file :

```
Ex.  PFX = "pri" | "su" | "nu" |
             ... .
```

Generic symbols may be recursive, that is, a generic symbol (ex. ExtSfxXV) may derived another one (ex. SfxV).

```
Ex.  SfxV = ExtSfxXV | { "d" ;
    SEMT(fact) } | { "st" ;
        SEMT(fact) }.
```

Generic symbols can also be associated to grammatical features shared by derived symbols. This property is very close to the concept of inheritance in object-oriented programming. For example, all the symbols derived from the generic symbol Pfx may inherit the value *prefix* (PFX) for the feature *morphological type* (MT) :

```
Ex.  (5, 5, { Pfx ; MT(PFX) ;
        [>PFX] }).
```

The last component of the complex symbol, operations on the context, is described in the next paragraph.

Value recording ALeksas is also extended by a grammatical recording device, which allows to carry relevant grammatical informations while progressing in the automaton. Such data are recorded in a register expressing the grammatical context. The register of ALeksas presents many similarities both in design and in purpose with the registers of Cohen-Sygal and Wintner (2006).

ALeksas defines four operations which may be carried on the register, two mutators and two accessors :

>X : adds the symbol X

<X : suppresses the symbol X

+X : asserts the presence of the symbol X

-X : asserts the absence of the symbol X

All these operations, which can be combined by &, appear in the third part of the complex transition symbol.

```
Ex.  (5, 5,  "si" ; REFL ;
    [+PFX&-REFL&>REFL] ).
```

The purposes of the register are :

1. to insure of more natural expression of some relations between morphological units;

2. to transfer information between the different levels (root automaton ↔ lexical automaton);

3. to minimize the automaton, especially in case of distant grammatical dependencies.

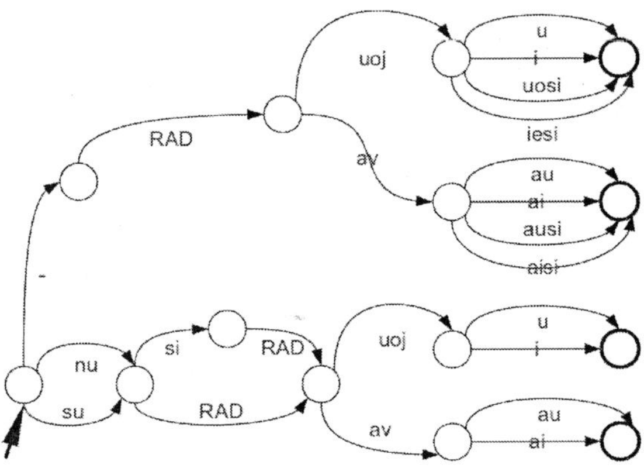

Figure 1: Sketch of an automaton

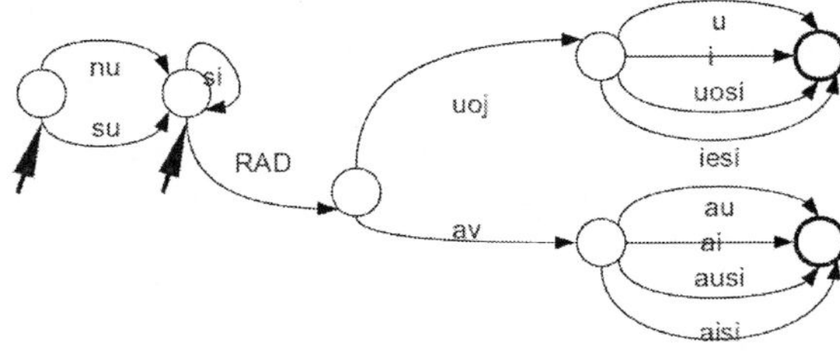

Figure 2: Corresponding compressed automaton

A characteristic example of the third point is given by the reflexive clitic. With a usual automaton, the structure (with a small illustrative subset) would be as in figure 1. The upper part of the figure describes unprefixed word forms, in which desinences can be either reflexive or not, while the lower part describes the prefixed verbal forms, reflexive or not, in which desinences cannot be reflexive. Obviously, the structure is partially double.

The use of the register and the mechanism of extended symbols, which are able to encode a part of the grammatical information, allows a significant reduction of the automaton, as shown in figure 2 (the rule of incompatibility between two elements with a REFL feature avoiding the conflict between a reflexive prefix and a reflexive ending).

However, such an enhancement from the point of view of expressivity involves a higher degree of complexity in processing and an increase in the time of execution.

5 Conclusion

Despite strong restrictions on the verbal patterns, which belong to two very different subsets, recognition and analysis of verb forms raise many problems. The challenge mostly arise from the fact that the simplest formal patterns are, to a great extent, shared by verbs and nouns and from multi-functional nature of many morphological elements.

The model has to be tested, in order to determine more precisely possible gaps in the description and to evaluate the efficiency of the proposed approach, especially by comparison with lexicon-based and statistical methods.

In further works, the question of lemmatization or, alternatively, the recognition of paradigmatically related verb forms, has to be addressed, so as to set the connections between word forms, which are essentially syntactic units, and lexemes, that is, lexical units.

References

Vytautas Ambrazas (red.). 1996. *Dabartinės lietuvių kalbos gramatika*. Mokslo ir enciklopedijų leidykla, Vilnius.

Loïc Boizou. 2009. Analyse lexicale automatique du lituanien. Master's thesis, Institut national des langues et civilisations orientales, Paris.

Michel Chicouène and Laurynas-Algimantas Skūpas. 1998. *Parlons lituanien*. L'Harmattan, Paris.

Yael Cohen-Sygal and Shuly Wintner. 2006. Finite state registered automata and their uses in natural languages. *Lecture Notes in Computer Science*, pages 43–54.

Danièle Corbin. 1986. *Morphologie dérivationnelle et structuration du lexique*. Max Niemeyer, Tübingen.

Tomáš Hoskovec. 2009. *Formální morfologie litevština ve funkčním popisu jazyka*. Slovanská ústav, Praha.

Françoise Kerleroux. 2005. Morpho-logie : la forme et l'intelligible. *Langage*, 152:12–32.

Jerzy Kuryłowicz. 1936. Dérivation lexicale et dérivation syntaxique. *Bulletin de la société linguistique de Paris*, 37:79–92.

Peter Matthews. 1991. *Morphology*. Cambridge university Press, Cambridge.

Erika Rimkutė and Gintarė Grigonytė. 2006. Automatizuotas lietuvių kalbos morfologinio daugiareikšmingumo ribojimas. *Kalbų Studijos*, 9:: 30–37.

Edward Stankiewicz. 1999. Grammatical categories and their formal patterns. *Travaux du Cercle linguistique de Prague*, (3):71–90.

ISSN 1736-6305 Vol. 11
http://hdl.handle.net/10062/16955

Semantic Search in Literature as an e-Humanities Research Tool: CONPLISIT – Consumption Patterns and Life-Style in 19th Century Swedish Literature

Lars Borin,[1] **Markus Forsberg,**[1] **Christer Ahlberger**[2]

[1]Språkbanken, Department of Swedish
[2]Department of Historical Studies
University of Gothenburg, Sweden
`lars.borin@svenska.gu.se`
`markus.forsberg@gu.se`
`christer.ahlberger@history.gu.se`

Abstract

We present our ongoing work on language technology-based e-science in the humanities, with a focus on text-based research in the historical sciences. Currently, we are working on the adaptation and integration of lexical resources representing different historical stages of Swedish into a lexical and morphological toolbox that will allow us to develop semantically oriented text search applications for historical research on Swedish text. We describe a semantic search prototype which was built using REST web services from this toolbox as components, and which has been evaluated by historians interested in using digitized 19th century novels as primary data for an historical investigation of the emerging consumer society in 19th century Sweden.

1 Introduction

Språkbanken[1] (the Swedish Language Bank), is a research unit at the University of Gothenburg in Sweden. It was established with government funding in 1975 as a national center with a remit to collect, process and store Swedish text corpora (i.e., large systematically compiled text collections). It also aims at making linguistic data extracted from the corpora and other linguistic resources, such as electronic lexicons and term lists, as well as the tools developed in-house for the purposes of linguistic processing of text, available to researchers and to the public.

Språkbanken's activities have traditionally been aimed at supporting (Swedish) linguistic research,

but over the last few years we have become increasingly interested in the potential of the language technology tools and language resources that we develop and maintain in Språkbanken for forming key components in a general e-science infrastructure for the humanities, social sciences and education, and not just linguistic research.

Currently, we are working on the adaptation and integration of lexical resources representing different historical stages of Swedish into a lexical and morphological toolbox that will allow us to develop semantically oriented text search applications for historical research on Swedish text. More specifically, the work we are presenting here is a project named *CONPLISIT, Consumption patterns and life-style in Swedish literature*, which is a collaboration with historians at our university and with the literature digitization initiative Litteraturbanken (see section 2.3 below), and the aim of which is to develop semantic search tools for investigating the emergence of the modern consumer society in Sweden using contemporary literary sources (Ahlberger, 2009).

To this end, we are currently extending and merging two lexical resources, SALDO and Dalin, and connecting them to the search API of Litteraturbanken.

The rest of this presentation is organized as follows. In section 2, we describe the existing language resources and tools that we have utilized and in some cases enhanced in order to accomplish our goals. Section 3 contains a description of the prototype semantic search application for historical research. In section 4, we report on the first user test of the application. In section 5 we sum up our work so far and outline our plans for future work.

---

[1]<http://spraakbanken.gu.se>

2 Existing language resources and tools

2.1 SALDO: a semantic lexical resource for present-day Swedish

SALDO (Borin, 2005; Borin and Forsberg, 2009; Borin et al., 2008; Borin and Forsberg, 2008), or SAL version 2, is a free modern Swedish semantic and morphological lexicon intended for language technology applications. The lexicon is available under a Creative Commons Attribute-Share Alike license and LGPL 3.0.

SALDO started its life as *Svenskt association-slexikon* (Lönngren, 1992) – 'The Swedish Associative Thesaurus', a so far relatively unknown Swedish thesaurus with an unusual semantic organization, reminiscent of, but different from that of WordNet (Borin and Forsberg, 2009). SAL has been published in paper form in two reports, from the Center for Computational Linguistics (Lönngren, 1998), and the Department of Linguistics (Lönngren, 1992), both at Uppsala University. Additionally, the headwords and their basic semantic characterizations have been available electronically, in the form of text files, from the very beginning.

The history of SAL has been documented by Lönngren (Lönngren, 1989) and Borin (Borin, 2005). Initially, text corpora were used as sources of the vocabulary which went into SAL, e.g., a Swedish textbook for foreigners and a corpus of popular-scientific articles. A small encyclopedia and some other sources provided the large number (over 3,000) of proper names found in SAL. Eventually, a list of the headwords from *Svensk ordbok* (SO, 1986) was acquired from the NLP and Lexicology Unit at the University of Gothenburg, and the second paper edition of SAL (Lönngren, 1992) contained 71,750 entries. At the time of writing, SALDO contains slightly over 104,000 entries, and new entries are added almost daily.

The central semantic relation of SALDO is *association*, a "non-classical" lexical-semantic relation (Morris and Hirst, 2004). SALDO describes *all* words semantically, not only the open word classes. By way of illustration, figure 1 shows the semantic 'neighbors' (rendered in blue/non-bold) in SALDO of the word *telefon* 'telephone (noun)'. It is associated i.a. with words like *samtala* 'hold a conversation', *telefonledes* 'by phone', *pulsval* 'pulse dialling', *ringa* 'call (verb)', *mobiltelefon* 'mobile phone', the proper name *Bell*, and many

others, as shown in figure 1.[2]

We soon realized that in order to be useful in language technology applications, SAL would have to be provided at least with part-of-speech and inflectional morphological information – both entirely absent from SAL in its original form – and SALDO was created. The morphological component of SALDO has been defined using Functional Morphology (FM) (Forsberg and Ranta, 2004; Forsberg, 2007), a tool that provides a development environment for computational morphologies. It is a tool with a flexible language for defining morphological rules together with a platform for testing, which is used to fend off resource degradation during development. Furthermore, it has a rich export system, targetting around 20 formats, and supports both (compound) analysis and synthesis.

SALDO is, as one of its distribution channels, published as REST web services, updated daily. Web services provide clean interfaces and instant updates, but are restricted to small amounts of data because of network latency. Presently available web services include incremental fullform lookup, semantic lookup, compound analysis, and an inflection engine service.[3]

2.2 Dalin: a lexical resource for 19th century Swedish

A.F. Dalin: Ordbok öfver svenska språket (1850–1855) (Dalin, 1853 1855) is a dictionary that has been digitized at our research unit, and is the starting point for our work on 19th century Swedish.

The language of Dalin – Late Modern Swedish according to the traditional linguistic periodization of Swedish used by Swedish linguists – is close to the modern language of SALDO, where the differences are in minor spelling variations, such as the use of the letter <f> instead of <v>, some morphological differences, such as inflection of verbs in person and number, completely absent in Present-Day Swedish. Moreover, there is a difference in the vocabulary, since the vocabulary of a dictionary reflects of the society it was produced in, e.g., many of the words in Dalin have to do either with agriculture or with religious matters.

We have created a morphology for Dalin by adapting the morphological component developed for SALDO. With a comparatively small effort we

---

[2]From <http://spraakbanken.gu.se/ws/saldo-ws/lid/html/telefon..1>

[3]See <http://spraakbanken.gu.se/eng/saldo>

lex:	telefon
l:	telefon+nn
fm:	samtala
fp:	PRIM
mf(19)	**PRIM:** fingerskiva hörtelefon kobra^2 pulsval ringa telefonautomat telefonera telefonledes telefonlur telefonör tonval **bild:** bildtelefon **knapp^3:** knapptelefon **lokal^2:** lokaltelefon **lyssna:** hörlur **mobil:** mobiltelefon **port:** porttelefon **trådlös:** radiotelefon **vägg:** vaggtelefon
pf(18)	**abonnent:** telefonabonnent **anrop:** telefonanrop **apparat:** telefonapparat **avgift:** teleavgift **central:** telefonstation **elledning:** telefonledning **fingerskiva:** petmoj **förbindelse:** teleförbindelse **katalog:** telefonkatalog **kontakt^2:** jack^2 **samtal:** telefonsamtal **signal:** telefonsignal **sladd:** telefonsladd **svara:** telefonsvarare telefonvakt **teknisk:** teleteknisk **ton:** kopplingston **uppfinnare:** Bell

Figure 1: Semantic neighbors (rendered in blue/non-bold) of *telefon* 'telephone (n)' in SALDO

have been able to provide most of the entries with an inflectional pattern based on the inflectional information provided in Dalin. However, the inflectional information in Dalin is underspecified, which means that there are erroneous word forms that we need to weed out. Also, the remainder of the entries will require a considerably larger effort, since part of the 19th century inflectional patterns cannot be automatically or almost automatically created by adaptation of the modern inflections; this holds for *inter alia* many pronouns and strong verbs. These comprise central, high-frequency vocabulary, important in practical text processing applications.

The linking of Dalin to SALDO has been done by analyzing modernized headwords of the entries in Dalin using SALDO. Connecting on the entry level is a first, over-generating, approximation, since the senses of Dalin is given within an entry. For the linking we were able to reuse an existing resource, as a manual spelling translation for the entries in Dalin had been made in an earlier project in our department and preserved in a database, which by a stroke of good luck still existed in one of our servers.

Since the vocabulary of Dalin reflects another time and another societal structure, many of its content words are not in SALDO. However, in a large number of cases they are compound words where the constituents of the compound are in SALDO. An example could be the headword *bäfverhund* with a modern spelling *bäverhund* 'beaver dog', meaning a dog used for hunting beavers, a word that would normally not find its way into a modern lexical resource – since the practice it refers to is no longer pursued – and adding the word to the modern resource would be unsatisfactory, since to a modern reader *bäverhund* would at most be a completely transparent compound, meaning 'a dog in some way connected to beavers', but without the conventionalized or lexicalized meaning the word had earlier.

In cases like this we instead choose another approach for linking the resources. Even though *bäverhund* is not in SALDO, both *bäver* 'beaver' and *hund* 'dog' are, so we use SALDO to do a compound analysis of *bäverhund* to *bäver+hund*, and link with respect to the head of the compound, i.e., *hund*.

The resulting entry for *bäfverhund*, which is analogous to the other linked entries in Dalin, is summarized in the table below. Every dictionary entry has been given an persistent identifier, here *bäfverhund..e.1*. We have the headword, its modern spelling, the inflectional information in Dalin, *m. 2.*, and the paradigm identifier it has been associated to, *nn_2m_ulf*. The paradigm identifier together with the headword defines the inflection table. Finally, we have the connection to the sense identifier in SALDO, *hund..1*.

headword	modern	pos	paradigm
bäfverhund	bäverhund	nn	nn_2m_ulf

gram. desc.	saldo	id
m. 2.	hund..1	bäfverhund..e.1

Dalin contains many verb entries consisting of prefix plus verb written as one word, which in Present-Day Swedish generally correspond to phrasal verbs, i.e., verb plus separate particle/ adverb. E.g., *påspäda* 'add to', where *på* 'on, onto' is the particle, would in modern Swedish be a phrasal verb, *späda på*, or in its more common short form, *spä på*. We deal with these cases by allowing adverbs as the first constituent of a compound, given that the head of the compound is a verb. For example:

headword	modern	pos	paradigm
påspäda	påspäda	vb	vb_2a_ärfva

gram. desc.	saldo	id
v. a. 2.	spä_på..1	påspäda..e.1

There is still much work to be done on the 19th century resource, but it is now in such a shape that we have been able to harvest the fruits of its creation, and the semantic search discussed in this article is one such fruit.

2.3 Litteraturbanken: a digital repository of classical Swedish fiction

Litteraturbanken[4] (the Swedish Literature Bank) is a national cultural heritage project financed by the Swedish Academy. It aims at making available online the full text of classical works of Swedish literature, in manually proofread digital versions of critical editions intended to be suitable for literary research and for the teaching of literature. There is also abundant commissioned ancillary material on its website, such as author presentations, bibliographies, and thematic essays about authorships, genres or periods, written by experts in each field. Currently, Litteraturbanken holds a bit less than 300 works in a fully searchable XML format (a variant of TEI P5), and about as much again in facsimile (image) and pdf format.

[4] <http://litteraturbanken.se/>

Similarly to many other literature digitization initiatives, most of the works in Litteraturbanken are such for which copyright has expired (under Swedish law this means that more than 70 years must have passed since the death of the author). At present, the bulk of the texts are from the 18th, 19th and early 20th centuries. However, there is also an agreement with the national organizations representing authors' intellectual property rights, allowing the inclusion of modern works according to a uniform royalty payment scheme.

The Litteraturbanken website provides a (string/ orthographic word) search function where search results are shown in a traditional concordance format, with links to the corresponding location in the digital full-text versions of the texts. However, there are also separate search (web service) APIs, both for displaying the results in the normal HTML format, and for retrieving a list of search hits for further processing.

3 Building a semantic search prototype

All the components needed for semantic search in 19th century literature are now at our disposal. A prototype was designed jointly by the language technology researchers in Språkbanken and the historians involved in the project. This was deliberately a low-stakes effort, since we would not like to put a lot of effort into a prototype which then would turn out not to be what the users desired. Our web service infrastructure supports this kind of rapid prototyping, which often becomes simply a matter of designing a couple of simple web pages acting as a kind of 'glue' joining REST web services which provide the needed functionality. Occasionally a new web service will have to be implemented, but it is our experience that in comparison to developing monolithic client-side applications, this web-service based approach allows very rapid construction and testing of quite sophisticated prototypes. Once the prototyping phase is over, it may turn out that this kind of architecture will not scale to meet production requirements due to, e.g., the inevitable network latency inherent in a web service setup. This is a separate problem, however, and its existence does in no way invalidate this approach to prototyping.

The semantic relation we decided to build a prototype around is the `md1` relation, which is the set of word senses at distance one from a target word sense in SALDO, i.e., semantically close senses.

The general idea behind the semantic search is the following: we look up up an input word form in the two morphologies of SALDO and Dalin. The SALDO senses associated to the input word form are collected, and all lexical entries in Dalin connected to these senses are listed.

The figure 2 shows the result of a search of the word form *soffa*[5] 'sofa', where there is only one sense identifier `soffa..1`,[6] connected to two entries in Dalin, `hvilosoffa..e.1` and `soffa..e.1`. Note that `hvilosoffa` has been connected to `soffa..1` through the compound analysis of its modernized form, *vilo+soffa* 'rest+sofa'. Clicking on either `soffa..e.1` or `hvilosoffa..e.1` gives a fullform search in Litteraturbanken.

There is only one md1 for both *soffa* and *hvilosoffa*, given by the connection to `soffa..1`. Figure 3 shows `soffa..1`'s md1,[7] where we can observe semantically related words such as *säng* 'bed' and *kanapé* 'couch', but also some erroneous ones due to the fact that the word *byrå* is homonymous, meaning both 'bureau' and 'dresser'. Clicking on any of the words in md1 gives a fullform search in Litteraturbanken.

Figure 4 shows the result of clicking on *relaterade ord*[8] 'related words', which is a concordance search of the words in md1. The words are linked to the place in Litteraturbanken where they occur.

4 Semantic search in historical research: Practical evaluation

The historians involved in the project have been interested primarily in investigating changing consumption patterns during the first half of the 19th century. Sweden was during this period undergoing a rapid integration into the emerging world capitalist economy. A fundamental part if this integration process was a profound change in patterns of consumption among ordinary people. This change in consumption patterns is the focus of the historical research questions addressed in the CONPLISIT project. Earlier research on this topic has utilized sources such as probate inventories and tax registers. Today we have a reasonably

good knowledge of the use of new commodities among social groups, sexes and age groups. On the other hand we still have very little knowledge of the contexts in which the new commodities were used. The methods and source material hitherto used in historical studies of emerging and changing consumption patterns simply has not allowed us to fully analyze and interpret the contexts of use of specific consumer items.

Hence, the research program of which our project forms a part has as one of its specific goals to develop new methods by the use of literature during the period 1830–1860 as a main source for understanding the context of consumption in this period. The prototype semantic search application is one such new method, which has undergone a small-scale formative evaluation conducted by two historians involved in the project. We now turn to the main impressions of this evaluation.

The historians initially searched for words like *porslin* 'porcelain, china', *spegel* 'mirror', *möbel* 'piece of furniture', *klocka* 'clock, watch' and so on. These items are example of the new way of living among average people. The novels also provide a context, which is how, why and by whom the new consumer items were used. The aim is to study the *new way of life* mirrored in contemporary literature and analyze the descriptions in the texts against what we know of actual consumption from other sources. Another important task for the research program is to reconstruct the new world-view and life-style of the emerging modern citizen.

The historians found the semantic search to be a good way of finding alternative search words that one would normally not think of, and it provides an overview of the variation in vocabulary choice. In this respect, it saves time and effort. An example is the search word *soffa* 'sofa', where the word *ottoman* 'ottoman' is one of the suggested words. This word had not occurred to the historians, and moreover provided an interesting surprise, since a search showed, contrary to expectation, that it is mainly used by authors in the late 19th century.

However, in some cases, such as for the search words *porslin* 'porcelain, china' and *tapet* 'wallpaper', there are many proposed words that are hard to consider relevant in the context, which was particularly true for the word *tapet*, where many of the related words are compounds with the head *vägg* 'wall', a word normally unrelated to consumption.

---

[5]<http://http://spraakbanken.gu.se/ws/dalin-ws/fl/html/soffa>

[6]The HTML rendering hides the suffix '`..1`'.

[7]<http://http://spraakbanken.gu.se/ws/dalin-ws/md1/html/soffa..1>

[8]<http://http://spraakbanken.gu.se/ws/dalin-ws/lb/html/250/soffa..1>

hvilosoffa..e.1	fullformssökning	**saldo:** soffa [möbel+sitta]	md1	relaterade ord
soffa..e.1	fullformssökning	**saldo:** soffa [möbel+sitta]	md1	relaterade ord

SOFFA
> f. 1. Möbel af trä att sitta eller ligga på, vanligen med stoppad sits äfvensom stoppade rygg- och sidodynor. Sitta, ligga på en s. — Ss. **Soffdyna** , **-karm** .

Figure 2: Word form lookup of *soffa* 'sofa'

uppmöblera	kanapé	bårstol	valkbord	tryckbord	tingsbord	tebord	svärtbord	strykbord	stigbord
spegelbord	skådebord	skärbord	skänkbord	ljusbord	kredensbord	kammarbord	hästskobord	herrskapsbord	färgbord
fällbord	friserbord	fortunabord	formbord	dambord	bröstbord	brädspelsbord	bord	bakbord	altarbord
tidningsbyrå	ottoman	kommissionsbyrå	klädesbyrå	divan	byrå	bord^2	affärsbyrå	adressbyrå	vändstol
väggbänk	vridstol	verkstol	verkbänk	vaskbänk	varpstol	varmbänk	valsstol	vaktbänk	understol
tvättstol	tvärbänk	torfbänk	sågbänk	svarfbänk	strumpstol	stol	sqvalbänk	spegelbänk	sofstol
soffstol	slipbänk	slagtbänk	slagtarbänk	skärbänk	skottstol	skjulstol	rörstol	ryggstol	rullbänk
rottingstol	reffelbänk	pressbänk	plantbänk	pinbänk	likstol	liggstol	kullerstol	korbänk	klädesstol
kardbänk	kalkbänk	häftstol	hvilostol	huggbänk	hjulstol	handstol	halmstol	gubbstol	gräsbänk
fogbänk	fallbänk	erkebiskopsstol	dufstol	dragstol	bönstol	bänk	brudbänk	borrstol	borrbänk
bordbänk	bokstol	biskopsstol	bibänk	bandstol	armstol	vaksäng	trädgårdssäng	säng	syskonsäng
spannssäng	skogssäng	sjuksäng	plantsäng	paulunsäng	negliksäng	melonsäng	löksäng	kryddsäng	korgsäng
gurksäng	fältsäng	dödssäng	bröllopssäng	blomsäng	blomstersäng	bergsäng	utdragssoffa	soffa	hvilosoffa
skeppsbord									

Figure 3: Words semantically related to *soffa* 'sofa'

190	begärligt förtärde sina kol. Ovanför en	ottoman	hängde en tavla, försedd med guldram	Kvartetten, som sprä...
191	bland kvinnotjusare att krypa upp på	soffan	, stiga in genom ramen och lägga sitt	Kvartetten, som sprä...
192	minnen, och satte sig gungande på	ottomanen	, varefter han fortsatte: – Den	Kvartetten, som sprä...
193	, på andra sidan bron. Där stodo gröna	bänkar	under träden, och jag erinrar mig	Kvartetten, som sprä...
194	av mig den höga hatten och lagt den på	bänken	bredvid mig, men alldeles plötsligt	Kvartetten, som sprä...
195	, och till sist satt jag ensam, satt i	sängen	och grät, så att det sjöng i resårerna.	Kvartetten, som sprä...
196	– herrar Backlund och Stoltz på någon	soffa	i en lämplig parkpassage, där folkfloden	Kvartetten, som sprä...
197	en väldig trasa avtorkade ett par små	bord	: – Avhöres något nytt, så meddelar vi	Kvartetten, som sprä...
198	Mussy hest fråga, där hon satt i sin	stol	och stötte med käppen i golvet. Då	Kvartetten, som sprä...
199	och lade sig på ett knä vid hennes	stol	, medan hon i barmen fiskade efter det	Kvartetten, som sprä...
200	. Doktorns höga gestalt syntes snart vid	sängen	, kring vilken anförvanterna rörde	Kvartetten, som sprä...
201	matsal. Det - ligt dukade	bordet	sken, rosorna doftade och kristal	Kvartetten, som sprä...
202	gick att intaga en hedrande plats vid	bordet	. När det omsider knackades i vinglaset	Kvartetten, som sprä...
203	åter stolsbenen på Häradshövdingens	stol	, då han med bakdelen sköt den ut på	Kvartetten, som sprä...
204	. Då han en afton, liksom nu, låg i	sängen	, medan tankarna travade omkring Guldkalven	Kvartetten, som sprä...

Figure 4: Related word search

The words that are proposed but get no hits in Litteraturbanken are in many cases especially interesting, since they define a set of words denoting items that may not have existed at the time, or were too uncommon, or just not interesting enough for the author. An example is *fickspegel* 'pocket mirror' that is mentioned in the literature, but only in the late 19th century. Since pocket mirrors where common already in the early 19th century, it raises the question why no writer mentioned them, especially in contrast to words such as *tapet* 'wallpaper' and *gardin* 'curtain', that show another pattern.

The function *relaterade ord* 'related words' that gives a search for all words in `md1` was judged by the historians as potentially very useful, but many irrelevant hits tended to drown the relevant ones. However, if it would be possible to remove some of the words before the search, it would make a good exploratory tool.

One of the strongest requirements by the historians was the addition of chronological information, i.e., enrichment of the metadata available for the works in Litteraturbanken, and the possibility to limit the search with respect to chronological information, as well as sort the search results chronologically by publication year.

5   Summary and future work

Summing up, in the CONPLISIT project so far we have accomplished the following:

- We have built a prototype semantic search application for 19th century Swedish text. This was possible to accomplish in reasonable time – even quite quickly – since we were able to reuse several existing language resources and tools through their standardized REST web service APIs, and only needed to provide simple HTML pages as 'glue' for the prototype application.
- We have conducted a small formative evaluation of this search application with historians involved in the project, who represent one intended end-user category. The results of the evaluation were encouraging, and indicated some directions for further development.-
- We would like to claim that we have been able to show how language resources and tools can be used with good effect for building new research tools for humanities scholars.

Given what we have already accomplished or are in the midst of carrying out, as well as the kinds of resources and expertise that we can bring to bear on the problem of language technology support for historical studies, there are some lines of research that are more natural than others for continuing our work:

- We have until now only tried one kind of semantic relation – that available already in SALDO – so a natural next step is to experiment with other relations. The lexical resources used in the CONPLISIT project are developed within the framework of a larger lexical project, Swedish FrameNet++.[9] As part of the larger project, we are also developing a Swedish wordnet. Because of the way our infrastructure is built, the wordnet relations will be only a web service away once the wordnet is in place.
- One of the strongest wishes on the part of the historians was to be able to search Litteraturbanken's works chronologically, by publication year. This requires that the corresponding metadata are added to Litteraturbanken, something which is on their agenda anyway.
- Obviously, user interface issues have taken second place in our work so far, and as the functionality of successive prototypes comes closer to fulfilling the basic requirements of the users, user interface design will become increasingly important.
- An interesting question is how to find good and convincing use cases where more sophisticated linguistic information would be required, e.g. named entity information or grammatical information such as part of speech or syntactic function.[10]

---

[9]See <http://http://spraakbanken.gu.se/eng/swefn>

[10]There are some indications in the literature that deeper linguistic processing of historical documents can be of help to humanities scholars (Rayson et al., 2007; Pilz et al., 2008).

On the other hand, and at the shallow end of the linguistic-processing scale, one anonymous reviewer pointed out the usefulness for large-scale investigations of historical texts of extremely knowledge-light approaches inspired by information retrieval technology, such as that of Michel et al. (2011), who investigate n-gram statistics in the enormous database collected in the Google Books project.

Acknowledgements

The research presented here was supported by the Swedish Research Council (the project *Safeguarding the future of Språkbanken* 2008–2010, VR dnr 2007-7430), the University of Gothenburg through its support of Språkbanken (the Swedish Language Bank), and CLARIN through its support of the CONPLISIT collaboration.

References

Christer Ahlberger. 2009. Consumption patterns and life-style in Swedish literature – novels 1830-1860 (CONPLISIT). CLARIN collaboration proposal, April.

Lars Borin and Markus Forsberg. 2008. Saldo 1.0 (svenskt associationslexikon version 2). Språkbanken, Göteborgs universitet.

Lars Borin and Markus Forsberg. 2009. All in the family: A comparison of SALDO and WordNet. Odense.

Lars Borin, Markus Forsberg, and Lennart Lönngren. 2008. The hunting of the BLARK – SALDO, a freely available lexical database for Swedish language technology. In Joakim Nivre, Mats Dahllöf, and Beata Megyesi, editors, *Resourceful language technology. Festschrift in honor of Anna Sågvall Hein*, number 7 in Acta Universitatis Upsaliensis: Studia Linguistica Upsaliensia, pages 21–32. Uppsala University, Department of Linguistics and Philology, Uppsala.

Lars Borin. 2005. Mannen är faderns mormor: *Svenskt associationslexikon* reinkarnerat. *LexicoNordica*, 12:39–54.

Anders Fredrik Dalin. 1853–1855. *Ordbok öfver svenska språket. Vol. I–II*. Stockholm.

Markus Forsberg and Aarne Ranta. 2004. Functional morphology. In *ICFP'04. Proceedings of the ninth ACM SIGPLAN international conference of functional programming*, Snowbird, Utah. ACM.

Markus Forsberg. 2007. *Three Tools for Language Processing: BNF Converter, Functional Morphology, and Extract*. Ph.D. thesis, Göteborg University and Chalmers University of Technology.

Lennart Lönngren. 1989. *Svenskt associationslexikon: Rapport från ett projekt inom datorstödd lexikografi*. Centrum för datorlingvistik. Uppsala universitet. UCDL-R-89-1.

Lennart Lönngren. 1992. *Svenskt associationslexikon. Del I-IV*. Institutionen för lingvistik. Uppsala universitet.

Lennart Lönngren. 1998. A Swedish associative thesaurus. In *Euralex '98 proceedings, Vol. 2*, pages 467–474.

Jean-Baptiste Michel, Yuan Kui Shen, Aviva Presser Aiden, Adrian Veres, Matthew K. Gray, The Google Books Team, Joseph P. Pickett and1 Dale Hoiberg, Dan Clancy, Peter Norvig, Jon Orwant, Steven Pinker, Martin A. Nowak, and Erez Lieberman Aiden. 2011. Quantitative analysis of culture using millions of digitized books. *Science*, 331(176):176–182.

Jane Morris and Graeme Hirst. 2004. Non-classical lexical semantic relations. In Dan Moldovan and Roxana Girju, editors, *HLT-NAACL 2004: Workshop on Computational Lexical Semantics*, pages 46–51, Boston. ACL.

T. Pilz, A. Ernst-Gerlach, S. Kempken, Paul Rayson, and Dawn Archer. 2008. The identification of spelling variants in English and German historical texts: Manual or automatic? *Literary and Linguist Computing*, 23:65–72.

Paul Rayson, Dawn Archer, A. Baron, J. Culpeper, and N. Smith. 2007. Tagging the bard: Evaluating the accuracy of a modern POS tagger on Early Modern English corpora. In *Proceedings of Corpus Linguistics 2007*, Birmingham. University of Birmingham.

SO. 1986. *Svensk ordbok*. Esselte Studium, Stockholm.

ISSN 1736-6305 Vol. 11
http://hdl.handle.net/10062/16955

Evaluation of Terminologies Acquired from Comparable Corpora : an Application Perspective

Estelle Delpech
Université de Nantes - LINA FRE UMRS 6249
2 rue de la Houssinière BP 92208, 44322 Nantes Cedex 3, France
estelle.delpech(at)univ-nantes(dot)fr
Lingua et Machina
c/o Inria Rocquencourt, BP 105 Le Chesnay Cedex 78153, France
ed(at)lingua-et-machina(dot)com

Abstract

This paper describes a protocol for the evaluation of bilingual terminologies acquired from comparable corpora. The aim of the protocol is to assess the terminologies' added-value in a task of specialized translation. The protocol consists in having specialized texts translated in various situations: without any specialized resource, with an domain-related bilingual terminology or using Internet. By comparing the quality of the segments translated using these various resources, we are able to assess the impact of our bilingual terminologies on the quality of the translation.

1 Introduction

Evaluation plays an important role in NLP developments: it assesses the quality of tools, brings out the progress made between two developments, spots the limitations and highlights possible lines of research. Regarding the evaluation of terminologies, Nazarenko et al. (2009) show that terminologies are complex objects and that their evaluation can be quite arduous. These authors distinguish between three evaluation modes:

evaluation through reference : the terminology is compared to a standard reference, the evaluation metric indicates the adequacy between the assessed terminology and the reference terminology.

evaluation through interaction : the evaluation aims at measuring the cost of the transformation of the raw terminology as outputted by the system into the final, validated, ready-to-use terminology.

evaluation through application : the evaluation's purpose is to compare the performance of a given application with and without the terminology, the metric indicates the added-value of the terminology and depends on the application.

Nazarenko et. al. (2009) propose protocols and metrics for the first two evaluation modes and focus on monolingual terminologies only. The aim of this paper is to propose a protocol for the evaluation through application of bilingual terminologies acquired from comparable corpora. The considered application is human specialized translation.

Terminologies acquired from comparable corpora are usually assessed using an evaluation through reference protocol (Fung, 1997; Sadat et. al., 2003; Koehn et. al., 2002). Algorithms which extract bilingual terminologies from comparable corpora output a list of 1-to-n alignments: each source term is aligned with the n best candidate translations, most of the time the *Top20* candidate translations. The output of the algorithm is compared to a reference lexicon and the evaluation metric is a precision score computed on the *Top1*, *Top10* or *Top20* candidates. For example, a 50% precision on the *Top20* candidates indicates that the correct translation is found among the first top 20 candidates for 50% of the source terms.

Although evaluation through reference is useful to monitor the effect of changes in the alignment algorithm and to compare the alignment techniques, we believe it is important to demonstrate the impact and the usefulness of terminologies and lexicons acquired from comparable corpora in real-life applications. Renders et al. (2003) showed the influence of such lexicons on cross-lingual information retrieval. We would like to determine the added-value of these bilingual terminologies when they are used in a task of human specialized translation.

Section 2 explains how terms are aligned in comparable corpora and examines the issue of translation quality assessment. The evaluation protocol is defined in section 3. The experimentation and results are described in section 4. Perspectives and future work are discussed in section 5.

2 Background

In this section, we describe the algorithm used for term alignment (section 2.1) and give a brief state-of-the-art survey in translation quality assessment (section 2.2).

2.1 Term alignment from comparable corpora

Comparable corpora are sets of texts written in two languages which are not translations of each other but which share a substantial part of their vocabulary, mainly because they are topic-related. The major advantage of comparable corpora is that it is much more available than parallel corpora and enables the processing of unprecedented language pairs. It is also often argued that the target language texts found in comparable corpora contain more spontaneous / natural terms and expressions than in parallel corpora because the target texts are not translations and they have not been influenced by the language of the source text.

Term alignment from comparable corpora was initiated by the work of Fung (1997) and Rapp (1995). The alignment algorithm is based on distributional linguistics and considers that two terms are probable translations if they occurr in similar contexts. The context of a term T is represented by a vector indicating the number of times T co-occurs with each word within a given contextual window (for instance: three words on the left of T and three words on the right of T). The cooccurrence frequencies are normalized using the log-likelihood ratio (Dunning, 1993). Words in the source context vectors are translated into the target language using a bilingual seed lexicon. Then, the source and target vectors are compared using a similiarity measure such as the Cosine similarity measure. The most similar the vectors, the most likely the target and source terms are translations of each other. Morin and Daille (2009) report that the correct translation is to be found among the top 20 best candidates for 42% to 80% of the source terms depending on corpus size, on the complex-

ity of the terms and whether the alignment is made using specialized corpora or general language corpora. As a consequence, the output lexicon is ambiguous and sometimes, the correct translation does not appear among the candidates.

2.2 Translation quality assessement (TQA)

Because we want to compare the quality of translations made by humans with and without bilingual terminologies, we need to find a way to assess human translation quality. If Machine Translation (MT) enjoys well-defined and rather consensual metrics to evaluate its quality, evaluation of human translation poses a real challenge. These two domains use different protocols for the assessment of translations. On the one hand, MT evaluation focuses on comparing the output of different MT systems. This evaluation is done in reference to one or several human translations. On the other hand, translation studies seek to assess the quality of a human translation on its own, without any reference to a standard translation. In fact, the only reference is the judge himself/herself.

2.2.1 TQA and machine translation

There are two ways of assessing machine translations. One is called *objective* or *automatic evaluation*. The other is called *subjective* or *human evaluation*.

In objective evaluation, translations are evaluated through a measure which is automatically computable and which has the advantadge of being reproducible. Examples of such measure are: BLEU (Papineni et al., 2002) which is based on the count of common n-grams between the assessed translation and reference translation(s) and METEOR (Banerjee and Lavie, 2005) which is similar to BLEU but leaves room for variation by including morphological variants and synonyms in the n-gram comparison. These metrics are in turn meta-evaluated by computing their correlation with human jugements. Though handy for the evaluation of MT systems on a daily basis, these metrics were not used in the shared translation tasks of the ACL Workshop on Statistical Machine Translation where they are perceived as imperfect substitutes of human assessment, see the work of Callison-Burch et al. (2009; 2010) for example.

MT evaluation campaigns led to the development of a series of protocols for what is called *subjective* or *human* evaluation of MT. Two evaluation protocols stand out :

judgement task The judge grades each translation independently. The grading scale can be quite complex, like 5 points scales over two criteria (fluency, adequacy) or simple binary judgements (correct/incorrect).

ranking task The judge ranks several translation of the same source segment from worse to best, each translation being produced by a different system.

These protocols are meta-evaluated using inter- and intra- annotator agreement measures which gives some indication on the coherence of the judgements. Experiments by Callison-Burch (2007) show that annotation tasks which involve complex sets of categories (e.g. 5 points scales over adequacy and fluency vs. binary judgements) and larger segments (sentences vs. phrases) tend to be more time-consuming and to result in lower agreement. The ranking task is considered easier and less time-consuming than the judgement task. It also yields a higher annotator agreement.

2.2.2 TQA and translation studies

In translation studies, TQA is mainly used by the translation industry as a way to monitor the quality of its products. Secară (2005) gives an overview of various translation grids. Although there is no consensus, all grids follow more or less the same methodology. Translation errors are categorized (e.g. spelling, grammar, terminology) and each error type is assigned a certain cost which is proportional to its gravity. A passage of a given length is randomly selected from the translation under assessment. Errors are marked and the cost points add up. If the sum of the points exceeds some threshold, the translation is deemed unacceptable.

These grids are criticised by theoretical approaches to TQA - see Williams (2001) for instance - because they stick to the lexical and syntactic levels and do not take into account higher linguistic levels like discursive or argumental structures. They are also monolithic and supposed applicable to any kind of text whereas authors like Reiss (1971) have argued that the evaluation criteria and their weight should be adapted to the text's function.

3 Protocol

The evaluation protocol is based on the ranking and judgement tasks used in MT subjective evaluation. These tasks were chosen because of their relative simplicity (compared to traditional 5-points scales) which also results in more reliable judgements as shown by Callison-Burch et al. (2007). Automatic evaluation metrics were discarded because their only advantage - reproducibility - is of no use in this kind of evaluation: the protocol includes a subtask which is not reproducible (the translation) which makes the overall evaluation non-reproducible anyway. Evaluation grids were also discarded because they are too complex to put in practice, difficultly available and scarcely documented.

The evaluation's protocol is as follows:

1. Translators translate specialized texts in three different situations which we call "situations of translation". These situations of translation share a common base of identical generic resources (two monolingual and one bilingual dictionnaries). Translation are made from second-language to native language:

   situation 0 : translate with *generic resources* only

   situation 1 : translate with generic resources + a *bilingual terminology* extracted from comparable specialized corpora.

   situation 2 : translate with generic resources + full access to *Internet* where the translator can find all sorts of translation aids

   Situation 0 acts as a baseline where the translator has no specialized resource. The terminology used in situation 1 is the terminology under assessment. In situation 2, the Web is considered as some sort of "super-" or "meta-" specialized resource, because the translator will have access to all the specialized lexicons and termbases that are available online.

2. Once the translations are done, translators note down the time they spent in translation as well as the terms or expressions that they found problematic to translate and which drove them to use a linguistic resource. They also note down which resources they used to make the translation.

3. For each problematic term, judges rank the translations produced in the different situations[1] (ranking task). They also judge each translation separately using three categories: exact, acceptable or wrong (judgement task).

4. The added-valued of the bilingual terminology (situation 1) is measured by the comparing the quality of the translations produced in situation 1 with the quality of the translations produced in situations 0 and 2.

We decided to restrict the evaluation to the problematic terms rather than evaluating the quality of the whole translation because it appears from works in translation studies (Williams, 2001; Reiss, 1971) that the overall quality of the translation of a text emerges from the complex interaction of various parameters (register, syntax, argumental structure, spelling, etc.) most of which terminologies have no influence upon. By focusing on the problematic terms and expressions, we isolate the part of the translation that terminologies are meant to improve. As a side effect, evaluating small segments also saves time and yields more reliable judgements as demonstrated by Callison-Burch et. al. (2007).

The judgement task is based on three categories presented in table 1. These categories were chosen in accordance with Reiss (1971) who states that the translation of "content-focused texts" (e.g. scientific and technical texts, manual for use...) should favor the transfer of the source text's meaning over the transfer of the source text's form. An *acceptable* translation is a translation which conveys the meaning of the source term. An *exact* translation is a translation which makes use of the expected, standard target term. In a way, the "meaning transfer" and "accurate form" criteria parallel the more classical "adequacy" and "fluency" criteria found in MT campaigns.

	meaning transfer	accurate form
exact	✔	✔
acceptable	✔	
wrong		

Table 1: Translation quality criteria

In order to leverage differences in the quality of the translations which would arise from the translator's expertise rather than from the quality of the

---

[1] Ties are allowed.

language resource, each situation of translation is evaluated on the basis of texts translated by several translators. In turn, one has to be cautious that translators do not translate texts from the same domain in different situations of translation. Indeed, if a translator translates a text from domain A in situation 1, he/she must not translate a text from domain A in situation 2: there is a risk that the translator re-uses some terms'translations he/she has learnt in the previous situation.

A critical point when judging the translation of technical texts is that the judges often lack domain expertise and that domain experts are rarely available. One can get round this trouble by choosing specialized texts which already have an existing translation, like research paper abstracts for example. Judges can also get help from general terminological databases such as *Termium* [2].

The consistency of the judgements can be improved by first running a blank evaluation on a small set of data and then discussing the disagreements with the judges (Blanchon and Boitet, 2007). In any case, it is necessary to provide the judges with clear instructions and examples of annotations on debatable cases.

4 Experimentation

This section describes the experimental framework (section 4.1) and the result of the evaluation (section 4.2).

4.1 Experimental framework

4.1.1 Data

Two bilingual terminologies were built for the evaluation. One was acquired from comparable corpora on BREAST CANCER and the other from comparable corpora on WATER SCIENCE . The WATER SCIENCE corpus is quite large (2M words per language) and its topic is coarse-grained. Texts are research papers from the journals *Sciences de l'eau*[3] and *Water Science and Technology*[4]. Conversely, the BREAST CANCER corpus is small (400k words per language) with a fine-grained topic. Texts come from various research papers of the publications portal *Elsevier* [5]. The texts to be translated belong to the same domains. They are divided into scientific texts and popular science

---

[2] http://www.termiumplus.gc.ca/
[3] http://www.rse.inrs.ca/
[4] http://www.iwaponline.com/wst/
[5] http://www.elsevier.com/

texts. The scientic texts are 2×3 research papers abstracts taken from *Elsevier* and the water science journals. The popular science texts are 2×1 webpages taken from bilingual websites on breast cancer[6] and water treatment[7]).

	BREAST CANCER	WATER SCIENCE
scientific	508	499
pop. science	613	425

Table 2: Size of texts to be translated (number of words)

4.1.2 Data processing

The algorithm described by Fung (1997) was applied to the terms and to every open-class word occurring more than 5 times in the corpus. Extra knowledge was automatically added to the terms and open-class words in order to help the translators: part-of-speech, frequency, collocations[8], variants[9], related terms[10], definitions[11], concordances. Translators could browse the terminology via a dedicated interface designed for terminologies acquired from comparable corpora (Delpech and Daille, 2010).

4.1.3 People involved

Due to the lack of human resources to perform the evaluation, there was some collisions in the roles of translator/judge and translator/organizer. Three persons were involved in the test of the protocol. The author of the paper, who is not a trained translator, translated the texts in the baseline situation (general resources only) and organized the evaluation. Two trained translators translated the texts in situation 1 (terminology) and 2 (Internet) and also judged the translations. The translations were anonymized and randomly shuffled so that the judges would not know the origin of the translations.

Texts, domains and situations were distributed as follows :

	BREAST CANCER	WATER SCIENCE
untrained translator	sit. 0	sit. 0
trained translator 1	sit. 1	sit. 2
trained translator 2	sit. 2	sit. 1

4.2 Results

4.2.1 Translators' feedback

It was difficult for translators to adapt to the ambiguity of the alignments. Although the aim and the context of the evaluation had been explained to them, they still expected the correct translation to appear "on click", just like it happens with the traditional languages resources they are accustomed to. Another obstacle was the coverage of the terminology, especially for the WATER SCIENCE domain whose topic was not refined enough. Table 3 shows the percentage of words of the texts to be translated which also appear in the terminology. Clearly, fined-grained corpora should be favored over large corpora.

	BREAST CANCER	WATER SCIENCE
EN texts	94%	14%
FR texts	67%	78%

Table 3: Terminology coverage of the vocabulary of the texts to be translated (EN) and their reference translation (FR)

4.2.2 Problematic terms

Problematic terms are terms or expressions that a translator found difficult to translate. Problematic terms retained for the evaluation are terms which were tagged problematic by at least 2 translators. We collected 148 problematic terms (26 tagged by 2 translators and 122 tagged by 3 translators). Table 4 shows the repartition of problematic terms among domains and types of corpora.

	BREAST CANCER	WATER SCIENCE
pop. science	34	10
specialized	43	51
total	87	61

Table 4: Problematic terms used for evaluation

4.2.3 Time

The texts to be translated amounted to 2,147 words. Translators were quicker in situation 0

---

[6]http://www.cbcf.org/

[7]http://www.lenntech.com/

[8]most remarkable cooccurrents, the association measure is the log-likelihood ratio (Dunning, 1993)

[9]phrases which have not been identified as terms by the term extractor but have words in common with the entry term

[10]terms which have words in common with the entry term

[11]either the Wikipedia or Wiktionary article if avalaible or a sentence extracted from the corpus and containg a very simple pattern like "A \$TERM is a..."

which is normal because they had less resources to browse (7.15 words/sec. on average). There is no significant time difference between situation 1 and situation 2 (11.18 and 11.6 words/sec. respectively).

4.2.4 Agreement between judges

Agreement was computed using the Kappa coefficient (Carletta, 1996) which takes into account the observed agreement $P(A)$ and the agreement which would have occurred by chance $P(E)$.

$$Kappa = \frac{P(A) - P(E)}{1 - P(E)}$$

Agreement was better for the ranking task: 0.65 (substantial) than for the judgement task: 0.36 (fair) which is consistent with the findings of Callison-Burch et. al. (2007). Agreement was better for the popular science texts: 0.57 (moderate) than for the scientific texts: 0.48 (moderate).

4.3 Judgement task

Table 5 gives quality judgements for the translations of the BREAST CANCER texts. The proportion of translations judged *wrong* is almost equivalent for all situations. Translations produced in situation 1 (with the terminology) are more often judged *exact* than the translations produced in situation 0 (only generic resources). Translations produced in situation 2 (with Internet) are the most accurate ones.

	sit.0	sit.1	sit.2
exact	38%	43%	47%
acceptable	42%	38%	35%
wrong	20%	19%	18%

Table 5: Translations' quality - BREAST CANCER domain

Table 6 gives quality judgements for the translations of the WATER SCIENCE texts. One can see that translations produced in situation 1 are of lesser quality than those produced in situation 0. This is unexpected because situation 1 and situation 2 share a common base of generic resources. Translations produced in situation 1 should be at least as good as translations produced in situation 0.

The fact is that the translators used the languages resources in different manners depending on the situation in which they performed the

	sit.0	sit.1	sit.2
exact	59%	56%	77%
acceptable	23%	23%	16%
wrong	18%	21%	7%

Table 6: Translations' quality - WATER SCIENCE domain

translations. Thanks to the data collected during the translation phase, we are able to tell, for each term translation if it was produced using the generic resource or the specialized resource (terminology/Internet) or relying on intuition (not exclusive). Table 7 shows that the translators who had access to a specialized resource scarcely used the generic resource. It might be because they felt the generic resource was useless to get the translation of technical terms and they preferred to use directly the specialised resource. But as the WATER SCIENCE terminology covers only a small part of vocabulary of the texts to translate, it was barely advantageous. A systematic exploitation of the generic resource in situation 1 would have led to translations at least as good as those produced in situation 0.

	sit.0	sit.1	sit.2
gen. ress.	43%	14%	3%
spec. ress.	-	25%	56%
intutition	79%	77%	44%

Table 7: Exploitation of the language resources depending on the situation of translation

4.4 Ranking task

The ranking task results are similar to those of the judgement task. When different translations of the same terms are compared, those produced in situation 2 are always better, whatever the domain. Those produced in situation 1 are better than the ones produced in situation 0 only for the BREAST CANCER domain, probably because of divergences in the exploitation of the language resources as explained above.

5 Discussion and future work

We have described a protocol which assesses the added-value of terminologies acquired from comparable corpora when used for specialized human translation. This protocol consists in comparing

	sit.0	sit.2
sit.1 better than	28%	26%
sit.1 as good as	47%	42%
sit.1 worse than	26%	32%

Table 8: Translations' ranking - Breast Cancer domain

	sit.0	sit.2
sit.1 better than	18%	16%
sit.1 as good as	49%	41%
sit.1 worse than	33%	43%

Table 9: Translations' ranking - Water Science domain

several situations of translation in which the translators have access to diverse language resources: only generic resources, generic resources and the evaluated terminology, generic resources and full access to Internet. The added-value of the terminology is supposed to be evidenced by the difference in the quality of the translations produced in the three situations. We have described in section 4 a first trial of the protocol. This first trial showed that some hitches in our procedure prevent us from clearly demonstrating the added-value of terminologies acquired from comparable corpora : we had contradictory results for the Breast Cancer and Water Science domains. Nonetheless, this first experimentation, although carried out with a small set of data and participants, allowed us to test the feasibility of the protocol and pinpointed problems which must be solved before launching a more thorough evaluation :

- The observed added-value of the terminology highly depends on its coverage of the texts used to evaluate it. Any measure of this added-value should also mention the adequacy between the assessed terminology and the texts to be translated, otherwise it is not interpretable. We determined this adequacy in a simple manner, by computing the proportion of words in the texts to be translated that also occurr in the terminology. This leaves some room for improvement. The comparability of the corpora used form terminology extraction and alignment must also be taken into account. For this, we are planning to use the comparability measure developped by Bo and Gaussier (2010).

- The joint use of several language resources seems to bias the results as the translators' behaviour changes in function of the resources he/she has as his/her disposal. It is better to have only one resource per situation of translation, for instance:

  - situation 0: no resources,
  - situation 1: assessed terminology only,
  - situation 2: Internet only.

- Translators should be prepared to translate in a situation which is unusual to them. Ideally, one shoud run at first a blank translation task so as to discuss it with the translators and help them apprehend these new situations and resources.

The next step is to scale-up the protocol. We will renew the experiment on a much larger scale (a whole class of students translators) and include all the improvements listed above.

Finally, even if it was not the goal of this work, this first evaluation gives rise to some lines of research to improve the usefulness of terminologies acquired from comparable corpora. First, we have seen that the acquisition corpus should be collected in function of the texts that are to be translated and that the topic should be fine-grained. Second, it is clear that the Internet is a huge repository of linguistic resources and translations. A nice development would be to add a new functionality to the terminology software which, when the queried term is not present in the database, would either automatically generate a translation and filter it on the Internet or search it in pre-selected online resources. However, the worth of Internet as a linguistic resource should not be overestimated. In most professional translations, translators have to translate texts whose vocabulary can not be found on the Internet. It is especially the case with corporate translations : companies use their own terminologies, which can only be found in the texts produced by the company itself. Thus, we can not expect to rely on Internet as a unique source of translations and still need to improve the term alignment program. For this, we are planning to use translation techniques relying on the compositionality of terms (Morin and Daille, 2009) in addition to the distribution-based approaches (Fung, 1997) presented in section 2.1 and which we used for this evaluation.

Acknowledgments

This work was funded by the company Lingua et Machina and the French National Research Agency (funding no. ANR-08-CORD-009). I would like to thank Clémence de Baudus and Mathieu Delage for their participation in the evaluation.

References

S. Banerjee and A. Lavie. 2005. METEOR: An Automatic Metric for MT Evaluation with Improved Correlation with Human Judgments *Proceedings of Workshop on Intrinsic and Extrinsic Evaluation Measures for MT and/or Summarization at the 43rd Annual Meeting of the Association of Computational Linguistics*, pp. 65–72.

H. Blanchon and C. Boitet. 2007. Pour l'évaluation externe des systèmes de TA par des méthodes fondées sur la tâche *Traitement Automatique des Langues*, 48(1):33–65.

L. Bo and E. Gaussier. 2010. Improving Corpus Comparability for Bilingual Lexicon Extraction from Comparable Corpora *23ème International Conference on Computational Linguistics*, pp. 23–27.

C. Callison-Burch, C. Fordryce, P. Koehn, C. Monz and J. Schroeder. 2007. (Meta-) Evaluation of Machine Translation *Proceedings of the 2nd workshop on Statistical Machine Translation*, pp. 136–158.

C. Callison-Burch, P. Koehn, C. Monz and J. Schroeder. 2009. Findings of the 2009 Workshop on Statistical Machine Translation *Proceedings of the Fourth Workshop on Statistical Machine Translation*, pp. 1–28.

C. Callison-Burch, P. Koehn, C. Monz, K. Peterson, M. Przybocki and O. Zaidan. 2010. Findings of the 2010 Joint Workshop on Statistical Machine Translation and Metrics for Machine Translation *Proceedings of the Joint Fifth Workshop on Statistical Machine Translation and Metrics MATR*, pp. 17–53.

J. Carletta. 1996. Assessing Agreement on Classification Tasks: The Kappa Statistic *Computational Linguistics*, 22(2).

E. Delpech. 2010. Dealing with lexicon acquired from comparable corpora : validation and exchange *Proceedings of the 2010 Terminology and Knowledge Engineering Conference (TKE 2010)*, pp. 211–223.

T. Dunning. 1993. Accurate Methods for the Statistics of Surprise and Coincidence *Computational Linguistics*, 19(1):61–74.

P. Fung. 1997. Finding Terminology Translations from Non-parallel Corpora *Proceedings of the 5th Annual Workshop on Very Large Corpora*, pp. 192–202.

P. Koehn and K. Knight. 2002. Learning a Translation Lexicon from Monolingual Corpora *Unsupervised Lexical Acquisition: Proceedings of the Workshop pf the ACL Special Interest Group on the Lexicon (SIGLEX)*, pp. 9–16. Association for Computational Linguistics. Philadelphia, Pennsylvania.

E. Morin and B. Daille. 2009. Compositionality and lexical alignment of multi-word terms *Language Resources and Evaluation (LRE)*, 44:79–95. P. Rayson, S. Piao, S. Sharoff, S. Evert, B. Villada Moirón (eds.) Springer Netherlands

A. Nazarenko, H. Zargayouna, O. Hamon and J. Van Puymbrouk. 2009. Évaluation des outils terminologiques : enjeux, difficultés et propositions *Traitement Automatique des Langues*, 50(1):257–281.

K. Papineni, S. Roukos, T. Ward and W.-J. Zhu. 2002. BLEU: A method for automatic evaluation of machine translation. *Proceedings of the 40th Annual Meeting of the Association for Computational Linguistics*, 311–318.

E. Planas. 2005. Similis : un logiciel d'aide à la traduction au service des professionnels. *Traduire*, 206:41–48.

R. Rapp. 1995. Identifying Word Translations in Non-Parallel Texts. *Proceedings of the 35th Annual Meeting of the Association for Computational Linguistics*, pp. 320–322.

K. Reiss. 1971. *Translation criticism, the potentials and limitations : categories and criteria for translation quality assessment.* St. Jerome Pub., Manchester, GB.

M. Renders, H. Djean and E. Gaussier. 1971. Assessing Automatically Extracted Bilingual Lexicons for CLIR in Vertical Domains: XRCE Participation in the GIRT Track of CLEF 2002 *Lecture Notes in Computer Science.*, pp. 363–371.

F. Sadat, M. Yoshikawa and S. Uemura. 2003. Learning Bilingual Translations from Comparable Corpora to Cross-Language Information Retrieval: Hybrid Statistics-based and Linguistics-based Approach *Proceedings of the 6th International Workshop on Information Retrieval with Asian Languages.*, 11:57–64

A. Secară. 2005. Translation Evaluation - a State of the Art Survey. *eCoLoRe / MeLLANGE Workshop*, 39–44.

M. Williams. 2005. The Application of Argumentation Theory to Translation Quality Assessment *Meta : journal des traducteurs / Meta: Translator's Journal*, 46(2):326–344.

ISSN 1736-6305 Vol. 11
http://hdl.handle.net/10062/16955

A Quantitative and Qualitative Analysis of Nordic Surnames

Eirini Florou
Institute of Informatics
and Telecommunications
NCSR 'Demokritos'
Athens, Greece
eirini.florou@gmail.com

Stasinos Konstantopoulos
Institute of Informatics
and Telecommunications
NCSR 'Demokritos'
Athens, Greece
konstant@iit.demokritos.gr

Abstract

Analysing Nordic persons' names with respect to language identification is a very hard task, as the chosen group of languages is closely related, but provides interesting insights into the structure of names; it is also a task that has many applications in information extraction, speech synthesis, and automatic transliteration. In this paper we present and discuss results obtained by statistical language modelling as well as by a hand-crafted definite clause grammar.

1 Introduction

Language identification is the task of predicting the language that a text or utterance is written or spoken in. Language identification is typically approached as a statistical text categorization task, where features are extracted by analysing different linguistic levels, from the acoustic and prosodic to the phonotactic or graphotactic.

In this paper we concentrate on identifying the language of written text and, in fact, the language of a *single person's name*, in isolation or in a document written in a different language. This is a much harder task than predicting the language of texts, even short ones, but also one that is interesting from the theoretical as well as the practical perspective: from the *onomastics* perspective, it leads to interesting insights into the internal structure of names; from the *computational linguistics* perspective, it helps us explore the limits of various modelling methods on a task that is both hard and well-understood; and, finally, this task has interesting *natural language processing* applications in information extraction, speech synthesis, and automatic transliteration.

We further focus our task to the surnames of people from Denmark, Norway, Sweden, Finland,

and Germany.[1] Surnames from Denmark, Norway, and Sweden form a cluster of particularly hard to separate surnames, while adding those from Finland and Germany leads to interesting conclusions as will be discussed later.

Our investigation builds on previous work on text categorization and, in particular, predicting the linguistic background of the bearer of a name (Section 2). To this end, we first apply statistical modelling (Section 3), the results of which guide us to propose a hypothesis (Section 4), which we validate by implementing as a definite clause grammar (Section 5). The paper closes drawing conclusions and outlining future work (Section 6).

2 Background

Guessing the language of a document falls under the larger area of *text categorization*, which aims at classifying a document as belonging to one (or more) out of certain, predefined categories or subject codes. Document language is one of the possible dimensions of categorization, interesting for various document organization, data mining, and information extraction tasks.

In their seminal paper, Cavnar and Trenkle (1994) report experiments on language categorization using a simple n-gram frequency algorithm. The language models consist of frequency counts of n-grams (up to 5-grams) for various languages. To classify a document, the frequency counts of n-grams in the document are calculated and their distribution compared against the distribution of n-grams in the language models. The model with the smallest distance from the distribution of the document, is assumed to be the language of the document.

---

[1]In the remainder of this paper we, somewhat arbitrarily and for lack of a perfectly-fitting term, collectively refer to these five classes as *Nordic*. We, furthermore, occasionally abbreviate them, in tables and elsewhere, as follows: DA (Denmark), NO (Norway), SV (Sweden), FI (Finland), and DE (Germany).

This algorithm was tested on Usenet postings from the `soc.culture` newsgroup hierarchy. An eight-language corpus was generated semi-automatically: a first pass operated under the assumption that the postings are in the language of the country or region under discussion in each newsgroup, and at a second pass discrepancies between the newsgroup's default language and the system's prediction were manually resolved.

With the 400 most frequent n-grams retained in the models, and postings of at least 300 characters of length, the system classified the test set almost perfectly, achieving an accuracy of 99.8%. The authors also report an accuracy of 99.3% for postings that are under 300 characters, without providing any further details of how accuracy drops with shorter test documents.

Cavnar and Trenkle's algorithm has seen various implementations and applications, the most notable probably being the TEXTCAT[2] implementation used in the SPAMASSASSIN[3] spam filter.

Although very accurate even for texts as small as two or three hundred characters, Cavnar and Trenkle's experiments did not test how well one can identify the language of a single word. Efforts in this, much harder, task originate in speech synthesis (Spiegel, 1985; Vitale, 1991; Font Llitjós and Black, 2001), with language identification used to select different pronunciation models for foreign names, depending on each name's origin.

Font Llitjós and Black (2001), in particular, note that language identification of isolated names is a difficult task, as they tried to manually tag 516 names and found that they could confidently tag only 43% of the data. For their speech synthesis experiment they used a simplification of the Cavnar and Trenkle algorithm which only counted 3-grams. They trained language models on general text (ranging from 255 thousand to 11 million words), and provided the classification results as features for the grapheme-to-phoneme models. Unfortunately they do not report results for the language identification part of their experiments.

Another field of application of the same general methodology is automatic transliteration of named-entities for the purposes of *information extraction* (Virga and Khudanpur, 2003) or *machine translation* (Huang, 2005). In Huang's experi-

ment languages were grouped together in clusters, guided by the effect each clustering had on the accuracy of the overall transliteration. The resulting clusters roughly corresponded to familiar language groupings (Chinese, Romance, English-and-Dutch, Nordic). Employing language identification models is reported to improve the accuracy of the overall task, but no results are provided for the language identification sub-task per se. Virga and Khudanpur (2003) report improved accuracy in recovering the original orthography of English-language named-entities in Chinese text by using a tri-gram model to first decide whether a Chinese string is an English-language name or not or selecting different transliteration model depending on his.

More recently, Konstantopoulos (2007) presented a corpus of European names compiled by harvesting information from the web. The corpus matches about 15 thousand names against their nationality and was used to compare the accuracy of n-gram modelling on language identification of a single name against language identification of common words of the same size, finding the former to offer themselves to significantly more accurate prediction. Konstantopoulos (2010) followed up with applying a series of statistical tests looking for the discriminative features in names that offer themselves to more accurate prediction, but without reaching any definite conclusions.

3 Statistical Modelling

As a first, exploratory, step we applied the TEXTCAT implementation of Cavnar and Trenkle's 5-gramm modelling method and tested the language models of the training set itself to derive confusion matrices. For this, we used the relevant parts of the corpus created by Konstantopoulos (2007). This corpus was created by harvesting the Transfermarkt website,[4] featuring various information about football players, including—most crucially for our purposes—their nationality. We extended this corpus with names harvested from lists of members of parliament. Because of the strictness of football associations' naturalization rules and the increased inertia in politics at the national level, these names delineate tightly, although not perfectly, the linguistic background of their bearers. In total, we were able to compile a corpus of 5568 names, distributed

---

[2] `http://www.let.rug.nl/~vannoord/TextCat/`

[3] `http://spamassassin.apache.org/`

[4] See `http://www.transfermarkt.de/`

Table 1: Confusion matrix of surnames, given as the fraction of predictions that a string is in each class (rows) for each of the actual classes (columns), so that the numbers along the diagonal (in bold) represent the *recall* achieved in each class. The absolute size of each class in the dataset is given in the bottom row of the table.

	Actual				
	DE	DA	NO	SV	FI
DE	**0.73**	0.24	0.13	0.16	0.07
DA	0.10	**0.54**	0.16	0.06	0.04
NO	0.10	0.17	**0.63**	0.16	0.10
SV	0.00	0.01	0.01	**0.64**	0.01
FI	0.07	0.04	0.06	0.04	**0.78**
Size	2608	678	987	629	666

among the five languages under consideration as shown on the last row of Table 1.

With respect to the choice of languages, we have chosen Swedish, Norwegian, and Danish because the form a cluster of closely related languages with similar orthographic conventions, making language identification a challenging task. German and Finnish were included in order to study interactions at the periphery of the three core target languages.

It should be noted that, since TEXTCAT language models comprise absolute frequency counts, we reduplicated names from the less populous name lists in order to have a balanced distribution of instances among classes and avoid having n-grams that are even moderately (in relative terms) frequent in German names dominate relatively frequent n-grams from other languages. We should also note that we have reduced all letters with diacritics to their plain Latin base letter. This was done for two reasons: in order to normalize orthography into a form that minimizes 'easy guesses' of the ø/ö kind, and in order to have an approach that fits named-entity recognition tasks in foreign-language contexts, where diacritics are often simply omitted, rather than transcribed into digraphs. That is, in such applications *å* typically becomes *a* rather than *aa*.

4 Discriminative Features

As Table 1 shows, this is a very hard task and the direct application of language modelling does not get us very hard, even when testing over the

training set. But, as noted before, this was only an exploratory stage, where the observation of the results and the frequencies recorded in the models helped us identify the features that best discriminate surnames as well as those that cause the most confusion. From this basis, we looked for further morphological and semantic features that, we postulate, improve discernability; we used these extra features to formulate a series of hypotheses about the structure of Nordic surnames, presented in this section and tested in Section 5.

4.1 Patronymic surnames

Arguably the most characteristic Nordic surnames are patronyms ending in *–sen* (DA, NO) or *–son* (SV) suffixed to a first name. As *–sen* is shared between Danish and Norwegian, accounting for 26% of Danish and 31% of Norwegian surnames, and since there is very little (if any) grounds for correctly classifying the first names, this explains most of the confusion between these two languages' surnames seen on Table 1.

Swedish patronyms, on the other hand, can be easily spotted as they follow a different pattern where the first name in genitive (marked by *–s*) is followed by *–son*. This leaves no margin for ambiguity within the scope of our experiments, as 'son' is spelt *Sohn* in German and is rarely found in surnames anyway. Even beyond the scope of this paper, Scottish surnames that often exhibit this pattern should be relatively easy to separate by first name.

4.2 Toponymic surnames

Ending in *–er* is a common feature of all Nordic surnames, in fact, words in general, and accounts for 17.4% of German, 6.6% of Danish, 4.3% of Swedish, 2.7% of Norwegian, and 1.2% of Finnish surnames. Although of low discriminative power by itself, the *–er* suffix is important in our observations when co-occurring with other features.

In our data, surname derivations are mostly applied to monomorphemic roots with the exception of German where surnames are often derived from roots that are themselves derivatives. More specifically, 362 out of the 2608 German surnames in our corpus exhibit this property, typically derived from placenames; *Pfeifenberger*, *Rasswalder*, and *Amerhauser* are characteristic examples.

A more marked observation, also typical of German surnames, is that they can be derived

Table 2: Some examples of surnames including the *n*-grams <ander> and <land>.

Swedish	Danish/Norwegian	German
Andersson	*Andersen*	*Ander*sohn
Se*lander*		*Lander*l
	Klit*land*/Hel*land*	Wei*land*

from surnames, as exemplified by *Husterer* and *Eibinger*.

A characteristic failure of our language models is with toponymic surnames where the placename ends in *–land*. In Swedish it is common to use *–er* to derive such toponymic surnames (example shown in second row of Table 2), adding considerably to the frequencies of the <ander> and <land> *n*-grams in the Swedish language model. As 5-gram models are unable to capture the distinction between <lander> and <ander>, this feature causes several misclassifications, as <ander> appears frequently in Danish, Norwegian, and German surnames. Some characteristic examples are shown on Table 2.

The problem is further aggravated by the frequent appearance of <land> across all four languages. For example, <land$>[5] is less characteristic of Swedish (i.e., more common across all languages) than <lander$>, which should make <land$> a weaker indicator than <lander$>. Because, however, <lander$> subsumes <land$>, the latter's weight in the Swedish language model is boosted causing misclassifications.

There are a lot of cases of Danish surnames that the *–er* occurs in the morpheme *–ager*. This suffix can be added to whatever monosyllabic lexeme of the same language which could be Danish first or last name.

Also, Nordic surnames, except for Finnish, are formed by adding the *–er* to each language's corresponding toponyms in order to denote the person who is descended from the certain local. A series of examples indicates this fact.

4.3   German and Danish surnames

Occupational surnames are one of the major factors of the misclassification of many Danish surnames as German. As one can observe on Table 1, the confusion is largely asymmetric,

the reason being the existence of many German-language occupational surnames in the Danish data, with the German orthography retained. One possible explanation is that these names were incorporated in Danish in the sixteenth and seventeenth centuries by the immigration of travelling guilds from Germany, who had already adopted occupational surnames.

Although the confusion can be somewhat alleviated by the fact that compounds such as *Rothbauer* and *Sommermayer* are only found in the German data, it is impossible to correctly classify surnames such as *Möller*, *Weber*, *Meyer*, and *Schmidt* found in the Danish data.

Another factor of confusion between German and Danish surnames, but also one that helps in the hard task of separating Danish from Norwegian, is the suffix *–ing* is almost exclusively found in German (2%) and Danish (2.5%). A differentiating factor is that in German *–ing* is sometimes part of a longer, uniquely German, morpheme such as *–ling* (e.g., *Emmerling*), and reduplication that might sometimes manifest this 4-gram can be easily spotted (as in, e.g., Danish *Balling*). Furthermore, a large class of German surnames in *–ing* are occupational surnames (e.g., *Möllering*) where Danish ones are placenames in Denmark (e.g., *Gjesing*, *Grønning*).

4.4   Compounding

Many Nordic surnames are formed by compounding a nominal modifier with natural or man-made features, such as *berg* 'mountain' (DE, SV) or 'iceberg' (DA) or *gaard* 'farm'. In the case of *berg*:

<nominal> + *berg*

where <nominal> is of the same language as the surname and in the case of Norwegian and German surnames can also be an adjective whereas in Swedish and Danish it is always a noun, possibly marked for plural or genitive (especially in Danish). Some indicative examples are given on Table 3. This is a fairly common pattern, matching 6% of the Swedish data and 2% of the Danish, Norwegian and German data. It should be noted that *Berg* also appears as the modifier in compounds such as *Bergqvist* (SV) or *Bergheim* (DE).

Another common pattern in Denmark and Norway is compounds with with *gaard*, accounting for 7% of Danish surnames, 4.5% of Norwegian sur-

---

[5]We use <$> to signify word boundaries, consuming one of the 5 characters of each entry in the language model.

Table 3: Examples of surnames in *–berg*

Norwegian	German	Swedish	Danish
Ny-*berg*	Stolz-en-*berg*	Ceder-*berg*	Co-*berg*
Skjon-s-*berg*	Grun-*berg*	For-s-*berg*	Falken-*berg*

Table 4: Surnames in *–gaard*

Danish	Norwegian
Abil*gaard*	Ost*gaard*
Bis*gaard*	Ny*gaard*
Song*gaard*	Kort*gaard*

names, and many misclassifications. As is the case with *berg*, Norwegian surnames can be spotted by adjective modifiers, whereas Danish only allows nouns, typically toponyms.

Moreover, surnames may be formed by compounding with *man(n)*, where German/Danish use *mann* and Swedish *man*. The percentages of Nordic surnames with the certain suffix are respectively: DA 2%, DE 4%, SV 3%. Furthermore, German (but not Danish) *mann* compounds are ofter formed with a derived modifier (e.g., *–er-mann*, *–el-mann*), helping us identify surnames like *Kellermann* as German. Simpler surnames such as Danish *Hermann* can be easily misclassified.

Another common pattern, setting Swedish surnames apart, is that Swedish compound surnames often use roots related to natural features, for instance *Lind* 'lime tree', *Ceder* 'cedar'.

4.5 Some observations on *–er* surnames

The n-gram analysis has shown that there is a series of n-grams which contribute to Nordic surnames ambiguation. However, there are other features which can help to cause disambiguation.

Typical case is the bigram *–er* which is a common feature of all Nordic surnames. But only German surnames can be derived from other already existed surnames while all Nordic surnames are formed by adding *–er* to corresponding toponyms. Moreover, the occupational surnames are very common in German and Danish language. However, there are German surnames which can be formed by adding an occupational name to another typical German first or last name. Furthermore, there are typical per language morphemes which include the certain suffix and as a consequence the

morpheme can bring better recognition results in contrast with the single suffix.

Apart from few exceptions, the majority of *n*-grams which cause Nordic surnames confusion have similarities with *–er* in their ability to identify the Nordic language in combination with other discriminative features.

5 Rule Modelling

Through statistical language modelling, we postulated a hypothesis about discriminative features of Nordic surnames that cannot be captured by 5-grams, either because the required context is too long or because they refer to morphological or semantic background knowledge.

As such dependencies and background can be more intuitively expressed as *definite clause grammars (DCG)*, we decided to use this framework to formalize and test out hypotheses. Besides long-distance dependencies and the ease of incorporation of external background knowledge, DCG also provide a declarative, intuitive representation that can more easily maintained and extended with new linguistic constructs.

This section presents the grammar and the results obtained over the data. Apart from the rules which are described below and which, arguably, capture general linguistic structures, our grammar also relies on a lexicon of entity names (first names, place names) and a lexicon of common words with part-of-speech annotations (adjectives, nouns, adverbs) as well as limited semantic annotations (e.g., words denoting geographic features). These resources were partially automatically created: regarding entity names we collected first names from the Konstantopoulos (2007) corpus and from a baby-names website[6] and toponyms from the Geonames database[7]. Other semantic classes have been manually compiled.

5.1 Some characteristic rules

As shown in the previous section, reference to part-of-speech and semantic class can correctly classify many difficult instances in our data. For instance, Norwegian and Danish *–gaard* compounds differ in that only Norwegian surnames use adjectives to modify *gaard*.

This is captured by the rules:

---

[6]http://www.babynames.com
[7]http://www.geonames.org

```
name(no) →lex(adj,_) gaard
name(da) →lex(plce(da),_) gaard
name(L)  →lex(_,L) gaard
```

The second argument of `lex/2` encodes the prediction obtained by n-gram modelling and the `plce(Country)` lexical category signifies the placenames acquired from the Geonames database. With these rules, we can override the n-gram prediction when part-of-speech or semantics (Danish placename) offers itself for a more certain guess. Another hard case, *berg* compounds, is treated by generalizing the rules above into compounding rules such as:[8]

```
name(no) →lex(adj,_) lex(geofeat,no)
name(de) →lex(adj,_) lex(geofeat,de)
name(da) →lex(plce(da),_) lex(geofeat,da)
name(L)  →lex(_,L) lex(geofeat,L)
```

where lexical category `geofeat` includes words such as *gaard* and *berg*.

Other rules override language modelling predictions in situations where n-grams, such as <ander>, are known to cause misclassifications in certain contexts. Referring to Section 4.2 above:

```
name(sv) →lex(_,_) land er
```

overrides any language modelling prediction made about the origin of the name. Surname-surname derivations can be recursively stipulated to be German irrespective of what the root surname is categorized as:

```
name(de) →name(_) er
```

5.2 Results

The n-gram modelling results (cf. Section 3), as well as the observation of the frequencies in the language models themselves, helped us identify discriminative and confusing features and drove our investigation into structure of surnames, culminating into a definite clause grammar that formalizes our observations.

This allowed a combination of n-grams results with morphological and semantic features that could be captured with n-gram modelling. Performance was evaluated in terms of *precision, recall* and the combined *F-measure*, as shown on Table 5. It should be noted that the test set is the training set itself, so that the predictive accuracy of the models is expected to be lower, but what is mostly relevant is the significant increase that

Table 5: Recall R, precision P and F-measure $F = 2RP/(R+P)$ obtained by the n-gram model and the definite clause grammar.

	n-gram model			DCG		
	R	P	F	R	P	F
DE	0.73	0.54	0.62	0.86	0.79	0.82
DA	0.54	0.57	0.55	0.72	0.58	0.64
NO	0.63	0.57	0.60	0.64	0.92	0.75
SV	0.50	0.94	0.65	0.63	0.84	0.72
FI	0.78	0.77	0.77	0.78	0.89	0.84

the DCG achieves. The only single measurement that is higher in the n-gram modelling experiment is precision over Swedish names, which is clearly due to the overspecificity of the model, as demonstrated by the low recall and the fact that the better balance between precision and recall in the grammar achieves a much higher F-measure.

Besides these qualitative results, we have shown above examples of rules and given qualitative explanations of why they capture patterns that cannot be modelled with n-grams. Furthermore, we should also note that the DCG is a sounder generalization of the data as, notwithstanding the lexical resources it has access to, it is considerably shorter (just below 60 rules comprising fewer than 200 terms) than the 400 n-grams *per language* that the statistical language models retain. The lexical resources (geographic names and terms, part-of-speech annotations) are, naturally, very voluminous but one can arguably claim that they are not part of these experiments' foreground as their are independently justified semantic and morphological annotations. This brings forwards one of the most advertised advantages of DCGs and explicit representations in general, that is, their ability to exploit background knowledge.

Another decisive factor is the ability to express long-distance dependencies. Consider, for example, our DCG treatment of surnames in *–er*, a suffix that occurs frequently across all investigated languages and is not, by itself, a useful discriminator: the characteristically German surname-from-surname derivation, the identification of larger contexts such as Swedish *–land-er*, and other similar longer-than-five-gram features have dramatically improved the performance of these surnames.

---

[8]We have taken some liberties with non-essential details of rules for the purpose conciseness and clarity of the presentation. The interested reader can contact either author to obtain the full grammar.

6   Conclusions and Future work

In this paper we approached the very hard problem of identifying the linguistic background of Nordic surnames from two angles: as a statistical machine learning task and as a grammar engineering task. The main contributions are providing the resources and establishing a methodology for formulating, formalizing, and testing hypotheses about name structure; demonstrating a concrete case where the combination of machine learning and grammar engineering has proved beneficial; and, finally, improving performance on a very hard task that can been used on a variety of natural language processing applications.

Our methodology proposes using statistical language modelling to 'map' the domain, examining the n-grams in the language models to identify those that are good discriminators and, most critically, misleading n-grams that, although frequent, often lead to misclassifications. Building on these insights, a definite clause grammar is created which analyses surnames in order to classify them. This grammar has access to morpheme annotations derived from a variety of resources and analysis tools, including graphotactic (the n-gram modelling predictions), morphological (part-of-speech annotations), and semantic (the Geonames hierarchy).

We have measured the performance of the definite clause grammar to be significantly higher than that achieved by statistical language modelling alone, demonstrating that it can make good use of the additional morphological and semantic background that was available.

Besides the methodology itself, our contribution extends to discovering certain aspects of the structure of Nordic surnames that have, to the best of our knowledge, not been previously reported, such surnames being derived from surnames being a characteristically German trait. We have also augmented the Konstantopoulos (2007) names corpus with further entries.[9]

Naturally, there is considerable room for further work. Initially, it would be interesting to examine name structure at a purely phonotactic level where no guesses can be made from orthographic conventions. Besides the theoretical interest, this would also make our work relevant to informa-

tion extraction from speech and spoken language machine translation tasks, where the orthography (even the simplified orthography we based our experiments on) is not recoverable before having recognized the language of the name.

It would also be interesting to compare grammars generated by a machine learning method, such as *inductive logic programming*, against our grammar, as well as surname recognizers against recognizers of other nominal classes, such as compounds. Such a survey would help us understand which of the structures we have discovered are characteristic of surnames and which are reflections of more general word-formation phenomena in these languages.

Acknowledgements

Stasinos Konstantopoulos wishes to acknowledge the support of the FP7-ICT project PRONTO.[10]

PRONTO develops methodologies for the analysis and interpretation of textual, audio, and video data, aiming at the extraction of operational knowledge supporting and improving resource management. In this context, the work described here is applied to the treatment of out-of-dictionary words in text and in audio transcriptions.

References

William B. Cavnar and John M. Trenkle. 1994. N-gram-based text categorization. In *Proceedings of Third Annual Symposium on Document Analysis and Information Retrieval (SDAIR 94), Las Vegas, 11–13 April 1994*, pages 161–175.

Ariadna Font Llitjós and Alan W. Black. 2001. Knowledge of language origin improves pronunciation accuracy of proper names. In *Proc. of Eurospeech 2001, Aalborg, Denmark*.

Fei Huang. 2005. Cluster-specific named entity transliteration. In *Proceedings Conf. on Human Language Technology and Empirical Methods in Natural Language Processing (HLT/EMNLP 2005), Vancouver, British Columbia, Canada*, pages 435–442.

Stasinos Konstantopoulos. 2007. What's in a name? In *Proc. RANLP Workshop on Computational Phonology, Borovets, Bulgaria, September 2007*.

---

[9]The augmented corpus and various scripts for its manipulation are available at `http://www.iit.demokritos.gr/~konstant/dload/tmc.tgz`

[10]See `http://www.ict-pronto.org`

Stasinos Konstantopoulos. 2010. Learning language identification models: a comparative analysis of the distinctive features of names and common words. In *Proc. 7th Intl Conf. on Language Resources and Evaluation (LREC-2010), 19–21 May, Valletta, Malta*, pages 3431–6.

Murray F. Spiegel. 1985. Pronouncing surnames automatically. In *Proc. Conf. of the American Voice Input/Output Society*, pages 109–132.

Paola Virga and Sanjeev Khudanpur. 2003. Transliteration of proper names in cross-lingual information retrieval. In *Proc. ACL Workshop on Multilingual and Mixed-language Named Entity Recognition*, pages 57–64.

Tony Vitale. 1991. An algorithm for high accuracy name pronunciation by parametric speech synthesizer. *Computational Linguistics*, 17(3):257–276.

ISSN 1736-6305 Vol. 11
http://hdl.handle.net/10062/16955

Experiments on Lithuanian Term Extraction

Gintarė Grigonytė, Erika Rimkutė, Andrius Utka and Loic Boizou
Centre of Computational Linguistics (http://donelaitis.vdu.lt)
Vytautas Magnus University
Kaunas, Lithuania
{g.grigonyte, e.rimkute, a.utka, l.boizou}@hmf.vdu.lt

Abstract

This paper explores the problem of extracting domain specific terminology in the field of science and education from Lithuanian texts. Four different term extraction approaches have been applied and evaluated.

1 Introduction

Term extraction nowadays is becoming automated and a well defined process that contains phases of NLP in the levels of morphology, syntax, and sometimes semantics (Sager, 1990; Cabre, 1992). Even though NLP tools have never reached very high reliability, there is a wide choice of term extraction applications for widely spread Indo-European languages like English (Pantel and Lin, 2001), French (Daille, 1994), Polish (Piskorski et al., 2004), and Russian (Mitrofanova and Zakharov, 2009).

The research strategies of term extraction can be divided into statistically-based and linguistically-based[1] (Cabre et al., 2001). Rarer languages often do not have the luxury of linguistic tools for automatic text processing. One can argue that a possible solution could be statistically-based tools, which are claimed to be language independent. However, there is a lack of evaluation of such tools for rare languages.

Even though there are some rapid advances in Lithuania's HLT[2], automatic term extraction is still quite a new and unexplored field. First attempts of using commercial term extraction tools for Lithuanian were described by Zeller (2005).

The present paper deals with the automatic extraction of Lithuanian domain specific terminology in the field of education and science. In the following subsections we will describe the terminology situation in Lithuania and several Lithuanian language specific pitfalls that are relevant for linguistically or statistically based term extraction systems.

1.1 Terminology Situation in Lithuania

The main volume of Lithuanian terminology is available at the Lithuanian Terminology bank[3].

The Terminology bank is being run and constantly updated by the Commission of the Lithuanian Language[4] together with the Office of Lithuanian Seimas[5]. Presently, the bank keeps records of 150 thousand terms and their definitions of various domains, e.g. machinery, computer science, medicine, etc. Naturally, there is a large number of domain specific databases and dictionaries in various institutions that do not always include officially accepted terms.

In Lithuania until now terms have been composed, chosen and approbated on the basis of inconsiderable amount of texts, intuition, and the norms of the Lithuanian language. This is a traditional prescriptive way of term definition that does not satisfy contemporary needs of the language.

However, there is a great urge for changes in the Lithuanian terminology, as now there is a constant lack of terms and a large number of incorrectly translated terms. Furthermore, new variants of terms occur much faster than the definition of a term. Quite often the standardized terms are not willingly accepted by the society.

Obviously this paper takes the descriptive path, as it is an attempt to find an efficient and robust way to extract a domain specific terminology without any prescriptive judgment.

---

[1]Hybrid approaches combine both strategies: usually linguistic analysis followed by statistical filtering.

[2]More about Lithuanian HLT in Marcinkevičienė and Vitkutė-Adžgauskienė (2010).

[3]http://terminai.vlkk.lt:10001/pls/tb/tb.search
[4]http://vlkk.lt/
[5]http://www.lrs.lt/

1.2 The Language Related Problem

Lithuanian is a highly inflective language. For example, Lithuanian nouns, adjectives and particles typically have 7 cases in singular and 7 in plural, which makes 14 different wordforms of a single-word. Additionally some Lithuanian nouns, adjectives, participles, pronouns, and numerals can be used in three different genders (feminine, masculine, and neuter), which again adds to a variety of forms. This proliferation of inflections makes the statistical automatic identification of terms more complicated, as distinct wordforms of terms appear very infrequently.

The solution for this is the morphological tagging, which again is complicated due to many morphological categories and morphological ambiguity, which exists in Lithuanian in spite of rich variety of wordforms. Unlike in other languages like for instance Malay morphological categories do not necessarily resolve ambiguity as ambiguity is present within lemmas, e.g., "laiko" (noun "time" and verb "hold"), and within wordforms, e.g. "prekės" (sing. noun gen. and pl. noun nom.).

Besides, the linguistic approach needs an answer to the question, which of grammatical categories are necessary for the successful extraction of term candidates and which can be ignored. One thing is obvious that the part-of-speech category is not enough for Lithuanian.

The categories of gender and number are not very helpful in distinguishing between terms and non-terms. For example, if we consider the most productive two-word term combination N + N in Lithuanian, then in the terms like *dėstytojų kompetencija* (competence of teachers), *studentų atstovybė* (students' organization) the first noun should have plural Genitive form, while in the terms like *fakulteto taryba* (faculty board), *universiteto autonomija* (autonomy of the university) the first noun should have singular Genitive form.

In other cases the second noun needs to be either in plural (*akademiniai įgūdžiai* (academic skills), *auditorinės darbo valandos* (class hours)) or in singular (*bendrasis priėmimas* (common enrollment), *mokslinis leidinys* (scientific publication)). The category of gender may not be a distinguishing feature either, as each constituent of a term can potentially be in feminine or masculine gender.

It seems that the only useful additional feature in the N + N combination is the Genitive case of the first constituent, as it remains stable across

many variants.

Additional complications arise with three-word or longer terms. For example, if we take the term *mokslinių tyrimų įstaigos atestacija* (certification of institution of scientific researches), then its structure is

A pl. Gen + N pl. Gen + N sg. Gen + N sg. Nom

Such long terms often consist of several combinations of words, where their syntactic relations might differ. For example, in the term *neformaliojo suaugusiųjų švietimo įstatymas* (law of informal education of adults) with a structure of A sg. G. + N pl. G. + N sg. G. + N sg. N syntactic relations are spread as follows: (figures indicate the elements of word combinations):

$1 \longleftarrow 3$

$2 \longleftarrow 3$

$[123] \longleftarrow 4$

Beside language related problems, there are some universal terminology identification problems typical to all languages. One of such problems is determining term boundaries. For example, the word combination *dėstytojų ir mokslininkų kvalifikacijos bei kompetencijos atitiktis* (correspondence of qualification and competence of teachers and scientists) may give birth to one term or several terms: 1) *dėstytojų kvalifikacijos bei kompetencijos atitiktis* (correspondence of qualification and competence of teachers), 2) *mokslininkų kvalifikacijos bei kompetencijos atitiktis* (correspondence of qualification and competence of scientists), 3) *dėstytojų ir mokslininkų kvalifikacijos atitiktis* (correspondence of qualification of teachers and scientists), 4) *dėstytojų ir mokslininkų kompetencijos atitiktis* (correspondence of competence of teachers and scientists) (more combinations of possible terms (concerning their boundaries) are possible).

Finally, the question, whether a particular stable word combination is a term or not, is faced by both human experts and computer programs. However, even if a word combination is a term, yet another judgment on its specificity, i.e. domain term vs. general term, is required. The solution of such problem is possible only with the help of an expert.

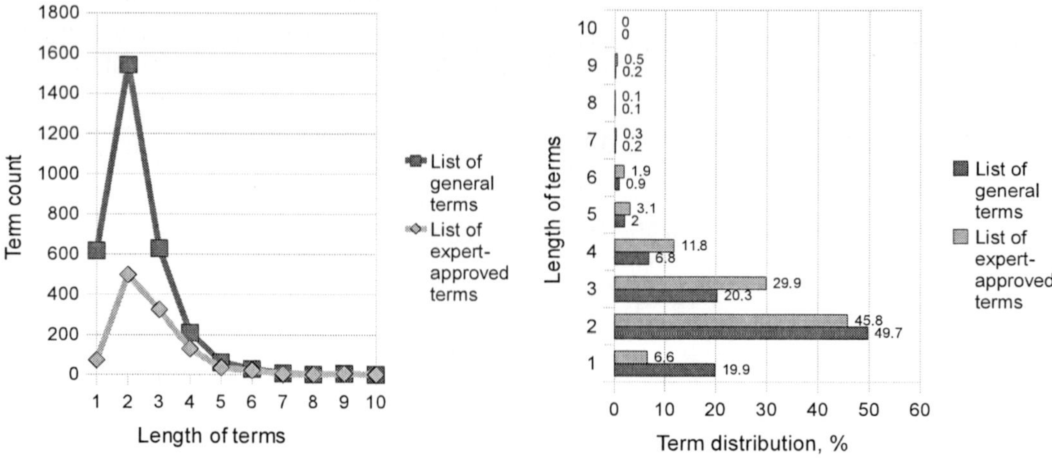

Figure 1: Absolute frequency distribution (1st part) and relative frequency distribution (2nd part) of term lengths.

2 Experimental Settings

2.1 The Corpus

An experimental 103,893 token corpus of education and science has been compiled specifically for term extraction experiments. This corpus consists of laws, orders, regulations, resolutions, memoranda, descriptions, overviews, notes, reports, newsletters, programmes, summaries, and standards. The texts mainly encompass the following topics: high education policy, research policy, continuous education, and professional education policy. Two reference lists have been manually created for the analysis of terms and evaluation purposes: the first one is a larger list of all general terms, and the second one is the special list of terms in the field of education and science.

Firstly, 5 linguists have identified a list of general terms (in total 3,106 lemmas). Problem cases and disagreements have been solved by consultation between the linguists. Then this provisional list has been further reviewed by the education expert, who has identified the terms of science and education. As a result of this review, the list has shrank to 1,085 terms. The expert mostly removed general administrative terms and terms that are not related to the previously mentioned topics.

The analysis of distribution of term lengths in the reference lists has been performed, as term length is very important characteristic to many term extraction methods. The analysis of term types has shown that the term length can vary from one to ten words (see Figure 1). Although two-

word terms are by far most frequent (49.7 % of the total number of terms), they cover only a half of all terminology.

In the expert list, the part of single and two-word terms has significantly decreased, while the part of three and four-word terms has significantly increased. The distribution of term lengths shows that terms with lengths from 1 to 4 words make up 96.7% of all terms in the general list and 94.1% in the expert list. Many extraction methods typically leave out single-word and four-word terms, although it is evident from this analysis that they are quite important in the overall coverage of terminology.

2.2 Statistical Approaches

Statistically-based term extraction aims at detecting syntagmatic collocations or keywords, which are relevant for the domain[6]. Many statistic measures can be applied for term extraction task starting with frequency rank, Mutual Information (Church and Hanks, 1989), Dice coefficient (Smadja et al., 1996), T-score (Church et al., 1991), Log-likelihood (Dunning, 1993), C-value (Frantzi and Ananiadou, 1996), and others.

A major advantage of statistical TE systems is that they do not require huge databases with term patterns constructed by humans and also do not require running through language analysis pipelines. The assumption in using statistical models in TE is that words which tend to co-occur together are related and therefore they are likely term candidates.

---

[6]These features are referred as unithood and termhood.

In this section, we will deal with three statistical approaches, namely keyword cluster identification, keyword extraction with machine learning, and collocation extraction.

2.2.1 Keyword Clusters

When analysing abilities of extracting terms by the linguistic program *WordSmith Tools* (Scott, 2008), the idea of extracting *keyword clusters* as terminology candidates has emerged. The idea is based on the assumption that the most frequent clusters of keywords in a given text may also point to terminology.

Keywords are identified by comparing a given text's frequency list to the frequency list of a large reference corpus by using Ted Dunning's (Dunning, 1993) log likelihood test. The final step is calculating keyword clusters that are two or more words, which are found repeatedly near each other (1-3 intervening words may be present). Below is the list of 10 most frequent keyword clusters and their frequencies:

mokslo [.] studijų (studies of science)	*524*
švietimo [.] mokslo (education science)	*522*
aukštojo mokslo (higher education)	*474*
mokslinių tyrimų (scientific research)	*390*
suagusiųjų švietimo (adult education)	*292*
lietuvos respublikos (lithuanian republic)	*284*
protų nutekėjimo (brain drain)	*228*
švietimo ministerija (ministery of education)	*220*
profesinio mokymo (professional teaching)	*184*
neformaliojo [.] švietimo (non-formal education)	*164*

Even though the resulting list seems very promising, the comparison in terms of precision and recall with the reference lists has not shown good results. The best result with the whole keyword list has produced 9.7% of recall and 1.8% of precision when compared to the expert's list and 7.5% of recall and 3.7% of precision when compared to the list of general terms (see Table 2 for all results).

2.2.2 Machine Learning: KEA

Many NLP tools require a process of machine learning, which allows the system to improve the quality of results by its own experience or the supervision of a human.

The keyword extractor KEA[7] implements such methods. The core of the KEA system is a statistically-based algorithm with a machine learning system generating an extraction model. The multi-featured algorithm rates keywords taking in account four components:

- degree of specificity;
- position in the text;
- length of the phrase;
- node degree.

The learning process, which is based on Naive Baysian Method using the software WEKA[8], requires a manual extraction of keywords from a training corpus. A clear overview of the whole system may be found in Medelyan (2005). Besides, the core may be extended by language specific Java components as a stop-words list and a stemmer.

From a terminological perspective, it must be noticed that a keyword is not the same as a term. However, in a corpus made of specialized texts, we may expect a significant matching between the set of keywords and the set of terms.

The task of machine learning has been based on a subset of the test corpus consisting of four texts, representing approximately 22,000 words, about 1/5 of the whole experimental corpus. The manually selected keywords have been the terms appearing in the sub-corpus. Given the highly inflected nature of the Lithuanian language, two attempts of machine learning have been carried out. In the first case, the list of manually extracted keywords has included only the main nominal forms (Nominative, Accusative and Genitive, if relevant singular and plural). In the second case, the list has been restricted to the base forms (lemma). The extraction results have been identical for both methods.

Once the extraction model has been built, three different approaches have been tested : 1) with no extension, 2) with a stop-words list and 3) with both a stop-words list and a stemmer. The first approach has produced results of insufficient quality with such terms as *mokslo ir* (science and). This has led to the conclusion that a stop-word list would enhance the quality. On the basis of the results given by the rough extraction, a list of more than one hundred stop-words has been compiled. In order to avoid an artificial *ad hoc* correction of the results, only words of some specific groups have been included in the stop-words list:

- grammatical words such as prepositions, con-

---

[7]http://www.nzdl.org/Kea/

[8]http://www.cs.waikato.ac.nz/ml/weka/

junctions, particles, some adverbs and frequent forms of pronouns;

- some expressions of quantity;
- main abbreviations;
- some general verb forms (to be, to show, modal verbs).

The use of this restricted stop-word list obviously has improved the results, avoiding some common mistakes of highly improbable terminological combinations.

Besides, the third variant adding a stemmer has also been tested, but the quality of the results has been the worst of all three. The Lithuanian results have appeared as a confirmation of a statement in the documentation of KEA's source code - "We have obtained better results for Spanish and French with NoStemmer".

Given the preliminary results of the different methods, the term candidates have been extracted on the basis of the second variant, that is, with a stop-words list only. Subsets of different sizes have been extracted (10,000, 5,000, 1000, 500 forms of term candidates).

2.2.3 Collocation Extraction Methods

Collocations and terminology are related concepts, but this relationship is not a synonymic or a simple one. It is a well known fact that the term of collocation is very broadly understood, and therefore it is important at the very start to define which notion of collocation is used in the current paper. In this paper we will deal only with statistical collocations, that is with sequences of words that co-occur more often than would be expected by chance.

Automatically extracted collocations have been used for terminology extraction process many times (e.g., Daille, 1996, Azé et al., 2005 etc.). As a rule, collocation extraction methods are used as the first step in creating a terminology candidate list, which is then further processed by ranking and extracting the relevant items. However, there are at least two problems associated with these methods. The first problem is that there is quite a large number of statistical collocation extraction methods (e.g. Azé et al., 2005 deal with 13 methods), and it is not a trivial task to choose the best one for the terminology extraction task. The second problem is that the majority of collocation extraction methods are limited to extracting two to three word collocations, while the range of term lengths,

as our analysis has shown, is rather more broad.

The latter statement can be supported by the analysis of term lengths in 103,893 word experimental corpus (see Figure 1).

Due to these reasons, it has been decided to try only the tools and methods that extract collocations of variant length, i.e. LICE (Gravity Counts)[9], and leave out other tools that extract fixed length collocations.

Gravity counts (Daudaravičius and Marcinkevičienė, 2004) is a method for determining borders or collocations. It is based on the idea that all words in a text are more or less tied, that is, the degree of attraction between them may be stronger or weaker. Gravity count G for two words x and y in this order is calculated according to the formula:

$$G(x,y) = \log\left(\frac{f(x,y)\cdot r(x)}{f(x)}\right) + \log\left(\frac{f(x,y)\cdot l(y)}{f(y)}\right) \tag{1}$$

where f(x) is the frequency of x, f(y) the frequency of y, f(x,y) the frequency of the two word co-occurring in this order, r(x) the number of different words to the right of x and l(y) the number of different words to the left of y.

The software LICE, which is designed to implement the gravity counts, has been used to collect collocations with the aim of comparing them with the set of terms manually extracted. It must be emphasized that LICE does not extract only multiword expressions, since the program is designed to indicate the limits of collocations. Thus, if a group of consecutive words shows a significant degree of attraction, they appear as a collocation, but words which are loosely tied to others appears separately in the results given by LICE.

The result given by LICE has been processed in order to extract the multiword expressions. Then, in order to improve the result in the same way it has been done for KEA, a stop-words list (the same as prepared for KEA) has been used as a second filter. It must be emphasized that even after the filtration the number of expressions remains very high (more than 16,000 terms).

2.3 Linguistically-based Approach

The process of linguistically-based term extraction is a pipeline that may include morphological analysis, syntactic parsing, and a module of linguistic rules (patterns) that describes terms.

---

[9]LICE is an experimental piece of software used for internal research at CCL VMU.

N Gen	N Nom			638
A Nom	N Nom			610
N Nom				484
A Gen	N Gen	N Nom		168
N Gen	N Gen	N Nom		145
A Nom	N Gen	N Nom		73
PART Nom	N Nom			66
A Nom	A Nom	N Nom		42
A Gen	N Gen	N Gen	N Nom	37
V inf				31

Table 1: Morphological patterns in the general list of terms (where N - noun, A - adj, PART - participle, Nom - Nominative, Gen - Genitive).

The approach is language dependent as terms in different languages have different morphological patterns. Morphological patterns may include part-of-speech categories for analytic languages (e.g. English), or additional grammatical categories such as cases for synthetic languages (e.g. Lithuanian), or syntactic categories (e.g. noun phrases).

Typically this approach requires an annotated corpus, which needs to have an appropriate annotation scheme (e.g. POS, POS+case, or syntax). The term extraction tools simply extract all occurrences of required patterns from the annotated corpus and produce a list of term candidates that can be manually reviewed, statistically processed, or filtered with the help of stop-word lists.

Linguistic rules can be coded as regular expressions and directly used for identifying term candidates. An example of such a rule for a single-word term is [noun], for two-word terms - [noun]+[noun] and [adjective]+[noun]. Morphological patterns that have not been coded into a term extractor will produce low recall, while nonterms that coincide with the programmed patterns will reduce precision. Lopes et al. (2010) have shown that linguistic approaches produce better results than statistical ones, besides they also emphasize the fact that linguistic approaches are more complicated in comparison to easy adaptable statistical methods.

For the present study, the manually extracted terminological list has been morphologically tagged[10] and a frequency list of morphological patterns has been built. In order to avoid unnecessary diversity of the patterns, only categories

of part-of-speech and case have been considered. The list of top ten grammatical patterns with frequencies of occurrence in the lemmatized list of general terms is given in Table 1.

A set of 27 morphological patterns has been selected for the extraction of term candidates from the annotated experimental corpus. The list of patterns includes mostly combinations of nouns and adjectives, sometimes with the intervening conjunction *ir* 'and'. In order to limit the noise, only multiword patterns have been considered. The maximal length of morphological patterns is five words. A Haskell function has been specially developed for this goal. Some deficiencies of this approach result from the tagging process which can give inaccurate analysis or fail to analyse an unknown word.

2.4 Evaluation

The evaluation of a term extraction system can be addressed with measuring against the *gold standard*. Two term reference lists have been set (see section 2.1) for the purpose of evaluating the four different term extraction approaches.

The quality performance of the term extraction system can be evaluated in terms of *precision* and *recall*. Which are the equivalent of inverted measures of *silence* and *noise* proposed by (Cabre et al., 2001).

2.5 Results

All the test results of the above tested methods and tools are summarized in the Table 2.

Concerning the recall, there are several objective reasons, which have negatively influenced the results. In case of KEA and the linguistic approach, candidate terms longer than 5 words have not been extracted, while these patterns represent between 1.4% and 2.8% of the manually extracted terms. Similarly, the linguistic, keyword clusters approach and LICE, have not taken into account single word terms, which represent between 6.6% and 19.9%.

Moreover, some discrepancy comes from terms in the expert's reference list, that actually have not been present the experimental corpus. The expert's reference list includes 158 items absent from the corpus, which represents 14.5% of the list and has a strong influence on the recall rates. Except for few direct additions, for example *akademikas*

---

[10]The tagging has been performed using the morphological analyzer developed at CCL VMU. Rimkutė and Daudaravičius (2007) have established that the precision of the tagger is 94% for establishing grammatical categories and 99% for lemmatisation.

Method	Tools	Reference	Candidates	Lemmas	Match*	Recall	Precision
Keyword clusters	WSmith	General list	10777	5959	219	7.5	3.68
			5000	3096	186	6.4	6
			1000	734	105	3.6	14.3
			500	397	69	2.4	17.4
		Expert list	10777	5959	105	9.7	1.8
			5000	3096	88	8.1	2.8
			1000	734	53	8.1	7.2
			500	397	35	3.2	8.8
Keywords	KEA	General list	10000	6398	865	29.7	13.5
			5000	3165	629	21.6	19.9
			1000	703	238	8.2	33.9
			500	381	157	5.4	41.2
		Expert list	10000	6398	269	24.8	4.2
			5000	3165	197	18.2	6.2
			1000	703	77	7.1	11
			500	381	51	4.7	13.4
Gravity Count	LICE	General list	16593	14627	1124	38.6	7.7
		Expert list	16593	14627	388	35.8	2.7
Linguistic approach	Tagger, scripts	General list	25058	18990	1801	61.8	9.5
		Expert list	25058	18990	713	65.7	3.8

*number of automatically extracted terms that match terms in reference lists.

Table 2: Evaluation of Terminology Extraction Tools.

'academician', it is mainly due to a significant process of normalization of terms occurring in the corpus by operations on the syntactic structure by the expert. For example, the terms *docento pedagoginis vardas* 'pedagogical title of docent', *vakariniai kursai* 'evening courses' and *priėmimas į universitetą* 'enrollment in university' appear respectively in the expressions *docento ir profesoriaus pedagoginiai vardai* 'pedagogical titles of docent and Professor', *kursai (dieniniai, vakariniai, tęstiniai, trumpalaikiai ir kt.)* 'courses (full-time, evening, continuing, short)' and *priėmimo į VU* 'enrollment in UV' (or *priėmimo į valstybines aukštąsias mokyklas* 'enrollment in public high schools'). None of these examples could be found by any of the tested extraction methods.

The number of extracted candidate terms has a strong influence on the level of precision. For example, with LICE and the linguistic approach, the number of extracted patterns is very high, with more than 15,000 lemmatized expressions, which has generated mechanically much noise in comparison with the manually extracted reference lists consisting of 1,085 and 3,106 terms. Besides, term candidates have not been rated by both of the methods, which does not allow to extract a meaningful subset of comparable number.

We are aware that results could be further evaluated, taking into account measures for partial matches, however the lack of necessary tools has not allowed us to include in the present paper.

The overall analysis of the results shows that the linguistic approach that extracts term candidates on the basis of morphological patterns has appeared to be quite reliable and most promising according to the measure of recall (61.8% and 65.7%). While in terms of precision, the keyword approach with machine learning has produced better results. Both these methods may be considered as the most perspective, as the linguistic approach could identify a thousand more correct terms than the keyword approach, and the keyword approach has picked up the smallest number of non-terms.

3 Conclusions

We have looked at the term extraction task for Lithuanian from the perspective of existing term extraction tools. Four different methods, i.e., three statistical and one linguistic, have been applied and evaluated against manually constructed reference lists.

The evaluation of term extraction methodology has lead to the following conclusions:

- Most of Lithuanian domain specific terms are two-word or three-word noun phrases.

- The majority of the Lithuanian terms are very rare.

- The best performing methods in terms of recall pick up low precision.

- The statistical modeling for term detection on such a tiny corpus is not very reliable. Thus linguistically based term candidate detection appeared to perform better, i.e. the combined recall and precision levels have been the highest with this method.

- The analysis has shown that all the methods have problems in extracting both multiword and single-word terms, as well as determining which terms are domain specific and which ones are general. The possible solution would be the combination of several methods for each of these tasks.

- Domain specificity of a term has not been analysed is this paper. A possible approach would be a statistical measure of specificity that expresses the difference of usage of a term between a general corpus and a domain specific corpus.

- An increased quality, i.e. increased precision, may be obtained by improving the linguistic filtering of noisy candidate term lists in order to extract only expressions matching the usual structure of Lithuanian terms.

- A significant improvement of the results may be expected for the machine learning method (KEA) with a more extensive learning process and a processing of each file of the corpus separately.

- Hybrid approaches have not been analysed in this paper, however they may turn out to be very useful in reducing the noise produced by the linguistic approach.

Acknowledgments

The presented research is funded by a grant (No. LIT-2-44) from the Research Council of Lithuania in the framework of the project "Švietimo ir mokslo terminų automatinis identifikavimas – ŠIMTAI 2" (Automatic Identification of Education and Science Terms). The authors would like to thank anonymous reviewers for their comments.

References

Azé J., Roche M, Kodratoff M., and Sebag M. 2005. *Preference Learning in Terminology Extraction: a ROC-based Approach*, Proceedings of Applied Stochastic Models and Data Analysis. p. 209-219.

Cabre T., Estopa R., and Vivaldi J. 2001. *Automatic term detection. Recent advances in computational terminology*. p. 53-88.

Cabre T. 1992. *Terminology: theory, methods and applications*. John Benjamins.

Church K.W., and Hanks P. 1989. *Word Association Norms, Mutual Information and Lexicography*. In Proc: ACL'89, p. 76-83.

Daille B. 1994. *Towards Automatic Extraction of Monolingual and Bilingual Terminology*. In Proc: COLING'94, p. 515-524.

Daille B., Habert B., Jacquemin C., and Royaut J. 1996. *Empirical observation of term variations and principles for their description*. Terminology, 3(2):197-258.

Daudaravičius V., and Marcinkevičienė R. 2005. *Gravity counts for the boundaries of collocations*. Corpus Linguistics, 9(2):321-348.

Dunning T. 1993. *Accurate Methods for the Statistics of Surprise and Coincidence*. Computational Linguistics, 19(1): 61-74.

Frantzi K., and Ananiadou S. 1996. *Extracting Nested Collocations*. In Proc: COLING'96, p. 41-46.

Lopes L., de Oliveira L. H. M., and Vieira R. 2010. *Portuguese Term Extraction Methods: Comparing Linguistic and Statistical Approaches*. In Proc: 9th Int. Conf. on Computational Processing of the Portuguese Language.

Marcinkevičienė R., and Vitkutė-Adžgauskienė D. 2010. *Developing the Human Language Technology Infrastructure in Lithuania*. In Proc: 4th Int. Conf. Human Language Technologies - The Baltic Perspective. IOS Press.

Medelyan O. 2005. *Automatic Keyphrase Indexing with a Domain-Specific Thesaurus*. Master Thesis. University of Freiburg, Germany.

Mitrofanova O., and Zakharov V. 2009. *Automatic Analysis of Terminology in the Russian Corpus on Corpus Linguistics*. In Proc: 5th Int. Conf. NLP, Corpus Linguistics, Corpus Based Grammar Research.

Pantel P., and Lin D. 2001. *A Statistical Corpus-Based Term Extractor*. In Proc: 14th conf. Advances in Artificial Intelligence. E. Stroulia and S. Matwin (Eds.). Springer-Verlag, London, p. 36-46.

Piskorski J., Homola P., Marciniak M., Mykowiecka A., Przepiorkowski A., and Wolinski M. 2004. *Information Extraction for Polish Using the SProUT Platform*. In Proc. of Intelligent Information Systems 2004. Springer Verlag.

Rimkutė E, and Daudaravičius V. 2007. *Morfologinis dabartinės lietuvių kalbos tekstyno anotavimas*. In Kalbų studijos, 11:30-35.

Sager J. 1990. *A Practical Course in Terminology Processing*. John Benjamins.

Scott M. 2008. *WordSmith Tools version 5*. Liverpool: Lexical Analysis Software.

Smadja F., McKeown K., and Hatzivassiloglou V. 1996. *Translating collocations for bilingual lexicons: a statistical approach*. Computational Linguistics, 22(1):1-38.

Zeller I. 2005. *Automatinis terminų atpažinimas ir apdorojimas*. PhD thesis, VMU, Lithuania.

ISSN 1736-6305 Vol. 11
http://hdl.handle.net/10062/16955

Fishing in a Speech Stream - Angling for a Lexicon

Peter Juel Henrichsen
Center for Computational Modelling of Language (CMOL)
Copenhagen Business School
`pjh.isv@cbs.dk`

Abstract

We present a learning device able to deduce a set of Danish color and shape terms. Only two data sources are available to the learner: A phonetic transcription of a human informant solving a description task, and a minimal formal model of the picture being described. The system thus contains no preconceived lexical, morphological, or semantic categories. The test data are from the phonetic corpus DanPASS, a standard Danish reference corpus. The learning device, called InShape-2, is an early result of an ambitious research programme at CMOL on data-driven language learning.

1   Introduction

Imagine a device able to learn the lexical units and linguistic structures occurring in a natural language discourse. The device would have access to data of only two sorts: a sound recording of a language user[1] and a formal representation of the scene (physical or mental) being talked about. In particular, the device would have no built-in language model, no grammatical or lexical expectations, no phonological bias. Such a device would not only be of practical value, it could also play a role as evidence in the still unsettled debate about linguistic universals and innate language capacities. In addition, it would have obvious use as an instrument for first language (L1) acquisition studies.

In this paper we present a toy system called InShape-2, intended as a small step towards the general learning device.[2] We begin with a short introduction of the speech data that we have used, followed by some methodological considerations, a presentation of our implementation, and some test results. The paper concludes with a discussion of the limitations of the current framework – and how to remove those limitations.

2   A learning experiment

We take our starting point in a simple-minded world of geometrical figures.

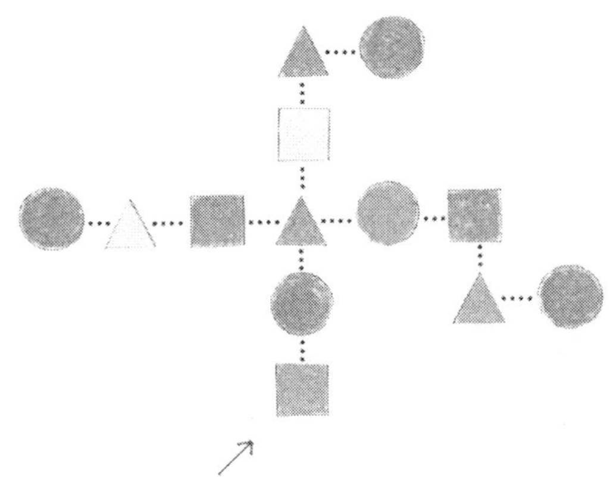

Figure 1. Corpus DanPASS: The geometrical network.[3]

The design in fig. 1 is borrowed from the phonetic corpus DanPASS (Danish Phonetically Annotated Spontaneous Speech, Grønnum (2009)). The corpus was collected and annotated by phonologists at Copenhagen University, and it has mainly been used for phonetic research. As a matter of fact, DanPASS comes with a disclaimer: "The intention was to supply a corpus for acoustic and perceptual phonetic investigations. That is, the primary goal is neither syntactic, pragmatic, socio-linguistic, psychological, nor whichever other aspect of spoken language one might wish to investigate." (http://www.danpass.dk). We are thus dealing with data that were not prepared for, or biased towards, experiments addressing lexical and semantic issues.

---

[1]   This paper, and the associated line of research, is primarily aimed at the auditory part of the speech situation, not the related visual and tactile cues (gestures, gaze directions, body movements, etc).

[2]   InShape-2, here presented for the first time, is a complete rewrite of the earlier program InShape-1 (Henrichsen 2010, now deprecated). More details below.

[3]   The 13 objects are colored; consult the original graph at http://www.cphling.dk/~ng/danpass_webpage/figs/geometry.pdf. Symbols e1..e13 are not included in the original.

DanPASS consists of a monologue part and a dialogue part, each containing a number of lab recordings of Danish informants solving various language tasks. The design in fig. 1, call it **G** (for "geometrical network"), was used in a series of description tasks. Eighteen male and female informants were asked to give a complete description of **G** as if to a person who could not see it. The informants were instructed to begin with the object pointed to by the arrow, but otherwise no clues were given as to what specific terms should be used for e.g. colors and shapes, nor to the sequence in which the objects should be named. As a result, the sessions vary considerably with respect to term selection, description strategy, rhetorical and grammatical style, informational redundancy, and duration. The shortest session is only 45 seconds, the longest more than four times longer.

The goal of the InShape-2 project was to design a robust learning device able to determine for each **G** session its basic vocabulary (the shape and color terms being used) and its temporal composition (the sequence of naming events) based on two information sources only, (i) the phonetic transcription data available with DanPASS and (ii) a minimal formal representation of **G**.

At this point we are not making claims of cognitive isomorphism. We simply wanted to demonstrate that linearly ordered phonetic data can be sufficiently rich for extraction of structured lexical and semantic information in a process governed by a specific learning purpose.

2.1 Formal preliminaries

We refer to the geometrical objects of **G** as **e1**, **e2**, .., **e13**, reading the branches of the network clockwise (see fig. 1). For reference to individual sessions, we use the DanPASS identifiers m_*n*_g (m='monologue', *n*=informant code, g='geometrical network').

For reasons of computational tractability, some basic constraints had to be hardwired into the implementation. Some of them concern the naming events of the sessions, i.e. those utterances by which informants refer to the particular objects. Examples of naming events are "en gul firkant" (a yellow square), "den lilla trekant" (the purple triangle), but also "en rund grøn" (a round green) using two adjectives instead of a standard noun phrase, and "en grøn tre- en blå trekant" (a green tri- a blue triangle) including a self-correction. Since the informants were instructed to include all objects in their descriptions, the naming

events are expected to occur in sequences of 13. Such a complete sequence referring to each object in turn, we call a path.

[e1,e2,e3,e7,e8,e9,e4,e5,e6,e10,e11,e12,e13]

The path above happens to be the one most frequently used by the informants, but by no means the only one. Perhaps surprisingly, no less than seven different paths are represented in the 18 sessions.

Formal requirements

- A session has (at least) one path consisting of 13 unambiguous naming events
- In any path, the first naming event denotes **e1**

In addition to the formal requirements, we also imposed some linguistic conditions for reasons to be discussed shortly.

Linguistic conditions

In any path, all color terms and shape terms must be used consistently in the following sense:

- no synonymy (i.e. no two distinct terms for one color or for one shape)
- no homonymy (no single term can denote a particular color *and* a shape)
- no material inclusion among the terms within a domain (no color term can be a part of another color term, excluding term pairs like "light green"+"green"; similarly for shapes)
- adjacency of terms for shape and color (e.g. not "a circle <u>in a</u> green color")

In **G** sessions there are often multiple naming events referring to one particular object, or several uses of the color and shape terms not referring to any object at all. Some naming events may even refer to non-existing objects, sometimes (but not always) followed by a self-correction. Most of this variation is not critical with respect to InShape learning (and shouldn't be!) as long as at least one well-formed path exists. It should be noticed, though, that the significant naming events may be very unevenly distributed; in session m_009_g, the initial naming event (**e1**) thus occurs after no less than 74 seconds.

Finally, to limit the search space an integrity constraint is adopted formalizing the observation that informants tend to move from object to adjacent object whenever possible rather than jumping arbitrarily around in the network. The constraint is defined in terms of *path complexity* (PC), defined informally as the minimal number of instructions in {'up', 'down', 'left', 'right', 'reset'} needed in an explanation. For instance, the path mentioned above can be explained as: "**e1** *UP* **e2 e3 e7 e8** *RIGHT* **e9** *RESET* **e3** *LEFT* **e4 e5 e6** *RESET* **e3** *RIGHT* **e10 e11** *DOWN* **e12** *RIGHT* **e13**", making PC=8 for this path. Only one other path has PC=8, while ten paths has PC=9. The PC<10 paths include all actually occuring DanPASS naming sequences with the sole exception of the quite entangled m_31_g (PC=10). Moreover, the PC=8 paths are generally preferred (7+3 cases) over the PC=9 (3+2+1+1+0+0+0+0+0+0), adding some psychological plausibility to the complexity measure.[4]

Integrity constraint

- Path complexities >9 are not considered

Following the requirements, conditions, and constraints, a number of sessions must be excluded from the InShape test material leaving a test corpus of 13 sessions. The excluded sessions (see table 1) do however play an important role as negative evidence in the testing of the implementation.

Session	Disqualifying feature
m_003_g	**e9** is wrongly described as "en gul cirkel" (*a yellow circle*)
m_005_g	**e10** is wrongly described as "en rød cirkel" (*a red circle*)
m_008_g	**e3** is wrongly described as "en firkantet lilla" (*a square violet*); the mistake is corrected, but too late to restore the path.
m_013_g	Homonymy: two terms for *square* ("firkant", "kvadrat")
m_031_g	Integrity constraint violation: Path is too entangled

Table 1. Discarded sessions.

It is worth mentioning that even the formally well-formed **G** sessions may be quite informal in style with lots of repetitions and quite verbose explanations. Several sessions contain one or more self-corrections, such as

"en violet en lilla trekant"   [m_007_g]
(*a violet a purple triangle*)

"en lilla nej en brun en brun firkant" [m_014_g]
(*a violet no a brown a brown square*)

"til en blå eller til en grøn cirkel"   [m_016_g]
(*to a blue or to a green circle*)

Deducing the lexical paradigms and semantic relations in **G** thus calls for parsing strategies that are not usually taught in courses on formal grammar.

2.2 Color blindness

A curious property of **G** – probably unintended by its designers – is the similarity of the left branch [**e4,e5,e6**] and the upper branch [**e7,e8,e9**] concerning shapes and colors. Both branches share the shape sequence [*square, triangle, circle*] while the color sequences are [X, Y, *green*] and [Y, X, *green*], respectively. As colors X and Y do not occur elsewhere in **G**, an inference engine needs to learn some location terms in order to deduce the intended terms for *red* and *yellow*. Picking the wrong color terms for X for Y, for the reasons mentioned, we shall refer to as *color blindness*.

3 InShape-2 – the implementation

Skipping over irrelevant programming details, we present the implementation as a pipeline of functional modules. The chain is strictly feed-forward (no backtracking between modules).

Extract_phones > Find_siblings > Assign_shapes > Assign_colors > Build_lex

Figure 2. The InShape-1 functional modules.

Each of the stations in fig. 2 is introduced below, with special emphasis on those implementing the semantic inference system, viz. Assign_shapes and Assign_colors. Other papers expanding on the data preprocessor (Extract_phones) and the growth of lexical structure (Build_lex) are in preparation; Find_siblings is treated at length in Henrichsen (2004).

---

[4]   In InShape-1 the set of well-formed paths were hardwired into the system whereas InShape-2 derives it directly from the **G**-geometry, preparing the system for experiments with varying geometries.

3.1 Extract_phones

The phonetic data are derived from the TextGrid files (Boersma 2001) included in the DanPASS corpus. Fig. 3 shows a sample from the orthographic tier of m_007_g.[5]

du starter nederst på papiret med= en= + blå firkant + dernæst går du= + opad= + mod toppen af papiret + og lægger en= grøn= cirkel + og endelig= lægger du= en = = violet en lilla + trekant + fortsætter du opad + og lægger en gul firkant + og en rød trekant + og til højre for den røde trekant men + på= niveau + med trekanten + lægger du en + grøn = cirkel + så vender du tilbage til den= + lilla + trekant= der nu er i midten + til højre + men= på niveau + med den lilla trekant + lægger du en + blå cirkel +

Figure 3. Orthographic transcription.

Extract_phones reads a TextGrid, returning the phonetic transcription in compact form excluding pauses, hesitation, stress pattern, stød, and syllabification, since these features tend to be less consistently annotated by transcribers than vowels and consonants. For m_007_g, the string returned thus begins with [dusdAd0neD0sp-cp0piCDmEDenblcfiRkant...].

3.2 Find_siblings

Which is the easier to learn, the shape domain or the color domain? Two observations on **G** suggest the answer. Firstly, there are six color types and only three shape types. Secondly, each shape type has a substantial amount of occurrences in the geometrical network (5+4+4), as opposed to the thinner spread of the colors (4+3+2+2+1+1). As data-driven learning typically relies on repetition and limited diversity, the shape domain should, arguably, be addressed first.

The phone stream from Extract_phones must be segmented into potentially meaningful units, interpreted as recurring substrings of phones. For the segmentation analysis we used

the Siblings-and-Cousins algorithm of Henrichsen (2004). Due to space limitations, we have to introduce the S&C algorithm very briefly; a thorough presentation is in the paper mentioned. Originally, S&C was suggested as a way of clustering the lexical items (words) occurring in an unannotated text corpus based on their distributional similarity. A main ingredient in the S&C framework is the *proximity* measure comparing the similarity of two types based on the distribution of their adjacent tokens in the corpus.

Modifying the S&C framework to accommodate the current data type, the proximity of two *n*-grams X and Y occurring in a phonetic transcription T is given by the *Prox* formula.

$$Prox(X,Y,T) = \frac{\sum_{z \in Voc} c(z) \cdot \left(1 - \frac{\left(L_1 - L_2\right)}{L_1 + L_2}\right)}{c(X)} \cdot \frac{\sum_{z' \in Voc} c(z') \cdot \left(1 - \frac{\left(R_1 - R_2\right)}{R_1 + R_2}\right)}{c(X)}$$

Figure 4. Proximity of two n-grams X and Y.

Voc is the set of all tokens in T, $c(g)$ is the T count function, i.e. the number of occurrences of *n*-gram g in T, and

$$L_1 = c([z\,X])/c([X]); \quad L_2 = c([z\,Y])/c([Y]);$$
$$R_1 = c([X\,z'])/c([X]); \quad R_2 = c([Y\,z'])/c([Y]).$$

Intuitively, *Prox* measures the similarity of two *n*-grams occuring in a transcription, based on their left and right context functions. *Prox*-values always range between 0 and 1 for valid input. Kindred *n*-grams (such as two color terms, or two shape terms) tend to score high, while less associated *n*-grams (such as one color term and one shape term) score lower. *Prox*=1 occurs for pairs of *n*-grams with identical distribution of tokens in their immediate surroundings, while a pair of *n*-grams not sharing a single left-side token or right-side token makes *Prox*=0.

```
#62             'f_i_R_k_a_n'        5
1.000000         f_i_R_k_a_n         5
0.321535         t_r_z_k_a_n         8
0.140000         s_i_R_g_0_l         5
0.124675         b_l_c               4
0.098937         z_R                 4
0.098209         t_C                 4
0.080672         g_r_Q_n_s_i_R_g_0_l 4
(...)
```

Figure 5. Sample from the S&C log for m_019_g

---

[5] '+' = pause, '=' = hesitation with phonation. English word-by-word gloss, with underlining of *significant* and *non-significant* naming events: *You start lowest on the-paper with= a= + blue square + thereafter go you= + upwards= + towards the-top of the-paper + and put a= green= circle + and finally= put you= a= = violet a. purple + triangle + continue you upwards + and put a. yellow square + and a red triangle + and at right of the red triangle but + at= level + with the-triangle + put you a + green = circle + then turn you back to the= + purple + triangle= that now is in the-middle + at right + but= at level + with the purple triangle + put you a + blue circle +

Sets of *n*-grams with mutually high *Prox*-values are informally called *siblings*. Consider the sample in fig. 5, quoted from the S&C analysis for *X*=`f_i_R_k_a_n`. As reported, this particular *n*-gram has five occurrences in the transcription, and it was analysed as the 62th item. In the quoted list, the *Y*s (i.e. the siblings of *X*) are sorted by their associated *Prox* values. Speakers of Danish will notice the difference between this phonetic string and the standard pronunciation for "firkant" (*square*), especially concerning the final part of the word. Whereas the Danish standard phonetic dictionary prescribes a final stop [d], the pronunciations in m_019_g show some variation, with [fiRkan] being the invariant part. Therefore (only) this part is suggested by the Find_siblings module as a potentially meaningful unit – and similarly for *triangle,* `t_r_z_k_a_n`.

Observe that the 10-gram `g_r_Q_n_s_i_R_g_0_l` (*greencircle*), even though it is not an acknowledged Danish lexeme, is also suggested as a potentially meaningful unit in the specific learning context of InShape. The prediction of `g_r_Q_n_s_i_R_g_0_l` as a semantic atom is an effect of the **G** model where circles are generally green, with only one exception. As we will argue, predictions like this should be seen as signs of lexical flair rather than just errors.

As demonstrated in fig. 5, lexical types belonging to the same semantic category, e.g. shape terms, color terms, or direction terms, tend to appear near each other in S&C log tables. This property is used by Find_siblings for output generation. All sets of three siblings above a certain *Prox* threshold (typically >0.1) are thus extracted and exported as input for the Assign_shapes module.

```
( f_i_R_k_a_n , t_r_z_k_a_n , s_i_R_g_0_l )
( f_i_R_k_a_n , t_r_z_k_a_n , b_l_c       )
( f_i_R_k_a_n , s_i_R_g_0_l , b_l_c       )
( t_r_z_k_a_n , s_i_R_g_0_l , b_l_c       )
             (...)
```

Figure 6. Exported tri-sets for m_019_g.

Of course, algorithms other than S&C could be used for segmentation and grouping of the phonetic data. Most of those known to us would however force us to split up the n-gram formation and the paradigm-formation in two more or less independent steps, which is why we settled on the S&C framework with its simultaneous and inter-dependent chunking and clustering. More discussion on the segmentation methodology is to follow in the final section.

3.3 Assign_shapes

The Assign_shapes algorithm is implemented in the programming language Prolog (e.g. Bratko 2000). In this language, propositional knowledge is particularly easy to formalize and to reason about, as exemplified by the **G** model below.

```
prop(color,blue,[e1,e10,e12]).
prop(color,green,[e2,e6,e9,e13]).
prop(color,red,[e4,e8]).
prop(color,yellow,[e5,e7]).
prop(color,purple,[e3]).
prop(color,brown,[e11]).

prop(shape,square,[e1,e4,e7,e11]).
prop(shape,circle,[e2,e6,e9,e10,e13]).
prop(shape,triangle,[e3,e5,e8,e12]).
```

Figure 7. Formal model of **G**.

The Assign_shape algorithm is perhaps best presented by an example. Consider a particular tri-set T3 of shape term candidates as delivered by Find_siblings, and transformed to the shape lexicon T3'.

```
T3 =
  (f_i_R_k_a_n, t_r_z_k_a_n, s_i_R_g_0_l)

T3' = ( square:   f_i_R_k_a_n ,
        circle:   s_i_R_g_0_l ,
        triangle: t_r_z_k_a_n )
```

We trace the program execution at a point where T3' is to be evaluated with respect to the session transcription, m_019_g, and a particular path *P'*.

```
P' = [e1,e2,e3,e7,e8,e9,e4,
      e5,e6,e10,e11,e12,e13]
```

Consulting `prop/3` (fig. 7), the Prolog engine infers that *P'* has the related shape sequence [*square, circle, triangle, square, triangle, circle, square, triangle, circle, circle, square, triangle, circle*], so T3' is evaluated by searching for a 13-section of the transcription m_019_g faithfully representing the shape sequence (that is, its T3' mapping). As it turns out, such a 13-section does exist, verifying T3' in this case.

In general, each tri-set delivered by Find_siblings is evaluated for each of its six permutations, and for each formally well-formed path (cf. 2.1). Each combination of path and tri-set for which a 13-section was found is then passed on to Assign_colors for further evaluation.

3.4   Assign_colors

In this part of the Prolog script, a partly instantiated variable `Table` is declared.

```
Table = [green:_,blue:_,red:_,
         yellow:_,purple:_,brown:_],
```

Using Prolog backtracking, a solution is sought in the form of a fully instantiated `Table` structure. A slightly simplified version of the central Prolog predicates is shown below (excluding some performance improving modifications).

```
eval(Tran,[T1,T2,T3]):-
  path(Path),
  perm(Shapes,[T1,T2,T3]),
  Table = [green:_,blue:_,red:_,
           yellow:_,purple:_,brown:_],
  traverse(Tran,Path,Shapes,[],Con),
  deduce_colors(Con,Table),
  write_result(Table,Path).

traverse( Tran_in, [E|Path],
          [Tr,Sq,Ci], ConIn,ConOut):-
  prop(color,Col,Colset),
  member(E,Colset),
  prop(shape,Shp,Shpset),
  member(E,Shpset), member(Shp:Shpname,
  [triangle:Tr,square:Sq,circle:Ci]),
  occur(Shpname,Tran_in,Tran_out,Con),
  traverse( Tran_out, Path, [Tr,Sq,Ci],
            [Col:Con|ConIn], ConOut
  ).
traverse(_,[],_,Con,Con).

deduce_colors([],_).
deduce_colors([Col:Txt|More],ColTable):-
  append(_,ColName,Txt),
  member(Col:ColName,ColTable),
  deduce_colors(More,ColTable).
```

Figure 8. Central Prolog predicates of Assign_colors

Two sessions contain small variations of the pronunciation for a specific color term, viz. m_029_g (*yellow*: g_u_l, g_u) and m_033_g (yellow: g_u_l, g_u_l_0). As these two are otherwise fit for InShape-2 analysis, we accommodate the phonetic variation replacing

```
Table = [green:_,blue:_,red:_,
         yellow:_,purple:_,brown:_],
```
by
```
( Table=[green:_,blue:_,red:_,yellow:_,
         purple:_,brown:_], Extra=none
;
```

```
Table=[green:_,blue:_,red:_,yellow:_,
       purple:_,brown:_,Extra:_]
),
```

in `eval/2` (fig. 8). Notice the logical disjunction (the connective `;/2`) ensuring that a proper one-to-one mapping (`Extra=none`), if any, is preferred over versions with an `Extra` color term. This way, a single unspecified lexical deviation can be accommodated in a controlled manner. Of course, more licenses could be issued by adding more `Extras` to the `Table` list, at a price of extra processing load.

4   Results

The inference engine delivers satisfactory results for all sessions, however with some interesting twists. Before we go into the details, we present an example of an output from the Assign_colors module.

```
  m_017_g

  triangle : [t,r,z,k,a,n,d]
  square   : [f,i,R,k,a,n]
  circle   : [s,i,R,g,0,l]

  blue     : [b,l,c]
  brown    : [C,t,0,h,Q,j,C,f,C,d,
             0,n,b,l,c,s,0,R,g,
             0,l,h,A,d,u,e,n,b,r,o,n]
  green    : [g,r,Q,n]
  purple   : [C,X,
             0,n,X,i,g,E,n,
             h,A,d,u,e,n,l,e,l,a]
  red      : [n,r,x,D]
  yellow   : [g,u,l]

  Extra = none

  PATH : [e1,e2,e3,e7,e8,e9,e10,
          e11,e4,e5,e6,e12,e13]
```

Figure 9. Output from Assign_colors.

The PATH is correctly identified: informant 017 did name the thirteen objects in the order shown. Concerning the deduced vocabulary, several unusual phonetic forms are encountered. Perhaps most surprising are the very long terms for colors *brown* and *purple*. With a little bit of reflection, it is easy to see why the inference engine, with each of these colors occuring only once among the significant naming events, has too sparse data to determine their usual delimitation. As expected, the standard color names are identified by the *right* edge of the proposed strings (shown in

bold in fig. 9). Like English, Danish usually has adjectives in pre-nominal position.

Notice also that *red* translates to [nrxD] rather than the expected form [rxD] due to the fact that the latter on all its occurrences in m_017_g is preceded by [n]. More examples in the same vein can be studied in table 2, showing the variety of color terms picked for *yellow*.

Such non-standard delimitations are the fingerprints of a truly data-driven learning automat. Of course, several cosmetic operations could be applied post festum, arriving at tokens much more like the dictionary forms – for example by relating the deduced color-terms to the frequency distribution of the *n*-grams in the S&C log. We have chosen not to do so. Actually, we find the deduced terms quite beautiful as they are.

The results of all **G** analyses are summarized in table 2. Paths are explained using the symbols A=[e1,e2,e3], B=[e4,e5,e6], C=[e7,e8,e9], D=[e10,e11], and E=[e12,e13].

Ses-sion	Path	Instantiation of yellow	Status	Dia-gnosis
003	ABDEC	-	*OKneg*	*Anomaly*
005	ABCDE	-	*OKneg*	*Anomaly*
006	ABDEC	[e,n,g,u,l]	*OK*	-
007	ACDEB	[n,r,x,D]	*OK*	*ColBlind*
008	ACDEB	-	*OKneg*	*Anomaly*
009	ABDEC	[g,u,l]	*OK*	-
013	ACBDE	-	*OKneg*	*Violation*
014	ACBDE	[g,u,l]	*OK*	-
016	ACBDE	[N,g,u,l]	*OK*	-
017	ACDBE	[g,u,l]	*OK*	-
018	ACBDE	[d,C,e,n,g,u,l]	*OK*	-
019	ACDEB	[e,n,r,x,D]	*OK*	*ColBlind*
021	ACBDE	[n,g,u,l]	*OK*	-
027	ACBDE	[e,n,g,u,l]	*OK*	-
029	ADEBC	[g,u,l] Extra:[g,u]	*OK*	-
031	AC/D BC2E	-	*OKneg*	*I.con.viol.*
033	ABCDE	[n,r,x,D]	*OK*	*ColBlind*

Table 2. Learning results for InShape-2

In table 2, 'ColBlind' stands for an instance of color blindness (cf. 2.2); 'Violation' for a violation of a linguistic constraint (2.1); 'I.con.viol.' for an integrity constraint violation; 'Anomaly' for a factual description error.

As seen, all sessions were successfully analysed, in the sense that the same paths were identified by the inference engine (IE) and by a human listener (HUM). The sessions are marked as *OK* if the vocabulary and the path deduced by IE is the same as those reported by HUM, modulo color blindness, i.e. possibly with confusion of the terms for *red/yellow* and the related confusion of branches B and C. Sessions for which no well-formed paths could be found either by IE or by HUM, are marked as *OKneg* . These anomalous cases either contain factual description errors with late or no self-correction, or are in conflict with the well-formedness criteria of 2.1.

4.1 Linguistic constraints revisited

From a general linguistic point of view, the conditions of 2.1 are not very attractive. Which language does not have instances of synonymy or homonymy? How, then, could an L1 acquisition model afford to reject it?

We did a few test runs with manufactured sessions copied from real ones, but with certain vital elements changed, e.g. replacing each occurrence of the term for *blue* by the term for *triangle* (creating homonymy), and replacing every second occurrence of the term for *green* by a fresh term (synonymy). As it turned out, the In-Shape-2 system is actually fully capable of learning homonymy in this sense, and even synonymy with one synonymous term allowed for each extra uninstantiated element in the `Table` structure of the Assign_colors module – however at the cost of a heavy overhead in processing loads, especially in the case of synonymy.

Concerning the adjacency condition and the material inclusion condition, these are perhaps even more weakly motivated than the synonymy and homonymy constraints from a linguistic point of view. Again it is easy to modify the program to make it accept non-contiguous naming events, but the processing cost is high.

5. Discussion

InShape-2 is a simple-minded learning device, but nevertheless quite successful on its own terms. Based on unbracketed strings of phones representing a great variety of speech styles, the system robustly derives a set of lexemes and semantic categories in a combined process of low-level data clustering and high-level semantic inference. However, still some refinement is needed. Only property terms were learned (in Danish mostly associated with adjectives and nouns) while locations and spatial relations were not (prepositions and adverbials), causing symptoms of color blindness. We are currently working on an enhanced learner with improved color vision, to be presented in the near future.

Greater challenges are waiting further ahead. Shifting from pre-digested phonetic symbols to uninterpreted acoustic data will soon force us to reconsider the whole regime of speech sound segmentation. It is by no means given that the phonematic level, of all possible levels, will provide the optimal domain for information extraction. In contrast, we expect that the most fertile segmental level will vary dynamically with the purpose of the learning session. "Meaningful units" thus cannot be identified a priori with phonemic or syllabic or prosodic elements, or any other independently defined domain, since the very meaning of *meaningful* depends crucially on the purpose and the success criteria of the task at hand. Simple examples of situated meaningful units are the terms extracted from the **G** sessions which did not always coincide with Danish dictionary items, simply because they were generated as handles for deductive reasoning under very specific conditions, rather than as speaker and purpose independent abstractions. We hence need to develop methods for sound analysis able to lock in on a particular domain of segmentation in a semantically informed feedback-loop. This means that the current phonetic transcription data must be abandoned and replaced by data derived from the sound signal directly (e.g. Henrichsen et al 2009).[6]

An acoustically based learning device would provide a number of interesting spin-offs, both of theoretical and practical nature. One of our immediate goals is to extend the InShape experiment to data from other languages. At CMOL, we have built a large collection of **G** session recordings for languages within the Indo-European family (German, Bulgarian, Hindi, ...)

as well as typologically unrelated languages (Tamil, Xhosa, Khmer, ...). For most of these recordings by far, we have no phonetic transcription, so sound-driven learning is the natural approach towards genuine language-independency.

Even more difficult than the segmentation problem is however the model-theoretic challenge. The scene around the purple triangle must eventually be replaced by something of greater psychological relevance in order for us to approach a claim of cognitive realism. This does not mean, however, that the use of very simple models should be frowned upon. Even infants begin their linguistic career by developing primitive, highly personal sound units as names for a small number of concrete objects.

References

Ando, R. and L. Lee. 2003. Mostly-Unsupervised Statistical Segmentation of Japanese Kanji Sequences. *Natural Language Engineering*, 9(2).

Belkin, M. and P. Niyogi. 2004. Semi-supervised learning on Riemannian manifolds. *Machine Learning, Special Issue on Clustering*, 209–239.

Boersma, P. 2001. Praat, a system for doing phonetics by computer. *Glot. International* 5:9/10, 341-345.

Bratko, I. 2000. *Prolog Programming for Artificial Intelligence.* Third Edition, Addison-Wesley.

Church, K.W. and P. Hanks. 1990. Word association norms, mutual information, and lexicography. *Computational Linguistics* 16(1), 22 29

Cover, T.M.; J.A. Thomas. 1991. *Elements of Information Theory.* Wiley Series in Telecommunications, New York.

Grønnum, N. 2009. A Danish phonetically annotated spontaneous speech corpus (DanPASS). *Speech Comm.* 51, 594-603.

Henrichsen, P. J. 2004. Siblings and Cousins, statistical methods for spoken language analysis. *Acta Linguistica Hafniensia*, 36, 7-33.

Henrichsen, P. J. 2010. Den lilla trekant - learning Danish shape and color terms from scratch. *Linguistic theory and raw sound. Copenhagen Studies in Language*, 40. 27-44.

Henrichsen, P. J. and T. U. Christiansen. 2009. Fishing for meaningful units in connected speech; Proceedings of *ISAAR-2009.*

---

[6] An interesting investigation which we leave for others to explore, would be to compare the current S&C based chunking algorithm to alternative unsupervised, statistical methods using mutual information (e.g. Cover et al 1991), *t*-score (e.g. Church et al 1990), or newer frameworks as Ando (2003) and Belkin (2004).

ISSN 1736-6305 Vol. 11
http://hdl.handle.net/10062/16955

The Impact of Part-of-Speech Filtering on Generation of a Swedish-Japanese Dictionary Using English as Pivot Language

Ingemar Hjälmstad
DSV, Stockholm University
Stockholm, Sweden
iingemar@gmail.com

Martin Hassel
DSV, Stockholm University
Stockholm, Sweden
xmartin@dsv.su.se

Maria Skeppstedt
DSV, Stockholm University
Stockholm, Sweden
mariask@dsv.su.se

Abstract

A common problem when combining two bilingual dictionaries to make a third, using one common language as a pivot language, is the emergence of false translations due to lexical ambiguity between words in the languages involved. This paper examines if the translation accuracy improves when using part-of-speech filtering of translation candidates. To examine this, two different Japanese-Swedish lexicons were created, one with part-of-speech filtering, one without. The results show 33 % less translation candidates and a higher quality lexicon when using part-of-speech filtering. It also resulted in a free lexicon of Swedish translations to 40 716 Japanese entries with a 90 % precision, and the conclusion that part-of-speech filtering is an easy way of improving the translation quality in this context.

1 Introduction

Bilingual dictionaries are specialized dictionaries used to translate words or phrases from one language to another. They aid us in understanding other languages, people and cultures – something that becomes more and more important in today's high paced Internet connected society.

The manual creation of bilingual dictionaries is very time consuming and requires hard work. Several automatic methods have been proposed to aid this work. The more common ones are statistical analysis of parallel corpora or by translating from one language to another through a common third language – the pivot language. These methods are, however, not perfect and this paper aims to investigate how to improve on these methods, in particular how part-of-speech filtering affects automatic generation of translation candidates when using a pivot language.

2 Background

An alternative to corpus based methods was proposed by Tanaka and Umemura (1994) where they showed that it is possible to automate the translation from source language to target language through a common intermediate language. Here a Japanese-English and an English-French dictionary were used to automatically generate translation candidates of Japanese-French translations. They discovered some false translations, however, and in order to filter out these *inverse consultation*—a method for assessing the quality of a translation candidate—was proposed.

One time inverse consultation is done by taking each translation candidate in the target language and translating it back to the intermediate language. These translations are then compared to the translations of the word from the source language into the intermediate language. The larger the number of common translations in the intermediate language, the better candidate. In this way it can be measured how close the meaning of the original word is to the meaning of the translation candidate. In two times inverse consultation, also proposed by Tanaka and Umemura (1994), the method is taken one step further and the translations in the intermediate language are translated back to the source language and compared to the source word.

Shirai and Yamamoto (2001) proposed a variant of Tanaka and Umemura's method where they used one time inverse consultation to create a Korean to Japanese dictionary. Here, the degree of similarity for the translation candidates was calculated using the Dice coefficient for the two sets of words in the intermediate language. One of the sets consisted of the translations of the source word from Korean to English and the other set consisted of translations back from the Japanese candidate to English.

Bond and Ogura (2008) combined several of the above methods when creating a Japanese-Malay dictionary. They also used matching of part-of-speech in the generation of translation candidates. Pairs were only accepted if they had the same part-of-speech which, according to Bond and Ogura, gave a marked reduction of false translations. It lowered the number of translation candidates with 15 %, out of which the majority of the candidates were wrong.

For Swedish, similar work on automated generation of bilingual dictionaries have been made by Sjöbergh (2005). This approach differed from earlier work by using a measure similar to inverse document frequency, and by allowing a source language word to be translated by a combination of two target language words.

Sjöbergh finally suggested an improvement in the method by examining the part-of-speech on the suggested translation candidate, to primarily distinguish between nouns and verbs. This was something which, according to Sjöbergh, gave rise to a number of erroneous suggestions for translations. Khanaraksombat and Sjöbergh (2007) used the same method as Sjöbergh (2005) with only a few small changes, including part-of-speech matching. However, many of the words had no part-of-speech marked, and they do not report on how the part-of-speech matching affected the results.

3 Problem

In aforementioned works the most common type of problems in automatic generation of bilingual dictionary with a pivot language are due to lexical ambiguity. Examples of different forms of lexical ambiguity are internal and external homographs and ambiguity in part-of-speech, referred to as polysemy.

Part-of-speech matching has previously been suggested as a possible improvement of the method. Zhang et al. (2007), Khanaraksombat and Sjöbergh (2007) as well as Bond and Ogura (2008) have used part-of-speech matching with positive results. However, it has not been investigated fully with Swedish as one of the included languages, probably due to the absence of a dictionary in which all entries have been marked with the part-of-speech. Since the data sources used here have all entries marked with the part-of-speech, matching will be performed on all the suggestions of the translation candidates in this work.

4 Method

This survey has been carried out with Japanese as source language, English as intermediate (pivot) language and Swedish as target language. The Japanese WordNet (Isahara et al., 2008) and the People's English-Swedish dictionary (Kann and Hollman, 2011) are used for Japanese-English and English-Swedish translation, respectively. These were selected since they are the largest available dictionaries for the languages involved that also have all entries marked with part-of-speech, and that are available in digital format for free download and use. Since the lexicons use different notations for part-of-speech, e.g. the Japanese Word-Net uses the abbreviation "nn" for nouns while the People's English-Swedish dictionary uses "n" for nouns, a mapping was done to a common part-of-speech notation for easier comparison in later stages.

4.1 Translation Candidate Generation

The method for generating translation candidates from Japanese to Swedish is based on the method by Tanaka and Umemura (1994) with a pivot language. Two sets of translation candidates were generated, one with part-of-speech matching and the other without.

Meta code to generate Japanese-Swedish translation candidates:

1. For each Japanese word in the Japanese WordNet, look up its English translations.

2. For each English translation, look up its Swedish translations in the People's lexicon.

3. For each Swedish translation, if it exists:

    (a) Perform part-of-speech filtering, that is compare part-of-speech in the Japanese and Swedish dictionaries and save as filtered translation candidate only if both words have the same part-of-speech.

    (b) Do not perform part-of-speech filtering, save as unfiltered translation candidate and continue with next.

This method differs from previous work in the same area by using part-of-speech filtering on all translation candidates, thus thoroughly examining the impact of the part-of-speech filtering step.

4.2 Translation Candidate Scoring

The method of scoring the automatically generated translation candidates is based on the method by Tanaka and Umemura (1994): one time inverse consultation. This method has been used successfully in a number of other works (Shirai and Yamamoto, 2001; Zhang et al., 2007; Bond and Ogura, 2008; Sjöbergh, 2005). One time inverse consultation requires an additional data source: a bilingual dictionary from the target language back to the intermediate language. For this the People's Swedish-English dictionary with 22 014 Swedish dictionary words has been used.

One time inverse consultation is carried out according to the following steps.

1. For each translation candidate, translate the word in the target language back to the intermediate language.

2. Translate the word in the source language into the intermediate language.

3. Count how many common translations there are in the intermediate language.

The more matches, the better translation candidate. To calculate the score for the proposal the formula from Shirai and Yamamoto (2001) is used. Points p for a translation candidate w are then, here, calculated using the following generalized formula, where s denotes the source language (in this case Japanese), t denotes the target language (here Swedish) and i denotes the intermediate language (here English).

$$p(w) = 2 * \frac{\text{Common translations}}{\text{Translations}_{s \to i} + \text{Translations}_{t \to i}}$$

The resulting $p(w)$ shows on a scale from 0 to 1 how good the proposed translation is, with 1 as the highest score.

Additional calculations of how good the translation candidate is can be done. Other methods are Sjöbergh's (2005) inverse document frequency, and Varga and Yokoyama's (2007) lexicological checks in WordNet or Bond and Ogura's (2008) matching through a second intermediate language. None of these methods have been used since they were not considered essential for the study of how part-of-speech filtering affects the outcome. One scoring is enough to show any differences in the quality of the resulting lexicon. Shirai and Yamamoto's method is also well proven (Zhang et al., 2007; Bond and Ogura, 2008).

4.3 Data

The People's English-Swedish dictionary (version 1.1) currently contains 46 762 English entries, which are carefully grouped by part-of-speech. The People's English-Swedish dictionary is freely available for use and download in XML format under the Creative Commons Attribution-ShareAlike 2.5 Generic license.[1] The Swedish-English part of the People's dictionary (version 2009-07-08) contains 22 014 Swedish entries. It has a similar breakdown of the part-of-speech groups as the English-Swedish part of the lexicon. It is, however, not yet available for free download.

The Japanese WordNet (version 0.92) is a semantic lexicon of the Japanese language. It is produced by the National Institute of Information and Communications Technology (NICT) in Japan and contains 87 133 unique Japanese entries with translations into English. All entries are marked by one of the following parts-of-speech: noun, verb, adjective or adverb. Bond and Ogura (2008) claim that they have reached a WordNet with reasonable coverage of most common Japanese words. They finish, however, with a caveat that 5 % of the lexicon's entries may contain errors, but that this is something they intend to correct manually while working with future versions. The Japanese WordNet is freely available for use, reproduction and distribution, and is available for download as an SQLite database.[2]

5 Evaluation

Precision and recall are the most common measures in evaluating the quality of automatically generated glossaries and variations of these have been used by Hara et al. (2008), Varga and Yokoyama (2007), Bond and Ogura (2008), Sjöbergh (2005) and Khanaraksombat and Sjöbergh (2007).

Precision is a measure used to evaluate systems for information retrieval and is defined as the proportion of retrieved relevant answers. The relevant answers in this case are all the suggestions for translations that are correct. Thus, the accuracy is the percentage of correct translation candidates compared to all translation candidates.

What is most interesting for this work, however, is the difference in quality of dictionaries pro-

---

[1] `http://folkets-lexikon.csc.kth.se/folkets/folkets.en.html`
[2] `http://nlpwww.nict.go.jp/wn-ja/`

duced without part-of-speech filtering compared to the lexicon produced using part-of-speech filtering. The precision p of a word w is calculated by the following formula:

$$p(w) = \frac{\text{Correct translation candidates}}{\text{All translation candidates}}$$

Accuracy is calculated by performing a sample survey. In addition, a stratified sample was made based on the translation candidate's score—calculated using Tanaka and Umemura's one time inverse consultation—to get an idea of whether the precision varies with the score of the translation candidate. This also shows what threshold could be appropriate to use when presenting results to users of the lexicon. The translation candidates were divided into 10 strata, from 0.0 to 1.0 points, where each stratum corresponds to 0.1 points. From each stratum a random sample of 100 words was then drawn by systematic sampling, that is every n suggested translation was chosen, where n is calculated by all units in the population divided by the size of the sample.

To determine whether a translation candidate is relevant, that is correctly translated, you can use native speakers of both source and target languages and have them manually correct the translations. This method has been successfully used by Khanaraksombat and Sjöbergh (2007). Since access to such persons was missing, the samples were instead evaluated by manually checking the English translations of the translation candidate and whether the English translation is consistent with its proposed Swedish translation. Manually performing an exhaustive survey of this kind is not reasonable, so a sample survey was carried out instead. This method has been used successfully by Sjöbergh (2005).

Recall is another commonly used measure in the evaluation of systems for information retrieval. When evaluating an automatically generated dictionary, it is not reasonable to check all translation candidates. Instead one can compare with a baseline set to a selection of entries from a printed manually constructed lexicon in which all words are assumed to be correctly translated. Recall is, then, calculated as follows:

$$r(w) = \frac{\text{Correct part-of-speech filtered candidates}}{\text{Correct baseline translation candidates}}$$

For this work, however, it is more interesting to examine the coverage of the method relative to

earlier methods. Therefore the correct translation candidates produced without part-of-speech filtering was set as the baseline. It was then examined whether the translations were among the proposals of translations produced with part-of-speech filtering. Thus a measure of the method's recall relative to the baseline method is calculated, which shows to what extent the method using part-of-speech filtering catches all the correct translations generated by the method not using part-of-speech filtering.

6 Results

Table 1 shows the number of translation candidates generated for various points in each range, with and without the use of part-of-speech filtering, as well as the difference in the number of translation candidates created using each method. By using part-of-speech filtering the total number of translation candidates created decreased by 578 387 words, or 33.04 %. The reduction of translation candidates varies depending on the score and range from 9.43 % to 34.73 %, with a tendency of more translation candidates with different parts-of-speech in target and source language in the lower scoring ranges. This is probably because most of the translation candidates with different parts-of-speech are wrong, partly filtered out by the one time inverse consultation.

A large part of the translation candidates have not received any score at all. This applies to 1 341 391 translation candidates generated without part-of-speech filtering and 875 527 for those with part-of-speech filtering. This is mainly because the Swedish entries were missing in the People's Swedish-English dictionary, which has relatively few Swedish dictionary entries, and no look-up means zero score. This has the effect that the generated Japanese-Swedish lexicon contains fewer good words and translations. This can hopefully be addressed if more extensive versions of the People's Swedish-English Dictionary are released, rendering more Swedish entries available.

6.1 Quality

The quality of the automatically generated dictionaries is measured by calculating the precision of the suggested translation candidates. Table 2 shows the estimated quality of the translation candidates generated without part-of-speech filtering, while Table 3 shows the estimated quality of the translation candidates generated with part-of-

Score (p)	Without pos-filtering	With pos-filtering	Difference	Diff (%)
0	1 341 391	875 527	465 864	34.73
$0.0 < p \leq 0.1$	69 015	47 646	21 369	30.96
$0.1 < p \leq 0.2$	150 142	105 400	44 742	29.80
$0.2 < p \leq 0.3$	79 937	58 671	21 266	26.60
$0.3 < p \leq 0.4$	57 479	43 397	14 082	24.50
$0.4 < p \leq 0.5$	25 917	20 096	5 821	22.46
$0.5 < p \leq 0.6$	3 989	3 462	527	13.21
$0.6 < p \leq 0.7$	14 914	11 654	3 260	21.86
$0.7 < p \leq 0.8$	1 665	1 508	157	9.43
$0.8 < p \leq 0.9$	176	154	22	12.50
$0.9 < p \leq 1.0$	6 078	4 801	1 277	21.01
Total	1 750 703	1 172 316	578 387	33.04

Table 1: Score from one time inverse consultation, divided in intervals, for translation candidates generated without and with part-of-speech filtering.

Score (p)	Quantity	Precision	$\neq$
$0.9 < p \leq 1.0$	6 078	0.73	19
$0.8 < p \leq 0.9$	176	0.87	10
$0.7 < p \leq 0.8$	1 665	0.90	7
$0.6 < p \leq 0.7$	14 914	0.72	18
$0.5 < p \leq 0.6$	3 989	0.82	15
$0.4 < p \leq 0.5$	25 917	0.71	17
$0.3 < p \leq 0.4$	57 479	0.54	28
$0.2 < p \leq 0.3$	79 937	0.66	23
$0.1 < p \leq 0.2$	150 142	0.46	32
$0.0 < p \leq 0.1$	69 015		
0	1 341 391		

Table 2: Precision for translation candidates generated without part-of-speech filtering. Each sample is 100 words, $\neq$ represents the number of translation candidates where both source and target language have different part-of-speech.

Score (p)	Quantity	Precision
$0.9 < p \leq 1.0$	4 801	0.93
$0.8 < p \leq 0.9$	154	0.94
$0.7 < p \leq 0.8$	1 508	0.94
$0.6 < p \leq 0.7$	11 654	0.90
$0.5 < p \leq 0.6$	3 462	0.92
$0.4 < p \leq 0.5$	20 096	0.92
$0.3 < p \leq 0.4$	43 397	0.91
$0.2 < p \leq 0.3$	58 671	0.92
$0.1 < p \leq 0.2$	105 400	0.70
$0.0 < p \leq 0.1$	47 646	
0	875 527	

Table 3: Precision for translation candidates generated with part-of-speech filtering. Each sample is 100 words.

speech filtering.

Most interesting for this paper is the difference in quality between the two generated lexicons. Figure 1 illustrates the difference in the quality of translation candidates (y-axis) generated without part-of-speech filtering compared to translation candidates generated with part-of-speech filtering. Quality is the precision, that is the number of correctly translated translation candidates compared to all translation candidates, divided into strata (x-axis) based on the translation candidate's score to illustrate how the precision varies with the score.

Figure 1 shows a higher precision for the translation candidates generated with part-of-speech

filtering than without for all tested strata. Each examined stratum has a sample size of 100 words. We also see a positive correlation ($r = 0.77$ without part-of-speech filtering, $r = 0.62$ with) that high values on the translation candidate's score correspond to high values for precision and that a low score equals low precision. All examined translation candidates where source and target languages are of different part-of-speech have been found incorrect.

Figure 1 also shows the threshold that is appropriate to use when presenting results to users. If you want a dictionary of good quality, you might choose precision 0.9 as threshold, which corresponds to a score of >0.7 with translation candidates generated without part-of-speech filtering, while you can go down to a score of >0.2

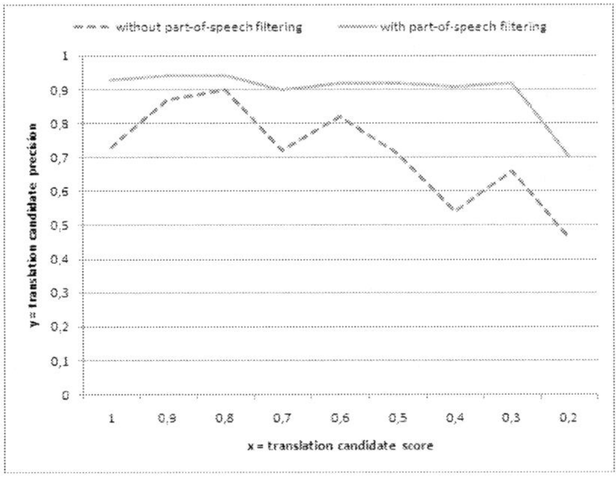

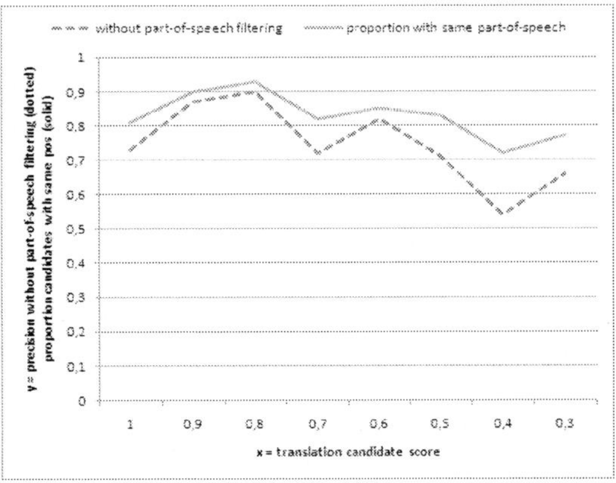

Figure 1: Score and precision for translation candidates generated without and with part-of-speech filtering.

Figure 2: Precision of translation candidates generated without part-of-speech filtering and the proportion of these with same part of speech.

with translation candidates generated with part-of-speech filtering. This would provide a dictionary with a maximum of 10 % false translation candidates, and with 143 743 translation candidates of 40 716 unique Japanese entries with an average of 3.5 candidates per entry. Without part-of-speech filtering a dictionary of comparable quality would only contain 7 919 translation candidates of 5 244 unique Japanese entries with an average of 1.5 candidates per entry. Summarized there is a ratio of 20 between the two configurations.

Because of declining precision, no translation candidates with a precision below 0.1 have been checked. A too poor precision is not interesting, therefore the manual survey was terminated before all translation candidates were checked.

Review of data from Table 2 also showed a positive correlation between proposal precision and the percentage of translation candidates that had the same part-of-speech in both source and target language ($r = 0.99$). This applies for all investigated strata, where each sample stratum is 100 words.

To illustrate this more clearly, the two graphs are overlaid on each other in Figure 2. The dashed curve is from Figure 1 and shows the quality, i.e. precision, of translation candidates (y-axis) generated without part-of-speech filtering. The solid curve shows the percentage of the checked translation candidates that have the same part-of-speech in both source and target language. The proportion of such proposals (y-axis) are shown for each stratum (x-axis).

The positive correlation between the percentage of translation candidates with same part-of-speech and the candidate's accuracy may also explain the irregular jagged curve, since the random sample selected by systematic sampling appears to have an uneven distribution of proposals with different parts-of-speech. A better idea might be to ensure that each stratum has the same proportion of translation candidates with and without the same part-of-speech as is the case in the complete population. For example the score range $0.9 < p < 1.0$ had 21 % words with different parts-of-speech, which should then also be the case in the sample.

A review of the translation candidates that were filtered away, i.e. the candidates that have different parts-of-speech in the source and target languages, showed that they were all wrong. This also suggests that the more candidates that have different parts-of-speech in the source and target languages, the lower the precision of the generated dictionary.

Recall has been calculated for all investigated strata. The correct translation candidates generated without part-of-speech filtering have been set as the baseline, then it was checked whether they were among the translation candidates generated with part-of-speech filtering. All the evaluated candidates were included. This shows that the recall of the method is 100 % relative to the baseline method, that is, all correctly translated translation candidates produced without part-of-speech filtering were among the candidates generated with part-of-speech filtering.

7 Discussion

The most common cause of erroneous suggestions for translations were lexical ambiguity and specifically due to homographs. This problem has been effectively reduced by using part-of-speech filtering of the translation candidates. The second most common cause is ambiguity within the same part-of-speech. These may be filtered by inverse consultation, but not always, which then requires manual checking afterwards.

Another problem is the different categorizations of part-of-speech in the different dictionaries. An example found when searching the database for translation candidates with another part-of-speech than the original word is the following: The Japanese character for one (1) is categorized by the Japanese WordNet as a noun, while the People's English-Swedish dictionary categorized the Swedish translation as a cardinal numeral. This appears to be due to differences in the languages, where the Japanese language categorizes numerals as nouns. By part-of-speech filtering this correct translation candidate was errornously purged. However, no such entries were discovered in the systematic sample evaluation of the translation candidates, which implies that they are rather uncommon in this language combination.

One problem with using English as the intermediate language is the difference between British and American English. During the manual evaluation it was found that the Japanese WordNet had both British and American spelling of some English translations. One way to solve this, which has been tried by Bond and Ogura (2008), is to use some sort of British / American English dictionary for finding alternate spellings, if you can not find a direct translation.

8 Conclusion

The purpose of this study was to examine the impact of part-of-speech filtering on automatic generation of a bilingual dictionary by means of a pivot language. For this purpose two Japanese-Swedish lexicons were created, one without part-of-speech filtering and the other with part-of-speech filtering.

A comparison of these two dictionaries showed that the method with part-of-speech filtering gave 33 % fewer translation candidates. The manual evaluation of the quality of the candidates showed a higher precision of the candidates generated with part-of-speech filtering for all investigated strata. The results also showed a positive correlation (r = 0.99) between the percentage of translation candidates that have the same part-of-speech in both source and target language and proposal precision. Method recall is 100 %, according to the systematic manual evaluation, but later searches in the database uncovered that certain types of words still can be filtered out incorrectly, for example, numerals which appear to have different parts-of-speech in Japanese and Swedish.

From these results it is concluded that part-of-speech filtering is a useful method that reduces the number of erroneous suggestions for translations, at least for the current language of the trio (Japanese, English and Swedish). Part-of-speech filtering effectively eliminates problems stemming from external homographs in the intermediate language. Given the data, it is a simple step to add to the automatic generation of suggestions for translations, resulting in clear improvements.

As a result of the study 143 743 Japanese-Swedish translation candidates were created for 40 716 unique Japanese entries. Through using the precision curve in Figure 1, a precision of 0.9 was suggested as an appropriate threshold, which corresponds to >0.2 in score for translation candidates generated with part-of-speech filtering. These candidates have an estimated 10 % false translations, therefore it is important to conclude by pointing out that methods to automatically generate bilingual dictionaries are not perfect. They are great as preliminary and highly time-saving work, which should be followed by manual checks and cleaning of the resulting material. The result is also largely dependent on the source material used for one time inverse consultation to work properly.

The resulting Japanese-Swedish lexicon and the Java code used to generate it will be released under a Distributed Creative Commons Attribution-ShareAlike 2.5 Generic license[3] for free usage, sharing and remixing of the work.

References

Francis Bond and Kentaro Ogura. 2008. Combining linguistic resources to create a machine-tractable Japanese-Malay dictionary. *Language Resources and Evaluation*, 42(2):127–136.

---

[3]`http://creativecommons.org/licenses/by-sa/2.5/`

Takahiro Hara, Maike Erdmann, and Shokiro Nishio.
2008. Extraction of bilingual terminology from a
multilingual web-based encyclopedia. *Journal of
Information Processing*, 16:68–79.

Hitoshi Isahara, Francis Bond, Kiyotaka Uchimoto,
Masao Utiyama, and Kyoko Kanzaki. 2008. Development of the Japanese WordNet. In *LREC*. European Language Resources Association.

Viggo Kann and Joachim Hollman. 2011. People's English-Swedish dictionary, version 1.1.
http://folkets-lexikon.csc.kth.se/folkets/om.en.html.
[Online; accessed 21-January-2011].

Wanwisa Khanaraksombat and Jonas Sjöbergh. 2007.
Developing and evaluating a searchable Swedish–
Thai lexicon. In *Proceedings of Nodalida 2007*,
pages 324–328, Tartu, Estonia.

Satoshi Shirai and Kazuhide Yamamoto. 2001. Linking english words in two bilingual dictionaries to
generate another language pair dictionary. In *19th
International Conference on Computer Processing
of Oriental Languages: ICCPOL-2001*, pages 174–
179.

Jonas Sjöbergh. 2005. Creating a free digital Japanese-
Swedish lexicon. In *Proceedings of PACLING 2005*,
pages 296–300, Tokyo, Japan.

Kumiko Tanaka and Kyoji Umemura. 1994. Construction of a bilingual dictionary intermediated by a third
language. In *Proceedings of the 15th conference on
Computational linguistics - Volume 1*, COLING '94,
pages 297–303, Stroudsburg, PA, USA. Association
for Computational Linguistics.

Istvan Varga and Shoichi Yokoyama. 2007. Japanese-
Hungarian dictionary generation using ontology resources. In *Machine Translation Summit XI*, pages
483–490.

Yujie Zhang, Qing Ma, and Hitoshi Isahara. 2007.
Building Japanese-Chinese translation dictionary
based on EDR Japanese-English bilingual dictionary. In *Machine Translation Summit XI*, pages
551–557.

ISSN 1736-6305 Vol. 11
http://hdl.handle.net/10062/16955

A Gold Standard for English–Swedish Word Alignment

Maria Holmqvist and Lars Ahrenberg
Department of Computer and Information Science
Linköping University, Sweden
`firstname.lastname@liu.se`

Abstract

Word alignment gold standards are an important resource for developing and evaluating word alignment methods. In this paper we present a free English–Swedish word alignment gold standard consisting of texts from Europarl with manually verified word alignments. The gold standard contains two sets of word aligned sentences, a test set for the purpose of evaluation and a training set that can be used for supervised training. The guidelines used for English–Swedish alignment were created based on guidelines for other language pairs and with statistical machine translation as the targeted application. We also present results of intrinsic evaluation using our gold standard and discuss the relationship to extrinsic evaluation in a statistical machine translation system.

1   Introduction

Translated texts are rich sources of information about language differences and translation. A fundamental step in extracting translation information from parallel text is to perform word alignment and determine which words and phrases are translations of each other in the source and target texts. Word alignment forms the basis of (phrase-based) statistical machine translation (PBSMT) but alignments are also used in other data-driven approaches to machine translation to extract bilingual dictionaries and learn translation rules.

The task of identifying corresponding words in a parallel text is difficult and manual word alignment can be time-consuming. Unsupervised methods for automatic word alignment have dominated the machine translation field (Och and Ney, 2003), but an increasing amount of research is devoted to improving word alignment quality through supervised training (e.g., Ayan and Dorr, 2006; Blunsom and Cohn, 2006; Ittycheriah and Roukos, 2005). Supervised methods require a set of high quality alignments to train the parameters of a discriminative word alignment system. These alignments are often hand-made alignment gold standards. Gold standards are also an important resource for evaluation of word alignment accuracy.

In this paper, we present an English–Swedish word alignment gold standard. It consists of 1164 sentence pairs divided into a training set and a test set. The training set was produced to be used as training data for supervised word alignment (Holmqvist, 2010) and the test set was created for the purpose of word alignment evaluation. The test set alignments have confidence labels for ambiguous links in order to be able to calculate more fine-grained evaluation measures. The gold standard and alignment guidelines can be downloaded from `http://www.ida.liu.se/~nlplab/ges` . Alignments are stored in NAACL format (Mihalcea and Pedersen, 2003).

This paper is organized as follows. In Section 2 we review available gold standards for English–Swedish and compare them to our newly created resource. The selection of parallel texts is described in Section 3 and the guidelines for manual word alignment are motivated and exemplified in Section 4. We then review recent research on word alignment evaluation in Section 5. In Section 6 we use our gold standard reference alignment to compare intrinsic evaluation with extrinsic evaluation in a phrase-based statistical machine translation system. Finally, Section 7 contains conclusions and directions for future work.

2 Related work

Gold standards consisting of parallel text with manually annotated word alignments exist for several language pairs including English–French (Och and Ney, 2003), Dutch–English (Macken, 2010) and English–Spanish (Lambert et al., 2005).

For some language pairs, parallel resources have been developed in the form of parallel tree-banks. Parallel treebanks consist of parallel syntactic trees that have manual alignments between corresponding words and phrases as well as between subtrees. The added effort of verifying syntactic structure and aligning subtrees makes treebanks even more labor-intensive to produce than alignment gold standards. However, word alignments from large parallel treebanks such as the English-Arabic treebank from LDC are also used to train and evaluate word alignment systems, (e.g., Gao et al., 2010).

Currently, available resources for English–Swedish word alignment include two parallel tree-banks, Smultron (Volk et al., 2009) and LinES (Ahrenberg, 2007). Smultron is a multi-lingual treebank consisting of 1500 sentences from three domains with subsentential alignments. The Smultron alignment guidelines are similar to our test data guidelines where two types of links are used, one for regular links and one for more fuzzy correspondences. LinES is an English–Swedish treebank containing 2400 sentences from four sub-corpora. This treebank was primarily designed to investigate and measure the occurrence of translation shifts and the word alignments in LinES are sparse. Furthermore, LinES is not an open resource, but it can be queried through a web interface. Another resource of free parallel English–Swedish data is OPUS, an open source collection of multilingual parallel data with automatic sentence and word alignments (Tiedemann, 2009).

Our gold standard is a freely available resource designed for the purpose of improving word alignment for statistical machine translation. First of all, it has the advantage that it contains over 1000 sentences with full-text word alignments from a single domain. The Europarl domain was chosen since it is an open source corpus that is large enough for training an English–Swedish SMT system. By building translation systems from different alignments we can measure the impact of the alignment on translation quality and compare it to intrinsic measures of word alignment accuracy.

Furthermore, the alignment guidelines used for our gold standard work is based on a similar effort by Lambert et al. (2005) to produce a gold standard for English–Spanish word alignment for machine translation. Especially the test data in the gold-standard was created based on their findings on how to build reference alignments that will strengthen the correlation between word alignment accuracy and translation quality.

3 Text Selection

The parallel texts in the gold standard were taken from the English–Swedish part of the Europarl[1] corpus (Koehn, 2005) with texts collected between the years 1997-2003. The texts from the 4th quarter of 2000 were not included in our corpus since these texts are commonly used as test sets for machine translation evaluation.

The corpus was sentence aligned (Gale and Church, 1991) and sentences longer than 40 words were removed. This step removed 20% of the sentence pairs resulting in a parallel corpus with 704852 parallel segments and about 1,5 million words per language.

A random sample of 1200 sentence pairs from the first 20 000 sentences was divided into a training set of 1000 sentence pairs and a test set of 200 sentence pairs. About 3% of the sentence pairs were removed from the data because their sentence alignment was incorrect. Table 1 shows the final size and characteristics of the training and test corpora in terms of sentences, word tokens and word types.

Corpus	Size	English		Swedish	
		Words	Types	Words	Types
Training	972	20340	3374	18343	4181
Test	192	4263	1332	3837	1395
Total	1164	24603	4706	22180	5576

Table 1: Corpus statistics for training and test data.

4 Manual Word Alignment

This section describes the manual word alignment process and presents guidelines for English–Swedish word alignment. Section 4.1 presents a range of factors that must be considered before settling on a set of word alignment guidelines and Section 4.2 and 4.3 presents the guiding principles for alignment of test and training data respectively.

---

[1]Europarl v. 2.0, http://www.statmt.org/europarl/archives.html.

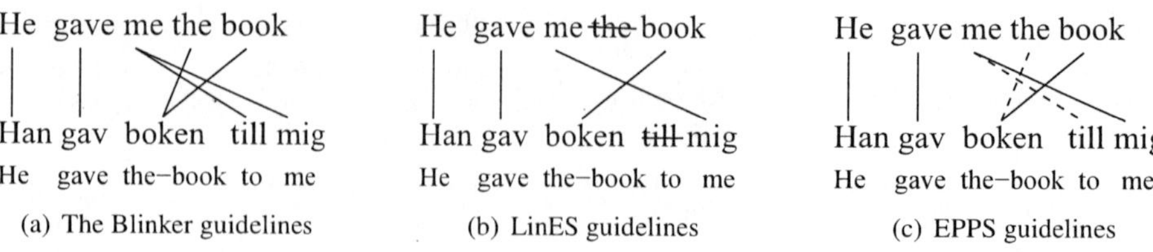

Figure 1: Example of word alignment guidelines. Lines represent Sure links, dashed lines represent Possible links and strikethrough represents null links.

4.1 Alignment Guidelines

Word alignment is an ambiguous task for human annotators as there can be several plausible options for linking words in a given sentence pair. In order to produce a gold standard alignment that is consistent and yet fair to different alignment strategies, it is common to let several human annotators perform the alignment task independently based on a set of guidelines that explains the alignment strategy. A strategy for word alignment must contain decisions on many levels, including:

Size of alignment units. Alignments can be more or less oriented to lexical items instead of larger segments such as phrases. Phrase alignments are usually created by linking each word in the source phrase to each word in the target phrase.

Alignment purpose and coverage. The final purpose of the alignment will influence alignment strategy and affect the need for coverage. For example, some applications only require alignment of a pre-determined set of words (translation spotting) instead of full-text alignment (Véronis, 2000).

Confidence labels. A label can be attached to each word link to distinguish between *sure* and *possible* links.

Criteria for correspondence. Criteria for translation correspondence can be biased in favor of semantic or structural correspondence.

Untranslated items. Some word alignment guidelines include a special link type for untranslated words, a null link, while others let these words be unaligned.

We will illustrate different alignment strategies with the relatively simple sentence *He gave me the book – Han gav boken till mig* which has been aligned using three different guidelines: Blinker (Melamed, 1998), LinES (Ahrenberg, 2007) and the guidelines of Lambert et al. (2005) (henceforth referred to as EPPS).

The Blinker guidelines in Figure 1(a) aim to align as small segments as possible including as many words as necessary to achieve semantic correspondence. Blinker allows two types of links, regular links and null-links.

The same link types are used in the LinES guidelines in Figure 1(b) but in these guidelines one-to-one links are strongly preferred over many-to-many links and function words are null-linked if they lack a corresponding token in the other language.

The EPPS guidelines in Figure 1(c) incorporates both alignment strategies by labeling unambiguous correspondences as *sure* links while the function words without corresponding tokens are labeled as *possible* links. When sure and possible labels are used in an alignment reference, sure alignments should be more important than possible alignments during evaluation. The EPPS alignment would therefore be fair to systems that follow either Blinker or LinES alignment guidelines.

4.2 Test Data Alignment

Word aligned test data is used as a reference when evaluating the quality of computed alignments. The guidelines for aligning English–Swedish reference data are based on the EPPS guidelines which are adapted to the task of producing full-text reference word alignments for alignment evaluation and machine translation (Lambert et al., 2005).

The basic correspondence criterion for English–Swedish word alignment follows the definition in Lambert et al. (2005) that "the correspondence between two lexical units should involve on both sides as few words as possible but as many words as necessary, with the requirement that the linked words or groups bear the same meaning." Correspondences between multiword units are created by linking each word in the source segment to each word in the target segment. The EPPS guidelines adds a confidence label to each word link in the reference where alignments labeled *sure* (S) are obligatory while alignments labeled *possible* (P) are acceptable alignments during evaluation. As shown in the previous section, confidence labels ensure that the reference alignment is reasonably fair to different alignment strategies.

The *alignment error rate* (AER) (Och and Ney, 2003) is a common evaluation measure for word alignment that takes the confidence label of the reference links into account when error rate is calculated (See section 5 for more details). Lambert et al. (2005) show that a large proportion of possible links in the reference will lead to an AER that favours high precision alignments. Since recall is just as, if not more, important than precision for statistical machine translation, the EPPS guidelines are designed to create reference alignments with a large proportion of sure links in order to increase the importance of alignment recall. Unlike the EPPS guidelines we also use explicit *null links* to mark words and phrases that have no translation in the other language.

The proper use of sure and possible links in our guidelines are illustrated by Figures 2 and 3. As a rule, two words or phrases correspond if they are semantically and structurally equivalent and alignments should be kept as fine-grained as possible. A word link is sure if the correspondence meets both semantic and syntactic criteria and possible if only one criterion is met, when a correspondence is uncertain or if a word has many alignment possibilities.

For example, Figure 2(a) contains a word-by-word translation of the noun phrase *the red car* annotated with S links. The noun phrase in Figure 2(b), however, lacks a Swedish lexical item corresponding to the definite article *the*, and since the definiteness instead is expressed with a Swedish definite suffix, the article is linked to the noun with a P link. In short, function words should be S linked to corresponding function words if possible. However, in cases where the syntactic function is expressed by a content word, a P link should be used between the function and content words. In Figure 2(c), for example, *om* has an attributive function and is P-linked to the English attribute *threshold*.

P links can also be used when two content words correspond on a structural level but not on the semantic level such as the words *worst* and *större* (*Eng.* larger) in Figure 3. These words cor-

respond in the given sentence but they might not work well as translations of each other in another context.

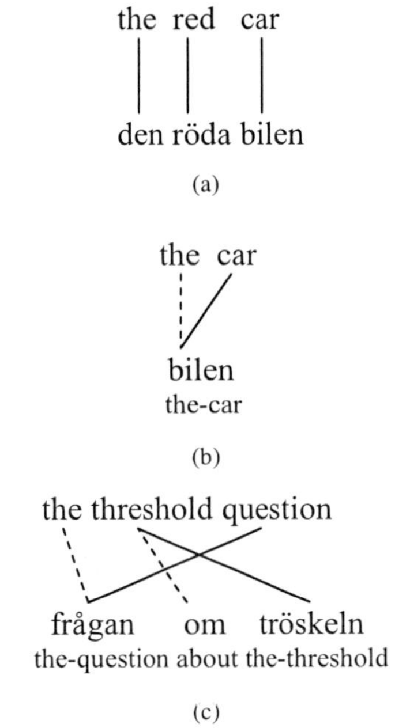

Figure 2: Noun phrase alignments.

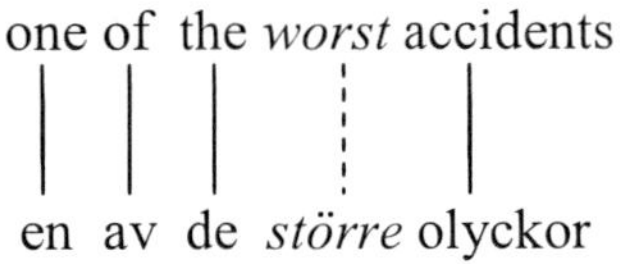

Figure 3: P-linked content words.

4.2.1 Inter-annotator Agreement

Two annotators, the authors of this paper, were given the task of drawing links between corresponding words and to give at least one link to all words in the sentence pair, using S, P and null links according to the guidelines. All links from both alignments were added to the final reference alignment. If annotators disagreed on a link or on the label of a link, that link was labeled P in the reference. If a word was null-linked by one annotator and linked to a word by the other annotator, the null link was removed and the word link was labeled P in the reference. The final reference alignment contains a large proportion of sure links (73% if not counting null-links). The proportion of each link type is shown in Table 2.

The alignment consistency between the two annotators was relatively high. Inter-annotator agreement shown in Table 3 was calculated as $AGR = 2*I/(A1+A2)$ where $A1$ and $A2$ is the sets of links created by the first and second annotator and I is the intersection of these sets. The agreement between A1 and A2 was 85.8% for labeled agreement and 91.3% for unlabeled agreement. Possible links were the link type on which annotators disagreed the most.

Reference	%S	%P	%Null	Links
A1	70.1	15.1	14.8	5527
A2	68.3	13.5	18.2	5086
Final	63.6	23.5	12.9	5254

Table 2: Alignment data.

Links	% Agreement
s	93.7
p	55.2
n	79.6
s+p (unlabeled)	87.1 (93.7)
s+p+n (unlabeled)	85.8 (91.3)

Table 3: Inter-annotator agreement per link type.

Ref	Alignment	F-score	AER
A2	A1	93.67	5.78
A1	A2	93.67	3.26
Final	A1	98.58	0.00
Final	A2	95.23	0.00

Table 4: Evaluation of each annotator.

We also evaluated each annotation with the final gold standard as reference (ignoring null-links). The result in Table 4 shows that these evaluations resulted in an alignment error rate of 0, which makes sense since both are perfectly valid human alignments. Table 4 also contains the result of evaluating each annotation with the other as reference which resulted in very low error rates.

4.3 Training Data Alignment

The training data guidelines were written to produce word alignments that cover as much of the text as possible while preserving the semantic and syntactic correspondence between aligned segments. The alignment followed the same principles as the test data alignment except that no confidence labels were used. A link is either a regular link or a null link. Words are the preferred unit of alignment and phrase alignments should be as small as possible. Training data alignment guidelines are similar to the Blinker guidelines although null links are used more often to avoid large phrase alignments. The training data was aligned by one annotator.

4.4 Alignment Annotation Tools

The manual alignments were produced using two tools, I*Link (Ahrenberg et al., 2003) and the Alpaco_sp editor[2] (Lambert et al., 2005). I*Link is a a tool for interactive word alignment that simplifies the manual alignment process by suggesting alignments which the user can choose to either accept or reject. The user can also override suggested alignments and add new ones. This method of alignment is relatively fast but I*link can not distinguish between possible and sure links, and it does not allow alignment of discontinuous segments such as when the two parts of a particle verb *låser upp* (*Eng.* unlock) are separated by a pronoun as in *låser* du *upp* – you *unlock*.

The Alpaco_sp alignment editor is a tool for manual word alignment with confidence labels. After aligning sure and continuous segments with I*Link, annotators used Alpaco to refine the alignments by adding possible links and links for discontinuous segments where appropriate.

5   Word Alignment Evaluation

Word alignment quality is evaluated either intrinsically by comparing alignments to a reference alignment or extrinsically by measuring the impact of the alignments in an application. In intrinsic evaluation, standard measures of precision (1), recall (2) and F-measure (3) are calculated by comparing a set of computed alignments A to a set of gold standard alignments G.

$$\text{Precision}(A,G) = \frac{|G \cap A|}{|A|} \qquad (1)$$

$$\text{Recall}(A,G) = \frac{|G \cap A|}{|G|} \qquad (2)$$

$$\text{F-measure}(P,R) = \frac{2PR}{P+R} \qquad (3)$$

Different weights can be assigned to precision and recall when calculating F-score by varying

---

[2] http://gps-tsc.upc.es/veu/personal/lambert/scripts/alpaco_sp.tgz

α in the general formulation of the F-measure, shown in (4).

$$\text{F-measure}(A, G, \alpha) = \cfrac{1}{\cfrac{\alpha}{Precision(A,G)} + \cfrac{(1-\alpha)}{Recall(A,G)}} \quad (4)$$

Setting $\alpha = 0.5$ results in the standard balanced F-measure that gives equal weight to precision and recall. A lower α-constant will weight recall higher and a larger constant will favor high precision.

Alignment Error Rate (5) is a quality measure that uses the confidence labels in the gold standard (Och and Ney, 2003). It takes into account the fact that sure links (S) should be more important to get right than possible links (P) when calculating alignment accuracy. It is based on a different formulation of precision and recall, where recall errors only can be made if the computed alignment lacks a sure link (6) and precision errors only when a computed link is not even a possible link in the reference (7). Sure links are by definition also possible.

$$\text{AER}(A,P,S) = 1 - \frac{|S \cap A| + |P \cap A|}{|S| + |A|} \quad (5)$$

$$\text{Recall}(A,S) = \frac{|S \cap A|}{|S|} \quad (6)$$

$$\text{Precision}(A,P) = \frac{|P \cap A|}{|A|} \quad (7)$$

5.1 Word Alignment and SMT

Researchers in statistical MT want to improve word alignment in order to produce better translations. However, several studies have shown that improvements in terms of AER often fail to result in improved translation quality, (e.g., Ayan and Dorr, 2006; Fraser and Marcu, 2006). Translation quality can be measured in terms of the Bleu metric (Papineni et al., 2001). One reason for this lack of correlation between intrinsic and extrinsic evaluation measures is that AER favours high-precision alignments. Fraser and Marcu (2006) found that although precision is important for translation systems trained on small corpora, the importance of recall increases as the amount of data grows and alignment quality improves. In a standard PBSMT system, word alignments control which phrases are extracted as possible translations. A sparse, high-precision alignment is more ambiguous and phrase extraction heuristics will

extract more alternative phrase translations. Especially for systems trained on small corpora the many alternative translations in the phrase table seem to be beneficial to translation quality (Lambert et al., 2009).

The connection between word alignment and phrase extraction suggests that other alignment characteristics than alignment precision and recall might be important for extracting the right phrases. For instance, correctly aligned discontinuous phrases such as German particle verbs can prevent the extraction of useful phrases from embedded words and removing these (correct) links improved translation quality (Vilar et al., 2006).

A better correlation between intrinsic measures of alignment quality and translation quality have been found by having a large proportion of S links in the reference (Lambert et al., 2005) or by only having S links (Fraser and Marcu, 2006). In addition, Fraser and Marcu, achieved better correlation for Arabic–English and French–English when using the general F-measure weighed in favor of recall as the intrinsic measure instead of AER.

6 Experiments on English–Swedish Europarl

In this section we use our gold standard to compare intrinsic alignment quality measures with translation quality for PBSMT systems built on the English–Swedish Europarl corpus. Our aim is to investigate how well alignment quality metrics and translation quality correlate for this corpus and how variables such as corpus size and translation direction affect the correlation.

Our alignment and translation experiments were performed on two corpora of different size, a small corpus containing 100K sentence pairs and a large corpus of 700K sentence pairs. We used the Giza++ word alignment system (Och and Ney, 2003) to create four alignments for each corpus with varying precision and recall. The four alignments were produced using different heuristics to create a single alignment from the source-to-target and target-to-source alignments produced by Giza++. The alignment with highest precision takes the *intersection* (I) of links from the two alignments, the alignment with highest recall takes the *union* (U), and heuristics *grow-diag* (GD) and *grow-diag-final* (GDF) create alignments from the intersection and add links from the union to increase alignment recall.

	small						large					
					Bleu%						Bleu%	
Align	P	R	F	AER	en-sv	sv-en	P	R	F	AER	en-sv	sv-en
I	95.6	56.4	71.0	16.3	22.9	28.3	96.5	60.8	74.6	12.9	23.7	30.0
GD	83.2	73.7	78.2	15.0	23.1	28.5	85.3	76.9	80.9	12.6	24.7	30.7
GDF	73.7	77.4	75.5	19.5	22.8	28.3	77.6	79.5	78.6	16.2	24.7	30.6
U	69.9	78.4	73.9	21.7	22.4	27.9	75.0	80.7	77.7	17.5	24.9	30.3

Figure 4: Intrinsic and extrinsic evaluation of Swedish–English word alignment.

Alignments were evaluated against the 192 sentences in the gold standard test set. To investigate the correlation between intrinsic quality measures and machine translation quality on our corpus, we built standard phrase-based SMT systems using Moses (Koehn et al., 2007), one for each alignment and translation direction, resulting in eight systems for each corpus size.

System parameters were tuned using a development set of 1000 sentence pairs. Each system was evaluated on a test set of 2000 sentences and translation quality was measured in Bleu. Table 4 contains alignment quality scores precision, recall, F-measure and AER and Bleu scores for each translation system.

The table shows that different alignments generally have a small effect on Bleu score. The change is 0.6-0.7 Bleu points for the small systems and 0.7-1.2 Bleu points for the large systems.

The alignment heuristic with the best AER (*grow-diag*) produces the best translation in most systems, but the correlation between AER and Bleu is not strong for all conditions and alignment heuristics. Table 5 shows the correlation between $1 - AER$ and Bleu measured by the Pearson product-moment correlation coefficient, r. This correlation is quite strong for the small dataset ($r = 0.92$ and $r = 0.84$), but negative for the larger dataset ($r = -0.59$ and $r = -0.01$). This is consistent with earlier findings that high-precision alignments which are favored by the AER measure tend to result in better translation quality when systems are trained on smaller corpora.

Higher correlation have been reported between F-score and Bleu. Fraser and Marcu (2006) found the highest correlation by adapting the precision/recall weights in the F-measure to different corpora sizes and language pairs.

To find the optimal weights of precision and recall for our data set we set α in (4) to different values in the range $0.1, .., 0.9$. Table 5 shows the

α that results in the best correlation with Bleu for each system. For the small dataset, the best correlation was found with a constant of 0.6 and for the large data set the best constant was 0.1 and 0.5 respectively. This also supports the hypothesis that precision is more important to systems trained on small corpora while recall is more important for systems trained on large corpora.

There are also differences in the optimal balance between precision and recall between the two translation directions for the system trained on the large corpus. Translation from English to Swedish seems to benefit from higher alignment recall, while the quality of Swedish to English translation depends more equally on precision and recall.

Corpus		Best α	Correlation r		
			F_α	$F_{0.5}$	1-AER
small	en-sv	0.6	0.91	0.45	0.92
	sv-en	0.6	0.87	0.48	0.84
large	en-sv	0.1	0.99	0.80	-0.59
	sv-en	0.5	0.99	0.99	-0.01

Table 5: Correlation between measures of word alignment accuracy and Bleu.

7 Conclusion

We have presented a freely available gold standard for English–Swedish word alignment which can be used to train and evaluate word alignment systems. We described the alignment guidelines for manual annotation that we developed for Swedish–English word alignment which were based on previous research in producing gold standards for other languages for the purpose of statistical machine translation.

In addition, we showed how the gold standard reference can be used to evaluate different word alignment methods and compared it to an external evaluation in a statistical machine translation system. We measured the correlation between alignment quality metrics and translation quality.

Our results support the findings for other language pairs that recall plays a more important role for MT systems trained on large corpora, while precision is more important for systems trained on smaller corpora. However, in the translation direction Swedish–English translation quality was not as dependent on alignment recall. We believe this observation warrants further investigation using a larger sample of alignments.

We also plan to investigate the relationship between alignment and translation by measuring other characteristics of the alignment which may affect translation quality, such as aligned word types and the number of discontinuous links.

References

Lars Ahrenberg, Magnus Merkel, and Michael Petterstedt. 2003. Interactive word alignment for language engineering. In *Proceedings of EACL 2003*, pages 49–52, Budapest, Hungary.

Lars Ahrenberg. 2007. LinES: An English-Swedish parallel treebank. In *Proceedings of Nodalida 2007*, pages 270–273, Tartu, Estonia.

Necip Fazil Ayan and Bonnie J. Dorr. 2006. A maximum entropy approach to combining word alignments. In *Proceedings of HLT-NAACL 2006*, pages 96–103, Morristown, NJ, USA.

Phil Blunsom and Trevor Cohn. 2006. Discriminative word alignment with conditional random fields. In *Proceedings of COLING-ACL 2006*, pages 65–72, Sydney, Australia.

Alexander Fraser and Daniel Marcu. 2006. Semi-supervised training for statistical word alignment. In *Proceedings of COLING-ACL 2006*, pages 769–776, Sydney, Australia.

William A. Gale and Kenneth W. Church. 1991. A program for aligning sentences in bilingual corpora. In *Proceedings of ACL 1991*, pages 177–184, Berkeley, California, USA.

Qin Gao, Nguyen Bach, and Stephan Vogel. 2010. A semi-supervised word alignment algorithm with partial manual alignments. In *Proceedings of WMT and MetricsMATR*, pages 1–10, Uppsala, Sweden.

Maria Holmqvist. 2010. Heuristic word alignment with parallel phrases. In *Proceedings of LREC 2010*, Valletta, Malta.

Abraham Ittycheriah and Salim Roukos. 2005. A maximum entropy word aligner for Arabic–English machine translation. In *Proceedings of HLT-EMNLP 2005*, pages 89–96, Vancouver, Canada.

Philipp Koehn, Hieu Hoang, Alexandra Birch, Chris Callison-Burch, Marcello Federico, Nicola Bertoldi, Brooke Cowan, Wade Shen, Christine Moran, Richard Zens, Chris Dyer, Ondrej Bojar, Alexandra Constantin, and Evan Herbst. 2007. Moses: Open source toolkit for statistical machine translation. In *Proceedings of ACL 2007, demo session*, Prague, Czech Republic.

Philipp Koehn. 2005. Europarl: A parallel corpus for statistical machine translation. In *Proceedings of MT Summit X*, Phuket, Thailand.

Patrik Lambert, Adrià de Gispert, Rafael Banchs, and José B. Mariño. 2005. Guidelines for word alignment evaluation and manual alignment. *Language Resources and Evaluation*, 39:267–285.

Patrik Lambert, Yanjun Ma, Sylwia Ozdowska, and Andy Way. 2009. Tracking relevant alignment characteristics for machine translation. In *Proceedings of MT Summit XII*, Ottawa, Canada.

Lieve Macken. 2010. An annotation scheme and gold standard for Dutch-English word alignment. In *Proceedings of LREC 2010*, Valletta, Malta.

I. Dan Melamed. 1998. Annotation style guide for the Blinker project, version 1.0. Technical report, University of Pennsylvania.

Rada Mihalcea and Ted Pedersen. 2003. An evaluation exercise for word alignment. In *HLT-NAACL 2003 Workshop: Building and Using Parallel Texts*, pages 1–10, Edmonton, Canada.

Franz Josef Och and Hermann Ney. 2003. A systematic comparison of various statistical alignment models. *Computational Linguistics*, 29(1):19–51.

Kishore Papineni, Salim Roukos, Todd Ward, and Wei-Jing Zhu. 2001. BLEU: A method for automatic evaluation of machine translation. In *Proceedings of ACL 2001*, pages 311–318, Philadelphia, Pennsylvania, USA.

Jörg Tiedemann. 2009. News from OPUS - A collection of multilingual parallel corpora with tools and interfaces. In *RANLP*, vol. V, pages 237–248. Borovets, Bulgaria.

David Vilar, Maja Popović, and Hermann Ney. 2006. AER: Do we need to "improve" our alignments? In *Proceedings of IWSLT 2006*, pages 205–212, Kyoto, Japan, November.

Martin Volk, Torsten Marek, and Yvonne Samuelsson. 2009. SMULTRON (version 2.0) - The Stockholm MULtilingual parallel TReebank. An English-German-Swedish parallel Treebank with sub-sentential alignments.

Jean Véronis. 2000. Evaluation of parallel text alignment systems: the ARCADE project. In *Parallel text processing: Alignment and use of translation corpora*, pages 369–388. Dordrecht: Kluwer Academic Publishers.

ISSN 1736-6305 Vol. 11
http://hdl.handle.net/10062/16955

Relevance Prediction in Information Extraction
using Discourse and Lexical Features

Silja Huttunen, Arto Vihavainen, Peter von Etter, Roman Yangarber
Department of Computer Science
University of Helsinki, Finland
`First.Last@cs.helsinki.fi`

Abstract

We present on-going work on estimating the relevance of the results of an Information Extraction (IE) system. Our aim is to build a user-oriented measure of utility of the extracted factual information. We describe experiments using *discourse-level features*, with classifiers that learn from users' ratings of relevance of the results.

Traditional criteria for evaluating the performance of IE focus on correctness of the extracted information, e.g., in terms of recall, precision and F-measure. We introduce subjective criteria for evaluating the quality of the extracted information: utility of results to the end-user.

To measure utility, we use methods from text mining and linguistic analysis to identify features that are good predictors of the relevance of an event or a document to a user. We report on experiments in two real-world news domains: business activity and epidemics of infectious disease.

1 Introduction

In this paper we present on-going work aimed at finding user-oriented relevance measures for information extracted from plain-text news articles. Measure for relevance has been created in collaboration with actual end users of our system. End users view and rate the utility of extracted events using our online news surveillance service.

We aim to show that by utilizing domain-specific and domain-independent sets of features we can build and train a system that is able to predict the utility of new information obtained by an Information Extraction system. We apply the methods on two domains in order to demonstrate that the approach is, in principle, domain independent, and easily adapted to different domains.

Our target domains are business news, with the focus on analyzing reports about corporate acquisitions and new product launches, and medical news, with the focus on outbreaks and spread of infectious diseases. These topics are actively researched in the IE community, e.g. (Grishman et al., 2003; Freifeld et al., 2008; Cvitas, 2010; Saggion et al., 2007).

The news extraction and relevance prediction works in three phases. The first phase identifies articles potentially relevant to a target domain using a broad keyword-based Web search – this is done continuously. The second phase employs IE to extract events from acquired articles, and the final phase then determines the *relevance* of the extracted events or articles for the end-user.

For the business domain the system extracts the names of the companies involved in the target activities (corporate acquisitions and product launches), date, location, value of the transaction (if any) and, for the product-launch scenario, the product type. An example of a sentence reporting a corporate acquisition event: *"Air New Zealand said Friday it has bought 14.9 percent of Australia's Virgin Blue for $143 million."* A product-launch event is found, e.g., in *"An executive at T-Mobile said the company was introducing its new DriveSmart service at the request of customers."* For the medical domain the system extracts which victims were affected by what diseases, where and when. An example sentence *"The HSE in Ireland has said that there have been a further four deaths from human swine flu in the past week"* induces an event, with attributes country, disease, number of casualties, and the time of occurrence.

In the next section, we briefly present the criteria for judging *quality* of extracted events, and present the approach taken in our system. Section 3 introduces the features we use for predicting utility. Section 4 discusses our experimental setup and gives a short system description of the relevance generation process. Section 5 presents our current experiments and results with automatic assignment of relevance scores. In the final section we discuss the results and outline next steps.

2 Quality measures

In IE research, performance has been traditionally measured in terms of *correctness*, counting how many of the fields in each record were correctly extracted by comparing the system's answers to a set of answers pre-defined by human annotators. In the MUC and ACE initiatives, e.g., this was computed mainly in terms of recall and precision, and F-measure, (Hirschman, 1998; ACE, 2004).

We would like to distinguish *objective* vs. *subjective* measures of quality. Objective measures take the perspective of the system in evaluating the obtained IE results in terms of correctness and confidence. Confidence has been studied to estimate the probability of the correctness of the system's answer, in e.g. (Culotta and McCallum, 2004). Our IE system, PULS, computes *confidence* using *discourse-level cues*, (Steinberger et al., 2008), such as: confidence decreases as the distance between the sentence containing the event and event attributes increases; confidence increases if a document mentions only one country.

Subjective measures reflect the end users' perspective, that is the relevance (or utility) of the extracted information, and the reliability[1] of the information found (von Etter et al., 2010).

Utility measures how *useful* the result is to the user *irrespective* of its correctness. An event may be correctly extracted, and yet be of low utility to the user.[2] Conversely, an event may have many incorrectly extracted attributes, and yet be of great *value* and interest to the user.

We focus specifically on relevance vs. correctness. The relevance ratings currently used in our

work are listed in Table 1. Our goal is, specifically to devise methods for automatic assignment of relevance scores to extracted events, and to the documents in which they are found.

Criteria	*Score*
New information highly relevant	5
Important updates, on-going developments	4
Review of current events, hypothetical, predictions	3
Historical/non-current background information	2
Non-specific, non-factive events, secondary topics	1
Unrelated to target domain	0

Table 1: Guidelines for relevance scores

The users assign the scores as presented in the Likert-like scale, Table 1. In the work and experiments reported in this paper, these scores are reduced for simplicity, into either a three-way classification—high (4–5), low (1–3) and irrelevant (0), or a binary classification— where events with high relevance are those with a score of 4–5, and low-relevance events have a score of 0–3. The binary classification is useful because one immediate purpose of introducing the relevance score is for the system to determine whether to present the extracted event to the end user on the main page of the site—which is a binary decision.

3 Linguistic Features

In this section we describe the features that we use in our system for predicting the relevance of an event. These features were devised through a detailed analysis of the domains and user-evaluated events, and were chosen based on their potential for relevance prediction.

Many features are characterized in terms of the event *trigger* and its *attributes*. Our IE system operates by pattern matching, (Grishman et al., 2002).[3] A trigger sentence is where an event pattern matches, signaling a mention of an event at that point in the document. For example, in the sentence "... *Department says there have been*

---

[1] *Reliability* measures whether the reported event is "true", or trustworthy. We include this criterion for completeness, since it is the ultimate goal of any news surveillance process. However, this requires pragmatic knowledge, including information that is obtainable by the user only through downstream verification, and is thus beyond the scope of this paper.

[2] Historical or hypothetical events, e.g., may not be useful for an analyst concerned with the current state of affairs.

[3] The system has a large set of domain-specific linguistic patterns, which map from surface-syntactic representation of the facts in the sentence to the semantic representation in the database records.

eight confirmed cases of measles, after an out-break at Royal Perth Hospital." a pattern is triggered by the phrase "cases of *disease*". The attributes of the event correspond to the fills in the database record, in this example, the name of the disease, the location, date, the number of cases, etc. Several events may appear in a news article.

We distinguish *discourse features* and *lexical features*. Discourse features are based on properties of the article text and of the events extracted from it. Lexical features are simpler low-level features based on bags of words, discussed in section 3.2. In essence, lexical features capture local information, while discourse features capture longer-range relationships within the document.

3.1 Discourse Features

Discourse features include information about the number of events, positioning of the event in the document, the compactness of the placement of the event's attributes (Bagga and Biermann, 1997; Huttunen et al., 2002), and the recency of event occurrence.

3.1.1 Layout and positioning

We introduce a set of features describing the position of the trigger sentence within the document. These help to quantify the assumption that important details of news topics are placed in the beginning of an article whereas less important details are stated later.[4] Layout features include the length of the document and the position of the trigger sentence in the document.

Figure 1 shows the distribution of the relative location of the event in the text, given that the event has a high relevance score (4-5), low relevance (1-3), or is completely irrelevant (score 0).

Figure 2 shows that high-relevance events favor the placement of the trigger sentence in the document *header*, i.e., in the headline or the first two sentences of the news article.

3.1.2 Event compactness

In a compact event, all the event attributes are situated close to the trigger in the text. The *compactness features* track the distance of mentions of event attributes from the event trigger. We model the effect of compactness on relevance of an event by, e.g., measuring the distance between the trigger and the disease name (for epidemics domain) or a company name (for business domain).

---

[4]The so-called "Inverted Pyramid" principle, (Bell, 1991)

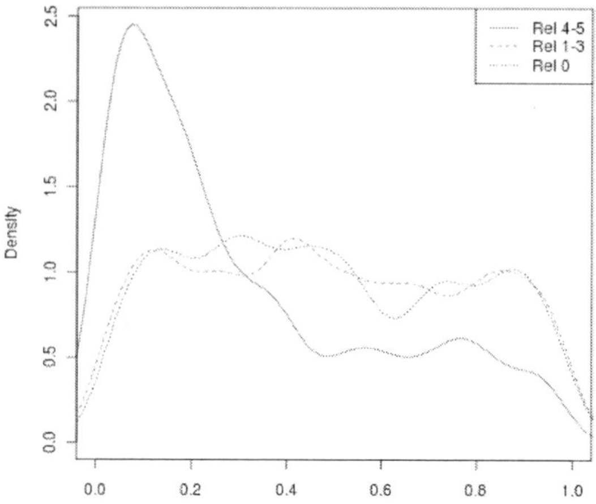

Figure 1: Distributions of relative trigger position in medical domain, given relevance class (high/low/zero)

The distance is measured as the number of bytes, words, or sentences. The "active" participating attributes of an event are here called *actors*.

Figure 3 shows the distribution of the distance in sentences (horizontal axis) between disease name and trigger (or absence of disease name in document) given high, low and zero relevance. The name of a disease is more likely to occur in a trigger sentence of a high-relevance event than in the trigger sentence of low-relevance event. For events that contain no actor at all, the feature receives a special value *NA*.

Content-repetition features test whether an important fill, such as an actor, is repeated in the document (likely affecting relevance positively). Conversely, features that count the number *distinct* actors mentioned in text may be good indicators of lower relevance—such as an article mentioning many different diseases or companies is less likely to be of high relevance.

3.1.3 Time and recency

Time features relate to the recency of an event, comparing the time attributes of an event with the publication date of the news article, i.e., the difference between publication date and the reported event date. The system may extract different kinds of events, including hypothetical events, and events with the event date in the future. Highly rel-

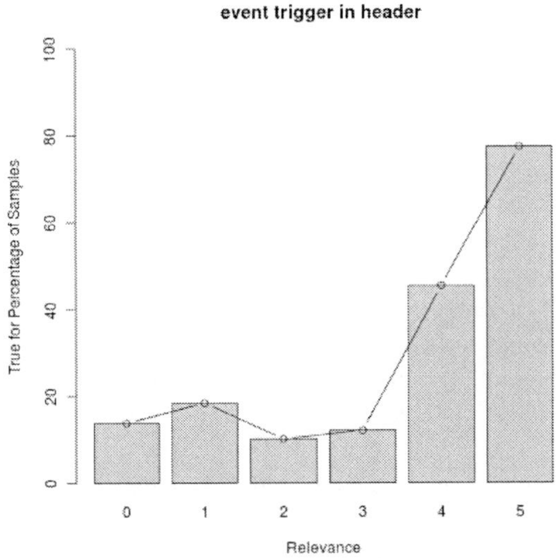

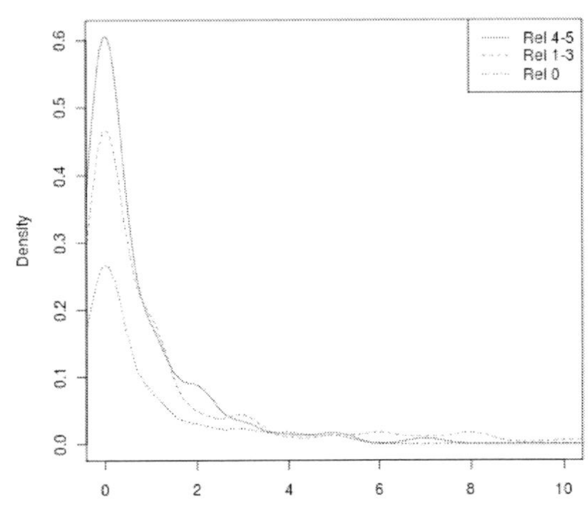

Figure 2: Probability that the trigger of the current event is in the header for medical domain, given the different relevance scores.

Figure 3: Distribution of distance from trigger to name of the disease. Instances with no disease, or with distance > 10 are mapped to the point distance $= 20$ (not shown in the figure).

evant articles, usually describe more recent events. Recency is a good indicator for relevance, as can be seen in Figure 4.

3.1.4 Indicators of irrelevant domains

For each domain, we devise a set of *blacklist features* that signal low relevance in respect to a given domain. Negative indicators for epidemic surveillance, may be, e.g., "vaccination campaign" and "obituary". The latter is a common source of false positives when the deceased suffered from illnesses during his/her lifetime, and the IE patterns fail to distinguish those from epidemics cases, on *local* cues alone.

In the business domain, an indicator of low relevance is, e.g., "President", possibly followed by a proper name, and a country. This mostly refers to a head of state, rather than head of a company.

The PULS system extracts "negative events", (called here *harm events*), as well, to catch events that frequently interfere with events of interest. For example, in the business domain, satellite/rocket launches may trigger patterns for finding product launches, since they are syntactically similar; natural disasters (flooding, earthquake, etc.) with casualties often interfere with patterns in for medical domain. The number of found harm events in a document is a discourse feature.

A missing attribute may also be an indication

of an irrelevant event. Events rejected or marked irrelevant by the user are more likely to be missing the name of a disease. The system also extracts victim names where possible, since obituaries, stories about public figures, and other items irrelevant from the epidemiological perspective, tend to name the victims.[5]

The number of unique actors preceding the trigger sentences is potentially correlated with irrelevance.[6] For example, if no disease names exist before the trigger sentence, then the document is likely to be irrelevant. On the other hand, important news events often mention only a single disease or company. The discourse features used in the experiments are listed in Table 2.

3.2 Lexical Features

Lexical features for an event consists of bags of words in the trigger sentence, and in the sentences immediately preceding and following the trigger sentence. The surrounding sentences provide additional context for disambiguation. For example,

---

[5]On the other hand, some news articles about genuine epidemic outbreaks may name the victims as well—to personalize them for the reader. All these features only capture tendencies and probabilities, and are not deterministic.

[6]PULS system normalizes and unifies variants of disease names and organization names, e.g., Swine Flu with H1N1; company full-names and acronyms.

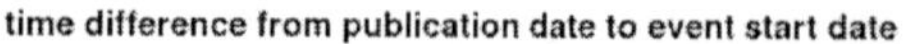

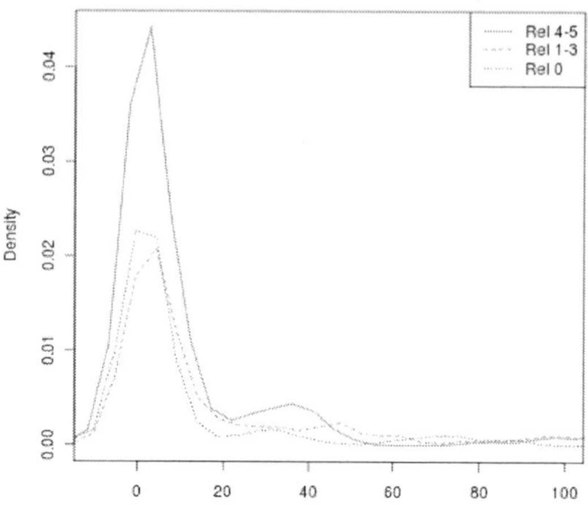

Figure 4: Distribution of the difference days from publication to event date in medical domain. Negative values indicate events in the future.

the trigger sentence may include deaths and injuries, but in principle the article could be about any kind of casualties.

3.3 Domain specificity

Some features are applicable directly to different domains. An example of such features are the recency features, which compare the event date to the publication date of the document. Other features are domain-specific, and make use of the domain-specific attributes. For example, we may check the position of an actor attribute, and see whether it appears in the headline. In the medical domain, such an attribute would be the disease name, in the business domain, we use the company name in an analogous fashion.

4 Experimental Setup and System Description

Next, we briefly describe how the relevance classifiers are built. We have an online news surveillance system that allows users to review, rate and correct events extracted from news articles. The work-flow for finding relevant events is as follows:

The system's information retrieval (IR) component continuously polls news sites, (Yangarber et al., 2007). News filtering is done using Boolean keyword-based queries. The result is a continuous

Layout features
event-trigger-is-in-header/headline
any-event-trigger-found-in-header/headline
trigger's-relative-location
actor-in-trigger/header/headline
country-in-trigger/header/headline
document-length
Compactness
Trigger-actor-distance
Is-actor-found-before-trigger-sentence-end
Num-uniq-countries/actors-in-trigger-sentence
Num-uniq-countries/actors-until-trigger-end
Num-uniq-countries/actors-in-document-events
Contains-valid-country/actor
Content-repeated-in-header/document
Num-of-events-in-document
Time
Event-has-time-of-occurrence
Distance-trigger-sentence-to-date-span
Time-diff-pubdate-event-start/end
Low relevance indicators
Is-blacklisted-data-in-header/
Headline/document
Num-of-harm-events-in-document
Domain-specific (epidemic domain)
Victim-count
Is-named-victim
Is-unspecified-illness

Table 2: Examples of discourse features

stream of potentially relevant documents, that is forwarded to the information extraction system.

Our IE system then extracts events of potential relevance from this stream of articles. The extracted information, i.e., the structured events with their attributes, is stored into a database. The IE component uses a large set of linguistic patterns, which in turn utilize general and domain-specific concepts, such as diseases, locations and organizations.

Once the attributes of an event have been extracted, the relevance classifier is invoked. Each event is converted to a feature vector, to which a classifier assigns a relevance score.

After the event receives a relevance score, it appears on the on-line server. Relevance predictions are highlighted with different colors, which enhances the user experience and allows easy notification of high relevance events.

The system's user interface (UI) provides a simple editing facility for the extracted events. In case of errors in the automatic extraction, the UI allows the user to correct erroneous fills, e.g., if a company name, country, or a disease name was extracted incorrectly. In addition to editing the event fills, the users can also assign or edit the relevance labels to the extracted events. The set of events that have been corrected and/or relevance-labeled manually by human users are used for training and testing the relevance classifiers.

In the business domain, we use a set of hand-labeled data, in which currently roughly 45% of the events are high-relevance, and 55% are low-relevance. In the medical domain, about 80% of examples are labeled with lower relevance. We experimented with building balanced and unbalanced classifiers for the medical domain; we took a sample from the complete labeled set, so that the class distribution in the sample is about even—i.e., the randomly sampled training subset is balanced so it contains about the same amount of low- and high-relevance events.

Since parts of the labeled data are actually corrected by the user, we obtain *two* parallel sets of events with relevance labels: the "raw" events, as extracted by the system, and corresponding "cleaned" events, i.e., the same events with corrections. The raw set is more noisy, since it contains the errors that were introduced by the system.

The relevance classifiers are built using the cleaned labeled data. For evaluation, we test the classifier performance against both the cleaned and the raw events. We focus on classification performance on the raw events, because ultimately the goal is to build a classifier that can be applied to the extracted event stream, which are not validated or corrected by the end-user. In any case, the IE system must assign the relevance score to each event, before a user examines it, and possibly validates it. Therefore, the "raw" scores in the evaluation give us an indication of what performance we can expect in the real-world setting.[7]

5   Evaluation Methodology and Results

The predictive power of our features is evaluated by using three different classifiers: Naive Bayes (John and Langley, 1995), SVM (Platt, 1999) and BayesNet (Bouckaert, 2004). We used

the implementations from the WEKA toolkit (Hall et al., 2009), which provides a collection of machine learning algorithms.

Evaluations are done using a 10-fold cross-validation. We evaluated the results using precision, recall, F-measure and accuracy for high/low-relevance classification. It is important to note that when we split the corpus into 10 parts, we make sure that for any given document, *all* events found in that document fall within the same split—to assure that a document never contributes events to both the training and the testing set.

5.1 Business domain

In the business domain, we use about 213 user-labeled events, in 127 documents. Table 3 shows classification performance achieved on discourse, lexical and combined features. Discourse feature construction is as described in section 3. We currently utilize roughly 40 discourse-level features.

In the table, we report the system's performance on *all* events in our labeled corpus, as well as only on events that appear *first* within a document (which may contain more than one event). The first-event evaluation is interesting since we can view it as an additional document-level *text-filtering* task, where the relevance of the first event is used to define the relevance of the entire document.

We train two types of binary classifiers: the high-vs-low classifiers separate between events labeled 4–5 and 0–3. The zero-vs-rest classifiers separate the zero-relevance (i.e., completely useless) events from the rest. In each case, the F-measure is calculated for predicting the higher-relevance class.

For each classifier, we show the performance using discourse features only, lexical features only, and the combined set of features. The classifiers are trained with feature selection using information gain. In the table, the bold score indicates the best score achieved for the given column.

5.2 Medical domain

Table 4 shows the classification results using the same strategy as in business domain. In most cases, discourse features perform better than lexical features, and combining the discourse and lexical features improves the predictive performance over both discourse and lexical features alone. These classifications were obtained on approximately 900 events, in 530 documents.

---

[7]Note that, on the other hand, it makes less sense to train the classifier on raw data, since it is inherently more noisy, degrades the classifier performance.

Business Domain

High-vs-low	Lexical		Discourse *(All events)*		Combined		Lexical		Discourse *(First events only)*		Combined	
SVM	72.2	(0.696)	84.6	(0.83)	**85.3**	**(0.833)**	70.4	(0.738)	81.8	(0.826)	81.4	(0.818)
Naive Bayes	74.3	(0.73)	75.7	(0.753)	82.5	(0.814)	70.3	(0.731)	81.7	(0.823)	82.2	(0.825)
Bayes Net	75.3	(0.73)	84.2	(0.823)	84.5	(0.823)	71.6	(0.718)	81.5	(0.822)	**82.8**	**(0.834)**
Zero-vs-rest												
SVM	81.0	(0.894)	84.8	(0.916)	82.6	(0.904)	84.0	(0.912)	84.4	(0.914)	84.7	(0.916)
Naive Bayes	84.8	(0.915)	83.0	(0.906)	**85.5**	**(0.92)**	**89.2**	**(0.94)**	83.6	(0.91)	86.2	(0.924)
Bayes Net	83.0	(0.908)	82.4	(0.903)	81.7	(0.899)	84.2	(0.915)	84.2	(0.915)	84.1	(0.914)

Table 3: Relevance classification results on business domain: accuracy and F-measure (in parentheses) for discourse features, lexical features, and combined features.

Medical Domain

High-vs-low	Lexical		Discourse *(All events)*		Combined		Lexical		Discourse *(First events only)*		Combined	
SVM	82.2	(0.537)	**85.1**	(0.618)	84.2	(0.613)	87.2	(0.625)	88.5	(0.664)	**89.6**	(0.71)
Naive Bayes	79.7	(0.64)	80.7	(0.598)	84.6	**(0.702)**	85.8	(0.679)	85.0	(0.639)	89.2	**(0.728)**
Bayes Net	80.6	(0.558)	79.1	(0.615)	79.5	(0.64)	82.6	(0.529)	82.0	(0.612)	82.5	(0.619)
Zero-vs-rest												
SVM	83.9	(0.907)	84.8	(0.913)	**85.9**	(0.917)	80.6	(0.888)	81.6	(0.895)	83.0	(0.897)
Naive Bayes	85.3	(0.915)	84.1	(0.908)	85.7	**(0.918)**	82.7	(0.898)	82.5	(0.895)	**83.8**	**(0.902)**
Bayes Net	82.4	(0.903)	81.7	(0.891)	82.1	(0.893)	78.3	(0.876)	78.8	(0.868)	78.2	(0.864)

Table 4: Initial relevance classification results on Medical domain. Accuracy and F-measure (in parentheses) for discourse features, lexical features, and combined features.

6 Discussion and Conclusions

As the quantity of information available from different news services increases rapidly, the capability to extract and highlight relevant news items becomes important. For intelligence officers such as business analysts and epidemiologists, it is important that they can limit the amount of time used to monitor extracted facts.

The relevance classifiers form a component of the on-line news monitoring, to predict the relevance of extracted events to the users. In the experiments in the business domain, the discourse features alone perform better than lexical features. In most cases for the business domain, combining discourse and lexical features helps the classifier. The nature of product launch and corporate acquisition news is typically such that most of the information is available in the first few sentences.

In medical domain, combining discourse and lexical features also generally helps classification performance. Information such as disease type, adjectives related to the event and other subtle hints (e.g. female victims are often described through their family relations) are missing from the discourse features, but have an effect on the classifier performance.

In certain knowledge-intensive domains—such as the ones studied here—missing a relevant news item carries a higher cost to the end-user. In our future work, we will also test classification with different precision-recall-ratio, by adjusting the classification threshold, to model the utility of the results to the users with a preference for high- or low-relevance news items.

To summarize the points addressed in the paper:

- We present prediction of relevance in the task of event extraction in the domains of public health and business intelligence, that we believe to be generalizable to different domains.

- We emphasize the importance of the user's perspective when estimating quality, not just the system's performance. *Relevance* to the user is at least as important as (if not more important than) correctness.

- For the present, we assume that users have the same notion of relevance of an event in a given domain. We do not model differences between individual users (as with collaborative filtering), and treat them as a single group with a shared perspective.

- We have presented experiments and an initial evaluation of assignment of relevance scores.

- Our experiments indicate that relevance is a *tractable* measure of quality, at least in the studied domains.

Our on-going work includes refining the classification approaches, especially exploring feature dependencies using Bayesian networks, extending the system to cover multiple languages, and exploring collaborative filtering to address users' and user-groups differing interests. We are currently working on applying our approach to other domains as well.

Acknowledgements

We thank the anonymous reviewers for their valuable feedback.

References

ACE. 2004. Automatic content extraction.

A. Bagga and A. W. Biermann. 1997. Analyzing the complexity of a domain with respect to an information extraction task. In *Proc. 10th Intl. Conf. on Research on Computational Linguistics (ROCLING X)*.

Allan Bell. 1991. *The Language of News Media*. Language in Society. Blackwell, Oxford, September.

R. Bouckaert. 2004. Bayesian network classifiers in Weka. Technical report.

A Culotta and A McCallum. 2004. Confidence estimation for information extraction. In *Proc. HLT-NAACL*.

A. Cvitas. 2010. Information extraction in business intelligence systems. In *MIPRO, 2010 Proceedings of the 33rd International Convention*.

C.C. Freifeld, K.D. Mandl, B.Y. Reis, and J.S. Brownstein. 2008. HealthMap: Global infectious disease monitoring through automated classification and visualization of internet media reports. *J. Am. Med. Inform. Assoc.*, 15(1).

R. Grishman, S. Huttunen, and R. Yangarber. 2002. Event extraction for infectious disease outbreaks. In *Proc. 2nd Human Language Technology Conf. (HLT 2002)*, San Diego, CA.

R. Grishman, S. Huttunen, and R. Yangarber. 2003. Information extraction for enhanced access to disease outbreak reports. *J. of Biomed. Informatics*, **35**(4).

M. Hall, E. Frank, G. Holmes, B. Pfahringer, P. Reutemann, and I. H. Witten. 2009. The WEKA data mining software: an update. *SIGKDD Explor. Newsl.*, 11(1).

L. Hirschman. 1998. Language understanding evaluations: Lessons learned from MUC and ATIS. In *Proc. First Int'l Conf. on Language Resources and Evaluation (LREC)*, Granada.

S. Huttunen, R. Yangarber, and R. Grishman. 2002. Complexity of event structure in information extraction. In *Proc. 19th Intl. Conf. Computational Linguistics (COLING 2002)*, Taipei.

G. H. John and P. Langley. 1995. Estimating continuous distributions in bayesian classifiers. In *Eleventh Conference on Uncertainty in Artificial Intelligence*, San Mateo. Morgan Kaufmann.

John C. Platt. 1999. Fast training of support vector machines using sequential minimal optimization. In *Advances in kernel methods: support vector learning*. MIT Press, Cambridge, MA, USA.

H. Saggion, A. Funk, D. Maynard, and K. Bontcheva. 2007. Ontology-based information extraction for business intelligence. In *Proc. Intl. Semantic Web Conf. and 2nd Asian Asian Semantic Web Conf.*, ISWC'07/ASWC'07, Berlin, Heidelberg. Springer-Verlag.

R. Steinberger, F. Fuart, E. van der Goot, C. Best, P. von Etter, and R. Yangarber. 2008. Text mining from the web for medical intelligence. In D. Perrotta, J. Piskorski, F. Soulié-Fogelman, and R. Steinberger, editors, *Mining Massive Data Sets for Security*. OIS Press, Amsterdam, the Netherlands.

P. von Etter, S. Huttunen, A. Vihavainen, M. Vuorinen, and R. Yangarber. 2010. Assessment of utility in web mining for the domain of public health. In *Proc. NAACL HLT 2010, Second Louhi Workshop on Text and Data Mining of Health Documents*, Los Angeles, CA.

R. Yangarber, C. Best, P. von Etter, F. Fuart, D. Horby, and R. Steinberger. 2007. Combining information about epidemic threats from multiple sources. In *Proc. RANLP-2007 MMIES Workshop*, Borovets, Bulgaria.

ISSN 1736-6305 Vol. 11
http://hdl.handle.net/10062/16955

What kind of corpus is a web corpus?

Janne Bondi Johannessen
Tektslab, ILN, University of Oslo
`jannebj@iln.uio.no`

Emiliano Raul Guevara
Tektslab, ILN, University of Oslo
`e.r.guevara@iln.uio.no`

Abstract

This paper discusses an investigation into the Norwegian NoWaC corpus. We have compared this web corpus with one corpus of spoken language and one of written language. For nearly all variables that we look at, the web corpus sides with the written corpus, not the spoken one. Thus, despite including language samples from blogs and web forums, NoWaC does not appear to be more speech-like. One exception is interjections, which it does have to some larger extent than the written corpus. It also has taboo words, lacking in the other two. The comparisons have been made purely on the basis of frequency lists, showing that this is a possible and simple way of comparing corpora. We use both a qualitative and quantitative method. In the latter, (log) relative frequency plots show an almost linear relation between NoWaC and the written corpus.

1 Credits

This work depends on the existence of four Norwegian corpora. We are grateful to those who have been central in compiling and developing them. These are: Anne Marit Bødal, Kristin Hagen, Signe Laake, Anders Nøklestad, Joel Priestley (all are former or present staff at the Text Laboratory), Øystein Alexander Vangsnes and Tor Anders Åfarli (central in the compilation of the Nordic Dialect Corpus, and in the network ScanDiaSyn), and the VD group at USIT, UiO, for computing assistance. Finally we want to acknowledge the Keywords for Language Learning for Young and adults alike, KELLY, with project leader Sofie Johansson Kokkinakis, which provided the funding for the compilation and processing of the NoWaC lemma frequency list.

2 Introduction

It is well known that spoken and written language differ from each other in a variety of ways. This has been discussed and shown in, e.g. Akinnaso (1982), Chafe and Tannen (1987), McCarthy (1998), Miller and Weinert (1998), Biber et al. (1999), a special issue of *Studia Linguistica* for spoken language (Johannessen 2008), for Swedish, Allwood (1998) and for Norwegian, Johannessen and Hagen (2008). For the same reason corpora based on written and on spoken language also differ from each other, and are thereby useful for different purposes.

Since the web started to be used as a corpus, and now when there are actual corpora built by mining it (cf. Baroni and Bernardini 2006, Baroni and Kilgariff 2006, Kilgariff 2007, and the workshop series Web as a Corpus), it is interesting to investigate what kind of language the web actually contains. No doubt this will differ from language to language, so we stress here that our investigation is based on Norwegian.

Our aim is two-fold. On the one hand we want to investigate the Norwegian web corpus NoWaC to try to uncover what kind of a corpus it is w.r.t. the spoken/written dimension. The other is to see whether using frequency lists is a useful method in order to determine the differences in genre/register between different corpora.

We will compare NoWaC with one written and one spoken language corpus. Our hypothesis is that NoWaC will be somewhat closer to the spoken language corpus than the written corpus. This is due to the fact that Internet is widely available (88 % of people aged 16/79 used Internet at home in 2010, according to Statistics Norway). In fact Norway was the first country after the USA to have Internet. One would therefore assume that a lot of the contents on the Norwegian web pages would be informal forums and blogs that are by hypothesis speech-like.

However, as we shall see, surprisingly, NoWaC is not like a spoken corpus, in fact it is in many ways even more formal linguistically than the written corpus.

3 Three corpora – three frequency lists

In order to investigate what kind of texts NoWaC contains, we will compare it with two other corpora, which we will describe in turn. But first, let us start with NoWaC.

NoWaC (for details about the methodological steps taken during the contruction of the corpus, see Guevara 2010) is a corpus mined from the web using the bootstrapping guidelines as described in Baroni and Bernardini (2006). It contains about 700 million words of Bokmål Norwegian. With the strict legislation in Norway (the Personal Data Act) and its implementation by the Privacy Ombudsman for Research, mining the web and keeping the data is not legal without special permission, which this corpus obtained from the Ministry of Culture. The version we have used here was tagged with a statistical tagger (Treetagger), trained on a small manually annotated corpus available at the Text Laboratory, UiO.

In addition we have used what we here choose to call the Written Language Corpus, although its official name is the Oslo Corpus of Written Norwegian Bokmål Texts (Johannessen et al. 2000). It has 18 million words, is tagged with the rule-based Oslo Bergen Tagger, and contains about 10 % fiction (in addition to 50 % newspaper and magazine texts and 40 % non-fiction).

Finally we use a combination of two speech corpora, here called the Spoken Language Corpus. These are the Nordic Dialect Corpus (Johannessen et al. 2009) and the NoTa-Oslo: Norwegian Speech Corpus - Oslo part (Johannessen et al. 2007). These contain approximately 2.2 million words from recordings of spontaneous speech in dialogue. They have been transcribed orthographically, and are thus immediately comparable with the written language corpus, and have been grammatically tagged with a statistical tagger.

From these corpora we have compiled frequency lists. Each list contains the 6000 most frequent lemmas of that corpus. It is these lists that we will use in the corpus comparisons in this paper.

Comparing corpora has been a common concern in computational linguistics and in corpus linguistics since the advent of large electronic corpora in the 1990's (see, among others, Hofland and Johansson 1982, Kilgarriff 1997, Rayson and Garside 2000). However, all the measures and methods proposed in the literature concentrate on one of the following two cases:

- comparing a sample (specialistic) corpus to a large(r) reference corpus
- comparing two corpora of roughly the same size

Our situation is different. We have a very large corpus of which we want to determine the linguistic variety, and two smaller reference corpora. In addition, some of the previous methods (e.g. Kilgariff's 1997 "Known Similarity Corpora") cannot be applied to our data without leaving out a substantial part of NoWaC. In what follows we will present a combination of qualitative and quantitative methods addressing our research question.

4 Comparing corpora through frequency lists: a qualitative point of view

Biber et al. (1999) use corpus analysis to distinguish the styles of spoken and written language. They focus on syntactic structures and collocations, which we will not do in this task. However, some syntactic constructions are accompanied by certain words. Biber et al. (op.cit, p.691) find that clauses introduced by *whether* are typically less common in spoken language than *if.*

Incidentally, Norwegian, too, has two words for the introduction of interrogative subordinate clauses, *om* and *hvorvidt.* The results from our three corpora are given in table 1. (Throughout this section, the number represents relative frequency, obtained by dividing the frequency count by corpus size, figures rounded for convenience.)

	Spoken	Written	NoWaC
om 'if'	0.00198	**0.00718**	0.00495
hvorvidt 'whether'	–	**0.00006**	0.00003

Table 1: Two subordinating conjunctions meaning 'whether'.

Hvorvidt has a more bookish feel to it, and this intuition is confirmed by the frequency lists, where it is absent in the spoken language corpus.

But notice that in NoWaC its frequency is relatively lower than in the written text corpus. *Om* confirms this point, showing a strong difference between the spoken corpus on one side, and the written corpus and NoWaC on the other side, but with NoWaC closer to the speech corpus.

Bick (2010) compares five English corpora going from chat, e-mail, to one formal and one informal speech corpus, plus a written text corpus, and shows that many features expected to be more typically informal are indeed so. For example, there is relatively little subordination in the chat corpus. Looking at the subordinator *at* ('that') our results again show that NoWaC is closer to the spoken corpus by a small margin. The written corpus is the most formal of all.

	Spoken	Written	NoWaC
At ('that')	0.00461	**0.01463**	0.00887

Table 2: The subjunction *at* 'that'.

A very interesting finding by Bick (2010:727) regards the distribution of pronouns. He finds that the chat corpus, with live (written) dialogue, has nearly three times as many 3p pronouns as 1p ones, and that the spoken corpus also scores high here, with about twice as many. This is also true of his written corpus, which contains a lot of fiction. The monologues that the e-mails consist of and the formal speeches in his formal speech corpus have very different figures, where the 1p pronouns are more frequent than the 3p ones.

We have tested our three corpora for the singular pronouns of all three grammatical persons. From Bick's paper we would expect our spoken corpus to show the same distribution as the chat corpus, and possibly the written corpus to be quite different, given what we have seen for the other categories above. For NoWaC we would expect it to be closer to the written corpus, on the basis of what we have seen above. The results are given in table 3.

	Spoken	Written	NoWaC
jeg ('I')	**0.02193**	0.01130	0.00875
du ('you')	**0.01147**	0.00429	0.00507
han ('he')	0.00409	**0.01300**	0.00290
hun ('she')	0.00214	**0.00717**	0.00144

Table 3: Personal pronouns

For ease of exposition we illustrate the numbers in the following chart, with the 3p shown cumulatively.

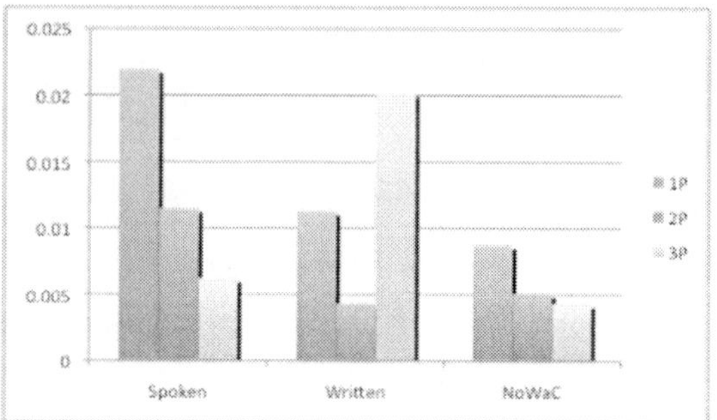

Fig 1: Personal pronouns as chart

However, we do not find quite the same as Bick. The spoken corpus, as expected, has very a high frequency for 1p and a relatively high frequency for 2p. On the contrary, the written corpus that has a relatively high number of 3p pronouns w.r.t. 1p and a lower frequency for 2p. NoWaC shows a mixed picture: it seems to pattern with the spoken corpus regarding 3p, but with the written corpus regarding 1p and 2p.

Why would this be the case? For the spoken corpus the answer has to be found in the way it was recorded. The informants were instructed carefully at the beginning of each session: they were told to avoid (for reasons to do with legal protection of individuals) talking about other people they knew – although they were for the most part also told that it would be acceptable to talk about people who were already in the public eye. This would be the reason that 3p pronouns are not as frequent as they would otherwise have been.

Several researchers look at the difference between spoken and written Norwegian language in Johannessen and Hagen (2008). Both Svein Lie's paper and Søfteland and Nøklestad's paper focus on the particular word *sånn* 'such', which is very typical of spoken language. Vangsnes argues that there is a systematic difference between the status of questions words, with *åssen* 'how' as the most colloquial. Fjeld's paper discusses the many lexical items that are hard to find in dictionaries, which often have a written bias, however implicit. In the table below we investigate words from these papers.

	Spoken	Written	NoWaC
sånn ('such')	**0.00781**	0.00037	0.00024
åssen ('how')	**0.00049**	0.00002	0.000004
do ('loo')	0.00003	0.00002	**0.00004**
dass ('loo')	**0.000004**	-	0.000003

Table 4: Norwegian words typical of spoken language

The first two words in table 4, which are grammatical words, show the same as we have seen earlier, too. NoWaC tends to pair off with the written corpus, while the spoken language corpus is in a different league. The last two words are typical words used in the spoken domain. It is surprising that they occur in the written corpus and NoWaC. We had to further investigate this, and found that both were mixed with other other lemmas that happened to be nouns according to our tags. For *do* 'loo', the less offensive of the two, about half the occurrences in the written corpus are parts of Vietnamese names (*Tranh Thi Le Do*), English phrases (*back/ so I gotta do now*), names of sports (*Tae Kwon Do*), which means that it really should have a much lower relative frequency.

The word *dass* 'loo' is very colloquial and it is not among the 6000 most frequent words in the written corpus. A closer look at the hits in NoWaC reveals that some of the occurrences refer to the surname of the hymn writer Petter Dass, which should of course have been excluded from the lists. It also has many examples of *dass* used in a metaphoric sense (in expressions like 'go down the drain'). To conclude, we find NoWaC to have a bit in common with spoken language w.r.t. *dass*, which is the most colloquial word, although the relative frequencies are rather low. For the other typical spoken words, it sides more with the written corpus.

Interjections are a category that obviously belongs to the spoken domain, so this a category worth looking into.

	Spoken	Written	NoWaC
Ja ('yes')	**0.02701**	0.00056	0.00025
Nei ('no')	**0.00737**	0.00042	0.00021
Oi ('oh')	**0.00019**	-	-
Uff ('oh')	**0.0001**	-	0.000004
Nja ('well')	**0.00007**	-	-
Jøss ('Jesus')	**0.00005**	-	-
Fy ('bad')	**0.00004**	-	-
Æsj ('yuck')	**0.00003**	-	-
Au ('auch')	**0.00003**	-	-

Table 5: Interjections

The interjections show that NoWaC does have some speech-like contents, w.r.t. 'yes' and 'no', but so does the written corpus, both with low figures, as does NoWaC for the one additional internjection it has: *uff* 'oh'. However, NoWaC does contain a lot of different interjections which did not make it into our list of the 6000 most frequent words in the corpus. Looking at the con-

cordances, it is obvious that it is without a doubt blogs and forums, i.e. kinds of dialogue, which are the text types where these interjections are found. An example is given in (1).

(1)   anonym : **æsj** , det suger
         anonymous: yuck, it sucks

Swearing and taboo words are very rare in serious, written texts, so this is an interesting test for NoWaC. The results are given in table 6.

	Spoken	Written	NoWaC
Faen ('devil')	0.00004	**0.00006**	0.00003
Herregud ('Lord God')	**0.00007**	0.00002	0.000009
Fitte ('female sexual organ')	-	-	**0.000007**
Pikk ('male sexual organ)	-	-	**0.000019**

Table 6: Swearing and taboo words

Unexpectedly, the first swear word has a relatively high position in the written material and in NoWaC, while the second one is much more common in the spoken corpus.

However, for taboo words – the last two rows in the table – the NoWaC corpus really differs from both corpora. It is the only corpus containing them, which makes it more informal than even the spoken language corpus.

One must ask why that is. For the spoken corpus the answer is easy: All recordings were done under controlled circumstances. All informants knew that they were being recorded and had a camera directed towards them. While it may be somewhat 'cool' to use swear words by some people (notably young men), swear words and taboo words are still embarrassing. For NoWaC, we had to investigate a bit further. Although we have not looked at all the examples, we have checked some, including googled them for their original context, and found that although clearly the taboo words sometimes occur on informal forums they very often are from porn sites.

To conclude: For typically written language variables, such as formal subordinators, NoWaC is like a written corpus. Looking at variables that will say something about the extent to which spoken topics are concerned, such as subordination, NoWaC is still like a written corpus, although by a small margin. Checking for spoken version words of those that have several variants, NoWaC is still also like a written corpus.

Typically colloquial elements like interjections, swear words and taboo words do not provide us with clear ways to distinguish the corpora and, actually, point out issues with the reliability and "naturalness" of the spoken corpus.

However, we should add that there are also many other interjections among the hundred most frequent words in the spoken corpus, which are not in NoWaC or the written corpus. These are typical discourse markers, especially OCMs (own communication management) used with turn-taking, which do not have a regular spelling, but they have to be regarded as words, indeed interjections, since they have a clearly identifiable phonology and semantics. One example is *mm* (disyllabic, with toneme 2), meaning: 'yes, I agree', which is the 30th most frequent word in the spoken corpus.

The relatively high proportion of taboo words does not necessarily show a speech-like quality of the corpus, but does show that the corpus contains some material not usually contained in carefully compiled corpora.

5 Comparing corpora through frequency lists: a quantitative point of view

As we pointed out in the introductory section, previous methods to compare linguistic corpora rely on the assumption that the comparison is made with corpora of at least the same size. In our case, however, the target of the study is over 300 times larger than the spoken reference corpus. We instead propose to systematically extend the kind of comparison that was presented in the previous section, that is, a correlation analysis between the relative frequencies of words in the different corpora.

In order to accomplish this, we first apply a logarithmic transformation to the frequency counts in the various corpora and create a data frame containing only the lemmas which are present in all the lists with the same POS tag (1810 items). Let us start by simply plotting the obtained data (see Fig. 2 and 3).

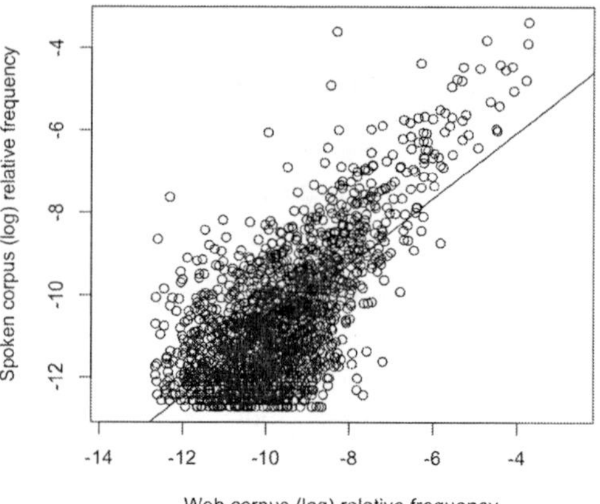

Fig. 2: A plot of corresponding frequencies in the spoken and web-based corpora

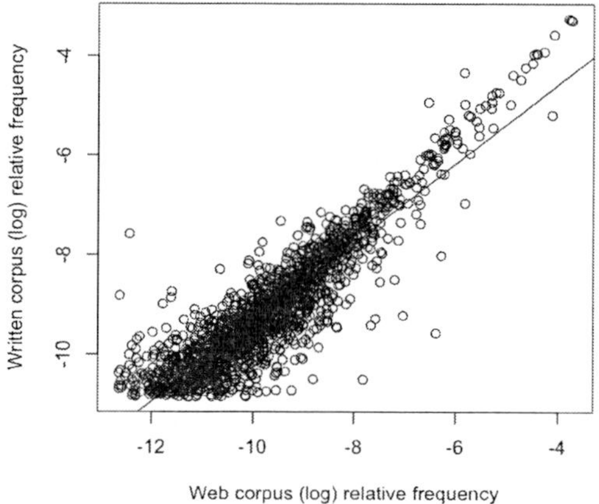

Fig. 3: A plot of corresponding frequencies in the written and web-based corpora

These simple plots already show that the frequencies from the NoWaC and the written corpus have an almost linear relation, while the comparison between web-data and the spoken corpus is much sparser. For an even more striking difference, compare the sparseness of the first cloud of data points with respect to the indicated regression line (simple linear regression).

In addition, the relation of the spoken data with our reference written corpus resembles very closely the cloud that we can see in the first figure above:

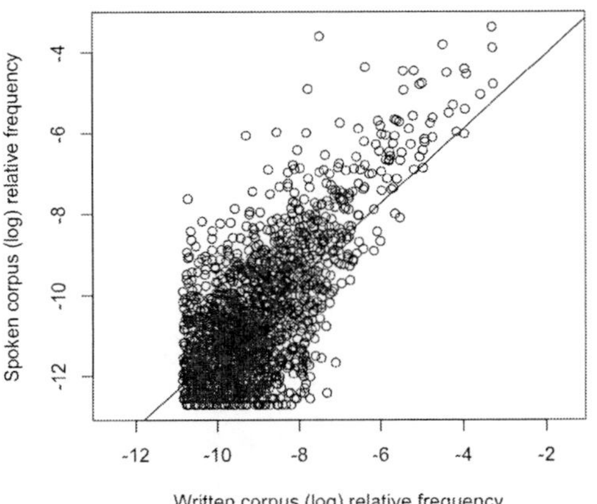

Fig. 4: A plot of corresponding frequencies in the spoken and written corpora

In other words, the spoken corpus seems to bear the same type of loosely linear relation to both the written corpus and NoWaC. On the other hand, NoWaC and the written corpus show a much tighter, linear correspondence which actually approximates quite closely a linear regression line.

To study these relations in depth we calculated Kendall's *tau* coefficient of correlation between the log frequencies obtained from NoWaC and each of the reference corpora. Kendall's *tau* is a robust non-parametric hypothesis test for statistical dependence that does not make any assumption about the distribution of the data. The test is a measure of rank correlation (related to Spearman's *rho*) that is able to deal with tied ranks in the data. We summarize the results in the following table:

Data	Correlation	p-value
NoWaC ~ Spoken	0.4098755	< 0.001
NoWaC ~ Written	**0.705881**	< 0.001
Spoken ~ Written	0.3955764	< 0.001

Table 7: Rank correlation

Clearly, the frequencies from all the used corpora are statistically correlated: this comes as no surprise, given that they share the same language and a great part of the vocabulary. However, the kind of language that was sampled in NoWaC is more closely correlated to the written corpus than to the spoken corpus (differences between the correlation coefficients statistically significant, two tailed p-value < 0.001).

In addition, we also calculated the correlation between the two reference corpora, whose result shows that there is less correlation between them than for each with NoWaC.

We interpret these results as indicating that our web corpus contains primarily a kind of language that is typical of the written register. However, some of its traits are in common with data from the spoken corpus.

In other words, if we consider the spoken and written reference corpora as two endpoints, NoWaC stands between them but not exactly half-way: it is significantly closer to the written end of language.

6 Conclusion

From a purely qualitative point of view, NoWaC is a written language corpus when it comes to proportions of typically written variables. Wherever a word exists in a formal and informal style, the formal style is by far the most common.

However, NoWaC does have interjections that are typical of dialogue, revealing this way that it does have some qualities shared with the spoken corpus. They are also considerably less frequent than in the spoken corpus. NoWaC also has a share of informal words and taboo words, showing that it contains texts that are not common in manually and carefully crafted written corpora, i.e. those that are based on texts from established publishing houses, legal documents etc.

These findings were further corroborated by a test of correlation between the frequencies from all three corpora. NoWaC shows a relatively stronger correlation to the written reference corpus, although it is also correlated significantly to spoken data.

The simple ideas and methods put forward in this paper provide us with plenty of novel insight. The web is the largest source of linguistic data, mostly text. We must be prepared to deal with the intricacies and peculiarities of this source. Although the web's register is primarily written (at least as it has been sampled in NoWaC), we might be witnessing the birth of a distinct register which contains elements of colloquiality and vocabulary from the spoken language.

References

Allwood, Jens. 1998. Some Frequency based Differences between Spoken and Written Swedish. In *Proceedings from the XVI:th Scandinavian Conference of Linguistics*, Department of Linguistics, University of Turku, Finland.

Akinnaso, F. 1982. On the differences between spoken and written language. *Language and Speech*, 25, 2, 97–125.

Baayen, R. Harald. 2008. *Analyzing Linguistic Data.* Cambridge, Cambridge University Press.

Baroni, Marco and Silvia Bernardini (eds.) 2006. *Wacky! Working papers on the Web as Corpus.* Bologna: GEDIT.

Baroni, Marco and Adam Kilgarriff. 2006. Large linguistically-processed web corpora for multiple languages. In *Proceedings of European ACL*, Trento, Italy.

Biber, Douglas, Stig Johansson, Geoffrey Leech, Susan Conrad, and Edward Finegan. 1999. *Longman Grammar of Spoken and Written English.* Pearson Education Ltd, Harlow, Essex, UK.

Bick, Eckhard. 2010. Degrees of Orality in Speech-like Corpora: Comparative Annonatio of Chat and E-mail Corpora. In Otoguro, Ryo; Ishikawa, Kiyoshi; Umemoto, Hiroshi; Yoshimoto, Kei; Harada, Yasunari (eds.): *Proceedings of the 24th Pacific Asia Conference on Language, Information and Computation.* Waseda University, Sendai, Japan: 721–729.

Chafe, William and Deborah Tannen. 1987. The relation between written and spoken language. *Annual Review of Anthropology* 16, 383–407.

Fjeld, Ruth E. Vatvedt. 2008. Talespråksforskningens betydning for leksikografien. In Johannessen and Hagen (eds.), 15–28.

Guevara, Emiliano. 2010. NoWaC: a large web-based corpus for Norwegian. In *Proceedings of the NAACL HLT 2010 Sixth Web as Corpus Workshop*, Los Angeles, California, 1–7.

Hofland, Knut and Stig Johansson. 1982. *Word Frequencies in British and American English.* The Norwegian Computing Centre for the Humanities, Bergen, Norway.

Johannessen, Janne Bondi, Anders Nøklestad and Kristin Hagen. 2000. A Web-Based Advanced and User Friendly System: The Oslo Corpus of Tagged Norwegian Texts. In Gavrilidou, M., G. Carayannis, S. Markantonatou, S. Piperidis and G. Stainhaouer (red.) *Proceedings, Second International Conference on Language Resources and Evaluation (LREC 2000)*, Aten, 1725-1729.

Johannessen, Janne Bondi; Hagen, Kristin; Priestley, Joel; Nygaard, Lars. 2007. An Advanced Speech Corpus for Norwegian. In: *NODALIDA 2007 PROCEEDINGS.* Tartu: University of Tartu 2007. s. 29-36.

Johannessen, Janne Bondi. 2008. *Studia Linguistica: Special issue on spoken language.* Vol. 62, issue 1.

Johannessen, Janne Bondi and Kristin Hagen (eds.). 2008. *Språk i Oslo. Ny forskning om talespråk.* [Language in Oslo. New Research on Spoken Language] Novus forlag, Oslo, Norway.

Johannessen, Janne Bondi, Joel Priestley, Kristin Hagen, Tor Anders Åfarli, and Øystein Alexander Vangsnes. 2009. The Nordic Dialect Corpus - an Advanced Research Tool. In Jokinen, Kristiina and Eckhard Bick (eds.): *Proceedings of the 17th Nordic Conference of Computational Linguistics NODALIDA 2009. NEALT Proceedings Series Volume 4.*

Kilgarriff, Adam. 1997. Using Word Frequency Lists to Measure Corpus Homogeneity and Similarity between Corpora. In "Proceedings of the Fifth Workshop on Very Large Corpora", Beijing and Hong Kong, China. Association for Computational Linguistics.

Kilgariff, Adam. 2007. Googleology is Bad Science. *Computational Linguistics* 33 (1): 147-151.

Lie, Svein. 2008. Veldig sånn festejente. In Johannessen and Hagen (eds.), 78–95.

McCarthy, Michael. 1998. *Spoken language and applied linguistics.* Cambridge University Press, Cambridge, UK.

Miller, Jim and Regina Weinert. 1998. *Spontaneous Spoken Language. Syntax and Discourse.* Oxford University Press, Oxford, UK.

Norway Statistics: http://www.ssb.no/

Rayson, Paul and Roger Garside. 2000. Comparing Corpora using Frequency Profiling. In Adam Kilgarriff and Tony Berber Sardinha (eds.) "Proceedings of the Workshop on Comparing Corpora", Hong Kong, China. Association for Computational Linguistics.

Søfteland, Åshild and Anders Nøklestad. 2008. Manuell morfologisk tagging av NoTa-materialet med støtte fra en statistisk tagger. In Johannessen and Hagen (eds), 226–234.

Vangsnes, Øystein Alexander Vangsnes. 2008. Omkring adnominalt åssen/hvordan i Oslo-målet. In Johannessen and Hagen (eds), 50–62.

Corpora

Nordic Dialect Corpus: http://www.tekstlab.uio.no/nota/scandiasyn/index.html Read about it in Johannessen et al. (2009).

NoWaC: http://www.hf.uio.no/iln/tjenester/sprak/korpus/skriftsprakskorpus/nowac/ Read about it in Guevara (2010).

NoTa-Oslo: Norwegian Speech Corpus - Oslo part: http://www.tekstlab.uio.no/nota/oslo/english.html Read about it in Johannessen et al. (2007).

The Oslo Corpus of Tagged Norwegian Texts: http://www.tekstlab.uio.no/norsk/bokmaal/english.html Read about it in Johannessen et al. (2000).

ISSN 1736-6305 Vol. 11
http://hdl.handle.net/10062/16955

Morphological analysis of a non-standard language variety

Heiki-Jaan Kaalep
University of Tartu
`Heiki-Jaan.Kaalep@ut.ee`

Kadri Muischnek
University of Tartu
`Kadri.Muischnek@ut.ee`

Abstract

This article introduces a corpus-based method for improving the process of automatic morphological analysis of a non-standard text variety. More precisely, our paper is concerned with the morphological analysis of Estonian chatroom texts. First, the morphological analyzer designed for the standard written Estonian is used for the analysis of chatroom texts. On the basis of output error analysis a method for improving the process is proposed. We take advantage of the fact that there are deviations with high token frequency, but low type frequency, on the one hand, and deviations with low token frequency, but high type frequency, on the other hand. The first group has to be manually compiled into a user lexicon, whereas the second group of errors can be taken care of by automatic means: automatic preprocessing of texts and automatic complementation of the user lexicon. As a result, the percentage of unknown tokens in the output of the morphological analyzer decreases from 27 to 10.5.

1   Introduction

Recently new text types have emerged where the language and orthography used differ considerably from the conventions of the standard written language. E-mails, chatroom texts, internet forums and blogs are some of the examples of these new text types. The expressions 'language of the computer-mediated communication', 'Internet language' or 'Netspeak' (e.g. Crystal 2001) are used to designate all of them.

Morphological analysis is an inevitable prerequisite for any kind of further automatic analysis of a morphologically complex language like Estonian. For standard written Estonian the automatic morphological analysis is nowadays more or less a solved problem (Kaalep, Vaino 2001), but the language and orthography of the aforementioned new text types differs considerably from that of the standard written Estonian and thus the morphological analyzer can be expected to perform poorly while analyzing the Internet language texts.

In this article we report on the experiments on the morphological analysis of the Estonian chatroom (or Internet Relay Chat, IRC) texts. We present the results of the automatic morphological analysis using a tagger meant for the standard written language, group and analyze the errors and introduce a corpus-based method for compiling a customized lexicon for the analyzer for the text currently at hand.

Estonian language belongs to the Finnic group of the Finno-Ugric language family. Typologically Estonian is an agglutinating language but more fusional and analytic than the languages belonging to the northern branch of the Finnic languages. Written Estonian uses phonemic orthography. One can find a detailed description of the grammatical system of Estonian in (Erelt 2003).

The rest of this article is structured as follows. Section 2 gives an overview of the material we have used: the corpus of Estonian chatroom texts and the morphological analyzer *etmrf*. Section 3 presents some related research on the linguistic properties and automatic morphological analysis of Internet language varieties. In Section 4 we analyze the main deviations of the language used in Estonian chatrooms from the standard written Estonian and in Section 5 we put forward different strategies for coping with these deviations, namely preprocessing of texts prior to the morphological analysis and compiling a user lexicon. In Section 6 we present the results of running the morphological analyzer together with preprocessor and user lexicon; in Section 7 we mention some perspectives for the future research and Section 8 concludes.

2 Material: corpus of chatroom texts and the morphological analyzer *etmrf*

For our experiments we used a corpus of Estonian chatroom texts from 2003 and 2006[1] consisting of ca 7 million tokens annotated according to the TEI P5 guidelines.[2] The annotation of the corpus dwells from the opinion that the chatroom conversation is like a kind of staged drama text: there are actors who enter the stage, produce their lines, and leave. All chatters i.e. their nicknames are annotated with the tag <speaker> and the text produced by the chatter is annotated with the paragraph tag <p>. The nicknames have not been changed in any way for anonymisation, but e-mail addresses, URLs and phone numbers have been masked (by substituting parts with 'xxxx').

These chatrooms are an environment for general leisurely chatting. The chatters try to be witty. Language play, including play with orthography and nicknames, is an integral part of this type of communication.

The sentences are not annotated. A sentence splitter developed for the standard written Estonian fails to find sentence boundaries in the chatroom texts, as a typical sentence there does not begin with a capital letter nor end with a punctuation mark. But the text entered by one chatter at one time and annotated as a paragraph is typically short and can be treated as one sentence for the morphological analysis.

For the morphological analysis we used *etmrf*, a tool developed by Filosoft Ltd; the demo version of the program can be found at www.filosoft.ee. *Etmrf* can be used both as a morphological analyzer and as a morphological disambiguator; we performed only morphological analysis.

Etmrf is a convenient tool for our purposes as its behaviour as a morphological analyzer can be modified with a customized user lexicon – a text file that contains word-forms and their preferred analyses. While analyzing a word-form in the text with a user lexicon, *etmrf* first turns to the user lexicon and only in the case the word-form is not present there, the ordinary process of morphological analysis

starts. Thus the user lexicon enables us to give analysis to the word-forms not present in the standard written language, or give alternative readings to word-forms which usage in chatroom texts differs from that of the standard written language, e.g. representing a different part of speech.

3 Internet language

From the linguistic and sociolinguistic point of view, David Crystal (2001) gives a comprehensive overview of the language used in the computer-mediated communication and some of its subtypes. He characterizes the language used on the Internet as identical neither to speech nor writing, but selectively and adaptively displaying properties of both (Crystal 2001: 47).

Crystal has a separate chapter on the language of the chatgroups, that is a generic term he uses for chatrooms, newsgroups, mailing lists and other multi-participant electronic discourse, whether real-time or not (Crystal 2001: 129).

Among the distinctive features of the language used in computer-mediated communication Crystal mentions distinctive graphology, especially the strong tendency to use lowercase everywhere, minimalist punctuation and multiplying of vowels and consonants to express the "ferocity" of the expression. He also notes that chatgroups make a great deal of use of phonetic spelling; and presents a long list of genre-specific abbreviations (2001: 85-86) compiled of the initial letters of the words in a phrase (e.g. *btw* 'by the way', *cu* 'see you').

In an overview of the Internet language, Naomi S. Baron (2003) lists the usage of emoticons, abbreviations and acronyms as distinctive features of the computer-mediated communication.

Lari Kotilainen (2002) analyzes the usage of English words and phrases in Finnish chatrooms. Finnish chatters like to use phonetic spelling while writing English text (e.g. *how aar juu*). Kotilainen shows that English in Finnish chatrooms is used mostly in the form of fixed expressions.

Mark Myslín and Stephan Th. Gries (2010) conduct a study of Spanish Internet orthography. They conclude that the spelling used by the "speakers" of Internet Spanish reflects two interrelated rules: 'modify words

---

[1] The corpus is available at
http://www.cl.ut.ee/korpused/segakorpus/uusmeedia/jututoad.php?lang=en
[2] http://www.tei-c.org/Guidelines/P5/

that have special pragmatic functions and if you are really determined to modify a common word then make big/several changes'.

Vincent Ooi (2002) has done work on the morphological analysis of English Internet Relay Chat texts. The author experiments with two taggers, namely CLAWS and AUTASYS, both probabilistic taggers.

Ooi notes the frequent usage of discourse particles (which he calls discourse markers) in the genre of IRC. Analyzing the output and listing frequent errors he mentions that the taggers he used could not handle emoticons or extra-linguistic acts like *lol* – an abbreviation for laughing out loud. Other frequent errors were caused by proper nouns beginning with a lower-case letter and therefore not recognized as proper nouns, non-standard spelling and using digits for syllables, e.g. *2* for *too*. Ooi concludes that clearly the lexicon of the part-of-speech tagger needs to be modified in order to handle the language of the computer-mediated communication.

We are not aware of any previous work, resulting in a large morphologically tagged corpus of internet language. Experiments have either led to an analysis of errors, as in (Ooi 2002), or to a manually corrected small corpus, as in (Forsyth, Martell 2007).

4 Main deviations from standard literary language

As an initial experiment, we performed morphological analysis of the chatroom texts using simply the morphological analyzer *etmrf* as it is. In the output text, 27% of the tokens were tagged as unknown words. This is much worse than the 2% reported for *estmorf* (a previous implementation of *etmrf*) for standard literary Estonian by (Kaalep, Vaino 2001).

By and large, our chatrooms show the same types of deviation from the standard written form as do other languages (cf Section 3).

4.1 Parts of Speech

4.1.1 Discourse particles

Discourse particles are a part of speech widely recognized in spoken language, but not present in the word-class system of *etmrf*. Analyzing the frequent word-forms that had received the label of an unknown token from *etmrf*, it was clear that we should follow the word-class system used for analyzing the spoken language (e.g. Hennoste et. al. 2002)

and create a special part-of-speech tag for discourse particles, i.e. these short or shortened word-forms that often constitute a clause alone and if used in a clause are not syntactically part of it. They have mostly no clear semantic content but a pragmatic (interactional or emotive) function, e.g. *tre* (a shortened form of *tere*) 'hello' or *kle* (a shortened form of *kuule*) 'hey, listen'. Discourse particles are a frequent part of speech in chatroom text making up 5.8% of the tokens.

```
(1)kle    krizzy   mis   teed
particle propname what do-
2.ps.sg
'hey krizzy, what are you
doing?'
```

4.1.2 Emoticons

Emoticons are iconic signs combined of punctuation marks that are used for expressing emotions, e.g. :P , :-) , :D. As emoticons contribute a certain meaning or a meaning nuance to the text, just like words do, it would be reasonable to analyze them as words and give them a word-class tag. If analyzed as word-forms, emoticons make up 3.2% of the tokens in chatroom texts.

4.2 Orthography

In languages with non-phonetic spelling like English and French, chatgroups make a great deal of use of phonetic spelling.

Estonian spelling, in contrast, is very close to phonetic. Still, dropping h from the beginning of a word (e.g. *ommik* for *hommik* 'morning') might be called an instance of pronunciation affecting spelling as the word-initial *h* is not articulated in spoken Estonian.

4.2.1 Character substitution

This is a wide-spread phenomenon in chatroom texts. Frequent substitutions include using *ff* for *hv* (e.g. *raffas* pro *rahvas* 'people'), *x* for *ks* (e.g. *näitex* pro *näiteks* 'for example'), *y* for *ü* (e.g. *kyll* pro *küll* 'enough'), *c* for *ts* (e.g. *täica* pro *täitsa* 'entirely'), *2* for *ä* (e.g. *h2sti* pro *hästi* 'well'), *6* for *õ* (e.g. *h6be* pro *hõbe* 'silver') and *8* for *ö* (e.g. *t88* for *töö* 'work').

The tradition of substituting non-ASCII characters like *äöüõ* with some other symbol has originally arisen from the wide usage of non-customized keyboards, but this need has largely disappeared as we can see for example from spellings like *ykskõik* pro *ükskõik* 'no matter'.

A question that this material brings forth is: what is the meaning of all these alternations? Why do the chatters bother to alternate the orthography of Estonian, although (differently from, say, English) it is phonetic already? Using *ff* for *hv* does not make the typing quicker or the orthography more phonetic. One explanation would be they need to signal the informality of chatroom communication as opposed to other registers of the written language.

Multiplication of characters, mostly in order to express emotion (e.g. *ahhhhh*) could also be included in this group.

The question important for compiling the user lexicon is, whether these substitutions occur in a closed set of frequent word-forms, or they are productive, i.e. used also in an open set of non-frequent word-forms. In the first case we could simply list them in the user lexicon of the morphological analyzer; in the second case we should think of some kind of an algorithm for normalizing the words prior to the standard morphological analysis.

A look at the frequency lists of words with these substitutions revealed that their frequency profiles differ from each other. For example *ff* is used for *hv* in only certain high-frequency word-forms, but *x* is used for *ks* in non-frequent as well as frequent word-forms, e.g. in the grammatical endings of the translative case of a noun (e.g. *kirurgix* 'surgeon-sg.transl') or subjunctive mood of a verb (e.g. *ärkax* 'awake-ps.subj).

4.2.2 Non-capitalized proper nouns

Proper nouns are typically not written with a capital letter in the chatroom texts (capitalization is used for other purposes, namely for emphasizing). Proper nouns make up 6.5% of the tokens in chatroom texts. They are so frequent because they are used as a direct address in order to explicitly show the adressee of the message and to catch the addressee's attention, e.g. *krizzy kle...* 'Krizzy (proper noun) listen...'

4.2.3 Typos

Typos are frequent in chatroom text as the messages are often typed in a hurry and there is no time and actually also no need for editing the text. Word-forms with typos are frequent as a class but this class consists mostly *of hapax legomena*.

4.3 Vocabulary

4.3.1 Foreign-language words

Foreign languages, mostly English, but also Russian and other languages are used in chatroom texts both in the form of single words or phrases in an Estonian sentence or whole foreign-language sentences. Similarly to Finnish (see Section 3), foreign-language text can be written with phonetic spelling, e.g. *luk huus tooking* 'look who's talking' as a certain form of language play.

There are no chatroom-specific abbreviations, compiled of the initial letters of the words in a phrase (e.g. English *btw* 'by the way', *cu* 'see you') for frequent Estonian phrases; English loans are used instead.

4.3.2 Neologisms and genre-specific vocabulary

The chatroom texts contain a lot of genre-specific (i.e. chatroom-specific) vocabulary, mostly fresh loanwords, but also innovative derivatives. Such vocabulary includes e.g. verbs *privama* 'hold a private conversation in chatroom' or *ruulima* 'rule'; nouns like *friik* 'freak', adjectives like *feik* 'fake' and adverbs like *loogish* 'logical'.

Of course, it is a bit complicated to make a clear distinction between a new loanword and a foreign word in an Estonian-language sentence, cf. e.g. (2). The governing principle has been to regard a word-form following the rules of Estonian inflection a loanword, e.g. the inflected form of the verb *chillima* 'chill' in (3). But the problem remains with uninflecting words like adverbs and inflecting words in a non-marked form, e.g. a nominal in nominative case like the adjective *cool* in (2).

```
(2) tahan  ka   cool olla
want-1.sg also cool be-inf
'I want to be cool too'
(3) no mis chillite siin
    so what chill-2.pl here
'so what are you chilling/doing
here?'
```

4.3.3 Dialect and colloquial word-forms

Dialect and colloquial, non-standard word variants are frequent in chatroom texts, perhaps signaling the informality of the interaction. Besides colloquial word-forms also colloquial inflectional endings are used. For example, the standard ending of the active past participle form of a verb is *–nud* (e.g. *teinud* 'done') but in chatroom texts often the colloquial form ending with *–nd* (e.g. *teind* 'done') is used. This ending is productive, i.e. used also for forming past participle forms of verbs occurring only 1-2 times in the corpus.

5 Strategies for achieving better morphological analysis

From the viewpoint of automatic processing, the non-standard word-forms described in Section 4 should be divided into two groups: those that have to be included in the user lexicon manually, and those that can be normalized using some kind of rewriting rules prior to the morphological analysis, or added to the user lexicon automatically. This division corresponds roughly to that of frequent, irregular, non-productive on one side, and infrequent, regular, productive morphological or orthographic changes, on the other side.

Further in this section we will present these two solutions in more detail. Words that are frequent in chatroom texts but not present in the standard written Estonian are included in the user lexicon. The automatic methods are twofold: preprocessing of texts prior to the morphological analysis and automatic complementing of the user lexicon.

5.1 Preprocessing

The preprocessing of the corpus started from the reducing of repeated characters or syllables. Such repetitions are frequently used in chatroom texts and their function is mostly intensification, e.g *eieieieieiei* (for intensive *ei* 'no') or *jaaaaaaaaaa* for intensive *ja* 'yes'). The fact of repetition (being an intensification) may be of importance for the further linguistic analysis but the exact number of repetitions is probably not. So we reduced all multiplied characters or syllables to three repetitions, so *eieieieieiei* became *eieiei*.

Analogous multiplying occurs in emoticons, whereas a punctuation mark in an emoticon could be repeated more than hundred times. These repetitions were also reduced to three during the preprocessing step, thus keeping the original intention of the chatter.

Next, we tried to eliminate flood, i.e. repeated chunks of text, often with nonsense meaning, entered by some of the chatters in order to disturb the conversation or simply as a bad joke. Distinctive features of the flood messages are their length and repetitions – they are usually longer than ordinary messages and/or have a distinctly repetitious nature. E.g. if a message contained three identical 20-character spans in a row, or a message was repeated at least 5 times, while being at least 110 characters long, then it was classified as flood.

Flood deletion erased 16,000 tokens, and repetition deletion diminished the word type count by 18,000, to 390,000.

5.2 User lexicon

As mentioned previously, *etmrf* is a convenient tool for our purposes as it has an in-built option of a user lexicon.

5.2.1 Manual complementation of the user lexicon

Among the groups described in Section 4, the discourse particles (Section 4.1.1) and emoticons (Section 4.1.2) are the most frequent ones in texts. The traditional system of the parts of speech of Estonian does not recognize particles (and of course not the emoticons), nor does the morphological analyzer *etmrf*. For the morphological analysis of chatroom texts two new part-of speech tags were introduced for them.

As for handling the variability of the particles (e.g. the particle with literary meaning 'listen' could be written as *kuule*, *kule* or *kle*), we assumed that it is better not to overgeneralize and kept the possible variants of particles apart, so *kuule*, *kule* and *kle* are tagged as three different particles, not variants of the same particle.

The treatment of particles in the output of etmrf with user lexicon is not very systematic, though. The user lexicon contains mostly those word-forms that had received the analysis of an unknown token during the morphological analysis of the chatroom corpus using *etmrf* without the user lexicon. Some word-forms, that on the basis of the usage in spoken Estonian could be suspected to be used as particles also in the chatroom texts, were checked in the corpus and if used as particles, added to the user lexicon.

So, for example the present plural 1st person form of the verb 'say' *ütleme* and the present conditional form of the same verb *ütleks* are used as particles in spoken Estonian and also in Estonian chatrooms. But a systematic study of the particles in chatroom texts has not been conducted, so there certainly are word-forms in the output text that are used as particles but have been tagged with some other part-of-speech tag.

The user lexicon also gives a special part-of-speech tag to the emoticons. There are 100 different emoticons in the user lexicon; this relatively great amount is due to the fact that during the preprocessing of the texts multiplied punctuation marks up to three repetitions were left as they were and more repetitions were diminished to three, so the user lexicon contains separate entries for :) , :)) and :)))

Frequent new loanwords (Section 4.3.2) were also entered into the user lexicon. As for foreign words and phrases (Section 4.3.1), we do not think that the user lexicon is a proper way to solve their problem. Instead, some kind of a language identification program should be used.

Dialectal and colloquial variants of standard words (Section 4.3.3) were entered into the user lexicon so that their lemmas are those of the standard written language. Neologisms and genre-specific words (Section 4.3.2), being out of standard written language vocabulary, naturally have their own lemmas in the lexicon.

One can easily see that drawing a strict line between these two groups is somewhat problematic. For example, is the word-form *plix* a genre-specific variant of the standard Estonian word *plika* 'girlie' or a different, genre-specific word which lemma should be *pliks*?

The manually complemented lexicon has less than 300 entries.

5.2.2 Automatic complementation of the user lexicon

The remaining groups of deviations from the Standard Written Estonian, namely lower-case proper nouns (Section 4.2.2) and word-forms written with character substitutions (Section 4.2.1), including the phonology-related word-forms with omitted initial *h*, show high type frequency, but low token frequency.

Proper nouns are as a rule not capitalized in the chatroom texts and are frequently used as direct address in order to catch the adressee's attention. Fortunately a program can scan a chatroom transcript prior to analyzing it morphologically and compile a list of proper nouns used as nicknames in every single chatroom, as the nicknames have been annotated in the corpus, as described in Section

2. This list can then be automatically turned into a subpart of the user lexicon.

If a nickname is homonymous with some Estonian word-form, the user lexicon leaves the word-form ambiguous between the readings of a proper noun and the other reading. If the chatter has entered his/her nickname with a capital letter, it still should be included in the user lexicon also with a small initial letter – other chatters tend not to use the capital letter while addressing her/him or chatting about her/him.

So, for example the examples (4-5) add three entries to the user lexicon:

Dammu as a proper noun

dammu as a proper noun

kakuke ('bun') as a general noun and a proper noun – the general noun reading is present in the actual lexicon of *etmrf*, but as the user lexicon "overrides" the original lexicon, we have to repeat it here.

```
(4) <speaker> Dammu </speaker>
<p> heihei </p>
(5) <speaker> kakuke </speaker>
<p> dammu mis teed </p>
```

The nicknames used in one chatroom are temporarily included in the user lexicon just for the morphological analysis of the same text only. The reason for this is that nicknames are a very heterogeneous class, containing also word-forms that are used as common nouns and/or even pronouns, e.g. *keegi* 'someone'. Thus, including them in the user lexicon for analysis of all the chatroom texts would result in a purposeless increase of ambiguity.

For non-standard word-forms with character substitutions, the user lexicon entries were generated in the following cyclical way.

Etmrf analyzed the text, using the user dictionary it had at the moment. The unknown words were collected, and modified with some character substitution rule reversed, thus undoing the substitutions, described in section 4.2.1, e.g. *c* was changed to *ts* in *kick* and *viici*. The examples resulted in word-forms *kitsk* (nonce word) and *viitsi* (present personal negative form of verb *viitsima* 'bother') and were given to *etmrf* for analysis again. If *etmrf* gave the word-form some analysis other than that of an unknown word, the original word-form and the analysis of its rewritten variant were made into an entry of the user lexicon. The process continued for several cycles, trying different character substitution rules in every cycle, from the more likely ones to less likely ones, and eventually making several substitutions on the same word, e.g. *viicix* pro *viitsik*s (present personal conditional form of the verb *viitsima* 'to bother').

Note that this cyclical process results in including in the user dictionary also the variants of a chatroom-specific word that has been included in the user dictionary manually, e.g. *sau, sauu, sauh, tsau, zauu, tzau* etc. for *tsau* ('ciao').

The result of this automatic complementation was a user lexicon of over 30 000 entries (excluding the nicknames) for the whole corpus.

The automatically generated part of the user lexicon is presumably not very useful for the analysis of new chatroom texts or the texts of the other genres of the new media. More likely, it is the methodology of creating the user lexicon that is of some value to the future work: rewriting the word-forms unknown for the morphological analyzer, possibly several times, until the morphological analysis succeeds, and using the annotation of nicknames for the analysis of only the text where they occur.

6 Experiment: morphological analysis with the user lexicon

Finally, we performed morphological analysis of the whole corpus of chatroom texts with *etmrf*, using preprocessing and the user lexicon, described in Section 5. That is, we used the same set of texts we had been using for developing the strategies in the first place.

In the output text, 10.5% of the tokens still remained tagged as unknown words. This is a clear improvement from the initial 27%, when we used *etmrf* "as is".

As for the types of the unknown words, the foreign-language word-forms, especially frequent English words like *the, is, to, in, my, it* etc constituted the most numerous group.

In order to evaluate the quality of the morphological analysis (in addition to coverage), we manually checked certain excerpts of the output. These excerpts, originating from different chatroom texts contained 3281 tokens altogether. 3.4% of these tokens had received a wrong analysis from our customized *etmrf*. We counted as errors also the occasions if a word-form had been attached the label of the part-of-speech it typically has in the standard written language,

but its usage in the chatroom text would have suggested another part-of-speech reading. For example, the most frequent error, making up ca 50% of all errors, concerned the word-form *tere* 'hello'. *etmrf* analyzed it as an interjection, in line with the grammar of standard literary Estonian, although it should be tagged as a particle, just like its shortened counterpart *tre* that was given the part-of-speech tag of a particle by means of the user lexicon.

As we worked only with lists of unknown tokens while compiling the user lexicon and developing the preprocessor, it could be anticipated that the other frequent type of errors was analysing a foreign-language word-form homonymous with some Estonian word-form like an Estonian one; e.g. *me* is a short form of 1st person plural pronoun 'we' in nominative or genitive case and *mind* is a partitive case form of 1st person singular pronoun 'I'; both of them are also frequent tokens in English text. So in the output text all instances of *me* and *mind* while part of an English phrase were erroneously tagged as Estonian pronouns.

Also, if a genre-specific version of some Estonian word-form coincides with a Standard Written Estonian word-form, it receives an erroneous reading during the morphological analysis. For example, *ikke*, a colloquial form of *ikka* 'still' is homonymous with singular genitive case form of the word *ike* 'yoke' and has been given that analysis by *etmrf*.

The tagged version of the chatroom corpus can be queried at http://www.keeleveeb.ee

7 Unsolved issues

In spite of the efforts to recognize and delete foreign-language passages during the compilation process of the chatroom corpus, the texts still contain a considerable amount of foreign sentences, also foreign phrases and words as parts of Estonian sentences. Foreign language written with phonetic spelling is also common enough to need some special attention. A solution could be applying a language identification program that could identify as short excerpts of non-Estonian text as possible. The foreign language written with phonetic spelling needs some special attention here; perhaps compiling a small corpus of such sentences for (re-)training a language identification program is needed.

The other problem we have not found a good solution is that of the typos. As described in Section 4.2.3, typos are frequent as a type of errors but infrequent as word-forms. Perhaps we should think of a solution similar to that we used for character alternations: for unknown word-forms make some changes for fixing the common types of typos and try to perform the morphological analysis again.

By common types of typos we mean changing the order of two adjacent characters, e.g. *tow* for *two*, typing a neighboring character from the keyboard, e.g. *teo* for *two* and misplacing the space, e.g. *twot imes* instead of *two times*.

8 Conclusion: lessons learnt

This article focused on the process of customizing the morphological analyzer originally designed for the purposes of standard written language to meet the needs of a non-standard language variety; namely that of the chatroom texts.

Our main contribution lies in proposing a practical solution for coping with massive deviations from standard language, using a tool designed for analysis of this standard language.

The language of chatrooms is a variant of written Estonian. At first sight, it looks very different from the standard literary language – over a quarter of the tokens could not be analysed by a program, meant for the standard literary Estonian. A closer look, however, reveals that, roughly speaking, the differences are either systematic or concern a small set of words. This is to be expected – a (sub)language has to be learnable and usable, meaning here that unsystematic deviations from the standard language have to be limited to a small set of high-frequency words, just like irregularly inflected words have to have a low type frequency and a high token frequency.

The idea that most of the deviations result from some regular, productive modifications of the standard orthography might serve as guidance for future work. The place for looking for these regular modifications is hapax legomenon, the set of tokens that occur in the corpus only once.

In a way the chatroom corpus is self-contained: one can extract data that can be used for analyzing the data itself. It is the frequency profiles of different words that let us decide which words should be added to a user lexicon manually, and what productive rules might be at work here. It is the nicknames of the chatters that give us clues for analyzing much of the vocabulary.

References

Baron, Naomi S. 2003. Language of the Internet. In: Ali Farghali (ed.) *The Stanford Handbook for Language Engineers.* Stanford:CSLI Publications, pp. 59-127

Crystal, David 2001. *Language and the Internet.* Cambridge:University Press

Forsyth, Eric N., Martell, Craig H. 2007. Lexical and Discourse Analysis of Online Chat Dialog. *International Conference on Semantic Computing*, Irvine, California, pp. 19-26

Erelt, Mati (editor) 2003. *Estonian Language.* Linguistica Uralica Supplementary Series vol 1. Estonian Academy Publishers, Tallinn.

Hennoste, Tiit, Liina Lindström, Olga Gerassimenko, Airi Jansons, Andriela Rääbis, Krista Strandson, Piret Toomet, Riina Vellerind 2002. Suuline kõne ja morfoloogiaanalüsaator. In: Pajusalu, R.; Hennoste, T. (eds). *Tähendusepüüdja.* Tartu: Tartu Ülikooli Kirjastus, pp. 161-171

Kaalep, Heiki-Jaan, Vaino, Tarmo 2001. Complete Morphological Analysis in the Linguist's Toolbox. *Congressus Nonus Internationalis Fenno-Ugristarum* Pars V, Tartu, pp. 9-16,

Kotilainen, Lari 2002. Moi taas, ai äm päk. Lauseet, tilanteet ja englanti suomenkielisessä chat-keskustelussa. In: Ilona Herlin, Jyrki Kalliokoski, Lari Kotilainen and Tiina Onikki-Rantajääskö (eds). *Äidinkielen merkitykset.* Helsinki: Suomalaisen Kirjallisuuden seura, pp. 191-209.

Myslín, Mark and Stefan T. Gries. 2010. k dixez? A corpus study of Spanish Internet orthography. *Literary and Linguistic Computing*, Vol. 25, No. 1, pp. 85-104.

Ooi, Vincent B. Y. 2002. Aspects of computer-mediated communication for research in corpus linguistics. In: Peters, P., Collins P., Smith, A. (eds.) *New Frontiers of Corpus Research: papers form the twenty-first International Conference on English Language Research on Computerized Corpora.* Amsterdam: Rodopi, pp. 91-104.

ISSN 1736-6305 Vol. 11
http://hdl.handle.net/10062/16955

Editing Syntax Trees on the Surface

Peter Ljunglöf
Department of Computer Science and Engineering
University of Gothenburg and Chalmers University of Technology
Gothenburg, Sweden
`peter.ljunglof@gu.se`

Abstract

We describe a system for interactive modification of syntax trees by intuitive editing operations on the surface string. The system has a graphical interface, where the user can move, replace, add, and in other ways modify, words or phrases. During editing, the sentence is kept grammatical, by automatically rearranging words and changing inflection, if necessary. This is accomplished by combining constraints on syntax trees with a distance measure between trees.

1 Introduction

In this paper we describe the underlying theory of a grammatical editing system, where the actions of the user are interpreted as constraints on the syntax tree. The different editing operations that the user performs on the surface string, are interpreted as constraints on the underlying syntax tree which is never shown to the user. The system then searches for the closest matching tree, in terms of a suitable tree distance measure.

We believe that our editing system is more intuitive and easy to use than a system where the syntax is shown explicitly. Then it can be a useful pedagogical tool for supporting language learning and training, for children with communicative disabilities, and for people learning a second language. We also hope that the ideas can be useful in touch screen devices, as an additional editing layer in text-based applications such as translation, email and chat.

The current system is a pedagogical tool for language learning, and is still work in progress. As of April 2011, there is a functioning demo system which needs more work to be useful for the intended audience.

2 System overview

2.1 No free text input

The editing interaction is purely graphical, which means that the user is not allowed to enter words, phrases or sentences from the keyboard. There are several reasons for this, but the main reason is to avoid problems with words and grammatical constructions that the system doesn't know anything about. Systems that are supposed to handle free text input sooner or later run into problems with unknown words or phrases (Heift, 2001).

Another reason for disallowing free text input is to make the system accessible to people with communicative and/or physical disabilities, or for alternative input methods such as mobile phone touch screens.

2.2 Interacting with the system

The words that the user is editing are icon-like objects that can be selected, inserted, moved around and deleted. A word is selected by clicking, and the selection can be increased to multi-word phrases. The selected word or phrase has an associated context-menu consisting of similar words or phrases, such as different inflection forms, or synonyms, homonyms, etc. When an item is selected from the context-menu, it replaces the old word or phrase, and if necessary, the nearby words are also modified and rearranged to keep the sentence grammatical.

The user can move the selection to another position in the sentence, and the system will automatically keep the sentence grammatical by rearranging the words and change inflection, if necessary. Phrases can be deleted from the sentence by dragging them away. The user can also add or replace words by dragging new words into the sentence. All the time, the sentence will adapt by rearranging and inflecting.

2.2.1 Example: Modifying a phrase

Assume that the system starts with the sentence "*all cats sleep*", and the user wants to see the possible alternatives to the determiner "*all*":

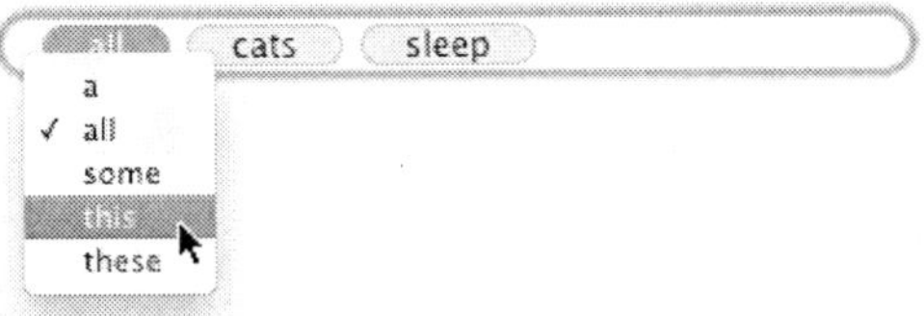

The user now changes "*all*" to the word "*this*" instead, thereby changing the number from plural to singular. Then the system automatically change the inflection of the other words in the sentence, so that it is kept grammatical:

2.2.2 Example: Inserting a phrase

Another alternative is to insert a new phrase into the sentence, by dragging it from a heap of possible phrases:

The system knows where the new phrase can be inserted and shows it by making room for it. On the other hand, the system does not react if the user tries to insert the phrase in an ungrammatical position:

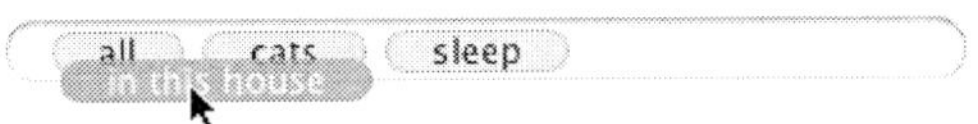

2.3 Implementation

The system consists of three implementation layers. The bottom layer is the GF grammar formalism (Ranta, 2009b). We use GF's multilingual resource grammar to define the different grammar modules (Ranta, 2009a). The surface strings are stored as GF syntax trees, and the GF linearisation algorithm is used for displaying the sentences to the user. We have no use of parsing the sentences, since the syntax trees are already known and there is no free text input.

On top of GF we implement an API for modifying syntax trees by specifying linearisation constraints. The API consists of functions that transform trees to obey the constraints, by using as few transformations as possible. An example of constraints can be that the linearisations of some given tree nodes must come in a certain order (e.g., when the user moves a word to a position between two other words). Another example is that the linearisation of a given node must be of a specified form (e.g., when the user selects a specific word form from the context menu).

The final layer is the graphical interface, which communicates with the API to decide which words can be moved where, and what their contextual menus should contain.

3 Grammatical Framework

GF is a two-level formalism, with an underlying abstract syntax and a surface concrete syntax (Ranta, 2009b). It is a high-level grammar formalism with good support for both multilingual and modular grammar writing (Ranta, 2009a). In this paper we focus on a simplified core language, which every grammar can be compiled into.

3.1 GF abstract syntax

The abstract syntax of a GF grammar consists of a finite number of typed functions. In the general framework, functions can be both higher-order and dependently typed, but most applications only use first-order functions with non-dependent types.

A GF function is declared by giving its type, $f : A_1 \ldots A_n \to A$. If $n = 0$, the function has no arguments, and is called a constant. From the function f we can create a *term* of type A by applying it to n terms of type $A_1, \ldots, A_n$. In other words, $f(t_1 \ldots t_n)$ is a term of type A whenever $t_1, \ldots, t_n$ are terms of types $A_1, \ldots, A_n$, respectively.

This is similar to how syntax trees are licensed by a context-free grammar, but instead of using nonterminals in the tree nodes, we use function names. In fact, the abstract syntax is equivalent to a context-free grammar without terminal symbols, where the nonterminals correspond to GF types, and where the grammar rules have names. A simple example grammar is shown in Figure 1. Two terms of type S licensed by this grammar are:

$$sleep(npp(all(cat), in(this(house))))$$
$$spp(sleep(all(cat)), in(this(house)))$$

Terms can be drawn as context-free syntax trees, where the nodes contain function symbols instead of nonterminals. The trees corresponding to the example terms above are shown in Figure 2.

$$
\begin{aligned}
cat, house \;&:\; N \\
this, all \;&:\; N \to NP \\
sleep \;&:\; NP \to S \\
in \;&:\; NP \to PP \\
npp \;&:\; NP, PP \to NP \\
spp \;&:\; S, PP \to S
\end{aligned}
$$

Figure 1: Example abstract grammar

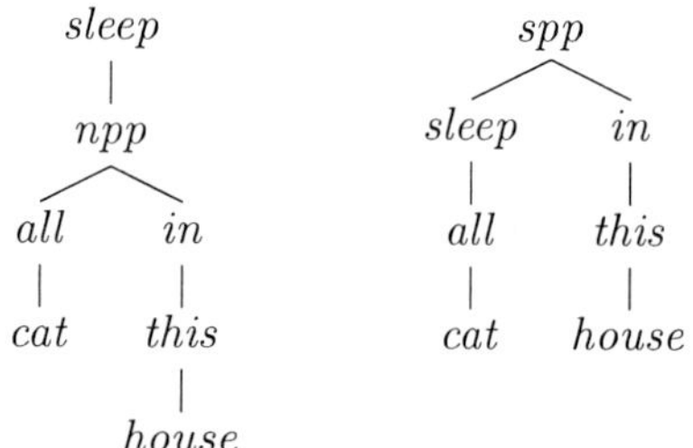

Figure 2: Trees licenced by the grammar

$$
\begin{aligned}
cat^\circ \;&=\; \langle \text{``cat''} ; \text{``cats''} \rangle \\
house^\circ \;&=\; \langle \text{``house''} ; \text{``houses''} \rangle \\
this^\circ(x) \;&=\; \langle \text{``this''} + x!1 ; 1 \rangle \\
all^\circ(x) \;&=\; \langle \text{``all''} + x!2 ; 2 \rangle \\
sleep^\circ(x) \;&=\; \langle x!1 + \langle \text{``sleeps''} ; \text{``sleep''} \rangle ! (x!2) \rangle \\
in^\circ(x) \;&=\; \langle \text{``in''} + x!1 \rangle \\
npp^\circ(x, y) \;&=\; \langle x!1 + y!1 ; x!2 \rangle \\
spp^\circ(x, y) \;&=\; \langle x!1 + y!1 \rangle
\end{aligned}
$$

Figure 3: Concrete syntax for the grammar

3.2 GF concrete syntax

The concrete syntax of a GF grammar is a compositional mapping from abstract terms to concrete terms, called the *linearisation*. The concrete terms can be quite complex and consist of strings, finite parameters, recursive records and inflection tables. We do not use the full concrete language in this paper, but instead use a simplified syntax which all GF grammars can be compiled into.

Every GF term is a tuple of strings and integer values. There are two operations; string concatenation and tuple selection:

$$
\begin{aligned}
\text{``}s_1\ldots\text{''} + \text{``}s_2\ldots\text{''} \;&=\; \text{``}s_1\ldots s_2\ldots\text{''} \\
\langle t_1; \ldots; t_k; \ldots; t_n \rangle ! k \;&=\; t_k
\end{aligned}
$$

This term language is similar to multiple context-free grammar (MCFG) (Seki et al., 1991), and indeed every GF grammar can be converted to an equivalent MCFG (Ljunglöf, 2004).

We write t° for the linearisation of t. Compositionality can then be formulated as,

$$
f(t_1 \ldots t_n)^\circ \;=\; f^\circ(t_1^\circ \ldots t_n^\circ)
$$

where f° is the linearisation function corresponding to the abstract function f. The concrete syntax of our example grammar is shown in Figure 3.

3.2.1 Example linearisation

To illustrate the linearisation algorithm, we here give the linearisation of the term $sleep(all(cat))$:

$$
\begin{aligned}
& sleep(all(cat))^\circ \\
=\; & sleep^\circ(all^\circ(cat^\circ)) \\
=\; & sleep^\circ(\langle \text{``all''} + cat^\circ !\,2 ; 2 \rangle) \\
=\; & sleep^\circ(\langle \text{``all''} + \langle \text{``cat''}; \text{``cats''} \rangle !\,2 ; 2 \rangle) \\
=\; & sleep^\circ(\langle \text{``all''} + \text{``cats''} ; 2 \rangle) \\
=\; & sleep^\circ(\langle \text{``all cats''} ; 2 \rangle) \\
=\; & \langle \langle \text{``all cats''}; 2 \rangle !\,1 + \\
& \quad \langle \text{``sleeps''}; \text{``sleep''} \rangle ! (\langle \text{``all cats''}; 2 \rangle !\,2) \rangle \\
=\; & \langle \text{``all cats''} + \langle \text{``sleeps''}; \text{``sleep''} \rangle !\,2 \rangle \\
=\; & \langle \text{``all cats''} + \text{``sleep''} \rangle \\
=\; & \langle \text{``all cats sleep''} \rangle
\end{aligned}
$$

Note that the numbers have different meaning in different linearisation terms: Both 2's in all° denotes plural, one for selecting the plural form of the noun and the other for remembering that the resulting NP is in plural. On the other hand, the 2 in $sleep^\circ$ is used to select the number of the NP, and then use that number to select the corresponding verb form.

4   Trees and tree editing

Formally, an ordered tree is a connected directed acyclic non-empty graph, in which every node $v \in V$ (where V denotes the set of nodes) has exactly one parent node $\uparrow v$, except the root node which has no parent. Furthermore, there is a precedence relation ($\prec$) defined on sibling nodes.

Each abstract GF term t is a tree where each node v has a label $\hat{v}$. The label values are GF functions. We write v° for the linearisation of the subtree rooted at v; i.e., $v^\circ = \hat{v}^\circ(v_1^\circ \ldots v_n^\circ)$ when $v_1 \ldots v_n$ are the children of v. Note that this is only meaningful if the tree is type-correct.

An example tree representing the term $t_c = sleep(all(cat))$ consists of the nodes a, b and c, where $\hat{a} = sleep$, $\hat{b} = all$, $\hat{c} = cat$, $a = \uparrow b$, and $b = \uparrow c$.

4.1   Tree edit distance

The *tree edit distance* is a distance measure between trees (Tai, 1979). It is a modification of the well-known Levenshtein string edit distance; the distance between two trees is the number of edit operations required to transform one of them into the other. The allowed operations are insertion, deletion and replacement:

- $insert(v, f, p, j, k)$ inserts a new node v with label f as the jth child of the node p. Furthermore, the new node becomes the parent of p's existing children j to $k - 1$.

- $delete(v)$ removes the node v. All children of v become children of v's parent node.

- $replace(v, f)$ replaces the label of v with f.

Note that the resulting tree after an editing operation is not guaranteed to be type-correct. In fact, for deletions and insertions, we always need at least two operations to get a new type-correct tree.

4.2   Constrained linearisation

In GF, not all strings in a linearisation of a subtree node have to be used in the linearisation of the full tree. In the example grammar, cat° contains two strings, but only one of them is used in $t = sleep(all(cat))^\circ$. In this paper we need to talk about only the parts of a linearisation that are used, and for this purpose we define the *constrained linearisation* $[\![v]\!]_t$ of a subtree node v in a tree t. The formal definition is a bit complex, but the intuition

is that $[\![v]\!]_t$ consists of the strings in v° that are actually used when calculating t°. For the example tree t_c with the node c representing the child, we get the constrained linearisation $[\![c]\!]_{t_c} = \langle \text{``cats''} \rangle$.

4.3   Constraints for automatic tree editing

Each GF grammar rule $f : B_1 \ldots B_n \to A$ can be seen as a constraint on f-labeled nodes and its children. Checking that a tree is grammatical according to the grammar, which in GF is the same as checking that the tree is type-correct, can then be implemented as a constraint satisfaction problem (Sulzmann and Stuckey, 2008). Furthermore, when we formulate the grammar as constraints on trees, we can add additional constraints for specifying in more detail how our intended tree should look like.

By using tree constraints and the notion of tree edit distance, we can describe a system for interactive tree editing. The system starts with a grammatical tree, and the user specifies additional constraints on the tree. Then the system searches for the closest grammatical tree (in terms of tree edit distance) that meets the constraints. This continues until the user is satisfied.

This approach lifts the level of tree editing from procedural to declarative: the user does not have to think about how to modify the tree, but instead what the tree should look like. First we have structural constraints on the tree:

- We can state that a node should be in the tree, $v \in V$, or should not be in the tree, $v \notin V$.

- We can state properties about node labels, $\hat{v} = f$, and node parents, $\uparrow v = v'$; as well as the order between node siblings, $v \prec v'$.

Since our final goal is to allow for editing directly on the concrete surface strings, we also need some linearisation constraints:

- We can specify that the (constrained) linearisation of a node should be, or should not be, a string (tuple): $[\![v]\!] = s$, resp. $[\![v]\!] \neq s$.

  A special case is $\neg[\![v]\!]$, meaning that the node is not realised in the final sentence; this is true either if it linearises to the empty string: $[\![v]\!] = \epsilon$, or if the node is removed completely: $v \notin V$.

- We can specify a linear precedence constraint: $[\![v]\!] \prec [\![v']\!]$ means that the rightmost word in $[\![v]\!]$ is adjacent to the leftmost word in $[\![v']\!]$; it also implies that both linearisations are non-empty.

Two special cases are $\epsilon \prec [\![v]\!]$ and $[\![v]\!] \prec \epsilon$, meaning that the linearisation comes first resp. last in the sentence.

4.3.1   Example: Modifying a phrase

The context-menu example, from section 2.2.1, can be explained like this. Assume that we start with the following tree t_c:

$$t_c = sleep(all(cat))$$
$$t_c^\circ = \text{``all cats sleep''}$$

This tree has the nodes a, b, c with the labels $sleep$, all, cat, respectively. Now we want to say that the second word (whose corresponding node is c) should be in its singular form. This can be specified by the constraint $[\![c]\!] = \text{``cat''}$. The system can then apply the tree editing operations to search for the closest type-correct tree t_c' which meets the constraint. In this case we need only one operation: we rename the b node from all to $this$:

$$t_c' = sleep(this(cat))$$
$$t_c'^\circ = \text{``this cat sleeps''}$$

4.3.2   Example: Inserting a phrase

Our second example, introduced in section 2.2.2, is when the user wants to insert a prepositional phrase $t_p = in(this(house))$ into the tree t_c. First we encode the whole subtree t_p as structural constraints:

$$\hat{d} = in \qquad \uparrow e = d$$
$$\hat{e} = this \qquad \uparrow f = e$$
$$\hat{f} = house$$

Now we can specify where t_p should be inserted by giving linearisation constraints:

- If we state that the phrase should come right after "sleeps", $[\![a]\!] \prec [\![d]\!]$, the system needs to first insert a spp-labeled node above a and then insert d as the 2nd child:

$$t_{cp} = spp(sleep(all(cat)), in(this(house)))$$
$$t_{cp}^\circ = \text{``all cats sleep in this house''}$$

- If we instead state that the phrase should come directly before "sleeps", $[\![d]\!] \prec [\![a]\!]$, the system inserts an npp-labeled node below a, and inserts d as the 2nd child:

$$t_{cp}' = sleep(npp(all(cat), in(this(house))))$$
$$t_{cp}'^\circ = \text{``all cats in this house sleep''}$$

4.4   Fine-tuning the search

When the grammar is large, there might be several possible syntax trees that are equally close to the original tree. One possible solution to this problem is to use a more fine-grained distance measure, where the cost of the editing operations depend on the nodes and the labels that are involved.

If the grammar used in example 4.3.1 contains the singular determiner $each$ in addition to $this$, then there will be two possible solution trees: $sleep(this(cat))$ and $sleep(each(cat))$. Our solution is to augment the grammar with distance values between different functions. In this case the grammar could state that replacing $all \mapsto each$ is cheaper than $all \mapsto this$, to force the resulting tree to be $sleep(each(cat))$.

We can introduce similar costs for deleting and inserting nodes; so that some functions prefer some other functions as parents, or siblings. This could be used, e.g., for PP attachment problems when inserting new phrases.

5   Syntactic editing of the surface string

Now we are ready to get rid of the syntax trees altogether, and introduce syntactic editing operations directly on the surface string. Our final goal is to implement a syntactic editor where the user does not need any knowledge of syntax trees. Therefore the text is presented to the user as a sequence of words, and in this section we define intuitive editing operations on the words.

To implement these operations, we only make use of three GUI "gestures": *select-click*, *context-click* and *drag*. In a 2-button mouse interface, they are commonly implemented by left-click, right-click, and click-and-hold. In a touch-screen interface, they can be implemented by touch-and-release, touch-and-hold, and touch-and-drag; but there are of course other possibilities.

5.1   Editing operations

Since the user only modifies the surface string, we need a way of translating surface editing operations onto the underying syntax tree. We use the fact that in GF, each surface word belongs to one and only one node in the syntax tree. So, when the user makes a gesture on a word $w \in [\![v]\!]_t$, we interpret it as a gesture on the underlying node v.

During editing, there is an information state consisting of the current tree, and a single node which is called *the selected node v^**. The selected node is displayed to the user by highlighting the words in $[\![v^*]\!]_t$. Sometimes there are other nodes v having the same linearisation, $[\![v]\!]_t = [\![v^*]\!]_t$. In that case we always select the *maximal* node, such that $[\![v^*]\!]_t \neq [\![\uparrow v^*]\!]_t$ always holds. The nature of GF grammars ensures that there always exist a unique maximal node.

5.1.1 Selecting a phrase

There are two possibilities when the user select-clicks a word w:

- If the word is unselected, $w \notin [\![v^*]\!]_t$, or if all words in the sentence are selected, the interpretation is that the user wants to start over, and select another node v such that $w \in [\![v]\!]_t$. The node v will be the maximal node with the minimal linearisation covering w. By "minimal linearisation" we mean that there is no descendant v' such that $w \in [\![v']\!]_t \neq [\![v]\!]_t$

- If the word is already selected, $w \in [\![v^*]\!]_t$, the interpretation is that the user wants to increase the selection. We do this by selecting the closest maximal ancestor v such that $[\![v]\!]_t \neq [\![v^*]\!]_t$.

Phrases can also be selected by context-clicking and dragging; if the user performs an operation on an unselected word, its covering node becomes selected before the operation is performed.

5.1.2 Displaying a context menu

When the user context-clicks a word w, the system displays a modification menu for the selected node v^*. Let $s = [\![v^*]\!]_t$ be the currently highlighted phrase.

The modification menu is calculated like this: We search for nearby trees satisfying the constraint $[\![v^*]\!] \neq s$, i.e., so that v^* is linearised different from the current linearisation. For each of these trees, we display a menu item consisting of its linearisation of v^*. If there are no such alternative linearisations, increase the selection and try again.

When the user selects a menu item, the current tree is replaced by the corresponding new tree. The selected node v^* remains selected. The example in section 4.3.1 shows what happens when the user selects the menu item "*cat*" for the selected word "*cats*".

5.1.3 Deleting a phrase

The user can delete the selected phrase by dragging it to the trash can. This introduces the linear constraint $\neg[\![v^*]\!]$, saying that either v^* should be removed, or that $[\![v^*]\!]$ should be empty. The system then searches for the closest tree satisfying the constraint.

5.1.4 Moving a phrase

The user can drag the selected phrase to another position in the sentence, which is interpreted as a linear precedence constraint on v^*. If the phrase is moved to between words w and w', we introduce the constraints $[\![v]\!] \prec [\![v^*]\!] \prec [\![v']\!]$, where $w \in [\![v]\!]_t$ and $w' \in [\![v']\!]_t$.

If the phrase is moved to the beginning or end of the sentence, instead of between two words, the constraints become $\epsilon \prec [\![v^*]\!] \prec [\![v']\!]$, or $[\![v]\!] \prec [\![v^*]\!] \prec \epsilon$, respectively

5.1.5 Inserting a phrase

We assume that somewhere on the screen there is a lexicon of phrases that the user can add to the sentence. If the user drags a phrase from the lexicon into the sentence between two words, we first deselect the currently selected node. Then we create new nodes and constraints representing the new phrase, as in the example in section 4.3.2, and select the topmost node. Finally we can add the same constraints as when moving a phrase, $[\![v]\!] \prec [\![v^*]\!] \prec [\![v']\!]$, but recall that v^* now denotes the topmost node in the inserted phrase, and not the previously selected phrase.

5.1.6 Replacing a phrase

Instead of inserting the user can replace phrases, by dragging a phrase from the lexicon and dropping it onto the selected phrase. As usual, if the user drops onto a currently unselected word, the system reselects it as explained in section 5.1.1.

All descendants $v_1, v_2, \ldots$ of the selected node v^* are removed by adding constraints $v_1, v_2, \ldots \notin V$. Furthermore, the new phrase should be added at v^*. We do this by letting v^* be the topmost node of the phrase, create new descendant nodes $v_1', v_2', \ldots$, and then add associated constraints:

$$\widehat{v^*} = f, \quad \widehat{v_1'} = a, \quad \uparrow v_1' = v^*, \quad v_1' \prec v_2', \quad \ldots$$

If there is no nearby tree matching the constraints, the system can increase the selection and try again.

6 Discussion

6.1 Grammar formalism

The underlying grammar formalism is GF, but there are of course other formalisms that can be used in the same way. The most important feature is the separation of abstract and concrete syntax, which several formalisms have in different ways. Formalisms such as HPSG and LFG are probably also well suited for surface string editing, but the theory of editing presented in this paper must of course be adapted to the underlying formalism.

6.2 Example applications

We hope that our grammatical editing system can be a useful pedagogical tool for supporting language learning and training, for children with communicative disabilities, and for people learning a second language. We also believe that the ideas can be useful in touch screen devices, as an additional editing layer in text-based applications such as translation, email and chat.

6.2.1 Touch screen devices

An example application can be a translation tool for a touch screen device such as a mobile phone, as a kind of interactive phrasebook. This kind of application is already being developed in the MOLTO project, but currently it has very limited editing facilities (Angelov et al., 2010). Other touch screen possibilities include chat and email, where the user can create messages by dragging around text blocks instead of writing with a error-prone touch screen keyboard. It could also work together with speech recognition, to correct mis-recognised phrases in a grammatical way.

6.2.2 Robust parsing

Another possible application can be robust parsing for limited-domain dialogue systems. It is possible to describe a dialogue system as a GF grammar (Ljunglöf, 2009), but the problem with GF is that the concrete syntax is not robust. Suppose that we use a statistical parser such as the MALT parser (Nivre et al., 2007). This returns a parse tree for every string, but in most cases, the tree is not grammatical. Then we can use the techniques in this paper for finding the closest grammatical tree, together with a confidence measure.

6.2.3 The GRASP project

The GRASP[1] project is developing another example application, an interactive system for Computer Assisted Language Learning (CALL). There are two intended target groups: one is children and adults trying to learn another language; another group is persons with communicative disabilities who are learning to read and write in their first language.

The idea of the final GRASP system is that it will work as an interactive textbook, where the user can read different texts and also experiment with and modify the texts. The system will be divided into modules dealing with different linguistic features, e.g., inflection, simple phrases and more advanced constructions. The modules can be used on their own, or can be combined for more advanced training.

The texts are stored as syntax trees in a multilingual GF grammar, which makes it possible to linearise the texts in parallel for several languages. This can be useful for second language learning, as the system can display the text in the user's first language in parallel. Multilinguality is also useful for first language learning, e.g., by displaying the parallel text in a symbol language such as Blisssymbolics.

6.3 Current status

The GRASP system is work in progress, and not all features described in this paper are implemented, as of April 2011. There is a functioning demonstration system, which needs more work to be useful for the intended audience. In particular, the implementation is still too slow and the demonstration grammar needs to be expanded.

The current demostration grammar is a small monolingual Swedish grammar, and the module system is not fully developed. The grammar handles noun phrase inflection, fronting of noun phrases, and verb inflection.

7 Acknowledgements

The author would like to thank three anonymous reviewers for their valuable comments on an earlier version of this paper. The GRASP project is financed by Sunnerdahls Handikappfond.

---

[1]GRASP is an acronym for "grammatikbaserad språkinlärning" (grammar-based language learning).

References

Krasimir Angelov, Olga Caprotti, Ramona Enache, Thomas Hallgren, and Aarne Ranta. 2010. The MOLTO phrasebook. In *SLTC'10, 3rd Swedish Language Technology Conference.*

Trude Heift. 2001. Intelligent language tutoring systems for grammar practice. *Zeitschrift für Interkulturellen Fremdsprachenunterricht*, 6(2).

Peter Ljunglöf. 2004. *Expressivity and Complexity of the Grammatical Framework.* Ph.D. thesis, University of Gothenburg and Chalmers University of Technology, Gothenburg, Sweden.

Peter Ljunglöf. 2009. Dialogue management as interactive tree building. In *DiaHolmia'09, 13th Workshop on the Semantics and Pragmatics of Dialogue*, Stockholm, Sweden.

Joakim Nivre, Johan Hall, Jens Nilsson, Gülşen Eryiğit, Sandra Kübler, Svetoslav Marinov, and Erwin Marsi. 2007. Maltparser: A language-independent system for data-driven dependency parsing. *Natural Language Engineering*, 13(2):95–135.

Aarne Ranta. 2009a. The GF resource grammar library. *Linguistic Issues in Language Technology*, 2.

Aarne Ranta. 2009b. Grammatical Framework: A multilingual grammar formalism. *Language and Linguistics Compass*, 3(5):1242–1265.

Hiroyuki Seki, Takashi Matsumara, Mamoru Fujii, and Tadao Kasami. 1991. On multiple context-free grammars. *Theoretical Computer Science*, 88:191–229.

Martin Sulzmann and Peter J. Stuckey. 2008. HM(X) type inference is CLP(X) solving. *Journal of Functional Programming*, 18(2):251–283.

Kuo-Chung Tai. 1979. The tree-to-tree correction problem. *JACM, Journal of the Association for Computing Machinery*, 26:422–433.

ISSN 1736-6305 Vol. 11
http://hdl.handle.net/10062/16955

Do wordnets also improve human performance on NLP tasks?

Kristiina Muhonen and **Krister Lindén**
Department of Modern Languages
University of Helsinki
kristiina.muhonen@helsinki.fi krister.linden@helsinki.fi

Abstract

FinnWordNet is a wordnet for Finnish that complies with the format of the Princeton WordNet (PWN) (Fellbaum, 1998). It was built by translating the Princeton WordNet 3.0 synsets into Finnish by human translators. It is open source and contains 117000 synsets. The Finnish translations were inserted into the PWN structure resulting in a bilingual lexical database.

In natural language processing (NLP), wordnets have been used for infusing computers with semantic knowledge assuming that humans already have a sufficient amount of this knowledge.

In this paper we present a case study of using wordnets as an electronic dictionary. We tested whether native Finnish speakers benefit from using a wordnet while completing English sentence completion tasks. We found that using either an English wordnet or a bilingual English-Finnish wordnet significantly improves performance in the task. This should be taken into account when setting standards and comparing human and computer performance on these tasks.

1 Introduction

Wordnets are lexical databases that group words of a language into synonym sets called synsets, provide general definitions of the synsets and encode the semantic relations between the synsets. Typically they are monolingual, but efforts have been made to produce multilingual wordnets as well, see e.g. Vossen (1998).

1.1 Building a New Wordnet

A wordnet for a new language can be constructed in several ways. First, it can be built from scratch. This requires extracting the synsets automatically from corpora or defining them manually. In order to ensure that the most common words of the language are actually present in the automatically collected synsets, a common strategy is to use a list with the central vocabulary of the language. Not only do the actual synsets need to be automatically extracted, also the semantic relations between the synsets must be encoded from the very beginning.

Second, the new wordnet can be translated from an existing wordnet. Translating a wordnet ignores the idea of every language being so different with such varying synonym groups and hierarchies that they have to be constructed separately for every language. However, like Lindén and Carlson (2010) note, most of the words in a language actually describe entities and phenomena present in most languages, although there are language specific differences in which nuances of a concept get a specific word capturing the distinctions in meaning.

The third way to construct a wordnet is a combination of automatic extraction and translation. First, the core of the new wordnet is built by translating 5000 central concepts from the PWN. This core can be extended with e.g. a thesaurus of the target language. Vossen (2004) describes how basing the wordnet on a common core enables linking wordnets to each other via the *Inter-Lingual-Index*.

1.2 The Finnish Wordnet

FinnWordNet (FiWN) is a direct translation of the synsets in the PWN 3.0. Choosing translation as the way to create the wordnet is motivated by the benefits it brings. Direct translation of an already existing wordnet results in a parallel arrangement of the synsets. This directly provides us with a wordnet that can be used as a bilingual dictionary. Also, most of the semantic relations from the PWN can be directly used in FiWN (Lindén and Carlson, 2010).

Choosing translation as the means of building FiWN has the downside of including many English-specific terms and concepts in the Finnish wordnet. However, English-specific or rare words in general are all welcome in an electronic version. Some synsets may seem problematic from a cultural perspective, e.g. *independence day* as synonymous with *4th of July*. In such cases, the less general concept can be made a hyponym with corresponding culture-specific terms as sister concepts.

1.3 Using Wordnets

Generally the research around wordnets revolves around NLP applications and less emphasis has been put on wordnets aiding human users. The usability of wordnets as lexical resources for NLP applications has long been established. In particular, wordnets have been found useful in improving the performance of systems for word sense disambiguation, information retrieval and automatic text classification, see e.g. Tanács et al. (2007).

The usability of wordnets for human users is a rather neglected topic. Since creating a wordnet consumes a lot of time and resources, the usability of wordnets should also be considered from a human perspective. The benefits humans get from an intuitively structured lexical database should be considered a prerequisite, not merely a positive side effect of the various wordnet projects implemented for different languages.

The focus of our study is to examine the usability of wordnets from a human perspective. We want to see how human users benefit from using wordnets as a lexical resource and compare the benefits they get from a regular electronic dictionary and first, a monolingual wordnet, and second, a bilingual one. We want to demonstrate that even a monolingual wordnet helps a non-native English speaker complete a sentence completion task at least as much as a regular dictionary does.

2   Method

The purpose of our study is to examine how wordnets aid human users. The experiment is conducted by asking Finnish native speakers to carry out sentence completion tasks in English using different lexical resources for assistance.

The test consists of SAT Reasoning Test style multiple choice sentence completion tasks. We

decided on using sentence completion rather than translation because it is more straightforward to assess the correctness of the answers. Had we chosen a translation task, we would have first had to decide what the ultimately best translation of a given English passage is, which is a complex issue reaching far beyond the scope of this paper.

We sought out the sample questions from a set of training questions for the SAT test[1]. We estimated that SAT-level English is sufficiently difficult for Finnish university students, so that the testees would not be able to get full scores on the test without using any help.

Sentence completions measure the testees vocabulary and understanding of sentence structure and require the testee to select one or two words that best complete the sentence. The questions are multiple choice and there are five options to choose from. In Figure 1 we display an example question from the test.

1. ___ by nature, Jones spoke very little even to his own family members.
A. garrulous
B. equivocal
C. taciturn
D. arrogant
E. gregarious

Figure 1: A sample question

There are 40 questions randomly grouped into sets of ten. Each set is completed with the help of a different aid.

2.1   Lexical Resources

The purpose of the experiment is to see which lexical aid helps the testee the most. In order to see this, we ask the testees to use three different tools: an electronic English dictionary, PWN and FiWN. One set of questions is answered without using any help so that we can establish the English vocabulary skills of the answerer.

2.1.1   Merriam-Webster

We chose the Merriam-Webster[2] English dictionary as the electronic dictionary since it is widely used and freely available. First off we thought of using an English-Finnish dictionary, but since the task is not about translation, the English dictionary better suits our needs. Using an English dictionary we can see what help the testees receive

---

[1] http://www.majortests.com/sat/sentence-completion.php
[2] http://www.merriam-webster.com

from a regular dictionary without Finnish translations. We assume this to be the most typical kind of lexical aid used. An abridged dictionary entry for "equivocal"[3] can be seen in Figure 2 with the boldface words being links to other entries.

equiv·o·cal

1.

a: subject to two or more **interpretations** and usually used to mislead or confuse <an equivocal statement>

b: uncertain as an indication or sign <equivocal evidence>

2.

a: of uncertain nature or classification <equivocal shapes>

b: of uncertain **disposition** toward a person or thing : **undecided** <an equivocal attitude>

c: of doubtful advantage, genuineness, or moral **rectitude** <equivocal behavior>

Examples of EQUIVOCAL

He responded to reporters' questions with *equivocal* answers. The experiment produced *equivocal* results.

Figure 2: A truncated Merriam-Webster dictionary entry

Merriam-Webster also includes information about the etymology of the word and a list of synonyms and antonyms. For conciseness sake we do not repeat the information here.

2.1.2 PWN

The second resource we use is the PWN. [4] We give a truncated PWN search result for the word *equivocal*[5] in Figure 3.

Overview of adj equivocal
The adj equivocal has 3 senses (first 1 from tagged texts)
1. (1) equivocal, **ambiguous** – (open to two or more interpretations; or of uncertain nature or significance; or (often) intended to mislead; "an equivocal statement"; [...])
2. equivocal – (open to question; "aliens of equivocal loyalty"; [...])
3. equivocal – (uncertain as a sign or indication; "the evidence from bacteriologic analysis was equivocal")

Figure 3: A truncated PWN entry: Overview

If the user only uses the "Overview" mode of the PWN, the use of the wordnet resembles that of a regular dictionary. Only when the user also views the "Similarity" information of the word,

does the structure of the wordnet benefit the user. This can be seen in Figure 4. The boldfaced words are again links to other entries.

Similarity of adj *equivocal*
Sense 1 *equivocal* (vs. **unequivocal**), **ambiguous**
=> **double, forked**
=> **evasive**
=> **indeterminate**
Also See-> **ambiguous#2**
Sense 2 *equivocal*
=> **questionable** (vs. **unquestionable**)
Sense 3 *equivocal*
=> **inconclusive** (vs. **conclusive**)

Figure 4: A truncated PWN entry: Similarity

It is also possible to view e.g. antonyms, pertainyms, derived forms and the polysemy count of the word, but for the task at hand the information presented in Figures 4 and 3 suffices.

We assume that using the English wordnet yields at least slightly better results in the sentence completion task than using an electronic dictionary. The assumption based on the intuitive grouping of the synsets.

2.1.3 FiWN

The third tool to be used in the test is the PWN with the Finnish translations visible, FiWN[6]. The search results are identical to the PWN, only the Finnish translations are added. The glosses and examples are still only in English. The overview of the translated adjective *equivocal* is shown in Figure 5.

Overview of adj equivocal
The adj equivocal has 3 senses (first 1 from tagged texts)
1. (1) equivocal [**kaksiselitteinen**], **ambiguous** [**monikäsitteinen, epäselvä, monimerkityksinen**] – (open to two or more interpretations; or of uncertain nature or significance; or (often) intended to mislead; "an equivocal statement"; [...])
2. equivocal [**epävarma, kyseenalainen**] – (open to question; "aliens of equivocal loyalty"; [...])
3. equivocal [**epävarma, kyseenalainen**] – (uncertain as a sign or indication; "the evidence from bacteriologic analysis was equivocal")

Figure 5: A truncated FiWN entry with translations: Overview

Correspondingly, Figure 6 shows the synsets with the Finnish equivalents.

We want to see whether the results get significantly better when the testee gets to use a bilingual wordnet. At first guess it can be assumed that the translations speed up the test taking and improve

---

[3]http://www.merriam-webster.com/dictionary/equivocal
[4]http://wordnet.princeton.edu/
[5]http://www.ling.helsinki.fi/cgi-bin/fiwn/search?wn=en&w=equivocal&t=all&sm=Search

[6]http://www.ling.helsinki.fi/cgi-bin/fiwn/search?

Similarity of adj *equivocal*
Sense 1 *equivocal* [**kaksiselitteinen**] (vs. **unequivocal** [**vastaansanomaton, selkeä**]), **ambiguous** [**monikäsitteinen, epäselvä, monimerkityksinen**]
=> **double** [**kaksimielinen**], **forked** [**kaksimielinen**]
=> **evasive** [**välttelevä, kartteleva**]
=> **indeterminate** [**epämääräinen**]
Also See-> **ambiguous#2** [**monikäsitteinen, epäselvä, monimerkityksinen**]
Sense 2 *equivocal* [**epävarma, kyseenalainen**]
=> **questionable** [**kyseenalainen**] (vs. **unquestionable** [**kiistaton**])
Sense 3 *equivocal* [**epävarma, kyseenalainen**]
=> **inconclusive** [**ei ratkaiseva**] (vs. **conclusive** [**ratkaiseva**])

Figure 6: A truncated FiWN entry with translations: Similarity

the results. Since we do not time the test taking, it is only possible to see whether the results get better.

2.2 The Test in Practice

We want to make sure that the randomly chosen questions are equally difficult and that the results are not influenced by one set of questions being easier or harder than the other. To ensure this, we circulate the tool used for each group as shown in Table 1.

QUESTIONS	1-10	11-20	21-30	31-40
TOOL USED	∅	M-W	PWN	FiWN
	FiWN	∅	M-W	PWN
	PWN	FiWN	∅	M-W
	M-W	PWN	FiWN	∅

∅= NO HELP

M-W= MERRIAM-WEBSTER

Table 1: Tool circulation

The test is conducted as an online query. The questions are organized in e-forms which are divided into four parts depending on what type of help the answerer can use. Due to the tool circulation, there are four different e-forms, the order of the tools corresponding to the lines in Table 1.

The test is conducted without supervision or timing. The lack of supervision is due to practical issues; the number of answers is higher when the testees can complete the task whenever it suits them best. This, however, means that the results can be faked. In order to make cheating in the task less tempting, the test is submitted anonymously.

3 Results

We got 34 responses to our query during three weeks with only one reminder. Though the number of testees is fairly small, we can still make general remarks on the usefulness of the three lexical aids as well as on their statistical significance.

Based on the 34 answers we can show that even using an English dictionary significantly improves the performance of the testee. This is a rather predictable outcome. The more interesting question is, whether using PWN as a dictionary improves the results further. And finally, whether a bilingual English-Finnish wordnet brings any further assistance compared to the English one.

Table 2 summarizes the results by showing the average of correct answers per tool. The maximum score is 10.

TOOL	MEAN	MEDIAN	MODE
∅	6.99	7	8
M-W	8.57	9	9
PWN	8.91	9	9
FWN	8.73	9	9

Table 2: Results per tool

Table 2 shows how different tools help users in completing the task. At first look it can already be seen that using any of the chosen tools improves the results, and that the difference between the tools is small.

From Table 3 we can deduce that the difficulty level of the groups is relatively even although the third group seems to have been slightly harder than the rest.

Based on this sample, we cannot draw any conclusions on whether the order of the tools used as an aid makes a difference to the result. We can only state that the results without any aid are always poorer than the results when the testees could use one of the given tools.

The slightly poorer average of the third group, WN-FW-∅-MW, can possibly be explained by the the most difficult question set (21-30) being answered without any help.

Had we gotten more responses, we might be able to better distinguish between the different question groups and whether the order of the tools used matters. With the sample size being 34, we can only make careful guesses on what trend the results could follow.

	N	1-10	11-20	21-30	31-40	MEAN (TOOLS)
		QUESTION GROUPS				
$\emptyset$-MW-PWN-FIWN	4	**8**	9	8.75	8.75	8.63
FIWN-$\emptyset$-MW-PWN	7	9.14	**6.86**	8.43	9.43	8.47
PWN-FIWN-$\emptyset$-MW	10	8.4	8.5	**5.7**	8	7.65
MW-PWN-FIWN-$\emptyset$	13	8.85	9.08	8.54	**7.38**	8.46
MEAN (QUESTIONS)		8.6	8.36	7.86	8.39	

$\emptyset$= NO HELP
MW= MERRIAM-WEBSTER
N= NUMBER OF ANSWERS

Table 3: Results per question group and tool order

From this test set-up, however, we can draw conclusions on the usefulness of the tools. On the average, all testees got 6.99/10 questions correct without using any aids. The number tells us that the difficulty level of the questions is apt; in fact only 4 testees got a full score without using any help.

Using the Merriam-Webster dictionary improved most testees' performance. The number of perfect answers rises up to 10 when the testees get to use a dictionary as their aid.

Using the monolingual PWN as assistance, yields highest results. On the average the testees got 8.9/10 with the help of PWN. 12 of the answers were perfect. Based on the test, getting the Finnish translations alongside the English PWN does not improve performance on the sentence completion task. The number of perfect answers is 11 with the help of FiWN. We conclude that the translations do not provide additional value to the PWN in this type of a task.

3.1 The Wilcoxon Two Sample Test

We choose the Wilcoxon Two Sample Test[7] as the means for calculating statistical significance of the results. We want to see whether there is a significant difference in the way the testees performed while using different aids. The Wilcoxon Test fits our need because it does not assume the data to be normally distributed and yields accurate results with even small data.

We run the Wilcoxon Test on the material pairwise to see which tools differ from each other significantly. The test is performed for all possible pairings of the tools, as shown below. With the Wilcoxon test we can assume that if p $<$0.05, it is

not likely that the two groups have the same distribution and median making the difference statistically significant.

a) $\emptyset$ vs. Merriam-Webster

b) $\emptyset$ vs. PWN

c) $\emptyset$ vs. FiWN

d) Merriam-Webster vs. PWN

e) Merriam-Webster vs. FiWN

f) PWN vs. FiWN

We formulate the null hypothesis in the following way:

H_0: *The data in groups x and y are independent samples from identical continuous distributions with equal medians.*

We carry out the Wilcoxon tests to see whether we have to reject the null hypothesis at the 5% significance level. The results are given in Table 4.

TOOL	p $<=$
a) $\emptyset$ vs. M-W	0.00085
b) $\emptyset$ vs. PWN	0.000034
c) $\emptyset$ vs. FiWN	0.00033
d) M-W vs. PWN	0.3706
e) M-W vs. FiWN	0.7452
f) PWN vs. FiWN	0.5852

Table 4: Results of the Wilcoxon Two Sample test

The figures in Table 4 tell us that with the sample size of 34 at the 5% significance level we have to reject the null hypothesis for pairs d, e, and f. However, for pairs a, b and c, we cannot reject the null hypothesis. From this follows that we can

---

[7]http://www.fon.hum.uva.nl/Service/Statistics/Wilcoxon_Test.html

assume that any of our chosen tools significantly helps the testee in completing the task.

Currently, the small number of responses prevents us from drawing firm conclusions on the significance of the difference between using wordnets and regular electronic dictionaries. However, the average performance using either of the two wordnets was better than using only an electronic dictionary.

4 Discussion and further work

The test gives us an insight into the usage of wordnets as dictionaries and into the way they can compete with traditional electronic dictionaries. The advantages a human user get from using a wordnet instead of a dictionary has so far not been widely studied.

We should extend the test with a larger sample of respondents to determine the significance of the improvement using wordnets over regular electronic dictionaries. Our number of responses is too small for making conclusions on which tool helps the testee most. Based on the experiment it is clear, however, that using any of our chosen tools helps the testee perform better.

Based on our study, it remains an open question whether the translations available in the FiWN bring any additional value to the testee. This could be better tested with a translation task, where the translated wordnet would probably be the most helpful tool. However, assessing the quality of the translations is difficult.

The average reported SAT results[8] in 2010 for the Critical Reading[9] part of the test for test takers with English as their first language are 64 percent.

Our sample consisted mainly of language students at the University of Helsinki and the sample performance of 69.9 percent on average conforms to the expectations when using no aids or tools. An initial concern that the performance boost is relevant only for non-native speakers therefore seems not to be the case.

Our experiment provided us feedback for development of the test and FiWN. After completing the test, the testees had the chance of leaving open feedback on both the testing method and the

tools. Most testees found the translated wordnet most helpful, their gut feeling was that that using it would yield best results. Only a few testees preferred using Merriam-Webster over using either one of the wordnets.

Typically NLP applications that use wordnets for semantic classification use human performance as the gold standard when evaluating the results. This is the case e.g. in Turney and Littman (2005). The authors implement an algorithm for corpus-based learning of analogies and semantic relations and compare the results against human performance in the SAT analogy questions. There system correctly answers 47% of the questions where the average SAT test taker gets about 57% of the questions right.

We have established that human performance on tasks like sentence completion significantly improves if wordnets can be used as lexical aids. This most likely also applies to solving verbal analogies, since they are even more context-sensitive. We therefore suggest that NLP applications using wordnets should in fact be compared with human performance when humans use the same lexical resources.

To conclude, some studies have used wordnets to boost computer program performance on word sense disambiguation. Our study suggests that human users should perhaps be given a similar advantage if we wish to compare the results in a fair way.

5 Conclusion

Typically wordnets are used as lexical resources in various NLP applications. Using wordnets as lexical databases for other information systems has been studied widely, but the advantage wordnet provides to a human user as an electronic dictionary has received less interest.

We assessed the advantage of using a wordnet instead of a traditional dictionary as help in completing an SAT-type sentence completion task. The test was conducted as an online query divided in four parts. The purpose of the experiment was to see which lexical resources aid a non-native speaker the most. The resources we chose for the test are the Merriam-Webster online dictionary for the first set, the English WordNet for the second, and the bilingual FiWN, which can be used as an English-Finnish (and Finnish-English) dictionary for the third set of questions. To establish the En-

---

[8]http://professionals.collegeboard.com/profdownload/2010-total-group-profile-report-cbs.pdf

[9]The results for sentence completion are not given separately, so we have to compare our results to the Critical Reading section consisting of sentence completions and reading comprehension.

glish vocabulary skills, one set of questions was answered without any help.

The experiment sought to give insight on how useful wordnets are to a human user. The testees used both the English wordnet, and the bilingual FiWN so that we could test whether the translations bring any additional help to a non-native English speaker.

We found that a wordnet significantly improves the performance of a human user on a sentence completion task and we found weak indications that a wordnet may be slightly better than a regular electronic dictionary for this purpose. This sets new standards for what we should require from computers on similar tasks when comparing them with humans if we boost the computer performance with wordnets or other lexical resources.

References

Christiane Fellbaum, editor. 1998. *WordNet: An Electronic Lexical Database*. The MIT Press, Cambridge/London/England.

Krister Lindén and Lauri Carlson. 2010. FinnWordNet – WordNet på finska via översättning. *LexicoNordica – Nordic Journal of Lexicography*, 17:119–140.

Attila Tanács, Dóra Csendes, Veronika Vincze, Christiane Fellbaum, and Piek Vossen, editors. 2007. *Proceedings of the Fourth Global WordNet Conference*. University of Szeged.

Peter D. Turney and Michael L. Littman. 2005. Corpus-based learning of analogies and semantic relations. *Machine Learning*, 60:251–278.

Piek Vossen, editor. 1998. *EuroWordNet: a multilingual database with lexical semantic networks for European Languages*. Kluwer, Dordrecht.

Piek Vossen. 2004. EuroWordNet: a multilingual database of autonomous and language-specific wordnets connected via an inter-lingual-index. *International Journal of Linguistics*, 17(2):161–173.

ISSN 1736-6305 Vol. 11
http://hdl.handle.net/10062/16955

Creating Comparable Multimodal Corpora for Nordic Languages

Costanza Navarretta
University of Copenhagen,
Centre for Language Technology
costanza@hum.ku.dk

Elisabeth Ahlsén
University of Gothenburg
elisabeth.ahlsen@ling.gu.se

Jens Allwood
University of Gothenburg
jens@ling.gu.se

Kristiina Jokinen
University of Helsinki and
University of Tampere
kristiina.jokinen@helsinki.fi

Patrizia Paggio
University of Copenhagen,
Centre for Language Technology
paggio@hum.ku.dk

Abstract

This paper describes the collection and annotation of comparable multimodal corpora for Nordic languages in a project involving research groups from Denmark, Estonia, Finland and Sweden. The goal of the project is to provide annotated multimodal resources to study communicative phenomena, such as feedback, turn-taking and sequencing in the languages involved in the project and to compare these phenomena. Studies so far include verbal expressions, head movements and facial expressions related to feedback.

1 Introduction

Human communication is multimodal, that is it involves speech and communicative body movements, such as facial expressions, head movements, body postures, gaze and hand gestures. All these behaviors occur naturally and have been claimed to be intertwined in communication (McNeill, 2002; Kendon, 2004). Investigating the characteristics of the various modalities and exploiting their interaction in various communicative and cultural situations has been the focus of a number of recent national and international projects and networks, such as AMI, CALLAS, CALO, CHIL, HUMAINE, ISLE, SPONTAL and SSPNET.

The present collaborative Nordic project is in line with these initiatives and involves research groups from Denmark, Estonia, Finland and Sweden. The main goals of the project are the following:

- providing comparative annotated multimodal data;

- using these data to investigate specific communicative phenomena such as feedback and turn-taking;

- developing, extending and adapting models of multimodal interactive communication management that can serve as a basis for interactive systems;

- applying machine learning techniques in order to test the possibilities for automatically recognizing or predicting hand gestures, head movements and facial expressions with different interactive communication functions.

In what follows we first present the data which we have collected so far (section 2), then we discuss the annotation model which is used and briefly describe annotation procedures and available annotations (section 3). In section 4 we present some of the data that have been extracted from the annotations until now and in section 5 we conclude and outline future work.

2 The corpora

The data we work with are video recordings of interactions from a number of social activities. These activities have different purposes and involve different numbers of participants with varying roles, degree of familiarity, position in the room etc. All these aspects can influence the participants' multimodal behaviors.

In the project, we will reuse existing resources, but we are also collecting new comparable data where the social activities recorded in the various languages are the same, and the recording settings are similar. Furthermore, the data are annotated following a common annotation model, which will allow a comparison of data and annotated phenomena. In this paper we will primarily focus on the new data, the annotation model and the studies carried out so far, differing from (Paggio et al., 2010) where we described the various corpora in the project.

The annotated data will be made available for research purposes through the project website (http://sskkii.gu.se/nomco/).

2.1 Corpora of first encounters

First encounters have been studied in intercultural studies (see i.a. Argyle, 1975; Kendon, 1999) because in these data it is possible to study central communicative aspects such as how different cultures deal with varying degrees of familiarity and liking as well as with social status and norms. A comparative multimodal study of first encounters in German and Japanese has been previously conducted in the CUBE-G project (Rehm et al., 2009) with the purpose of generating and testing behavioral models for virtual agents in the two cultures.

Our comparable corpora of first encounters are studio-recorded conversations and are presently available for Swedish and Danish, but a corresponding corpus for Finnish is being collected.

The first encounters corpora are interesting because Nordic cultures are generally regarded as relatively similar, and our data will provide us with empirical evidence for similarities as well as differences in a first-meeting scenario.

The interactions in both the Swedish and Danish first encounters corpora involve two subjects who are standing in front of a light background. The participants were instructed to get to know each other in a short interaction, as they might do at a party or a reception. After the recording they answered a questionnaire about their reactions to both the interlocutor and the interaction setting.

Additional first encounter data has also been collected to compare Swedish and Danish data with data from more distant cultures as well as intercultural communication situations. A number of Chinese-Chinese interactions in Chinese and a number of Swedish-Chinese interactions in English have been recorded. There is also a comparable dataset of first encounter recordings in German, recorded in Austria (Csokor, 2010).

The Swedish first encounters corpus

The Swedish first encounters corpus consists of 39 videorecordings of interactions in Swedish, each approximately 8-10 minutes long, in total about 5 hours. In terms of gender, 19 of the interactions are male-female, 11 are male-male and 9 are female-female. The age range is 19 to 34 with a mean age of 25.

The Chinese corpus consists of 6 videorecorded Chinese-Chinese first encounter interactions in Chinese, in total about 1 hour (with a mean duration about 10 minutes), containing 3 male-female, 2 male-male and 1 female-female encounters.

The intercultural Swedish-Chinese corpus contains 10 videorecorded Swedish-Chinese first encounters in English, in total 1½ hour (mean duration about 9 minutes). Four of these interactions are male-female, 3 are male-male and 3 are female-female.

The Danish first encounters corpus

The Danish corpus of first encounters consists of approximately one hour of video-recordings, comprising 12 interactions of approximately 5 minutes each and involves 12 speakers, six males and six females, all between 21 and 36 years old. Each speaker participated in two interactions, one with a male and one with a female.

The answers to the questionnaire show that the participants were in general positive about the interaction. They report that they felt well-liked and free to express their opinions. They judged the conversations as interesting although they were aware that the setting was not completely natural (Paggio et al., 2010).

The corpus has been orthographically transcribed and a set of gestures (i.e. communicative body movements) have been annotated as it will be described in section 4.

2.2 Corpora of group interactions

Besides two-person dialogues we have also video recordings of multiparty interactions. Some of these recordings have been collected under this project, while others were already available to the involved research groups.

When the number of participants increases, interaction management becomes more complex as the responsibility of smooth communication is divided among all of them: interlocutors have both pair-wise and shared interactions, and some of them can simply act as onlookers and not take an active role in the activity. The use of multimodal means in communication is thus expected to differ from two-party dialogues, and the observational studies in conversation analysis and sociolinguistic studies have indeed shown how different non-verbal signals and spatial proximity work in the coordination and control of group interactions (Goffman 1963; Hall 1966; Kendon 1990).

The group meeting corpora aim to provide comparable data for studying conversational activity in multiparty communications. However, we want to emphasise that our current group meeting corpora do not form a similar uniform set of corpora across the languages as the first encounters. We thus do not aim at the "sameness" of the group meeting corpora but regard similarity as an abstract concept which requires semantic interpretation of the actual context: similarity can be loosely characterized in terms of the number of participants, the activities that they are involved in and the viewpoints from which the events are looked at. Our goal is thus to collect a large variety of group meetings so as to provide as wide a basis for conversations studies as possible, and thus unravel comparable features of the group communication. We assume that this can be best achieved by using the same annotation scheme for the various group meeting corpora. In our case, we have used the MUMIN annotation scheme (section 3).

A Swedish corpus of group meetings in different social activities, which is a subcorpus of the Gothenburg Spoken Language Corpus (GSLC) (Allwood et al., 2000) is available for use in the project. The corpus consists of 82 video- or audiorecorded meetings of in total 122 hours, containing 636 268 word tokens, according to the GTS 6.4 Transcription Standard (Nivre, 2004). The corpus contains arranged and naturally occurring discussions, formal and informal meetings, and dinner discussions. The number of speakers range between 2 and 12 per recording, with a mean of 7-8 speakers. The total number of speakers is 502, with a total number of 255 males, 224 females and 23 participants unidentified for gender.

A Danish corpus of informal meetings between people that are well acquainted (friends or family members) are being annotated according to the annotation model described in section 3. The videos are collected and transcribed by the University of South Denmark, and will be available through the Danish CLARIN homepage[1].

They involve varying numbers of speakers of different age who are recorded while talking informally. In all the recordings the participants are sitting around a sofa table at private homes.

The Estonian corpus of group interactions contains two 30 minutes long conversations among three participants. The participants perform according to their designated roles in scenarios which concern the planning and inspection of a new school building. Despite the acted scenarios, the participants behave fairly naturally.

The Finnish group interactions consist of card-playing interactions among four participants and conversations between a Finnish teacher and an immigrant student. The Finnish interactions are collected by Minna Vanhasalo.

3 The annotation model

Data are annotated according to a common model which is an adaptation of the MUMIN model (Allwood et al. 2007). This model has been used to annotate communicative non-verbal behavior and its relation to speech in various languages, e.g. Greek (Koutsombogera et al. 2008), Danish (Paggio and Navarretta, 2010; Navarretta and Paggio, 2010), Estonian (Jokinen and Ragni, 2008) and Japanese (Jokinen et al. 2009). The model describes the shape and the communicative function of gestures, including head movements, facial expressions, hand gestures and body postures in terms of pre-defined behavior attributes and values.

The main focus in the model, according to Allwood et al. (2007), is on the communicative function of gestures. The description of the shape of gestures provided in the model is coarse-grained, but can be refined according to specific requirements in different studies.

---

[1] https://infra.clarin.dk/clarindk/forside.jsp.

The communicative functions which have been dealt with in the MUMIN model are feedback, turn management and sequencing. Furthermore, each gesture can be assigned a semiotic type following Peirce's (1931) classification, which distinguishes between indexical, iconic and symbolic signs.

Gestures can also be assigned a value indicating the attitude they show[2] and can be connected to a word or more words if the annotators judge that there is a semantic relation between the gestures and the words.

Gestures can be multifunctional, thus several categories can be assigned to the same gesture, e.g. a nod can indicate feedback-giving and turn taking at the same time.

We have slightly modified the MUMIN model to fit the project's specific goals, and the granularity of the attributes might change depending on the phenomena we are focusing on. For example, we have simplified the linking of gestures to words using a single link type, called *MMRelationSelf*, which connects a gesture produced by a participant to the word(s) produced by the same participant, while in MUMIN four relations were recognized following (Poggi and Caldognetto, 1996).

As an example of the annotation categories used in the project to describe the shape of gestures, we show the values and attributes defined for head movements in table 1. These gestures are annotated with two attributes: the first attribute indicates the type of movement while the second one records whether a movement occurs once (*Single*) or more times (*Repeated*).

Behavior attribute	Behavior value
HeadMovement	Nod
	Tilt
	Jerk (Up-nod)
	Shake
	Waggle
	SideTurn
	HeadBackward
	HeadForward
	Other
HeadRepetition	Single
	Repeated

Table 1: Attributes and values for head movements

Table 2 contains the attributes and values accounting for the communicative function of feedback. The first attribute in the table, *FeedbackBasic*, indicates whether there is feedback or not. The second attribute, *FeedbackDirection*, describes whether a subject is giving or asking for feedback. The last attribute, *FeedbackAgreement*, is used when an interaction participant agrees or disagrees with what stated by the interlocutors.

Behavior attribute	Behavior value
FeedbackBasic	Contact/ Perception/ Understanding(CPU)
	Other (C, CP)
FeedbackDirection	Give
	Elicit
	Give-Elicit
FeedbackAgreement	Agree
	Disagree

Table 2: Attributes and values for feedback

4 The Swedish Annotated Data

In what follows we describe the Swedish corpora currently annotated and the procedures used to perform the annotations. The Swedish corpora have all been transcribed using the GTS (Gothenburg Transcription Standard (Nivre, 2004) and MSO 6 (Modified Standard Orthography) for the Swedish data (Nivre, 1999).

4.1 The first encounters data

So far, 13 of the Swedish first encounters are fully transcribed and checked by an independent transcriber.

Coding of communication management oriented gestures (head gestures, facial expressions and hand gestures) will be done using a modified version of the MUMIN coding schema.

A small corpus of Swedish-Swedish, Chinese-Chinese and Swedish-Chinese interactions has been transcribed and given a preliminary coding of feedback related gestures.

For a number of the Swedish recordings, some of the basic prosodic features of feedback expressions (pitch, F0 shapes, timing and duration) have been analyzed with the purpose of investigating the relation between prosodic features of feedback and head movement as feedback. Experimental and naturalistic feedback data is also being analyzed with respect to emotional and attitudinal features.

---

[2] The list of attitudes and emotions is open-ended.

A study focusing on repeated head movements (head nods and head shakes) and the speech co-occurring with them in the Swedish first acquaintance corpus showed that the main function of such repeated head movements is communicative feedback. This is also the most frequent function of the speech co-occurring with the head movements. However, there is mostly no 1-1 relation between repetition in head movement and vocal words. Repeated head movements are more often accompanied by single than repeated words. Both repeated head movements and repeated vocal words can also occur without accompaniment in the other modality. Also in these cases, the most frequent function for the head movements is communicative feedback. However, the most frequent function of repeated words without accompaniment in the other modality is own communication management. Frequent functions of repeated head movements, besides feedback, are emphasis, self-reflection, citation, self-reinforcement and own communication management.

Other findings in the study are that affirmative repeated head nods mostly start with an upward movement and involve two repetitions (Boholm & Allwood, 2010).

First acquaintance recordings of 4 Chinese-Chinese, 4 Swedish-Swedish and 8 Chinese-Swedish recordings, where the Chinese-Swedish interactions took place in English, were analyzed.

Some of the preliminary results are (i) that in both the Swedish and the Chinese interactions, unimodal vocal feedback is more common than unimodal gestural feedback, (ii) that both the Swedes and the Chinese use gestural feedback more multimodally than unimodally. Some differences are that the Chinese do not have a special word which exactly corresponds to yes in vocal feedback. The most common vocal feedback is "n". In gestural feedback, they use more laughter, "gaze around", gaze sideways and covering their mouth with hands. The Swedes use more vocal "m" and ingressive feedback sounds and in gestural feedback only the Swedes have up-nods and tilts. Both Swedes and Chinese use more feedback gestures when they speak English in the intercultural interactions (Allwood & Lu, 2010).

4.2 The group interaction data

Parts of the Swedish group interaction data corpus have been coded, for example for communicative acts, main addressee and group decision processes in previous studies. Gestures are only coded when judged to be especially important for the interaction by the transcribers.

5 The Danish annotated data

The Danish data annotated so far are described below.

5.1 First encounters data

The Danish corpus of first encounters has been transcribed in PRAAT (Boersma and Weenik, 2009) following the guidelines provided by Grønnum (2006) for the DanPASS project. The transcriptions are orthographic and, in addition, contain information on word stress, pauses and filled pauses. They have been made by a coder and checked by a second coder and consist of approx. 17500 tokens, of which a 16150 are running words, 550 are onomatopoeic expressions such as "hmm" and "øh" and 800 are pauses.

The transcriptions are imported into the ANVIL tool (Kipp, 2004), which is used to create the multimodal annotations.

Three coders have annotated the communicative body movements and their relation to speech following a common annotation manual. So far, head movements and face expressions have been annotated, together with the communicative function of feedback and the links connecting gestures to words in the orthographic transcription.

The annotation procedure has been the following: each video is annotated by one coder and the annotation is then revised by a second coder. Disagreements are discussed and an agreed upon annotation version is created. In cases where it is not possible to reach an agreement, a third coder resolves the disagreement.

Two inter-coder agreement experiments have been run in order to test to which extent the three coders identified the same gestures and assigned the same categories to the recognized gestures. The first experiment was run in the beginning of the annotation process, and the second one when half of the data had been annotated. In both experiments a video was annotated independently by the three annotators and then the annotations were automatically compared in ANVIL, which tests both gesture segmentation and category assignment.

The results of the latest experiment in terms of Cohen's kappa (Cohen, 1960) show an agreement in-between 60-80%. The agreement for head movements is in general higher than for face expressions. The highest disagreement values are mainly due to disagreement in the segmentation of facial expressions. Deciding where exactly a smile starts and ends, for example, is often more difficult than doing the same for a side turn.

The intercoder agreement figures improved for nearly all categories in the second experiment, partly because the coders had achieved more experience, partly because the annotation manual had been revised establishing clearer distinction criteria for problematic categories. The final agreement scores are in line with those achieved in similar annotation tasks, e.g. (Jokinen et al., 2008).

So far the first 5 annotated videos have been analyzed. The gestures annotated in the first five videos are approximately 2000, of which 40% have been judged to have a feedback function.

The direction of most feedback gestures is *Give* and there are only few feedback eliciting gestures. This is probably due to the type of social activity, but comparison with videos belonging to other types of activities will confirm this hypothesis.

The most used behavior for the expression of feedback is *HeadMovement* (61%), followed by *Face* (28%) and *Eyebrows* (11%). However, if we look at specific movement and expression types, we see that *Smile* is the type most often used to give feedback (17%), followed by *RepeatedNod* (13%). The frequency of all other types in conjenction with feedback is below 10%.

A comparative study of feedback in the Danish first encounters corpus and in similar Japanese data is being carried out aiming to investigate differences and similarities in the way Danish and Japanese people communicate feedback in this type of social interaction (Paggio et al., forthcoming).

5.2 The informal meetings data

So far, four videos with two and three participants have been orthographically transcribed in PRAAT and then imported into ANVIL. The transcriptions of these interactions consist of approx. 5,300 running words. The multimodal annotations comprise facial expressions, head movements, hand gestures and body postures. The following communicative functions have been included: feedback, turn management, sequencing and deixis. The multimodal annotations comprise the following types of communicative body movements: 110 facial expressions, 1,051 head movements, 368 hand gestures and 89 body postures. How often these behaviors have been judged to express feedback varies. Thus, a feedback function is assigned to 58% of the facial expressions, 60.5% of the head movements, 7.5% of the hand movements and 29% of the body postures.

6 The Estonian/Finnish data

About 20 minutes of the Estonian group conversations (10 minutes of each conversation) have been annotated using the MUMIN annotation scheme, which was adapted to three person interactions. The data has been used in comparing Estonian and Danish dialogue strategies (Jokinen et al., 2008), and in investigating meta-gesturing or conversation control, e.g. stand-up gestures (Jokinen and Vanhasalo, 2009).

Annotations were produced in several passes with kappa agreement ranging between 40-80%. The final annotations comprise 151 utterances, 657 facial display elements, 442 hand gesture elements, and 380 body posture elements. Facial display elements make about 44% of all non-verbal communication, confirming the importance and frequency of facial expressions in communication. The data indicate a clear correlation between speaking and non-verbal communication: the participant who talks most (produce most utterances) also seems to produce most nonverbal behaviors. Furthermore, facial displays seem to be evenly distributed while there are individual differences in the use of hand gestures and body posture.

The Finnish card-playing conversations have been analyzed with focus on gesturing. Salo (2002) studied pointing gestures as deictic elements but emphasized that the use of pointing gestures is richer and more complicated. In line with this research Jokinen and Vanhasalo (2009) show how pointing gestures also function as an effective means to control and coordinate the dialogue.

7 Conclusions and future work

In the paper we have described the first phase of the creation of comparable multimodal annotated corpora for Danish, Estonian, Finnish and Swedish. These corpora comprise video recordings of different types of social activities, such as the first encounter interactions, recorded in the same way for the different languages, but also group meetings in different contexts, which provide a rich variation of interaction data. We have also provided a preliminary analysis of how feedback is expressed through gestures and speech in the first encounter data, and how they compare with similar data for Chinese and Japanese. Further coding and analysis of the corpora will provide a basis for additional studies of multimodal interactive communication management on feedback, but also on other phenomena such as turntaking and sequencing.

Acknowledgments

This work is done under the NOMCO project, which is funded by the NORDCORP programme under the Nordic Research Councils for the Humanities and the Social Sciences (NOS-HS).

References

Allwood, Jens, Maria Björnberg, Leif Grönqvist, Elisabeth Ahlsé,n and Cajsa Ottesjö, (2000). The Spoken Language Corpus at the Dept of Linguistics, Göteborg University. *FQS - Forum Qualitative Social Research*, Vol. 1, No. 3. - Dec. 2000, pp 22.

Allwood, Jens, Loredana Cerrato, Kristiina Jokinen, ostanza Navarretta, and Patrizia Paggio (2007). The MUMIN coding scheme for the annotation of feedback, turn management and sequencing phenomena. In J.-C. Martin, P. Paggio, P. Kuehnlein, R. Stiefelhagen, and F. Pianesi (Eds.), *Multimodal Corpora for Modelling Human Multimodal Behaviour*, Volume 41 of *Special issue of the International Journal of Language Resources and Evaluation*, pp. 273–287. Springer.

Allwood, Jens and Jia Lu (2010). Chinese and Swedish multimodal communicative feedback. Paper presented at the 5:th International Conference on Multimodality. University of Technology, Sydney. Dec 1-3, 2010.

Boersma, Paul and David Weenink (2009). Praat: doing phonetics by computer (version 5.1.05). Retrieved May 1, 2009, from http://www.praat.org/.

Boholm, Max and Jens Allwood (2010). Repeated head movements, their function and relation to speech. In M. Kipp et al. (Eds.) *Proceedings of the Seventh International Conference on Language Resources and Evaluation (LREC 2010) Workshop Multimodal Corpora: Advances in Capturing, Coding and Analyzing Multimodality*, Malta, 17 May 2010, http://www.lrec-conf.org/proceedings/lrec2010/index.html.

Cohen, Jacob A. (1960). A coefficient of agreement for nominal scales. *Educational and Psychological Measurement*, 20, 37-46.

Csokor, Laurentz (2010). *Feedback in Mixed-Sex Conversation Settings.* Master Thesis at the Faculty of Life Sciences, University of Vienna, Austria.

Grønnum, Nina (2006). DanPASS - A Danish Phonetically Annotated Spontaneous Speech Corpus. In N. Calzolari, K. Choukri, A. Gangemi, B. Maegaard, J. Mariani, J. Odijk and D. Tapias (Eds.), *Proceedings of the Fifth International Conference on Language Resources and Evaluation (LREC-06)*, Genova, Italy, May.

Goffman, Erwin (1963). *Behaviour in public places: notes on the social order of gatherings.*The Free Press, New York.

Hall, Edward T. (1966). *The Hidden Dimension: man's use of space in public and private*, New York: Doubleday.

Kendon, Adam (1990). Spatial organization in social encounters: the F-formation system, In Kendon, A: *Conducting Interaction: Patterns of behavior in focused encounters*, Studies in International Sociolinguistics, Cambridge University Press.

Jokinen, Kristiina, Costanza Navarretta and Patrizia Paggio (2008). Distinguishing the communicative functions of gestures. In *Proceedings of the 5th Joint Workshop on Machine Learning and Multimodal Interaction*, 8-10 September 2008, Utrecht, The Netherlands.

Jokinen, Kristiina and Minna Vanhasalo (2009). Stand-up Gestures – Annotation for Communication Management. In *Proceedings of the NODALIDA 2009 Workshop Multimodal Communication: from Human Behaviour to Computational Models.* Odense, Denmark, May 2009, pp. 15-20.

Koutsombogera, Maria, Lida Touribaba and Harris Papageorgiou (2008) Multimodality in Conversation Analysis: A Case of Greek TV Interviews. In *Proceedings of the Sixth International Conference on Language Resources and Evaluation (LREC 2008) Workshop on Multimodal Coorpora from Models of Natural Interaction to Systems and Applications*, Marrakesh, May 2008, pp. 12-15.

Navarretta Costanza and Patrizia Paggio. Classification of Feedback Expressions in Multimodal Data. *Proceedings of the 48th Annual Meeting of the Association for Computational Linguistics* (ACL 2010), Uppsala, Sweden, Juli 11-16, 2010, pp. 318-324.

Nivre, Joakim (1999). *Modifierad Standardortografi, Version 6 (MSO6)*. Department of Linguistics, University of Gothenburg.

Nivre, Joakim (2004). *Göteborg Transcription Standard. (GTS) V. 6.4*. Department of Linguistics, University of Gothenburg.

Paggio, Patrizia, Jens Allwood, Elisabeth Ahlsén, Jristiina Jokinen & Costanza Navarretta (2010). The NOMCO Multimodal Nordic Resource – Goals and Characteristics. In Calzolari, N, Choukri, K. Maegaard, B, Mariani, J., Odijk, J, Piperidis, S, Rosner, M. & Tapias, D. (Eds.) *Proceedings of the Seventh International Conference on Language Resources and Evaluation (LREC'10)* Valetta, Malta May 19-21. ELRA. http://www.lrecconf.org/proceedings/lrec2010/index.html

Paggio, Patrizia, Kristiina Jokinen and Costanza Navarretta (forthcoming). Head movements, facial expressions and feedback in first encounters interaction. To appear in the *Proceedings of HCI International 2011*, Orlando Florida, July 9-14.

Paggio Patrizia and Costanza Navarretta. Feedback in Head Gestures and Speech. In M. Kipp et al. (Eds.) In *Proceedings of the Seventh International Conference on Language Resources and Evaluation (LREC 2010) Workshop Multimodal Corpora: Advances in Capturing, Coding and Analyzing Multimodality*, Malta, May 17 2010, pp. 1-4.

Peirce, Charles S. (1931). *Collected Papers of Charles Sanders Peirce, 1931–1958*, 8 vols. Edited by C. Hartshorne, P. Weiss and A. Burks. Cambridge, MA: Harvard University Press.

Poggi, Isabella and Emanuela Magno Caldognetto (1996). A score for the analysis of gestures in multimodal communication. In *Proceedings of the Workshop on the Integration of Gesture and Language in Speech*. Applied Science and Engineering Laboratories. L. Messing, Newark and Wilmington, Del, pp. 235–244.

Rehm, Matthias, Elisabeth Andre, Nikolaus Bee, Birgit Endrass, Michael Wissner, Yukiko Nakano, Afia Akhter Lipi,Toyoaki Nishida, and Hung-Hsuan Huang (2008). Creating Standardized Video Recordings of Multimodal Interactions across Cultures. In Kipp et al (eds.) *Multimodal Corpora. From Models of Natural Interaction to Systems and Applications*. LNAI 5509. Springer, pp.138–159.

Salo, Minna (2002). Puhujan eleiden kuvailu: eleiden muoto ja merkitys sekä ajoitus. ("Description of the speaker's gestures: the form and meaning of gestures and their timing") Master's Thesis.

Department of Finnish and General Linguistics. University of Tampere.

ISSN 1736-6305 Vol. 11
http://hdl.handle.net/10062/16955

Estimating Language Relationships from a Parallel Corpus.
A Study of the Europarl Corpus

Taraka Rama, Lars Borin
Språkbanken, Department of Swedish
University of Gothenburg, Sweden
taraka.rama.kasicheyanula@gu.se
lars.borin@svenska.gu.se

Abstract

Since the 1950s, linguists have been using short lists (40–200 items) of basic vocabulary as the central component in a methodology which is claimed to make it possible to automatically calculate genetic relationships among languages. In the last few years these methods have experienced something of a revival, in that more languages are involved, different distance measures are systematically compared and evaluated, and methods from computational biology are used for calculating language family trees. In this paper, we explore how this methodology can be extended in another direction, by using larger word lists automatically extracted from a parallel corpus using word alignment software. We present preliminary results from using the Europarl parallel corpus in this way for estimating the distances between some languages in the Indo-European language family.

1 Introduction

Automatic identification of genetic relationships among languages has gained attention in the last few years. Estimating the distance matrix between the languages under comparison is the first step in this direction. Then a distance based clustering algorithm can be used to construct the phylogenetic tree for a family. The distance matrix can be computed in many ways. Lexical, syntactic and semantic features of the languages can be used for computing this matrix (Ringe et al., 2002). Of these, lexical features are the most widely used features, most commonly in the form of *Swadesh lists*.

Swadesh lists are short lists (40–200 items) of basic senses which are supposed to be universal. Further, the words expressing these senses in a language are supposed to be resistant to borrowing. If these two assumptions hold, it follows that such lists can be used to calculate a numerical estimate of genetic distances among related languages, an endeavor referred to as *lexicostatistics*. A third assumption which was often made in the older literature was that the replacement rate of this basic vocabulary was constant and could be expressed as a constant percentage of the basic vocabulary being replaced over some unit of time (exponential decay). This third assumption has generally been abandoned as flawed and with it the body of research that it motivated, often referred to as *glottochronology*.

In lexicostatistics, the similarity between two languages is the percentage of shared cognates between the two languages in such a list. In the terminology of historical linguistics, cognates are words across languages which have descended independently in each language from the same word in a common ancestor language. Hence, loanwords are not cognates. Cognates are identified through regular sound correspondences. For example, English $\sim$ German *night* $\sim$ *Nacht* 'night' and *hound* $\sim$ *Hund* 'dog' are cognates. If the languages are far enough removed in time, so that sound changes have been extensive, it is often far from obvious to the non-expert which words are cognates, e.g. English $\sim$ Greek *hound* $\sim$ *kuon* 'dog' or English $\sim$ Armenian *two* $\sim$ *erku* 'two'.

In older lexicostatistical work (e.g. Dyen et al. 1992), cognates are manually identified as such by experts, but in recent years there has been a strong interest in developing automatic methods for cognate identification. The methods proposed so far are generally based on some form of orthographic similarity[1] and cannot distinguish be-

---

[1] Even though the similarity measures used in the literature all work with written representations of words, these written representations are often in fact phonetic transcriptions, so that we can say that we have a phonetic similarity measure. For this reason we will use "orthographic" and "phonetic" interchangeably below.

tween cognates on the one hand and loanwords or chance resemblances on the other. Confusingly, the word pairings or groups identified in this way are often called cognates in the computational linguistics literature, whereas the term *correlates* has been proposed in historical linguistics for the same thing (McMahon and McMahon, 2005). In any case, the identification of such orthographically similar words is a central component in any automatic procedure purporting to identify cognates in the narrower sense of historical linguistics. Hence, below we will generally refer to these methods as methods for the identification of cognates, even if they actually in most cases identify correlates.

There have been numerous studies employing string similarity measures for the identification of cognates. The most commonly used measure is normalized edit distance. It is defined as the minimum number of deletions, substitutions and insertions required to transform one string to another. There have also been studies on employing identification of cognates using string similarity measures for the tasks of sentence alignment (Simard et al., 1993), statistical machine translation (Kondrak et al., 2003) and translational lexicon extraction (Koehn and Knight, 2002).

The rest of this paper is structured as follows. Section 2 discusses related work. Section 3 explains the motivation for using a parallel corpus and describes the approach.

2   Related work

Kondrak (2002) compares a number of algorithms based on phonetic and orthographical similarity for judging the cognateness of a word pair. His work surveys string similarity/ distance measures such as *edit distance*, *Dice coefficient* and *longest common subsequence ratio* (LCSR) for the task of cognate identification. The measures were tested on vocabulary lists for the Algonquian language family and Dyen's (1992) Indo-European lists.

Many studies based on lexicostatistics and phylogenetic software have been conducted using Swadesh lists for different language families. Among the notable studies for Indo-European are the lexicostatistical experiments of Dyen et al. (1992) and the phylogeny experiments of Ringe et al. (2002) and Gray and Atkinson (2003). In another study, Ellison and Kirby (2006) used intra-language lexical divergence for measuring the inter-language distances for the Indo-European

language family.

Recently, a group of scholars (Wichmann et al., 2010; Holman et al., 2008) have collected 40-item Swadesh word lists for about two thirds of the world's languages.[2] This group uses a modified Levenshtein distance between the lexical items as the measure of the inter-language distance.

Singh and Surana (2007) use corpus based measures for estimating the distances between South Asian languages from noisy corpora of nine languages. They use a phonetics based similarity measure called *computational phonetic model of scripts* (CPMS; Singh et al. 2007) for pruning the possible cognate pairs between languages. The mean of the similarity between the pruned cognate pairs using this measure is estimated as the distance between the languages.

Bergsma and Kondrak (2007) conduct experiments for cognate identification using alignment-based discriminative string similarity. They automatically extract cognate candidate pairs from the Europarl corpus (Koehn, 2005) and from bilingual dictionaries for the language pairs English–French, English–German, English–Greek, English–Japanese, English–Russian, and English–Spanish. Bouchard-Côté et al. (2007) also use the Europarl corpus to extract cognates for the task of modeling the diachronic phonology of the Romance languages. In neither case is the goal of the authors to group the languages genetically by family, as in the work presented here. The previous work which comes closest to the work presented here is that of Koehn (2005), who trains pair-wise statistical translation systems for the 11 languages of the Europarl corpus and uses the systems' BLEU scores for clustering the languages, under the assumption that ease of translation correlates with genetic closeness.

3   Our approach

As noted above, automatic identification of cognates is a crucial step in computational historical linguistics. This requires an approach in which cognates have to be identified with high precision. This issue has been discussed by Brew et al. (1996). They were trying to extract possi-

---

[2]Their collaboration goes under the name of the *Automated Similarity Judgement Program (ASJP)* and their current dataset (in late 2010) contains word lists for 4,820 languages, where all items are rendered in a coarse phonetic transcription, even for those languages where a conventional written form exists.

ble English-French translation pairs from a multilingual corpus for the task of computational lexicography. Two issues with the automatic methods is the presence of *false friends* and *false negatives*. False friends are word pairs which are similar to each other but are unrelated. Some examples of false friends in French and English are *luxure* 'lust' ~ *luxury*; *blesser* 'to injure' ~ *bless*. False negatives are word pairs which are actually cognates but were identified as unrelated. For our task, we focus on identifying cognates with a high precision – i.e., few false friends – and a low recall – i.e., many false negatives. The method requires that the word pairs are translations of each other and also have a high orthographic similarity.

Section 4 introduces the use of the Europarl corpus for cognate identification. We extract the cognate pairs between a pair of languages in the following manner. For every language pair, the corpus is word aligned using GIZA++ (Och and Ney, 2003) and the word pairs are extracted from the alignments. Word pairs with punctuation are removed from the final set. Positive and negative training examples are generated by thresholding with a LCSR cutoff of 0.58.

The cutoff of 0.58 was proposed by Melamed (1999) for aligning bitexts for statistical machine translation. The reason for this cutoff is to prevent the LCSR's inherent bias towards shorter words. For example, the word pairs *saw/osa* and *jacinth/hyacinthe*[3] have the same LCSR of $2/3$ and $4/6$ which is counter-intuitive. If the words are identical, then the LCSR for the longer pair and the short pair are the same. A word alignment tool like GIZA++ aligns the words which are *probable translations of each other* in a particular sentence.

Given cognate lists for two languages, the distance between two languages l_a, l_b can be expressed using the following equation:

$$Dist(l_a, l_b) = 1 - \frac{\sum_i sim(l_a^i, l_b^i)}{N} \quad (1)$$

$sim(l_a^i, l_b^i)$ is the similarity between the ith cognate pair and is in the range of $[0, 1]$. String similarities is only one of the many possible ways for computing the similarity between two words. N is the number of word pairs being compared. Lexicostatistics is a special case of above equation where the range of the sim function is $0|1$. The choice of the similarity function is a tricky one. It would

be suitable to select a function which is symmetric. Another criterion that that could be imposed is $sim(x, y) \rightarrow [0, 1]$ where x, y are two strings (or cognate pairs).

To the best of our knowledge, there is no previous work using these lexical similarities for estimating the distances between the languages from a parallel corpus. Section 4 describes the creation of the dataset used in our experiments. Section 5 describes the experiments and the results obtained. Finally the paper concludes with a direction for future work.

4   Dataset

The dataset for these experiments is the publicly available Europarl corpus. The Europarl corpus is a parallel corpus sentence aligned from English to ten languages, Danish, Dutch, Finnish, French, German, Greek, Italian, Portugese, Spanish, and Swedish. Greek was not included in this study since it would have to be transliterated into the Latin alphabet.[4] The corpus was tokenized and the XML tags were removed using a dedicated Perl script. The next task was to create parallel corpora between all the 45 pairs of languages. English was used as the bridge language for this purpose. For each language pair, a sentence pair was included, if and only if there is a English sentence in common to each sentence. Only the first 100,000 sentence pairs for every language pair were included in these experiments. Sentence pairs with a length greater than 40 words were not included in the final set.

All the languages of the Europarl corpus belong to the Indo-European language family, with one exception: Finnish is a member of the Finno-Ugric branch of the Uralic language family, which is not demonstrably related to Indo-European. The other languages in the Europarl corpus fall under three different branches of Indo-European:

1. Danish, Dutch, English, German and Swedish are Germanic languages and can be further subgrouped into North Germanic (or Scandinavian) – Danish and Swedish – and West Germanic – Dutch, English and German, with Dutch and German forming a more closely related subgroup of West Germanic;

---

[3]Taken from Kondrak (2005)

[4]This is a task for the future.

	pt	it	es	da	nl	fi	fr	de	en
sv	3295	4127	3648	12442	5568	**2624**	3159	3087	5377
pt		10038	13998	2675	2202	**831**	6234	1245	6441
it			11246	3669	3086	**1333**	7692	1738	7647
es				3159	2753	**823**	6933	1361	7588
da					6350	**2149**	3004	3679	5069
nl						**1489**	2665	3968	4783
fi							955	1043	**1458**
fr								1545	6223
de									2206
sv : Swedish, **pt** : Portugese, **it** : Italian, **es** : Spanish, **da** : Danish, **nl** : Dutch **fi** : Finnish, **fr** : French, **de** : German								

Table 1: Number of cognate pairs for every language pair.

2. French, Italian, Portuguese and Spanish are Romance languages, with the latter two forming a more closely related Ibero-Romance subgroup, joining French at the next level up in the family tree, and Italian being more distantly related to the other three;

3. Greek forms a branch of its own (but was not included in our experiment; see above).

We would consequently expect our experiments to show evidence of this grouping, including the isolated status of Finnish with respect to the other Europarl corpus languages.

5 Experiments

The freely available statistical machine translation system MOSES (Koehn et al., 2007) was used for aligning the words. The system also extracts the word alignments from the GIZA++ alignments and computes the conditional probabilities for every aligned word pair. For every language pair, the word pairs that have an LCSR value smaller than the *cutoff* are discarded. Table 1 shows the number of pairwise cognates.

We experiment with three string similarity measures in this paper. Levenshtein distance and LCSR are described in the earlier sections. The other measures are *Dice* and *LCSR*. *Dice* is defined as twice the total number of shared character bigrams between two words divided by the total number of bigrams. In the next step, the normalized Levenshtein distance (NLD) between the likely cognate pairs are computed for every language pair. The Levenshtein distance between two words is normalized by the maximum of the length

of the two words to account for the length bias. The distance between a language pair is the mean of all the word pairs' distances. The distance results are shown in table 2. *Dice* and *LCSR* are similarity measures and lie in the range of $[0, 1]$.

We use these distances as input to a hierarchical clustering algorithm, UPGMA available in PHYLIP (Felsenstein, 2002), a phylogeny inference package. UPGMA is a hierarchical clustering algorithm which infers a *ultrametric* tree from a distance matrix.

6 Results and discussion

Finnish is clearly the outlier when it comes to shared cognate pairs. This is shown in bold in table 1. Not surprisingly, Finnish shares the highest number of cognates with Swedish, from which it has borrowed extensively over a period of several hundred years. Table 2 shows the pair-wise language distances. The last column shows the language that has the maximum and minimum similarity for each language and distance.

Figures 1, 2 and 3 show the trees inferred on the basis of the three distance measures. Every tree has Spanish, Portugese and Italian under one subgroup, and Danish, Swedish and German are grouped together in all three trees. Finnish is the farthest group in all the trees except in tree 2. The closest languages are Danish and Swedish which are grouped together. Spanish and Portugese are also grouped as close relatives. The trees are not perfect: For instance, French, English and Dutch are grouped together in all the trees.

One can compare the results of these experiments with the tree inferred using Swadesh lists,

	pt	it	es	da	nl	fi	fr	de	en	max	min
sv	0.2994	0.2999	0.306	0.2012	0.2806	0.3131	0.2773	0.2628	0.282	da	fi
	0.5849	0.5876	0.5869	0.6805	0.61	0.6215	0.6187	0.634	0.6195	da	pt
	0.7321	0.7272	0.7264	0.8127	0.7516	0.7152	0.7496	0.7577	0.7424	da	fi
pt		0.2621	0.187	0.2944	0.2823	0.3234	0.2747	0.2783	0.2895	es	fi
		0.6147	0.6824	0.5892	0.6102	0.5709	0.5711	0.5958	0.6008	es	fi
		0.7646	0.8289	0.7289	0.7529	0.7109	0.7541	0.7467	0.7405	es	fi
it			0.2611	0.2923	0.2858	0.3418	0.2903	0.283	0.2802	es	fi
			0.6137	0.5871	0.5916	0.5649	0.5725	0.5847	0.6065	pt	fi
			0.7638	0.7321	0.7474	0.6954	0.7397	0.7448	0.7473	pt	fi
es				0.2965	0.2918	0.3265	0.2725	0.2756	0.2841	it	fi
				0.5924	0.5992	0.5746	0.5799	0.5967	0.6084	pt	fi
				0.7298	0.7444	0.7081	0.7601	0.75	0.7475	pt	fi
da					0.2829	0.3174	0.2596	0.2648	0.269	sv	fi
					0.6064	0.6196	0.6208	0.6164	0.6201	sv	fi
					0.7518	0.7127	0.7639	0.7618	0.7509	sv	fi
nl						0.3343	0.2452	0.2699	0.268	fr	fi
						0.5743	0.6457	0.5971	0.6207	fr	fi
						0.7058	0.7843	0.765	0.7616	fr	fi
fi							0.3369	0.3389	0.3218	sv	it
							0.5525	0.5817	0.6093	sv	fr
							0.7027	0.7135	0.7072	sv	it
fr								0.2734	0.2328	en	fi
								0.5964	0.6505	en	fi
								0.7555	0.7905	en	fi
de									0.2733	sv	fi
									0.6082	sv	fi
									0.749	da	fi

Table 2: The first, second and third entry in each cell correspond to Levenshtein distance, Dice and LCSR distances.

e.g. the results by Dyen et al. (1992), which on the whole agree with the commonly accepted subgrouping of Indo-European (except that according to their results, English is equally far apart from Dutch/German and Danish/Swedish). However, for its successful application to language subgrouping problems, Swadesh lists rely on a large amount of expert manual effort, both in the compilation of a Swadesh list for a new language[5] and in making the cognacy judgements required for the method used by Dyen et al. (1992) and others.

Working with corpora and automated distance measures, we are in a position both to bring more languages into the comparison, and avoiding the admitted subjectivity of Swadesh lists,[6] as well as

potentially being able to draw upon both quantitatively and qualitatively richer linguistic data for the purposes of genetic classification of languages.

Instead, we compare our results with the only similar previous work that we are aware of, viz. with the tree obtained by Koehn (2005) from BLEU scores. Koehn's tree gets the two major branches of Indo-European – Germanic and Romance – correct, and places Finnish on its own. The subgroupings of the major branches are erroneous, however: Spanish is grouped with French instead of with Portugese, and English is grouped

---

[5]It is generally not a straightforward task to determine which item to list for a particular sense in a particular language, whether to list more than one item, etc.

[6]The Swadesh lists were originally compiled on the ba-

sis of linguistic experience and intuition about which senses should be universally available as words in languages and which words should be most resistant to replacement over time. These assumptions are only now beginning to be subjected to rigorous empirical testing by typological linguists, and it seems that both may be, if not outright false, then at least too simplistic (Goddard, 2001; Evans and Levinson, 2009; Haspelmath and Tadmor, 2009).

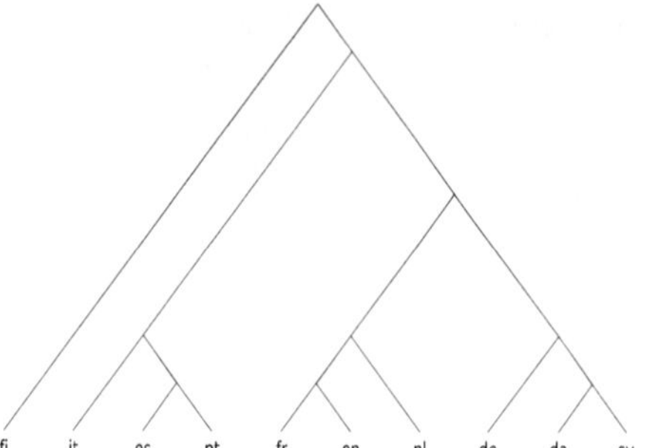

Figure 1: UPGMA clustering for Levenshtein distance scores

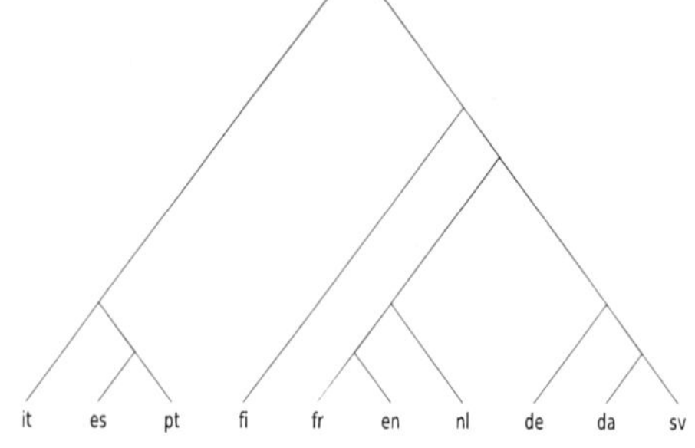

Figure 2: UPGMA clustering for Dice distance scores

with Swedish and Danish instead of forming a group with German and Dutch.

Using corpora rather than carefully selected word lists brings noise into the comparison, but it also promises to bring a wealth of additional information that we would not have otherwise. Specifically, moving outside the putative core vocabulary, we will pick up evidence of language contact in the form of borrowing of vocabulary and historical spread of orthographical conventions. Thus, one possible explanation for the grouping of Dutch, English and French is that the first two have borrowed large parts of the vocabulary used in the Europarl corpus (administrative and legal terms) from French, and additionally in many cases have a spelling close to the original French form of the words (whereas French loanwords in e.g. Swedish have often been orthographically adapted, for example French *jus* ∼ English *juice* ∼ Swedish *sky* 'meat juice').

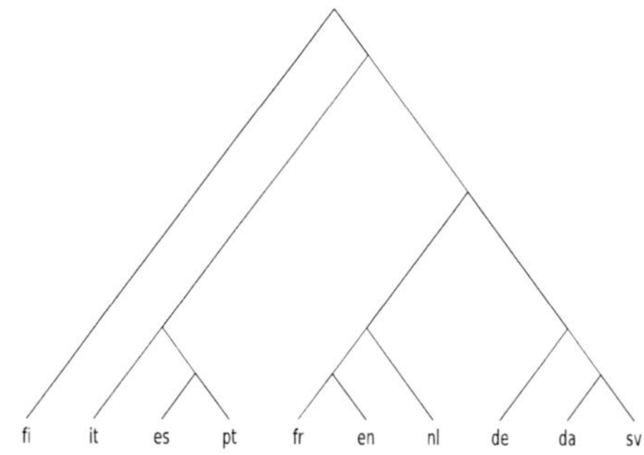

Figure 3: UPGMA clustering for LCSR distance scores

7   Conclusions and future work

We have presented preliminary experiments with different string similarity measures over translation equivalents automatically extracted from a parallel corpus for estimating the genetic distances among languages. The preliminary results indicate that a parallel corpus could be used for this kind of study, although because of the richer information that a parallel corpus provides, we will need to look into, e.g., how cognates and loanwords could be distinguished. This is an exciting area for future research.

In this study, only the lexical features of the parallel corpora have been exploited, following the tradition of Swadesh list based language comparison. However, using corpora we can move well beyond the lexical level, as corpora can also be used for comparing other linguistic features. Consequently, we plan to experiment with syntactic features such as POS tags for estimating the similarity among languages. Not only the orthographic similarity but also the co-occurrence context vectors for the words could be used to estimate the similarity between translationally similar words.

References

S. Bergsma and G. Kondrak. 2007. Alignment-based discriminative string similarity. In *AN-NUAL MEETING-ASSOCIATION FOR COMPU-TATIONAL LINGUISTICS*, volume 45, page 656.

A. Bouchard-Côté, P. Liang, T.L. Griffiths, and D. Klein. 2007. A probabilistic approach to diachronic phonology. In *Empirical Methods in Natural Language Processing*.

C. Brew, D. McKelvie, et al. 1996. Word-pair extraction for lexicography.

I. Dyen, J.B. Kruskal, and P. Black. 1992. An Indoeuropean classification: A lexicostatistical experiment. American Philosophical Society.

T.M. Ellison and S. Kirby. 2006. Measuring language divergence by intra-lexical comparison. In *Proceedings of the 21st International Conference on Computational Linguistics and the 44th annual meeting of the Association for Computational Linguistics*, pages 273–280. Association for Computational Linguistics.

Nicholas Evans and Stephen C. Levinson. 2009. The myth of language universals: Language diversity and its importance for cognitive science. *Behavioral and Brain Sciences*, 32:429–492.

J. Felsenstein. 2002. PHYLIP (phylogeny inference package) version 3.6 a3. *Distributed by the author. Department of Genome Sciences, University of Washington, Seattle*.

Cliff Goddard. 2001. Lexico-semantic universals: A critical overview. *Linguistic Typology*, pages 1–65.

R.D. Gray and Q.D. Atkinson. 2003. Language-tree divergence times support the Anatolian theory of Indo-European origin. *Nature*, 426(6965):435–439.

Martin Haspelmath and Uri Tadmor, editors. 2009. *Loanwords in the world's languages: A comparative handbook*. De Gruyter Mouton.

E.W. Holman, S. Wichmann, C.H. Brown, V. Velupillai, A. Müller, and D. Bakker. 2008. Explorations in automated language classification. *Folia Linguistica*, 42(3-4):331–354.

P. Koehn and K. Knight. 2002. Learning a translation lexicon from monolingual corpora. In *Proceedings of the ACL-02 workshop on Unsupervised lexical acquisition-Volume 9*, pages 9–16. Association for Computational Linguistics.

P. Koehn, H. Hoang, A. Birch, C. Callison-Burch, M. Federico, N. Bertoldi, B. Cowan, W. Shen, C. Moran, R. Zens, et al. 2007. Moses: Open source toolkit for statistical machine translation. In *Proceedings of the 45th Annual Meeting of the ACL on Interactive Poster and Demonstration Sessions*, pages 177–180. Association for Computational Linguistics.

P. Koehn. 2005. Europarl: A parallel corpus for statistical machine translation. In *MT summit*.

G. Kondrak, D. Marcu, and K. Knight. 2003. Cognates can improve statistical translation models. In *Proceedings of the 2003 Conference of the North American Chapter of the Association for Computational Linguistics on Human Language Technology: companion volume of the Proceedings of HLT-NAACL 2003–short papers-Volume 2*, pages 46–48. Association for Computational Linguistics.

G. Kondrak. 2002. Algorithms for language reconstruction.

G. Kondrak. 2005. Cognates and word alignment in bitexts. *Proceedings of the Tenth Machine Translation Summit (MT Summit X)*, pages 305–312.

A.M.S. McMahon and R. McMahon. 2005. *Language classification by numbers*. Oxford University Press, USA.

I.D. Melamed. 1999. Bitext maps and alignment via pattern recognition. *Computational Linguistics*, 25(1):130.

Franz Josef Och and Hermann Ney. 2003. A systematic comparison of various statistical alignment models. *Computational Linguistics*, 29(1):19–51.

D. Ringe, T. Warnow, and A. Taylor. 2002. Indo-European and Computational Cladistics. *Transactions of the Philological Society*, 100(1):59–129.

M. Simard, G.F. Foster, and P. Isabelle. 1993. Using cognates to align sentences in bilingual corpora. In *Proceedings of the 1993 conference of the Centre for Advanced Studies on Collaborative research: distributed computing-Volume 2*, pages 1071–1082. IBM Press.

A.K. Singh and H. Surana. 2007. Can corpus based measures be used for comparative study of languages? In *Proceedings of Ninth Meeting of the ACL Special Interest Group in Computational Morphology and Phonology*, pages 40–47. Association for Computational Linguistics.

Anil Kumar Singh, Harshit Surana, and Karthik Gali. 2007. More accurate fuzzy text search for languages using abugida scripts. In *Proceedings of ACM SIGIR Workshop on Improving Web Retrieval for Non-English Queries*, Amsterdam, Netherlands.

S. Wichmann, E.W. Holman, D. Bakker, and C.H. Brown. 2010. Evaluating linguistic distance measures. *Physica A: Statistical Mechanics and its Applications*.

ISSN 1736-6305 Vol. 11
http://hdl.handle.net/10062/16955

Improving Sentence-level Subjectivity Classification through Readability Measurement

Robert Remus

Dept. of Computer Science, NLP Group
University of Leipzig, Germany
rremus@informatik.uni-leipzig.de

Abstract

We show that the quality of sentence-level subjectivity classification, i.e. the task of deciding whether a sentence is subjective or objective, can be improved by incorporating hitherto unused features: readability measures. Hence we investigate in 6 different readability formulae and propose an own. Their performance is evaluated in a 10-fold cross validation setting using machine learning. Thereby, it is demonstrated that sentence-level subjectivity classification benefits from employing readability measures as features in addition to already well-known subjectivity clues.

1 Introduction

Wiebe et al. (2004) refer to *subjectivity* in natural language as "aspects of language used to express opinions, evaluations, and speculations". For example, an utterance like

> "In the end, though, it is only mildly amusing when it could have been so much more."

clearly bears an opinion, i.e. is subjective, whereas an utterance like

> "The movie takes place in mexico, 2002."

clearly does not[1]. *Readability* is usually refered to as "the degree to which a given class of people find certain reading matter compelling and, necessarily, comprehensible" (cf. McLaughlin (1969)). So whereas the meaning of a sentence like

> "Nanometer-sized single crystals, or single-domain ultrafine particles, are often referred to as nanocrystals."

is quite difficult to grasp, a sentence like

> "Wills and Kate get into marriage mode."

is much easier to understand[2]. Why is that? The former sentence not only exhibits a more complex syntactic structure than the latter, but also extensively utilises domain-specific terminology that many readers would not be familiar with.

Although counter-intuitive on first sight, we pose the following hypothesis: There is a *connection between subjectivity and readability* in natural language text. If so, we may assume that knowing about its readability possibly yields valuable information regarding its subjectivity.

1.1 Related Work

To our best knowledge, readability measures have not been used to assess the subjectivity of any lexical units so far, be it word forms, phrases, sentences or whole documents. However, there is Hoang et al. (2008)'s work on evaluating the *quality* of user-created documents, and recent work on grading the *helpfulness* of reviews by (O'Mahony and Smyth, 2010), both incorporating readability measures. Close to our research is Nishikawa et al. (2010)'s study on *sentiment summarisation* which utilises measures both for informativeness and readability. Very recent support in favour of our hypothesis is provided by (Lahiri et al., 2011), who measure a correlation between *informality* and readability.

As subjectivity classification poses many interesting challenges and has many applications in NLP including genre detection, flame recognition and information extraction, the identification of

---

[1]Both sentences are taken from (Pang and Lee, 2004)'s *subjectivity data set v1.0*.

[2]The first sentence is taken from the Wikipedia article http://en.wikipedia.org/Nanoparticles, the second is taken from Sun Daily News' homepage http://www.thesun.co.uk, both accessed on January 8th, 2011.

features for subjectivity classification and the classification itself has been extensively studied. Especially Wiebe et al. contributed a lot to the field: Wiebe (2000) learns subjective adjectives from corpora in a semi-supervised fashion, while Wiebe et al. (2001) identify other subjectivity clues using collocations. Riloff et al. (2003) and Riloff and Wiebe (2003) present ways to mine extraction patterns for subjective expressions. Wiebe et al. (2004) summarise these findings and show how different features work "together in concert". Wiebe et al. (2005) introduce a scheme for annotating opinions and the like in Wiebe et al. (2003)'s English-language *Multi-Perspective Question Answering* (MPQA) corpus. Wilson et al. (2004) assess the strength of deeply-nested opinions. Wiebe and Riloff (2005) create high-precision classifiers for distinguishing between subjective and objective sentences and use them as a source for learning additional subjectivity clues.

Yu and Hatzivassiloglou (2003) perform both document- and sentence-level subjectivity classification using Naïve Bayes classifiers and several unsupervised approaches. Pang and Lee (2004) use a graph-based formalism to first tell subjective and objective sentences apart, then perform a polarity classification employing both Naïve Bayes classifiers and Support Vector Machines.

1.2 Outline

This paper is structured as follows: In the next section, we describe our method by presenting hitherto unused features for subjectivity classification: readability measures. In Section 3 we describe our experimental setup and evaluate its performance. Finally, we draw conclusions and point out possible directions for future work in Section 4.

2 Method

Following our assumption that knowing about the readability of natural language text possibly yields valuable information regarding its subjectivity, we will try to measure readability and later exploit this information for *sentence-level subjectivity classification*.

According to Klare (1974)'s survey there are 3 possible solutions to "tell whether a particular piece of writing is likely to be readable to a particular group of readers": A first solution is simply to guess. A second solution are tests, manually built and refined. A third solution are *readability measures*. We will assess readability by such measures for the obvious reason that some of them are automatically computable.

2.1 Readability Measures

We chose 6 different readability formulae from the large body of available readability measures. All measures we chose are automatically computable and *do not* depend on lexical resources like word lists and the like. We solely present the 6 formulae themselves. The reader interested in their underlying ideas, their development and the derivation of their constants and variables may be refered to the aforementioned Klare (1974), or the original work cited below.

Additionally, we propose an easy to calculate formula that embodies our own intuition for assessing readability.

2.1.1 Devereux Readability Index

The *Devereux Readability Index* D was introduced by Smith (1961) and is calculated as shown in Equation 1,

$$D = 1.56 \times wl + 0.19 \times sl - 6.49 \qquad (1)$$

where wl is the average word length in characters and sl is the average sentence length in words. The Devereux formula was designed to cover school grades 4 to 12. Hence, the higher the value of D, the less readable the graded text according to the formula.

2.1.2 Easy Listening Formula

The *Easy Listening Formula* EL was introduced by Fang (1966) and is calculated simply as shown in Equation 2,

$$EL = npsw \qquad (2)$$

where $npsw$ is the average number of polysyllabic words per sentence, i.e. words with more than just one syllable. The Easy Listening Formula is, as the name suggests, tailored to "listenability" rather than readability. Therefore, the higher the value of EL, the less "listenable" the graded text according to the formula.

2.1.3 Fog Index

The *Fog Index* was introduced in Gunning (1952) and reformulated by Powers et al. (1958). It is calculated as shown in Equation 3,

$$FI = 3.068 + 0.0877 \times sl + 0.0984 \times nosw \qquad (3)$$

where sl is the average sentence length in words and $nosw$ is the average number of one-syllable words per sentence. The higher the value of FI, the less readable the graded text according to the formula.

2.1.4 FORCAST

The *FORCAST* formula F was introduced in Caylor et al. (1973). It is calculated as shown in Equation 4,

$$F = 20.41 - 0.11 \times nosw \qquad (4)$$

where $nosw$ is the average number of one-syllable words per sentence. The higher the value of F, the less readable the graded text according to the formula.

2.1.5 New Reading Ease Index

The *New Reading Ease Index* NREI was introduced by Farr et al. (1951) and is calculated as shown in Equation 5,

$$NREI = 1.599 \times nosw - 1.015 \times sl - 31.517 \qquad (5)$$

where $nosw$ is the average number of one-syllable words per sentence and sl is the average sentence length in words. The higher the value of NREI, the less readable the graded text according to the formula.

2.1.6 SMOG

The *SMOG* grading S was introduced by McLaughlin (1969) and is calculated as shown in Equation 6,

$$S = 3 + \sqrt{npsw} \qquad (6)$$

where $npsw$ is the number of polysyllabic words. Again, the higher the value of SMOG, the less readable the graded text according to the formula.

2.1.7 An Own Formula

Following our intuition for how to assess readability, we propose an easy to calculate formula, shown in Equation 7.

$$W = wl \times sl \times ntop \qquad (7)$$

Here, wl is the average word length per sentence, sl is the average sentence length in words and $ntop$ is the average number of words in each sentence, that are not among the top 1,000 most frequent words of a large reference corpus. This list was automatically extracted from

	D	EL	FI	F	NREI	S	W
wl	×						×
sl	×		×		×		×
$nosw$			×	×	×		
$npsw$		×				×	
$ntop$							×

Table 1: Comparison of language characteristics captured by the presented readability formulae. wl denotes the average word length, sl the average sentence length in words, $nosw$ the average number of one-syllable words per sentence, $npsw$ the average number of polysyllabic words per sentence.

an English-language newspaper corpus of University of Leipzig's *Wortschatz*[3] project consisting of 49,628,893 distinct sentences, 4,785,862 word types and 926,766,504 word tokens. The idea behind $ntop$ is, that high-frequency words are common to all readers, whereas medium- to low-frequency words are not necessarily. The more unfamiliar words a reader encounters in a text, the less readable it is. wl and sl basically capture the same idea: both longer sentences and longer words lead to less readable text. Just as for all the other formulae, the higher the value of W, the less readable the graded text according to our formula.

2.1.8 Other Formulae

There are other well-known readability formulae we did not investigate in yet, e.g. Lorge (1939) and Lorge (1948)'s *Lorge formula*, Flesch (1944)'s *Flesch formula* and Dale and Chall (1948)'s *Dale-Chall formula*. These rely on lexical resources some of which are not publicly available and additionally introduce stronger language dependency.

2.2 Summary

Different readability formulae capture different language characteristics, as summarised in Table 1. Not only do they differ in their encoded features, but also in their intended outcome. Whereas some aim to determine a school grade, some refer to tables for further interpretation. For those reasons, the readabilities calculated by the presented measures are not comparable in general, although they do have in common, that higher values signalise less readable (or less listenable) text.

---

[3] http://wortschatz.informatik. uni-leipzig.de/

3 Evaluation

In order to evaluate whether the presented readability measures indeed yield possibly valuable information regarding a natural language text's subjectivity or not, we perform a sentence-level subjectivity classification using readability formulae as features: i.e., given a sentence, extract its features and classify it as being either subjective or objective.

3.1 Experimental Setup

The evaluation data set, the features and the text classifier we used in our experiments are now briefly described.

3.1.1 Evaluation Data Set

To ensure comparability and reproducibility of our results we use Pang and Lee (2004)'s publicly available *subjectivity data set v1.0*[4]. This widely-used data set consists of 5,000 sentences marked as "subjective" and 5,000 sentences marked as "objective".

3.1.2 Features

Our baseline features are *subjectivity clues* provided by Wilson et al. (2005). Their freely available English-language lexical resource encompasses 8,221 word forms, each manually annotated for being either a strong or a weak subjectivity clue and for its polarity being either positive, negative or neutral. We only used the 5,569 *strong* subjectivity clues to form a solid baseline. Examples of strong subjectivity clues include *disagree*, *love* and *overstate*.

Our additional features are the readability formulae presented in Section 2. Although most of them were developed to capture readability of whole texts, we apply them to single sentences. Their minima, maxima, averages and standard deviances measured in the 5,000 subjective and 5,000 objective sentences are shown in Table 4.

3.1.3 Text Classifier

The actual text classification is performed by Support Vector Machines (SVMs) (cf. Vapnik (1995) and Cortes and Vapnik (1995)). SVMs are known for being able to handle large feature spaces while simultaneously limiting overfitting. Because of the large number of baseline features at hand, SVMs were a natural choice. The SVMs were

Feature(s)	P	R	F
Clues	**0.849**	0.158	0.263
D	0.695	0.558	0.618
EL	0.654	0.443	0.527
FI	0.652	**0.868**	**0.743**
F	0.524	0.767	0.623
NREI	0.651	0.859	0.739
S	0.603	0.810	0.680
W	0.630	0.754	0.685

Table 2: Precision P, recall R and f-score F of all single features.

Feature(s)	P	R	F
EL, F, NREI	**0.806**	0.870	0.825
D, EL, FI, F, S	0.636	**0.961**	0.760
D, EL, F, NREI, W	0.806	0.910	**0.845**
Clues, FI, F	**0.870**	0.258	0.396
Clues, D, F, S	0.702	**0.695**	0.694
Clues, FI, F, NREI, S	0.743	0.681	**0.704**

Table 3: Precision P, recall R and f-score F of the best performing feature combinations with and without (Wilson et al., 2005)'s strong subjectivity clues.

trained using an radial basis function kernel as provided by *LibSVM* (cf. Chang and Lin (2001)).

Even though it is highly probable that some of the baseline features are either redundant, misleading, or both, no feature selection (cf. for example Weston et al. (2001)) was carried out.

3.2 Results

As we use 8 features (7 readability formula and a "feature package" consisting of 5,569 strong subjectivity clues), there are $\sum_{k=1}^{8} \binom{8}{k} = 255$ possible feature combinations. For each feature combination a SVM was trained and tested in a 10-fold cross validation setting.

In this paper we only report on the best performing feature combinations regarding precision, recall and f-score plus each single feature on its own. The results of all feature combinations will be made accessible through the author's web site[5] by the time of the publication of this work.

Results of single features are shown in Table 2, results for best performing feature combinations are shown in Table 3.

---

[4]http://www.cs.cornell.edu/People/ pabo/movie-review-data/

[5]http://www.asv.informatik. uni-leipzig.de/staff/Robert_Remus

Formula	Minimum		Maximum		Average			Std.-Dev.	
	Subjective	*Objective*	*Subjective*	*Objective*	*Subjective*	*Objective*	*Difference*	*Subjective*	*Objective*
D	-1.86	1.06	10.81	16.43	4.62	5.06	9.58%	1.94	2.25
EL	0.0	0.00	22.0	35.0	7.12	8.15	**14.38%**	3.81	4.46
FI	3.27	3.35	7.87	10.14	4.78	5.13	7.46%	0.76	0.92
F	16.36	14.71	20.32	20.32	19.16	19.0	0.87%	0.58	0.68
NREI	-85.21	-111.79	-32.18	-33.09	-49.78	-53.82	8.18%	8.74	10.68
S	3.13	3.13	6.74	8.55	4.93	4.82	2.32%	0.68	0.79
W	7.0	7.6	75.84	114.75	31.74	36.24	14.19%	10.86	14.22

Table 4: The minima, maxima, averages and standard deviances of the presented readability formulae.

3.3 Discussion

Although the presented measures may be considered as rather crude approximations of readability, it is quite clear from the results shown in Table 2 and Table 3 that they provide a valuable source of information regarding the sentence-level subjectivity.

Whereas for "single features" the strong subjectivity clues perform best in regards to precision, every single readability formula significantly outperforms them in regards to both recall and f-score as shown in Table 2. The best performing readability measure in terms of precision is the Devereux Readability Index, the Fog Index performs best in recall and f-score. Even though these results look promising on their own, it is noteworthy that a classifier that simply always chooses the same class reaches P = 0.5, R = 1.0 and F = 0.67 on the given data set.

Combinations of different readability formulae show *considerable improvement* in precision, recall and f-score over single readability formula features as shown in Table 3. Finally, combining different readability formulae with strong subjectivity clues shows further improvement and outperforms using these clues alone in precision, recall and f-score, as also shown in Table 3.

It is remarkable that FORCAST appears in every single feature combination shown in Table 3, both with and without the subjectivity clues. Noticeably Easy Listening Formula only appears in feature combinations without the subjectivity clues. Fog Index, the best performing single readability formula, appears only in combinations including the subjectivity clues. Our own formula does not contribute a lot – it only appears once.

Comparison

(Pang and Lee, 2004) report 92% *accuracy* on sentence-level subjectivity classification using Naïve Bayes classifiers and 90% accuracy using SVMs on the same data set. (Wiebe et al., 2004) report 94% accuracy on *document-level* subjectivity classification using the *k-nearest-neighbour* algorithm. Although these results are not directly comparable to ours, our approach seems to perform not as good as theirs.

4 Conclusion & Future Work

We have shown that using readability formulae and their combinations as features in addition to already well-known subjectivity clues leads to significant quality improvements in sentence-level subjectivity classification. Therefore, one might argue in favour of our initial hypothesis and say that there is a connection between readability and subjectivity. We will carry out a detailed error analysis to shed light on their relationship.

Although our approach does not yet perform as good as current state-of-the-art, we believe that readability is a feature with *less language dependency* and a greater generalisation power than the pure presence or absence of certain word n-grams. Thus, it looks promising to further investigate in readability formulae as features for subjectivity classification. Thereby, it is possibly worthwhile to choose more complex formulae, e.g. ones that incorporate syntactic knowledge like the depth of parse trees or the number of subtrees of parse trees (cf. Schwarm and Ostendorf (2005)). Such formulae might be more reliable predictors of readability than the one used in our current work.

Questions still remaining open include: do we need readability formulae themselves or is it sufficient to just use the language characteristics captured by them? Are readability formulae independent from each other, and if so, to what degree? Are our results reproducible on other data sets, in other domains and even for languages other than English? If so, is there a plausible linguistic explanation for a correlation between subjectivity and readability? We will address these points in future work.

Acknowledgements

I'm grateful to Bo Pang and Lilian Lee, Chih-Chung Chang and Chih-Jen Lin as well as Theresa Wilson, Janyce Wiebe and Paul Hoffmann for making their data sets, their software and their lexical resources publicly available. Special thanks go to the anonymous reviewers whose useful comments and suggestions considerably improved the original paper.

References

John S. Caylor, Thomas G. Sticht, Lynn C. Fox, and J. Patrick Ford. 1973. Methodologies for Determining Reading Requirements of Military Occupational Specialties. Technical Report 73-5, HUMRO Western Division.

Chih-Chung Chang and Chih-Jen Lin, 2001. *LIB-SVM: a Library for Support Vector Machines.* Software available at http://www.csie.ntu.edu.tw/~cjlin/libsvm.

Corinna Cortes and Vladimir Vapnik. 1995. Support-vector Networks. *Machine Learning*, 20(3):273–297.

Edgar Dale and Jeanne S. Chall. 1948. A Formula for Predicting Eeadability. *Educational Research Bulletin*, pages 11–28.

Irving E. Fang. 1966. The "Easy Listening Formula". *Journal of Broadcasting & Electronic Media*, 11(1):63–68.

James N. Farr, James J. Jenkins, and Donald G. Paterson. 1951. Simplification of Flesch Reading Ease Formula. *Journal of Applied Psychology*, 35(5):333–337.

Rudolf Flesch. 1944. Marks of Readable Style: A Study in Adult Education. *The Teachers College Record*, 45(6):422–423.

Robert Gunning. 1952. *The Technique of Clear Writing*. McGraw-Hill New York.

Linh Hoang, Jung-Tae Lee, Young-In Song, and Hae-Chang Rim. 2008. A Model for Evaluating the Quality of User-created Documents. In *Proceedings of the 4th Asia Information Retrieval Conference on Information Retrieval Technology*, pages 496–501.

George R. Klare. 1974. Assessing Readability. *Reading Research Quarterly*, 10(1):62–102.

Shibamouli Lahiri, Prasenjit Mitra, and Xiaofei Lu. 2011. Informality Judgment at Sentence Level and Experiments with Formality Score. pages 446–457.

Irving Lorge. 1939. Predicting Reading Difficulty of Selections for Children. *Elementary English Review*, 16(6):229–33.

Irving Lorge. 1948. The Lorge and Flesch Readability Formulae: a Correction. *School and Society*, 67:141–142.

G. Harry McLaughlin. 1969. SMOG Grading: A New Readability Formula. *Journal of Reading*, 12(8):639–646.

Hitoshi Nishikawa, Takaaki Hasegawa, Yoshihiro Matsuo, and Genichiro Kikui. 2010. Optimizing Informativeness and Readability for Sentiment Summarization. In *Proceedings of the 18th Annual Meeting of the Association for Computational Linguistics (ACL)*, pages 325–330.

Michael P. O'Mahony and Barry Smyth. 2010. The Readability of Helpful Product Reviews. In *Proceedings of the 23rd International Florida Artificial Intelligence Research Society Conference (FLAIRS)*.

Bo Pang and Lillian Lee. 2004. A Sentimental Education: Sentiment Analysis using Subjectivity Summarization Based on Minimum Cuts. In *Proceedings of the 42nd Annual Meeting of the Association for Computational Linguistics (ACL)*.

Richard D. Powers, W.A. Sumner, and Bryant E. Kearl. 1958. A Recalculation of Four Adult Readability Formulas. *Journal of Educational Psychology*, 49(2):99–105.

Ellen Riloff and Janyce Wiebe. 2003. Learning Extraction Patterns for Subjective Expressions. In *Proceedings of the 8th Conference on Empirical Methods in Natural Language Processing (EMNLP)*, pages 105–112.

Ellen Riloff, Janyce Wiebe, and Theresa Wilson. 2003. Learning Subjective Nouns Using Extraction Pattern Bootstrapping. In *Proceedings of the 7th Conference on Natural Language Learning at HLT-NAACL*, pages 25–32.

Sarah E. Schwarm and Mari Ostendorf. 2005. Reading Level Assessment using Support Vector Machines and Statistical Language Models. In *Proceedings of the 43rd Annual Meeting on Association for Computational Linguistics (ACL)*, pages 523–530.

Edgar A. Smith. 1961. Devereux Readability Index. *The Journal of Educational Research*, 54(8):298–303.

Vladimir Vapnik. 1995. *The Nature of Statistical Learning*. Springer New York, NY.

Jason Weston, Sayan Mukherjee, Olivier Chapelle, Massimiliano Pontil, Tomaso Poggio, and Vladimir Vapnik. 2001. Feature Selection For SVMs. *Advances in Neural Information Processing Systems*, pages 668–674.

Janyce Wiebe and Ellen Riloff. 2005. Creating Subjective and Objective Sentence Classifiers from Unannotated Texts. In *Proceedings of the Sixth International Conference on Intelligent Text Processing and Computational Linguistics (CICLing)*, pages 486–497.

Janyce Wiebe, Theresa Wilson, and Matthew Bell. 2001. Identifying Collocations for Recognizing Opinions. In *Proceedings of the ACL Workshop on Collocation: Computational Extraction, Analysis, and Exploitation*, pages 24–31.

Janyce Wiebe, Eric Breck, Chris Buckley, Claire Cardie, Paul Davis, Bruce Fraser, Diane Litman, David Pierce, Ellen Riloff, Theresa Wilson, David Day, and Mark Maybury. 2003. Recognizing and Organizing Opinions Expressed in the World Press. In *Working Notes – New Directions in Question Answering (AAAI Spring Symposium Series)*.

Janyce Wiebe, Theresa Wilson, Rebecca Bruce, Matthew Bell, and Melanie Martin. 2004. Learning Subjective Language. *Computational Linguistics*, 30(3):277–308.

Janyce Wiebe, Theresa Wilson, and Claire Cardie. 2005. Annotating Expressions of Opinions and Emotions in Language. *Language Resources and Evaluation*, 1(2):165–210.

Janyce Wiebe. 2000. Learning Subjective Adjectives from Corpora. In *Proceedings of the National Conference on Artificial Intelligence*, pages 735–741.

Theresa Wilson, Janyce Wiebe, and Rebecca Hwa. 2004. Just How Mad Are You? Finding Strong and Weak Opinion Clauses. In *Proceedings of the National Conference on Artificial Intelligence*, pages 761–769.

Theresa Wilson, Janyce Wiebe, and Paul Hoffmann. 2005. Recognizing Contextual Polarity in Phrase-level Sentiment Analysis. In *Proceedings of the Conference on Human Language Technology (HLT) and Empirical Methods in Natural Language Processing (EMNLP)*, pages 347–354.

Hong Yu and Vasileios Hatzivassiloglou. 2003. Towards Answering Opinion Questions: Separating Facts from Opinions and Identifying the Polarity of Opinion Sentences. In *Proceedings of the 8th Conference on Empirical Methods in Natural Language Processing (EMNLP)*, volume 3, pages 129–136.

ISSN 1736-6305 Vol. 11
http://hdl.handle.net/10062/16955

Iterative, MT-based Sentence Alignment of Parallel Texts

Rico Sennrich and **Martin Volk**
Insitute of Computational Linguistics
University of Zurich
Binzmühlestr. 14
CH-8050 Zürich
{sennrich,volk}@cl.uzh.ch

Abstract

Recent research has shown that MT-based sentence alignment is a robust approach for noisy parallel texts. However, using Machine Translation for sentence alignment causes a chicken-and-egg problem: to train a corpus-based MT system, we need sentence-aligned data, and MT-based sentence alignment depends on an MT system. We describe a bootstrapping approach to sentence alignment that resolves this circular dependency by computing an initial alignment with length-based methods. Our evaluation shows that iterative MT-based sentence alignment significantly outperforms widespread alignment approaches on our evaluation set, without requiring any linguistic resources other than the to-be-aligned bitext.

1 Introduction

Given a parallel text, i.e. the same text in two (or more) languages, aligning the different language versions on a sentence level is a necessary first step for corpus-based machine translation (e.g. statistical MT (SMT) or example-based MT), but also for building translation memories from existing parallel texts or other forms of multilingual analysis. Some parallel texts can be aligned with comparative ease. Parliamentary Proceedings such as Europarl or the Canadian Hansards, which are frequently used for MT, provide markup information to identify the different speakers; such markup information provides useful anchor points for an alignment, and allows for accuracies above 95% (Gale and Church, 1993).

However, sentence alignment is significantly harder for other texts, as will be illustrated in section 3. Since SMT systems depend on relevant training data for their performance, it is not sufficient to only use easily accessible and alignable texts as training material for SMT systems; ideally, SMT systems should be trained on texts that are similar to those one wishes to translate. This warrants continued research on more robust sentence alignment algorithms.

Bleualign is a sentence alignment algorithm that, instead of computing an alignment between the source and target text directly, bases its alignment search on an MT translation of the source text. It has been shown that Bleualign can robustly align texts for which other algorithms perform poorly (Sennrich and Volk, 2010). The quality of sentence alignment has an effect on the performance of SMT systems (Lambert et al., 2010), but high quality is also desirable for other purposes, e.g. when building a translation memory from a text corpus. The main disadvantage of an MT-based algorithm is that it requires an existing MT system. For resource-poor language pairs, this requirement makes the algorithm unattractive.

We have investigated the bootstrapping of MT-based sentence alignment with an MT system trained on the to-be-aligned corpus. For this first MT system, a length-based sentence alignment algorithm is used which requires no linguistic resources. Such an iterative approach can supersede the dependence of the algorithm on existing MT systems.

(Sennrich and Volk, 2010) have demonstrated that the sentence alignment quality of their MT-based algorithm depends on the quality of the MT system. If we can produce a superior MT system using Bleualign, it is worthwhile to test if the resulting MT system can in turn be used for an even better sentence alignment.

2 Related Work

The first sentence alignment algorithms by (Brown et al., 1991) and (Gale and Church, 1993) are based on a length-comparison between source and target text and work without language-specific information.[1] A second strand of sentence alignment algorithms work with lexical correspondences. This is either done on the basis of correspondence rules (Simard et al., 1993), with external dictionaries (Varga et al., 2005), or using a translation model trained on the parallel text itself (Moore, 2002; Varga et al., 2005). The latter requires a preliminary sentence alignment of the parallel text, usually performed with a length-based algorithm. After this first pass, a translation model can be trained (e.g. an IBM Model 1 in the case of (Moore, 2002), a dictionary-based translation model in (Varga et al., 2005)), which is then used for the alignment in a second pass.

(Sennrich and Volk, 2010) describe an alignment algorithm based on the automatic translation of one language portion of the parallel text. They use existing MT systems to translate the to-be-aligned parallel text, then try to find an alignment between the translated source text and the target text that maximizes the BLEU score. Since sentence alignment is required to build an SMT system, being dependent on existing MT systems for sentence alignment causes a chicken-and-egg problem.

Circular dependencies as the one relating to MT-based sentence alignment are a well-known problem, for instance for word alignment. Word translation probabilities can only be estimated from a word-aligned parallel text, and to word-align the parallel text, we need a translation model. Brown et al. (Brown et al., 1993) use an iterative Expectation-Maximization algorithm for word alignment in the still widely-used IBM models.

In this paper, we investigate if the algorithm lends itself to an iterative approach similar in spirit to the one by (Brown et al., 1993), in order to avoid the dependency on pre-existing MT systems

for sentence alignment[2], while obtaining equal or better results.

3 The Parallel Text

We conduct our experiments on the parallel part of the Text+Berg corpus, a collection of Alpine texts (Volk et al., 2010). As of now, the collection consists of the yearbooks of the Swiss Alpine Club from 1864 to 1995. Since 1957, the yearbook has been published in two parallel editions, German and French. This results in about 3 million tokens of parallel text which can be used for Statistical Machine Translation.

The Text+Berg corpus is characterized by its thematic homogeneity. The topic of most if not all texts are the mountains. However, there is a wide range of text types represented in the corpus. We will illustrate this with some examples from the 1975 yearbook. Most typical are reports on mountain expeditions: *Schreckhorn-Nordwand im Winter* (English: *Schreckhorn North Face in winter*). We also find poems (one called *Praise of Nature*, one on the alphorn), a historical account on the extermination and reintroduction of ibex in the Swiss Alps, and articles that capture current trends or innovations, such as *Segelflieger im Gebirge* (English: *Gliders in the Mountains*). Recurring articles include chronicles of Himalaya expeditions, and scientific reports on the periodic variations of the glaciers in the Swiss Alps.

The corpus poses interesting challenges for Machine Translation. The terminology used in the text is very specific and is translated badly by SMT systems trained on out-of-domain data. In a set of 1000 Text+Berg sentences, 11% of tokens, or 31.4% of types, are out-of-vocabulary items for a SMT system trained on the Europarl corpus. These unseen words can be roughly divided into the following categories: named entities (*Nadelhorn*; *Selbstsanft*), domain-specific vocabulary (*Pickel*, English: *pick-axe*; *Basislager*, English: *base camp*), Swiss spelling variations (*gross* instead of *groß*, English: *big*), and OCR errors (*iweimal* instead of *zweimal*, English: *twice*). Of course, we can expect a certain proportion of unseen words in any text, especially in German, where compounds and inflected word forms abound[3]. Domain-specific vocabulary is the most

---

[1]To be precise, Gale & Church's algorithm does contain a priori probabilities for deletions and insertions estimated from the Canadian Hansards (Gale and Church, 1993). However, these parameters are usually left untouched (Danielsson and Ridings, 1997).

[2]We use open source tools to build the SMT systems; we do not, however, use any training data other than the parallel text we wish to align.

[3]We measured 0.8% unseen tokens, 4.8% unseen types in

prevalent category in the list of unseen words, and is the strongest reason for adapting MT systems to new domains with in-domain training data – not only to reduce the number of unseen words, but also to learn domain-specific translations of polysemous terms. For instance, the German term *Führer* is usually translated into French as *dirigeant* in Europarl (English: *leader*), but as *guide* in Text+Berg.

Aligning the Text+Berg corpus on a sentence level is surprisingly difficult. The texts are aligned semi-automatically on an article level. Within each article, there are no reliable structural markers: the number of paragraphs is different for the two language versions; page breaks are at different places in the text. With an average article length of approximately 200 sentences (which is about 6 pages of text), the search space for possible alignments is significantly larger than for the small segments in Europarl which are delimited by commentary tags.

Additionally, the ratio of 1-to-1 aligned sentences (We will subsequently call any n-to-m alignment a *bead*) is very low in the articles which we manually aligned for evaluation purposes. Out of the 422 beads found in a manually aligned article, only 58.3% are 1-to-1 beads. This is a striking contrast to earlier publications on the topic of sentence alignment, which reported on texts with over 90% 1-to-1 beads (Manning and Schütze, 1999). In the hand-aligned article, 19.5% of the beads are 1-to-2 or 2-to-1, 9.7% deletions (0-to-1 or 1-to-0), and the remaining 12.6% beads of higher order (2-to-2, 1-to-many, many-to-1, many-to-many).

The two main reasons for the low number of 1-to-1 beads are the joining or splitting of sentences by the translators, and errors in the digitization of the corpus. The 1-to-4 bead shown in table 1 is an example of a German sentence being split up into several French ones. In the article we hand-aligned, the translator frequently splits or joins sentences in this way. We cannot claim that the article is representative of the whole corpus, however, hence we do not exactly know how pervasive this problem is[4]. Other 1-to-many alignments are artifacts of the digitization process, e.g. OCR, tokenization, or sentence boundary detection errors.

In summary, sentence alignment is considerably more difficult for the Text+Berg corpus than e.g.

a Europarl test set, with a Europarl training set.

[4]In a independent hand-aligned set of 1000 sentences by various authors, we found 74% 1-to-1 alignments.

for Europarl, both because there are few anchor points, and because the number of 1-to-1 beads is low.

4 Iterative Sentence Alignment

Technically, iterative sentence alignment is simple, given freely available tools for SMT and sentence alignment. Each iteration consists of the following steps:

1. Sentence-align the parallel training corpus.

   - In the first iteration, use an implementation of the Gale & Church algorithm (or any other sentence alignment tool that does not require additional resources).
   - In all subsequent iterations:
     - Automatically translate the corpus using the SMT system trained in the last iteration.
     - Align the texts using Bleualign and this translation.

2. Train an SMT system on the sentence-aligned corpus.

The language model needs only be trained once; we use SRILM (Stolcke, 2002). The SMT system is built with GIZA++ (Och and Ney, 2003) and Moses (Koehn et al., 2007). The most time-consuming part of each iteration is typically the automatic translation of the training set.

In the remainder of this section, we will discuss how the alignment algorithm works, and what potential problems the iterative approach brings.

4.1 The Sentence Alignment Algorithm

The sentence alignment algorithm, first described in (Sennrich and Volk, 2010), is a two-pass approach. In the first pass, dynamic programming is used to find a set of 1-to-1 beads that maximizes BLEU score in the document without violating the monotonic order of sentence pairs. In the second pass, unaligned sentences are either added to beads found in the first pass (if warranted by increasing BLEU scores), aligned using a length-based algorithm (if possible without violating the monotonic order of sentence pairs), or discarded.

It was shown that the algorithm is very sensitive to the quality of the automatic translation (Sennrich and Volk, 2010). If no translation is provided, performance is actually worse than if the texts are aligned using the algorithm by Gale &

s_1	Aber hinter dem grossen Turm wird der Schnee grundlos, keiner von der ganzen Seilschaft hat sicheren Stand, die Spur wird zu einem tiefen Graben, der Mann an der Spitze wühlt sich 30, höchstens 40 Schritte aufwärts und tritt dann wortlos zur Seite, um dem nächsten Platz zu machen. [But behind the great tower, the snow becomes groundless; noone in the rope team has a secure footing. The track becomes a deep trench; the man in the vanguard climbs through the snow for 30, no more than 40 steps and then silently steps aside to make room for the next person.]
t_1	Mais au delà de la grosse tour, la neige est sans consistance;
t_2	aucun des membres de la cordée ne peut assurer solidement.
t_3	La trace devient une vraie tranchée;
t_4	le premier patauge péniblement pendant 30 , au maximum 40 pas, puis, sans un mot, tire de côté pour laisser place au suivant.

Table 1: Example of a 1-to-4 alignment. s is the German source text; t the French target text. English translation ours.

Church. This may happen if the BLEU-based first pass yields wrong beads, for instance if there are recurring names or dates.

4.2 Pruning

Let us consider the effect of misaligned sentence pairs. With the word alignment and phrase extraction algorithms that the Moses system uses, wrong phrase translations will be learned if sentences are misaligned. Such wrong phrase translations are normal in SMT, and usually not a big problem. For frequent phrases, every wrong phrase translation tends to be much rarer (and thus less probable) than correct ones. Rare phrases that are mistranslated are unlikely to occur again in the to-be-translated text.

Unfortunately, this last point does not hold true for an iterative approach where the training text is also the to-be-translated text. The type *AlbertEggler*, an artifact caused by OCR, only occurs once in the Text+Berg corpus. It is part of the sentence - *AlbertEggler :*, which is misaligned in the first sentence alignment pass to the sentence *1954 , Helmut Heuberger en géographie ;*. Consequently, the training algorithm estimates via Maximum Likelihood Estimation that the phrase - *AlbertEggler :* is translated to *1954 , Helmut Heuberger en géographie ;* with a probability of $1.$[5] Hence, the sentence is mistranslated during the next iteration. The problem is that such mistranslations may cause the same alignment errors to be made in subsequent iterations.

In order to prevent random misalignments to be fossilized, we prune the translation model using the approach by (Johnson et al., 2007). The pruning is based on computing whether the co-occurrence frequency of phrase pairs in the translation model is statistically significant, or to be expected by chance. All phrase pairs whose significance value fall below a predefined threshold are discarded. We chose the significance threshold $\alpha + \epsilon$, which among others discards all phrase pairs that co-occur only once.[6]

5 Evaluation

For the evaluation of alignment quality, we manually aligned an article consisting of 468 and 554 sentences (German and French, respectively). This manual alignment serves as a gold standard to which the automatic sentence alignments will be compared. The alignment test set is a subset of the training set. This unusual choice was made because it mirrors the conditions of the iterative approach: the text that is to be translated serves as training set for the SMT system, which potentially causes errors (see section 4.2). To test whether pruning mitigates the problem, we will perform the evaluation both with and without pruning.

Because of the high proportion of 1-to-many alignments, we will use two different truth conditions, which are evaluated on a per-alignment basis. Under the strict truth condition, we demand an exact match between the gold alignment and the hypothesis. Under the lax condition, a hypothesis is true if there is an overlap with a gold alignment on both language sides. This means that a 2-to-2 alignment that is misrecognized as two 1-to-1

---

[5]The term *phrase* is used to denote arbitrary word sequences in SMT, without syntactic implications. In this case, the whole sentence is treated as a single phrase by the SMT system.

[6]with $\alpha = log(N)$ and ϵ an "appropriately small positive number" (Johnson et al., 2007).

Algorithm	Alignment based on	Alignment quality		BLEU
		F_1 strict	F_1 lax	
G&C	-	0.2%	0.2%	15.54
Bleualign	Europarl	69.5%	94.4%	16.38

Table 2: Baseline scores: Sentence alignment quality and MT performance (with pruning). G&C: Gale & Church algorithm.

alignments will count as two false positives under the strict condition, but two true positives under the lax condition.

While sentence alignment may serve various goals, our main interest is using the aligned corpus for SMT, and obtaining better translation systems from better-aligned corpora. Hence, we measure translation performance of all SMT systems trained through BLEU (Papineni et al., 2002). The systems, built with SRILM (Stolcke, 2002), GIZA++ (Och and Ney, 2003) and Moses (Koehn et al., 2007), will be evaluated on a test set of 1000 sentences, held-out from training. The training set consists of 3 300 000 German and 3 740 000 French tokens, measured before sentence alignment.[7] We test translation performance in the direction DE–FR, and use a language model trained on 9 511 000 tokens of in-domain text. We did not perform Minimum Error Rate Training, which is typically the most time-intensive step of training an SMT system, in order to limit the computational cost of the iterative approach. Statistical significance is tested with paired bootstrap resampling (Koehn, 2004).

5.1 Results

We first establish baseline scores achieved by either using the Gale & Church algorithm or Bleualign with an out-of-domain MT system, shown in table 2. For a wider comparison of different sentence alignment algorithms, see (Lambert et al., 2010).

On the alignment test set, Gale & Church's algorithm fails almost entirely; only 1 out of 468 alignment hypotheses is correct. The reason for the bad performance of the Gale & Church algorithm in this evaluation is that errors tend to propagate, since misaligned sentences may cause neighbouring sentences to be misaligned as well. This is one of the reasons why anchor points – article

boundaries in our case – are so important; they serve as boundaries to the alignment algorithm and stop the propagation of errors from one article to the next.

For the iterative approach, the results obtained by aligning the Text+Berg training corpus with Bleualign, based on a translation of the corpus with a SMT system trained on Europarl[8], serve as the baseline. We observe an F_1 score of 69.5% (strict condition) and 94.4% (lax condition) in the evaluation of alignment quality. With 16.38 BLEU points, it is significantly better in terms of MT performance than the system aligned with the Gale & Church algorithm (15.54 BLEU points).[9]

It might seem surprising that MT performance of the system that is based on the Gale & Church alignment is still acceptable, despite most alignments in the alignment test set being wrong. However, note that the MT quality evaluation is based on the entire Text+Berg corpus, whereas the alignment quality evaluation is based on a relatively small test set of about 500 setences; there are articles for which Gale & Church alignment performs better. In terms of how difficult the test set is to align, this evaluation is complementary to the one by (Sennrich and Volk, 2010), who evaluated alignment algorithms on a test set of seven shorter articles. Having a difficult-to-align test set is important for the second part of our evaluation; the high error rate of the Gale & Church algorithms for this test set allows us to observe whether and to what degree misalignments are self-reinforcing, as we outlined in section 4.2.

Table 3 shows SMT and alignment performance for each of 5 iterations. Table 4 does the same, but before re-translating the training text, the system is pruned according to (Johnson et al., 2007). Note that we are interested in the effects of pruning on the alignment of training data, not in the direct effect of pruning on SMT results. This is why even for the unpruned experiment (table 3), we show MT results both with and without pruning. The effect of pruning is especially strong in the first iteration (which is identical to the baseline Gale & Church system): pruning accounts for an increase in BLEU score from 13.72 to 15.54

---

[7]The final number used for training may vary, depending on the number of sentences discarded during alignment, and the number of sentence pairs filtered because of sentence length.

[8]Approximately 25 000 000 tokens per language for training the translation model, 47 000 000 French tokens for the language model.

[9]Note that the training corpus is the same for all experiments; only the alignment algorithm and the system used to translate the corpus change between experiments.

i	Algorithm	Alignment based on	Alignment quality F_1 strict	Alignment quality F_1 lax	BLEU no pruning	BLEU pruning
1	G&C	-	0.2%	0.2%	13.72	15.54
2	Bleualign	$i\,1$	36.7%	63.8%	15.26	15.98
3	Bleualign	$i\,2$	56.7%	86.1%	15.56	16.27
4	Bleualign	$i\,3$	63.9%	92.8%	15.83	16.50
5	Bleualign	$i\,4$	65.3%	94.0%	15.69	16.44

Table 3: Sentence alignment quality and MT performance after i iterations. For each alignment, the *unpruned* MT system from the previous iteration is used. G&C: Gale & Church algorithm.

BLEU points. In later iterations, the difference is between 0.7 and 0.8 BLEU points.

We can see that the alignment quality improves after each iteration in the experiment without pruning (table 3). However, after 4 iterations, it is still lower than in the baseline experiment with an SMT system trained on Europarl. The systems in the experiment with pruning reach a higher alignment quality, and reach it after fewer iterations. We cannot explain this difference away through the general quality increase through pruning. In the third and fourth iteration without pruning, MT performance on the held-out test set is higher than in the first iteration with pruning. Still, the pruned system leads to a higher alignment quality in the subsequent iteration. We conclude that a self-reinforcement of misalignments, as described in section 4.2, does indeed occur if we do not prune the SMT systems, and that pruning successfully combats this effect.

In this experiment, an iterative alignment (with pruning) only requires two iterations to reach a stable level both in alignment quality and SMT performance. SMT performance of the second iteration of the experiment with pruning is significantly better than both baselines, and significantly better than the fifth iteration without pruning. Compared to the baseline with the Europarl SMT system, the increase is relatively small, from 16.38 to 16.67 BLEU points. At least in this experiment, the main advantage of the iterative approach lies not in a performance increase, but in being independent from external MT systems.

5.2 Interpretation and Usage Recommendations

Having to translate the entire training corpus for sentence alignment is a costly requirement, even if the iterative algorithm does not rely on external MT systems. It is thus positive that, with our SMT tools and the well-known pruning approach by (Johnson et al., 2007), we reach the highest qual-

i	Algorithm	Alignment based on	Alignment quality F_1 strict	Alignment quality F_1 lax	BLEU
1	G&C	-	0.2%	0.2%	15.54
2	Bleualign	$i\,1$	76.1%	97.6%	16.67
3	Bleualign	$i\,2$	76.7%	97.6%	16.60
4	Bleualign	$i\,3$	76.1%	97.5%	16.64
5	Bleualign	$i\,4$	76.4%	98.0%	16.52

Table 4: Sentence alignment and MT performance quality after i iterations (with pruning). G&C: Gale & Church algorithm.

ity after just two iterations, meaning that the training corpus only needs to be translated once. Still, we do not recommend iterative sentence alignment with Bleualign for all purposes.

Aspects worth considering for the choice of sentence alignment algorithm are:

1. The accuracy of computationally less expensive sentence alignment algorithms such as Gale & Church's on the parallel text. The lower their accuracy, the more promising it is to perform a sentence alignment with Bleualign.

2. The size of the parallel text. If the amount of parallel text is too small to train an adequate MT system with it, we recommend using Bleualign with a pre-existing MT system or a different alignment algorithm altogether. On the other hand, if the amount of parallel text is very large, this slows down the iterations considerably, both because of the large amount of text to be translated and the increase in training/decoding time resulting from more data. Using only a subsection of the parallel text to build the first, non-final SMT system will speed up the process.

3. The availability of language-specific resources. Whether the recommended resources are dictionaries (Varga et al., 2005), or MT systems (Sennrich and Volk, 2010), they might be unavailable or lacking in qual-

ity for a given alignment task. The iterative sentence alignment approach described in this paper is especially suitable for language pairs with few existing resources.

6 Conclusion

In (Sennrich and Volk, 2010), Bleualign was established as a well-performing sentence alignment tool given a sufficiently good existing MT system. In this paper, we show that a similar performance can be achieved without the use of language-specific resources other than the to-be-aligned parallel text. We do this by training an SMT system on the to-be-aligned text, using a length-based sentence alignment algorithm. This SMT system is then used to translate the source side of the parallel training corpus; on this translation, Bleualign bases its sentence alignment.

The biggest weakness of an iterative sentence alignment approach is that misaligned sentences lead to errors in the translation model, which tend to cause the same alignment errors in the next iteration. We show that pruning singleton phrase pairs improves the quality of iterative sentence alignment tremendously, leading to the best results after just two iterations.

Acknowledgments

This research was funded by the Swiss National Science Foundation under grant 105215_126999.

References

Peter F. Brown, Jennifer C. Lai, and Robert L. Mercer. 1991. Aligning sentences in parallel corpora. In *Proceedings of the 29th annual meeting on Association for Computational Linguistics*, pages 169–176, Morristown, NJ, USA.

P.F. Brown, V.J. Della Pietra, S.A. Della Pietra, and R.L. Mercer. 1993. The Mathematics of Statistical Machine Translation: Parameter Estimation. *Computational Linguistics*, 19(2):263–311.

Pernilla Danielsson and Daniel Ridings. 1997. Practical presentation of a "vanilla" aligner. In *TELRI Workshop on Alignment and Exploitation of Texts*, Ljubljana. Institute Jozef Stefan.

William A. Gale and Kenneth W. Church. 1993. A program for aligning sentences in bilingual corpora. *Comput. Linguist.*, 19(1):75–102.

Howard Johnson, Joel Martin, George Foster, and Roland Kuhn. 2007. Improving translation quality by discarding most of the phrasetable. In *Proceedings of the 2007 Joint Conference on Empirical Methods in Natural Language Processing and Computational Natural Language Learning (EMNLP-CoNLL)*, pages 967–975, Prague, Czech Republic, June. Association for Computational Linguistics.

Philipp Koehn, Hieu Hoang, Alexandra Birch, Chris Callison-Burch, Marcello Federico, Nicola Bertoldi, Brooke Cowan, Wade Shen, Christine Moran, Richard Zens, Chris Dyer, Ondřej Bojar, Alexandra Constantin, and Evan Herbst. 2007. Moses: Open Source Toolkit for Statistical Machine Translation. In *Proceedings of ACL 2007*, pages 177–180, Prague, Czech Republic, June.

Philipp Koehn. 2004. Statistical significance tests for machine translation evaluation. In *Proceedings of EMNLP 2004*, Barcelona, Spain.

Patrik Lambert, Sadaf Abdul-Rauf, Mark Fishel, Sandra Noubours, and Rico Sennrich. 2010. Evaluation of sentence alignment systems. Fifth MT Marathon. Le Mans, France.

Christopher Manning and Hinrich Schütze. 1999. *Foundations of Statistical Natural Language Processing*. MIT Press, Cambridge, MA, USA.

Robert C. Moore. 2002. Fast and accurate sentence alignment of bilingual corpora. In *AMTA '02: Proceedings of the 5th Conference of the Association for Machine Translation in the Americas on Machine Translation: From Research to Real Users*, pages 135–144, London, UK. Springer-Verlag.

Franz Josef Och and Hermann Ney. 2003. A systematic comparison of various statistical alignment models. *Computat. Linguist.*, 29(1):19–51.

Kishore Papineni, Salim Roukos, Todd Ward, and Wei-Jing Zhu. 2002. BLEU: a method for automatic evaluation of machine translation. In *Proceedings of ACL 2002*, pages 311–318, Morristown, NJ, USA.

Rico Sennrich and Martin Volk. 2010. MT-based sentence alignment for OCR-generated parallel texts. In *The Ninth Conference of the Association for Machine Translation in the Americas (AMTA 2010)*, Denver, Colorado.

Michel Simard, George F. Foster, and Pierre Isabelle. 1993. Using cognates to align sentences in bilingual corpora. In *CASCON '93: Proceedings of the 1993 conference of the Centre for Advanced Studies on Collaborative research*, pages 1071–1082. IBM Press.

A. Stolcke. 2002. SRILM – An Extensible Language Modeling Toolkit. In *Seventh International Conference on Spoken Language Processing*, pages 901–904, Denver, CO, USA.

Dániel Varga, László Németh, Péter Halácsy, András Kornai, Viktor Trón, and Viktor Nagy. 2005. Parallel corpora for medium density languages. In *Proceedings of the RANLP 2005*, pages 590–596.

Martin Volk, Noah Bubenhofer, Adrian Althaus, Maya Bangerter, Lenz Furrer, and Beni Ruef. 2010. Challenges in building a multilingual alpine heritage corpus. In *Proceedings of the Seventh conference on International Language Resources and Evaluation (LREC'10)*, Valletta, Malta. European Language Resources Association (ELRA).

ISSN 1736-6305 Vol. 11
http://hdl.handle.net/10062/16955

Combining Statistical Models for POS Tagging using Finite-State Calculus

Miikka Silfverberg
Helsinki University
Helsinki, Finland
miikka.silfverberg@helsinki.fi

Krister Lindén
Helsinki University
Helsinki, Finland
krister.linden@helsinki.fi

Abstract

We introduce a framework for POS tagging which can incorporate a variety of different information sources such as statistical models and hand-written rules. The information sources are compiled into a set of weighted finite-state transducers and tagging is accomplished using weighted finite-state algorithms. Our aim is to develop a fast and flexible way for trying out different tagger designs and combining them into hybrid systems. We test the applicability of the framework by constructing HMM taggers with augmented lexical models for English and Finnish. We compare our taggers with two existing statistical taggers TnT and Hunpos and find that we achieve superior accuracy.

1 Introduction

Part-of-Speech (POS) tagging, and other sequential labeling tasks like named entity recognition and chunking, constitute core tasks of language technology. Highly successful POS taggers for English have been constructed both using rule-based methods e.g. finite-state constraints used by Voutilainen (1995) and statistical methods e.g. Hidden Markov Models (HMM) used by Brants (2000).

Besides HMMs, other statistical models such as Conditional Random Fields and Maximum Entropy Models have recently been used to construct POS taggers, but HMMs remain one of the most widely used in practice. Though the more recent models surpass HMMs in accuracy, the great tagging speed and a fast development cycle of HMMs ensure a continuing popularity.

Accuracies for state of the art statistical taggers for English newspaper text surpass 97%, but results for applying these models on other languages are not always as encouraging. E.g. Dredze and Wallenberg (2008) report an accuracy 92.06% on tagging Icelandic using bidirectional sequence classification.

Low accuracy is partly due to the lack of sufficiently large tagged corpora, which can be used as training material. Reduction of accuracy can also result from the fact that the syntax and morphology of many languages differ substantially from English syntax and morphology. E.g. many languages do not have as rigid word order as English and many languages incorporate far more extensive morphological phenomena. Thus models, which have been developed for English, may not work well on many other languages.

These practical and theoretical problems associated with constructing POS taggers for virtually all of the world's languages, demonstrate the need for POS tagging models, which can incorporate a variety of different information sources including different kinds of statistical models but also more linguistic models like the ones utilized by Voutilainen (1995). Ideally the linguistic models could be used to fine-tune the result of the statistical tagging.

We propose a general framework for building POS taggers, where various kinds of statistical models and other POS tagging models can be combined using weighted finite-state calculus. Using this framework, developers can test a variety of models for tagging a language and apply the models in parallel. E.g. a statistical model trained with insufficient training data can be augmented with hand-made or machine-learned rules for common tagging errors.

In order to test the framework, we trained standard second order HMMs for Finnish and English and augmented these with extended lexical models using tag context.

We train and evaluate the English tagger using the Wall Street Journal (WSJ) corpus from Penn

Treebank II (Marcus et al., 1994). We compare the accuracy obtained by our model with the well known and widely used HMM tagger TnT (Brants, 2000) and a more recent open-source HMM tagger Hunpos (Halácsy et al., 2007), which also utilizes an extended lexical model. After improving upon the lexical model of Hunpos, our tagger obtains an accuracy of 96.67%, outperforming both TnT (96.46%) and Hunpos (96.58%).

For training and testing the Finnish tagger, we use morphologically analyzed and disambiguated newspaper text. The optimization of the model for Finnish requires some changes in the model. Together these changes improve the accuracy from a baseline second order HMM by more than 1%. We also train a Hunpos tagger for Finnish and compare it with our own tagger. The 96.02% accuracy, we obtain on the Finnish material, clearly outperforms Hunpos (95.62%).

We implemented all taggers using the freely available HFST-interface for weighted finite-state transducers (Lindén et al., 2009). An open-source interface for constructing taggers in our framework will be made publicly available.

This paper is structured in the following way. We first review some earlier work on enhancing the accuracy of HMMs. We then introduce our framework for constructing taggers in section 4. In section 5 we introduce an HMM tagger augmented with contextual lexical probabilities, which we implemented for English and Finnish in our framework. We then evaluate the English and Finnish taggers using corpus data and compare them with TnT and Hunpos. Following evaluation, we present a brief discussion on our results and future work. Finally we conclude the paper.

2 Previous Work

Statistical POS tagging is a common task in natural language applications. POS taggers can be implemented using a variety of statistical models including Hidden Markov Models (HMM) (Church, 1999; Brants, 2000), Maximum Entropy Models (Tsuruoka et al., 2005) and Conditional Random Fields (Lafferty et al., 2001).

HMMs are probably the most widely used technique for POS tagging and one of the best known imlpementations of an HMM is TnT by Brants (2000). When tagging the WSJ corpus using the splits introduced by Collins (2000), TnT achieves an accuracy of 96.46%. Although more recent statistical techniques result in improved accuracy, HMMs have remained in use chiefly because of the speed of both developing a tagger and tagging.

Recently Banko and Moore (2004) and Halácsy et al. (2007) have worked on improving the accuracy of HMMs by adding tag context into the lexical model of the HMM. The technique was pioneered by Toutanova et al. (2003) in the context of Conditional Markov Models.

The strength of Banko and Moore (2004) is that their lexical models use both left and right context when determining the conditional probability which should be associated to a wordform given a tag. The Hunpos tagger by Halácsy et al. (2007) uses only the left tag context, but it does not require a full lexicon, which makes it very practical.

We combine the left and right tag context in lexical models with a guesser for unknown wordforms. Our approach differs from Hunpos in that we only use contextually dependent lexical probabilities for known words.

Besides evaluating our approach to POS tagging by constructing a tagger for English text, we also test our approach on Finnish. Work with statistical POS tagging for Finnish seems to be virtually non-existent. Silfverberg and Lindén (2010) derive a Finnish POS tagger for the Finnish Europarl corpus (Koehn, 2005), which achieves high accuracy i.e. 96.63%, but these results could be contested on the grounds that the Europarl corpus is translated into Finnish from other languages. Silfverberg and Lindén (2010) also use an extremely large (25 million tokens) corpus. We use Finnish newspaper text to train and evaluate the tagger. Our training corpus is comparable in size to the Wall Street Journal corpus.

3 Note on Terminology

We use the terms *analysis*, *POS tag* and *tag* interchangeably to refer to POS tags, which are given for words. The *correct tag* or *analysis* refers to the intended analysis of a word in a gold standard corpus. By the term an *analysis of a sentence*, we signify one possible way to assign a unique POS tag to each of the words in the sentence. We use the term *correct analysis of a sentence* to denote the unique analysis where all of the words receive their correct analyses.

The term *analysis or tag profile of a word* refers to the set of tags which can occur as its POS analyses.

If all of the analyses of a sentence are compiled into a transducer, the paths of the transducer correspond exactly to the analyses of the sentence. In this setting, we use the terms analysis and path interchangeably. We call the transducer, compiled from the tag profiles and associated probabilities, the *sentence transducer*.

4 A Framework for Constructing POS Taggers

Our framework factors POS tagging into two tasks: (i) assigning tag profiles and probabilities $p(w|t)$ to each word w in a sentence and each of its possible analyses t and (ii) re-scoring the different analyses of the entire sentence using parallel weighted models for word and tag sequences.[1]

In the first task, the tag profile for a word w and the probabilities $p(w|t)$ for each of its tags is estimated from a training corpus. The probabilities are independent of surrounding words and tags. For unknown words u, a number of guessers can be included. These estimate the probabilities $p(u|t)$ using the probabilities $p(s|t)$ for the suffixes of u. The suffix probabilities can be estimated from a training corpus.

A number of guessers can be used to estimate the distribution of analyses for different kinds of unknown words. Like Hunpos and TnT, we always include different guessers for upper case words and lower case words, which improves accuracy.

The tag profiles of words along with tag probabilities are compiled into a weighted finite-state transducer, which associates a probability for every possible analysis of the sentence. The probability assigned to a path at this stage is the product of lexical probabilities.

After assigning tag profiles and probabilities for words, the second task is to re-score the paths of the sentence transducer. Different models can be used to accomplish this. Each of the models adds some weight to each of the analyses of the sentence and their combined effect determines the best path i.e. the most probable path. We could also incorporate models which forbid some analyses. This means that the analyses are discarded in favor of other analyses which initially seemed less

likely. Such models could be used to correct systematic errors stemming from the statistical models.

The result of applying the re-scoring models to the tag profiles is computed using weighted intersecting composition by Silfverberg and Lindén (2009). After re-scoring, a best paths algorithm (Mohri and Riley, 2002) is used to extract the most probable analysis for the sentence.

5 Augmented HMM POS Tagger for English and Finnish

For English and Finnish we constructed POS taggers based on traditional second order HMMs augmented with models, which re-score lexical probabilitites according to tag context (this is the factor $p(w_i|t_{i-1}, t_i, t_{i+1})$ in the formula below). For the sentence w_i, ..., w_n, the taggers attempt to maximize the probability $p(t_1, ..., t_n|w_i, ..., w_n)$ over tag sequences t_1, ..., t_n. Because of the data sparseness problem, it is impossible to compute the probability directly, so the tagger instead maximizes its approximation

$$\prod_{i=1}^{n} p(t_i|t_{i-1}, t_{i-2})p(w_i|t_{i-1}, t_i, t_{i+1})p(w_i|t_i)$$

where the tag sequences t_1 ..., t_n ranges over all analyses of the sentence. The term $p(t_i|t_{i-1}, t_{i-2})$ is the standard second order HMM approximation for the probability of the tag t_i. The term $p(w_i|t_{i-1}, t_i, t_{i+1})$ conditions the probability of the word w_i on its tag context. Finally the term $p(w_i|t_i)$ is the standard HMM lexical probability.

In order to get the indices to match in the formula above, three additional symbols are needed, i.e. t_{-1}, t_0 and t_{n+1} denote sentence boundary symbols, which are added during training and tagging for improved accuracy. Using sentence boundary symbols is adopted from Brants (2000).

In order to get some estimates for the probability of tag trigrams, which did not occur in the training data, we use tag bigram $p(t_i|t_{i-1})$ and tag unigram $p(t_i)$ models in parallel to the trigram model. Similarly we use models which assign probability $p(w_i|t_{i-1}, t_i)$ and $p(w_i|t_i, t_{i+1})$ in order to deal with previous unseen tag trigrams and wordforms. Of course the lexical model also weights analyses of words, serving as a backup model even in the case where the tag bigrams with the wordform were previously unseen.

---

[1]Although the probabilities $p(t|w)$ would seem like a more natural choice in the lexical model, the approximation for probabilities used in the HMM model of the tagger require the inverted probabilities $p(w|t)$. For a more thorough discussion of HMMs see Manning and Schütze (1999).

5.1 Lexical Models

For each tag t and word w, our lexical model estimates the probability $p(w|t)$. For unknown words, we construct similar guessers as Brants (2000) and Halácsy et al. (2007). The guessers estimate the probability $p(w|t)$ using the probabilities $p(s_i|t)$ for each of the suffixes of w. These can be computed from training material. The estimate $p(w|t)$ is a smoothed sum of the estimates for all of the suffixes, as explained by Brants (2000).

Like Brants (2000), we train separate guessers for upper and lower case words. For Finnish, we additionally train a guesser for sentence initial words, because preliminary tests revealed that there were a lot of unknown sentence initial words. Using a separate guesser for these words yielded better results than using the upper case or the lower case guesser. For English, a separate guesser for sentence initial words does not improve accuracy.

For Finnish another modification was needed in addition to the added guesser. For unknown words, it seemed beneficial to use only the 10 highest ranking guesses. For English, reducing the number of guesses also reduces accuracy. The maximum number of guesses is therefore a parameter which needs to be estimated experimentally and can vary between languages.

5.2 Tag Sequence Models

We construct a set of finite-state transducers whose effect is equivalent to an HMM. For the sake of space reduction, we do not compile a single transducer equivalent to an HMM. Instead we split the HMM into component models, each of which weights n-grams of wordforms and tags in the sentence. We give a short overview here and refer to Silfverberg and Lindén (2010) for a more thorough discussion on how this is done.

We simulate the tag n-gram models of a second order HMM using six models compiled into transducers. We use one transducer which assigns probabilitites for the tag unigrams in the sentence, two transducers which assign probabilitites for tag bigrams and three transducers assigning probabilities for tag trigrams.

As an example of how the transducers operate, we explain the structure of the three transducers which assign probabilities to tag trigrams. As explained above: After lexical probabilities have been assigned to the words in a sentence, the

words and their analyses are compiled into a finite-state transducer, which assigns probabilities to the possible analyses of the entire sentence. Each of the three component models of the trigram model re-weight the paths of this transducer.

The first one of the models starts with the first three words (1st, 2nd and 3rd word) of the sentence and assigns a probability for each analysis trigram of the word triplet. It then moves on to the next three words (4th, 5th and 6th word) and their analyses, and so on. Hence the first model assigns a probability for each triplet of words and its analyses, which begins at indices $3k + 1$ in the sentence.

The second model skips the first word of the sentence, but after that it behaves as the first model re-scoring first the analyses of the triple (2nd, 3rd and 4th) and going on. As a result, it assigns probabilities to trigrams starting at indices $3k + 2$ in the sentence. By skipping the first two words, the third trigram model assigns weight to triplets beginning at indices $3k$. The net effect is that each trigram of wordforms and tags gets weighted once by the trigram model.

The models re-weighting tag bigrams and tag unigrams are constructed in an analogous way to the tag trigram models and the unigram bigram and trigram probabilities are smoothed using deleted interpolation, as suggested by Brants (2000).

Each of the models assigns a minimum penalty probability $1/(N + 1)$ to unknown tag n-grams. Here N is the size of the training corpus.

5.3 Context Dependent Lexical Models

In addition to the transducers making up the HMM model, we construct context dependent lexical models, which assign probabilities

$$p(w_i|t_{i-1}, t_i, t_{i+1}), \ p(w_i|t_{i-1}, t_i), \ p(w_i|t_i, t_{i+1})$$

to word and tag combinations in analyses. The models which assign probabilities to word and tag bigram combinations are included in order to estimate the probability $p(w_i|t_{i-1}, t_i, t_{i+1})$ when the combination of w_i with tags t_{i-1}, t_i and t_{i+1} has not been seen during training.

The context dependent lexical models are only applied to known words, but they do also provide additional improvement for tagging accuracy of unknown words by directly using neighboring words in estimating their tag profiles and probabilities. This is more reliable than using tag sequences.

The choice to only apply the models on known words is a convenient one. For known words context dependent lexical models were very easy for us to compile, since they are quite similar to ordinary tag n-gram models. Integrating them with the transducers making up the HMM model did not require any extra work besides estimating experimentally three coefficients which weight the models w.r.t. the HMM and each other. Weighted intersecting composition can be used to combine the sentence transducer and the re-scoring models regardless of how many models there are.

Similarly as in the HMM, unknown combinations of tags and words receive probability $1/(N+1)$, where N is the training corpus size.

6 Data

We trained taggers for English and Finnish using corpora compiled from newspaper text.

For English we used the Wall Street Journal Corpus in the Penn Treebank. We adopted the practice, introduced by Collins (2000), to use sections 0-18 for training lexical and tag models, sections 19-21 for fine tuning (like computing deleted interpolation coefficients) and sections 22-24 for testing.

For Finnish, we used a morphologically analyzed and disambiguated corpus of news from the 1995 volume of Helsingin Sanomat, the leading Finnish newspaper[2] (We used the news from the KA section of the corpus).

The morphological tagging in the Finnish corpus is machine-made and it has not been checked manually. This soon becomes evident when one examines the corpus, since there are a number of tagging errors. Thus our results for Finnish have to be considered tentative.

Table 1 shows the number of tokens in the training, fine-tuning and test materials used to construct and evaluate the taggers. The tokenization of the corpora is used as is and all token counts include words and punctuation. As the table shows, token counts for the Finnish and English corpora are comparable.

	English	Finnish
Training	969905	1027514
Tuning	148158	181437
Testing	171138 (2.43%)	156572 (10.41%)

Table 1: Summary of token counts for the data used for evaluation. The counts include words and punctuation. The amount of words, which were not seen during training, is indicated in parentheses.

	English	Finnish
POS Tags	81	776

Table 2: Number of POS tags in the Finnish and English corpora.

The amount of unknown words in the test corpus for Finnish is high. This is to be expected given the extensive morphology of the language. The extensive morphology is also reflected in the tag counts in table 2, which shows that the tag profile of the Finnish corpus is nearly ten times as large as the tag profile of the WSJ.[3]

Of the tags, in the Finnish corpus, 471 occur ten times or more, 243 occur one hundred times or more and 86 occur one thousand times or more. We conclude that there is a large number of tags which are fairly frequent. The corresponding figures for English are 58 tags occurring ten times or more, 44 tags occurring one hundred times or more and 38 tags occurring one thousand times or more.

The average number of possible analyses for words in the English corpus is 2.34. In the Finnish corpus, a word receives on average 1.45 analyses. The high number of analyses in the English corpus is partly explained by certain infrequent analyses of the frequent words "a" and "the". When these words are excluded, the average number of analyses drops to 2.06.

When reporting accuracy, we divide the number of correctly tagged tokens with the total number of tokens in the test material, i.e. accuracy counts include punctuation. In this we follow the ACLWiki State of the Art page for POS tagging[4]. All re-

---

[2]Information about the corpus is available from `http://www.csc.fi/english/research/software/ftc`. It was compiled by The Research Institute for the Languages of Finland and CSC - IT Center for Science Ltd. The corpus can be obtained for academic use.

[3]There are 45 unique POS markers (such as NN and JJ) used in WSJ, but there are some unresolved ambiguities left in the corpus. That is why some words have POS tags consisting of more than one marker (eg. VBG|NN|JJ) making the total number of POS tags 81.

[4]`http://www.aclweb.org/aclwiki/`

sults on accuracy are reported for the test materials, which were not seen during training.

7 Evaluation

We trained four separate taggers both for English and Finnish. The accuracies for the different models are shown in table 3.

	1	2	3	4
Eng	96.42%	96.55%	96.70%	96.77%
Fin	95.56%	95.87%	95.98%	96.02%

1. Second order HMM.

2. Second order HMM augmented with lexical probabilities $p(w_i|t_{i-1}, t_i)$.

3. Second order HMM augmented with lexical probabilities $p(w_i|t_{i-1}, t_i)$ and $p(w_i|t_i, t_{i+1})$.

4. Second order HMM augmented with lexical probabilities $p(w_i|t_{i-1}, t_i)$, $p(w_i|t_i, t_{i+1})$ and $p(w_i|t_{i-1}, t_i, t_{i+1})$.

Table 3: Summary of tagging accuracies using different models. For Finnish, a separate guesser is used for sentence initial words.

The first tagger is a standard second order HMM. The only divergence from the HMM introduced by Brants (2000) is training a separate guesser for sentence initial words for Finnish and limiting the number of guesses to 10 for Finnish. This considerably improves the accuracy of the tagger from 94.91% to 95.56%.

The second tagger, we evaluate, is an HMM augmented by lexical probabilities conditioned on left tag context $p(w_i|t_{i-1}, t_i)$. This model roughly corresponds to the model Hunpos uses for POS tagging. As pointed out in section 5.3, the difference is that we do not estimate context dependent lexical probabilities for unknown words. This seems to lead to a slight reduction in accuracy.

In the third tagger, we add lexical probabilitites conditioned on right context $p(w_i|t_i, t_{i+1})$ and in the fourth tagger we add the final statistical model, which additionally uses lexical probabilities conditioned on both right and left tag context $p(w_i|t_{i-1}, t_i, t_{i+1})$.

The second tagger performs nearly as well as Hunpos and the third and fourth taggers perform better. This is to be expected, since the taggers in-

```
index.php?title=POS_Tagging_
(State_of_the_art)
```

corporate right lexical context, which Hunpos cannot utilize.

	Seen	Unseen	Overall
TnT	96.77%	85.19%	96.46%
Hunpos	96.88%	86.13%	96.58%
Hfst	97.13%	83.72%	96.77%

Table 4: Summary of tagging accuracies for WSJ using TnT, Hunpos and Hfst. The accuracies are given for seen, unseen and all tokens. Hfst is our own tagger.

Table 4 shows accuracies for TnT, Hunpos and the best of our models, which we call **Hfst**, when tagging WSJ. It clearly performs the best out of all the taggers on all tokens and it has very high accuracy on known tokens. For unknown words, its accuracy is nevertheless somewhat lower than for TnT and Hunpos.

	Seen	Unseen	Overall
Hunpos	98.06%	76.83%	95.62%
Hfst	97.98%	81.04%	96.02%

Table 5: Summary of tagging accuracies for the Finnish test corpus using Hunpos and Hfst. The accuracies are given for seen, unseen and all tokens. Hfst is our own tagger.

Table 5 shows accuracies for Hunpos and Hfst on the Finnish test corpus. The accuracy on known words is markedly high for both taggers. This is probably partly due to the low average number of analyses per word, which makes analyzing known words easier than in English text. Conversely, the accuracy on unknown words is quite low and much lower for Hunpos than for Hfst.

By increasing the number of guesses from 10 to 40 for unknown words, we accomplish a similar reduction in accuracy on unknown words (from 81.04% to 79.29%) for Hfst as Hunpos exhibits. This points to the direction that the problems Hunpos encounters in tagging unknown Finnish words are in fact due to its unrestricted guesser.

In conclusion, the Hfst tagger has better overall performance than both Hunpos and TnT.

8 Discussion and Future Work

Because of extensive and fairly regular morphology, words in Finnish contain a lot of information about their part-of-speech and inflection. Hence words which share long suffixes are probably more likely to get the same correct POS analysis in Finnish than in English.

By considering more guesses for a Finnish unknown word, one at the same time considers more guesses which were suggested on basis of words with short suffixes in common with the unknown word. This problem is worsened by smoothing, which reduces the differences between the probabilities of suggestions. In fact we believe that this implies that the kind of guesser suggested by Brants (2000) and used in Hunpos is not the ideal choice for Finnish. And an architecture which makes it possible to try out different guesser designs, could make a tagger toolkit adaptable for a larger variety of languages than a traditional HMM.

The need for an added guesser for sentence initial words in Finnish can be understood rather easily by examining the test corpus. Sentences are fairly short, on average 10.3 words. The number of unknown words in the corpus is high and sentence initial words are not an exception. Both using the guesser for lower case words and upper case words produces poor results, because the first one underestimates the number of proper names among sentence initial words and the second one grossly overestimates it. Hence a guesser trained either on all words in the test material or only sentence initial words is needed.

The need for a sentence initial guesser in fact speaks in favor of Hunpos, since it incorporates a contextually dependent lexical model also for unknown words. Therefore it needs no special tweaks in order to perform well on sentence boundaries. Still, our baseline second order HMM achieves 95.56% which is extremely close to Hunpos 95.62%. The baseline model uses context dependent lexical probabilities only in the sense that it uses the separate guesser for sentence initial words. Perhaps this is indeed the only place where a context sensitive guesser has added effect in the Finnish corpus.

There is a lot of work left with the Hfst tagger. The accuracy of the guesser needs to be improved even when tagging English. There should not be any reason why it could not be made at least as accurate as the guesser in TnT.

Another improvement would be a rule compiler which compiles hand-written rules into sequential models, that are compatible with the statistical models which are used currently. Especially for Finnish, such a rule compiler would be a significant asset, because e.g. the disambiguation of analyses of verb forms often leads to long distance dependencies, which n-gram models capture poorly. It is not evident how TnT or Hupos could be adapted to using e.g. hand-written tagging rules in order to improve performance. But it would be an easy task for Hfst, if only there existed a suitable rule compiler.

A third direction of future work, would be to try the framework for other sequential labelling tasks such as tokenizing, chunking and named entity recognition.

9 Conclusion

We have demonstrated a framework for constructing POS taggers, which is capable of incorporating a variety of knowledge sources for POS tagging. We showed that it is possible, even straight forward, to combine different statistical models into one tagger. We hope that we have also demonstrated that it would be fairly straight forward to incorporate other kinds of models as well.

We constructed taggers for English and Finnish, which obtain superior accuracy compared to two widely known and used taggers TnT and Hunpos based on HMMs. For Finnish we modified the guessers used to tag unknown words in order to achieve added accuracy. Because of the modular design of our system, this did not require changes in any of the other models. We believe that the accuracy on tagging Finnish 96.02% shows that our taggers can be successfully adapted to languages which differ substantially from English.

Acknowledgments

We thank the HFST team for their support. We would also like to thank the anonymous reviewers of this paper. Their comments were appreciated. Miikka Silfverberg was financed by LangNet the Finnish doctoral programme in language studies.

References

Michelle Banko and Robert C. Moore. 2004. *Part of Speech Tagging in Context*. Proceedings of the 20th international conference on Computational Linguistics, COLING-2004, Stroudsburg, PA, USA.

Thorsten Brants. 2000. *A Statistical Part-of-Speech Tagger*. Proceedings of the sixth conference on

Applied natural language processing, ANLP-2000, Seattle, USA.

Kenneth Church. 1988. *A Stochastic Parts Program and Noun Phrase Parser for Unrestricted Text.* Proceedings of the second conference on Applied natural language processing, ANLP-1988, Austin, Texas, USA.

Michael Collins. 2002. *Discriminative Training Methods for Hidden Markov Models: Theory and Experiments with Perceptron Algorithms.* Proceedings of the ACL-02 conference on Empirical methods in natural language processing, EMNLP-2002, Philadelphia, USA.

Dóra Csendes, János Csirik and Tibor Gyimóthy. 2004. *The Szeged Corpus: A POS tagged and Syntactically Annotated Hungarian Natural Language Corpus.* Proceedings of the 7th International Conference on Text Speech and Dialogue, TSD-2004, Brno, Czech Repulic.

Mark Dredze and Joel Wallenberg. 2008. *Icelandic data driven part of speech tagging.* Proceedings of the 46th Annual Meeting of the Association for Computational Linguistics on Human Language Technologies, HLT-2008, Stroudsburg, PA, USA.

Péter Halácsy, András Kornai and Csaba Oravecz. 2007. *HunPos – An Open Source Trigram Tagger.* Proceedings of the 45th Annual Meeting of the Association of Computational Linguistics, ACL-2007, Prague, Czech Republic.

Philipp Koehn. 2005. *Europarl: A Parallel Corpus for Statistical Machine Translation.* Machine Translation Summit, MTS-2005, Phuket, Thailand.

John Lafferty, Andrew MacCallum and Fernando Pereira. 2001. *Conditional Random Fields: Probabilistic Models for Segmenting and Labeling Sequence Data.* Proceedings of the Eighteenth International Conference on Machine Learning, ICML-2001, Williamtown, MA, USA.

Krister Lindén, Miikka Silfverberg and Tommi Pirinen. 2009. *Hfst Tools for Morphology – an Efficient Open-Source Package for Construction of Morphological Analyzers.* Workshop on Systems and Frameworks for Computational Morphology, SFCM-2009, Zürich, Switzerland.

Christopher Manning and Hinrich Schütze. 1999. *Foundations of Natural Language Processing.* The MIT Press, Massachusets, USA.

Mitchell Marcus, Grace Kim, Mary Ann Marcinkiewicz, Robert MacIntyre, Ann Bies, Mark Ferguson, Karen Katz and Britta Schasberger. 1994. *The Penn Treebank: Annotating Predicate Argument Structure.* ARPA Human Language Technology Workshop, ARPA-1994, Plainsboro, New Jersey, USA.

Mehryar Mohri and Michael Riley. 2002. *An Efficient Algorithm for the n-Best-Strings Problem.* 7th International Conference on Spoken Language Processing, ICSLP-2002, Denver, USA.

Miikka Silfverberg and Krister Lindén. 2010. *Part-of-Speech Tagging Using Parallel Weighted Finite-State Transducers.* 7th International Conference on Natural Language Processing, ICETAL-2010, Reykjavik, Iceland.

Miikka Silfverberg and Krister Lindén. 2009. *Conflict Resolution Using Weighted Rules in HFST-TwolC.* The 17th Nordic Conference of Computational Linguistics, NODALIDA-2009, Odense, Denmark.

Kristina Toutanova, Dan Klein, Christopher Manning, and Yoram Singer. 2003. *Feature-Rich Part-of-Speech Tagging with a Cyclic Dependency Network.* Proceedings of the 2003 Conference of the North American Chapter of the Association for Computational Linguistics on Human Language Technology, HLT-NAACL-2003, Edmonton, Canada.

Yoshimasa Tsuruoka, Yuka Tateishi, Jin-Dong Kim, Tomoko Ohta, John McNaught, Sophia Ananiadou and Jun'ichi Tsuji. *Developing a Robust Part-of-Speech Tagger for Biomedical Text, Advances in Informatics.* 10th Panhellenic Conference on Informatics, PCI-2005, Volos, Greece.

Atro Voutilainen. *A Syntax-Based Part-of-Speech Analyser.* Proceedings of the seventh conference on European chapter of the Association for Computational Linguistics, EACL-1995, Dublin, Ireland.

ISSN 1736-6305 Vol. 11
http://hdl.handle.net/10062/16955

Toponym Disambiguation in an English-Lithuanian SMT System with Spatial Knowledge

Raivis Skadiņš
Tilde SIA
Vienibas gatve 75a,
Riga, Latvia

Tatiana Gornostay
Tilde SIA
Vienibas gatve 75a,
Riga, Latvia

Valters Šics
Tilde SIA
Vienibas gatve 75a,
Riga, Latvia

`raiviss@tilde.lv` `Tatiana.Gornostay@tilde.lv` `Valters.Sics@tilde.lv`

Abstract

This paper presents an innovative research resulting in the English-Lithuanian statistical factored phrase-based machine translation system with a spatial ontology. The system is based on the Moses toolkit and is enriched with semantic knowledge inferred from the spatial ontology. The ontology was developed on the basis of the GeoNames database (more than 15 000 toponyms), implemented in the web ontology language (OWL), and integrated into the machine translation process. Spatial knowledge was added as an additional factor in the statistical translation model and used for toponym disambiguation during machine translation. The implemented machine translation approach was evaluated against the baseline system without spatial knowledge. A multifaceted evaluation strategy including automatic metrics, human evaluation and linguistic analysis, was implemented to perform evaluation experiments. The results of the evaluation have shown a slight improvement in the output quality of machine translation with spatial knowledge.

1 Introduction and Background

During recent decades the corpus-based strategy has become dominant for machine translation, as it has proven to be more effective both from the point of view of time and labour resources and the quality of the output. The statistical approach has occupied the leading position with the first research results performed in the late 1980s. Since then statistical machine translation (SMT) has become the major focus for many research efforts due to its cost effectiveness doubled with the availability of such open source tools as GIZA++ (Och and Ney, 2003) and Moses (Koehn et al., 2007), as well as parallel text resources on the Internet.

Pure SMT methods (Brown et al., 1993; Koehn et al., 2003) do not use any linguistic knowledge (e.g. morphological information). As a result, they perform better for analytical languages, such as English, with little inflection. Although English and Lithuanian are Indo-European languages and share some grammatical features, they have a wealth of differences. English belongs to the Germanic language group while Lithuanian belongs to the group of Baltic languages. Also, in the morphological typology English is an analytical language in contrast to a synthetic Lithuanian with a rich set of inflections. SMT for synthetic languages with high inflection (e.g. Lithuanian, Latvian, Russian and others) requires larger amounts of training data and additional knowledge to get the same level of performance.

Modern SMT methods use different kinds of additional knowledge (e.g. morphological or syntactical) to build more sophisticated statistical models and improve the output quality of machine translation (see, for example, factored SMT (Koehn et al., 2007), tree-based SMT (Chiang 2007; Marcu et al., 2006; Li et al., 2009); treelet SMT (Quirk et al., 2005). This paper presents an innovative research resulting in an English-Lithuanian statistical factored phrase-based machine translation system based on the Moses toolkit and enriched with semantic knowledge inferred from the spatial ontology.

Using semantic knowledge in rule-based machine translation is not new in the field. In SMT, however, there has been little research in this area[1]. The implemented SMT system that is de-

---

[1] See, for example, the research on extracting phrasal correspondences that are approximately semantically equivalent for building a full-sentence paraphrasing model that then is applied to a single good reference translation for each sentence in a statistical machine translation development set (Madnani et al., 2008).

scribed in this paper uses semantic knowledge to improve the quality of translation, in particular with regard to the disambiguation of geographical names, or toponyms. Spatial knowledge is added to toponyms in the source text as additional semantic tags, or factors. By adding factors into the source text, the translation accuracy is improved. This is the result of resolving semantic ambiguities in the source language.

The first part of the paper overviews the system design including a description of its functionality and implementation with spatial knowledge. In the second part we focus on the system multifaceted evaluation and its results, as well as potential limitations of the system. Finally, we present conclusions and future plans.

2 System Design

2.1 Functionality

In the overall machine translation theory and in practice English-Lithuanian toponym translation problems have not been researched before. The core functionality of the presented system is a disambiguation of toponyms during the machine translation process. Toponyms are geographical names, or names of places (hydronyms, oronyms, geonyms, oeconyms, etc.). A natural language is ambiguous and toponyms are not exceptions. This fact makes toponyms difficult for processing (e.g. resolution, cross-language information retrieval, human translation and especially machine translation), and due to their linguistic and extra-linguistic nature toponyms require special treatment (Gornostay and Skadiņa, 2009).

There are cases when real-world geographical knowledge is required for the resolution of ambiguous toponyms. The implemented SMT system deals with two types of ambiguity (see Leidner (2007) for the description of possible types of toponym ambiguity). The first type is a referential ambiguity, where a toponym may refer to more than one location of the same type, for example:

- *Georgia* as the US state and the country in Caucasus (English);

- *Riga* as the populated place and the capital of Latvia and as the populated place in the USA, state Michigan (Latvian);

- *Šveicarija* as the village in Lithuania and as the country in Europe (Lithuanian).

The second type of ambiguity is a feature type ambiguity, where a toponym may refer to more than one place of a different type, for example:

- *Tanfield* refers to the populated place as well as the castle in the United Kingdom (English);

- *Gauja* refers to the populated place as well as the river in Latvia (Latvian);

- *Šventoji* as the town near the Baltic Sea as well as the name of 3 different rivers in Lithuania (Lithuanian).

In the implemented system the two described types of toponym ambiguity are resolved using semantic knowledge inferred from the spatial ontology.

2.2 Baseline SMT System

The baseline system was a statistical phrase-based machine translation system based on the Moses toolkit and trained on the following publicly available and proprietary corpora:

- DGT-TM parallel corpus[2] – a publicly available collection of legislative texts in 22 languages of the European Union;

- OPUS parallel corpus – a publicly available collection of texts from the web in different domains[3] (Tiedemann, 2004; Tiedemann, 2009).

- Localization parallel corpus obtained from translation memories that have been created during the localization of software, user manuals and helps.

We also included word and phrase translations from bilingual dictionaries and term translations from EuroTermBank[4] to increase word coverage.

Monolingual corpora for the training of language models were prepared from corresponding monolingual parts of parallel corpora, as well as Lithuanian news articles collected from the web. Bilingual and monolingual resources prepared and used for the baseline SMT system development are represented in Table 1.

Monolingual corpus	Units
Lithuanian side of parallel corpora	~4,04 mil.

---

[2] http://langtech.jrc.it/DGT-TM.html
[3] We chose the EMEA (medical domain) and KDE4 (IT domain) sentence-aligned corpora.
[4] www.eurotermbank.com

Web news	~5,22 mil.
Total	**~9,26 mil.** (filtered)
Bilingual corpus	**Parallel units**
Localization TM	~5,21 mil.
DGT-TM	~1,08 mil.
OPUS EMEA	~1,04 mil.
Dictionary data	~0,27 mil.
EuroTermBank data	~0,1 mil.
KDE4	~0,05 mil.
Fiction	~0,01 mil.
Total (used for the baseline system)	**~7,76 mil.** (filtered)

Table 1. Training corpora.

2.3 Spatial Ontology

The spatial ontology to be integrated into the machine translation process was developed using the ontology language, designed and implemented in the web ontology language (OWL) using RCC-8 properties (Region Connection Calculus) (Randell et al., 1992), and tools developed in the SOLIM project[5]. RCC-8 properties are as follows: externally connected (EC), disconnected (DC), covered by/tangential proper part (TPP), inside/non-tangential proper part (NTPP), equal (EQ), partial overlap (PO), covers/tangential proper part inverse (TPPi), and contains/non-tangential proper part inverse (NTPPi).

The spatial ontology consisted of three sub-ontologies: basic and two language ontologies. The basic ontology contained concepts and spatial properties. The two language ontologies contained English and Lithuanian toponyms. Words in language ontologies were matched with concepts in the basic ontology (e.g. *United States*, *US* and *USA* represent the same concept *USA*). All locations in language ontologies were represented by a *geo-info.owl* code and lexically represented by a *hasLexrep* relation.

A list of instances was created on the basis of the GeoNames database[6] (7 continents, 193 countries, 51 USA states, 6359 USA cities, 6955 Lithuanian place names, 1869 cities from top 10 cities of other countries). The GeoNames database contains information about continents, countries and cities and it contains information about spatial relations between these objects. RCC-8 relations were extracted from the GeoNames database.

To query the spatial ontology we used the function *GetSpatialRelations(A,B)* to get spatial knowledge about relations between A and B. This information can be inferred from the spatial ontology, whereas we cannot get false or unknown information, for example:

- *GetSpatialRelations(Georgia,Armenia)=* "EC" only if there is enough information in the ontology to infer this relation;

- *GetSpatialRelations(Georgia,Latvia)=* "DC" if this relation can be inferred;

- *GetSpatialRelations(Georgia, Latvia)=* "", if there is not enough information in the ontology to infer the DC relation.

2.4 Implemented SMT System with Spatial Knowledge

For the implemented system with spatial knowledge we used the same training corpora as for the baseline system, as well as prepared two more corpora from the ontology – a translation dictionary (~0,02 mil. units) and spatial relation dictionary (~0,42 mil. units).

The developed baseline SMT system was a pure phrase-based SMT system which dealt only with surface forms of words. Its translation model contained simple probabilities like:

- *P(Georgia|Gruzija)* – a probability that *Georgia* is the English translation of the Lithuanian word *Gruzija*;

- *P(Georgia|Džordžija)* – a probability that *Georgia* is the English translation of the Lithuanian word *Džordžija*.

It also contained probabilities for all morphological variants of Lithuanian words and phrases. However, it was difficult to choose the correct Lithuanian translation of a given ambiguous English toponym since both probabilities were similar:

$$P(Georgia|Gruzija) \cong P(Georgia|Džordžija).$$

The factored phrase-based SMT (Koehn and Hoang, 2007) is an extension of the phrase-based approach. It contains an additional annotation at a lexical unit level. The lexical unit is no longer just a token, but a vector of factors that represent different levels of annotation. The training data (a parallel corpus) has to be annotated with additional factors. For instance, it is possible to add lemma or part-of-speech information on source and target sides.

---

[5] www.solim.eu
[6] www.geonames.org

The implemented SMT system was based on the Moses toolkit that features factored translation models allowing the integration of additional layers of data directly into the process of translation. Spatial knowledge was used during training and translation processes as additional semantic factors integrated with the source language data. All toponyms in the source text were analysed and tagged (annotated) with semantic factors (spatial knowledge) inferred from the spatial ontology with a reasoner. For example, a toponym *Georgia* is ambiguous: it can refer to the USA state or the Caucasian country. See the example sentences:

- There are Lithuanians living in Georgia, Florida and other states.

- Experts have failed to travel to Georgia at the Tbilisi airport.

In the first sentence *Georgia* refers to the USA state, while in the second one it refers to the Caucasian country. To resolve this type of ambiguity, spatial knowledge was used to determine spatial relations between corresponding toponyms within one sentence. For example, in the first sentence *Georgia* was annotated with *EC.Florida* since that information had been inferred from the spatial ontology (*Georgia* is externally connected to *Florida*). In the second sentence *Georgia* was annotated with *NTPPi.Tbilisi* (*Tbilisi* is a city in *Georgia*). We searched a sentence for toponyms and queried the spatial ontology for their relations. If there were more than two toponyms in a sentence we used just one (the first found, but not DC) annotation to each toponym. Compared with a simple unfactored translation model, that kind of factored translation model contained more useful information for toponym disambiguation since it might contain probabilities like:

- *P(Georgia/EC.Florida|Džordžija)* – a probability that *Georgia* is the English translation of a Lithuanian word *Džordžija* given that *Georgia* is externally connected to *Florida*;

- *P(Georgia/NTPPi.Tbilisi|Gruzija)* – a probability that *Georgia* is the English translation of Lithuanian word *Gruzija* given that *Georgia* encloses *Tbilisi*.

The translation model with probabilities about words and phrases with spatial knowledge helped to perform more accurate toponym disambiguation, because spatial context was included in the translation model. For example, if we have almost equal probabilities for *Georgia*, being a translation of both *Gruzija* and *Džordžija* in the translation model of the baseline system, probabilities with spatial knowledge are significantly different:

P(Georgia/EC.Armenia|Gruzija) ≫
   P(Georgia/EC.Armenia|Džordžija)

P(Georgia/EC.Florida|Džordžija) ≫
   P(Georgia/EC.Florida|Gruzija)

Thus, during the machine translation process semantic factors inferred from the spatial ontology provide additional information for the Moses decoder. As a result, it helps in choosing the appropriate translation equivalent. Therefore, SMT training data annotated with the proposed kind of spatial knowledge leads to a better machine translation quality.

It should also be mentioned that two SMT systems with spatial knowledge were trained. The first system (later referred as Spatial-8) was trained using corpora annotated with all eight RCC-8 spatial relations. The second system (later referred as Spatial-7) was trained using only seven RCC-8 relations since initial experiments, proved with the linguistic analysis, showed that using the *DC:disconnected* relation did not help in toponym disambiguation.

3 Evaluation and Limitations

A multifaceted strategy with three procedures was applied to the evaluation of the output quality of machine translation performed by the implemented system with spatial knowledge:

- automatic (black-box) evaluation;

- human evaluation;

- linguistic analysis.

3.1 Automatic Evaluation

For the automatic evaluation the two most popular and widely used metrics BLEU (Papineni et al., 2002) and NIST (Doddington, 2002) were used. Automatic metrics are cost-effective and do not require much human intervention. They allow comparisons of two and more systems, as well as different versions of one system in the process of its implementation and improvement as many times as necessary.

A balanced test set of 500 English sentences was developed for the automatic evaluation purposes. Sentences were manually collected from the web and translated into Lithuanian by a professional translator (a reference set to be compared with). The breakdown of topics in the corpus is presented in Table 2.

Domain	Percentage
General information about the EU	12%
Specification and manuals	12%
Popular scientific and educational	12%
Official and legal documents	12%
News and magazine articles	24%
Information technology	18%
Letters	5%
Fiction	5%

Table 2. Testing set.

The procedure of the automatic evaluation consists of several sub-processes and the main idea, in general, is in the comparison of machine translation and reference sets. The higher the automatic scores are, the better the machine translation output quality is. BLEU and NIST scores for the baseline system were 27,35 and 5,90 correspondingly. BLEU and NIST scores for the implemented system with spatial knowledge were 27,97 (BLEU) and 5,97 (NIST) for the system "Spatial-8" and 27,47 (BLEU) and 5,91 (NIST) for the system "Spatial-7" (see Table 3).

System	BLEU	NIST
Baseline	27,35	5,90
Spatial-8	27,97	5,97
Spatial-7	27,47	5,91

Table 3. Results of the automatic evaluation.

As a result, a slight improvement in the output quality of machine translation with spatial knowledge can be observed. In general, this improvement is not high and is not sufficient for the objective and an integrated evaluation procedure. Results of the automatic evaluation can be explained so that general-purpose development and evaluation corpora used for the evaluation did not contain many ambiguous geographical names. Therefore, the evaluation with the task-specific evaluation corpus was performed during the human evaluation. Nevertheless, automatic scores were set as a threshold for further experiments.

3.2 Human Evaluation

A test set of 464 English sentences containing ambiguous toponyms was developed for human

evaluation purposes. A ranking of translated sentences relative to each other was used for the manual evaluation of systems. This was the official determinant of translation quality used in the 2009 Workshop on Statistical Machine Translation shared tasks (Callison-Burch et al., 2009).

A web-based human evaluation environment (Skadiņš et al., 2010) was used where source sentences and translation outputs of the two SMT systems could be uploaded as simple txt files. Once the evaluation of the two systems was set up, a link to the evaluation survey was sent to evaluators. Evaluators were evaluating the systems sentence by sentence. Evaluators saw the source sentence and the translation output of the two SMT systems – baseline and the one implemented with spatial knowledge. The frequency of preferring each system based on evaluators' answers and a comparison of the sentences was calculated. About 20 evaluators participated, each comparing translations of 50 sentences.

The manual comparison of the two systems (Baseline vs. Spatial-8)[7] has shown that the implemented SMT system with spatial knowledge is slightly better than the baseline system: in 50,66% of cases evaluators judged its output to be better than the output of the baseline system. Results of the human evaluation do not allow us to say with certainty either the spatial SMT system is significantly better or it is disambiguating toponyms better, since the difference is not convincing and evaluators have been comparing sentences using subjective criteria and not paying a special attention to the translation of toponyms.

3.3 Linguistic Evaluation of Toponym Disambiguation

A detailed linguistic analysis of toponym disambiguation during the machine translation process was performed. The same corpus as for the human evaluation was used and the accuracy of the toponym translation was evaluated. The accuracy of the baseline system was 84,09%. The accuracy of the Spatial-8 system was 83,87%. Since results for the baseline system were better, it was decided to analyse the impact of each spatial relation to toponym disambiguation. It was discovered that the accuracy could be increased to 88.00% if the DC:*disconnected* relation was ignored (system Spatial-7).

---

[7] The human evaluation of the system Spatial-7 is in progress at the moment and will be presented in the final version of the paper.

4   Conclusions and Future works

In the paper we have presented how toponyms can be disambiguated in the process of statistical machine translation using spatial knowledge by the example of the English-Lithuanian system. We have overviewed the system design including the description of its functionality, baseline and implementation with spatial knowledge, as well as focused on the system multifaceted evaluation and its results.

We can see that the quality of machine translation can be improved by using the semantic information from the spatial ontology. Nevertheless improvement is not big and further more detailed evaluation would be necessary to assess whether this improvement is statistically significant.

It was noticed during linguistic evaluation that some RCC-8 properties seem to be much more useful than others (e.g. *EC:externally connected* and *EQ:equal*). But a detailed evaluation of the impact of each relation has not been done yet. The EQ property can be used for machine translation of toponyms which are synonyms, for example, a full name and an abbreviation – *the United States of America* and *USA*. The same property can be used for the so-called exonyms (names of places used by other groups, not locals) as *Praha* for its inhabitants and *Prague* for the English (for other examples, see Leidner (2007)).

It should be also noted, that the best version of the implemented system with the spatial ontology is not dealing with *DC:disconnected* relations, e.g. *Georgia* is disconnected from *California* or *Hawaii*. In this case, other types of information in the spatial ontology may be used in further experiments, e.g. the ontology class *State* and its instances.

Moreover, the spatial ontology was not used for disambiguation of common nouns since they were not represented in the ontology. However, a morpho-syntactic type of toponym ambiguity, when a word itself can be a toponym or a common noun in a language) and its resolution can be performed with the help of the spatial ontology, for example:

- *Hook* refers to the populated place in the UK and *hook* is a common noun (English);

- *Liepa* refers to the populated place in Latvia and *liepa* (lime-tree) is a common noun (Latvian);

- *Batą* refers to the populated place in Lithuania and *batą* (shoe) is a common noun (Lithuanian).

The proposed approach to toponym disambiguation is not limited to:

- machine translation *per se* and can be regarded as generic, i.e. it can be also applied to other fields of natural language processing, e.g. information retrieval;

- use of spatial knowledge only: other types of implicit or inferred knowledge can be used in a similar way.

References

Brown P., Della Pietra S., Della Pietra V., Mercer R. 1993. The mathematics of statistical machine translation: Parameter estimation. *Computational Linguistics*, 19(2), pp. 263–311.

Callison-Burch C., Koehn P., Monz C., Schroeder J. 2009. Findings of the 2009 Workshop on Statistical Machine Translation. *Proceedings of the Fourth Workshop on Statistical Machine Translation*, 1-28, Athens, Greece.

Chiang D. 2007. Hierarchical Phrase-Based Translation. *Computational Linguistics*, 33(2), pp. 201-228.

Koehn P., Och F. J., Marcu D. 2003. Statistical phrase based translation. Proceedings of the Joint Conference on Human Language Technologies and the Annual Meeting of the North American Chapter of the Association of Computational Linguistics (HLT/NAACL).

Koehn P. and Hoang H. 2007. Factored Translation Models. *Proceedings of EMNLP '07*.

Li Z., Callison-Burch C., Dyer C., Ganitkevitch J., Khudanpur S., Schwartz L., Thornton W., Weese J., Zaidan O. 2009. Joshua: An Open Source Toolkit for Parsing-based Machine Translation. *Proceedings of the Workshop on Statistical Machine Translation (WMT09)*.

Marcu D., Wang W., Echihabi A., Knight K.. 2006. SPMT: statistical machine translation with syntactified target language phrases. *Proceedings of the 2006 Conference on Empirical Methods in Natural Language Processing*, Sydney, Australia, July 22-23. ACL Workshops. Association for Computational Linguistics, pp. 44-52.

Quirk C., Menezes A., Cherry C. 2005. Dependency Treelet Translation: Syntactically Informed Phrasal SMT. *Proceedings of ACL 2005*.

Papineni K., Roukos S., Ward T. et al. 2002. BLEU: a Method for Automatic Evaluation of Machine

Translation. *ACL '02: Proceedings of the 40th Annual Meeting on Association for Computational Linguistics*, Philadelphia, Pensilvania. Morristown, NJ: Association for Computational Linguistics, pp. 311-318.

Doddington G. 2002. Automatic Evaluation of Machine Translation Quality Using N-gram Co-Occurrence Statistics. *HLT 2002: Human Language Technology Conference: Proceedings of the Second International Conference on Human Language Technology Research*, San Diego, California. San Francisco: Morgan Kaufmann Publishers, pp. 138-145.

Tiedemann J. and Nygaard L. 2004. The OPUS corpus – parallel & free. *Proceedings of the Fourth International Conference on Language Resources and Evaluation (LREC'04)*, Lisbon, Portugal, May 26-28.

Tiedemann J. 2009. News from OPUS – A Collection of Multilingual Parallel Corpora with Tools and Interfaces. *Recent Advances in Natural Language Processing*, vol. V, John Benjamins, Amsterdam/Philadelphia, pp. 237-248.

Randell D. A., Cui Z., Cohn A. G. 1992. A spatial logic based on regions and connection. *Proceedings of the 3rd International Conference on Knowledge Representation and Reasoning,* Morgan Kaufmann, San Mateo, pp. 165–176.

Skadiņš R., Goba K. and Šics V. 2010. Improving SMT for Baltic Languages with Factored Models. *Proceedings of the Fourth International Conference Baltic HLT 2010*, Riga, Latvia, pp. 125-132.

Och F. J. and Ney H. 2003 A Systematic Comparison of Various Statistical Alignment Models. *Computational Linguistics*, (29)1, pp. 19-51, 2003.

Koehn P., Federico M., Cowan B., Zens R., Duer C., Bojar O., Constantin A., Herbst E. 2007 Moses: Open Source Toolkit for Statistical Machine Translation. *Proceedings of the ACL 2007 Demo and Poster Sessions*, Prague, pp 177-180.

Madnani Nitin, Resnik Philip, Dorr Bonnie, Schwartz Richard. 2008. Applying Automatically Generated Semantic Knowledge: A Case Study in Machine Translation. *Proceedings of the Symposium on Semantic Knowledge Discovery, Organization and Use.*

Leidner Jochen L.. 2007. *Toponym Resolution in Text: Annotation, Evaluation and Applications of Spatial Grounding of Place Names.* PhD thesis. Institute for Communicating and Collaborative Systems School of Informatics, University of Edinburgh.

Gornostay T. and Skadiņa I. 2009. English-Latvian Toponym Processing: Translation Strategies and Linguistic Patterns. *EAMT-2009: Proceedings of the 13th Annual Conference of the European Association for Machine Translation*, May 14-15, Universitat Politècnica de Catalunya, Barcelona, Spain, pp. 81-87.

ISSN 1736-6305 Vol. 11
http://hdl.handle.net/10062/16955

Automatic Summarization As Means Of Simplifying Texts, An Evaluation For Swedish

Christian Smith and Arne Jönsson
Santa Anna IT Research Institute AB
Linköping, Sweden
chrsm@ida.liu.se, arnjo@ida.liu.se

Abstract

We have developed an extraction based summarizer based on a word space model and PageRank and compared the readability of the resulting summaries with the original text, using various measures for Swedish and texts from different genres. The measures include among others readability index (LIX), nominal ratio (NR) and word variation index (OVIX). The measures correspond to the vocabulary load, idea density, human interest and sentence structure of the text and can be used to indicate the difficulty a reader might have in processing the text. The results show that the summarized texts are more readable, indicating that summarization can be used to reduce the effort to read a text.

1 Introduction

Many persons have, for various reasons, problems assimilating long complex texts. Not only persons with visual impairments or dyslexia, but also, for instance, those having a different mother tongue or persons in need of a quick summary of a text. In the project EasyReader we are developing an interactive tool for automatic summarization of texts from different genres.

Automatic summarization can be done in various ways. A common distinction is extract versus abstract summaries. An extract summary is created by extracting the most important sentences from the original text. An abstract summary on the other hand is a summary where the text has been broken down and rebuilt as a complete rewrite to convey a general idea of the original text. Furthermore, the summaries can be indicative (only providing keywords as central topics) or informative (content focused) (Firmin and Chrzanowski,

1999). The former might be more usable when a reader needs to decide whether or not the text is interesting to read and the latter when a reader more easily needs to get a grasp of the meaning of a text that is supposed to be read.

For various user groups it can also be beneficial if the text is easy to read and not only shorter. There are numerous measures of readability and readability for a number of different summarization techniques has been investigated by, for instance, Margarido et al. (2008). The difficulty of the text or the readability can also be measured by several automatic measures. Vadlapudi and Katragadda (2010) present an investigation on automatic evaluation of various aspects of readability for summaries. Readability has also been used, to, for instance, re-rank webpages to better suit a particular user (Newbold et al., 2010).

In this paper we will examine the readability of automatically created summaries by comparing them to the readability of the original full-length text. First, we describe the techniques used by the summarizer. Second, an overview of readability and some valid measures is presented. Third, we present results from the automatic readability evaluation of the generated summaries.

2 The summarizer

The summarizer used in our investigations is called COGSUM (Jönsson et al., 2008b; Jönsson et al., 2008a). It is an extraction based summarizer, using the word space model random indexing (RI), c.f. Hassel (2007) and a modified version of PageRank (Brin and Page, 1998).

2.1 The word space model

The word space model, or vector space model (Eldén, 2007), is a spatial representation of a word's meaning that can reduce the linguistic variability and capture semantically related concepts by taking into account the positioning of words in a multidimensional space, instead of looking at only shallow linguistic properties. This facilitates the creation of summaries, since the positioning in the word space can be used to evaluate the different passages (words or sentences for instance) in relation to a document with regards to informational and semantic content.

Every word in a given context occupies a specific point in the space and has a vector associated to it that can be used to define its meaning.

Word spaces are constructed according to the distributional hypothesis and the proximity hypothesis. In the distributional hypothesis, words that occur in similar contexts have similar meanings so that a *word* is the sum of its contexts and the *context* is the sum of its words, where the *context* can be defined as the surrounding words or the entire document. The proximity hypothesis states that words close to each other in the word space have similar meaning while those far from each other have dissimilar meaning.

The word space is constructed from a matrix where text units are columns and the words in all text units are rows in the matrix. A certain entry in the matrix is nonzero iff the word corresponding to the row exists in the text unit represented by the column. The resulting matrix is very large and sparse which makes for the usage of techniques for reducing dimensionality. Latent Semantic Analysis is one such technique that, however, can be computationally expensive unless used with alternative algorithms (Gorrell, 2006).

2.2 Random Indexing (RI)

Random Indexing (Sahlgren, 2005; Kanerva, 1988) is a dimension reduction technique based on sparse distributed representations that provides an efficient and scalable approximate solutions to distributional similarity problems. The basic idea of Random Indexing is to accumulate context vectors based on the occurrence of words in contexts. This technique can be used with any type of linguistic context, is inherently incremental, and does not require a separate dimension reduction phase as for instance Latent Semantic Analysis.

Random Indexing can be described as a two-step operation:

Step 1 A unique d-dimensional *index vector* is assigned and randomly generated to each context (e.g. each document or each word).

These index vectors are sparse and high-dimensional. They consist of a small number, ρ, of randomly distributed +1s and -1s, with the rest of the elements of the vectors set to 0.

Step 2 *Context vectors* are produced on-the-fly. As scanning the text, each time a word occurs in a context (e.g. in a document, or within a sliding context window, w), that context's d-dimensional index vector is added to the context vector for the word. Words are thus represented by d-dimensional context vectors that are effectively the sum of the index vectors of all the contexts in which the word appears.

In COGSUM the vectors for whole sentences and the similarity between these and the average document vector are of interest. The average document vector is calculated by dividing the total document vector, which consists of the sum of all unique words' context vectors, with the number of unique words in the document, Equation 1.

$$\vec{doc} = \frac{1}{N}\sum_{i=1}^{N}\vec{w_i} \qquad (1)$$

where N denotes the number of unique words.

The sentence vectors are then calculated by subtraction of the average document vector from the context vectors of the words in the sentence which are summed together and divided by the number of words in the sentence, Equation 2.

$$\vec{sent_j} = \frac{1}{S}\sum_{i=1}^{S}(\vec{w_i} - \vec{doc}) \qquad (2)$$

where S denotes the number of words in sentence j.

2.3 PageRank

COGSUM uses the Weighted PageRank algorithm in conjunction to its RI-space to rank the sentences (Chatterjee and Mohan, 2007). PageRank is a graph-based ranking algorithm which originally was used to rank home pages automatically and objectively in the Google search engine (Brin and Page, 1998). To use PageRank for summaries we create an undirected fully connected graph where a vertex depicts a sentence in the current text and an edge between two different vertices is assigned a weight that depicts how similar these are based on a cosine angle comparison of their meaning vectors, see Figure 1. As it is fully connected, all vertices are connected with each other.

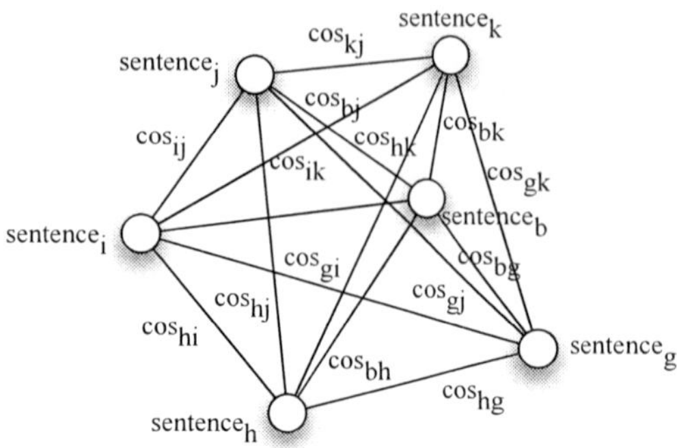

Figure 1: A simplified graph where sentences are linked and weighted according to the cosine values between them.

The algorithm rank ingoing and outgoing links to pages depending on the number of links as follows:

$$PR^W(s_i) = \frac{1-d}{N} + d \times \sum_{s_j \in In(s_i)} \frac{PR^W(s_j)}{Out(s_j)} \quad (3)$$

where s_i is the sentence under consideration, $In(s_i)$ are the set of sentences that link to s_i, $Out(s_j)$ are the set of sentences that link from s_i and N is the total number of sentences. d is the damping factor.

The damping factor is originally set to account for the possibility of a surfer clicking a random web link when he gets bored (Brin and Page, 1998). With regards to the ranking of sentences, we see the damping factor as the possibility of a sentence containing some implicit information that a certain reader might consider more important at the time. The computation is carried out on all sentences iteratively until node weights converge.

Sentences with similar content will then contribute with positive support to each other. This does not exclusively depend on the number of sentences supporting a sentence, but also on the rank of the linking sentences. This means that a few high-ranked sentences provide bigger support than a greater number of low-ranked sentences. This leads to a ranking of the sentences by their importance to the document at hand and thus to a summary of desired length only including the most important sentences.

2.4 Achieving a summary

CogSum, see Figure 2, takes as input only the text to be summarized along with a list of stop words (common function words such as prepositions). When the text has been processed using RI and PageRank, the most important sentences are extracted, for instance 30% of the original text, resulting in a condensed version of the original text with the most important information intact. Since all sentences are ranked, the length of the summary is easy to specify, in CogSum this is implemented as a simple slider. CogSum is designed for informative summaries, but it is also possible to have indicative summaries by clicking a "keywords" check box, see Figure 2.

It it important to note that the algorithm only takes the current document as total context and the information within the document, without any knowledge from an outside corpus (other than a list of stop words). This makes it highly portable to different domains, genres and languages (Mihalcea, 2004).

Evaluations of CogSum with human users show that summaries produced by CogSum are useful, considered informative enough and readable (Jönsson et al., 2008a). CogSum has also been evaluated on gold standards for news texts and authority texts showing that it is better than another Swedish summarizer (SweSum, (Dalianis, 2000)) on authority texts and almost as good on news texts, texts that the other summarizer was especially adapted to handle (Gustavsson and Jönsson, 2010).

3 Readability

Generally, easy-to-read material is characterized by simple straightforward language without necessarily being simplistic or childish. Such material can be considered more readable and comprehensible by a person (Mühlenbock and Kokkinakis, 2009). Readability can, however, be seen from various angles. In part, it is the extent to which the reader can understand a written text, and the psychological processes involved within the reader. Here, focus lies on individual shortcomings with regards to perception and understanding of the written text and not on the text itself. Readability can also be seen as a measurable property of a given text. Then, the individual prerequisites in terms of psychological abilities are often neglected.

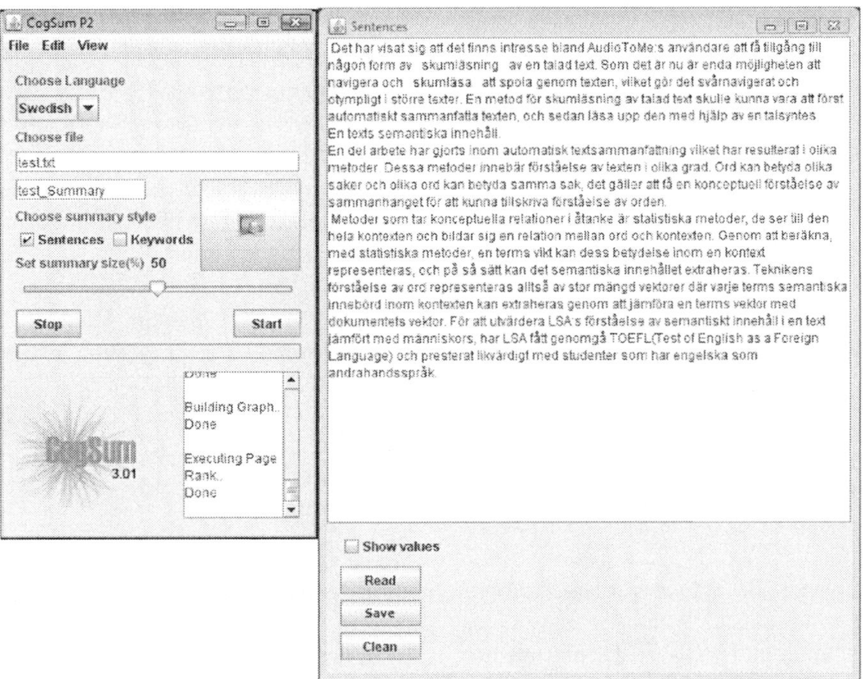

Figure 2: The CogSum interface.

Chall (1958) included the reader and concluded that there are four types of elements that seem to be significant for a readability criterion; vocabulary load, sentence structure, idea density and human interest. By mapping these psychological criteria of the individual with measurable readability properties of a text, several automatic measures of readability have been proposed.

3.1 Automatic measures

Automatic measures of readability for English is abundant, e.g. The Flesch Reading Ease Formula, Flesch-Kincaid, Dale-Chall, the Coleman-Liau test, Gunning Fog and SMOG (DuBay, 2004). For Swedish we have for instance: LIX, NR and OVIX (Mühlenbock and Kokkinakis, 2009; Rybing et al., 2010).

The Flesch Reading Easy score can be computed as:

$$Score = 206.835 - (1.015 \times \frac{n(w)}{n(s)}) - (84.6 \times ASW)$$

(4)

where $n(w)$ denotes the number of words, $n(s)$ the number of sentences and ASW the number of syllables.

The measures correspond to how understandable a text is, e.g. a Flesch Reading Easy score between 70 and 80 is "Fairly Easy" which means that the text can easily be understood by a (U.S.) 7th grade student. The Flesch-Kincaid Grade level is a U.S. grade level version that normalises (4) to correspond to readability for students in various grades.

For Swedish, being an inflecting and compounding language, the readability index LIX (Björnsson, 1968) is almost exclusively used. LIX measures the number of words per sentence and also the number of long words (> 6 characters) in the text through the formula:

$$LIX = \frac{n(w)}{n(s)} + (\frac{n(words > 6\ chars)}{n(w)} \times 100)$$

(5)

where $n(s)$ denotes the number of sentences and $n(w)$ the number of words.

Contrary to Flesch's original formula (and many of its modifications) the LIX formula does not consider syllables but instead word length. As LIX only considers ratios, sentence length and proportion of long words, it does not depend on text length.

A text with many long words and long sentences is considered more complex and therefore more difficult to read. A high LIX value indicates this, see Table 1.

Table 1: LIX-values for different genres, from Mühlenbock and Kokkinakis (2009)

LIX value	Text genre
-25	Children's books
25-30	Easy texts
30-40	Normal text/fiction
40-50	Informative text
50-60	Specialist literature
> 60	Research, dissertations

In an effort to enhance the LIX formula, Mühlenbock and Kokkinakis (2009) have included an additional parameter called Extra Long Words (XLW). Extra Long Words are words with more than 14 characters and indicates a larger proportion of compounds of usually three or more stems, relatively common in Swedish. LIX has however been considered insufficient for a complete readability assessment of a text, since target groups of readers often are highly heterogeneous. By taking into account additional parameters, a better view of a text's readability can be achieved. This is done by mapping Chall's elements of readability to automatic measures (Mühlenbock and Kokkinakis, 2009). LIX is for instance, together with the amount of extra long words, mapped to *vocabulary load*.

Lexical variation or OVIX (word variation index) measures the ratio of unique tokens in a text and is used to indicate the *idea density*, in conjunction with the nominal ratio (NR). OVIX is calculated as:

$$OVIX = \frac{log(n(w))}{log(2 - \frac{log(n(uw))}{log(n(w))})} \tag{6}$$

where $n(w)$ denotes the number of words and $n(uw)$ the number of unique words. OVIX does not depend on text length (Lundberg and Reichenberg, 2009).

NR is calculated by dividing the number of nouns, prepositions and participles with the number of pronouns, adverbs and verbs:

$$NR = \frac{n(noun) + n(prep) + n(part)}{n(pro) + n(adv) + n(v)} \tag{7}$$

where $n(noun)$ denotes the number of nouns, $n(prep)$ the number of prepositions, $n(part)$ the number of participles, $n(pro)$ the number of pronouns, $n(adv)$ the number of adverbs, and $n(v)$ the number of verbs.

A higher NR indicates a more professional and stylistically developed text, while a lower value indicate more simple and informal language. In some contexts a low NR can indicate a narrative style, such as in children's books. NR should not depend on text length.

The degree of *human interest* is measured simply through the proportion of proper nouns (PN) and by measuring the length of sentences (ASL), *sentence structure* can broadly be gathered (Mühlenbock and Kokkinakis, 2009).

4 Evaluation

We have evaluated summarized texts from a readability perspective by creating summaries of texts from different genres and compared their readability to the original text.

We use three types of texts representing three different genres:

- **DN**. Newspaper texts from the Swedish newspaper "Dagens Nyheter"; ca 25,000 words divided in 130 articles.

- **FOF**. Popular science texts from the Swedish Magazine "Forskning och Framsteg"; ca 20,000 words divided in 31 articles.

- **FOKASS**. Authority texts from the Swedish Social Insurance Administration (Sw. Försäkringskassan); ca 25,000 words from 2 brochures. The brochures were divided so that each chapter was an article resulting in a total of 35 "articles"

The texts were summarized using CoGSum with a random index dimensionality, d, of 100, a focus window size, w, of 4 (2 left, 2 right) and $\rho = 4$, i.e. 2 positive 1:s and 2 negative 1:s, in line with Chatterjee and Mohan (2007). The texts were also stemmed using the snowball algorithm (Swedish) and stop words were removed. The PageRank damping factor was set to .85 (Brin and Page, 1998) and the number of iterations when the weights converged was below 50.

The texts were extracted from the concordances at Språkbanken (2011), except for the authority texts which were taken from the Swedish Social Insurance Administration's web page (Försäkringskassan, 2011). They were summarized to different lengths (30%, 50% and 70%) and compared with the originals (100%) with regards to the different readability measures.

The summaries were evaluated using 7 measures, see Table 2. The values of the measures of the summaries were also compared to the full length texts using a paired-samples T-test.

5 Results

Table 2 shows the mean values for the various readability measures used on the different texts. Roughly, low values on any readability measure means that the text is more readable. The table also includes values on average word length (AWL).

The following significant differences were found:

DN For newspaper articles LIX got a lower score on all the summaries, (p<.05):

	Length	t(122)	Mean	SD
	30%	-8.092	43.60	10.14
LIX	50%	-9.147	45.21	8.70
	70%	-7.393	47.04	8.16
	100%		49.34	7.35

OVIX got a higher value for the 30% summary, (p<.05):

	Length	t(122)	Mean	SD
OVIX	30%	2.483	81.24	30.62
	100%		75.48	11.00

At 50% of the original text the words are also shorter on average (AWL) (p<.05):

	Length	t(122)	Mean	SD
AWL	50%	-3.4642	4.74	0.51
	100%		4.83	0.41

The sentences also became shorter (ASL) for all summarization lengths (p<.05):

	Length	t(122)	Mean	SD
	30%	-4.817	16.12	5.09
ASL	50%	-3.331	16.85	5.98
	70%	-5.115	17.04	4.27
	100%		18.00	3.91

FOF For popular science LIX was lower on all summarization lengths (p<.05):

	Length	t(30)	Mean	SD
	30%	-6.933	53.65	9.84
LIX	50%	-6.270	55.90	8.61
	70%	-5.327	57.57	8.36
	100%		59.92	7.81

At 50% and 70% OVIX got a lower score (p<.05):

	Length	t(30)	Mean	SD
	50%	-7.136	64.26	9.67
OVIX	70%	-6.017	66.26	8.89
	100%		69.24	7.94

At 30% and 50% we had lower average word length, (p<.05):

	Length	t(30)	Mean	SD
	30%	-2.234	4.86	0.36
AWL	50%	-2.465	4.89	0.27
	100%		4.94	0.23

We had a smaller proportion of extra long words for all summarization lengths (p<.05):

	Length	t(30)	Mean	SD
	30%	-2.689	0.01	0.01
XLW	50%	-2.458	0.01	0.01
	70%	-2.464	0.01	0.01
	100%		0.02	0.01

FOKASS Authority texts also displayed a lower LIX for all summarization lengths (p<.05):

	Length	t(34)	Mean	SD
	30%	-8.497	46.28	12.76
LIX	50%	-5.939	50.53	13.39
	70%	-4.642	52.92	13.09
	100%		55.46	13.00

OVIX was lower for 70% summarizations (p<.05):

	Length	t(34)	Mean	SD
OVIX	70%	-2.209	46.77	9.55
	100%		48.19	8.69

The sentences were longer at 50% and at 70% (p < .05):

	Length	t(34)	Mean	SD
	50%	2.144	15.10	3.55
ASL	70%	2.606	14.87	2.61
	100%		14.27	2.41

No significant differences could be observed in nominal ratio (NR) or proper nouns (PN) for any text genre or summarization length.

6 Discussion

A significantly lower LIX could be observed across the board of summaries, regardless of length and genre. This shows that the complexity of the text is reduced when the text is summarized by the summarizer.

A lower LIX presents together with the amount of extra long words the vocabulary load required to read the text (Mühlenbock and Kokkinakis, 2009). For popular science, this seems the most prominent, as not only LIX but also the amount of extra long words decreased for all summarization

Length	TEXT	LIX		OVIX		NR		AWL		ASL		XLW		PN	
		Mean	SD	Mean	SD	Mean	SD	Mean	SD	Mean	SD	Mean	SD	Mean	SD
0,30	DN	**43,60**	10,14	*81,24*	30,62	1,39	0,72	4,76	0,62	**16,12**	5,09	0,02	0,02	0,09	0,07
	FOF	**53,65**	9,84	65,29	16,46	1,56	0,33	**4,86**	0,36	17,46	4,40	**0,01**	0,01	0,03	0,03
	FOKASS	**46,28**	12,76	48,22	14,17	1,23	0,62	4,84	0,63	15,22	4,30	0,04	0,03	0,02	0,03
0,50	DN	**45,21**	8,70	74,41	16,45	1,37	0,61	**4,74**	0,51	**16,85**	5,98	0,02	0,02	0,09	0,07
	FOF	**55,90**	8,61	**64,26**	9,67	1,59	0,36	**4,89**	0,27	17,15	3,32	**0,01**	0,01	0,03	0,02
	FOKASS	**50,53**	13,39	47,96	14,61	1,29	0,71	4,89	0,58	*15,10*	3,55	0,04	0,03	0,02	0,03
0,70	DN	**47,04**	8,16	74,33	12,74	1,37	0,54	4,79	0,44	**17,04**	4,27	0,02	0,02	0,09	0,06
	FOF	**57,57**	8,36	**66,26**	8,89	1,56	0,28	4,90	0,25	17,01	3,27	**0,01**	0,01	0,03	0,02
	FOKASS	**52,92**	13,09	**46,77**	9,55	1,25	0,54	4,90	0,51	*14,87*	2,61	0,04	0,03	0,01	0,02
1,00	DN	49,34	7,35	75,48	11,00	1,35	0,44	4,83	0,41	18,00	3,91	0,02	0,01	0,09	0,06
	FOF	59,92	7,81	69,24	7,94	1,53	0,24	4,94	0,23	16,74	2,82	0,02	0,01	0,03	0,02
	FOKASS	55,46	13,00	48,19	8,69	1,25	0,63	4,89	0,47	14,27	2,41	0,04	0,05	0,01	0,02

Table 2: Means of the measured readability scores, LIX, NR, and OVIX. AWL is the average length of the words in the text, ASL is the average sentence length, XLW is the proportion of words longer than 14 characters, and PN is the proportion of proper nouns in the text. Means that are significantly better than the original texts of the same genre are in bold, whereas means that are worse are in italics.

lengths. Thus, for popular science, the vocabulary load decreased when articles were summarized.

OVIX also seems to be most effectively reduced for popular science texts when summarized, indicating that idea density is also reduced.

The average sentence length can be seen as a way of analyzing the structure of the sentence, without adopting syntactic parsing (Mühlenbock and Kokkinakis, 2009). This seems to be most prominent in newspaper articles. Newspaper texts had a high idea density from the start (by a high variation in words, OVIX) and a low LIX. They benefitted from summarization by getting a lower value on average sentence length, or sentence structure, for all summarization lengths.

Authority texts did not benefit as much from summarization, for all summarization lengths, as the other genres. OVIX was lower for 70% summaries but sentences got, for instance, longer for long summaries (50% and 70%).

No significant differences were found for any text on the amount of proper nouns (PN) and NR. A low NR might indicate a stylistically simple text such as narrative children's books while a higher NR is more common in advanced texts and since the summarizer at this point does nothing to rewrite sentences, a change in NR is not to be expected.

To conclude; there seems to be a difference between different genres in how a summary is affecting the readability of the texts. Popular science seems to benefit most by being summarized, followed by newspaper articles. The vocabulary load and complexity of sentence structure can be lowered in newspaper articles and popular science, where also idea density in addition can be lowered.

7 Summary and future research

We have shown that automatic summarization have a positive impact on readability for texts from different genres and with different summarization lengths. This shows that summarization can be used as a promising means to make a text more easy to read and may work well as a first step in an effort to make texts available with reduced difficulties across several target domains for different types of texts.

The evaluations were done using a number of automatic measures of readability. A next step is to conduct experiments with humans to gain further insights on readability of the summaries. For instance, a general problem with extract summarizations is that the sentences that are extracted can refer to a sentence that hasn't been extracted, resulting in a fragmentation of the text that may increase the workload required by the reader.

Rewriting the text automatically based on syntactical properties of a target easy-to-read corpus, such as presented by Rybing et al. (2010), will probably further increase readability, and will also be investigated in future studies. Future research also include investigations on the interaction effects, found in this study, between various readability measures.

Acknowledgement

This research was partly supported by a research grant from The Swedish Post and Telecom Agency (PTS). The authors are grateful to Henrik Danielsson for many fruitful discussion and valuable help with the analyses.

References

C.H. Björnsson. 1968. *Läsbarhet*. Stockholm: Liber.

Sergey Brin and Lawrence Page. 1998. The anatomy of a large-scale hypertextual web search engine. *Computer Networks and ISDN Systems*, 30(1-7):107–117.

J.S. Chall. 1958. *Readability: An appraisal of research and application*. Columbus, OH: Ohio State University Press. Reprinted 1974. Epping, Essex, England: Bowker Publishing Company.

Nilhadri Chatterjee and Shiwali Mohan. 2007. Extraction-based single-document summarization using random indexing. In *Proceedings of the 19th IEEE international Conference on Tools with Artificial intelligence – (ICTAI 2007)*, pages 448–455.

Hercules Dalianis. 2000. Swesum – a text summarizer for swedish. Technical Report TRITA-NA-P0015, IPLab-174, NADA, KTH, Sweden.

William H. DuBay. 2004. *Smart language: Readers, Readability, and the Grading of Text*. Costa Mesa:Impact Information.

Lars Eldén. 2007. *Matrix Methods in Data Mining and Pattern Recognition*. Society for Industrial & Applied Mathematics (SIAM).

Thérese Firmin and Michael J Chrzanowski, 1999. *An Evaluation of Automatic Text Summarization Systems*, volume 6073, pages 325–336. SPIE.

Försäkringskassan. 2011. Försäkringskassans website, January. http://www.forsakringskassan.se.

Genevieve Gorrell. 2006. *Generalized Hebbian Algorithm for Dimensionality Reduction in Natural Language Processing*. Ph.D. thesis, Linköping University.

Pär Gustavsson and Arne Jönsson. 2010. Text summarization using random indexing and pagerank. In *Proceedings of the third Swedish Language Technology Conference (SLTC-2010), Linköping, Sweden*.

Martin Hassel. 2007. *Resource Lean and Portable Automatic Text Summarization*. Ph.D. thesis, ISRN-KTH/CSC/A–07/09-SE, KTH, Sweden.

Arne Jönsson, Mimi Axelsson, Erica Bergenholm, Bertil Carlsson, Gro Dahlbom, Pär Gustavsson, Jonas Rybing, and Christian Smith. 2008a. Skim reading of audio information. In *Proceedings of the The second Swedish Language Technology Conference (SLTC-08), Stockholm, Sweden*.

Arne Jönsson, Bjarte Bugge, Mimi Axelsson, Erica Bergenholm, Bertil Carlsson, Gro Dahlbom, Robert Krevers, Karin Nilsson, Jonas Rybing, and Christian Smith. 2008b. Using language technology to improve interaction and provide skim reading abilities to audio information services. In *Proceedings of eChallenges e-2008, Stockholm, Sweden*.

Pentii Kanerva. 1988. *Sparse distributed memory*. Cambridge MA: The MIT Press.

Ingvar Lundberg and Monica Reichenberg. 2009. *Vad är lättläst?* Socialpedagogiska skolmyndigheten.

Paulo R. A. Margarido, Thiago A. S. Pardo, Gabriel M. Antonio, Vinícius B. Fuentes, Rachel Aires, Sandra M. Aluísio, and Renata P. M. Fortes. 2008. Automatic summarization for text simplification: Evaluating text understanding by poor readers. In *Companion Proceedings of the XIV Brazilian Symposium on Multimedia and the Web*.

Rada Mihalcea. 2004. Graph-based ranking algorithms for sentence extraction, applied to text summarization. In *Proceedings of the ACL 2004 on Interactive poster and demonstration sessions*, ACLdemo '04, Morristown, NJ, USA. Association for Computational Linguistics.

Katarina Mühlenbock and Sofie Johansson Kokkinakis. 2009. Lix 68 revisited – an extended readability measure. In *Proceedings of Corpus Linguistics*.

Neil Newbold, Harry McLaughlin, and Lee Gillam. 2010. Rank by readability: Document weighting for information retrieval. In Hamish Cunningham, Allan Hanbury, and Stefan M. Rüger, editors, *Advances in Multidisciplinary Retrieval, First Information Retrieval Facility Conference, IRFC 2010, Vienna, Austria, May 31, 2010. Proceedings*, volume 6107 of *Lecture Notes in Computer Science*, pages 20–30. Springer.

Jonas Rybing, Christian Smith, and Annika Silvervarg. 2010. Towards a rule based system for automatic simplification of texts. In *Proceedings of the third Swedish Language Technology Conference (SLTC-2010), Linköping, Sweden*.

Magnus Sahlgren. 2005. An Introduction to Random Indexing. *Methods and Applications of Semantic Indexing Workshop at the 7th International Conference on Terminology and Knowledge Engineering, TKE 2005*.

Språkbanken. 2011. Concordances of språkbanken, January. http://spraakbanken.gu.se/konk/.

Ravikiran Vadlapudi and Rahul Katragadda. 2010. On automated evaluation of readability of summaries: Capturing grammaticality, focus, structure and coherence. In *Proceedings of the NAACL HLT 2010 Student Research Workshop*.

ISSN 1736-6305 Vol. 11
http://hdl.handle.net/10062/16955

Using Graphical Models for PP Attachment

Anders Søgaard
Center for Language Technology
University of Copenhagen
Njalsgade 142
DK-2300 Copenhagen
`soegaard@hum.ku.dk`

Abstract

PP attachment has attracted considerable interest the last two decades. The standard set-up has been to extract quadruples of verbs, direct objects, prepositions and prepositional complements from the Wall Street Journal and classify them as either low or high attachments. State-of-the-art results almost equal human performance in the standard set-up. Recently, however, Atterer and Schütze (2007) has questioned this methodology. In this paper, we show that state-of-the-art results can be achieved by simpler means than what has previously been shown, using graphical models, but also that state-of-the-art parsers perform insignificantly worse than state-of-the-art PP attachment classifiers. This questions the usefulness of previous studies of PP attachment, even if the methodology in these studies is sound.

1   Introduction

One of the main challenges in parsing has for a long time been assumed to be the resolution of ambiguity. One frequently studied type of ambiguity is prepositional phrase (PP) attachment. Given a quadruple of a verb, a direct object, a preposition and a prepositional complement (the head of the NP2 embedded in the PP), PP attachment – or PP re-attachment – is the task of determining whether the PP should attach to the verb (V) or the direct object (N). PP attachment is thus construed as a binary classification problem, typically with labels N and V.

The standard features for PP-attachment used in Ratnaparkhi et al. (1994) and subsequent studies are listed in Figure 1. The seven features are the ones in rows 2–8. A distributional cluster is a set of words that have similar distributions according to a hierarchical clustering algorithm, typically based on probabilities in a bigram language model. The granularity of clusters varies, but we will use a 1000 clusters in our experiments below.

Example. To see the complexity of this learning problem, consider the following four examples:

(1) (Andy Warhol) painted paintings with 3D-glasses.

(2) (Andy Warhol) painted [portraits with 3D-glasses].

(3) (Andy Warhol) painted [paintings with ice-cream].

(4) (Andy Warhol) painted portraits with ice-cream.

The square brackets indicate likely low attachment, i.e. that the prepositional phrase most naturally modifies the noun. Note that the four data points have an XOR-like distribution in two-dimensional space:

3D-glasses	V	N
ice-cream	N	V
	paintings	portraits

The distributional cluster features are of no help here, since there is a function from words to clusters. In sum, the learning problem has few dimensions, but variables are highly interdependent.

The interdependence of the variables given the class, illustrated by the examples above, was initially ignored in studies such as Ratnaparkhi et al. (1994) and Collins and Brooks (1995). However, it was the interdependence of the variables that motivated Toutanova et al. (2004) (who report the best result

1	label (N or V)
2	verb
3	verb (distributional cluster)
4	direct object
5	direct object (distributional cluster)
6	preposition
7	prepositional complement
8	prepositional complement (distributional cluster)

Figure 1: Standard features in PP-attachment.

in the literature on the standard Wall Street Journal dataset for English PP attachment) to consider graphical models.

The most important of our seven features is undoubtedly the prepositions (feature 6). This has been noted before, for example by Collins and Brooks (1995) who base their backed-off estimate on this observation (Sect. 6): "A key observation in choosing between these tuples is that the preposition is particularly important to the attachment decision." Moreover, selecting PP attachment site only by the preposition typically provides a relatively strong baseline. This observation was also central in the models used by Toutanova et al. (2004).

Previous studies are reviewed in Sect. 2. Atterer and Schütze (2007) recently questioned the methodology used in these studies, however. We briefly summarize their discussion in Sect. 3.

Sect. 4 presents two PP attachment algorithms based on graphical models that are simpler than the one proposed by Toutanova et al. (2004), yet perform as well as theirs. This is an interesting empirical result independently of whether the methodology in re-attachment studies is sound or not.

Sect. 5 qualifies the discussion in Atterer and Schütze (2007), showing that state-of-the-art dependency parsers perform about as well as state-of-the-art re-attachment classifiers on the standard PP attachment dataset. This strengthens the claim in Atterer and Schütze (2007) that PP re-attachment studies are of little practical relevance.

2 Previous studies

Collins and Brooks (1995) use a simple backed-off estimate for modeling PP attachment. In a way similar to nearest-neighbor learning, they first look for identical quadruples in the training data, then for

triples and then for pairs. They report a score of 84.5% on the Wall Street Journal dataset. This is identical to the score reported with cross-product features above. It is also similar to what was reported in Abney et al. (1999) (84.6%). It is also similar to what was achieved by Vanschoenwinkel and Manderick (2003) using SVMs and kernel methods (84.8%).

Toutanova et al. (2004) present an approach to PP attachment similar to ours. They manually construct a Markov chain Bayesian network with only two independence assumptions, namely, that given a verbal attachment, the second noun is independent of the first noun, and that given a nominal attachment, the second noun is independent of the verb. The parameters of the graphical model are learned discriminatively by random walks. In addition to the training data, Toutanova et al. (2004) use large amounts of automatically parsed quadruples from the BLLIP corpus (Charniak, 2000). They also use morphological analysis and WordNet features to achieve the best reported results in the literature. Without these additional resources they report an accuracy of 85.9%. Using morphological analysis they achieve 86.2%, and using all features, incl. WordNet features, they achieve 87.6% which is very close to human performance. One of the algorithms proposed below will be similar to this algorithm, but we will learn the graph structure automatically from the training data using no additional resources.

In this paper we will only consider results obtained without additional manually constructed resources. It should be mentioned that Zhao and Lin (2004) report a result of 86.5% on this data set, using more advanced distributional clusters and nearest neighbor classification. Their study is exploratory, and they report several results for the test data, ranging from 83.1% to 86.5%.

Finally, there has been some work in what has been referred to as "unsupervised" PP attachment (Ratnaparkhi, 1998; Kawahara and Kurohashi, 2005). The idea in this work is to extract unambiguous examples of triples or quadruples from large amounts of raw data, typically based on automatically inferred part-of-speech. The methods subsequently used are standard supervised techniques, so in a way this can be seen as supervised learning with outlier detection on large amounts of data. It is therefore not that surprising that results are good. Ratnaparkhi (1998), who pioneered this approach, report an accuracy of 81.9% (compared to 81.6% in his earlier work), and Kawahara and Kurohashi (2005) report an impressive 87.3%, but in an explorative study where different results are reported.

3   Is re-attachment sound?

Previous studies of PP attachment have, as should be clear now, assumed an oracle that provides preliminary syntactic structure, i.e. extracts the relevant quadruples from gold-standard parse trees. The task is then to re-attach the involved PPs. PP attachment classifiers perform considerably worse in the absence of oracles, however.

Atterer and Schütze (2007) present empirical evidence for this and discuss the difficulties with the standard methodology of using extracted quadruples. One problem arises if the parser does not find the direct object and the prepositional phrase and then does not recognize the ambiguity. It is also harder to decide low or high attachment if the head words of the direct object and the prepositional complement are not correctly identified. Accuracy without oracles drops about 5%.

Atterer and Schütze (2007) also argue that state-of-the-art parsers do almost as good attachment decisions as re-attachers in realistic scenarios, i.e. in the absence of oracles. In Sect. 5 we show that state-of-the-art *also* do almost as good attachment decisions as attachment classifiers when oracle quadruples are provided.

4   Using graphical models for PP attachment

Graphical models (Jordan, 1998) are a happy marriage between probability theory and graph theory, and graphical models are best understood as a framework for talking about and generalizing over various known models, including mixture models, factor analysis, hidden Markov models, Kalman filters and Ising models. Graphical models are also ways of compactly representing joint probability distributions. Their discriminative analogues, conditional random fields (Lafferty et al., 2001), which model conditional probabilities directly rather than joint probabilities, will also be included under the term graphical models here. We will refer to generative graphical models as Bayesian networks, and to discriminative graphical models as conditional random fields. In general, graphical models are graphs in which each node represents a variable whose distribution is to be inferred, and edges represent dependencies.

4.1   Bayesian networks with cross-product of features

Using Bayesian networks we need a method for learning directed graphs over our variables and a method for doing inference in them. This is in contrast to Toutanova et al. (2004) who designed the Bayesian network by hand, guided by linguistic intuition. In the experiments below, we focus on *hill climbing* for learning graphs (Jordan, 1998). Estimation or inference is simple. The choice of using hill climbing is primarily motivated by replicability and computational efficiency, but our initial experiments showed that more advanced methods such as K2 or conditional independence tests did not lead to better results on development data. We also restrict ourselves to Bayesian networks where all nodes have at most one parent. In other words, our graphical models are unordered trees. Experiments showed that allowing for two or three parents did not lead to better results either. This means that our graphical models are much simpler than the ones used in Toutanova et al. (2004).

The *estimation* method is simply to compute

$$\arg\max_{y} P(Y = y | \mathbf{parents}(Y))$$

1	x_i
2	x_{i+1}
3	x_{i+2}
4	$c_i(x_i)$
5	$c_{i+1}(x_{i+1})$
6	$c_{i+2}(x_{i+2})$
7	$c_j(x_{i-1})$

Figure 2: Feature template used in all experiments for classifier c_j.

Finally, we take the cross-product of the standard features (Figure 1). Since some of these feature pairs may be irrelevant, we use a particle swarm approach to assign weights to each feature. In particular, we use the RapidMiner 4.6 implementation of particle swarm feature weighting with a default parameter setting of 40 generations of size 6.[1]

4.2 Stacked conditional random fields

In conditional random fields, each node in our graphs has an exponential family distribution. Some variables are observed, whereas others are to be inferred (in our case using a quasi-Newton approach). In classification, there is really only one hidden variable, but we will pretend that there are as many as there are observable variables. The new hidden variables will just be copies of this variable.

In particular, we will assume chain graphs, i.e. a subclass of the graphs considered in Bayesian networks. In addition, we will condition each hidden variable on the corresponding observed variables and the two *succeeding* observable variables.[2] The full set of features is presented in Figure 2. A feature $c_i(x_i)$ means the prediction of the classifier trained on sequences of length i prediction for node i (its final prediction). Note that these features are orthogonal to the features of the underlying classification problem (Figure 1). The features of the classification problem only affect the length of the sequences that are given to our stacked sequential labeler.

Our learning algorithm C2C transforms an n-dimensional classification problem to a sequence labeling task for sequences of m length with $m \leq n$. In some cases we will group two or more variables

together in nodes, which is why m may be smaller than n. This happens, for example, if we use both word forms and distributional clusters to represent words in PP attachment (in a way similar to Ratnaparkhi et al. (1994)). Each node is then represented by two features, so $m = \frac{n}{2}$. Note also that all sequences in our data will have the same length, i.e. the number of attributes in the original classification data set. Note also that the special case where we group n variables together reduces to standard classification.

Otherwise (when $m = n$) we will transform a classification data set with data points:

$$y^i \quad x^i_1 \quad x^i_2 \quad \ldots \quad x^i_n$$

into a sequence labeling task for sequences $x^i_1 \ldots x^i_n$.

The idea is then to train n many models; the smallest model will be trained on sequences of length 1 (the first feature x^i_1 paired with the class label), the next smallest model on sequences of two nodes (x'_1, x'_2), and so on. The largest model will be trained on the full length sequences. Each node will be augmented with a prediction feature initialized as 'NULL' for all nodes. Each model on sequences of length j will be used to set the value of the prediction feature of node i in each sequence, basically representing the class prediction this far in the sequence.

So our model is in a way similar to ensemble-based methods or corrective modeling, i.e. a form of stacking (Wolpert, 1992). The smallest model in PP-attachment may try to guess low or high attachment based on the verb, for example. The next model sees the next word, say the object noun, but also the class predicted by the smaller model and tries to guess whether the PP attaches to the verb or to the object noun. The next model then sees the preposition also and possibly corrects the guess, and finally the larger model produces the final class prediction. Note that the bigger models when predicting the label of node x^i_j *both* have access to the predictions of the smaller models and its own last prediction for x^i_{j-1}. Herein lies the strength of our model.

The overall algorithm is sketched in Figure 3. In the first line, we simply rewrite our classification training and test sets, respectively T_0 and T_1, as sequential labeling data sets. If $m = n$, this amounts to pairing the class label with all attributes and see-

---

[1] http://rapid-i.com/

[2] The intuition here is that the preceding observable variables are reflected in the previous classifier's predictions; see below.

```
 1: $T_t = \tau(T_0), T_s = \tau(T_1)$
 2: for $1 \le i < m$ do
 3:     $c_i = \mathbf{train}(\{\mathbf{x}_1 \ldots \mathbf{x}_i | \mathbf{x}_1 \ldots \mathbf{x}_m \in T_t\})$
 4:     $y_1 \ldots y_i = c_i(\mathbf{x}_1 \ldots \mathbf{x}_i)$
 5:     $\mathbf{x}_i[i] = y_i$ # update prediction feature
 6: end for $c_m = \mathbf{train}(T_t)$
 7: for $\mathbf{x}_1 \ldots \mathbf{x}_m \in T_s$ do
 8:     for $1 \le i < m$ do
 9:         $y_1 \ldots y_i = c_i(\mathbf{x}_1 \ldots \mathbf{x}_i)$
10:         $\mathbf{x}_i[i] = y_i$ # update prediction feature
11:     end for
12:     $y_1 \ldots y_m = c_m(\mathbf{x}_1 \ldots \mathbf{x}_m)$
13:     return $y_m$
14: end for
```

Figure 3: C2C.

ing the pairs of attributes and class labels as sequences. We then do $m-1$ iterations. In each iteration, we train a sequential labeler c_i on sequences of i length in T_0, $1 \le i < m$ (line 3). The sequential labeler is then applied to partial sequences, and the final prediction (for node i) is used to update the prediction feature of this node. This information is then used for training the classifier in the next iteration. We return the prediction for the last node in the sequences of length m in the test data.

4.3 Data

In our experiments we use the PP attachment dataset presented in Ratnaparkhi et al. (1994).[3] The dataset contains 20,801 quadruples from the syntactically annotated Wall Street Journal (Penn Treebank 0.5) with attachment decisions for training, 4,039 for development, and 3,097 for testing. Each quadruple consists of a verb, a direct object, a preposition and a prepositional complement, e.g.:

prepare	dinner	for	family	(V)
shipped	crabs	from	province	(V)
ran	broadcast	on	way	(N)
is	apartment	with	floors	(N)

Remember the label N means low attachment, while V means that the preposition is a complement of the verb. The quadruples are extracted from the Wall Street Journal relying on manual annotation. Consider some suggested lower and upper bounds

on this dataset:

	Acc (%)
Majority baseline	59.0
Most likely for each preposition	72.2
Human (quadruples)	88.2
Human (sentences)	93.2

Majority baseline is the accuracy of a system that always predict low attachment. Here, 'Most likely for each preposition' means use the attachment seen most often in training data for the preposition seen in the test quadruple. The human performance results are taken from Ratnaparkhi et al. (1994), and are the average performance of three treebanking experts on a set of 300 randomly selected test events from the Wall Street Journal corpus, first looking at the four head words alone, then using the whole sentence. The results are thus not directly comparable to those obtained using the test section.

Ratnaparkhi et al. (1994) use the standard features listed in Figure 1, but also suggest to use n-gram features ($1 \le n \le 4$) over words and Brown clusters. Ratnaparkhi et al. (1994) used logistic regression to learn from these presentations.

In our experiments, we only use unigrams. Our feature vectors are therefore very short; we use eight features in the standard representation, namely words and clusters of verbs, direct objects, prepositions and prepositional complements, and four and ten features in the two alternative representations. Actually, since all prepositions belong to the same cluster in our hierarchical clustering, we only need to consider seven variables in the standard representation. For reproduceability, we use the Brown clusters available on the website that accompanies Turian et al. (2010) with $C = 1000$, to build our feature representations.

4.4 Results

We compare Bayesian networks and C2C with previous studies of PP attachment. Ratnaparkhi et al. (1994) used logistic regression on standard features. Since we do not use exactly the same hierarchical clusters as they did, we include both his reported results and results obtained with our feature representations using generalized iterative scaling (GIS).[4] Our graphical models are learned using

---

[3] ftp://ftp.cis.upenn.edu/pub/adwait/PPattachData/

[4] http://homepages.inf.ed.ac.uk/lzhang10/LogReg_toolkit.html

hill climbing and with the restriction that each node has at most one parent (P=1).

Our results are presented in Figure 4. Note that both our approaches perform as good as the approach in Toutanova et al. (2004).

5 How well do parsers perform?

PP attachment became an interesting topic with Ratnaparkhi et al. (1994) at a time where most parsers were grammar-based, and statistical PP attachment was necessary for ambiguity management. Statistical parsers of course do PP attachment themselves finding the most probable parse, but re-attachment may still improve the overall quality of parsers if attachment classifiers are trained specifically to deal with this problem.

Atterer and Schütze (2007) showed that attachment classifiers are only a little better than modern statistical parsers in realistic scenarios where quadruples are not known. Here we show that modern parsers are almost as good as re-attachment classifiers, even when quadruples *are* known.

To cast the re-attachment task as a dependency parsing problem, we convert the labeled quadruples into dependency structures the following way:

In a low attachment the preposition, which is the head of the prepositional complement and thereby head of the PP, is a dependent of the noun, and the dependency between them is labeled MOD for modifier. If the label is V, the preposition is a dependent of the verb, and the dependency is labeled OBL for oblique.

Consider, for example, the dependency structure in Figure 5. The black dependencies are correct and predicted dependencies. The blue dependency is correct, and the red is predicted. In other words, this quadruple, which is the first in the test section of our dataset, is annotated as V, but a low attachment is predicted.

The information available to the dependency parser in Figure 5 is words and hybrid POS tags and clusters. POS tags are obviously redundant on their own. In general, we tried three different feature representations: using only words, using words and clusters, and using words and hybrid POS tags and clusters. Note that the hybrid setting is similar to what was used for semi-supervised dependency

Parser	Acc (%)	Toutanova et al. (significance)
MaltParser	83.1	< 0.01
MSTParser	84.1	> 0.05
Opt. MaltParser	**85.1**	> 0.05
Bikel	83.7	< 0.05

Figure 6: PP re-attachment accuracy of state-of-the-art parsers.

	FORM	CPOSTAG
Input	0,1	1
Stack	0,1	0,1

Figure 7: Features used in Opt. MaltParser. 0 is the first word on the buffer (Input) or stack; 1 the second, and so on.

parsing in Koo (2008). This setting led to the best results on the development data.

We trained two different parsers on the converted PP attachment dataset, namely MaltParser (Nivre et al., 2007) and MSTParser (McDonald et al., 2005). We report results for the two parsers with default parameters and a result for MaltParser with a feature model partially optimized on development data; all results are listed in Figure 6. The optimized feature model is presented in Figure 7.[5] The third column reports significance compared to the results in Toutanova et al. (2004), using χ^2 test. The result of the Bikel parser (Bikel, 2004) is taken directly from Atterer and Schütze (2007).

It follows that state-of-the-art dependency parsers are *not* significantly worse than state-of-the-art PP attachment classifiers. This questions the usefulness of PP attachment classifiers in statistical parsing.

6 Conclusions

We have contributed to the PP attachment literature in two ways. First we have presented two new algorithms that equal state-of-the-art in their performance on the standard Wall Street Journal dataset. One is based on Bayesian networks, the other is based on conditional random fields. Second we have strengthened the claim in Atterer and Schütze (2007)

---

[5]Optimization was performed by greedily removing features from the default feature model for the arc-eager parsing algorithm. All other features were left unoptimized.

Learning algorithm	Method	Params/Ref	Acc (%)
LogReg	GIS	Standard	80.4
LogReg	RRRR94	Standard	81.6
Backed-off estimate	CB95	Words	84.5
Boosting	ASS99	Standard	84.6
Bayesian networks	TMN04	Words	**85.9**
Bayesian networks	Hill climbing, P=1	Cross-product	85.8
c2c	-	Standard	**85.9**
Human (quadruples)			88.2

Figure 4: Results.

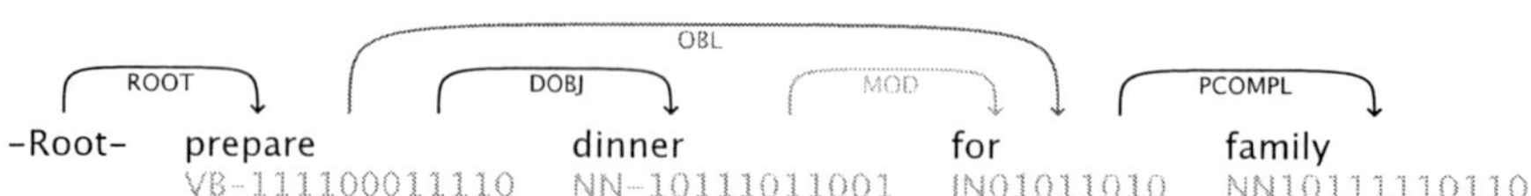

Figure 5: PP re-attachment as parsing problem.

that statistical parsers can do PP attachment almost as good as specialized classifiers in the absence of oracles. In fact, we have shown that state-of-the-art dependency parsers are insignificantly worse than such classifiers even in the presence of oracles. In particular, we showed that the difference between a statistical parser and the best re-attachment classifiers was less than 0.8%.

References

Steven Abney, Robert Schapire, and Yoram Singer. 1999. Boosting applied to tagging and PP-attachment. In *EMNLP*.

Michaela Atterer and Hinrich Schütze. 2007. Prepositional phrase attachment without oracles. *Computational Linguistics*, 33(4):469–476.

Daniel Bikel. 2004. Intricacies of collins parsing model. *Computational Linguistics*, 30(4):479–512.

Eugene Charniak. 2000. A maximum entropy-inspired parser. In *NAACL*.

Michael Collins and James Brook. 1995. Prepositional phrase attachment through a backed-off model. In *Workshop on Very Large Corpora*.

Michael Jordan, editor. 1998. *Learning in graphical models*. MIT Press.

Daisuke Kawahara and Sadao Kurohashi. 2005. Pp-attachment disambiguation boosted by a gigantic volume of unambiguous examples. In *IJCNLP*.

Terry Koo, Xavier Carreras, and Michael Collins. 2008. Simple semi-supervised dependency parsing. In *ACL*.

John Lafferty, Andrew McCallum, and Fernando Pereira. 2001. Conditional random fields: probabilistic models for segmenting and labeling sequence data. In *ICML*.

Ryan McDonald, Fernando Pereira, Kiril Ribarov, and Jan Hajič. 2005. Non-projective dependency parsing using spanning tree algorithms. In *HLT-EMNLP*.

Joakim Nivre, Johan Hall, Jens Nilsson, Atanas Chanev, Gülsen Eryigit, Sandra Kübler, Svetoslav Marinov, and Erwin Marsi. 2007. MaltParser: a language-independent system for data-driven dependency parsing. *Natural Language Engineering*, 13(2):95–135.

Adwait Ratnaparkhi, J Reynar, and S Roukos. 1994. A maximum entropy model for prepositional phrase attachment. In *ARPA Workshop on Human Language Technology*.

Adwait Ratnaparkhi. 1998. Statistical models for unsupervised prepositional phrase attachment. In *COLING*.

Kristina Toutanova, Christopher Manning, and Andrew Ng. 2004. Learning random walk models for inducing word dependency distributions. In *ICML*.

Joseph Turian, Lev Ratinov, and Yoshua Bengio. 2010. Word representations: a simple and general method for semi-supervised learning. In *ACL*.

B Vanschoenwinkel and B Manderick. 2003. A weighted polynomial information gain kernel for resolving pp attachment ambiguities with support vector machines. In *IJCAI*.

David Wolpert. 1992. Stacked generalization. *Neural Networks*, 5:241–259.

S Zhao and Dekang Lin. 2004. A nearest-neighbor

method for resolving PP-attachment ambiguity. In
IJCNLP.

ISSN 1736-6305 Vol. 11
http://hdl.handle.net/10062/16955

Corrective re-synthesis of deviant speech using unit selection

Sofia Strömbergsson
Dep. Of Speech, Music and Hearing,
KTH (Royal Institute of Technology),
Stockholm, Sweden
`sostr@csc.kth.se`

Abstract

This report describes a novel approach to modified re-synthesis, by concatenation of speech from different speakers. The system removes an initial voiceless plosive from one utterance, recorded from a child, and replaces it with another voiceless plosive selected from a database of recordings of other child speakers. Preliminary results from a listener evaluation are reported.

1 Background

Modified re-synthesis of recorded speech can be used for different purposes. For example, modification through linear predictive coding (LPC) parameter manipulation has been used to create ambiguous realizations of speech sounds for experiments of categorical perception, and to create extrapolated realizations of speech sounds to exaggerate the difference between two phonemes (Protopapas, 1998). A similar technique has also been used to generate "corrected" versions of children's deviant /r/ productions (Shuster, 1998). Here, children and adolescents listened to recordings of themselves and of other children, where half of the words were incorrectly produced, and the other half "corrected" by LPC parameter modification. For each word, the children judged the correctness of the /r/ and the identity of the speaker. However, as manipulations were done manually, there was a time span of 1-2 weeks between recording of the children and listening, and this gap could partly explain the difficulties the children had recognizing their own recordings. Thus, in order to fully understand how children (or adults) react to hearing corrected versions of their recorded incorrect speech, corrective re-synthesis should preferably be done in real-time.

A method for re-synthesizing segmentally modified versions of recorded speech could be valuable not only in speech and language intervention for children with deviant speech, but could also be used e.g. in second language learning. However, for these purposes, the technique must not only allow modification and re-synthesis of recorded speech in real-time, but the generated speech must also be conceivable realizations of speech that might have been produced by the recorded speaker himself/herself. In earlier studies involving re-synthesized speech, characteristics other than naturalness and preservation of perceived speaker identity have been prioritized, e.g. controlling intonation and syllabic rhythm (Ramus & Mehler, 1999) and increasing intelligibility of poorly articulated speech (Kain et al, 2007). In these studies, re-synthesis was done through diphone synthesis and formant synthesis, respectively. If naturalness and preservation of speaker identity are prioritized, however, other synthesis methods are better suited.

The present study describes a novel approach to modified re-synthesis of phonemic segments, by standard methods of unit selection and concatenative synthesis, but where the concatenated speech segments come from different speakers. The purpose of the study was to find out if this re-synthesis method can be used to generate natural and comprehensible speech.

2 Method

2.1 Speech data

A corpus of recordings of 74 children producing one word utterances was used as a speech database. The recording script used for all children contained 19 words, with 10 beginning with /kV/ and the other 9 beginning with /tV/ (see Appendix). The recorded children were 4 to 9 years old.

60 of the children had normal speech and 14 of the children were diagnosed with phonological impairment (PI), and had problems with deviant production of either /k/ or /t/, which were often produced as [t] or [k], respectively.

The recordings were made at different schools and pre-schools, and always took place in a separate room with limited noise. All recordings were made by a Sennheiser m@b 40 headset, using a 16-kHz sampling rate and 16-bit resolution.

The total number of utterances in the speech corpus was 1406 utterances. 132 of these were produced by the children with PI and judged by the author as having a deviant initial plosive.

2.2 Preparation of speech data

All data in the speech corpus was segmented and aligned with the HMM-based nAlign (Sjölander, 2003). A concatenation position was defined at the middle of the first vowel in the utterance. At this position, three sets of acoustic features were extracted. F0, log power and MFCCs (13 Mel-Frequency Cepstrum Coefficients).

2.3 Unit selection

The task for the unit selector was to find an initial segment u_{i-1} in the speech database that would best match a given remainder segment u_i. The concatenation cost C^c between these segments was calculated as follows (Hunt & Black, 1996):

$$C^c(u_{i-1}, u_i) = \sum_{j=1}^{q} w_j^c C_j^c(u_{i-1}, u_i)$$

Three sub-costs C_j were used in the unit selection (i.e. $q = 3$):

- Euclidean distance (Taylor, 2008) in F0

- Euclidean distance in log power

- Mahalanobis distance (Taylor, 2008) for the MFCCs

Different weights w_j were assigned to the different sub-costs. These weights were derived from a weight optimization procedure (described below). High penalties were given to combinations of segments where the vowel in u_{i-1} did not match the vowel in u_i, to avoid combinations of mismatching vowels. The segment u_{i-1} with the lowest concatenation cost was then selected from the speech corpus as the optimal segment for concatenation with u_i.

2.4 Concatenation

Concatenation positions in u_i and u_{i-1} were adjusted to the zero-crossings closest to the middle of the vowel (within a range of 15 samples before or after), where the direction of the slope (negative or positive) was the same for u_i and u_{i-1}, to preserve wave continuation.

2.5 Weight optimization

15 original recordings were held out from the speech corpus and used as training material. To arrive at an optimal set of weights for the sub-costs for F0, log power and MFCC distance, a weight space search (Hunt & Black, 1996) was performed. Three different values were attempted for the different weights, in all possible combinations ($3^3 = 27$). For each weight set, the 15 training utterances were re-synthesized with the best fitting initial segment in the speech corpus. (The initial segments in the training material were never eligible for selection.)

The Mel-Cepstral Distance (MCD; Kubichek, 1993) was used as an objective measure of the difference between synthesized utterances and training utterances. MCD was calculated frame-by-frame, as follows (for the frame k):

$$MCD(k) = \sqrt{\sum_{i=1}^{13} \left[MC_x(i,k) - MC_y(i,k) \right]^2}$$

where $MC_x(i,k)$ and $MC_y(i,k)$ are the ith Mel-Cepstral coefficients of the vowel in the synthesized and the original (training) utterance, respectively. As the remainder part of the synthesized utterances is always identical to the remainder part of the training utterances, MCD was only calculated for the vowel part of the utterances. When the number of frames in the synthesized vowel and the training vowel was different, comparison was only performed up to the last frame of the shortest segment. An average MCD was calculated for all frames in the vowel to represent the difference between the synthesized utterance and the training utterance. The weight set that generated the set of synthesized utterances that were most similar to the set of training utterances was then selected as the optimal weight set.

2.6 Evaluation

A listening script of 60 stimuli was generated automatically, without supervision, from the speech corpus, with the restriction that 20 stimuli were original recordings (10 normal and 10 deviant), and 40 stimuli were modified. In all modified stimuli, the initial consonant was replaced by a different initial consonant (/t/ for /k/ and vice versa). Through this re-synthesis, 20 of the modified stimuli were "corrected" and 20 were "impaired". An online listening test was constructed to first present 3 training stimuli, and then the 60 stimuli in random order (different for different listeners). The task for the listeners was to report what they heard (by typing) and to judge whether the stimulus was an original recording or a modified recording. 38 adult listeners participated in the experiment.

3   Results

As a measure of intelligibility of the stimuli, the listeners' identification accuracy of the initial consonants was used. (As half of the stimuli were produced with deviant speech, and as such, most often nonsense words, inconsistency in the listeners' spelling was expected. Therefore, only the initial consonant was regarded in the analysis.) Inter-rater agreement of the listeners' perception of the initial consonants was measured by Fleiss' kappa at 0.64. Figure 1 shows that original deviant consonants are ambiguous to the listeners, whereas for all other stimulus types, the identification accuracy is around 80% or higher.

As a measure of naturalness, the listeners' judgment of whether a stimulus was an original or a modified recording was used. Here, inter-

rater agreement was measured by Fleiss' kappa at 0.13. As shown in Table 1, 62% of the synthesized stimuli were perceived as original recordings. For comparison, 24% of the original recordings were actually perceived as modified.

	Actual	
Perceived	Original	Modified
Original	76%	62%
Modified	24%	38%

Table 1. Relative distribution of the listener's perception of original and modified recordings.

4   Discussion

The finding that around 80-90% of the synthesized stimuli are perceived correctly (by their initial consonant) indicates that the generated speech is intelligible. For the intended use with children with deviant speech, the difference in consonant identification accuracy between original deviant recordings and corrected re-synthesized recordings is perhaps the most interesting. Whereas the listeners' perception of the initial consonants in original deviant recordings is quite equivocal, corrected re-synthesized recordings are perceived as much less ambiguous. This suggests that correction by re-synthesis could be a way of generating unambiguous speech targets for children with deviant speech.

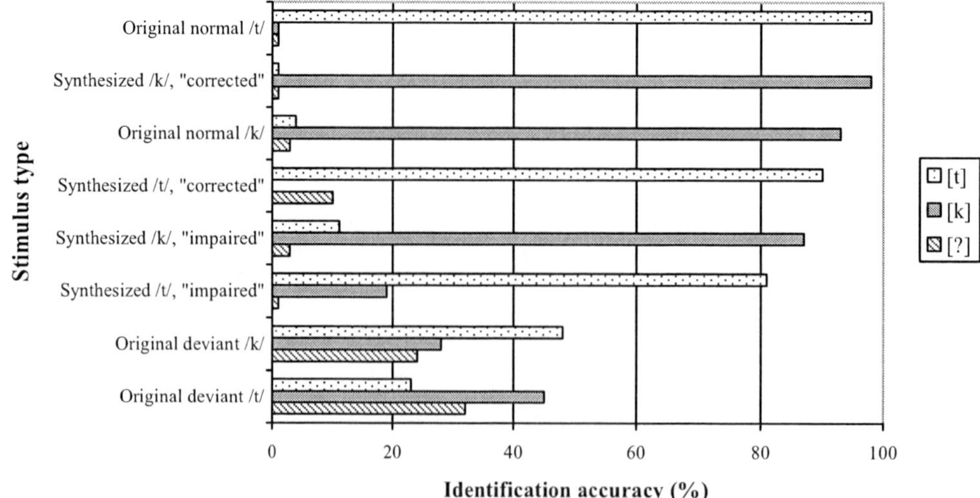

Figure 1. The listeners' identification accuracy of initial consonants, across the eight different types of stimuli, in descending order of accuracy. The different bars represent the three perceptual categories [t], [k] and [?] (any other sound), respectively.

Most of the modified stimuli were perceived as original recordings. This finding, together with the low degree of agreement between the listeners (Fleiss' kappa at 0.13), are indications that it was difficult for the listeners to distinguish between original and modified stimuli. Thus, it is indeed possible to generate natural speech by concatenating speech from different speakers. But even if listeners were able to detect that an utterance has been modified, it is not clear whether this is really a problem in the intended use with children with deviant speech, assuming that the generated speech is still intelligible.

An additional conclusion that can be drawn from the results in this study is that quite good results can be achieved with recordings of suboptimal quality. The recordings in this study were all done with rather simple recording equipment, and in naturalistic settings, rather than in a sound-proof studio. As these are conditions one could expect in a clinical setting, the technique (together with the speech corpus) could easily be implemented into a speech and language therapy tool. Such a tool would allow the generation of speech production targets that are tailor-made for each individual child, and for each individual utterance. Assumably, this would be a valuable resource in speech and language therapy.

Acknowledgements

The web experiment was implemented and administered by PhD Christoph Draxler at the Institute of Phonetics and Speech Processing in Munich, Germany.

References

Andrew J. Hunt & Alan W. Black. 1996. Unit selection in a concatenative speech synthesis system using a large speech database. *Proceedings of IEEE International Conference on Audio, Speech and Signal Processing ICASSP-96*, Atlanta, GA, USA.

Alexander B. Kain, John-Paul Hosom, Xiaochuan Niu, X, Jan P. H. van Santen, Melanie Fried-Oken, and Janice Staehely. 2007. Improving the intelligibility of dysarthric speech. *Speech Communication*. 49(9): 743-759.

Robert F. Kubichek. 1993. Mel-cepstral distance measure for objective speech quality assessment. *IEEE Pacific Rim Conference on Communications, Computers and Signal Processing*.

Athanassios Protopapas. 1998. Modified LPC re-synthesis for controlling speech stimulus discriminability. *136th Annual Meeting of the Acoustical Society of America*. Norfolk, VA, USA.

Franck Ramus and Jacques Mehler. 1999. Language identification with suprasegmental cues: A study based on speech resynthesis. *Journal of the Acoustical Society of America*, 105(1): 512-521.

Linda I. Shuster. 1998. The Perception of Correctly and Incorrectly Produced /r/. *Journal of Speech Language and Hearing Research*, 41(4): 941-950.

Kåre Sjölander. 2003. An HMM-based system for automatic segmentation and alignment of speech. *Proc of Fonetik 2003*, Umeå University, Sweden.

Paul Taylor. 2009. *Text-to-Speech Synthesis*. Cambridge University Press, Cambridge, UK.

Appendix A. Recording script

	Word	Pronounced	In English
1	k	/ko:/	*(the letter k)*
2	kaka	/kɑːka/	*cake*
3	kam	/kam/	*comb*
4	karta	/kɑːʈa/	*map*
5	katt	/kat/	*cat*
6	kavel	/kɑːvəl/	*rolling pin*
7	kopp	/kɔp/	*cup*
8	korg	/kɔrj/	*basket*
9	kulle	/kɵlə/	*hill*
10	kung	/kɵŋ/	*king*
11	tåg	/to:g/	*train*
12	tak	/tɑːk/	*roof*
13	tant	/tant/	*lady*
14	tavla	/tɑːvla/	*picture*
15	tomte	/tɔmtə/	*Santa Claus*
16	topp	/tɔp/	*top*
17	tumme	/tɵmə/	*thumb*
18	tunga	/tɵŋa/	*tongue*
19	tupp	/tɵp/	*rooster*

ISSN 1736-6305 Vol. 11
http://hdl.handle.net/10062/16955

Psycho-acoustically motivated formant feature extraction

Bea Valkenier
University of Groningen
Groningen, the Netherlands
b.valkenier@ai.rug.nl

Dirkjan Krijnders
University of Groningen
Groningen, the Netherlands
j.d.krijnders@ai.rug.nl

Ronald A.J. van Elburg[1]
University of Groningen
Groningen, the Netherlands
RonaldAJ@vanElburg.eu

Tjeerd C. Andringa[1]
University of Groningen
Groningen, the Netherlands
t.c.andringa@ai.rug.nl

[1]These authors contributed equally.

Abstract

Psycho-acoustical research investigates how human listeners are able to separate sounds that stem from different sources. This ability might be one of the reasons that human speech processing is robust to noise but methods that exploit this are, to our knowledge, not used in systems for automatic formant extraction or in modern speech recognition systems. Therefore we investigate the possibility to use harmonics that are consistent with a harmonic complex as the basis for a robust formant extraction algorithm. With this new method we aim to overcome limitations of most modern automatic speech recognition systems by taking advantage of the robustness of harmonics at formant positions. We tested the effectiveness of our formant detection algorithm on Hillenbrand's annotated American English Vowels dataset and found that in pink noise the results are competitive with existing systems. Furthermore, our method needs no training and is implementable as a real-time system which contrasts many of the existing systems.

1 Introduction

Formants are the resonance frequencies of the vocal tract; they change as the shape of the vocal tract changes. As such, formants are important acoustical cues for the description and identification of phonemes.

The task of automatic formant frequency estimation is traditionally investigated by methods based on LPC. Such representations accurately estimate formant positions and formant developments (Vargas and McLaughlin, 2008) in clean speech. However, efforts that focus on formant detection in noise (de Wet et al. 2004; Mustafa and Bruce, 2006; Yan et al. 2007) show results that deteriorate quickly in noise. One exception to this can be found by the system that was recently developed by Glaeser et al. (2010); their method shows a major improvement with regard to other methods.

Human listeners can detect and recognize speech in uncontrolled environments with relatively little hindrance of background noises (O'Shaughnessy, 2008). Psycho-acoustical research suggests that human listeners use Bregmans grouping cues (Bregman, 1990) to recombine components of sounds into a single percept. Provided the individual components are separable from background noise these grouping principles can be applied in automatic methods. Those methods were first investigated by Duifhuis et al. (1982). In general, systems based on grouping of harmonics are applicable in uncontrolled environments and do not rely on training. However, harmonic mismatches or missed detections sometimes occur.

Here, we investigate whether we can use the extractions of a harmonic grouping algorithm to extract robust formants without the need of training. Our results show that formant position estimates are stable over different noise conditions for a simple database. The results indicate that a renewed investigation of the problem of harmonic complex extraction can be a key to solving the lack of robustness in features for applications such as automatic speech recognition.

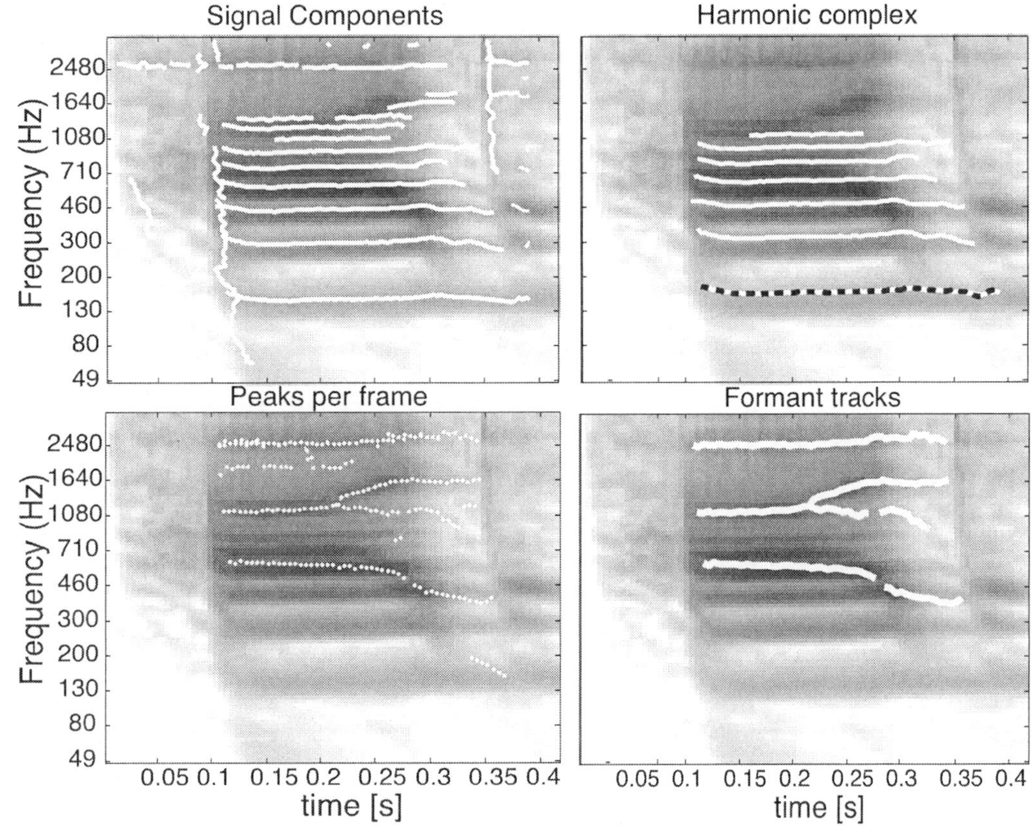

Figure 1: *Results of the different steps in the algorithm represented on a cochleogram of a male speaker pronouncing [hud]. (top left) Energetic signal components; (top right) selected HC, the fundamental frequency is given by the dashed line; (bottom left) formant detections based on this fundamental frequency and its overtones that fall below 4000Hz; (bottom right) selected formants*

2 Methods

2.1 Algorithm

In order to reach a close estimation of the resonance frequencies of the vocal tract we perform peak interpolation over harmonics in a harmonic complex (HC). First, the time signal is converted to the time-frequency domain by a gamma-chirp filterbank (Irino and Patterson, 1997). Its filter coefficients (h_{gc}) are defined by,

$$h_{gc} = at^{N-1}e^{-2\pi bB(f_c)t}e^{j(2\pi f_c t + c\log(t))} \qquad (1)$$

where N = 4 is the order of the gammachirp. The coefficients (a = 1, b = 0.71, c = -3.7) are based on Irino and Patterson (1997) but were adjusted such that the response is narrower in frequency such that the tonal components become emphasized. The frequency range f_c is fully logarithmic from 67 to 4000 Hz over 100 channels. The band-

width (B) of the filters is given by (9),

$$B(f_c) = 24.7 + 0.108 f_c \qquad (2)$$

We call the averaged and logarithmically compressed result a cochleogram.

Second, harmonics are extracted from the cochleogram using tone fit. Here we only give a global description of tone fit (see Krijnders and Andringa (submitted) and Krijnders et al. (2009) for details). The tone fit is a measure how well the cochleogram matches a tone at that time-frequency location. This measure is calculated with a filter derived from the response of the cochleogram to a perfect tone. Connected locations that match the filter well (with high tone-fit values) are extracted and are described as a line through the best matching location. We call such a description a signal component (Figure 1, top left).

The final step before the formant extraction combines signal components into HCs (Figure 1, top right). To that end, HC hypotheses are generated from energetic signal components (Figure 1, top right) that partly overlap in time and have an approximately harmonic frequency relation to each other. Initially a hypothesis consists of a fundamental frequency (f_0) estimate and energetic signal components. Additional signal components are added later to each hypothesis if they increase the score of that hypothesis. This score is defined as (Krijnders et al., 2009; Niessen et al., 2009):

$$S = n_{sc} + b_{f0} + n_h - \sum_{sc} rms_{sc} - \sum_{sc} \Delta f_{sc} \quad (3)$$

where n_{sc} is the number of signal components in the group, b_{f0} is one or zero depending on the existence of a signal component at the f_0, n_h is the number of sequential harmonics in the group, rms_{sc} are the root mean square values of the differences of the signal component f_0 after the mean frequency difference is removed, and Δf_{sc} is the mean frequency difference divided by harmonic number. To reduce octave errors additional hypotheses at octaves above and below each hypothesis are added and scored. In the formant extraction phase only the hypothesis with the highest score is used.

The resonance frequencies of the vocal tract might be located between two harmonics. Therefore, a three point quadratic interpolation over the harmonics around the harmonic with (local) maximum energy is used to estimate the formant location (Figure 1, bottom left). Subsequently, formant estimates with minimal distance in the adjacent frames in the time-frequency plane are connected into formant tracks. Only tracks of sufficient duration (7 frames or more, Figure 1, bottom right) are kept. These long formant tracks constitute our final formant estimate.

2.2 Material

The formant extractor was tested on the American English Vowels dataset (AEV) HillenBrand (1995). The dataset consists of 12 vowels pronounced in /h-V-d/ context by 48 female, 45 male and 46 child speakers. The AEV dataset is automatically annotated and subsequently hand-corrected for the first four formants at 8 points in time for each vowel, which makes it a suitable ground truth. We added pink noise in decreasing signal to noise ratios (SNRs), from 30dB to -6dB SNR. Pink noise was chosen because it masks speech evenly.

2.3 Evaluation

As we do not extract exactly three formants we cannot calculate error scores that represent the distance of the extracted formant to the annotated formant. The annotations are determined in clean speech and therefore we compare our results to the annotations for the clean speech condition. In order to evaluate the robustness of the system, we compare our results in noise to our results in clean speech as this gives the best estimate of noise robustness of the features.

2.3.1 Detections in clean speech

We specify two performance measures that together indicate how useful the features are for classification and calculate those for the features extracted in clean speech. The usefulness for classification is based on extraction of informative features on the one hand and neglecting non-informative features on the other hand.

The r_d gives the fraction of annotated formants that is consistent with our detections,

$$r_d = \frac{\#detected \cap \#annotated}{\#annotated} \quad (4)$$

We consider a detection to be consistent with the annotation if the relative error falls within the range of 15% (1st formant), 12% (2nd formant) and 8% (3rd formant). This equals a mean accepted error of respectively 95Hz, 316Hz and 266Hz. The range is chosen such that formants that were considered correct by the authors according to visual inspection were included.

The ratio spurious peaks (r_{sp}) is a measure for the detected formants that cannot be related to the annotated formants. It gives the ratio between the number of extra detected formants at the annotated positions, and the number of annotated points,

$$r_{sp} = \frac{\#detected - (\#detected \cap \#annotated)}{\#annotated} \quad (5)$$

The r_d and the r_{sp} are used to compare our results in clean speech to the annotations of the database. The robustness of the features is not determined with regard to the annotations but by comparing the results to itself.

2.3.2 Precision and recall in noise

The robustness is calculated by the precision and recall of the findings in clean speech. The precision reflects whether the extracted formants are

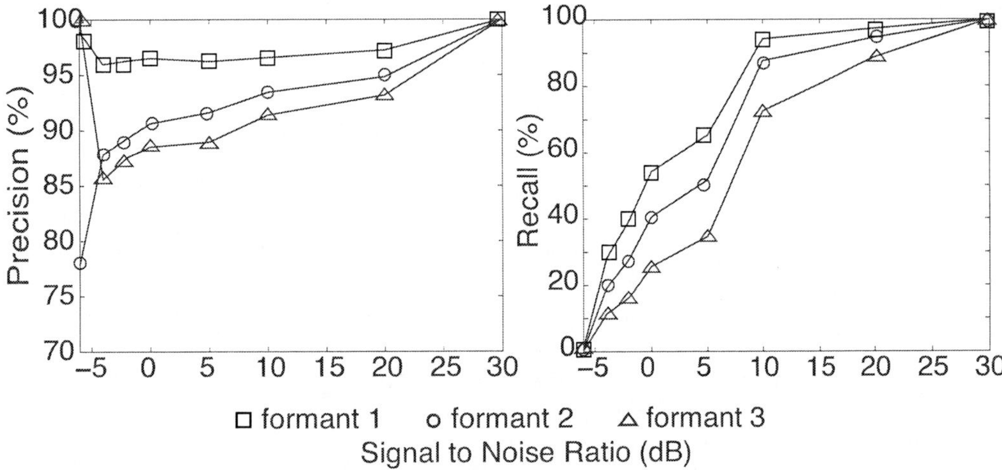

Figure 2: *Left panel: Percentage of correctly extracted formants (i.e. relative error falls within the range of 15% (1st formant) 12% (2nd formant) and 8% (3rd formant) in increasing SNR levels in pink noise. Right panel: Percentage not detected formants in increasing SNR levels in pink noise.*

relevant (with regard to the ground truth), it gives the amount of correct detections relative to the total amount of detections for a noise condition.

$$precision = \frac{\#truepositive}{\#truepositive + \#falsepositive} \quad (6)$$

The recall gives the amount of not detected formants relative to the total amount of detections for a noise condition reflecting whether the formants in the ground truth are extracted in noise as well.

$$recall = \frac{\#truepositive}{\#truepositive + \#falsenegative} \quad (7)$$

3 Results

3.1 Detections in clean speech

The detection rates (r_d) and proportion of spurious peaks (r_{sp}) are calculated for clean speech with regard to the annotated formants. In clean conditions, 90% correct detections are made for all three speaker classes for the first formant, and 75% correct for the second and third formants. The level of spurious peaks is found at 10%.

Table 1: *Type of mismatch for detection of the harmonic complex for male, female and child speakers in pink noise. For male speakers more harmonic complexes are missed and more octave errors are made.*

	SNR(EdB)	30	10	0	-4	-6
female	not extracted	0	1	18	35	51
	octave error	1	3	10	13	11
male	not extracted	2	8	41	74	81
	octave error	8	10	7	3	3
child	not extracted	0	1	17	39	51
	octave error		2	4	9	8

3.2 Precision in noise

In Figure 2 the precision of the findings is plotted against an increasing SNR in pink noise (left panel). Formants consistent with the ground truth can still be extracted at negative SNR values. Performance stays very high for the first formant and remains above 75% for both the second and the third formant.

3.3 Recall in noise

The right panel in Figure 2 shows that the recall is high above 10dB SNR and decreases rapidly in higher noise levels. The main reason for this is that harmonic complexes are not, or not correctly extracted. To provide a better insight in the results of the HC extraction stage, table 1 shows the occurrences of HCs that are not detected and the occurrences of HCs that exhibit an octave error in pink noise, calculated on the f0 annotations in Hillenbrand (1995).

4   Discussion

We described and tested a method to automatically extract formants based on robust parts of the acoustic signal, namely the harmonics at formant positions. The robustness of harmonics at formant positions allows us to develop a method to extract similar feature values in varying SNR. Because the harmonics have high energy levels the influence of noise is relatively small. The energetic harmonics provide a solid bases for the extraction of formants that are important acoustical cues for the identification of phonemes. With the aim of developing a system for robust phoneme identification speech features derived from harmonics are a good starting position. We showed that it is possible to extract formant feature values over SNRs from 30dB to -6dB in pink noise, that uses the robustness of harmonics at formant positions in human hearing. These initial results support the believe that harmonic grouping can be used as a basis for speech processing.

Recently Glaeser et al. (2010) presented a method that robustly estimates formant positions. In 0dB SNR they find mean relative error scores of approximately 24%, 17% and 10%, which is slightly worse than our results probably because it was tested on a more challenging database. One important difference of their method is that it is based on the enhancement of harmonics instead of grouping. We expect therefore that our method is better suited for data with mixed sources such as competing speakers.

Because the extraction of harmonic complexes poses some unsolved problems such as misses and octave errors we argue that the problem of the extraction of harmonic complexes should be systematically investigated. If this problem can be solved we have access to extremely robust features for speech coding with the advantage that training on a specific noise condition is not needed.

4.1   Conclusion

We showed that it is possible to develop an automatic method to extract formant feature values over SNRs from 30dB to -6dB in pink noise, that uses the robustness of harmonics at formant positions in human hearing. These initial results support the believe that harmonic grouping can be used as a basis for speech processing.

5   Acknowledgements

BV was supported by STW grant DTF 7459, JDK was supported by NWO grant 634.000.432. The authors would like to thank Odette Scharenborg, Jennifer Spenader, Maria Niessen, Hedde van de Vooren and three anonymous reviewers for their useful comments on earlier versions of this manuscript.

References

Bregman, A.S., "Auditory scene analysis: The perceptual organization of sound", Cambridge, Massachusetts: The MIT Press 1990.

Glaeser,C., Heckmann, M., Joublin, F. and Goerick,C. "Combining auditory preprocessing and bayesian estimation for robust formant tracking," IEEE trans. on audio, speech and language processing, 18(2), pp. 224 - 236, 2010

Hillenbrand, J.M., Getty, L.A., Clark, M.J. and Wheeler, K. "Acoustic characteristics of American English vowels," J Acoust Soc Am, 97, pp. 3099 - 3111, 1995

Irino, T. and Patterson, R.D. "A time-domain, level-dependent auditory filter: The gammachirp," J Acoust Soc Am, 101(1), pp. 412 - 419, Jan 1997.

Krijnders, J.D., Niessen, M.E. and Andringa,T.C. "Sound event recognition through expectancy-based evaluation of signal- driven hypotheses," Pattern Recognition Letters, accepted 2009.

Krijnders, J.D. and Andringa, T.C. "Tone, pulse, and chirp decomposition for environmental sound analysis," Submitted

Moore, B.C.J. "A revision of Zwicker's loudness modell." Acustica, 82(2), pp. 335 - 345(11), 1996.

Mustafa, K. and Bruce, I.C. "Robust Formant Tracking for Continuous Speech With Speaker Variability," IEEE trans. on audio, speech and language processing, 14(2), pp. 435 - 444, 2006

Niessen, M., Krijnders, J.D., and Andringa, T.C. "Understanding a soundscape through its components". Proceedings of Euronoise 2009

O'Shaughnessy, D. "Invited paper: Automatic speech recognition: History, methods and challenges," Pattern Recognition 41(10), 2965 - 2979, 2008

Vargas, J. and McLaughlin, S."Cascade Prediction Filters With Adaptive Zeros to Track the Time-Varying Resonances of the Vocal Tract," IEEE trans. on audio, speech and language processing, 16(1), pp. 1 - 7, 2008

Wet, F., Weber, K., Boves, L., Cranen, B., Bengio, S. and Bourlard, H. "Evaluation of formant-like features on an automatic vowel classification task," J Acoust Soc Am 116, pp. 1781 - 1791, 2004.

Yan, Q., Vesghi, S., Zavarehei, E., Milner,B., Darch,J., White, P. and Andrianakis, I. "Formant tracking linear prediction model using HMMs and Kalman filters for noisy speech processing," Computer speech and language 21, pp. 543 - 561, 2007

ISSN 1736-6305 Vol. 11
http://hdl.handle.net/10062/16955

Random Indexing Re-Hashed

Erik Velldal
Department of Informatics
University of Oslo, Norway
`erikve@ifi.uio.no`

Abstract

This paper introduces a modified version of Random Indexing, a technique for dimensionality reduction based on random projections. We here describe how RI can be efficiently implemented using the notion of universal hashing. This eliminates the need to store any random vectors, replacing them instead with a small number of hash-functions, thereby dramatically reducing the memory footprint. We dub this reformulated version of the method Hashed Random Indexing (HRI).

1   Introduction

Random indexing (RI) is a technique for dimensionality reduction that was initially introduced by Kanerva et al. (2000) for constructing compact word-by-context vector spaces for modeling the semantic similarity of words. The method is related to a family of techniques based on *random projections*, but comes with several particular advantages in terms of computational simplicity and incrementality. In this paper we introduce a modified version of RI which we call *hashed random indexing* (HRI), where we replace the so-called index vectors by a small set of *hash functions*.

We will start by describing the basic methodology of random indexing as introduced by Kanerva et al. (2000), also highlighting the relation to random projections. In Section 3 we then describe the notion of *universal families of hash functions*, and in particular *multiplicative universal hashing* (Dietzfelbinger et al., 1997), before finally showing how RI can be efficiently implemented using hash functions drawn from such families. In Section 4 we also include some general caveats regarding dimensionality reduction based on random projections. Finally, Section 5 provides an overview of other related work based on feature hashing, as well as discussing possible future directions.

2   Random Indexing

Random indexing was initially introduced by Kanerva et al. (2000) for reducing the dimensionality of word-by-document vector spaces, modeling the semantic similarity of words in terms of their contextual distribution. Proving an attractive alternative (or complement) to more costly dimensionality reduction techniques such as singular value decomposition (SVD), it has since been extensively used for constructing compact semantic space models (Karlgren and Sahlgren, 2001; Sahlgren, 2005; Widdows and Ferraro, 2009). Beyond this setting of distributional word similarity, Velldal (2010) applied RI as a general means of reducing the feature space of a classification problem. Working with SVM-based uncertainty detection, Velldal (2010) showed that RI could compress the feature space by two orders of magnitude without sacrificing classifier performance.

As the current paper has more of a theoretical focus, we will not assume any particular type of data or application. We will, however, assume that each data item is represented by a d-dimensional feature vector $\vec{f_i} \in \Re^d$. Given n examples and d features, the vectors can be thought of as rows in a matrix $F \in \Re^{n \times d}$. The purpose of RI is to avoid working with the original (possibly huge) feature matrix $F \in \Re^{n \times d}$, replacing it instead with a smaller matrix $G \in \Re^{n \times k}$ where $k \ll d$. The RI method constructs this compressed representation of the data in G by *incrementally accumulating* so-called *index vectors* assigned to each of the d features (Sahlgren, 2005). The process can be described by the following two simple steps:

- When a new feature is instantiated, it is assigned a randomly generated vector of a fixed dimensionality k, consisting of a small number of -1s and $+1$s (the remaining elements being 0). This is then the so-called *index vector* or *random label* of the feature.

- The vector representing a given training example (the jth row of G represents the jth example) is then constructed by simply summing the random index vectors of its features.

The parameters of RI that need to be specified are the number of non-zeros (ϵ) and the dimensionality (k) of the ternary index vectors. As noted by Sahlgren (2005), if the index vectors had been specified to consist of only one position of value 1 for each feature, i.e. *orthogonal* vectors of $k=d$ dimensions, the two steps above would have produced the standard feature matrix F. With RI, one instead uses randomly initialized k-dimensional index vectors. As observed by Hecht-Nielsen (1994), high-dimensional vectors having random directions are very likely to be *close to orthogonal*, and the matrix G can in this sense be viewed as an approximation of F (in terms of the relative distances of rows). Moreover, we can expect this approximation to be better the higher we set k.

Note that, in the traditional setting of semantic space modeling, RI is applied on the *type level*, accumulating global context vectors that represent the aggregated distribution of words across a corpus. When used more generally for compressing the feature space of a learning problem as in (Velldal, 2010), RI can also be applied at the *token level*, producing a compact representation of each training instance.

Mathematically, RI can be seen as part of a larger family of dimension reduction techniques based on *random projections*, and in particular the "neuronal" version described by Vempala (2004). Such methods work by multiplying the feature matrix $F \in \Re^{n \times d}$ by a random matrix $R \in \Re^{d \times k}$, for $k \ll d$, thereby reducing the number of dimensions from d to k:

$$FR = G \in \Re^{n \times k} \qquad \text{with } k \ll d \qquad (1)$$

Given that k is sufficiently high (logarithmic in n), the Johnson-Lindenstrauss lemma (Johnson and Lindenstrauss, 1984) tells us that the pairwise distances in F can be preserved with high probability within the lower-dimensional space G (Li et al., 2006). While much work on random projections for producing such so-called JL-embeddings assume r_{ij} having a standard normal distribution, Achlioptas (2001) shows that the only requirement on r_{ij} is that they are i.i.d. with zero mean and unit variance.

With RI, the index vector of the ith feature corresponds to the ith row of R in Equation 1. Moreover, for ϵ non-zeros, the entries of the index vectors $r_{ij} \in \{+1, 0, -1\}$ will then be distributed with probabilities corresponding to $\{\frac{\epsilon/2}{k}, \frac{k-\epsilon}{k}, \frac{\epsilon/2}{k}\}$.

One important advantage of the particular random indexing approach is that the full $n \times d$ feature matrix F never needs to be explicitly computed or represented (Karlgren and Sahlgren, 2001). As described above, with RI we construct the representation of the data in G by *incrementally accumulating* the index vectors assigned to each feature. This means that the dimension reduction is only *implicit*, in the sense that the compressed representation in G is constructed directly. With the introduction of *hashed* random indexing below, we also eliminate the need to explicitly represent R.

3 Indexing by Universal Hashing

In the traditional implementation of RI, a randomly generated index vector is assigned to each feature as it is first encountered. If the same feature is encountered again later, that same index vector is simply retrieved by look-up. For each of the d distinct features (which for typical NLP problems can number hundreds of thousands or millions), a separate index vector must be stored.

An attractive feature of RI is that is it allows us to think about dimensionality reduction in terms of data structures, rather than as a separate process. In fact, taking a step back, the accumulated index vectors in the reduced space G are reminiscent of probabilistic data structures like *Bloom filters* and various *sketch* representations. These are *hash-based* data structures, however, designed for compactly representing things like set membership and frequency counts in an approximate way. In a similar fashion, we here propose to save resources in RI by using a small set of *hash functions* to implicitly represent the index vectors. As we shall see, this eliminates the need for storing the random vectors in $R \in \Re^{d \times k}$.

Let h be a hash function that maps from a set of hash keys U into some smaller set of hash codes C. We here assume both U and C to be *integers* (without loss of generality as strings can be converted to integers). More precisely, U will correspond to the dimensions of the original input space F, and C will correspond to dimensions in the lower-dimensional index vectors. Given that the RI method relies on a one-to-many mapping from features into index vector positions, we need to use *multiple distinct hash functions*. For this purpose, the notion of *universal families of hash functions* comes in handy. This concept, introduced by Carter and Wegman (1979), refers to a method for randomly generating hash functions $h_i : U \rightarrow C$ from a family of functions H that also comes with certain guarantees on the probability of *collisions* (i.e. the chances of h_i mapping two distinct keys into the same code). There exists several approaches to defining such universal classes, typically based on computations seeded by some large prime, as in the original proposal by Carter and Wegman (1979). For the implementation of HRI, however, we propose to instead select functions from the particularly simple class of *multiplicative universal hashing* introduced by Dietzfelbinger et al. (1997), which provides mappings that can be evaluated very efficiently.

More precisely, Dietzfelbinger et al. (1997) define a universal family of mappings from *l-bit keys* to *m-bit indices*. Let $U = \{0, \ldots, 2^l - 1\}$ and $C = \{0, \ldots, 2^m - 1\}$. Furthermore, let A be the set of positive odd l-bit numbers, i.e. $A = \{a \mid 0 < a < 2^l \text{ and } a \text{ is odd}\}$. This then defines a family of universal hash functions $H_{l,m} = \{h_a \mid a \in A\}$, with h_a computed as:

$$h_a(x) = (ax \bmod 2^l) \text{ div } 2^{l-m} \quad \text{for } x \in U \quad (2)$$

where mod refers to the modulo operation and div means integer division. By randomly picking a number $a \in A$, we generate a new hash function h_a from the set of 2^{l-1} distinct hash functions in the class $H_{l,m}$. Note that, as the bits of the keys are typically assumed fixed to some value like $l = 32$, we will write $H_{l,m}$ as simply H_m.

As noted by Dietzfelbinger et al. (1997), the fact that the arithmetic involved in Equation 2 is based on powers of two, allows the mapping to be efficiently implemented at the level of simple bitwise operations.[1] Dietzfelbinger et al. (1997) also prove that H_m is so-called *2-universal*. This means that, for two distinct keys x and y, the function h_a obeys the following lemma:

$$Prob\left(h_a(x) = h_a(y)\right) \leq \frac{1}{2^{m-1}} \quad (3)$$

Returning to the method of random indexing, we now have a principled way of very efficiently computing and representing the random index vectors. Any set of d index vectors R in $k = 2^m$ dimensions[2] and with ϵ non-zero elements can now be *implicitly represented* by a set of hash functions $H^\epsilon = \{h_{a^1}, \ldots, h_{a^\epsilon}\} \subset H_m$. Each hash function $h_a \in H^\epsilon$ computes one non-zero element position. We randomly pick $\frac{\epsilon}{2}$ of the functions to indicate -1s, and label the remaining half $+1$s. Let σ_k correspondingly evaluate to $+1$ or -1, depending on whether h_k is selected to map into index positions with positive or negative values. In the compressed representation G, an entry corresponding to the jth dimension for the ith data item can then be formally described as

$$G_{ij} = \sum_{h_k \in H^\epsilon} \sum_{l:h_k(l)=j} \sigma_k f_{il} \quad (4)$$

Procedurally speaking, G is constructed in the incremental fashion described in Section 2, and without the need to first construct the full feature count matrix F: As a feature is instantiated, we update G according to the values and positions indicated by the hash functions. Evaluating the hash functions is very cheap and done in constant time. Most importantly, however; storing the full set of index vectors—corresponding to the $d \times k$ random matrix R in Equation 1—now simply amounts to storing the few random seed numbers (the as) for generating the hash functions. In terms of this implicit representation of R, no extra overhead is associated with increasing the dimensionality of the feature space (d) or the reduced space (k), or the number of training examples (n).

In theory, implementing the random index vectors in terms of universal hashing means introducing some new dependencies in our mappings. The lemma in Equation 3 gives the probability of a given hash-function mapping two different given keys to the same value, i.e. $h_i(x) = h_i(y)$. However, given that each index assignment assumes a one-to-many mapping, we would also like to avoid that two different functions map the same key to the same value, i.e. $h_i(x) = h_j(x)$. In practice, this proves to be a minimal concern, with collisions of this sort occurring with an observed probability of roughly $\frac{1}{2^m}$.

---

[1] The modulo operation can be computed as bit-wise AND (e.g. $y \bmod 2^l = y$ AND $(2^l - 1)$), and the integer division can be done by simple bit-shifting (e.g. y div $2^x = y$ RIGHT-SHIFT-BY x).

[2] Note that the dimensionality k will always be specified as a power of two, given the definition of the multiplicative hash functions in Equation 2.

Note that, the incrementality of RI means that the method generally lends itself well to *parallelization* or *stream processing*. For example, to combine or update different context vectors accumulated for a given word, we simply add them together. This presupposes that the assignment of index vectors is shared and known across subtasks or machines, however (to ensure coherent mappings). With HRI, parallelization is even simpler, as the only knowledge that needs to be shared is the seed numbers for the hash functions.

So far we have occupied ourselves with a particular method for *computing* a reduced space G. In the next section we shift focus slightly and turn to look at some potential pitfalls of *working within* such a reduced space, as produced by random projection based methods in general.

4 Caveats

Although methods based on random projections, such as random indexing, typically come with the promise of reducing memory load and computational cost, there are certain limitations and possible caveats that are worth bearing in mind and that are often overlooked in the literature.

First, if the original input space F is very *sparse*, as is indeed often the case in NLP settings, the reduced space G will typically be much more dense—the exact degree depending on the number of non-zero entries specified in R. In other words, the absolute number of non-zero elements will then be higher for the reduced space than the original space. In practice, the cost of storing a given matrix depends not on its dimensionality alone, but its number of non-zero elements. The reason, of course, is that any zero-valued element can simply be ignored. This means that storing the reduced space might actually end up requiring *more* memory than storing the original non-reduced space.

Naturally, the same line of argument also applies to computational aspects. Assuming a non-naive implementation, the computational cost of many vector operations depends less on the total number dimensions and more on the number of non-zero elements of the vectors. This means that certain common operations such as dot-products, euclidean distance, etc., might take *longer* to compute in the reduced (but more dense) space compared to the non-reduced (but more sparse) space.

5 #Hashing—A Trending Topic

There has recently been a series of papers in the NLP and ML literature on the use of hashing for constructing faster and more compact models. Several authors have explored the use of hash-based randomized data structures for storing approximate frequency counts for large data sets, such as the generalized notion of a *Bloom filter* used by Talbot and Osborne (2007) and Durme and Lall (2009) in the context of language modeling, or the *Count-Min sketch* used by Goyal et al. (2010) for computing web-scale distributional similarities. More closely related to the work presented in the current paper perhaps, is the notion of *hash kernels* introduced by Shi et al. (2009) and Weinberger et al. (2009) in the context of SVM-based spam filtering and topic categorization. With hash kernels, high-dimensional input vectors are compressed using a single hash function that maps the original features into a smaller range of indices, and dot-products are then computed between these hash maps. For an input vector $f \in \Re^d$, and for some hash functions $h : U \to C$ and $\xi : U \to \{\pm 1\}$, the ith element of a hash map $\phi(f)$ is defined as

$$\phi_i^{(h,\xi)}(f) = \sum_{j:h(j)=i} \xi(j)f_j \tag{5}$$

Each element in the hash map is given by a signed sum of all coordinates with the same hash code (Weinberger et al., 2009). Shi et al. (2009) argue that by using only a single hash function, hash kernels *preserve sparsity*. However, to reduce the information loss caused by collisions in the hash map, the original features are explicitly *duplicated* prior to hashing (Weinberger et al., 2009). Each level of duplication will incur a doubling in the dimensionality d of the original feature space F. In contrast, with the RI methodology, the same effect is achieved by simply increasing the ratio of non-zeros in the index vectors. On this background, we see that the signed sum in the hash kernel of Weinberger et al. (2009) is essentially equivalent to the result of adding ternary index vectors in the random indexing approach of Kanerva et al. (2000). Moreover, when comparing hash kernels to the general approach of random projections, Weinberger et al. (2009) note that one advantage of the former is that there is no need for storing the random matrices. With hashed RI, however, we need not store neither the random projection matrix R nor the original feature matrix F.

Another line of work bearing resemblance to (H)RI is the use of *Locality Sensitive Hashing* (LSH) for identifying semantically similar words by Ravichandran et al. (2005). LSH is a method for fast but approximate nearest neighbor search based on compact *bit signatures* created for each data point or vector. These signatures are created by applying multiple binary hash functions to each point in a way so that close items are hashed to the same buckets with a high probability. The cosine similarity of the original word vectors is then approximated by the hamming distance of their bit signatures. In the work of Ravichandran et al. (2005), the value of each hash function ($\{0,1\}$) is defined by the sign of the dot product between each word vector and a random vector. The bit signatures produced by LSH can be viewed as similar to the reduced representations produced by HRI, although the underlying perspective on the process itself can at first seem rather different: While the LSH approach of Ravichandran et al. (2005) defines hash functions over points in terms of random projections, HRI defines random projections in terms of hash functions over dimensions. Moreover, a modified version of projection-based LSH is presented by Van Durme and Lall (2010) for on-line generation of bit signatures for data *streams*. Taking advantage of the fact that the operations in the dot products between the data vectors and the random "hash vectors" are linear, Van Durme and Lall (2010) replace the dot products with individual additions corresponding to the random values associated with each feature as it is encountered in the stream, thereby taking a step towards the incrementality that we have several times pointed out in relation to random indexing above.

The final example of related work that we will be discussing is the feature hashing approach of Ganchev and Dredze (2008). Targeting NLP applications on resource constrained devices, Ganchev and Dredze (2008) suggest *eliminating the symbol-table* (also known as the alphabet, dictionary, etc.), replacing it instead with a hash function. Tests on a range of tasks (sentiment analysis, spam detection, topic labeling, etc.) shows "tolerable" degradation of performance relative to savings in storage (Ganchev and Dredze, 2008). A similar approach was taken by Bohnet (2010), who uses feature hashing for speeding up

the feature handling in a data-driven dependency parser. It is important to note that, rather than being primarily aimed at dimensionality reduction, the approach of Ganchev and Dredze (2008) aims to save resources by discarding the symbol-table. In fact, in order to reduce the chances of collisions, the assumed dimensionality is instead sometimes greatly *increased* using this approach, as in the dependency parsing experiments of Bohnet (2010).

An interesting direction for future work would be to combine HRI with the feature hashing approach of Ganchev and Dredze (2008), i.e. applying HRI on the symbolic feature representations directly. It should be noted that when learning a model that is to be applied to unseen test examples, the expected savings in terms of storage would likely come at the cost of reduced accuracy. The reason is that the space of possible features instantiated by our feature templates is typically not closed, in the sense that we might expect to instantiate features during testing that were not observed during training (e.g. unseen n-grams). Usually such unseen features will be filtered out and discarded as they will not correspond to an entry in the model's symbol-table. However, when by-passing the symbol-table and applying the feature hashing directly on the string level, we risk introducing some noise by mapping such previously unknown features into our feature vectors. If, on the other hand, we are to work within the "closed" vector space itself (for example, searching for nearest neighbors among given points in a semantic space model, as opposed to using the space as input for estimating a classifier), such worries would not arise. Although it would mean giving up the possibility to assign meaning to specific dimensions, that is something we have already done when applying random indexing in first place.

6 Conclusion

While random indexing (RI) is a well-established technique for dimensionality reduction, this paper has described a novel reformulation of the method, dubbed hashed random indexing (HRI), that eliminates the need to store any random vectors, thereby substantially reducing the memory footprint of the method. This is accomplished by replacing the so-called index vectors or random labels with a set of hash-functions. We furthermore suggest that these functions are drawn from the family of multiplicative universal hash functions described by Dietzfelbinger et al. (1997). Finally, we have also noted some general caveats regarding dimensionality reduction methods based on random projections, random indexing included, as well as discussed the relation of (H)RI to other approaches employing various notions of feature hashing.

References

Dimitris Achlioptas. 2001. Database-friendly random projections. In *Proceedings of the Twentieth ACM SIGMOD-SIGACT-SIGART Symposium on Principles of Database Systems*, Santa Barbara, USA.

Bernd Bohnet. 2010. Top accuracy and fast dependency parsing is not a contradiction. In *Proceedings of the 23rd International Conference on Computational Linguistics*, Beijing, China.

Larry Carter and Mark N Wegman. 1979. Universal classes of hash functions. *Journal of Computer and System Sciences*, 18(2).

Martin Dietzfelbinger, Torben Hagerup, Jyrki Katajainen, and Martti Penttonen. 1997. A reliable randomized algorithm for the closest-pair problem. *Journal of Algorithms*, 25(1).

Benjamin Van Durme and Ashwin Lall. 2009. Probabilistic counting with randomized storage. In *Proceedings of the 21st International Joint Conference on Artifical Intelligence*, Pasadena, USA.

Kuzman Ganchev and Mark Dredze. 2008. Small statistical models by random feature mixing. In *Proceedings of the ACL-2008 Workshop on Mobile Language Processing*, pages 19 – 20, Columbus, USA.

Amit Goyal, Jagadeesh Jagarlamudi, Hal Daumé III, and Suresh Venkatasubramanian. 2010. Sketch techniques for scaling distributional similarity to the web. In *GEometrical Models of Natural Language Semantics Workshop (GEMS) at ACL*, pages 51 – 56, Uppsala, Sweden.

Robert Hecht-Nielsen. 1994. Context vectors: General purpose approximate meaning representations self-organized from raw data. In J. M. Zurada, R. J. Marks II, and C. J. Robinson, editors, *Computational Intelligence: Imitating Life*. IEEE Press, Orlando, USA.

William Johnson and Joram Lindenstrauss. 1984. Extensions of Lipschitz mappings into a Hilbert space. *Contemporary Mathematics*, 26.

Pentti Kanerva, Jan Kristoferson, and Anders Holst. 2000. Random indexing of text samples for latent semantic analysis. In *Proceedings of the 22nd Annual Conference of the Cognitive Science Society*, Pennsylvania.

Jussi Karlgren and Magnus Sahlgren. 2001. From words to understanding. In Y. Uesaka, P. Kanerva, and H. Asoh, editors, *Foundations of Real-World Intelligence*. CSLI Publications, Stanford.

Ping Li, Trevor Hastie, and Kenneth Church. 2006. Very sparse random projections. In *Proceedings of the Twelfth ACM SIGKDD International Conference on Knowledge Discovery and Data Mining*, Philadelphia, USA.

Deepak Ravichandran, Patrick Pantel, and Eduard Hovy. 2005. Randomized algorithms and nlp: using locality sensitive hash function for high speed noun clustering. In *Proceedings of the 43rd Meeting of the Association for Computational Linguistics*, Michigan, USA.

Magnus Sahlgren. 2005. An introduction to random indexing. In *Proceedings of the Methods and Applications of Semantic Indexing Workshop at the 7th International Conference on Terminology and Knowledge Engineering (TKE)*, Copenhagen, Denmark.

Qinfeng Shi, James Petterson, Gideon Dror, John Langford, Alex Smola, Alex Strehl, and Vishy Vishwanathan. 2009. Hash kernels. In *Proceedings of the 12th International Conference on Artificial Intelligence and Statistics*, Florida, April.

David Talbot and Miles Osborne. 2007. Smoothed Bloom Filter language models: Tera-scale LMs on the cheap. In *Proceedings of the 2007 Conference on Empirical Methods in Natural Language Processing*, Prague, Czech Republic.

Benjamin Van Durme and Ashwin Lall. 2010. Online generation of locality sensitive hash signatures. In *Proceedings of the 48th Meeting of the Association for Computational Linguistics*, Uppsala, Sweden.

Erik Velldal. 2010. Detecting uncertainty in biomedical literature: A simple disambiguation approach using sparse random indexing. In *Proceedings of the Fourth International Symposium on Semantic Mining in Biomedicine (SMBM)*, Cambridgeshire, UK.

Santosh S. Vempala. 2004. *The Random Projection Method*, volume 65 of *DIMACS Series in Discrete Mathematics and Theoretical Computer Science*. American Mathematical Society, RI, USA.

Kilian Weinberger, Anirban Dasgupta, John Langford, Alex Smola, and Josh Attenberg. 2009. Feature hashing for large scale multitask learning. In *Proceedings of the 26th Annual International Conference on Machine Learning*, Montreal, Canada.

Dominic Widdows and Kathleen Ferraro. 2009. Semantic vectors: a scalable open source package and online technology management application. In *Proceedings of the 6th International Conference on Language Resources and Evaluation*, Marrakech, Morocco, May.

ISSN 1736-6305 Vol. 11
http://hdl.handle.net/10062/16955

Evaluating the Effect of Word Frequencies in a Probabilistic Generative Model of Morphology

Sami Virpioja and **Oskar Kohonen** and **Krista Lagus**

Aalto University School of Science

Adaptive Informatics Research Centre

P.O. Box 15400, FI-00076 AALTO, Finland

{oskar.kohonen,sami.virpioja,krista.lagus}@tkk.fi

Abstract

We consider generative probabilistic models for unsupervised learning of morphology. When training such a model, one has to decide what to include in the training data; e.g., should the frequencies of words affect the likelihood, and should words occurring only once be discarded. We show that for a certain type of models, the likelihood can be parameterized on a function of the word frequencies. Thorough experiments are carried out with Morfessor Baseline, evaluating the resulting quality of the morpheme analysis on English and Finnish test sets. Our results show that training on word types or with a logarithmic function of the word frequencies give similar scores, while a linear function, i.e., training on word tokens, is significantly worse.

1 Introduction

Unsupervised morphology learning is concerned with the task of learning models of word-internal structure. By definition, a probabilistic generative model describes the joint distribution of morphological analyses and word forms. An essential question is whether the morphological model represents *types*, that is, disregarding word frequencies in corpora, or *tokens*, i.e. fully appreciating the word frequencies. It has been observed that for the well-known Morfessor Baseline method (Creutz and Lagus, 2002; Creutz and Lagus, 2007), training on types leads to a large improvement in performance over tokens, when evaluating against a linguistic gold standard segmentation (Creutz and Lagus, 2004; Creutz and Lagus, 2005). A similar effect for a more recent method is reported by Poon et al. (2009). However, intuitively the corpus frequencies of words should be

useful information for learning the morphology. In support of this intuition, behavioral studies regarding storage and processing of multi-morphemic word forms imply that the frequency of a word form plays a role in how it is stored in the brain: as a whole or as composed of its parts (Alegre and Gordon, 1999; Taft, 2004). In addition, the optimal morphological analysis may depend on the task to which the analysis is applied. In Morpho Challenge evaluations (Kurimo et al., 2010b), the winners of the different tasks are often different algorithms. For example, in machine translation, the reason might be that the frequent inflected word forms do not benefit from being split. However, it is not trivial to utilize token counts in generative models, since word tokens follow a power-law distribution (Zipf, 1932), and thus naive approaches will over-emphasize frequent word forms.

In this article, we consider whether the frequency information is inherently useful or not in unsupervised learning of morphology. We show that for a certain class of generative models, including those of the Morfessor methods, the word frequency acts as a weight in the likelihood function. We explicitly modify the distribution of words that the model approximates, also allowing choices *between* types and tokens.

Related to our approach, Goldwater et al. (2006) define a Bayesian two-level model where the first level generates word forms according to a multinomial distribution and the second level skews the distribution towards the observed power law distribution. For extreme parameter values of the second level process, the multinomial is trained with either types or tokens. For intermediate values, frequent words are emphasized, but not as much as when using token counts directly. They find experimentally that in morphological segmentation the best results are achieved when the parameter value is close to using only types, but emphasizes frequent words slightly. Their approach is elegant but computationally demanding. In contrast, our method is based on transforming the observed frequencies with a deterministic function, and therefore can be performed as a quick preprocessing step for existing algorithms.

Another intermediate option between types and tokens is given by Snyder and Barzilay (2008). Their morphological model generates bilingual phrases instead of words, and consequently, it is trained on aligned phrases that consist up to 4–6 words. The phrase frequencies are applied to discard phrases that occur less than five times, as they are likely to cause problems because of the noisy alignment. However, training is based on phrase types. Considering the frequencies of the words in this type of data, the common words will have more weight, but not as much as if direct corpus frequency was used.

We study the effect of the frequency information on the task of finding segmentations close to a linguistic gold standard. We use Morfessor Baseline, which is convenient due to its fast training algorithm. However, it has a property that causes it to arrive at fewer morphemes per words on average when the size of the training data grows (Creutz and Lagus, 2007). This phenomenon, which we refer to as undersegmentation, happens also when the model is trained on token counts rather than types, but it is not inherently related to the word frequency weighting in the class of models studied. Recently, Kohonen et al. (2010) showed how the amount of segmentation can be controlled by weighting the likelihood. In their semi-supervised setting, optimizing the weight improved the results considerably. This results in state of the art performance in Morpho Challenge 2010 (Kurimo et al., 2010a). In order to evaluate the effect of the frequency information without the problem of undersegmentation, we apply a similar likelihood weighting.

Another potential use for frequencies is noise reduction. Corpora often contain misspelled word forms and foreign names, but they are likely to occur very infrequently and are therefore removed if one discards rare word forms. It has been observed that pruning words that occur fewer times than a given threshold sometimes improves results in linguistic evaluations (Virpioja et al., 2010). We examine to what extent this improvement is explained by noise reduction, and to what extent it is explained by improving on undersegmentation.

2　Methods

In this section, we first consider generative probabilistic models in the task of learning morphology. We show that by making some simple assumptions, the data likelihood function can be parameterized on a function of the word frequencies. Then we describe the Morfessor Baseline model in this general framework.

2.1　Generative models of morphology

A generative model of morphology specifies the joint distribution $P(A = a, W = w \mid \boldsymbol{\theta})$ of words W and their morphological analyses A for given parameters $\boldsymbol{\theta}$.[1] W is an observed and A a hidden variable of the model. Here we assume that an analysis is a list of morpheme labels: $a = (m_1, \ldots, m_n)$. The probability of an analysis for a given word can be obtained by

$$P(A = a \mid W = w, \boldsymbol{\theta})$$
$$= \frac{P(A = a, W = w \mid \boldsymbol{\theta})}{\sum_{\bar{a}} P(A = \bar{a}, W = w \mid \boldsymbol{\theta})}. \tag{1}$$

Generative models can be trained with unlabeled data $\boldsymbol{D}$. For model classes with a large number of parameters, estimating the posterior probability of the parameters of a model, $P(\boldsymbol{\theta} \mid \boldsymbol{D}) \propto P(\boldsymbol{\theta}) P(\boldsymbol{D} \mid \boldsymbol{\theta})$, may be difficult. An alternative is to use a point estimate of the model parameters, θ^*, and apply that in Eq. 1. Instead of the simplest point estimate, *maximum likelihood* (ML), it is often better to apply *maximum a posteriori* (MAP), where a prior distribution is used to encode possible prior information about the model parameters:

$$\boldsymbol{\theta}^{\mathrm{MAP}} = \arg\max_{\boldsymbol{\theta}} \left\{ P(\boldsymbol{\theta}) \times P(\boldsymbol{D} \mid \boldsymbol{\theta}) \right\}. \tag{2}$$

Let $\boldsymbol{D}_W$ be a set of training data containing word forms. Assuming that the probabilities of the words are independent, the likelihood of the data can be calculated as

$$P(\boldsymbol{D}_W \mid \boldsymbol{\theta}) = \prod_{j=1}^{|\boldsymbol{D}_W|} P(W = w_j \mid \boldsymbol{\theta})$$
$$= \prod_{j=1}^{|\boldsymbol{D}_W|} \sum_a P(A = a, W = w_j \mid \boldsymbol{\theta}). \tag{3}$$

---

[1] We denote random variables with uppercase letters and their instances with lowercase letters.

Using the chain rule,

$$P(A = a, W = w \mid \boldsymbol{\theta})$$
$$= P(A = a \mid \boldsymbol{\theta}) P(W = w \mid A = a, \boldsymbol{\theta})$$
$$= P(A = a \mid \boldsymbol{\theta}) \, \mathrm{I}(\mathrm{w}(a, \boldsymbol{\theta}) = w), \tag{4}$$

where $\mathrm{w}(a, \boldsymbol{\theta})$ indicates the word form produced by the analysis a, and $\mathrm{I}(X) = 1$ if X is true and zero otherwise. Thus, the choice for $P(A = a \mid \boldsymbol{\theta})$ and $\mathrm{w}(a, \boldsymbol{\theta})$ defines the model class.

If we assume that the training data has $|\boldsymbol{D}_W|$ word types w_j with their respective counts c_j, the logarithm of the corpus likelihood is

$$\sum_{j=1}^{|\boldsymbol{D}_W|} c_j \ln \sum_a P(A = a, W = w_j \mid \boldsymbol{\theta}). \tag{5}$$

Using types or tokens for training the model can be seen as modifying the counts c_j with a function $f()$, where $f(c_j) = 1$ corresponds to training on types and $f(c_j) = c_j$ on tokens. Generally, this results in the *weighted log-likelihood*

$$\sum_{j=1}^{|\boldsymbol{D}_W|} f(c_j) \ln \sum_a P(A = a, W = w_j \mid \boldsymbol{\theta}), \tag{6}$$

where $f()$ maps the counts into non-negative values. In other words, if we assume that each instance of a word form is generated independently, the modified frequency $f(c_j)$ of that form becomes a proportional weight in the likelihood function. Thus, when training on tokens, the model aims to give higher probabilities to frequent word types compared to rare word types.

2.2 Morfessor Baseline

Morfessor Baseline (Creutz and Lagus, 2002; Creutz and Lagus, 2005; Creutz and Lagus, 2007) is a method for morphological segmentation: The analysis of a word is a list of its non-overlapping segments, morphs. The method is inspired by the Minimum Description Length (MDL) principle by Rissanen (1978) and tries to encode the words in the training data with a lexicon of morphs. It applies the two-part coding variant of MDL, which is equivalent to MAP estimation using a particular type of prior. The MDL derived priors prevent overfitting by assigning a low prior probability to models with a large number of parameters.

Following the notation by Kohonen et al. (2010), the model parameters $\boldsymbol{\theta}$ are:

- Morph type count, or the size of the morph lexicon, $\mu \in \mathbb{Z}_+$

- Morph token count, or the number of morphs tokens in the observed data, $\nu \in \mathbb{Z}_+$

- Morph strings $\sigma_1, \ldots, \sigma_\mu, \sigma_i \in \Sigma^*$

- Morph counts $(\tau_1, \ldots, \tau_\mu), \tau_i \in \mathbb{Z}_+$, $\sum_i \tau_i = \nu$.

With non-informative priors, μ and ν can be neglected when optimizing. The morph string prior is based on the morph length distribution $P(L)$ and distribution $P(C)$ of characters over a character set Σ using the assumption that the characters are independent. For morph counts, the implicit non-informative prior $P(\tau_1, \ldots, \tau_\mu) = 1/\binom{\nu-1}{\mu-1}$ can be applied when μ and ν are known.

Each morph m_i in the lexicon has a probability of occurring in a word, $P(M = m_i \mid \boldsymbol{\theta})$, estimated from the count τ_i. A word is a sequence of morphs and the morph probabilities are assumed to be independent, so $\mathrm{w}(a, \boldsymbol{\theta}) = m_1 m_2 \ldots m_{|a|}$ and the probability of the analysis a is

$$P(A = a \mid \boldsymbol{\theta}) = \prod_{i=1}^{|a|} P(M = m_i \mid \boldsymbol{\theta}), \tag{7}$$

where m_i:s are the morphs in the analysis a.

The training algorithms of Morfessor apply the likelihood function only conditioned on the analyses of the observed words $\boldsymbol{A}$, $P(\boldsymbol{D}_W \mid \boldsymbol{A}, \boldsymbol{\theta})$. As before, an instance of $\boldsymbol{A}$ for the j:th word is a sequence of morphs: $a_j = (m_{j1}, \ldots, m_{j|a_j|})$. Furthermore, each word is assumed to have only a single analysis. For a known a, the weighted log-likelihood (Eq. 6) is thus

$$\ln P(\boldsymbol{D}_W \mid \boldsymbol{A} = a, \boldsymbol{\theta})$$
$$= \sum_{j=1}^{|\boldsymbol{D}_W|} f(c_j) \sum_{i=1}^{|a_j|} \ln P(M = m_{ji} \mid \boldsymbol{\theta}), \tag{8}$$

where m_{ij} is the i:th morph in word w_j. The number of morphs in the analysis, $|a_j|$, has a large effect on the probability of the word. Therefore the model prefers using a small number of morphs for words with a large $f(c_j)$.

The training algorithm of Morfessor Baseline minimizes the cost function $L(\boldsymbol{\theta}, a, \boldsymbol{D}_W) = -\ln P(\boldsymbol{\theta}) - \ln P(\boldsymbol{D}_W \mid a, \boldsymbol{\theta})$ by testing local changes to a. The training algorithm is described, e.g., by Creutz and Lagus (2005). In the semi-supervised weighting scheme by Kohonen et al. (2010), the log-likelihood is weighted by a positive constant α, which is optimized for the chosen evaluation measure using a development set. After training, a Viterbi-like algorithm can be applied to find the optimal analysis for each word given the model parameters; a description of the procedure is provided, e.g., by Virpioja et al. (2010).

3   Experiments

The goal of our experiments is to find an optimal function $f()$ for the weighted log-likelihood in Eq. 6. We consider the following set of functions for the counts c_j:

$$f(x) = \begin{cases} 0 & \text{if } x < T \\ \alpha g(x) & \text{otherwise} \end{cases} \quad (9)$$

If $\alpha = 1$ and $g(x) = 1$ we train on word types (lexicon); if $\alpha = 1$ and $g(x) = x$, we train on tokens (corpus). In addition, we test a logarithmic function $g(x) = \ln(1 + x)$. The frequency threshold T can be used for pruning rare words from the training data. The global weight α modifies the balance between the likelihood and the model prior as in Kohonen et al. (2010). Both T, α and the function type $g(x)$ can be optimized for a given data set and a target measure. To ensure that we do not overlearn the data set for which we optimize the function parameters, we use a separate test set for the final evaluations.

We use Morfessor Baseline in the experiments, as it is fast enough for training a large number of models even with large training corpora. Our implementation was based on the Morfessor 1.0 software (Creutz and Lagus, 2005). The format of the input data is a list of words and their counts, so the function $f()$ is, in principle, trivial to apply as preprocessing. However, because the Morfessor prior assumes integer counts, the parameter α was implemented as a global weight for the likelihood. Otherwise, we modified the training data according to the respective function before training. The result of the logarithmic function was rounded to the nearest integer. We used the standard training algorithm and implicit morph length and frequency priors. For words not present in the training data, we applied the Viterbi algorithm to find the best segmentation, allowing new morphs with the approximate cost of adding them into the morph lexicon.

3.1   Data and evaluation

We used the English and Finnish data sets from Competition 1 of Morpho Challenge 2009 (Kurimo et al., 2010b). These languages were chosen because of their different morphological characteristics. Both sets were extracted from a three million sentence corpora. For English, there were $62,185,728$ word tokens and $384,903$ word types. For Finnish, there were $36,207,308$ tokens and $2,206,719$ types. The complexity of Finnish morphology is indicated by almost ten times larger number of word types than for English, while the numbers of word tokens are much closer.

We applied also the evaluation method of the Morpho Challenge competition.[2] The results of the morphological segmentation were compared to a linguistic gold standard analysis for a set of word types. Precision measures whether the word types that share morphemes in the proposed analysis have common morphemes also in the gold standard. Recall is calculated analogously by swapping the roles proposed and gold standard analyses. The final score is the F-measure, the harmonic mean of precision and recall.

Finnish gold standard was based on the morphological analyzer FINTWOL from Lingsoft, Inc., that applies the two-level model by Koskenniemi (1983). English gold standard was from the CELEX database. We applied the same final test sets as in Morpho Challenge, based on $10,000$ English word forms and $200,000$ Finnish word forms. For tuning the parameters of the weight function, we sampled a development set that did not contain any of the words in the final test set. The development set included $2,000$ word forms for English and $8,000$ word forms for Finnish.

3.2   Results

We trained Morfessor Baseline with the word frequencies set according to the three different function types. For each type, we optimized the cutoff parameter T and the weight parameter α by choosing values that gave the optimal F-measure on the development set. When $\alpha = 1.0$ and $T = 1$, the results correspond to those of the standard Morfessor Baseline. First, we varied only one parameter while the other one was fixed at one. Figure 1 shows the results for English and Figure 2

---

[2] Both the training data and evaluation scripts are available from the Morpho Challenge 2009 web page: `http://www.cis.hut.fi/morphochallenge2009/`

for Finnish using precision-recall curves. The best results are in the top-right corner. In solid lines, $\alpha = 1$ and T varied; in dashed lines, $T = 1$ and α varied. When precision is high and recall is low, the algorithm undersegments. With the constant function, either reducing α or increasing T improved recall at the expense of precision. In other words, pruning improves the results mostly by preventing undersegmentation, not by removing noise. With logarithmic or linear counts, increasing the frequency threshold did not improve recall, but there was no such problem with decreasing α. Especially for English, the linear counts did not provide as good results as the others.

Next, we optimized the F-measure for each function type by varying both T and α. Every parameter combination was not computed, but we concentrated on the areas where the locally optimal results were found. The results for English are presented in Tables 1–3 and the results for Finnish in Tables 4–6. If frequency information is useful for the model, we should see an improvement in results for the linear and logarithmic function over the constant one when the weight α and the threshold T are optimal. While the linear function performed worse than the others even with the optimal weighting, the logarithmic function provided small improvements over the constant function for both languages.

The optimal α was the largest for the constant function, smaller (English) or the same (Finnish) for the logarithmic function, and the smallest for the linear function. Smaller α means that the algorithm would undersegment more without the weight. The weights for Finnish were smaller than for English, which is explained by a larger number of word types in the training set. A possible reason for the same $\alpha = 0.01$ for Finnish when using constant and logarithmic functions is that the most of the likelihood cost is anyway due to the word forms observed only once, and the logarithmic function does not affect that.

Regarding the cutoff parameter T for English, the optimal frequency threshold was around 10–20 for constant and logarithmic functions, but only one for the linear function. A possible explanation is that rare words do not contain new morphological information, as they typically are uncommon nouns with no or only a single suffix. With the linear function, they get a very low weight in any case and cause no problems, but with the other func-

tions, they are best to be excluded. For the Finnish data, the optimal frequency threshold was one for all three function types, so also the word forms occurring only once were useful for the algorithm. In an agglutinative language, such as Finnish, many valid inflected forms are very rare and therefore pruning does not remove only noise. While our results imply that it is better to use a smaller α than to prune, pruning infrequent words may still be useful in reducing computation time without sacrificing much accuracy.

Table 7 shows the results on the final test set. Again, using the word frequencies without optimized α and T clearly increase the problem of undersegmentation. In optimized cases, the results are more even. Note that unbalanced precision and recall imply that the tuning of the parameters did not completely succeed. For English, logarithmic counts gave higher F-measure also for the test set, but the difference to constant was not statistically significant according to the Wilcoxon signed-rank test. Linear counts gave clearly the worst results both for precision and recall. For Finnish, logarithmic counts did not give the improvement that the development set results promised: constant was slightly but significantly better. However, the slight undersegmentation indicates that it could be improved by fine tuning α. With linear counts, the F-measure was close, but still significantly lower.

Function	Opt	Pre	Rec	F-m
		English		
constant	no	76.13	48.97	**59.60**
logarithmic	no	87.76	31.77	46.65
linear	no	84.93	12.00	21.03
constant	yes	62.04	62.27	62.16
logarithmic	yes	57.85	67.62	**62.35**
linear	yes	53.96	56.42	55.16
		Finnish		
constant	no	89.50	15.70	**26.72**
logarithmic	no	91.24	11.95	21.13
linear	no	91.82	6.75	12.57
constant	yes	53.77	45.16	**49.09**
logarithmic	yes	57.87	42.06	48.72
linear	yes	48.86	47.37	48.10

Table 7: Precision (pre), recall (rec) and F-measure (F-m) on the final test set with the different function types for word frequencies. In optimized cases (opt), T and α are selected according to the best F-measure for the development set.

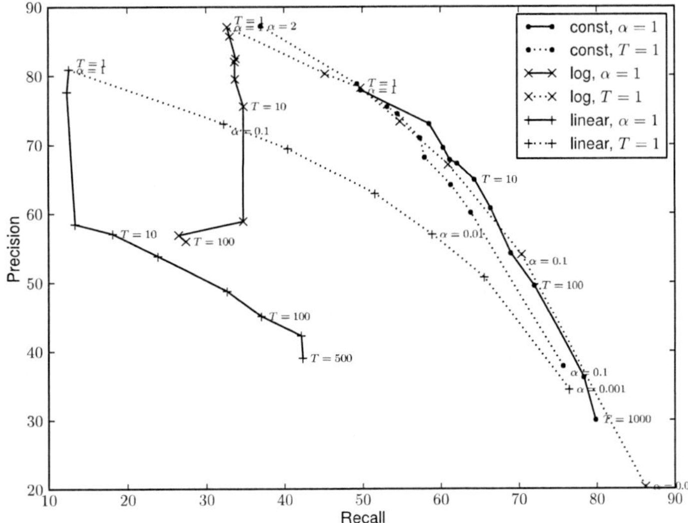

Figure 1: Precision-recall curves for English with constant (const), logarithmic (log), and linear frequency function types and varying function parameters α or T.

$T \setminus \alpha$	2	1.5	1.2	1.1	1	0.9	0.8	0.7	0.6
1	51.88	-	-	60.64	60.73	62.42	62.95	**63.46**	62.65
2	-	-	-	64.14	**64.97**	64.30	-	-	-
3	-	-	-	64.27	**64.60**	63.81	-	-	-
4	-	-	-	64.26	**64.30**	64.30	-	-	-
5	-	-	-	64.53	**64.55**	63.85	-	-	-
10	-	63.88	64.68	<u>**65.30**</u>	64.58	-	-	-	-
20	62.58	64.53	**65.29**	64.38	63.42	-	-	-	-
50	61.65	**63.13**	62.68	62.31	60.70	-	-	-	-

Table 1: Optimization results for English with $g(x) = 1$. Local optimum for each row (T) is written in boldface. The overall best results is underlined.

$T \setminus \alpha$	1	0.5	0.4	0.3	0.2	0.1
1	47.50	57.85	60.81	62.76	**63.88**	61.10
2	47.66	58.47	-	63.56	**63.80**	60.79
3	47.91	60.79	-	63.66	**64.12**	59.66
4	47.68	60.81	-	63.18	**64.53**	59.52
5	47.32	-	-	63.44	**64.47**	59.10
10	47.58	-	62.65	**64.87**	64.75	57.61
20	43.64	-	-	64.70	<u>**65.57**</u>	56.86
50	36.05	-	-	62.40	**63.93**	54.03

Table 2: Optimization results for English with $g(x) = \ln(1 + x)$.

$T \setminus \alpha$	1	0.1	0.05	0.02	0.01	0.005	0.001
1	21.75	44.73	51.10	56.69	<u>**57.92**</u>	57.19	47.45
2	21.24	-	-	56.31	**57.75**	57.07	-
5	21.67	-	-	55.98	**57.82**	57.03	-
10	27.48	-	-	56.11	**57.69**	56.40	-
20	33.01	-	-	55.67	57.50	-	-
50	39.09	-	-	-	57.10	-	-
100	40.64	-	-	-	-	-	-
200	42.19	-	-	-	-	-	-
500	40.60	-	-	-	-	-	-

Table 3: Optimization results for English with $g(x) = x$.

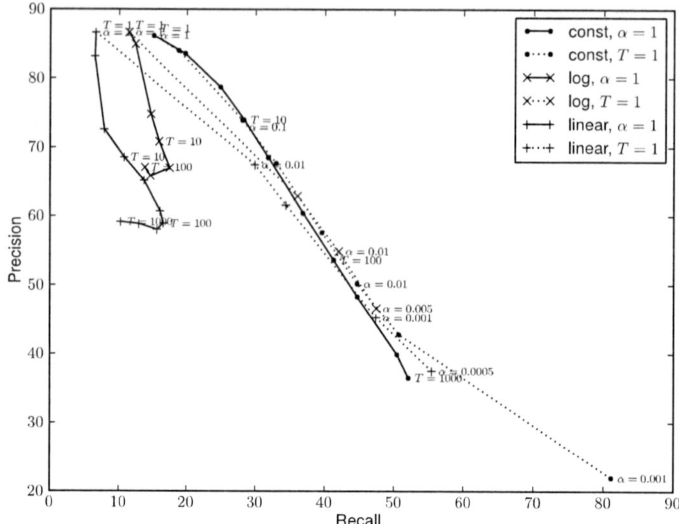

Figure 2: Precision-recall curves for Finnish with constant (const), logarithmic (log), and linear frequency function types and varying function parameters α or T.

$T \setminus \alpha$	1.2	1.1	1.0	0.5	0.2	0.1	0.05	0.02	0.01	0.005
1	-	-	25.83	30.74	-	40.64	44.35	46.91	**__47.27__**	46.40
2	-	-	31.96	36.86	-	45.07	**46.96**	46.80	45.35	-
5	-	-	37.75	41.89	46.15	**47.23**	46.83	-	39.10	-
10	-	-	40.92	44.37	**46.93**	46.61	-	-	33.85	-
20	-	-	43.49	46.15	**47.04**	45.88	-	-	-	-
50	-	-	45.75	**46.82**	45.70	42.17	-	-	-	-
100	-	46.29	**46.65**	46.50	-	-	-	-	-	-
200	46.19	**46.45**	46.43	-	-	-	-	-	-	-
500	44.69	**44.82**	44.54	-	-	-	-	-	-	-
1000	42.63	**43.17**	42.92	-	-	-	-	-	-	-

Table 4: Optimization results for Finnish with $g(x) = 1$. Local optimum for each row (T) is written in boldface. The overall best results is underlined.

$T \setminus \alpha$	1.0	0.5	0.2	0.05	0.02	0.01	0.005
1	20.20	-	-	-	45.81	**__47.60__**	47.02
2	21.62	29.81	36.74	44.43	46.96	**47.26**	46.28
5	24.66	-	-	46.03	**46.97**	46.28	-
10	26.11	-	-	-	46.70	-	-
20	27.80	-	-	-	-	-	-
50	24.03	-	-	-	-	-	-

Table 5: Optimization results for Finnish with $g(x) = \ln(1 + x)$.

$T \setminus \alpha$	1.0	0.1	0.01	0.005	0.001	0.0005
1	12.21	-	41.44	44.12	**__46.30__**	44.73
2	11.94	28.80	41.78	43.97	**45.94**	44.36
5	14.10	-	41.91	44.13	45.50	-
10	18.59	-	42.06	44.01	-	-
20	22.73	-	42.08	-	-	-
50	25.55	-	-	-	-	-
100	25.97	-	-	-	-	-
200	24.73	-	-	-	-	-
500	21.21	-	-	-	-	-

Table 6: Optimization results for Finnish with $g(x) = x$.

4   Conclusions

We showed that for probabilistic models, where word forms are generated independently, the word frequency acts as a relative weight in the likelihood function, changing how important the probabilities of the forms are to the likelihood. In the case of Morfessor Baseline, words with a large relative weight are segmented less, and vice versa. In the experiments, we trained Morfessor Baseline using three types of functions—constant, logarithmic, and linear—for the corpus frequencies of the words. Constant corresponds to learning on word types and linear on tokens, whereas logarithmic is between them. To overcome the model's tendency to undersegment, we used a likelihood weight optimized to give the best F-measure on a development set. While earlier results implied that learning on word types is the best option for this model when evaluated against linguistic gold standards, we showed that results of the same quality can also be obtained with logarithmic counts. In contrast, using corpus frequencies in a linear manner does not work as well. We also optimized a pruning threshold for the infrequent words. Pruning is simple and fast, but appears to work well only with the constant function type.

Acknowledgments

This work was funded by Graduate School of Language Technology in Finland and Academy of Finland.

References

Maria Alegre and Peter Gordon. 1999. Frequency effects and the representational status of regular inections. *Journal of Memory and Language*, 40:41–61.

Mathias Creutz and Krista Lagus. 2002. Unsupervised discovery of morphemes. In *Proceedings of the ACL-02 Workshop on Morphological and Phonological Learning*, pages 21–30, Philadelphia, Pennsylvania, USA.

Mathias Creutz and Krista Lagus. 2004. Induction of a simple morphology for highly-inflecting languages. In *Proceedings of the 7th Meeting of the ACL Special Interest Group in Computational Phonology*, pages 43–51, Barcelona, July.

Mathias Creutz and Krista Lagus. 2005. Unsupervised morpheme segmentation and morphology induction from text corpora using Morfessor 1.0. Technical Report A81, Publications in Computer and Information Science, Helsinki University of Technology.

Mathias Creutz and Krista Lagus. 2007. Unsupervised models for morpheme segmentation and morphology learning. *ACM Transactions on Speech and Language Processing*, 4(1), January.

Sharon Goldwater, Tom Griffiths, and Mark Johnson. 2006. Interpolating between types and tokens by estimating power-law generators. In *Advances in Neural Information Processing Systems 18*, pages 459–466. MIT Press, Cambridge, MA.

Oskar Kohonen, Sami Virpioja, and Krista Lagus. 2010. Semi-supervised learning of concatenative morphology. In *Proceedings of the 11th Meeting of the ACL Special Interest Group on Computational Morphology and Phonology*, pages 78–86, Uppsala, Sweden, July.

Kimmo Koskenniemi. 1983. *Two-level morphology: A general computational model for word-form recognition and production*. Ph.D. thesis, University of Helsinki.

Mikko Kurimo, Sami Virpioja, and Ville T. Turunen (Eds.). 2010a. Proceedings of the Morpho Challenge 2010 workshop. Technical Report TKK-ICS-R37, Aalto University School of Science and Technology, Department of Information and Computer Science, Espoo, Finland, September.

Mikko Kurimo, Sami Virpioja, Ville T. Turunen, Graeme W. Blackwood, and William Byrne. 2010b. Overview and results of Morpho Challenge 2009. In *Multilingual Information Access Evaluation I. Text Retrieval Experiments*, volume 6241 of *Lecture Notes in Computer Science*, pages 578–597. Springer.

Hoifung Poon, Colin Cherry, and Kristina Toutanova. 2009. Unsupervised morphological segmentation with log-linear models. In *Proceedings of NAACL HLT 2009*, pages 209–217.

Jorma Rissanen. 1978. Modeling by shortest data description. *Automatica*, 14:465–471.

Benjamin Snyder and Regina Barzilay. 2008. Unsupervised multilingual learning for morphological segmentation. In *Proceedings of ACL-08: HLT*, pages 737–745, Columbus, Ohio, June.

Marcus Taft. 2004. Morphological decomposition and the reverse base frequency effect. *The Quarterly Journal of Experimental Psychology*, A 57:745–765.

Sami Virpioja, Oskar Kohonen, and Krista Lagus. 2010. Unsupervised morpheme analysis with Allomorfessor. In *Multilingual Information Access Evaluation I. Text Retrieval Experiments*, volume 6241 of *Lecture Notes in Computer Science*, pages 609–616. Springer.

George Kingsley Zipf. 1932. *Selective Studies and the Principle of Relative Frequency in Language*. Harvard University Press, Cambridge, MA.

ISSN 1736-6305 Vol. 11
http://hdl.handle.net/10062/16955

Disambiguation of English Contractions
for Machine Translation of TV Subtitles

Martin Volk and Rico Sennrich
University of Zurich, Institute of Computational Linguistics
Zurich, Switzerland
{volk|sennrich}@cl.uzh.ch

Abstract

This paper presents a disambiguation method for English apostrophe+s contractions. They occur frequently in subtitles and pose special difficulties for Machine Translation. We propose to disambiguate these contractions in a pre-processing step and show that this leads to improved translation quality.

1 Introduction

Ideally, film and TV subtitles are created for each language independently, but for efficiency reasons they are often translated from a source language to one or more target languages. To support the efficient translation we have teamed up with a Scandinavian subtitling company to build Machine Translation (MT) systems. The systems are in extensive practical use today. Because of the established language sequence in the company we have first built translation systems from Swedish to Danish and to Norwegian. After the successful deployment of these two systems, we have worked on other language pairs including English, German and Swedish.

When dealing with English as source language, we have noticed an interesting phenomenon. English subtitles contain a high percentage of contractions. In particular, contractions comprise the short forms of auxiliary and modal verbs: *are* and *were* → *'re*, *shall* and *will* → *'ll*, *had* and *would* → *'d*. By far the most prominent are the apostrophe+s contractions *is*, *was* and *has* → *'s*, which also include contractions of the pronoun *us* (as in *let's do it*) all of which are homographic with the possessive marker. The following table lists the most frequent apostrophe-letter sequences in our corpus of 1 million English subtitles. Note that the last two are dialectal contractions that lead to strange

"words" when tokenized at the apostrophe.[1]

172,571	cases of 's	*is,has,us*, possessive
117,869	cases of 't	*not* as in *don't, won't*
53,587	cases of 'm	*am* as in *I'm*
50,219	cases of 're	*are, were*
36,245	cases of 'll	*shall, will*
22,743	cases of 've	*have*
16,576	cases of 'd	*had, should, would*
1,335	cases of 'am	*ma'am*
749	cases of 'all	*y'all*

In this paper we will only be concerned with apostrophe+s contractions because they are the most frequent and the most ambiguous contractions.

Contracted forms are popular in subtitles for several reasons. They are closer to the spoken language of the video, and they are shorter, thus saving precious character space on the screen. Unfortunately, these contractions introduce additional ambiguities into the subtitles which make automatic translation more difficult. We have noticed cases like the following where the English possessive marker *'s* is mistaken by the MT system for the copula verb *is* and therefore mistranslated into Swedish and German.

(1) Oh my gosh, Nicole**'s** dad is the coolest.
SV: Herregud, Nicole **är** pappa är coolast.
DE: Mein Gott, Nicole **ist** Papa ist der coolste.

We have therefore developed a method to disambiguate English apostrophe+s contractions before training the Statistical MT (SMT) system. This paper describes the method and presents the disambiguation results. But first we set the scene

---

[1]Note that these numbers were computed before lowercasing. The corpus contains also capitalized subtitles like CLEOPATRA'S BEAUTY SALON which we have not counted here.

"

by describing some related disambiguation work and then our MT systems for subtitles.

2 Related Work on Word Sense Disambiguation for MT

Our approach can be seen as a special type of word sense disambiguation (WSD) for MT. Many researchers have worked on this topic before with varying success. For example, (Carpuat and Wu, 2005) reported that they could not find "significant better translations" when using Chinese WSD in Chinese-English MT. But two years later the same authors (Carpuat and Wu, 2007) come to the conclusion that the incorporation of WSD within a typical SMT system "consistently improves translation quality" for Chinese-English. They claim that a disambiguation of phrasal units rather than words leads to these improvements. They report on gains of up to 0.5 BLEU points. These findings are in line with (Chan et al., 2007) who have also shown WSD to be beneficial for Chinese to English translation.

Basic research on WSD for MT is presented in various papers. For example (Specia et al., 2005) work with automatically derived rules for WSD of seven highly ambiguous verbs in English-Portuguese MT. (Apidianaki, 2009) questions the sense inventory which is frequently used in WSD and argues for a semantic analysis based on parallel corpora Greek-English in order to better tailor the sense inventory to MT. (Vickrey et al., 2005) investigate WSD for word translation French-English.

Our work is also similar to other preprocessing suggestions such as (El-Kahlout and Yvon, 2010). They work on the opposite translation direction and prepare the German input text before training and translation to English. When testing various normalization steps, they obtained the biggest improvements on compound splitting.

3 Our MT Systems for TV Subtitles

MT systems for subtitles date back to the work by Popowich et al. (2000) on English to Spanish translation. We have built Machine Translation systems for translating film and TV subtitles from English to Swedish and from Swedish to Danish and Norwegian in a commercial setting. Some of this work has been described earlier by Volk and Harder (2007) and Volk (2008).

Most films are originally in English and receive English or Swedish subtitles in a first manual step. The subtitler uses the English video and audio (sometimes accompanied by an English transcript).

The target language translator subsequently has access to the original English video and audio but also to the source language subtitles and the time codes. In most cases the translator will reuse the time codes and insert the target language subtitle. She can, on occasion, change the time codes if she deems them inappropriate for the target language text.

We have built SMT systems that produce Danish, Norwegian and Swedish draft translations to speed up the translators' work. This project benefited from three favorable conditions:

1. Subtitles are short textual units with little internal complexity.

2. We are dealing with closely related languages. The grammars are similar, however orthography differs considerably, word order differs somewhat and, of course, one language avoids some constructions that the other language prefers.

3. We have access to large numbers of subtitles in multiple languages. The cross-language correspondences can easily be established via the time codes which leads to an alignment on the subtitle level.

There are other aspects of the task that are less favorable. Subtitles are not transcriptions, but written representations of spoken language. As a result the linguistic structure of subtitles is closer to written language than the original (English) speech, and the original spoken content usually has to be condensed by the subtitler.

The task of translating subtitles also differs from most other machine translation applications in that we are dealing with creative language, and thus we are closer to literary translation than technical translation. This is obvious in cases where rhyming song-lyrics or puns are involved, but also when the subtitler applies his linguistic intuitions to achieve a natural and appropriate wording which blends into the video without standing out. Finally, the language of subtitling covers a broad variety of domains from educational programs on any conceivable topic to exaggerated modern youth language.

We have built SMT systems in order to shorten the development time (compared to a rule-based system) and in order to best exploit the existing translations. We have trained our SMT systems by using standard open source SMT software.

Our corpus consists of TV subtitles from soap operas (like daily hospital series), detective series, animation series, comedies, documentaries, feature films etc. For example, for the Swedish-Danish system we had more than 14,000 subtitle files (= single TV programmes) in each language, corresponding to more than 5 million subtitles (equaling more than 50 million words).

When we compiled our corpus we included only subtitles with matching time codes. If the source and target language time codes differed more than a threshold of 15 TV-frames (0.6 seconds) in either start or end-time, we suspected that they were not good translation equivalents and excluded them from the subtitle corpus. In this way we were able to avoid complicated alignment techniques. Most of the resulting subtitle pairs are high-quality translations thanks to the controlled workflow in the commercial setting. Note that we are not aligning sentences. We work with aligned subtitles which can consist of one or two or three short sentences. Sometimes a subtitle holds only the first part of a sentence which is finished in the following subtitle.

We split our subtitle corpus into training and test set in the usual way. Before the training step we tokenized the subtitles (e.g. separating punctuation symbols from words), converting all upper-case words into lower case, and normalizing punctuation symbols, numbers and hyphenated words.

This resulted, for instance, in BLEU scores of over 50 for the Swedish-Danish system. To better appreciate the translation quality we also calculated exact matches and character-based Levenshtein-5 matches, i.e. subtitles that differ from the human translation by 5 keystrokes or less. We obtained 9% exact matches and 30% Levenstein-5 matches when comparing against a prior human translation. We also ran a number of experiments with post-editors. They got our system output, and we asked them to correct this translation draft into a production-quality subtitle file. When we averaged over 6 post-editors we computed 22% exact matches and 43%

Levenstein-5 matches.

In (Volk et al., 2010) we describe the results in more detail. We also present the lessons learned in the process of building the MT systems and integrating them into the workflow of the subtitle company. The systems for Swedish-Danish and Swedish-Norwegian have been in productive use since early 2008 and translate large volumes of subtitles every day. Subsequently we have built a system for English-Swedish translation which went into production in 2010. It was during this latter development that we ran into the problem of contraction ambiguities.

4 The Contraction Ambiguity

In our English-Swedish MT system we observed errors like in example 1 (in the introductory section) which pointed to the problem of translating the various alternatives of apostrophe+s contractions. We started our investigation by manually classifying the occurrences of s-contractions in our subtitle corpus. We identified the following seven variants. An apostrophe+s can be

1. the possessive marker. This case is characterized by the *'s* following a name or a noun and occurring in the beginning of a noun phrase in the article position (i.e. typically in front of a noun or an adjective plus noun; it hardly ever occurs in front of a name). There are rare cases when *'s* follows an indefinite pronoun.

(2) I'm gonna buy Buzzy's store.
     You wouldn't say that if we were going after the world's hottest guy.
     You even finish each other's sentences.

2. an abbreviation for **the copula 'is'** (or 'was'). This is the most frequent case. It mostly occurs in front of a noun phrase or an adjective (phrase). The distinction between present tense 'is' and the past tense 'was' is only possible in rare sentences with multiple verbs.

(3) Hey, what's your dream, sweetie?
     When's the last time you left this place?
     -Anything under 60's really slutty.

3. an abbreviation for **the auxiliary 'is'** (or 'was'). This case can be identified by a following verb in present participle form, with perhaps a 'not' or an adverb intervening.

(4) He's trying to find a job.

Michael's thinking about changing his hair.
He's not kidding.
The CIA's still trying to download Dasha...

4. an abbreviation for **the auxiliary 'has'**. This variant occurs in front of a past participle verb form, with perhaps a 'not' or an adverb intervening.

(5)   The guy's been really depressed.
For some reason it's lost its magic.

5. an abbreviation for **the auxiliary 'does'** This case is characterized by a question and a verb that is neither a present participle nor a past participle. It is so rare that we do not deal with it.

(6)   -What the hell's it look like?

6. an abbreviation for **the pronoun 'us'**. This occurs only after 'let' and can thus trivially be identified.

(7)   Let's not rush into this, okay?

7. the plural marker for abbreviations, acronyms and numbers.

(8)   I take AP classes and I get all straight A's.
Let me hear those ABC's I taught you.
-With two E's or E-A? -Two E's.
I tolerate them no better on the bench in my 40's.
You know how many number 12's there are on Cold Street?

This plural marker case is difficult to identify. There are many instances of upper-case word plus apostrophe+s or number plus apostrophe+s that do not fall in this category.

(9)   Who do you know in the DA's office?
CHP's the last place I belong.
Flight 52's position report is overdue.
Air Traffic Control, flight 52's coming in.

We found that a reliable distinction for acronyms and abbreviations plus apostrophe+s is only possible if they follow a number (*two, three, ...*) or plural indicator like *all* or *many*, or if it occurs at the end of the sentence. For numbers plus apostrophe+s the best indicator is also sentence-final position.

Given these heuristics we identified 131 apostrophe+s occurrences as plural markers after

acronyms (upper-case words) and another 546 cases of upper-case word plus apostrophe+s which classify as one of the above alternatives 1-4. For numbers plus apostrophe+s we identified only 15 plural marker cases and 47 others. Since the number of occurrences of both variants is relatively small, we do not handle these cases in our disambiguation.

The most frequent and most difficult ambiguities are between the possessive marker and the copula 'is/was'. The distribution in both cases is similar, and a parse of the sentence would be needed for a precise distinction. All other cases can be disambiguated based on local context and Part-of-Speech (PoS) tags.

5   Disambiguation Method

Since we need PoS information for the disambiguation, we tested different English PoS taggers. It turned out that they do not reliably distinguish the kinds of contractions we are after. For example, the TreeTagger[2] distinguishes between possessive marker (POS), 3rd person singular of the verbs *to be* (VBZ) and *to have* (VHZ),[3] but it never tags apostrophe+s as a pronoun or a plural marker (there isn't even a tag for this). Unfortunately, the TreeTagger does not reliably assign the three tags. For example, it tends to tag apostrophe+s as VBZ (a form of *be*) instead of VHZ when there is an adverb between the contraction and the past participle (see example 10). This is explicable because of the tagger's limited context window. But surprisingly it sometimes also tags the apostrophe+s immediately after the personal pronouns *it* and *he* as possessive markers which can never be correct.

(10)   That 's/VBZ always/RB been/VBN a dream of mine.
It/PP 's/POS Sunday morning, ...

Therefore we have developed the following approach:

1. Run a PoS tagger over the subtitles. We used the TreeTagger with the standard English language model.

2. Run a correction script over the tagged subtitles that fixes the apostrophe+s contractions

---

[2] www.ims.uni-stuttgart.de/projekte/corplex/TreeTagger/
[3] The TreeTagger distinction between VBZ and VHZ is a refinement of the Penn Treebank tag set, which has only one tag for the 3rd person singular form of all verbs.

according to the rules which we sketched in the previous section in the listing of the seven interpretations.

For example, the correction script will turn the apostrophe+s into *is* when it is followed by a word that has been tagged as present participle (*-ing* form). Alternatively it will convert the apostrophe+s into *has* when it is followed by a word that has been tagged as past participle (*-ed* form). Every apostrophe+s that follows *let* is turned into the pronoun *us*. Example 11 shows a subtitle with a copula and a possessive marker before and after disambiguation.

(11) It's always about someone's mother.
It **is** always about someone**'s** mother.

6 Evaluation of the Disambiguation Module

We have tested our disambiguation method on both English-Swedish and English-German SMT systems with similar results. Here we report on our experiments for English-German. For these experiments we obtained 1 million subtitle pairs English-German from our subtitle partner company. The subtitles are of high quality and perfectly aligned on the basis of the time codes. As a first step we tokenized the subtitles by separating punctuation symbols from the words, and by removing the tags for italics and line breaks. This means we do not split or join the subtitles into sentences, instead we regard each subtitle as a translation unit. All subtitles were lower-cased. After tokenization we have 10.3 million tokens in the English subtitles and 8.2 million tokens on the German side.

We checked how many of the English tokens are apostrophe+s tokens. We found a total of 172,571 occurrences of such tokens in 158,328 subtitles. This means around 15% of all subtitles have at least one occurrence of apostrophe+s. These occurrences account for 1.8% of all tokens. After PoS tagging the distribution is as follows. Even if we account for a certain error rate in PoS tagging, it becomes clear that the vast majority of cases are not possessive markers but contractions of auxiliaries and the pronoun *us* (which happens to be tagged as VBZ most of the time).

28,529	tagged as possessive marker (POS)
138,754	tagged as 3rd singular of *be* (VBZ)
5,288	tagged as 3rd sing. of *have* (VHZ)
172,571	Total

In order to appreciate this distribution we compare it to the Penn Treebank. The differences are striking. The Wall Street Journal sections (0-24) of the Penn Treebank have a total of 1.2 million tokens out of which 11,538 are apostrophe+s tokens (0.9% compared to 1.8% in the subtitle corpus). But out of the 49,206 sentences in this treebank, 21% (10,134 sentences) contain such a token. The distribution of their functions is very different from our subtitle corpus. The vast majority (87%) are cases of possessive markers.[4]

10,025	marked as possessive marker (POS)
1,490	marked as 3rd sing. of *be* or *have*
11	marked as personal pronoun (PRP)
12	marked with miscellaneous tags
11,538	Total

From our subtitle corpus we extracted a test set and a development set, around 6500 subtitles each, from across the corpus. The rest (around 990,000 subtitles) was taken as the training set.

Using Moses, we built two SMT systems for English $\rightarrow$ German translation. The first system was trained on the original subtitles, and the second system was trained on the disambiguated English subtitles and the same German subtitles as before. The disambiguation step changed the English subtitles in the following way:

9493	cases of let's $\rightarrow$ let us
270	cases of pronoun + 's $\rightarrow$ has
3644	cases of pronoun + 's $\rightarrow$ is
1196	cases of other + 's $\rightarrow$ has
618	cases of other + 's $\rightarrow$ is

This means, a total of 15,221 PoS tags for apostrophe+s tokens (around 9% of all such tokens) were changed, so that we have the following distribution in our subtitle corpus after correction.

23,540	tagged as possessive marker (POS)
132,788	tagged as 3rd singular of *be* (VBZ)
6,750	tagged as 3rd sing. of *have* (VHZ)
9,493	tagged as personal pronoun (PP)
172,571	Total

In the disambiguation step all occurrences of apostrophe+s that are not tagged as possessive marker (POS) are turned into *is*, *has*, or *us*. Thus our disambiguation substitutes 149,031 oc-

---

[4]One might wonder whether there are no apostrophe+s occurrences functioning as plural markers in the Penn Treebank. In fact these have been marked with POS, too.

currences (86%) and reduces the apostrophe+s occurrences to the 23,540 possessive markers. Remember that we ignore the apostrophe+s plural markers because they are rare.

Automatic evaluation of both our systems (before and after disambiguation) against the test set of 6510 subtitles resulted in BLEU scores of 28.9. Obviously, BLEU has its limits when tracking small changes in translation. This finding is in line with observations by (Callison-Burch et al., 2006).

Therefore we performed a manual evaluation of the relevant subtitles. Out of the 6510 subtitles in the test set, 1024 subtitles contained apostrophe+s in the original English subtitle. Of these 1024 subtitles our disambiguation module changed 902. This means, in these 902 subtitles an apostrophe+s was turned into *is*, *has* or *us*. But only 224 of these 1024 subtitles have resulted in a different translation than before. We have examined these 224 subtitles in detail and checked whether the translation of the sentences after disambiguation is better than before.

In the following example tables, EN marks the original English subtitle, DE-REF indicates the human-created German reference translation, DE-MT is the output of our MT system before disambiguation. EN-DIS marks the disambiguated English subtitle and DE-DIS-MT the resulting system output.

We found clear cases of improvement as in example table 1. Interestingly, the improvement in this example does not show at the changed copula-apostrophe+s but at the possessive. This is probably due to the fact that the original English subtitles lead to a high translation probability of the apostrophe+s with German *ist* ($prob(ist|'s) = 0.605$), as this is by far the most frequent translation correspondence. This results in the erroneous translation of the apostrophe+s with the German copula *ist*. After disambiguation the probability of apostrophe+s (= possessive marker) with *ist* is much lower (0.319), thus paving the way for the correct German translation with the genitive form of the indefinite pronoun *jemand*.

There are other cases of improvement that are directly related to the disambiguation. Example table 2 shows an improvement for the translation of *'s been* after it has been turned into *has been*. The sentence is still not perfectly translated (mainly because the English word *block* needs to be translated differently in this context), but the

translation of the copula verb and the subsequent word order are clearly better.

There are other examples that show worse translations. In particular we find worse translations in connection with *let's* (as in example table 3). We suspect that *let's* is so idiomatic that a split will give too much significance to the pronoun *us* and "disturb" the translation probabilities.

It is also striking that sometimes the disambiguation leads to translations that are different but as good (or bad) as before. Obviously the disambiguation step leads to slight shifts in the translation probabilities that result in changed preferences for one translation over the other. Example 4 is such a case in point with a good idiomatic translation both before and after the disambiguation. Note that the latter translation will receive much higher BLEU scores because of its almost perfect overlap with the reference translation.

Table 5 contains the numerical results of the manual evaluation. Almost 26% of the examined subtitles show an improved translation in relation to apostrophe+s. This stands against about 6% that show a worse translation. So this is a net improvement for 20% of the examined subtitles (which account only for 22% of the subtitles with apostrophe+s in the test set).

Interestingly, we also find translation improvements that are seemingly unrelated to the apostrophe+s in the subtitle since they appear in a different part of the subtitle. We identified 16.5% improvements versus 12% degradations in this class. This adds to the positive overall effect of the disambiguation. The remaining 39% of the subtitles have resulted in translations that are different than before but are judged as being of equal quality (as in example table 4).

These numbers refer only to those 22% of the apostrophe+s-containing subtitles whose MT output had changed after the disambiguation. But the apostrophe+s disambiguation influences also the translation of subtitles without apostrophe+s because of differing word alignments. In order to see how the disambiguation step influences those subtitles, we also manually checked 224 subtitles with changed MT output in this class. There we found no statistically significant difference in translation quality before and after disambiguation.

EN:	it 's always about someone 's mother .
DE-REF:	es hat immer mit der mutter zu tun .
DE-MT:	es geht immer nur um jemand ist mutter .
EN-DIS:	it **is** always about someone 's mother .
DE-DIS-MT:	es geht immer nur um jemandes mutter .

Table 1: Example of improved MT for the possessive marker

EN:	this car 's been on my block for a week .
DE-REF:	seit einer woche steht ein auto in meiner straße.
DE-MT:	das auto ist auf mich block für eine woche .
EN-DIS:	this car **has** been on my block for a week .
DE-DIS-MT:	das auto war auf dem block für eine woche .

Table 2: Example of improved MT for *'s been → has been*

EN:	now , let 's step into the bar .
DE-REF:	treten sie ein .
DE-MT:	also , gehen wir in die bar .
EN-DIS:	now , let **us** step into the bar .
DE-DIS-MT:	lass uns in der bar .

Table 3: Example of worse MT for *let's → let us*

EN:	he 's out of his mind .
DE-REF:	er hat wohl den verstand verloren .
DE-MT:	er ist durchgeknallt .
EN-DIS:	he **is** out of his mind .
DE-DIS-MT:	er hat den verstand verloren .

Table 4: Example of equally good MT for an idiomatic expression

subtitles	percent	human judgement
58	25.9%	better translation related to apostrophe+s
14	6.3%	worse translation related to apostrophe+s
37	16.5%	better translation but not related to apostrophe+s
27	12.1%	worse translation but not related to apostrophe+s
88	39.3%	translation is different, but as good or as bad as before

Table 5: Results of the manual evaluation of 224 subtitles

7 Conclusion

We have shown that film and TV subtitles in general are well suited for MT. But they also have specific properties that make MT more difficult than for other genres. As an example of this, we have investigated apostrophe+s contractions in English that are frequent in subtitles and introduce additional ambiguities.

We have presented a method that disambiguates these contractions based on PoS tags assigned by a general-purpose PoS tagger. We found that this disambiguation has a positive impact on the translation quality of the respective subtitles (although this impact is not visible in the BLEU scores).

On the practical side we plan to investigate whether we can train a PoS tagger to reliably classify the apostrophe+s contractions directly so that we no longer need a separate disambiguation module. One option would be to train a special-purpose PoS tagger on the automatically corrected output of the general-purpose PoS tagger.

In a broader perspective our work reopens the question of whether other disambiguation steps in pre-processing (e.g. for other contraction types) will be similarly beneficial for MT.

Acknowledgments

We would like to thank Nicole Michel for help in assessing the MT output quality.

References

Marianna Apidianaki. 2009. Data-driven semantic analysis for multilingual WSD and lexical selection in translation. In *Proceedings of the 12th Conference of the European Chapter of the Association for Computational Linguistics (EACL)*, pages 77–85, Athens.

Christopher Callison-Burch, Miles Osborne, and Philipp Koehn. 2006. Re-evaluating the role of BLEU in machine translation research. In *Proceedings of the Thirteenth Conference of the European Chapter of the Association for Computational Linguistics*, Trento.

Marine Carpuat and Dekai Wu. 2005. Word sense disambiguation vs. statistical machine translation. In *Proceedings of the 43rd Annual Meeting of the ACL*, pages 387–394, Ann Arbor.

Marine Carpuat and Dekai Wu. 2007. Improving statistical machine translation using word sense disambiguation. In *Proceedings of the 2007 Joint Conference on Empirical Methods in Natural Language Processing and Computational Natural Language Learning*, pages 61–72, Prague.

Yee Seng Chan, Hwee Tou Ng, and David Chiang. 2007. Word sense disambiguation improves statistical machine translation. In *Proceedings of the 45th Annual Meeting of the Association for Computational Linguistics (ACL-07)*, pages 33–40, Prague.

Ilknur Durgar El-Kahlout and Francois Yvon. 2010. The pay-offs of preprocessing for German-English statistical machine translation. In *Proceedings of the 7th International Workshop on Spoken Language Translation*, Paris.

Fred Popowich, Paul McFetridge, Davide Turcato, and Janine Toole. 2000. Machine translation of closed captions. *Machine Translation*, 15:311–341.

Lucia Specia, Maria das Graças V. Nunes, and Mark Stevenson. 2005. Exploiting rules for word sense disambiguation in machine translation. *Procesamiento del Lenguaje Natural*, (35):171–178.

David Vickrey, Luke Biewald, Marc Teyssier, and Daphne Koller. 2005. Word-sense disambiguation for machine translation. In *Proceedings of Human Language Technology Conference and Conference on Empirical Methods in Natural Language Processing (HLT/EMNLP)*, pages 771–778, Vancouver.

Martin Volk and Søren Harder. 2007. Evaluating MT with translations or translators. What is the difference? In *Proceedings of Machine Translation Summit XI*, Copenhagen.

Martin Volk, Rico Sennrich, Christian Hardmeier, and Frida Tidström. 2010. Machine translation of TV subtitles for large scale production. In *Proceedings of the Second Joint EM+/CNGL Workshop on "Bringing MT to the User: Research on Integrating MT in the Translation Industry"*, pages 53–62, Denver.

Martin Volk. 2008. The automatic translation of film subtitles. A machine translation success story? In Joakim Nivre, Mats Dahllöf, and Beáta Megyesi, editors, *Resourceful Language Technology: Festschrift in Honor of Anna Sågvall Hein*, volume 7 of *Studia Linguistica Upsaliensia*, pages 202–214. Uppsala University, Humanistisk-samhällsvetenskapliga vetenskapsområdet, Faculty of Languages.

ISSN 1736-6305 Vol. 11
http://hdl.handle.net/10062/16955

Probabilistic Models for Alignment of Etymological Data

Hannes Wettig, Roman Yangarber
Department of Computer Science
University of Helsinki, Finland
`First.Last@cs.helsinki.fi`

Abstract

This paper introduces several models for aligning etymological data, or for finding the best alignment at the sound or symbol level, given a set of etymological data. This will provide us a means of measuring the quality of the etymological data sets in terms of their internal consistency. Since one of our main goals is to devise automatic methods for aligning the data that are as objective as possible, the models make no a priori assumptions—e.g., no preference for vowel-vowel or consonant-consonant alignments. We present a baseline model and successive improvements, using data from Uralic language family.

1 Introduction

We present work on induction of alignment rules for etymological data in a project that studies genetic relationships among the Uralic language family. Our interest is in methods that are as objective as possible, i.e., rely only on the data rather than on prior assumptions or "universal" principles about the data, possible rules and alignments. Another goal is to derive measures of quality of data sets in terms of their internal consistency—a data-set that is more consistent should receive a higher score. We seek methods that analyze the data automatically in an unsupervised fashion. The question is whether a complete description of the correspondences can be discovered automatically, directly from raw etymological data—sets of cognate words from languages within the language family. Another way of looking at this is: what alignment rules are "inherently encoded" in a data-set (the *corpus*) itself. Thus, at present, our aim is to analyze given etymological data-sets, rather than to construct one from scratch.

Several approaches to etymological alignment have emerged over the last decade, summarized in section 2. In prior work, it was observed that etymology induction may have potential applications, among them aiding machine translation systems for resource-poor languages. Our interest is somewhat more theoretical; we are at present less interested in applications than in building models that are principled and avoid building ad-hoc heuristics into the models from the outset.

We review related work in Section 2, present a statement of the etymology alignment problem in Section 3, our models in Section 3, results in Section 5, and the next steps in Section 6.

1.1 Computational Etymology

Etymology involves several problems, including: determination of genetic relations among groups of languages, from raw linguistic data; discovering *regular sound correspondences* across languages in a given language family; reconstruction of proto-forms for a hypothetical parent language, from which the word-forms found in the daughter languages derive.

Computational etymology is interesting from the point of view of computational linguistics and machine learning. Computational methods can provide valuable feedback to the etymological/linguistic community. The methods can be evaluated by whether they perform certain aspects of etymological analysis correctly, that is, whether automatic analysis—at least in some cases—is able to produce results that match the theories established by manual analysis.

Why is computational etymology useful—can results obtained by automatic analysis clarify or improve upon established theories?

First, even if computational methods yield no new insights from the linguistic point of view, and only validate previously established theories, that would still be a useful result. Because computational approaches differ in nature from traditional linguistic methods, a matching result would serve

"

as a non-trivial, independent confirmation of correctness of traditional methods.

Second, while some major language families have been studied extensively from the etymological perspective, many have not. Language families such as the Indo-European have received more attention than others and have been studied in greater detail, mainly because more relevant data has been collected and available to scholars for a longer time. For the less-studied language families, automatic analysis will allow linguists to bootstrap results quickly, to provide a foundation for further, more detailed investigation.

Third, the significant matter of uncertainty: Most etymological resources—dictionaries and handbooks—label certain relationships as "dubious," to a varying degree, usually due to violation of some expected regularity. Different (re)sources contain different decisions, which result in conflicts, because they are based on different theories. There is currently no way to objectively assess the relative likelihood of competing theories. Uncertainty is typically not quantified in a disciplined way, making it difficult for the linguist to know just how un/likely a particular relationship may be.

When etymology is approached by computational means, decisions are made within a rigorous framework, which makes it possible to state in probabilistic terms how likely any decision is to be correct given the data, and the relative likelihood of competing hypotheses.

Finally, a serious problem in manual etymological analysis is the potential bias of the human investigator. Bias may arise for many reasons; for example, at the time when a certain relationship is accepted as valid, some relevant data may be unknown or unavailable to the researcher, or may be available but ignored. Automatic analysis has the advantage of using all available data, without bias.

2 Related Work

We use two digital Uralic etymological resources, *SSA—Suomen Sanojen Alkuperä* ("The Origin of Finnish Words"), (Itkonen and Kulonen, 2000), and StarLing, (Starostin, 2005). StarLing was originally based on (Rédei, 1988 1991), and differs in several respects from SSA. StarLing has under 2000 Uralic cognate sets, compared with over 5000 in SSA, and does not explicitly indicate dubious etymologies. However, Uralic data in Star-Ling is more evenly distributed, because it is not

Finnish-centric like SSA is—cognate sets in Star-Ling are not required to contain a member from Finnish. StarLing also gives a *reconstructed* form for each cogset, which may be useful for testing algorithms that perform reconstruction.

We are experimenting with the Uralic data by implementing algorithms modeling various etymological processes. A method due to Kondrak, (Kondrak, 2002) learns one-to-one regular sound correspondences between pairs of related languages in the data. The method in (Kondrak, 2003) finds attested complex (one-to-many) correspondences. These models are somewhat simplistic in that they operate only on one language pair at a time, and do not model the *contexts* of the sound changes, while we know that most etymological changes are conditioned on context. Our implementation of (Bouchard-Côté et al., 2007) found correspondence rules with correct contexts, using more than two languages. However, we found that this model's running time did not scale if the number of languages is above three.

In validating our experiments we use rules found in, e.g., (Lytkin, 1973; Sinor, 1997).

The Uralic language family has not been studied by computational means previously.

3 Aligning Pairs of Words

We start with pairwise alignment: aligning two languages means aligning a list of pairs of words in the two languages, which our data set claims are related. The task is *alignment*, i.e., for each pair of words, finding which symbols correspond to each other. We expect that some symbols will align with themselves, while others have gone through changes over the time that the two related languages have been evolving separately. The simplest form of such alignment at the symbol level is a pair $(s, t) \in \Sigma \times T$, a single symbol s from the *source alphabet* Σ with a symbol t from the *target alphabet* T. We denote the sizes of the alphabets by $|\Sigma|$ and $|T|$, respectively.

Clearly, this type of atomic alignment alone does not enable us to align a source word **s** of length $|\mathbf{s}|$ with a target word **t** of length $|\mathbf{t}| \neq |\mathbf{s}|$.[1] We also need to allow *insertions* and *deletions*. We augment both alphabets with the empty symbol, denoted by a dot, and write $\Sigma_.$ and $T_.$ to refer to the augmented alphabets. We can now align word pairs such as *kaikki—kõik* (meaning "all" in

---

[1] We use boldface to denote words, as vectors of symbols.

Finnish and Estonian), for example, as either of:

$$
\begin{array}{cccccc}
k & a & i & k & k & i \\
| & | & | & | & | & | \\
k & \tilde{o} & i & k & . & .
\end{array}
\qquad
\begin{array}{ccccccc}
k & a & . & i & k & k & i \\
| & | & | & | & | & | & | \\
k & . & \tilde{o} & i & k & . & .
\end{array}
$$

The alignment on the right consists of the pairs of symbols: (k:k), (a:.), (.:õ), (i:i), (k:k), (k:.), (i:.).

Note that we speak of "*source*" and "*target*" language for convenience only—our models are completely symmetric, as will become apparent.

3.1 The Baseline Model

We wish to encode these aligned pairs as compactly as possible, following the Minimum Description Length Principle (MDL), see e.g. (Grünwald, 2007). Given a data corpus $D = (s_1, t_1), \ldots, (s_N, t_N)$ of N word pairs, we first choose an alignment of each word pair (s_i, t_i), which we then use to "transmit" the data, by simply listing the sequence of the atomic pairwise symbol alignments.[2] In order for the code to be uniquely decodable, we also need to encode the word boundaries. This can be done by transmitting a special symbol # that we do not use in any other context, only at the end of a word.

Thus, we transmit objects, or *events e*, from the event space E, in this case:

$$
E = \Sigma \times T \cup \{(\# : \#)\}
$$

We do this by means of Bayesian Marginal Likelihood (Kontkanen et al., 1996), or *prequential* coding, giving the total code length as:

$$
\begin{aligned}
L_{base}(D) = & -\sum_{e \in E} \log \Gamma\big(c(e) + \alpha(e)\big) \\
& + \sum_{e \in E} \log \Gamma\big(\alpha(e)\big) \\
& + \log \Gamma\left[\sum_{e \in E} \big(c(e) + \alpha(e)\big)\right] \\
& - \log \Gamma\left[\sum_{e \in E} \alpha(e)\right]
\end{aligned}
\tag{1}
$$

The *count* $c(e)$ is the number of times event e occurs in a complete alignment of the corpus; in particular, $c(\# : \#) = N$ occurs as many times as there are word pairs. The alignment counts are maintained in a corpus-global *alignment matrix*

M, where $M(i, j) = c(i : j)$. The $\alpha(e)$ are the (Dirichlet) priors on the events. In the baseline algorithm, we set $\alpha(e) = 1$ for all e, the so-called uniform prior, which does not favour any distribution over E, *a priori*. Note that this choice nulls the second line of equation 1.

Our baseline algorithm is simple: we first randomly align the entire corpus, then re-align one word pair at a time, greedily minimizing the total cost in Eq. 1, using dynamic programming.

In the Viterbi-like matrix below in Figure 1, each cell corresponds to a partial alignment: reaching cell (i, j) means having read off i symbols of the source and j symbols of the target word. We iterate this process, *re-aligning* the word pairs; i.e., for a given word pair, we subtract the contribution of its current alignment from the global count matrix, then re-align the word pair, then add the newly aligned events back to the global count matrix. Re-alignment continues until convergence.

Re-alignment Step: align a source word σ consisting of symbols $\sigma = [\sigma_1 ... \sigma_n] \in \Sigma^*$ with a target word $\tau = [\tau_1 ... \tau_m]$. We fill in the matrix via dynamic programming, e.g., top-to-bottom, left-to-right:[3]

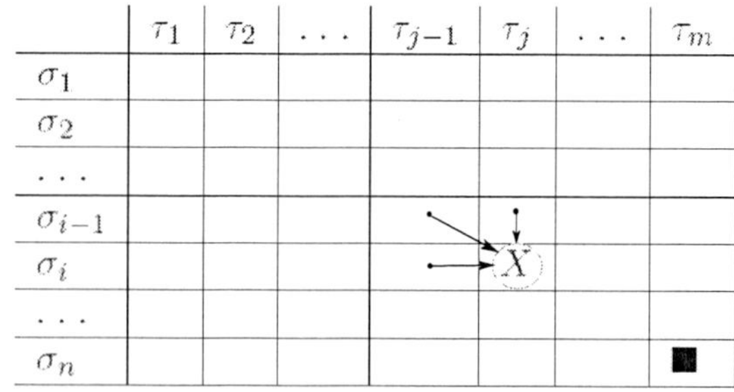

Figure 1: Dynamic programming matrix to search for most probable alignment.

Any alignment of σ and τ must correspond in a 1-1 fashion to some path through the matrix starting from top-left cell and terminating in bottom-right cell, moving only downward or rightward.

Each cell stores the probability of the *most probable* path to that point: the most probable way to have scanned the source word σ up to symbol σ_i and the target word up to τ_j, marked X in Figure 1.

$$V(\sigma_i, \tau_j) = \min \begin{cases} V(\sigma_i, \tau_{j-1}) & +L(.\,:\tau_j) \\ V(\sigma_{i-1}, \tau_j) & +L(\sigma_i :\,.) \\ V(\sigma_{i-1}, \tau_{j-1}) & +L(\sigma_i :\tau_j) \end{cases} \quad (2)$$

In each case, the term $V(.)$ has been computed earlier by the dynamic programming; the term $L(.)$—the cost of aligning the two symbols—is a parameter of the model, computed in equation (3).

The parameters $L(e)$ or $P(e)$, for every observed event e, are computed from the *change* in the total code-length—the change that corresponds to the cost of adjoining the new event e to the set of previously observed events E:

$$L(e) \quad = \quad \Delta_e L = L\big(E \cup \{e\}\big) - L(E)$$

$$P(e) \quad = \quad 2^{-\Delta_e L} = \frac{2^{-L\big(E\cup\{e\}\big)}}{2^{-L(E)}} \quad (3)$$

Combining eqs. 1 and 3 gives the probability:

$$P(e) = \frac{c(e) + 1}{\sum_{e'} c(e') + |E|} \quad (4)$$

In particular, the cost of the most probable *complete* alignment of the two words will be stored in the bottom-right cell, $V(\sigma_n, \tau_m)$, marked ■.

3.2 The Two-Part Code

The baseline algorithm has revealed two problems. First, the algorithm seems to get stuck in local optima, and second, it produces many events with very low counts (occurring only once or twice).

To address the first problem we use simulated annealing with a sufficiently slow cooling schedule. This yields a reduction in the cost, and a better—more sparse—alignment count matrix.

The second problem is more substantial. Events that occur only once clearly have not got much support in the data. In theory, starting out from a common ancestor language, the number of changes that occurred in either language should be small. This does not necessarily mean many self-alignments of a symbol with itself, since a change may apply to many occurrences, e.g., all occurrences of the sound h at the end of a word have disappeared in Finnish. However, we still expect *sparse* data: we expect a relatively small portion of all *possible* events in E^+ to actually ever occur.

We incorporate this notion into our model by means of a two-part code. We first encode which events have occurred/have been observed: we first send the number of non-zero-count events—this costs $\log(|E| + 1)$ bits—and then transmit which subset E^+ of the events have non-zero counts—this costs $\log\binom{|E|}{|E^+|}$ bits. This first part of the code is called the *codebook*. Given the codebook, we transmit the complete data using Bayesian marginal likelihood. The code length becomes:

$$L_{tpc}(D) = \log(|E| + 1) + \log\binom{|E|}{|E^+|}$$
$$- \sum_{e\in E^+} \log \Gamma\big(c(e) + 1\big) \quad (5)$$
$$+ \log \Gamma\left[\sum_{e\in E^+} \big(c(e) + 1\big)\right] - \log \Gamma(|E^+|)$$

where E^+ denotes the set of events with non-zero counts, and we have set all $\alpha(e)$'s to one. Optimizing the above function with Simulated Annealing yields very good quality alignments.

3.3 Aligning Multiple Symbols

Multiple symbols are aligned in (Bouchard-Côté et al., 2007; Kondrak, 2003). In Estonian and Finnish appear frequent geminated consonants, which correspond to single symbols/sounds in other languages; diphthongs may align with single vowels. We allow correspondences of at most two symbols on both the source and the target side. Thus, the set of admissible kinds of events is:

$$K = \left\{ \begin{array}{lll} (\# : \#), & (\sigma :\,.), & (\sigma\sigma' :\,.), \\ (.\,: \tau), & (\sigma : \tau), & (\sigma\sigma' : t), \\ (.\,: \tau\tau'), & (\sigma : \tau\tau'), & (\sigma\sigma' : \tau\tau') \end{array} \right\} \quad (6)$$

We do not expect correspondences of the different types to behave similarly, so we encode the occurrences of all event kinds separately in the codebook part of the two-part code:

$$L_{mult}(D) \quad = \quad L(CB) + L(D|CB) \quad (7)$$

$$L(CB) \quad = \quad \sum_{k\in K}\left[\log(N_k + 1) + \log\binom{N_k}{M_k}\right] \quad (8)$$

$$L(D|CB) = -\sum_{e\in E} \log \Gamma\big(c(e) + 1\big) \quad (9)$$
$$+ \log \Gamma\left[\sum_{e\in E} \big(c(e) + 1\big)\right] - \log \Gamma(|E|)$$

where N_k is the number of possible events of kind k and M_k the corresponding number of such events actually present in the alignment; by definition $\sum_k M_k \equiv |E|$.

Then, the parameters $P(e)$, for every observed event e, are again computed from the *change* in the code-length, eq. 3. But e may be of a kind that has been already observed previously, or it maybe of a new kind. Eq. 4 gives the formula for probability when $c(e) > 0$—that is, if $e \in E$—whereas

$$P(e) \;=\; \frac{1}{\displaystyle\sum_{e'} c(e') + |E|} \cdot$$

$$\cdot \frac{|E|}{\displaystyle\sum_{e'} c(e') + |E| + 1} \cdot \frac{M_k + 1}{N_k - M_k} \tag{10}$$

when $e \notin E$, and e is of kind k. If the event e has been already observed, the value of $P(e)$ is computed by plugging equation (9) into eq. (3)— yielding eq. (4); if this is the first time e is observed, $P(e)$ is computed by plugging *both* eq. (9) and eq. (8) into eq. (3), since then the codebook also changes—yielding eq. (10).

Again we optimize this cost function by means of Simulated Annealing.

4   3-Dimensional Alignment

The baseline models section we restricted ourselves to aligning two languages. The alignment models allow us to learn 1-1 patterns of correspondence in the language family. The model is easily extensible to *any* number of languages. Other methods for aligning more than two languages were presented in (Bouchard-Côté et al., 2007).

We extend the 2-D model to three-dimensions as follows. We seek an alignment where symbols correspond to each other in a 1-1 fashion, as in the 2-D baseline. A three-dimensional alignment is a triplet of symbols $(\sigma : \tau : \xi) \in \Sigma \times T \times \Xi$. For example, (*yhdeksän* : *üheksa* : *veχksa*)— meaning "9" in Finnish, Estonian and Mordva, can be aligned *simultaneously* as:

```
y  .  h  d  e  k  s  ä  n
|  |  |  |  |  |  |  |  |
ü  .  h  .  e  k  s  a  .
|  |  |  |  |  |  |  |  |
v  e  χ  .  .  k  s  a  .
```

In 3-D alignment, the input data contains all examples where words *in at least two* languages

are present[4]—i.e., a word may be *missing* from one of the languages, (which allows us to utilize more of the data). Thus we have two types of examples: *complete* examples, those that have all three words present (as "9" above), and *incomplete* examples—containing words in only two languages. For example, the alignment of (*haamu*:—:*čama*)—meaning "ghost" in Finnish and Mordva—is an example where the cognate Estonian word is missing.

We must extend the 2-D alignment matrix and the 2-D Viterbi matrices to 3-D. The 3-D Viterbi matrix is directly analogous to the 2-D version. For the alignment counts in 3-D, we handle complete and incomplete examples separately.

4.1   Marginal 3-D Model

The "marginal" or "pairwise" 3-D alignment model aligns three languages simultaneously, using *only* the marginal 2-D matrices, each storing pairwise 2-D alignments. The marginal matrices for three languages are denoted $M_{\Sigma T}$, $M_{\Sigma \Xi}$ and $M_{T\Xi}$. The algorithm optimizes the total cost of the complete data, which is defined as the *sum* of the three 2-D costs obtained from applying prequential coding to the marginal alignment matrices.

When computing the cost for event $e = (\sigma, \tau, \xi)$, we consider complete and incomplete examples separately. In "incomplete" examples, we use the counts from the corresponding marginal matrix directly. E.g., for event count $c(e)$, where $e = (\sigma, -, \xi)$, and $-$ denotes the missing language, the event count is given by: $M_{\Sigma \Xi}(\sigma, \xi)$, and the cost of each alignment is computed as in the baseline model, directly in 2 dimensions.

In case when the data triplet is complete—fully observed—the alignment cost is computed as the *sum of the pairwise 2-D costs*, given by three marginal alignment count matrices:

$$\begin{aligned} L(\sigma : \tau : \xi) \;=\;& L_{\Sigma T}(\sigma : \tau) \\ +\;& L_{\Sigma \Xi}(\sigma : \xi) \\ +\;& L_{T\Xi}(\tau : \xi) \end{aligned} \tag{11}$$

The cost of each pairwise alignment is computed using prequential two-part coding, as in sec. 3.2.

Note that when we register a complete alignment (σ, τ, ξ), we register it in *each* of the base

---

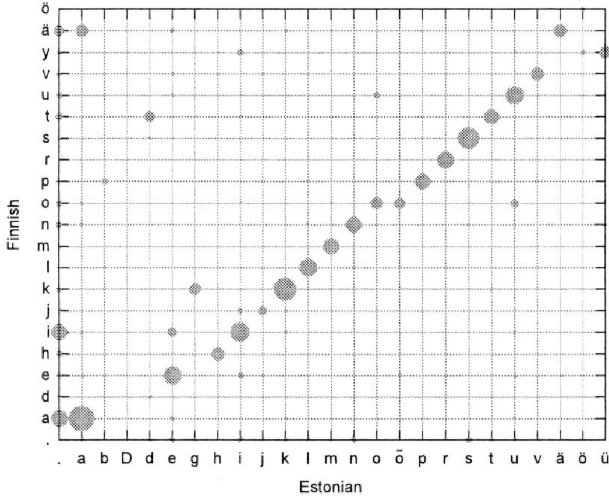

Figure 2: Alignment count matrix for Estonian-Finnish, using the two-part code.

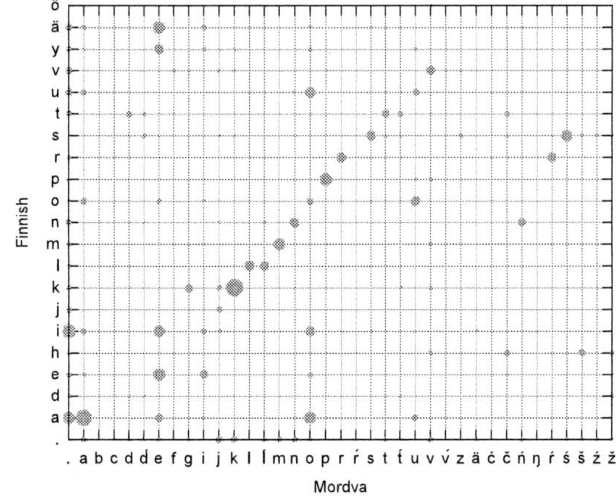

Figure 3: Mordva-Finnish 2-part code alignment.

matrices—we increment each of the marginal counts: $M_{\Sigma T}(\sigma, \tau)$, $M_{\Sigma\Xi}(\sigma, \xi)$, and $M_{T\Xi}(\tau, \xi)$. To deregister, we decrement all three counts.

To calculate the transition costs in the Viterbi algorithm, we also have two cases, complete and incomplete. For incomplete examples, we perform Viterbi in 2-D, using the costs directly from the corresponding marginal matrix, equation (5).

Note that in 3-D a non-empty symbol in one language may align to the deletion symbol "." in two languages, e.g., (.:.:d) in the 3-D example above. This means that the alignment (.:.) can now have non-zero count and marginal probability, as any other 1-1 alignment.[5]

Re-alignment: the re-alignment phase for the *complete* examples in 3-D is analogous to the re-alignment in 2-D, equation (2). The cell in the re-alignment matrix $V(\sigma_i, \tau_j, \xi_k)$—the cumulative cost of the cheapest path leading to the cell (i, j, k)—is calculated via dynamic programming, from the symbol-alignment costs $L(\sigma : \tau : \xi)$:

$$V(\sigma_i, \tau_j, \xi_k) =$$
$$\min \begin{cases} V(\sigma_{i-1}, \tau_j, \xi_k) & +L(\sigma_i : . : .) \\ V(\sigma_i, \tau_{j-1}, \xi_k) & +L(. : \tau_j : .) \\ V(\sigma_i, \tau_j, \xi_{k-1}) & +L(. : . : \xi_k) \\ V(\sigma_{i-1}, \tau_{j-1}, \xi_k) & +L(\sigma_i : \tau_j : .) \\ V(\sigma_i, \tau_{j-1}, \xi_{k-1}) & +L(. : \tau_j : \xi_k) \\ V(\sigma_{i-1}, \tau_j, \xi_{k-1}) & +L(\sigma_i : . : \xi_k) \\ V(\sigma_{i-1}, \tau_{j-1}, \xi_{k-1}) & +L(\sigma_i : \tau_j : \xi_k) \end{cases}$$

---

[5]NB: this count is always zero in 2-D alignments, and remains impossible when aligning incomplete examples in 3-D.

5 Results

Evaluation of the results of the alignment algorithms is not a simple matter. One way to evaluate thoroughly would require a *gold-standard* aligned corpus; the algorithms produce alignments, which should be compared to the alignments that we would expect to find. We currently have linguists working on a gold-standard alignment for the Uralic data. Given a gold-standard alignment, we can measure performance quantitatively, e.g., in terms of accuracy.

Alignment: We can still perform qualitative evaluation, by checking how many correct sound correspondences the algorithm finds, by inspecting the final alignment of the corpus and the alignment matrix. Sample matrices for 2-D alignments of Finnish-Estonian and Finnish-Mordva (Erzä di-

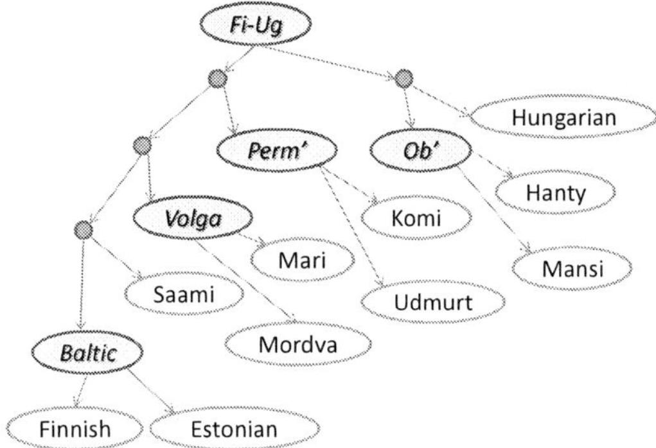

Figure 4: The Finno-Ugric sub-family of Uralic.

	est	*fin*	*khn*	*kom*	*man*	*mar*	*mrd*	*saa*	*udm*	*ugr*
est		**.372**	.702	.704	.716	.703	.665	.588	.733	.778
fin	.372		.731	.695	.754	.695	.635	.589	.699	.777
khn	.702	.719		.672	**.633**	.701	.718	.668	.712	.761
kom	.698	.703	.659		.675	.656	.678	.700	**.417**	.704
man	.702	.711	.633	.649		.676	.718	.779	.688	.752
mar	.715	.694	.731	.671	.746		**.648**	.671	.674	.738
mrd	.664	.624	.658	.678	.713	.648		.646	.709	.722
saa	.643	.589	.733	.706	.733	.621	.660		.686	.760
udm	.684	.712	.697	.417	.644	.694	.623	.677		.759
ugr	.780	.778	.761	.714	.755	.721	.743	.766	.741	

Table 1: Pairwise normalized compression costs for Finno-Ugric sub-family of Uralic, in StarLing data.

alect) are in figures 2 and 3. The size of each ball in the grid is proportional to the number of alignments in the corpus of the corresponding symbols.

Finnish and Estonian are the nearest languages in StarLing, and we observe that the alignment shows a close correspondence—the algorithm finds the *diagonal*, i.e., most sounds correspond to *"themselves"*. It must be noted that the algorithm has no *a priori* knowledge about the nature of the symbols, e.g., that Finnish *a* has any relation to Estonian *a*. The languages could be written, e.g., with different alphabets—as they are in general (we use transcribed data). This is evident in the Finnish-Estonian correspondence *y*~*ü*, which is the same sound written using different symbols. The fact that the model finds a large number of "self" correspondences is due to the algorithm.

The model finds many Finnish-Estonian correspondences—according to rules we find in handbooks, e.g., (Lytkin, 1973; Sinor, 1997). For example, *ä*~*a* or *ä*~*ä* about evenly: this reflects the rule that original front vowels (as *ä*) become back in non-first syllables in Estonian. Plosives *t, k* become voiced *d, g* in certain contexts in non-initial positions. Word-final vowels *a, i, ä* are often deleted. These can be observed directly in the alignment matrix, and in the aligned corpus.

In the Finnish-Mordva alignment, the diagonal is not as pronounced, since the languages are further apart and sound correspondences more complex. Many more sounds are deleted, there is more entropy than in Finnish-Estonian; for example, many Finnish vowels map correctly to Erzä *e*, especially the front and high vowels; the back vowels do so much less often. Finnish *h* is mapped correctly to *č* or *š*. There is a (correct) preference to align *o* to *u*, and vice versa.

Compression: We can evaluate the quality of the alignment indirectly, through distances between languages. We align all languages in StarLing pairwise, using the two-part code model. We can then measure the *Normalized Compression Distance* (Cilibrasi and Vitanyi, 2005):

$$\delta(\mathbf{a}, \mathbf{b}) = \frac{C(\mathbf{a}, \mathbf{b}) - \min(C(\mathbf{a}, \mathbf{a}), C(\mathbf{b}, \mathbf{b}))}{\max(C(\mathbf{a}, \mathbf{a}), C(\mathbf{b}, \mathbf{b}))}$$

where $0 < \delta < 1$, and $C(\mathbf{a}, \mathbf{b})$ is the compression cost—i.e., the cost of the complete aligned data for languages A and B.[6] The pairwise compression distances are shown in Table 1. Even with the simple 1x1 baseline model we see emerging patterns that mirror relationships within the Uralic family tree, shown in Fig. 4, e.g., one adapted from (Anttila, 1989). For example, scanning the row corresponding to Finnish, the compression distances *grow* as: Estonian .372, Saami .589, Mordva .635, Mari .695, Komi .695, Udmurt .699, Hanty .731, Mansi .754, and Hungarian .777, as the corresponding distance within the family tree also grows. The same holds true for Estonian.

In bold figures are sister languages, identified as being closest within their rows, (top to bottom): the Baltic, Ob', Permic, and Volgaic sub-branches.

Although the distances are not perfect (for some languages, the estimates are not 100% accurate) this confirms that the model is able to compress better—i.e., find *more regularity*—between languages that are are more closely related.

---

[6] $C(\mathbf{a}, \mathbf{a})$ is a monolingual "alignment" of a language with itself—which is very primitive, since the 1x1 model is then able to model only the symbol frequencies.

6 Current Work and Conclusions

We have presented several models of increasing complexity for alignment of etymological datasets. The baseline 1x1 model is improved upon by introducing a two-part coding scheme and simulated annealing—this helps reduce the cost and improves the alignment. Introducing 2x2 alignment helps to reduce the cost further, but produces many spurious symbol pairs, because certain combinations of sounds appear frequently within a single language. We conclude that the proper way to handle this is by modeling context explicitly, as described above. The powerful extension of the baseline to multiple languages performs well in terms of costs and resulting alignments—these will be tested against a gold-standard in future work. An interesting consequence of the MDL-based alignment procedure, is the ability to use the alignment costs as a measure of language relation, as shown in Table 1.[7]

Although the simulated annealing heuristic already yields useful results, the algorithm still tends to end up in different final alignment states—even with a slow cooling schedule—which differ in quality in terms of the cost function, eq. 7.

We are currently extending the alignment model in two ways: by modeling context—assigning different probabilities to the same event in different environments, and by using the phonetic feature representation of the alphabet symbols.

The presented methods are not intended to replace traditional methods for etymological analysis. We are addressing only a narrow slice of the problem of etymological analysis. However, we believe these models provide an initial basis for building more interesting and complex models in the future. In particular, we can use them to approach the question of comparison of "competing" etymological data-sets or theories. The cost of an optimal alignment obtained over a given data set gives an indication of the internal regularity within the set, which can be used as an indication of consistency and quality.

We have not begun to address many important questions in etymology, including borrowing and semantics, etc. We initially focus on phonological phenomena only. Earlier work, (Kondrak, 2004) has shown that even semantics can begin to be approached in a rigorous way by computational means. Borrowing will require building models that can span across language families, which will require more mature models in the future.

Acknowledgements

Research supported by the Uralink Project of the Academy of Finland, Grant 129185. We thank Arto Vihavainen and Suvi Hiltunen for their contribution to the implementation and testing of the algorithms. We are grateful to the anonymous reviewers for their comments and suggestions.

References

R. Anttila. 1989. *Historical and comparative linguistics*. John Benjamins.

A. Bouchard-Côté, P. Liang, T.Griffiths, and D. Klein. 2007. A probabilistic approach to diachronic phonology. In *Proc. EMNLP-CoNLL*, Prague.

R. Cilibrasi and P.M.B. Vitanyi. 2005. Clustering by compression. *IEEE Transactions on Information Theory*, 51(4).

P. Grünwald. 2007. *The Minimum Description Length Principle*. MIT Press.

E. Itkonen and U.-M. Kulonen. 2000. *Suomen Sanojen Alkuperä (The Origin of Finnish Words)*. Suomalaisen Kirjallisuuden Seura, Helsinki, Finland.

G. Kondrak. 2002. Determining recurrent sound correspondences by inducing translation models. In *Proceedings of COLING 2002*, Taipei.

G. Kondrak. 2003. Identifying complex sound correspondences in bilingual wordlists. In *A. Gelbukh (Ed.) CICLing*, Mexico. Springer LNCS, No. 2588.

G. Kondrak. 2004. Combining evidence in cognate identification. In *Proceedings of Canadian-AI 2004*, London, ON. Springer-Verlag LNCS, No. 3060.

P. Kontkanen, P. Myllymäki, and H. Tirri. 1996. Constructing Bayesian finite mixture models by the EM algorithm. Technical Report NC-TR-97-003, ESPRIT Working Group on NeuroCOLT.

V. I. Lytkin. 1973. *Voprosy Finno-Ugorskogo Jazykoznanija (Issues in Finno-Ugric Linguistics)*, volume 1–3. Nauka, Moscow.

K. Rédei. 1988–1991. *Uralisches etymologisches Wörterbuch*. Harrassowitz, Wiesbaden.

Denis Sinor, editor. 1997. *The Uralic Languages: Description, History and Foreign Influences (Handbook of Uralic Studies)*. Brill Academic Publishers.

S. A. Starostin. 2005. Tower of babel: Etymological databases. http://newstar.rinet.ru/.

---

[7] To save space, we focus on the Finno-Ugric sub-family of Uralic, and leave out the Samoyedic branch.

ISSN 1736-6305 Vol. 11
http://hdl.handle.net/10062/16955

Convolution Kernels for Subjectivity Detection

Michael Wiegand and **Dietrich Klakow**
Spoken Language Systems
Saarland University
D-66123 Saarbrücken, Germany
{Michael.Wiegand|Dietrich.Klakow}@lsv.uni-saarland.de

Abstract

In this paper, we explore different linguistic structures encoded as convolution kernels for the detection of subjective expressions. The advantage of convolution kernels is that complex structures can be directly provided to a classifier without deriving explicit features. The feature design for the detection of subjective expressions is fairly difficult and there currently exists no commonly accepted feature set. We consider various structures, such as constituency parse structures, dependency parse structures, and predicate-argument structures. In order to generalize from lexical information, we additionally augment these structures with clustering information and the task-specific knowledge of subjective words. The convolution kernels will be compared with a standard vector kernel.

1 Introduction

One of the most prominent subtasks in sentiment analysis is the detection of subjectivity. Given some expression in a particular context, one is to decide whether this expression conveys some subjective meaning:

1. The United States and its principal allies have acted with **exceptional** caution over recent weeks to the **unbelievable provocation** of the 11 September attacks.

2. General Lucas Rincon held a brief news conference to say Mr Chavez' resignation had been **demanded** and **accepted**.

Though there are several words, such as *horrible* or *ambitious*, that are subjective a priori, there are many ambiguous expressions being subjective only in particular contexts, such as the word *reactions* which is subjective in Sentence 3 but is not subjective in Sentence 4. These examples also illustrate that the contextual information is very helpful in order to decide whether a target word is subjective or not. In Sentence 3, the words that are syntactically related to the target word, e.g. the modifier *healthy* or its governing predicate *provokes*, are particularly predictive as they can be considered subjective expressions themselves.

3. That is a bitter pill to swallow in a thoroughly non-militaristic society such as ours, where the clash of weapons provokes healthy **reactions** of repulsion.

4. Although computers with DNA input and output have been made before, they have always involved a laborious series of *reactions*, each requiring human supervision.

In this paper, we explore different linguistic structures encoded as convolution kernels for the detection of such subjective expressions. We assume that contextual information of structures other than lexical units is useful for this task. The advantage of convolution kernels is that complex structures can be directly provided to a classifier without deriving explicit features. The feature design for the detection of subjective expressions is fairly difficult and there currently exists no commonly accepted feature set. Therefore, we assume that the usage of convolution kernels for this task may be suitable.

We consider various linguistic levels of representation commonly used for classification and extraction tasks in natural language processing, such as constituency parse structures, dependency parse structures, and predicate-argument structures. In order to generalize from lexical information, we additionally augment these structures with clustering information and the task-specific knowledge of subjective words. The convolution kernels will be compared with a standard vector kernel.

2   Related Work

Convolution kernels have been shown to be effective in various tasks in natural language processing, ranging from relation extraction (Bunescu and Mooney, 2005; Zhang et al., 2006; Nguyen et al., 2009), semantic role labeling (Moschitti et al., 2008) to question answering (Zhang and Lee, 2003; Moschitti, 2008). In sentiment analysis, this method has been successfully applied on opinion holder extraction (Wiegand and Klakow, 2010).

There is no general agreement as to whether linguistic information is useful for text classification tasks in sentiment analysis (which next to subjectivity detection also comprises polarity classification[1]). For supervised document-level analysis, traditional word-level features (i.e. bag of words/n-grams) are usually sufficient (Ng et al., 2006). The usage of more expressive features has been found more effective on fine-grained sentiment analysis, in particular, the classification at word/phrase level (Wilson et al., 2005; Karlgren et al., 2010; Johansson and Moschitti, 2010). The features used in those works have been manually designed and comprise various levels of representation, such as grammatical relations or predicate-argument structures. Johansson and Moschitti (2010) also use a tree kernel encoding dependency parse trees, however, there is no significant improvement achieved by that structure.

In this work, we not only consider dependency parse trees for convolution kernels but also other linguistic levels of representation. Moreover, we also consider appropriate substructures rather than the structures derived from an entire sentence. The latter approach has already been proved effective in opinion holder extraction (Wiegand and Klakow, 2010).

3   Data

As a labeled corpus, we use the Multi-Perspective Question Answering Corpus (MPQA-2.0)[2] which is a widely used corpus annotated with fine-grained information, such as expression-level subjectivity annotation. As subjective expressions, we consider nouns, (full) verbs, and adjectives being

labeled as a *direct subjective* or *expressive subjectivity*. We excluded those expressions with *low* or *implicit* subjectivity.[3] Please note that the expressions that are labeled as subjective need not be individual words but can also be phrases. For our approach, we will then consider each word of this phrase being either a noun, verb, or adjective separately, e.g. for Sentence 5 we will consider *biggest* and *story* as two subjective words.

5. You're making us leave as the **biggest story** gets here.

4   Method

4.1   Support Vector Machines and Kernel Methods

Support Vector Machines (SVMs) are one of the most robust supervised machine learning techniques in which training data instances $\vec{x}$ are separated by a hyperplane $H(\vec{x}) = \vec{w} \cdot \vec{x} + b = 0$ where $w \in \mathbb{R}^n$ and $b \in \mathbb{R}$ (Joachims, 1999). The hyperplane can be reformulated with a kernel function $K : X \times X \to \mathbb{R}$ that computes the similarity of two data instances $\vec{x}_i$ and $\vec{x}_j$ ($\vec{x}_i \wedge \vec{x}_j \in X$). While in a standard vector kernel these instances are represented by manually defined features, such as bag of words, in a convolution kernel the instances can be described by more complex discrete structures, such as trees or sequences. A convolution kernel function is an algorithm that specifies how the similarity of two instances represented by such discrete structures can be computed.

The convolution kernels we evaluate in this work are two tree kernels: Subset Tree Kernel (STK) (Collins and Duffy, 2002) and Partial Tree Kernel (PTK_{basic}) (Moschitti, 2006). We will focus exclusively on tree structures since they largely outperform other kernels, such as sequence kernels (Wiegand and Klakow, 2010). In a tree kernel, the similarity of two trees is computed by counting the number of common tree fragments. In STK, a tree fragment can be any set of nodes and edges of the original tree provided that every node has either all or none of its children. This constraint makes that kind of kernel well-suited for constituency trees (Zhang et al., 2006; Nguyen et al., 2009; Wiegand and Klakow, 2010) that have

---

[1]Polarity classification is the task of distinguishing between positive and negative opinions.

[2]`www.cs.pitt.edu/mpqa/databaserelease`

[3]Beyond the experiments presented in this paper, we also experimented with other definitions, e.g. also including *low* subjective expressions. Though these definitions usually result in different absolute numbers in the evaluation, the relation between the different methods remains similar.

been generated by context free grammars since the constraint corresponds to the restriction that no grammatical rule must be broken. For example, STK enforces that a subtree, such as *[VP [VBZ, NP]]*, cannot be matched with *[VP [VBZ]]* since the latter *VP* node only possesses one of the children of the former.

PTK_{basic} is more flexible since the constraint of STK on nodes is relaxed. This makes this type of tree kernel less suitable for constituency trees. We, therefore, apply it only to trees representing dependency trees (thus following Johansson and Moschitti (2010)) and predicate-argument structures (thus following Moschitti (2008)).

4.2 Bag of Words

The simplest form of contextual information to be used for our task is lexical information, i.e. bag of words. Even though it is extremely simple and cheap to produce, this level of representation is known to be fairly robust for different kinds of text classification tasks. We will examine several context windows and encode this representation in a standard vector kernel.

4.3 Convolution Kernels

The following subsections present the different kinds of tree structures that are used for convolution kernels.

4.3.1 Constituency Parse Structures (CON)

Wiegand and Klakow (2010) showed for opinion holder extraction that using the entire constituency parse tree of a sentence produces very low performing classifiers. Structures derived from an entire sentence contain too much irrelevant information for such a task at expression level. We assume that the same is true for the detection of subjectivity. Wiegand and Klakow (2010) use subtrees derived from scopes. The best performing subtree is the tree with the predicate scope, i.e. a subtree with the boundaries being the candidate or target expression and the nearest predicate. We also assume that this structure is meaningful for our task. As already discovered in previous work on the detection of subjective expressions (Riloff and Wiebe, 2003; Riloff and Wiebe, 2003; Wilson et al., 2005), discriminant patterns often encode a relation between the target expression and the nearest predicate. An illustration of this substructure is given in Figure 1(a). We use the Stanford

Parser (Klein and Manning, 2003) for obtaining constituency parse trees.

4.3.2 Dependency Parse Structures (DEP)

Apart from manually designed features, Johansson and Moschitti (2010) also test a tree kernel for subjectivity detection using a dependency parse. However, the entire parse comprising a sentence is considered. The resulting tree kernel does not show any significant improvement (again presumably because of the large amount of irrelevant information). The usefulness of particular (usually direct) relations, however, has been found effective on other related tasks in sentiment analysis (Jakob and Gurevych, 2010; Wiegand and Klakow, 2010). We therefore only consider the subtree exclusively containing the lexical units that are connected to the target word by a direct syntactic dependency relationship (i.e. direct parent and direct children). The precise encoding of the pertaining information (i.e. part-of-speech, grammatical relation, and lexical information) in the resulting tree is taken from (Johansson and Moschitti, 2010). An illustration of this substructure is given in Figure 1(b). Again, we use the Stanford Parser (Klein and Manning, 2003) for obtaining dependency parse trees.

4.3.3 Predicate-Argument Structures (PAS)

Predicate-argument structures (PAS), in particular, semantic role labeling has been shown to be effective for many information extraction tasks, including opinion holder extraction (Kim and Hovy, 2006; Wiegand and Klakow, 2010) and opinion target extraction (Kim and Hovy, 2006). Johansson and Moschitti (2010) also examine this level of representation for subjectivity detection. However, they employ manual features derived from these structures rather than using a corresponding tree kernel.

We follow Wiegand and Klakow (2010) for the encoding of these structures as tree kernels, that is we restrict ourselves to structures in which the target word is either a predicate or some argument. We derive our predicate-argument structures from a semantic parse based on the Prop-Bank annotation scheme (Kingsbury and Palmer, 2002). Semantic roles are obtained by using the parser by Zhang et al. (2008). A special property of PAS is that a data instance, i.e. the information regarding one target word and its particular context, is represented by a set of those structures rather than a single structure. Thus, the actual partial tree kernel function we use for this task, PTK, sums over all possible pairs PAS_l and PAS_m of two data instances x_i and x_j: $PTK(x_i, x_j) = \sum_{PAS_l \in x_i} \sum_{PAS_m \in x_j} PTK_{basic}(PAS_l, PAS_m)$. An illustration of these substructures is given in Figure 1(c).

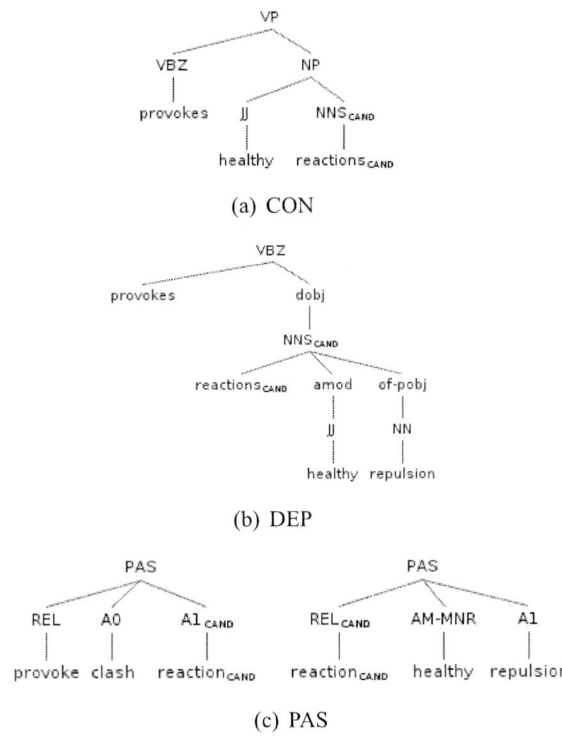

(a) CON

(b) DEP

(c) PAS

Figure 1: Illustration of the different tree structures employed for convolution kernels derived from Sentence 3 with *reactions* as the target word.

4.3.4 Augmentation with Clustering

A common type of unsupervised generalization is clustering. Words which co-occur with each other are automatically grouped into clusters. Ideally, a cluster thus contains words with similar syntactic/semantic properties. The cluster membership of individual words is induced from a large unlabeled corpus.

As the context windows of our target expressions contain fairly sparse lexical information, the additional usage of the cluster membership might be useful. Turian et al. (2010) have shown that for named-entity recognition, i.e. a task which faces similar lexical sparseness, features based on such a cluster membership improve the overall performance. For clustering, we chose Brown cluster-

ing (Brown et al., 1992) which is the best performing algorithm in (Turian et al., 2010). This algorithm induces clusters with the help of co-occurrence statistics of bigrams. We augment our structures with the clustering information. We add the node with a cluster label in such a way that it directly dominates the pertaining lexical node.

As a software we use SRILM (Stolcke, 2002) with the default algorithm. The clusters are induced on the North American News Text Corpus (LDC95T21). We chose this corpus as it contains news texts similar to our evaluation corpus (i.e. MPQA). Following Turian et al. (2010), we induced 1000 clusters.

As many names of persons and organizations can be very domain-specific, they may not appear in the corpus from which clusters are induced. Consequently, these expressions cannot be assigned to a cluster. We try to compensate this by incorporating the knowledge about named entities in tree kernels, i.e. instead of assigning some expression to a cluster we assign it to a named entity type. Named-entity information is obtained by the Stanford tagger (Finkel et al., 2005).

4.4 The Different Settings

We want to examine the behavior of the different kernel types under different circumstances. The first setting $NoTW$ considers a prediction for unseen target words. We assume that having observed a particular target word frequently in the training data (in particular if it is fairly unambiguous) makes it easy for the classification when it is observed as a test instance, i.e. due to the prior knowledge about the lexical unit the consideration of context is less critical. If a word, however, has not been observed in the training data the consideration of context becomes much more important. For instance, an unknown word that is modified by an intensifier *extremely* is more likely to contain a subjective meaning (as in *extremely **nice***) than a word that is not modified by such an expression. The question arises whether in these cases structural context has an even larger impact than lexical context. For reasons of simplicity, we simulate unseen target words by discarding the vector kernel features indicating the lexical unit of the target word and replacing the label of the corresponding leaf node in the tree kernels by a generic symbol. The second setting TW is the main setting we use for most experiments. In this setting, the target word is considered, i.e. we have dedicated features (original word form + lemma[4]) in the vector kernel and we retain the label of the leaf node representing the target word in the tree kernels.

The final setting $TW+OP$ also incorporates the knowledge about subjective expressions. For the vector kernel, we add features indicating whether the target word is either a weak or strong subjective expression. Moreover, we include two features indicating whether the context (i.e. the words surrounding the target word in its context window) contains either at least one weak or strong subjective expression. The knowledge about subjective expressions is drawn from a given sentiment lexicon. We use the Subjectivity Lexicon from the MPQA project (Wilson et al., 2005). Table 1 summarizes the different settings with regard to the respective features in the vector kernel and the encoding of the convolution kernels. An illustration of the different settings on a constituency parse tree (CON) is displayed in Figure 2.

5 Experiments

We used 400 documents of the MPQA corpus for five-fold cross-validation and 133 documents as a development set. We will exclusively report the results that are averages over cross-validation. We report statistical significance on the basis of a paired t-test using 0.05 as the significance level.

As there is a heavy class imbalance between positive and negative data (e.g. for nouns, more than 85% of the data instances are negative examples), we evaluate with F-Score rather than accuracy. In order to achieve an optimal F-Score, we tuned the cost parameter j (Morik et al., 1999) on the development set using our baseline classifier, i.e. VK.[5] This cost parameter allows to specify a higher penalty on false negative errors. Thus, on data sets with an imbalanced class distribution better models assigning less conservatively labels of the minority class can be produced. We set $j = 4$.

As far as tree kernels are concerned, we used the parameter settings from Moschitti (2008). Kernels were combined using plain summation.

For all experiments apart from those presented in Section 5.3 will be based on our main setting, i.e. TW (see Section 4.4).

---

[4]The lemma feature is important for normalizing inflectional forms. From the parts of speech that we consider verbs mostly benefit from such a normalization.

[5]Note that the cost parameter is the only parameter tuned on the development set.

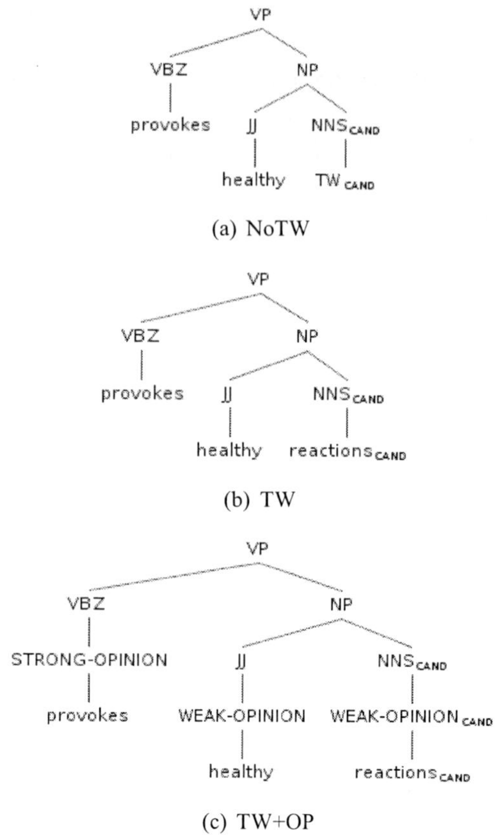

Figure 2: Illustration of the different settings (as defined in Table 1) on a constituency parse tree (CON).

5.1 Different Vector Kernel Configurations

Table 2 displays the performance (F-Score) of the vector kernel with different configurations. We vary the window size[6] and the kernel type, i.e. linear or polynomial kernel. We use a second degree polynomial kernel as we obtained the best performance with that type. The table shows that, usually the polynomial kernel always outperforms the linear kernel. Moreover, the best window size is between 5 and 10. The difference between those two window sizes using a polynomial kernel is, however, never statistically significant.

5.2 Different Convolution Kernel Configurations

Table 3 displays the performance of the different convolution kernels. As far as individual kernels are concerned, CON and DEP are fairly similar, PAS performs much worse. Overall, the best

---

[6]Window size n means that n words both preceding and following the target word are taken into consideration.

Setting	Vector Kernel (Features)	Convolution Kernel (Encoding)
NoTW	context words within window	label of target word node is replaced by generic *TW*
TW *(default)*	*all features from NoTW +* target word lemma of target word	label of target word node is not changed
TW+OP	*all features from TW +* is target word a weak/strong subjective word? has context more than one weak/strong subjective word?	label of target word node is not changed augment trees if weak/strong subjective words are present

Table 1: The different settings with the design of the corresponding kernel types.

	Noun		Verb		Adj	
WS	linear	poly	linear	poly	linear	poly
2	53.66	54.77	59.05	62.34	63.23	64.51
5	**55.90**	**59.29**	61.58	63.63	64.16	**66.52**
10	55.68	58.87	62.34	**64.46**	**64.52**	66.38
20	54.76	55.90	**62.68**	63.42	62.79	64.33

Table 2: F-Score of vector kernels using different window sizes (WS) and kernel types (using default setting TW).

combination is CON and DEP. A combination of PAS with the other convolution kernels only has a notable positive impact for verbs, which does not come as a surprise since semantic role labeling is clearly verb-centred (still, it is too sparse to be used as a kernel on its own). With the exception of verbs, a combination of all convolution kernels is not necessary, i.e. the combination of CON and DEP suffices (there is no significant improvement achieved by also adding PAS).

We were surprised that in spite of the fact that PAS as an individual kernel performs very poorly, it never harms performance when it is added to another kernel type and occasionally also causes some improvement. We ran some more experiments and found that the low performance of PAS is mainly due to the fact that a default value for the depth parameter μ (Zhang and Lee, 2003) was used. With an increased depth parameter (e.g. $\mu = 0.8$) which more suitably accounts for the low depth of flat predicate-argument structures, PAS performs much better. However, since for combined structures, the optimized parameter has only a marginal impact and we only use a default μ for all other configurations, for reasons of consistency we just use PAS with default settings.

Finally, the usage of tree augmentation using clustering (i.e. *best aug*), is always beneficial. Table 4 lists the content of three clusters that are induced. All three of them mostly contain expressions one would intuitively label as subjective expressions. This means that to a certain extent, clustering is able to group subjective expressions and objective expressions into different clusters.

We also ran some experiments using different structures than those presented in Section 4.3. Though for opinion holder extraction, a combination of scopes is useful for the constituency parse trees (Wiegand and Klakow, 2010), we found that for this task adding other scopes does not help. Further extensions of the dependency structure, e.g. by also including indirect syntactic dependency relationships (grandparent and grandchildren of the target word) did not help either. These results suggest that for this task there is little room for improvement by applying state-of-the-art convolution tree kernels on other structures than the one presented in this paper.

5.3 Comparing Vector Kernels with Convolution Kernels

Table 5 compares the best vector kernel (VK) for each respective part of speech and the combination of the best convolution kernel (CKs) with a vector kernel. As from the results for the individual vector kernels on the setting TW (Table 2) it is not obvious which window size is best (i.e. 5 or 10), we always tested both sizes and will report the best result in Table 5. For the combination with CKs, we always chose a vector kernel with the window size of 10 as, unlike the experiments on VK, we observed that this window size was consistently better than using the window size of 5.

We examine this combination on all three set-

Kernels	Noun			Verb			Adj		
	Prec	Rec	F	Prec	Rec	F	Prec	Rec	F
CON	53.49	52.23	52.84	47.15	68.89	55.98	57.07	67.49	61.83
DEP	46.43	59.57	52.17	43.68	79.94	56.49	49.72	74.78	59.72
PAS	21.12	39.39	12.04	**54.91**	12.08	18.56	29.97	49.51	29.87
CON+DEP	**52.81**	57.84	55.23	49.01	74.41	59.10	57.06	72.40	63.80
CON+PAS	52.00	56.94	54.34	48.90	78.25	60.18	56.88	68.19	62.01
DEP+PAS	47.78	59.85	53.12	45.89	81.14	58.76	50.25	73.44	59.66
all	52.23	59.57	55.64	49.60	77.75	60.65	**57.09**	71.96	63.65
best aug	52.60	**61.90**	**56.80**	50.30	77.99	**61.16**	56.74	**75.25**	**64.69**

Table 3: Performance of the different convolution kernels (using default setting TW).

tings, i.e. $NoTW$, TW and $TW{+}OP$ (see Section 4.4). The table shows that the overall performance of $NoTW$ is worst and that of $TW{+}OP$ is best, which is quite intuitive as it corresponds to the amount of knowledge encoded in the configurations. The gap between $NoTW$ and TW is the largest indicating that the knowledge of the target word itself is extremely important. The knowledge of subjective expressions $TW{+}OP$ helps but the degree of improvement is smaller.[7]

As far as the relation between vector kernels and convolution kernels is concerned, the combination of vector kernel and convolution kernels is mostly beneficial. With the exception of verbs, we always obtain a significant improvement over just using the best vector kernel.

If we compare the relation between vector kernel and the combination of vector kernel and convolution kernels across the different settings, we also observe that the less is known about the target word, the more helpful the information is that can be drawn from the convolution kernels. For example, when CKs are added to VK on nouns, there is an improvement of 5 percentage points while on the other settings the improvement is usually less than 2 percentage points. In other words, if we have test data in which many target words are unknown, then the structural context information is much more important than if the target words have mostly appeared in the training data.

acclaim, admiration, backing, benefit, contempt, disdain, disregard, disrespect, doom, finesse, gratitude, harm, praise, redress, refrain, rent, respect, ridicule, support, sympathy
anticipate, attribute, believe, confess, detest, expect, imply, indicate, liken, mean, owe, presume, pretend, resent, suggest, swear
decent, fantastic, good, handy, lousy, mediocre, miserable, nice, nostalgic, pleasant, shrewd, smart, terrific, wise, wonderful

Table 4: Some automatically induced clusters.

6   Conclusion

In this paper, we examined the usage of convolution kernels for the detection of subjective expressions and compared it to the performance of a vector kernel trained on bag-of-words features. The polynomial vector kernel is a hard baseline. For nouns and adjectives, however, the performance can be significantly increased if in addition to the vector kernel a pair of convolution kernels encoding a constituency parse subtree with predicate scope and a dependency parse subtree encoding the direct relationships between the target word and other words in a sentence is used. Additionally, the trees can be effectively augmented with cluster-membership information.

Acknowledgements

This work was funded by the BMBF project "Software-Cluster" (contract no.: *01IC10S01O) and the German research council DFG through the International Research Training Group. The authors would like to thank Yi Zhang for processing our data with his SRL system and Alessandro Moschitti for providing his toolkit SVMLight-TK.

---

[7]Since we expected a greater improvement by adding knowledge of subjective words, we ran some more exploratory experiments. We found that if we run SVMs with a default configuration that assigns the equal cost to the different classes , i.e. setting the cost parameter $j = 1$, the relative improvement from TW to $TW{+}OP$ is considerably larger (though in absolute numbers, the F-Scores are much lower than by using the optimized parameter).

Setting	Kernels	Noun			Verb			Adj		
		Prec	Rec	F	Prec	Rec	F	Prec	Rec	F
NoTW	VK	43.70	60.75	50.85	48.86	76.97	59.77	52.46	73.78	61.32
NoTW	VK+CKs	50.55	63.27	56.19*	48.45	79.56	60.22	54.83	76.80	63.98*
TW	VK	56.33	62.61	59.29	55.21	77.44	64.46	61.70	72.16	66.52
TW	VK+CKs	57.01	65.92	61.12*	53.46	78.90	63.73	61.51	77.21	68.47*
TW+OP	VK	56.01	65.57	60.41	55.59	78.45	65.07	62.62	75.36	68.39
TW+OP	VK+CKs	57.98	67.34	62.29*	55.16	79.36	65.08	62.61	77.93	69.43*

Table 5: Comparison of the (best) vector kernel and convolution kernels using different settings (*: significantly better than VK with $p \leq 0.05$).

References

P. F. Brown, P. V. deSouza, R. L. Mercer, V. J. Della Pietra, and J. C. Lai. 1992. Class-based n-gram models of natural language. *Computational Linguistics*, 18:467–479.

R. C. Bunescu and R. J. Mooney. 2005. Subsequence Kernels for Relation Extraction. In *Proc. of NIPS*.

M. Collins and N. Duffy. 2002. New Ranking Algorithms for Parsing and Tagging. In *Proc. of ACL*.

J. R. Finkel, T. Grenager, and C. Manning. 2005. Incorporating Non-local Information into Information Extraction Systems by Gibbs Sampling. In *Proc. of ACL*.

N. Jakob and I. Gurevych. 2010. Extracting Opinion Targets in a Single- and Cross-Domain Setting with Conditional Random Fields. In *Proc. of EMNLP*.

T. Joachims. 1999. Making Large-Scale SVM Learning Practical. In B. Schölkopf, C. Burges, and A. Smola, editors, *Advances in Kernel Methods - Support Vector Learning*. MIT Press.

R. Johansson and A. Moschitti. 2010. Syntactic and Semantic Structure for Opinion Expression Detection. In *Proc. of CoNLL*.

J. Karlgren, G. Eriksson, O. Täckström, and M. Sahlgren. 2010. Between Bags and Trees - Constructional Patterns in Text Used for Attitude Identification. In *Proc. of ECIR*.

S. Kim and E. Hovy. 2006. Extracting Opinions, Opinion Holders, and Topics Expressed in Online News Media Text. In *Proc. of the ACL Workshop on Sentiment and Subjectivity in Text*.

P. Kingsbury and M. Palmer. 2002. From TreeBank to PropBank. In *Proc. of LREC*.

D. Klein and C. D. Manning. 2003. Accurate Unlexicalized Parsing. In *Proc. of ACL*.

K. Morik, P. Brockhausen, and T. Joachims. 1999. Combining statistical learning with a knowledge-based approach - A case study in intensive care monitoring. In *Proc. in ICML*.

A. Moschitti, D. Pighin, and R. Basili. 2008. Tree Kernels for Semantic Role Labeling. *Computational Linguistics*, 34(2):193 – 224.

A. Moschitti. 2006. Efficient Convolution Kernels for Dependency and Constituent Syntactic Trees. In *Proc. of ECML*.

A. Moschitti. 2008. Kernel Methods, Syntax and Semantics for Relational Text Categorization. In *Proc. of CIKM*.

V. Ng, S. Dasgupta, and S. M. Niaz Arifin. 2006. Examining the Role of Linguistic Knowledge Sources in the Automatic Identification and Classification of Reviews. In *Proc. of COLING/ACL*.

T.-V. T. Nguyen, A. Moschitti, and G. Riccardi. 2009. Convolution Kernels on Constituent, Dependency and Sequential Structures for Relation Extraction. In *Proc. of EMNLP*.

E. Riloff and J. Wiebe. 2003. Learning Extraction Patterns for Recognizing Subjective Expressions. In *Proc. of EMNLP*.

A. Stolcke. 2002. SRILM - An Extensible Language Modeling Toolkit. In *Proc. of ICSLP*.

J. Turian, L. Ratinov, and Y. Bengio. 2010. Word Representations: A Simple and General Method for Semi-supervised Learning. In *Proc. of ACL*.

M. Wiegand and D. Klakow. 2010. Convolution Kernels for Opinion Holder Extraction. In *Proc. of HLT/NAACL*.

T. Wilson, J. Wiebe, and P. Hoffmann. 2005. Recognizing Contextual Polarity in Phrase-level Sentiment Analysis. In *Proc. of HLT/EMNLP*.

D. Zhang and W. S. Lee. 2003. Question Classification using Support Vector Machines. In *Proc. of SIGIR*.

M. Zhang, J. Zhang, and J. Su. 2006. Exploring Syntactic Features for Relation Extraction using a Convolution Tree Kernel. In *Proc. of HLT/NAACL*.

Y. Zhang, R. Wang, and H. Uszkoreit. 2008. Hybrid Learning of Dependency Structures from Heterogeneous Linguistic Resources. In *Proc. of CoNLL*.

ISSN 1736-6305 Vol. 11
http://hdl.handle.net/10062/16955

Explorations on Positionwise Flag Diacritics in Finite-State Morphology

Anssi Yli-Jyrä

Department of Modern Languages, PO Box 3, 00014 University of Helsinki, Finland
`anssi.yli-jyra@helsinki.fi`

Abstract

A novel technique of adding *positionwise flags* to one-level finite state lexicons is presented. The proposed flags are kinds of morphophonemic markers and they constitute a flexible method for describing morphophonological processes with a formalism that is tightly coupled with lexical entries and rule-like regular expressions. The formalism is inspired by the techniques used in two-level rule compilation and it practically compiles all the rules in parallel, but in an efficient way. The technique handles morphophonological processes without a separate morphophonemic representation. The occurrences of the allomorphophonemes in latent phonological strings are tracked through a dynamic data structure into which the most prominent (i.e. the best ranked) flags are collected. The application of the technique is suspected to give advantages when describing the morphology of Bantu languages and dialects.

1   Introduction

Computational morphology continues to be an area of challenges when it comes to the construction of exact models for many under-resourced languages whose grammar is not fully known. The purpose of this paper is to introduce a new flexible technique to finite state morphology: *positionwise flag diacritics* (or shortly: *positionwise flags, p-flags*). P-flags can be combined with the usual *flag diacritics* (Beesley and Karttunen, 2003) that are based on left-to-right inheritance. They are, however, directionless and relate the paths at a position rather than the positions on a path. As such, they capture phenomena for which morphophonological rules are often preferred to the usual flag diacritics.

The description of morphophonological processes is often delegated to SPE-inspired rewriting rules that are implemented as a sequence of finite transducers (Beesley and Karttunen, 2003). Such rules are particularly handy when describing suppletion or regular alternations that span over several segments.

Two-level systems (Koskenniemi, 1983) consist of parallel rules while being equally capable with transducer sequences. Since these systems have only one underlying representation, the ordering problems characterizing the transducer cascades are now avoided. However, over-constrained two-level systems are often difficult to debug or relax, especially when they involve multi segmental alternations and complex morphological conditions.

An ideal conflict resolution scheme is to ensure that each rule applies only in those string positions where the linguist wanted them to apply; if they apply more often, the risk for conflicting effects increases. In the typical implementations of two-level systems, the rules are separated from the description of the relevant morphemes. This makes it difficult to maintain coherence between the components of the system. There is thus a need for a better interface between the lexicon and the morphophonological rules.

An alternative approach avoids the morphophonological component by using the formalism of flag diacritics (Beesley and Karttunen, 2003). However, there remain morphophonological processes that are easier to describe with rules. We are thus posed with a question: *What is between the rules and flag diacritics.*

The main contribution of this article is the novel scheme of *positionwise flag diacritics* whose best practice involves capturing rule-like behaviour and elsewhere conditions. The second important contribution of the article is the idea of a normalized lexicon as a data structure that contains the latent phonological strings and their most prominent positionwise flags. Finally, the alleged relevance of the methods to computational description of *Bantu varieties* is made apparent.

1.1 The Prior Art

The flag diacritics described by Beesley and Karttunen (Beesley and Karttunen, 2003) implement an idea of expanding the state space of an automaton with a vector of flag value registers. During the construction of the networks, the flag diacritics are like ordinary multicharacter symbols. When a flag diacritic is encountered as a transition label during a lookup, it is interpreted (Table 1) and the symbol does not consume any input. A transition on a flag diacritic fails to exist if its success condition is not satisfied by the current flag value. Certain flag diacritics have side-effects on the flag values.

diacritic	succeeds if f is	side effect
@P.f.v@	*anything*	$f \leftarrow (v, +)$
@N.f.v@	*anything*	$f \leftarrow (v, -)$
@C.f@	*anything*	$f \leftarrow undef$
@U.f.v@	*undef*, $(v, +)$ or $(\overline{v}, -)$	$f \leftarrow (v, +)$
@D.f.v@	*undef*, $(\overline{v}, +)$ or $(v, -)$	
@D.f@	*undef*	
@R.f.v@	$(v, +)$	
@R.f@	*anything but undef*	

Table 1: The conditions and side-effects of flag diacritics

The flag diacritics are designed the left-to-right scanning of the string in mind. The pattern (@U.f.v@...@U.f.v@) is typically used as a means to cope with effects that depend on a class, declension, conjugation, stem type alternation or a harmony. The patterns (@P.f.v@...@R.f.v@) and (...@D.f.v@) are typically used to check that a certain prefix is present and absent, respectively. The problem with this is that one ends up adding flag diacritics to such paths that *cannot* co-occur with the given prefix. Further mechanisms similar to the flag diacritics have been proposed in the literature (Blank, 1989; Blåberg, 1994; Kornai, 1996; Kiraz, 1997; Amtrup, 2004; Schmid, 2005; Trón et al., 2006; Cohen-Sygal and Wintner, 2006).

In the sequel, some prior knowledge of the two-level morphology (Koskenniemi, 1983) and the calculus of regular relations (Kaplan and Kay, 1994; Beesley and Karttunen, 2003) is assumed. Table 2 lists some crucial regular expression operators used in this paper. The rules used in two-

operator	type	meaning
ϵ	nullary	empty string
:	infix	cross product
	infix	concatenation
*	postfix	Kleene star
$\cap$	infix	union
$\vert$ or $\cup$	infix	union
$-$	infix	asymmetric difference
$\circ$	infix	composition
$\Rightarrow$	infix	context restriction
$\Leftarrow$	infix	surface coercion
$\Leftrightarrow$	infix	the double arrow rule
Id()	function	convert to an identity relation

Table 2: regular expression operators

level morphology provide a well understood basis for morphophonological grammars. In two-level rules, it is common to refer to a set of symbol pairs through an underspecific notation: e.g. :C refers to all correspondence pairs with a surface consonant.

According to Koskenniemi and Silfverberg (2010), a state-of-the-art compilation method for morphophonological two-level rules is based on the *generalized restriction (GR)* operation (Yli-Jyrä and Koskenniemi, 2004). The operation is based on temporary markers that are added to a few positions of the strings during the construction. Besides its practical relevance to the compilation of individual rules, the GR operation provides theoretical means to compile and combine the set of disjunctively ordered constraints and the lexicon at the same time (Yli-Jyrä, 2008). Such a holistic approach relies on the determinization and complementation of finite automata. These operations are potential sources for high state and transition complexities.

2 Bantu Phonology

The Bantu languages refer to a group of a few hundred languages and dialects in Southern Africa. The languages share many common aspects such as rich affix morphology and reduplication. In phonology, the most common assimilatory process is the vowel height harmony of front and back vowels (Nurse and Philippson, 2003, p.46). The *Front Height Harmony (FHH)* process comes in two flavors that correspond to the rules such as follows:

(1) Front Height Harmony (FHH)

    a. General: $/i/:[e] \Leftrightarrow [\{o, e\} \; C] \_$

    b. Extended: $/i/:[e] \Leftrightarrow [\{o, e, a\} \; C] \_.$

The General FHH rule reads: "an underlying /i/ is realised as [e] if the vowel of the preceding syllable is [o] or [e]." The Extended FHH is more effective and it alters /i/ also after [a].

The General and Extended FHH rules are in conflict when /i/ is preceded with [a]. This kind of conflict is not to be resolved on the basis of rules per se, but by considering additional context information. The relevant context-dependency is neatly illustrated by the derivative extensions of verb stems in (Oshi)Kwanyama and (Otji)Herero varieties as described in (Halme, 2004) and (Möhlig and Kavari, 2008).

In Herero (HER), the inflectional stem of an applicative (APPL) verb (2-b) is formed by extending the inflectional stem (2-a) with the suffix /-ir/ that precedes the final vowel /-a/. In Kwanyama (KWA), the corresponding suffix is /-il/. In both cases, the sound /i/ is subject to the Extended FHH and the consonant is altered in nasal contexts (2-c).

(2) a. [*túng-a*]   (HER)'build'-FV

    b. [*túng-ir-a*]   (HER)'build'-APPL-FV

    c. [*món-en-á*]   (KWA)'see'-APPL-FV

On the other hand, the Neuter verb (NEUT) is formed in both languages with the suffix /-ik/ (3-a). The /i/ sound in this suffix is subject to to General FHH in Kwanyama (3-b), but not in Herero (Möhlig and Kavari, 2008).

(3) a. [*túng-ik-á*]   (KWA)'build'-NEUT-FV

    b. [*kómb-ek-á*]   (KWA)'sweep'-NEUT-FV

The grammatical tone of the derivative extensions cannot be discussed here due to space constraints.

In sum, the Bantu phonology shows that the sound changes depend on the variety (HER-KWA), the morpheme position (root-verbal extension) and the grammatical category of a morpheme (APPL~NEUT). Such dependency can be described through the concept of morphophonemes.

3 Morphophonology

3.1 Morphophonemes by Variation

A technique for identifying morphophonemes has been given (Austerlitz, 1967). Another technique (Koskenniemi, 1991) would provide the Applicative and Neuter morphemes of Kwanyama with the following morphophonological structures where individual morphophonemes are wrapped in angle brackets (they must not be confused with the brackets that denote an orthographic string):

(4) a. $|\langle \text{i-e}\rangle\langle \text{l-n}\rangle|$

    b. $|\langle \text{i-e}\rangle\langle \text{k}\rangle|$

Both derivative extensions involve the same morphophoneme, $|\langle \text{i-e}\rangle|$, which is distinguished from the morphophoneme $|\langle \text{i}\rangle|$ that occurs e.g. in verb roots. The morphophoneme helps thus to focus the application of the phonological rules on extensions (in contrast to verb roots).

The morphophoneme $|\langle \text{i-e}\rangle|$ is indifferent with the grammatical category of the extension. Therefore, the harmony rules need an additional condition to account the difference between APPL and NEUT. Reducing the morphological condition to the segmental structure of the morphemes does not seem to be a well-motivated option. Adding arbitrarily chosen lexical features (Koskenniemi, 1983, p.40) to the morphophonological strings is also a weakly motivated approach. Conditioning the rules with grammatical categories (Trost, 1991; Kiraz, 1997) is perhaps the most solid but also the heaviest approach. Conceptually, it leads to the following pair of realisation rules for the morphophoneme $|\langle \text{i-e}\rangle|$:

(5) a. $|\langle \text{i-e}\rangle|:/i/ \Rightarrow \_$

    b. $|\langle \text{i-e}\rangle|:/e/ \Leftrightarrow /\{e,a,o\} \; C/ \_(\text{APPL}),$
                         $/\{e,o\} \; C/ \_(\text{NEUT}).$

The use of the grammar categories in rules is a complication that we want to avoid or make simpler.

3.2 Morphophonemes by Contexts

Recently, Koskenniemi and Silfverberg (2010) have shown that the multi context rules like (5-b) can be compiled as two separate rules by using the variants of the phonemes:

(6) a. $|\langle \text{i-e}\rangle|:/\!/e_1/\!/$
        $\Leftrightarrow /\!/\{e_1,e_2,a,o\} \; C/\!/ \_(\text{APPL})$

    b. $|\langle \text{i-e}\rangle|:/\!/e_2/\!/$
        $\Leftrightarrow /\!/\{e_1,e_2,o\} \; C/\!/ \_(\text{NEUT}).$

The method requires that there is an additional mapping that replaces $/\!/e_1/\!/$ and $/\!/e_2/\!/$ with /e/.

It is worth observing that the multi context rules can be split in two different ways. By applying the splitting to the underlying rather than the surface level, one captures the morphological distinction differentiated by the context conditions. This simplifies the contexts of the rules into more elegant rules:

(7) a. $|\langle \text{iE-eE}\rangle|{:}/e/ \Leftrightarrow /\{e,a,o\}\,C/\ \_$
     b. $|\langle \text{iG-eG}\rangle|{:}/e/ \Leftrightarrow /\{e,o\}\,C/\ \_.$

In this case, there is no need for an additional mapping, because the refined morphophonemes can be used directly in the lexicon.

3.3 The GR-Based Compilation Method

A practical two-level grammar compilation method (Yli-Jyrä and Koskenniemi, 2006) reduces the traditional rules into *Generalized Restriction (GR)* rules. Accordingly, the double arrow rule (7-b) is first split into two subrules:

(8) $|\langle \text{iE-eE}\rangle|{:}/e/ \Rightarrow /\{e,a,o\}\,C/\ \_$

(9) $|\langle \text{iE-eE}\rangle|{:}/e/ \Leftarrow /\{e,a,o\}\,C/\ \_.$

The subrules are then reduced into two GR rules of the form $W \overset{2\diamond}{\Rrightarrow} W'$. Each GR rule involves two argument languages, $W, W' \subseteq \Sigma^*\diamond\Sigma^*\diamond\Sigma^*$. For the moment, Σ is the set of feasible morphophoneme-phoneme pairs. The argument languages specify when the rule is triggered (W) and what the triggered rule then requires (W'). In the strings of these languages, the marker $\diamond$ is a string element indicating which morphophoneme-phoneme pair is in the focus.

In fact, the form of the GR rules can be simplified to $W \overset{1\diamond}{\Rrightarrow} W'$ if we ignore certain epenthetic rules and are not interested in a length-based rule conflict resolution scheme that is supported by the full compilation method. In this case the argument languages W and W' are subsets of $\Sigma^*\diamond\Sigma^*$.

Under the simplification, the rules (8) and (9) give rise to the GR rules (10) and (11). In these rules, the *dots* symbol $\ldots$ denotes the language Σ^*.

(10) $\ldots\diamond\,\langle \text{iE-eE}\rangle{:}e\ldots \overset{1\diamond}{\Rrightarrow}$
      $\ldots\{{:}e,{:}a,{:}o\}\,{:}C\diamond\,\langle \text{iE-eE}\rangle{:}e\ldots$

(11) $\ldots\{{:}e,{:}a,{:}o\}\,{:}C\diamond\,\langle \text{iE-eE}\rangle{:}\ldots \overset{1\diamond}{\Rrightarrow}$
      $\ldots\{{:}e,{:}a,{:}o\}\,{:}C\diamond\,\langle \text{iE-eE}\rangle{:}e\ldots.$

One of the nice features of the GR-based approach is that the GR rules can be combined before they are compiled into finite automata over Σ. In other words, given the rules $W_1 \overset{2\diamond}{\Rrightarrow} W_1'$ and $W_2 \overset{2\diamond}{\Rrightarrow} W_2'$, there is an easy way to choose W_3 and W_3' in such a way that $W_3 \overset{2\diamond}{\Rrightarrow} W_3'$ equals to the intersection of the first two rules.

Using this closure property of GR rules, we can represent the rules (7-a) and (7-b) with a single GR rule:

$$(12)\quad
\left\{
\begin{array}{c}
\cdots\diamond_E\,\langle \text{iE-eE}\rangle{:}e\ldots \\
\ldots\{{:}e,{:}a,{:}o\}\,{:}C\diamond_E\,\langle \text{iE-eE}\rangle{:}\ldots \\
\cdots\diamond_G\,\langle \text{iG-eG}\rangle{:}e\ldots \\
\ldots\{{:}e,{:}o\}\,{:}C\diamond_G\,\langle \text{iG-eG}\rangle{:}\ldots
\end{array}
\right\}
\overset{1\{\diamond_E,\diamond_G\}}{\Rrightarrow}
\left\{
\begin{array}{c}
\ldots\{{:}e,{:}a,{:}o\}\,{:}C\diamond_E\,\langle \text{iE-eE}\rangle{:}e\ldots \\
\ldots\{{:}e,{:}o\}\,{:}C\diamond_G\,\langle \text{iG-eG}\rangle{:}e\ldots
\end{array}
\right\}.$$

3.4 One-Level Morphology

There is a striking redundancy in the GR rule (12). Namely, the type of the harmony process, i.e. 'E' vs. 'G', is indicated in every string twice: by the morphophoneme and by the marker.

Due to this observation, there is a motivation to replace the marked morphophoneme-phoneme correspondence pair like $\diamond_E\langle \text{iE-eE}\rangle{:}e$ with a marked phoneme $\diamond_E e$, reduce the two-level rules into *one-level rules* and redefine the alphabet Σ as a set of phoneme symbols (and some other symbols).

The key insight for valuing the resulting *one-level grammar* is that the morphophonemes and the markers specify the same underlying segmental positions. Roughly speaking, they are just two means to signal the associated variation and morphological contexts. The first is collective while the second is distributive. In order to switch fully to the one-level representation, we have to introduce a couple of useful ideas.

The *first idea* makes the one-level representation richer and sufficient for linguistically appropriate morphological analysis. In Bantu linguistics, the linguistically appropriate detail is often synonymous with phonemic transcriptions and the associated interlinear morpheme glosses. The format of the glossed linguistic examples is currently well regulated by the Leipzig Glossing Rules (Bickel et al., 2008).

A possible scheme for conflating the transcription and the glosses into a one-level string has been drafted by the author (Yli-Jyrä, 2011). This scheme would encode the example (2-c) as the following string where a white space separates individual symbols.

(13)   m ó n ::(KWA) :'see' - e n ::APPL
        - á ::FV

The *second idea* is to open the GR rule in such a way that the markers in W and W' are more transparent and the lexicon can predetermine at least some of the marker positions. The markers can specify the positions of the morphophonemes and simultaneously avoid postulating a single underlying string of morphophonemes. The goal of transparency is achieved by elaborating the notion of markers.

4 Positionwise Flags

Like the conventional flags (Beesley and Karttunen, 2003), the positionwise flag diacritics are designed for use in the lexicon. The positionwise flags are, however, in some sense more general because they have a further use in the morphophonological rule component. They correspond to the markers of the GR rule and can therefore be viewed as user's interface to the internals of the GR operation.

Let p be a name for a morphophonological *process* and k an even number of *ranks* in the positionwise flags. Based on these parameters, we define a set of markers and positionwise flags according to Table 3. Let P be the set of all names of morphophonological processes. For every such name, there is a series of ranked markers and flags. The p-flags and the corresponding markers are semantically equivalent, but used in different notations: The p-flags resemble the conventional flags and can be used in finite state lexicon formalisms whereas the corresponding markers are associated with the GR-based compilation formulas and its mathematical presentation. All ranked markers/p-flags constitute the set M.

marker	p-flag	feeded by	successful?
$\diamond_{1.p}$	@1.p@		yes
$\diamond_{2.p}$	@2.p@		no
$\diamond_{3.p}$	@3.p@	rank 2	yes
$\diamond_{4.p}$	@4.p@	rank 3	no
$\vdots$	$\vdots$	$\vdots$	$\vdots$
$\diamond_{k.p}$	@k.p@	rank $k-1$	no

Table 3: Markers and positionwise flag diacritics

The integer number in each marker/flag specifies the respective rank. Previously, Frank Liang (Liang, 1983) have proposed ranked hyphenation patterns that lie at odd- and even-numbered levels. Following the same idea, an odd-ranked marker is used to indicating a position of a *successful* (or valid) allomorphophoneme while an even-ranked marker is used to represent a *failing* (or invalid) allomorphophoneme.

Beyond the rank 1, the markers that have a low rank *feed* the markers that have an immediately higher rank. This means that a higher marker has the power only if it has an overriding effect. In the context of hyphenation patterns (Liang, 1983), this is so obvious that one does not even think of it. In the current context, the principle of such feeding can greatly simplify the specification of contexts in the case of rule exceptions. Still, it does not lead to similar problems as the rule ordering of transducer cascades, because the feeding order correlates now with the disjunctive ordering of parallel rules rather than the multiple levels of phonological representation.

Explaining the meaning of the p-flags requires some related mathematical definitions. The function $h : (\Sigma \cup M)^* \to \Sigma^*$ is a string projection that essentially deletes the markers M in its input strings. The strings with a successful marker form the languae $S = \{x\diamond_{i.p}y \mid xy \in \Sigma^*, i \in \{1, 3, ..., k-1\}, p \in P\}$. The strings with an unsuccessful marker form the language $F = \{x\diamond_{i.p}y \mid xy \in \Sigma^*, i \in \{2, 4, ..., k\}, p \in P\}$. Finally, the strings with markers of rank 1 and 2 form the language $B = \{x\diamond_{i.p}y \mid xy \in \Sigma^*, i \in \{1, 1\}, p \in P\}$.

4.1 Flags and Markers in the Lexicon

An *uncompiled lexicon L* defines a subset of $(\Sigma \cup M)^*$. The format of this lexicon is such that strings may contain several markers. Such markings will be distributed in the *normalized lexicon N_0* by reducing the number of markers in the string. The normalized lexicon is given by
$$N_0 = h(L) \cup \{h(x)\, m\, h(y) \mid m \in M, xmy \in L\}$$
and it contains three components:

$$\boxed{N_0 \cap \Sigma^*} \quad \boxed{N_0 \cap F} \quad \boxed{N_0 \cap S}.$$

Define the relation $\mu : \Sigma^* M \Sigma^* \times \Sigma^* M \Sigma^*$ as the set $\{(x \diamond_{i.p} y, x \diamond_{j.p} y) \mid 1 \leq j < i \leq k, p \in P, x, y \in \Sigma^*\}$. Now the lexicon with positionwise flags is compiled into a set of unmarked strings by applying the GR rule as follows:

$$[N_0 \cap \Sigma^*] \cap [(N_0 \cap F) \overset{1M}{\Rightarrow} \mu(N_0 \cap S)].$$

By the definition of the GR rule (Yli-Jyrä and Koskenniemi, 2006), this reduces to

$$[N_0 \cap \Sigma^*] - h((N_0 \cap F) - \mu(N_0 \cap S)).$$

4.2 Flags and Markers in the Grammar

The normalized lexicon N_0 is accompanied by the *one-level grammar* $G \subseteq S \cup F$ that consists of marked strings. The set of marked strings is used in some sense like the more familiar notion of a rule set. Formally, this means that the grammar is itself a language. This language consists of two components:

$$\boxed{G \cap B} \quad \boxed{G - B}.$$

The first component is automatically activated for application to the strings, while the second component waits for joining the application when the lexicon or previously applied marked strings exhibit flags that could trigger further marked strings.

The application of the first component of the grammar gives rise to the second generation of the normalized lexicon:

$$N_1 = [N_0 \cup [G \cap B]] - \mu(N_0 \cup [G \cap B]).$$

The activation of the remaining marked strings in the grammar is based on the *increment* relation $\iota : \Sigma^* M \Sigma^* \times \Sigma^* M \Sigma^*$ defined as the set $\{(x \diamond_{i.p} y, x \diamond_{i+1.p} y) \mid 2 \leq i < k, p \in P, x, y \in \Sigma^*\}$. Through this, any further generation of the normalized lexicon is obtained as

$$N_{i+1} = [N_i \cup [G \cap \iota(N_i)]] - \mu(N_i \cup [G \cap \iota(N_i)]).$$

The number of ranks k determines how many generations of the normalized lexicon need to be computed. Because the second generation, N_1, can still introduce markers whose rank is 1, the last normalized lexicon to be computed is N_k. When this has been computed, we obtain the markerless language of (glossed) transcriptions by evaluationg the formula:

$$[N_k \cap \Sigma^*] - h((N_k \cap F) - \mu(N_k \cap S)).$$

4.3 The Lexicon-Grammar Teamwork

Due to the shared positionwise flags / markers, the lexicon and the grammar can help each other. The lexicon specifies the default allomorphophonemes and the grammar can implement the alternations that choose alternative allophonemes.

Consider the morphophoneme $\langle$iE-eE$\rangle$. In the one-level lexicon this morphophoneme becomes an ambiguity class $\{\diamond_{1,E}$i, $\diamond_{2,E}$e $\}$. In a finite-state lexicon formalism, this ambiguity class could correspond to a user-defined constant symbol that denotes a regular expression `[@1.E@i | @2.E@e]`. The elements of the ambiguity class signal, on one hand, that the default allomorphophoneme is /i/ and that the allomorphophoneme /e/ is not acceptable by default. On the other, the markers/p-flags attached to the allomorphophonemes establish positions to which the grammar can refer. The grammar then alters the prominency of the marked allomorphophonemes by increasing their ranks through such marked strings that represent the appropriate environments of the non-default allomorphophonemes.

In practice, the grammar is given through some finite-state formalism that is now extended with the p-flag notation. In this formalism, the FHH rules are given through the regular expressions

$$\text{(14)} \qquad \texttt{...[e|o] C [@2.G@i|@3.G@e]...}$$
$$\texttt{...[e|a|o] C [@2.E@i|@3.E@e]...}$$

whose union expresses the string set

$$\text{(15)} \qquad \left\{ \begin{array}{l} \Sigma^*\{e,o\}C\{\diamond_{2.G}i, \diamond_{3.G}e\}\Sigma^* \\ \Sigma^*\{e,a,o\}C\{\diamond_{2.E}i, \diamond_{3.E}e\}\Sigma^* \end{array} \right\}.$$

The regular expressions should match full-fledged one-level representations, but the simplified expressions in (14) concern only the phonemic content. The first pattern in (14) states that if an allomorphophoneme /i/ governed by the General FHH process occurs after /e/ or /o/, it is wrong (rank 2 means a failure), but the allomorphophoneme /e/ in the same position is perfect (rank 3 means a success).

If one wishes, the regular expressions like (14) can be written with a more intuitive notation that mimics the rules of generative phonology but are actually born in the currently used one-level representation:

$$\text{(16)} \qquad \begin{array}{l} \texttt{i}_{2.G} \rightarrow \texttt{e}_{3.G} \ / \ \{e,o\} \ C \ \underline{\quad} \\ \texttt{i}_{2.E} \rightarrow \texttt{e}_{3.E} \ / \ \{e,a,o\} \ C \ \underline{\quad}. \end{array}$$

5 Reflections and Further Work

It is noteworthy that the new grammar (14) is substantially simpler and more intuitive than the one in (12). It seems to express the linguistic generalizations such as (1) compactly and directly (but as a morphophonological rather than a phonological process). These are just a few reasons that suggest that the positionwise flags may help increase the simultaneous human- and machine-readability of computational descriptions.

Another interesting thing is that the normalized lexicon is a dynamic data structure that contains latent phonological strings and their known allo-morphophonemes. The resulting adaptability of the lexicon may have uses in machine learning and computational typology. The normalized lexicon is also a very efficient debugging tool if some rules are missing or too strict.

The current method does not support rules whose environment conditions refer to morpho-phonemic contexts. Further investigations are needed to find out how severe a restriction this is since sufficiently precise conditions are still often expressible through the surface string and the interspersed glosses. If necessary, the support for markers in the contexts can be added although this would complicate the current method. Another extension would allow the normalized lexicon to contain pairs of positions i.e. substrings too. Such a data structure could define autosegments such as tones and metrical structures and support feature spreading and other suprasegmental processes, for example. There is, however, a danger that such an extension would make the system intractable.

In order to use simpler GR rules in compilation, the current presentation ignored the epenthesis rules. It turns out that the one-level representation is closely related to the model of the Item and Arrangement morphology (Hockett, 1954). In the IA model, epenthesis is not a real problem.

The surface orientation of the system is not necessarily a bad thing from the methodological point of view. One-level rules are easier to write, especially when segments are governed by more than one morphophonological process. The processes have the minimum impact on each other's alphabet because the surface string and the glosses are not split into separate cases.

Further research can find specialized and more efficient algorithms for the manipulation of markers/p-flags. It is also possible to optimize the representation of the one-level grammar G. Rules whose context conditions contain gaps are currently expensive because they can have a big effect on the state complexity. The problem arises only in rules that have not been constrained with a lexicon.

The author has discovered that the finite-state representation of the grammar can be optimized through on-demand compilation techniques. For example, one should avoid the eager expansion of the dots symbol '...' when compiling the regular expressions in the grammar G. To compute the original semantics of the intersection $G \cap N_i$, one can compute the image of the regular relation $(\mathrm{Id}(G) \circ T_1) \circ (T_2 \circ \mathrm{Id}(N_i))$ where the intermediately composed relation T_1 substitutes the occurrences of the symbol ... with the language ...* and the relation T_2 substitutes the occurrences of the symbol ... with the alphabet Σ. Both compositions in the parentheses have only a small effect on the size of the automata and the final composition is then computed in a very efficient way. However, this approach works only if the regular expressions do not contain negations. Therefore, the author is looking for ways to generalize the optimization to regular expressions that contain negations.

Although the positionwise flags can be combined with the conventional flag diacritics, this might be an error-prone activity, at least without a careful design step during which the possible interactions are properly managed.

In the context of computational Bantu morphology (Bosch, 2010), conventional flag diacritics and morphophonological rules have been proven very useful. This may suggest that also the positionwise flags have relevance to the Bantu morphophonology and morphotactics.

The author has started to evaluate the applicability of the currently presented formalism in the context of the computational description of tonal Bantu languages such as Kwanyama as well as in the construction of synchronic computational models of some closely related Bantu dialects. In this context, the one-level representation that reflects the Leipzig Glossing Rules (Bickel et al., 2008) is instrumental in fixing the desired morphosyntactic representation. The increased transparency of the grammar and the described strings is likely to support the notion of literate programming in the language documentation context.

References

Jan W. Amtrup. 2004. Efficient finite state unification morphology. In *Proceedings of the 20th international conference on Computational Linguistics,*

COLING '04, Stroudsburg, PA, USA. Association for Computational Linguistics.

Robert Austerlitz. 1967. The distributional identification of Finnish morphophonemes. *Language*, 43(1):20–33.

Kenneth R. Beesley and Lauri Karttunen. 2003. *Finite State Morphology*. CSLI Studies in Computational Linguistics. CSLI Publications, Stanford, CA, USA.

Balthasar Bickel, Bernard Comrie, and Martin Haspelmath. 2008. The Leipzig Glossing Rules. Conventions for interlinear morpheme by morpheme glosses. Max Planck Institute for Evolutionary Anthropology, Dept. of Linguistics. Retrieved 2011-02-15 from http://www.eva.mpg.de/lingua/resources/glossing-rules.php.

Olli Blåberg. 1994. *The Ment model. Complex states in finite-state morphology*. Number 27 in Reports from Uppsala University, Linguistics (RUUL). Department of Linguistics, Uppsala University, Uppsala, Sweden.

Glenn David Blank. 1989. A finite and real-time processor for natural language. *Communications of the ACM*, 32(10):1174–1189, October.

Sonja Bosch. 2010. Rule-based morphological analysis: Shared challenges, shared solution. In Karsten Legère and Christina Thornell, editors, *Bantu Languages: Analyses, Description and Theory*, volume 20 of *East African Languages and Dialects*, pages 1–15, Köln. Rüdiger Köppe Verlag.

Yael Cohen-Sygal and Shuly Wintner. 2006. Finite-state registered automata for non-concatenative morphology. *Computational Linguistics*, 32(1):49–82.

Riikka Halme. 2004. *A Tonal Grammar of Kwanyama*, volume 8 of *Namibian African Studies*. Rüdiger Köppe Verlag, Köln.

Charles Hockett. 1954. Two models of grammatical description. *Word*, 10:210–231.

Ronald M. Kaplan and Martin Kay. 1994. Regular models of phonological rule systems. *Computational Linguistics*, 20(3):331–378, September.

George Anton Kiraz. 1997. Compiling regular formalisms with rule features into finite-state automata. In *35th ACL 1997, 8th EACL 1997, Proceedings of the Conference*, pages 329–336, Madrid, Spain.

András Kornai. 1996. Vectorized finite state automaton. In András Kornai, editor, *Extended Finite State Models of Language, Proceedings of the ECAI'96 Workshop*, Studies in Natural Language Processing, pages 36–41. Cambridge University Press.

Kimmo Koskenniemi and Miikka Silfverberg. 2010. A method for compiling two-level rules with multiple contexts. In *Proc. 11th ACL-SIGMORPHON, ACL 2010*, pages 38–45, Uppsala, Sweden, 15 July.

Kimmo Koskenniemi. 1983. *Two-level morphology: a general computational model for word-form recognition and production*. Number 11 in Publications. Department of General Linguistics, University of Helsinki, Helsinki.

Kimmo Koskenniemi. 1991. A discovery procedure for two-level phonology. In A. Zampolli, L. Cignoni, and C. Peters, editors, *Computational Lexicology and Lexicography: A Special Issue Dedicated to Bernard Quemada*, volume I, pages 451–46. Giardini Editori e stampatori, Pisa.

Franklin Mark Liang. 1983. *Word Hy-phen-a-tion by Com-pu-ter*. Ph.D. thesis, Stanford University, Department of Computer Science, August.

Wilhelm J. G. Möhlig and Jekura U. Kavari. 2008. *Reference Grammar of Herero (Otjiherero)*. Number 3 in Southern African Languages and Cultures. Rüdiger Köppe Verlag, Köln.

Derek Nurse and Gérald Philippson. 2003. *The Bantu languages*. Routledge, New York.

Helmut Schmid. 2005. A programming language for finite state transducers. In Anssi Yli-Jyrä, Lauri Karttunen, and Juhani Karhumäki, editors, *FSMNLP*, volume 4002 of *LNCS/LNAI*, pages 308–309. Springer.

Viktor Trón, Péter Halácsy, Rebrus Peter, András Rung, Péter Vajda, and Simon Eszter. 2006. Hunmorph.hu: Hungarian lexical database and morphological grammar. In *Proceedings of LREC 2006*, pages 1670–1673.

Harald Trost. 1991. Recognition and generation of word form for natural language understanding systems: Integrating two-level morphology and feature unification. *Applied Artificial Intelligence*, 5(4):411–457.

Anssi Yli-Jyrä and Kimmo Koskenniemi. 2004. Compiling contextual restrictions on strings into finite-state automata. In Loek Cleophas and Bruce W. Watson, editors, *The Eindhoven FASTAR Days, Proceedings*, number 04/40 in Computer Science Reports, Eindhoven, The Netherlands. Technische Universiteit Eindhoven.

Anssi Yli-Jyrä and Kimmo Koskenniemi. 2006. Compiling generalized two-level rules and grammars. In Tapio Salakoski, Filip Ginter, Sampo Pyysalo, and Tapio Pahikkala, editors, *FinTAL*, volume 4139 of *LNCS*, pages 174–185. Springer.

Anssi Yli-Jyrä. 2008. Applications of diamonded double negation. In *Finite-State Methods and Natural Language Processing, 6th International Workshop, FSMNL-2007, Potsdam, Germany, September 14–16, Revised Papers*. Potsdam University Press, Potsdam.

Anssi Yli-Jyrä. 2011. Lifting interlinear morpheme glosses into plain strings in computational morphology. Manuscript 14p. Submitted in March 2011.

ISSN 1736-6305 Vol. 11
http://hdl.handle.net/10062/16955

III Regular Short Papers

Experiments to Investigate the Utility of Nearest Neighbour Metrics Based on Linguistically Informed Features for Detecting Textual Plagiarism

Per Almquist and Jussi Karlgren
Swedish Institute of Computer Science (SICS), Stockholm*
peralmq@kth.se jussi@sics.se

Abstract

Plagiarism detection is a challenge for linguistic models — most current implemented models use simple occurrence statistics for linguistic items. In this paper we report two experiments related to plagiarism detection where we use a model for distributional semantics and of sentence stylistics to compare sentence by sentence the likelihood of a text being partly plagiarised. The result of the comparison are displayed for visual inspection by a plagiarism assessor.

1 Plagiarism detection

Plagiarism is the act of copying or including another author's ideas, language, or writing, without proper acknowledgment of the original source. Plagiarism analysis is a collective term for computer-based methods to identify plagiarism. (Stein et al., 2007a) Plagiarism analysis can be performed *intrinsically* — a text is examined for internal consistency, to detect suspicious passages that appear to diverge from the surrounding text, or *externally* — a text is inspected with respect to some known corpus to find passages with suspiciously similar content to other text.

In external plagiarism detection, it is assumed that the source document d_{src} for a given plagiarized document d_{plg} can be found in a target document collection D. Typically, plagiarism detection then proceeds in three stages:

1. candidate selection through retrieval of a set of candidate source documents D_{src} is retrieved from D_{plg};

2. candidates d_{src} from D_{src} is compared passage by passage with the suspicious document d_{plg} and every case where a passage from d_{plg} appears to be similar to some passage in some d_{src} is noted;

3. followed by some post-processing to remove false hits.(Stein et al., 2007b; Potthast et al., 2010)

2 PAN workshop series

A series of workshops on Plagiarism Analysis, Authorship Identification, and Near-Duplicate Detection, organised since 2007, have provided the field with a shared task and test materials in the form of gold standard text collections with manually and automatically constructed plagiarised sections marked for experimental purposes. Some of the plagiarised sections are *obfuscated* with word replacement, edits, and permutations. The research results from the workshops are comparable, since they are to a large extent performed on the same materials using the same starting points and same target measures.

Example results relevant to this study (and on the whole none too surprising) are that unobfuscated plagiarism can be detected with a reasonable accuracy by the top plagiarism detectors. The recall decreases slightly with increasing obfuscation and that longer stretches of plagiarised material are easier to detect than shorter segments.(Potthast et al., 2010)

3 Our experimental set-up

The base of the experiment described here is to test a finer-grained analysis of plagiarised texts than other previous work. We use a sentence-by-sentence comparison of the suspicious text (d_{plg}) with all sentences of each target text (d_{src}) in D_{src} using two different similarity measures: one based

This work is performed at SICS, supported by the Swedish Research Council (Vetenskapsrådet) through the project "Distributionally derived grammatical analysis models" as part of Per Almquist's M Sc program at the Royal Institute of Technology (KTH), Stockholm

Table 1: Stylometric sentence features

Name	Description
arg	argumentative (*merely, for sure, ...*)
cog	cognitive process (*remember, think, ...*)
com	complex (average word length > 6 characters or sentence length > 25 words)
date	one or more date references
fin	money symbols or percentage signs
fpp	first person pronouns
le	named entities (person, organization)
loc	location expression
neg	grammatical negations
num	numbers
pa	place adverbials (*inside, outdoors ...*)
pun	punctuation inside sentence
se	split infinitives or stranded prepositions
spp	second person pronouns
sub	subordinate clauses
ta	time adverbials (*early, presently, soon ...*)
tim	one or more time expressions
tpp	third person pronouns
uni	symbols representing units of measurement

on overall semantic similarity, the other on specific stylometric measures.

The experiment is not a full scale evaluation of our method but is intended to test the practicability of our approach. Given that we have a suspicious text and some reasonable number of candidate source texts (through some retrieval procedure) — can we detect the likelihood of plagiarism in a text by inspecting the sentence sequence of the suspicious text one by one? This paper reports a selected plot dry run of the methodology performed over a number of sample texts.

3.1 Data

The experiments are performed on the PAN-PC-09(Potthast et al., 2009)[1] corpus since it can be used free of charge for research and contains plagiarized passages which has previously been marked and labeled as plagiarism, so that we know beforehand which passages are plagiarism.

The corpus is divided in two sets, one for training and one for test. The training set is further divided into three parts (D_{plg}, D_{src}, and L). D_{plg} contain the documents that are suspicious and might plagiarize documents in D_{src}, where D_{src} contain only orginal documents that make out the sources of any plagiarism in D_{plg}, and L is the solution, the labeling that tells us which sentences in D_{plg} that plagiarize what sentence in D_{src}.

---

[1] http://www.uni-weimar.de/cms/medien/ webis/research/corpora/pan-pc-09.html

3.2 Nearest neighbour metrics

We use cosine similarity (as defined in equation 1) to represent how similar two vectors are.

$$sim_{COS}(\vec{x}, \vec{y}) = \frac{\vec{x} \cdot \vec{y}}{|\vec{x}||\vec{y}|} = \frac{\sum_{i=1}^{n} x_i y_i}{\sqrt{\sum_{i=1}^{n} x_i^2} \sqrt{\sum_{i=1}^{n} y_i^2}} \quad (1)$$

For every sentence $s \in d_{plg}$ its nearest neighbour score (as defined in equation 2) is calculated.

$$\max(sim_{COS}(s, x)) \text{ for all sentences } x \in D_{src} \quad (2)$$

The nearest neighbour metric has the fortunate feature that a value of 1 describes identical or duplicate vectors. So if we were to find nearest neighbour values of 1 those two sentences would be very alike and therefore we would be able to assume that the newer sentence plagiarizes the older sentence.

In this experiment two settings for the experiment were used. In experiment one below we evaluate how well the nearest neighbour metric of two vectors in a semantic *word-space model* manage to detect plagiarism. In experiment two below we evaluate how well the nearest neighbour metric of two binary vectors based on 19 different stylometric features manage to detect plagiarism.

3.3 Target plots

As an example plagiarism inspection mechanism we plot the nearest neighbour metric with the sentences of a text along the x-axis against the score of the sentence. The objective is to find a stretch of material where several sentences have high nearest neighbour scores. As a comparison we will plot the gold standard plagiarism labeling of respective sentence and let the label for a sentence being plagiarism have value 1 and 0 otherwise. Now we can just plot our nearest neighbour scores and our modified labels against the sentences in the corpus.

3.4 Experiment 1: semantic similarity

The sentences of d_{plg} were compared by semantic similarity using a word-space model (Schütze, 1993) as a base for computing similarity between sentences. Each sentence was represented by the centroid of its constituent words in a word-space trained on the entire test corpus. The implementation was based on previous work on effective word-space models.

> "The word-space model is a computational model of word meaning that utilizes the distributional patterns of words collected over large text data to represent semantic similarity between words in terms of spatial proximity." (Sahlgren, 2006).

Obfuscation	Semantic space	Stylometric space
none		
low		
high		

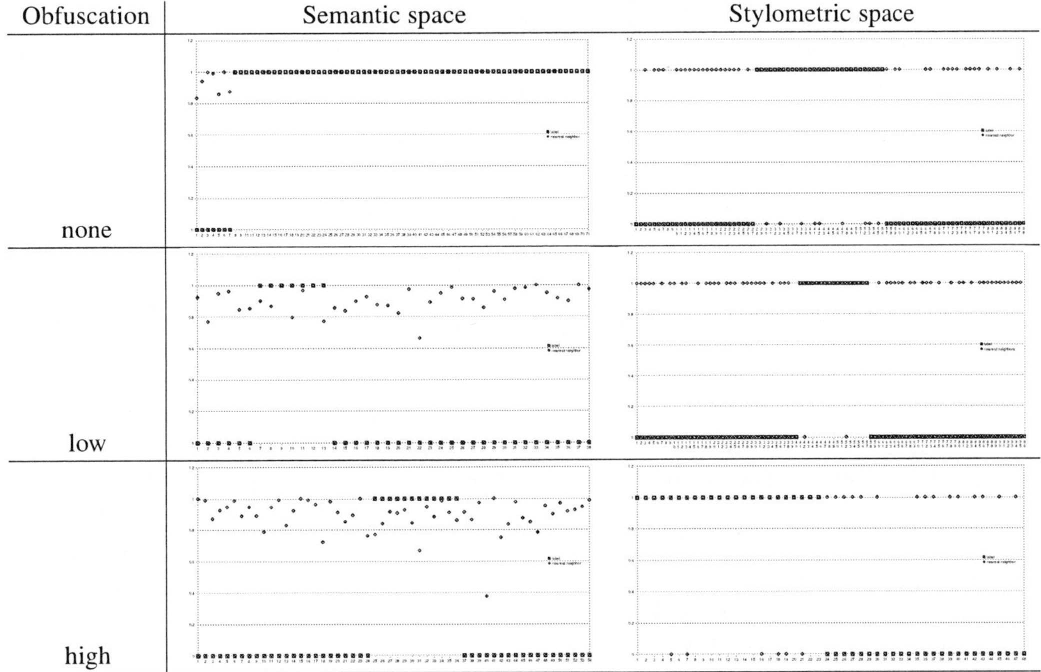

Table 2: Plots of semantic and stylometric similarity for texts with known plagiarized sections

The word-space model, from the work in (Kanerva, 1988) and (Sahlgren, 2006), models the meaning of words according to their distribution, creating a representation of their semantics based on where and how in the text the words appear. The word-space is a high dimensional vector space where every word is represented by a vector. Two words are semantically similar if their respective vectors are similar. For example the words "yellow" and "green" could be argued to have similar semantic meaning. So the vectors for yellow and green should be expected to be similar as seen in figure 1.

Figure 1: The vectors for the words "yellow" and "green" in a semantic space.

The word-space model is, as its name implies, mainly used to model words. It can however be used to model other linguistic entities such as sentences and documents using workarounds. A sentence can be represented by taking the centroid of the sentence's individual word's vectors. Therefore if the sentence "A yellow car." was changed to "A green car." the centroid ought not to change too much since the only change to the centroid would be one vector that in the first case represented the word "yellow" and in the second case the word "green" and these vectors should be fairly similar, as seen in figure 2. In our model we use a semantic word-space to model sentences under the hypothesis that if a sentence were to be obfuscated its semantic similarity would be kept. We build a semantic space for the corpus under consideration and assign each sentence a representative centroid vector of 3000 real dimensions for every sentence in the corpus. We then perform, for every sentence vector $\vec{s}$ from D_{plg}, the nearest neighbour search $nn(\vec{s}, \vec{s_{src}})$ against all the vectors $\vec{s_{src}}$ in D_{src}.

Figure 2: A centroid of a changed sentence.

3.5 Experiment 2: stylometric similarity

The 19 stylometric features that were chosen can be seen in table 1, and were chosen based on the work in (Biber, 1988) and (Karlgren, 2000). Our intention was to capture the authors' writing styles. We tried to find features that would not change if another author were to copy the text and even obfuscate it. Therefore we chose features that

- binds the texts to its topic, such as numbers or units of measurement.

- anchors the text to its context, i.e. named entities, location or time.

- captures peculiarities in the author's writing style: split infinitives or stranded prepositions.

- indicates how complex the language is, such as long sentences or subordinate clauses.

For every sentence in D_{plg} we extracted the stylometric features into a 19th dimensional binary vector $\vec{f}$. We then extracted 470 unique 19th dimensional binary vectors $\mathbf{F}_{src}$, based on the same stylometric features, from D_{src}. Then we performed the nearest neighbour search $nn(\vec{f}, \vec{f}_{src})$ against all the vectors $\vec{f}_{src}$ in $\mathbf{F}_{src}$.

4 Results and Conclusions

Table 2 shows the results for the nearest neighbour scores for both experiments, run on a test text with a known plagiarized section with the corresponding source text. We have three plots representing different levels of obfuscation of plagiarism, namely; a high level of obfuscation, a low level of obfuscation, and no obfuscation. To determine the effectiveness of each nearness measure, the results (red rhomboids) are displayed together with an indication of which section of the text is plagiarized (blue squares) noted with a score of 1 and a score of 0 for the non-plagiarized sections.

4.1 Experiment 1: semantic similarity

We find that the semantic space model (1) is a good detector for no obfuscation; (2) does not hold up for obfuscated materials, neither for low or high obfuscation since it is based on the presence of each word in the text; and consequentially (3) needs tuning so that specifically topical terms are weighted up compared to less topical terms. This should be done specifically for the topic in the candidate document being examined, since presumably the topic under consideration is the most likely topic to be plagiarized.

4.2 Experiment 2: stylometric similarity

We find that the stylometric similarity score (1) which is a dramatic dimensionality reduction unsurprisingly gives a large number of false positives for all levels of obfuscation; and (2) gives a comparatively high precision even for a high level of obfuscation.

4.3 Directions

Coming experiments will establish whether the combination of the two knowledge sources and the preservation of sequence information in the candidate source texts might provide effective results for a plagiarism detection task. Previous experiments on sequence encoding of stylistic information seem to indicate that sequential information can contain the right type of information to distinguish writing style. (Karlgren and Eriksson, 2007)

References

Douglas Biber. 1988. *Variation across Speech and Writing*. Cambridge University Press.

Pentti Kanerva. 1988. *Sparse Distributed Memory*. MIT Press, Cambridge, MA, USA.

Jussi Karlgren and Gunnar Eriksson. 2007. Authors, genre, and linguistic convention. In *SIGIR Workshop on Plagiarism Analysis, Authorship Identification, and Near-Duplicate Detection*.

Jussi Karlgren. 2000. *Stylistic Experiments In Information Retrieval*. Ph.D. thesis, Stockholm University.

Martin Potthast, Andreas Eiselt, Benno Stein, Alberto Barrón-Cedeño, and Paolo Rosso. 2009. PAN Plagiarism Corpus PAN-PC-09.

Martin Potthast, Alberto Barrón-Cedeño, Andreas Eiselt, Benno Stein, and Paolo Rosso. 2010. Overview of the 2nd international competition on plagiarism detection. In Martin Braschler and Donna Harman, editors, *Notebook Papers of CLEF 2010 LABs and Workshops*. CLEF, Padua, Italy.

Magnus Sahlgren. 2006. *The Word-Space Model*. Ph.D. thesis, Stockholm University.

Hinrich Schütze. 1993. Word space. In *Proceedings of NIPS'93*, San Francisco. Morgan Kaufmann.

Benno Stein, Moshe Koppel, and Efstathios Stamatatos. 2007a. Plagiarism analysis, authorship identification, and near-duplicate detection (PAN 07). *SIGIR Forum*, 42(2):68–71.

Benno Stein, Sven Meyer zu Eissen, and Martin Potthast. 2007b. Strategies for retrieving plagiarized documents. In *Proceedings of SIGIR 07*. ACM.

ISSN 1736-6305 Vol. 11
http://hdl.handle.net/10062/16955

CFG Based Grammar Checker for Latvian

Daiga Deksne
Tilde
Vienības gatve 75a, Riga, Latvia
LV1004
daiga.deksne@tilde.lv

Raivis Skadiņš
Tilde
Vienības gatve 75a, Riga, Latvia
LV1004
raivis.skadins@tilde.lv

Abstract

This paper reports on the implementation of the Latvian grammar checker. It gives a brief introduction of the project scope − Latvian language, the previous implementation of the grammar checker and its limitations. Then, it describes the proposed approach. This paper also describes the Latvian parser used for this project and the quality measurement methods used for the quality assessment of the grammar checking system. Finally, the current state of the grammar checker work is presented.

1 Introduction

The grammar checker described in this paper is not the first implementation of a Latvian grammar checker. The first Latvian and Lithuanian grammar checkers were implemented in 2004 (Mackevičiūte, 2004). Grammar checkers where implemented using an advanced pattern matching. There were almost 200 rules such as:

- If there is any verb in the imperative mood followed by an adverb 'lūdzu' (please), then suggest inserting comma between these words.

- If there is a noun in the nominative followed by a (i) comma, (ii) preposition "uz" and (iii) pronoun "kurš" in the singular genitive or plural dative AND genders of noun and pronoun are different; then suggest changing the gender of the pronoun to be equal with the gender of the noun.

These rules highlighted many grammar errors, but the grammar checker had many deficiencies; the most significant were:

- This format did not describe long distance errors and errors that describe complex syntactic structures. Only patterns matching near words were allowed.

- Many rules had to be disabled because they matched false errors caused by high morphological ambiguity.

- The pattern matching algorithm was quite slow and each new grammar rule made the grammar checker slower and slower.

All the obstacles mentioned above led to the work presented in this paper. A new Latvian grammar checker has been built based on more powerful techniques.

2 Chosen approach

2.1 Main principles

As Latvian is highly inflected language with a high morphological ambiguity there are many long distance agreements between words and phrases in a sentence for which we need a deep syntactic analysis of phrases and sentence to find possible errors. The new implementation of the Latvian grammar checker is based on a parser. The parser works with two sets of rules:

- Rules describing Latvian grammar, e.g. correct syntactic structures (G rules);

- Rules describing grammar errors (E rules).

If parser would work only with G rules it would fully parse grammatically correct sentences and partly parse ungrammatical sentences and also sentences whose syntactic structure is too complex. For example, if we parse the Latvian text "Manam piemēram ir jābūt skaidram. Piemēram es saprotu to." (My example must be clear. For example I understand it) we get a parse as in Figure 1. The first sentence is fully parsed therefore we can consider it to be grammatical, the second sentence is only partially parsed therefore it is either ungrammatical or it is too complex to be fully parsed with a current set of G rules.

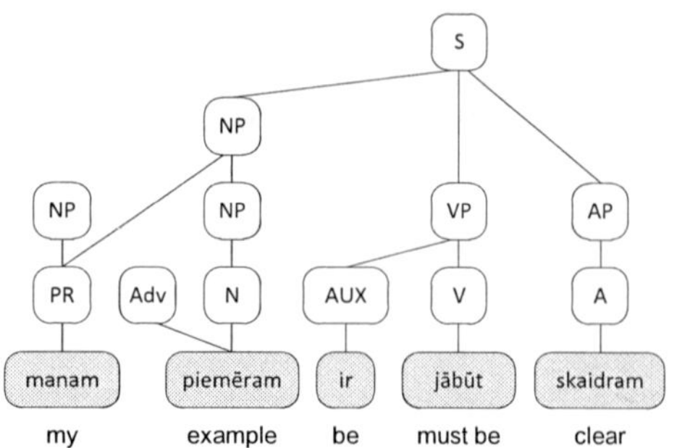

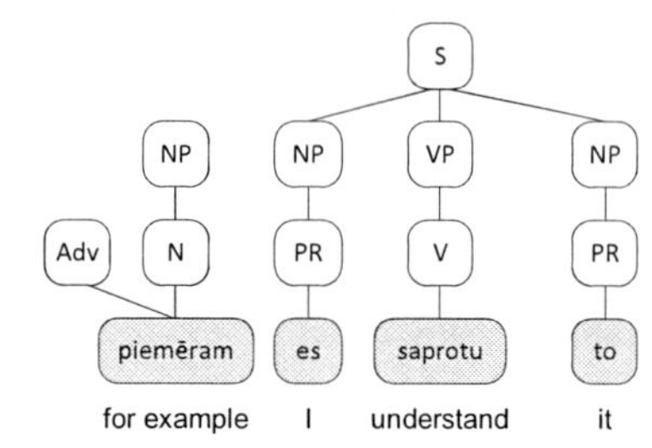

Figure 1. Result of parsing when parsing with G rules only.

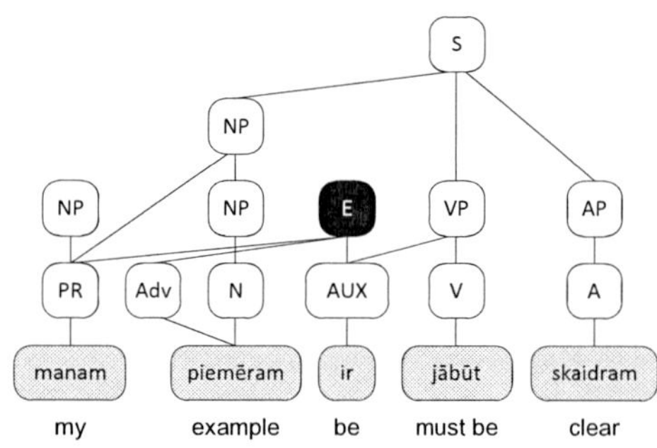

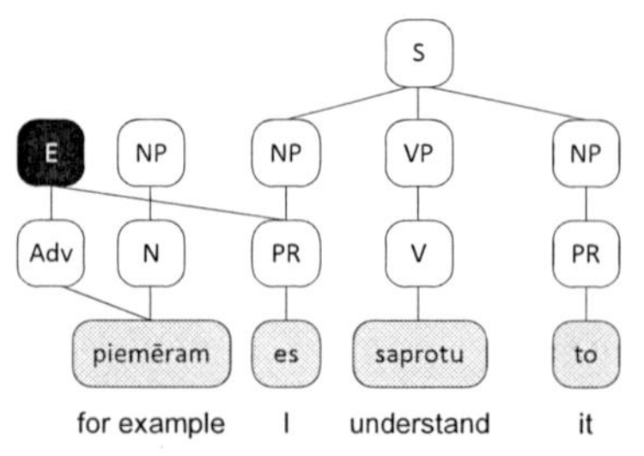

Figure 2. Result of parsing when parsing with both G and E rules.

If we add rules that also describe syntactic errors (E rules) we get a parse as in Figure 2. We get a similar result as before. The second sentence still is not fully parsed, but the parser has applied an error rule which finds the adverb

'piemēram' followed by pronoun. The parser has applied a similar error rule in the first sentence too. We can ignore this error rule in the first sentence because we know that that sentence is fully parsed (grammatical). But an error rule in the second sentence really marks a grammar error as the sentence (or phrases containing words marked by error rule) has not been fully parsed.

2.2 Parser

There are some requirements for the parser in order to use it to find grammar errors in the way described above. (i) The parser must be robust and return partial parses if the sentence cannot be fully parsed; (ii) The parser must be able to return all possible parses not only the one. As seen in Figure 2 error rules are not a part of parse trees; (iii) The parser must mark as correct only syntactic structures which really are correct; (iv) As we are working with Latvian, the parser rules must be powerful enough to deal with high morphological variance and ambiguity, word agreement and a rather free word order.

For the purposes of grammar checking we used the Latvian parser developed for machine translation purposes (Skadiņš *et al.*, 2007). The parser is using adapted CFG grammar (Chomsky, 1956) and it is based on the CYK algorithm (Younger, 1967) which allows partial parsing if the sentence cannot be fully parsed. The CYK algorithm is extended to support attributes for both terminals and non-terminals.

2.3 Rule format

As Latvian is a morphologically rich language Latvian grammar cannot be described with simple CFG rules like NP →N; NP →N N; S→NP V NP. The CFG used in the Latvian parser uses attributes for terminal and non-terminal symbols. For example, the noun phrase NP has attributes number, gender, case, person and some more. The error rules operate with terminals and phrases which were created with correct grammar rules. In the rule body there are usually some agreement or disagreement statements between attributes of several in itself correct phrases. There also might be an attribute comparison with an exact value. Also, lexical parts might figure in such rules. Often there is a correct grammar rule with the same right side constituents as in some error rule, only the comparison operators are different. See sample of a correct grammar and an error rule in Figure 3. The error rules have a section where the correct attribute values are assigned and instructions for suggestion generation are given.

```
NP -> attr:CAP main:NP
      Agree(attr:CAP, main:NP, Case,
Number, Gender)


ERROR-1 -> attr:CAP main:NP
      Disagree(attr:CAP,main:NP,
Case, Number, Gender)
GRAMMCHECK MarkAll
      attr:CAP.Gender=main:NP.Gender
      attr:CAP.Number=main:NP.Number
      SUGGEST(attr:CAP+main:NP)
```

Figure 3. Error and correct grammar rules.

If all comparison operators in the error rule are true, it does not guarantee that this error will be flagged as seen in Figure 2. For an error rule to succeed, the phrase it covers must be larger than the phrase for which the correct grammar rule works.

We also have a second grammar containing only error rules. It does not rely on correct grammar phrases. Capitalization and incorrect writing style errors enclose shorter phrases often with exact lexical values. The CapPattern operator defines the correct capital/noncapital letter usage in phrases with special meaning like organization, institution names, country names, job titles, etc. (See Figure 4). If the capitalization pattern is different for a phrase in the text, an error rule is triggered.

```
ERROR-14 -> attr:N attr:G main:N
      attr:N.Case==genitive
      attr:N.Number==singular
      attr:G.AdjEnd==definite
      main:N.Number==plural
      Agree(attr:G, main:N, Case,
Number, Gender)
      CapPattern fff
  LEX Amerika savienots valsts
```

Figure 4. Capitalization error rule.

3 The grammar checker architecture

The grammar checking system consists of separate components each having its own task. Most of them must be called in a certain order as each component relies on data structures prepared by the previous component.

The incoming text is split into separate token objects and sentence boundaries are detected in a tokenizer module. Subsequent components work only with a sentence, not with all incoming text at once. One of the following token types is assigned to every token object: word, abbreviation,

punctuation and numeric. In a simple error location module simple formatting errors are located using regular expressions. The analyzer module adds morphological analysis to every token. The parser component performs parsing using a given rule set. The parse walker component extracts the error trees from the parse result matrix and generates suggestions for error fixing. Results from this component and from the simple error locator are passed to the result preparation module which merges results and returns to a calling application.

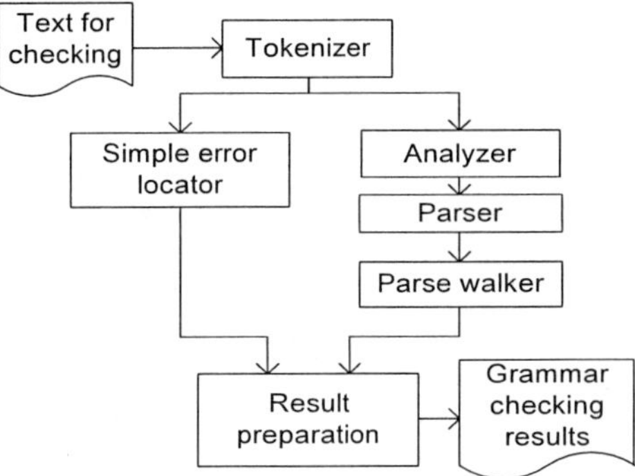

Figure 5. Grammar checker architecture.

4 The quality measuring methods

Test and development corpora are prepared to measure the quality of grammar and to have an assurance that the grammar checker works with approximately the same quality on any text. The test corpus is used only to measure the current quality of the grammar checker and rule developers do not see its content; the development corpus is also used in the process of tuning the rules.

Both corpora contain a variety of texts. About an equal amount of texts from every type are included in both corpora. We assume that potential users of the grammar checker will want to use it for checking grammar in the following types of texts: high school student essays, university student papers, blogs (qualitative, but not edited), e-mails (qualitative, but not edited), non-edited marketing texts, non-edited written texts from non-native Latvian speakers with good Latvian language knowledge, news texts, draft of some project tender (not edited), the works of new (amateur) writers, texts from the specialists in certain fields (teacher of physics, programmer, doctor, lawyer, geographer, psychologist, …)

The information about errors and expected corrections for each sentence is stored in a Golden Standard. The Golden Standard can be updated in two ways:

- A human annotator marked the sentences with error types prior to the grammar checking in the development corpus;

- After the grammar checking of both corpora, results are compared with the Golden Standard. Previously unseen cases are given to the human evaluator for the evaluation. The evaluator checks whether the error found by the grammar checker and the suggested correction is correct or not. Based on this information the Golden Standard is updated.

Several measurement values – recall, precision, f-measure, confidence interval for the precision – are calculated for every error type. The value of recall shows the possibility of finding all existing errors in the text. The recall is a number of correctly found errors (of type x) divided by number of errors (of type x) in corpus.

$$R(x) = tp(x)/(tp(x)+fn(x))$$

The value of precision shows the possibility of correctly finding errors in the text. The precision is a number of correctly found errors (of type x) divided by number of correctly and incorrectly found errors (of type x) in corpus.

$$P(x) = tp(x)/(tp(x)+fp(x))$$

Improvement of grammar rules is done based on the development corpus, the Golden Standard and evaluation results; the recompiled grammar is used for repeated evaluation and elaboration.

The test corpus contains 4814 sentences, the development corpus - 9364 sentences. Recall is given only for the development corpus, as the test corpus was not previously marked.

5　Results

So far our grammar checking system works with two grammars. The first one contains rules describing incorrect capitalization patterns in phrases and style errors. It contains 260 rules. The second is made of a set of 477 syntactically correct constructions describing rules and 237 error rules. Errors are classified with 21 error types. Precision and recall measures for eight most common error types are seen in Table 1.

The recall and precision values might be influenced by the fact that a sentence can contain several errors. Human evaluator is marking sentence with only a single error type. The grammar checking system is also selecting a single error per sentence – the one which covers the largest

phrase. The error types of the human evaluator and the grammar checking system might not match.

Error type	Recall	Precision	
	Dev. corp	Dev. corp.	Test. corp.
Agreement between words	0.247	0.543	0.426
Punctuation error at the end of sentence	0.240	0.957	—
Words must be written together	0.761	0.962	1.000
Comma error in insertions	0.563	0.913	0.892
Comma error in participial phrase	0.427	0.704	0.660
Wrong writing style	0.397	1.0	0.950
Comma error in equal parts of sentence	0.140	0.773	0.583
Comma error in sub clause	0.329	0.773	0.758
All error types	**0.290**	**0.833**	**0.710**

Table 1. Grammar checker results for development and test corpus.

The developed grammar checker is integrated in Microsoft Word and OpenOffice Writer text editors, it works as a background process and it is fast enough for real everyday use. An evaluation of user satisfaction showed that users find it helpful. The evaluation also showed that users prefer a grammar checker with a high precision rather than a high recall.

Reference

Chomsky, N. 1956. Three models for the description of language. Information Theory, IEEE Transactions 2 (3): 113–124.

Mackevičiūtė, J. 2004. Lithuanian morphological analysis system and grammar checker: Tilde's technologies in practice. In Proc. HLT'2004, Riga, Latvia

Skadiņš R., Skadiņa I., Deksne D., Gornostay T. 2007. English/Russian-Latvian Machine Translation System. In Proc. HLT'2007, Kaunas, Lithuania

Younger, D. 1967. Recognition and parsing of context-free languages in time n3. Information and Control 10(2): 189–208.

ISSN 1736-6305 Vol. 11
http://hdl.handle.net/10062/16955

Query Constraining Aspects of Knowledge
A Case Study

Ann-Marie Eklund
University of Gothenburg
Gothenburg, Sweden
`ann-marie.eklund@svenska.gu.se`

Abstract

In this paper we present a first analysis towards better understanding of the query constraining aspects of knowledge, as expressed in the most used public medical bibliographic database MEDLINE. Our results indicate that new terms occur, but also that traditional terms are replaced by more specific ones and decrease in use as major defining keywords, even though they are still used in abstracts. In other words, as knowledge, including terminology, evolve over time, queries and search methods will have to adapt to these changes to enable finding recent as well as older research papers in databases.

1 Introduction

When on-line databases are queried, answers are automatically derived from the contents of the database. For instance, MEDLINE (National Library of Medicine, 2010b) is a bibliographic database containing 18 million records from over 5000 biomedical journals, and for researchers in life science and medicine it is one of the most important on-line sources of new knowledge. Queries posted to the database are matched against bibliographic records of unstructured text (abstracts), titles and associated keywords. Each record aims at reflecting the knowledge of a given paper and its authors, and the best matching records are returned as answers to a query. In this case the answers are constrained by the bibliographic data. This data also has an impact on which terms would be the most efficient ones to use in a query. Since MEDLINE users, compared to users of general web search engines, are more persistent in their search for information and often reformulate their queries (Dogan et al., 2009), improved understanding of search behaviour may

be of importance for automatic query optimisation. Another interesting question that rises in infodemiology, i.e. "the study of the determinants and distribution of health information" (Eysenbach, 2006), is how the data, hence the encapsulated knowledge, residing in a database, impacts the querying process.

In this paper we will present the first steps of an ongoing work towards better understanding of the constraining aspects of a database, by analysing a subset of MEDLINE records corresponding to the publications on the obesity-related protein adiponectin. This analysis indicates that new terms occur, but also that traditionally used terms are replaced by more specific ones and decrease in use as major defining keywords, even though they are still used in abstracts.

2 Materials and Methods

We used a corpus of 5851 MEDLINE (National Library of Medicine, 2010b) records (1993-2009) of bibliographic data, containing the term adiponectin[1] in title, abstract or keywords. We call this term an *anchor term* due to its role of defining the corpus. From each record we used title, abstract, year of publication and keywords. The keywords consist of Medical Subject Headings (MeSH) (National Library of Medicine, 2010a), which is NLM's controlled vocabulary thesaurus organised in a hierarchical structure.

The implementation[2] was done in Python using the Natural Language Toolkit (NLTK) (tokenization and lemmatization) and Biopython (data retrieval and management). The analysis of data was done using Microsoft Excel in combination with R

---

[1]We chose the term adiponectin because it is unambiguous and without synonyms, and due to its relatively new appearance in life science the corresponding corpus becomes rather easy to analyse.

[2]The program and result files can be obtained from the author on request.

(visualisation of data)[3]. Since this study is only an intitial analysis of the existing data, we have not utilised any other analysis methods than manual inspection of the data.

3   Results

In the adiponectin context, around 4500 different MeSH terms, or keywords, have been used since the first adiponectin paper in 1993. The abstracts contain around 20,000 different words, stopwords not included, and only a small part of the terms have been examined here. The emphasis in this section is on findings related to uses of the corpus anchor term (adiponectin), hyponyms of the words/terms used in the context of adiponectin, and the introduction of new terms over time.

3.1   Use of the anchor term

One interesting aspect of knowledge and its expression is if and when it becomes common, thereby more seldom explicitly stated in communication.

The first MEDLINE record containing the term *adiponectin* is from 1993, but before the year 2000 there are not many papers in MEDLINE mentioning *adiponectin* (figure 1, top). The number of papers containing *adiponectin* in title, abstract or keywords has increased every year since 1999, but more and more of the papers do not have *Adiponectin* as a keyword, (figure 1, bottom).

Hence, it seems like the use of the anchor term as a keyword has decreased over time.

3.2   Use of terms and their hyponyms

Since the MeSH keywords are hierarchically organised, it is possible to study if, and how, the use of more general (hypernym) and specific (hyponym) terms changes over time.

The percentage of papers having *Obesity* as a keyword decreased from around the year 2000. A corresponding decrease can be found in titles and abstracts, where we also have a percentage decrease in the use of the word *obese* (which is not by itself a MeSH term). The keyword *Obesity, Abdominal* is a hyponym of the term *Obesity* and can be found in the papers from the last two years. In the abstracts we see a frequent use of the word *abdominal* since 2003.

Other adiponectin related keywords, *Diabetes Mellitus* and its hyponym *Diabetes Mellitus, Type*

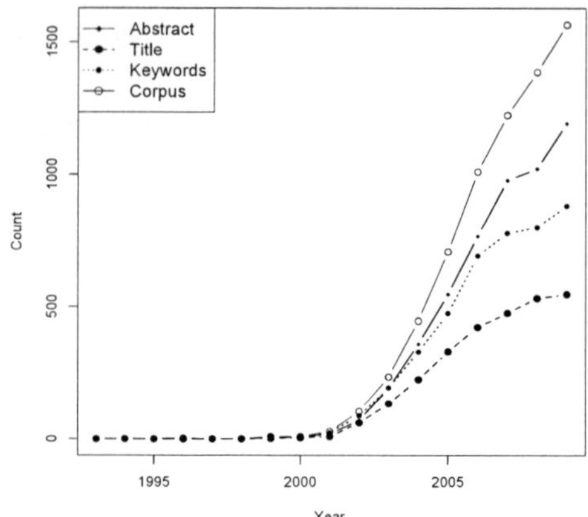

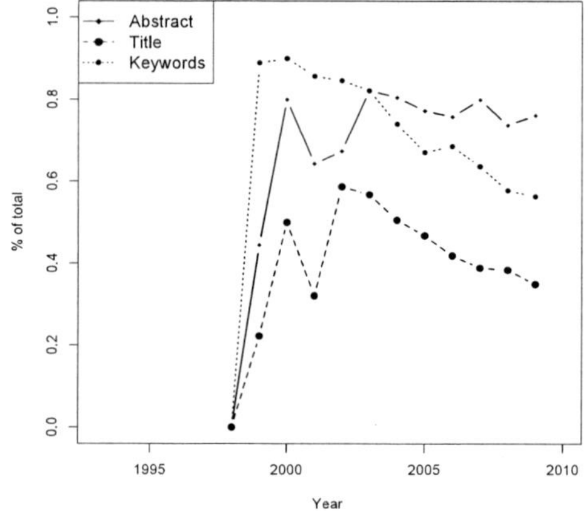

Figure 1: Number of MEDLINE records containing the term *adiponectin* in abstract, title or keywords (top), and the percentage of papers in the adiponectin corpus having the term in abstract, title and keywords respectively (bottom).

2, both first appeared in 2000 and both show a percentage decrease, although they increase in numbers. In titles and abstracts there is a percentage decrease for the term *diabetes*, but it is not as significant as for the keywords.

The keywords *Adipose Tissue* and *Adipocytes* were used in the first paper from 1993. They are both still in use as keywords, but there is a percentage decrease every year (figure 2). From 2007 *Adipocytes, White* and *Adipocytes, Brown* are being used as keywords. They are both hyponyms of the term *Adipocytes*. Similarly for *Adipose Tissue*, there are the hyponyms *Adipose Tissue, Brown*, first seen in 2002, and *Adipose Tissue,*

---

[3]nltk.org, biopython.org, r-project.org

White, which first occurred in 2006.

To conclude, by these examples we have seen indications of a shift over time in the use of traditionally used adiponectin related terms like *adipocytes*, *obesity* and *adipose tissue* towards the use of more specific terms (hyponyms).

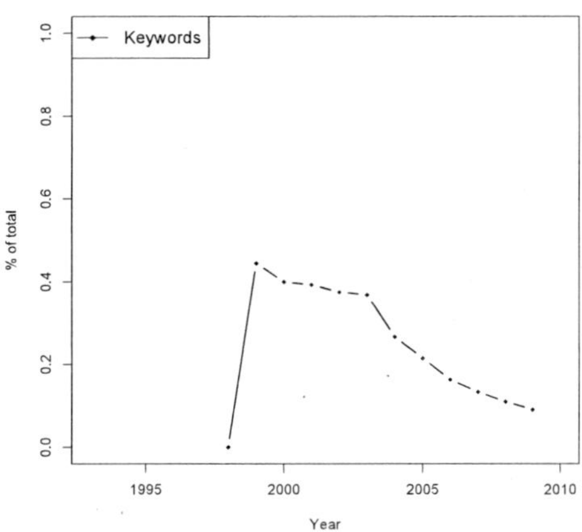

Figure 2: Percentage of papers indexed with keyword *Adipose Tissue*.

3.3 Use of new terms

If we assume that new knowledge and interests of a researcher are reflected in terms and keywords used in a paper, it is interesting to study if new words appear in our adiponectin corpus.

One interesting example of this is the increased use of words like *older*, *middle* and *aged* (figure 3) that we see in titles since their first occurrence in 2004. In abstracts *older* first appeared in 2003, and *middle* and *aged* in 2002. The keywords *Aged* and *Middle Aged* occurred for the first time in 1999, and since then both of them have been in frequent use. The keyword *Young Adult* is much used in 2009.

Another example is the plant related keywords. The keyword *Plant Extracts* has increased slightly since it was first used in 2005, and the keyword *Seeds* can also be found in a few papers every year since 2007 (*Seeds* is a descendant of *Plant Structures* or of *Food and Beverages* in the MeSH hierarchy). The last two years the keywords *Plant*, *Plant Stems*, "*Plants, Medicinal*" and *Plant Preparations* have appeared. In the last few years the words *plant* and *seed* have occurred mainly in abstracts, but also in a few titles.

Hence, by our analysis it is also possible to trace the occurrence of new terms, related to for instance age and plant concepts.

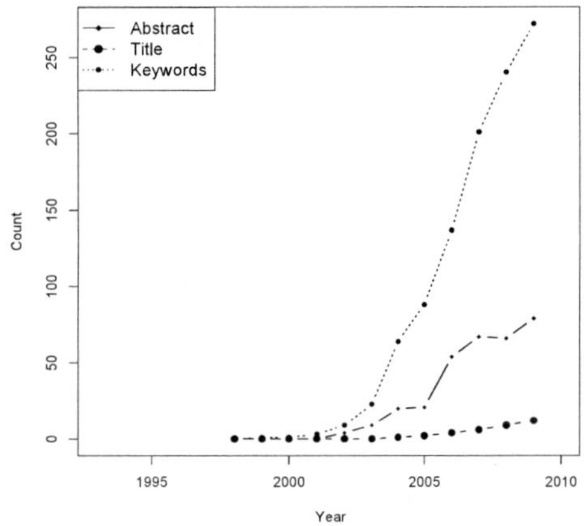

Figure 3: Number of occurrences of the term *aged*.

3.4 Other reflections

In addition to the topics above we have noted some variations of the term *adiponectin*.

Even in reviewed papers, misspellings of the anchor term adiponectin can be found in the abstracts, for example *adiponetin*, *adipnectin* and *adyponectin*. Another interesting aspect is that, based on the old term, new words have been created, e.g. *adiponectinaemia*, *adiponectinemic*, *hyperadiponectinemia*, which have all appeared after 2001.

4 Discussion

In this section we will discuss the uses of the corpus anchor term (*adiponectin*), hyponyms of terms and the introduction of new terms over time in the context of the results presented above. However, first we will elaborate on some aspects of the materials and methods used in this paper.

4.1 Materials and methods

Since MeSH is designed to reflect knowledge and use of terms in the field of biomedicine, a term may have been used in titles and abstracts for some time before it is introduced into the MeSH ontology and is available for use as an indexing term. Thereby, basing a trend analysis on only keywords may not reflect the actual use of terms, or expressed knowledge. We have not taken into account the year of introduction of a keyword into the MeSH ontology. When we find a keyword for the first time in the adiponectin context we do not know if this is the first time it is available as an indexing term or if it has been a MeSH term for some time. This may be slightly misleading when comparing the use of terms as keywords to their use in abstracts and titles.

In this study we only look at the term itself, and not at the term in combination with its hypernyms and hyponyms. If we took into account the terms above and below in the MeSH hierarchy, we might be able to see even more clear tendencies. For instance, by analysing the plant related terms and their hypo-/hypernyms together, we would add their different contributions, thereby making the new plant related aspect clearer.

In the light of the above limitations, our continued discussion will focus on the use of hyponyms and new terms.

4.2   Use of terms and hyponyms

In the examples in Results (section 3) we have seen indications of keywords becoming more specific, the annotations seem to have become more detailed, for example in the case of *Adipocytes* which decrease while its hyponyms *Adipocytes, White* and *Adipocytes, Brown* have started to be used as keywords. The use of more specific terms could indicate more detailed knowledge of a subject. To describe the new more detailed knowledge, new words may need to be used in the text, which may have led to the use of other more specific keywords to reflect that.

Another reason for the decrease in the use of for example terms like *Obesity* could be that obesity is already a given premise in this context and does not need to be stated explicitly anymore - terms become common knowledge, cf the above discussion on decreased use of the anchor term adiponectin.

4.3   Use of new terms

By studying the occurrence of new terms not used before in the adiponectin context, we find that terms related to completely new concepts appear. One example is the plant related terms, which correspond to an introduction of a new aspect into the research field. We can also see an increased age aspect, with terms like *Aged* and *Young Adult* being more and more common. New aspects like these often originate in the analysis of earlier study

results, where new connections can be seen in the data and lead to new angles to study. When new terms appear, like the plant or age related terms in the adiponectin context, it could reflect new knowledge and new interests within the field. The increased use of plant related terms seen in the last few years could indicate an increasing interest in plants in medicine.

5   Conclusions

In the examples above, we have presented indications of a shift over time in the use of terms towards more specific terms (hyponyms), where the use of more specific terms could indicate a more detailed knowledge of a subject. There was also a decrease in the use of some keywords which are closely connected to the anchor term *adiponectin*. This decrease could indicate that the concepts described by these terms are already given in this context and that the concepts have become common knowledge. We have also seen examples of the appearance of new terms related to concepts not previously occurring in this context. This could be an indication of new knowledge being added to the existing one.

To summarise, in this paper we have tried to exemplify how the use of terms in bibliographic records changes over time, and how this may be related to the evolution of new knowledge. As a consequence, as knowledge evolve over time, queries and search methods will have to adapt to these changes, so that the search terms which are used reflect the actual contents of the papers in the database.

References

Rezarta Islamaj Dogan, G. Craig Murray, Aurelie Neveol, and Zhiyong Lu. 2009. Understanding PubMed user search behavior through log analysis. *Database (Oxford)*, 2009:bap018.

Gunther Eysenbach. 2006. Infodemiology: tracking flu-related searches on the web for syndromic surveillance. *AMIA Annu Symp Proc*, pages 244–248.

National Library of Medicine. 2010a. Fact sheet Medical Subject Headings (MeSH).

National Library of Medicine. 2010b. Fact sheet Medline.

ISSN 1736-6305 Vol. 11
http://hdl.handle.net/10062/16955

A First Effort to Create a Categorization Scheme for Analyzing a Handbook of Swedish Writing Rules

Jody Foo
Linköping University
Linköping, Sweden
`jody.foo@liu.se`

Abstract

Today, spelling and grammar checkers are integrated into modern word processing environments. In some contexts of writing however, these components are not sufficient. In companies that write technical documentation, or when writing a research paper for a specific scientific community, style guides that can only be found in handbooks need to be followed. If such rules are to be implemented in a language-checking framework, they need to be analyzed to identify the requirements on the framework. A categorization scheme for such analysis does not seem to exist, hence the contribution of this paper – a first attempt at a scheme for classifying style guide rules for future implementation.

1 Background

There are many kinds of errors that can be made in written texts and there have been many attempts to automate the detection and correction of such errors. The most common kind of language checkers are spelling and grammar checkers for general language, e.g., those included in many word processing applications today. However, there are cases where a more restricted or specialized written language is needed, e.g., in companies that produce technical documentation (Almqvist & Hein) written in Simplified Technical English[1] (or similar controlled language), and when writing research publications that have to follow certain style guides such as APA style[2]. Such guidelines and rules for writing mostly exist in the form of written handbooks. Handbooks are however not that practical during the actual writing. The writer needs to keep an active knowledge of the guidelines and rules to be able to use them.

Analysis of writing rules contained in handbooks is needed to develop a framework capable of incorporating such guidelines.

To the author's knowledge, no research has been conducted concerning the problem of transforming written rules from style guides and handbooks into rules used in a language checker.

In this paper, we discuss a categorization scheme for analysis of such written rules for future implementation.

2 Rule/Error Types

There are many kinds of errors that can be found in written text. Below, a top-level categorization of these error types is presented. It should be noted that a classification scheme applied to errors is also applicable to rules. For example a spelling error is the result of breaking a spelling rule, e.g., using a word not contained by the dictionary. Categorization schemes exist for spelling errors and grammar errors but these are often considered separate problems from an implementation point of view (Domeij, Knutsson, Carlberger, & Kann, 1999). The scheme presented below combines some previous efforts but also contributes by taking into account the experiences from the analysis described in section 4.

- **Spelling errors** are ideally errors produced from misspelling a word. In the ideal case, the language checking software also suggests the correct spelling. However, the case might also be that the word is correctly spelled but not included in the software dictionary.

- **Grammar errors** can be divided into two types (Bustamante & León, 1996), (Sågvall Hein, 1998); a) A *structural grammar errors* and *b) non-structural errors*. A *structural error* can be corrected by inserting, deleting, or moving one or

---

[1] http://www.asd-ste100.org/
[2] http://www.apastyle.org/

more words. A *non-structural error* can be corrected by replacing an existing word with a different one.

- **Style errors** are errors that do not fit into the spelling and grammar categories according to (Naber, 2003). Examples include catching complicated sentence structures and uncommon words. Other style related rules and errors can be associated with specific corporate language and language used in a certain genre of writing.

- **Semantic errors** (Naber, 2003) are concerned with the truth and logic of a sentence. An example of a sentence containing semantic errors is "*I love to drive my potato to the song every year.*"

In many cases, the difference between two error categories is clear. However, in some cases such as with the rule *"sentences should start with a capital letter"*, the assignment of an error category is not as clear – is it a style error, or a grammar error? In addition to the referred error types I would like to add the following error/rule types.

- **Word formation/derivation**: How should new words be constructed? This is perhaps more pertinent to languages such as Swedish where noun-verb transformation is more complex than in e.g. English. Example: *Google (N), Googla (V)*. Another example of word formation/derivation is creating nouns from proper names in Swedish: *Amerika* → *amerikanisera, Finland* → *finlandism*

- **Terminological error**: A terminological error occurs when a forbidden term is used instead of the approved term. To detect terminological errors and correct them, access to a term bank is needed. For example, when documenting a particular operating system, the term *"directory"* may be forbidden and should be replaced with *"folder"*.

- **Typographic error**: Using the wrong glyph, spacing e.g. use of regular quotes rather than smart quotes, using the wrong spacing or dash glyphs, using three separate periods instead of an ellipsis glyph.

The word formation/derivation category could be grouped into the *style error* category or the *spelling* category. Whether or not it is a sub-

category to or a proper category is a minor issue however. The point of including it as a separate category is because of its *productive nature*. The category deals with how new words are constructed which in essence means defining a dynamic dictionary, but also rules of style regarding concerned with why one alternative is better than another e.g. choosing "*icke-kemisk*" over "*ickekemisk*" (Eng. *Non-chemical*).

3   Information Levels

In addition to error classification I would also like to propose classification of the information level needed to detect different errors. There are two aspects of information that are relevant when implementing a language checker – *feature* and *access*. Features are attribute values that can be assigned to e.g. a token or a phrase. Access is about how many tokens can be considered by the system – a single token, a single token and its predecessor and successor, any token in a sentence, tokens from multiple sentences, tokens from the whole document?

For example, the two categories of grammatical errors previously mentioned (structural and non-structural) are good linguistic error categories, but when building a system that implements these rules, the linguistic categorization scheme is not enough. Detecting different structural grammar errors requires different features, i.e. two different kinds of structural grammar errors may need two separate feature sets.

Depending on the available *document markup*, certain features may or may not be available. In some cases, there are workarounds. For instance, even though a sentence is not marked up as being part of a numbered list, it may be possible to deduce this by looking at the first characters of the previous and following sentences. If information about whether or not a sentence is part of a list is available, the access requirement is single sentence. However, if such information is not available, the access requirement is multi-sentence. The information features and access scope levels are presented in the listing below.

3.1   Orthographic features

- characters in token: `o_token-chars`

The characters that each token is composed of is the most basic feature.

3.2   Morpho-Syntactic features

- part-of-speech of token: `m_token-pos`

- token chunks/phrases: `m_chunk`

- clause, sub clause: `m_tree`

There are of course many more linguistic features that can be considered. However, these three should suffice in most cases.

3.3   **Document structure features**

- lower-cased alphabetic-numbered-list: `s_low-alpha-num-list`

- sentence is heading: `s_heading`

- part of table: `s_table`

- list: `s_list`

- quote: `s_quote`

Document structure related features contain information on the document semantics of a token or a token sequence, e.g., if the current sentence is a heading, or a list item. Depending on where the sentence is found in the document, different rules may apply. When writing in English, capitalizing nouns is acceptable in headings but not in body text. Document structure related features are in most cases provided by the authoring environment (e.g., a word processor). Whether or not they are present in the text to be analyzed by the language checker has a huge impact on how rules need to be implemented as demonstrated in the previous example related to capitalization in headings.

3.4   **Semantic features**

- date: `s_date`

- time: `s_time`

- is the word a geographic proper name: `s_prop-geo`

- language exception, e.g., a Swedish word in English text: `s_language`

- word is an abbreviation: `s_abbrev`

- word is a contraction: `s_contract`

- internet link, e.g., e-mail or URL: `s_internet`

- lexical semantic information: `s_lexsem`

All semantic features except the last feature are document structure-related. The last feature, *"lexical semantic information"* is a catchall feature for information such as knowing whether the word *"bank"* refers to a financial institution, a

location near a river in the sentence *"I went to the bank."* The availability of semantic features has a huge impact on how rules can be implemented. Semantic information is usually not inferred using algorithmic analysis, but might rather be available to the language checker e.g. in a corporate CMS environment where items such as telephone numbers, part numbers etc. are explicitly marked up in the source text.

3.5   **Information scope/access**

- serial access to tokens, i.e. one token at the time is processed: `a_serial`

- random access to all information of all tokens in a sentence: `a_sent-tokens`

- random sentence spanning information: `a_multi-sent`

In the access scheme above, it is assumed that access categories include lower numbered access categories as well, e.g., `a_multi-sent` access includes `a_sent-tokens` access.

4   Brief analysis of *"Skrivregler för svenska och engelska från TNC"*

The guidelines used in this paper were taken from the Swedish handbook *"Skrivregler för svenska och engelska från TNC"*[3] (*"Rules writing Swedish and English from TNC"* (SR-TNC)). In SR-TNC there are 216 paragraphs concerning the Swedish language. However, these paragraphs may contain more than one actual rule to implement. The guidelines in SR-TNC are written with technical documentation in mind. All 216 paragraphs were considered, but not all 216 paragraphs were chosen for analysis.

Instead, a selection of 30 of the 216 paragraphs was selected. The categorization scheme was iteratively revised as the analysis progressed.

5   Examples and discussion of analyzed rules

In **Table 1** an example is given of how the categorization scheme was applied. An example of a grammar rule can be found in SR-TNC paragraph 16 which states that a comma should be used after the conjunctions *och*, *eller*, *men* and

---

[3] Terminologicentrum (TNC), is a Swedish organization working to improve and technical writing. TNC has published several handbooks and dictionaries and also acts as advisors in terminological issues.

src-id	rule type	feature	access	rule name	description
tnc-2	style	o_token-chars	a_sent-tokens	ingen-extra-punkt-när-mening-avslutas-med-förkortning	Om en mening slutar med en förkortning försedd med punkt utelämnas meningens avslutningspunkt.
tnc-6	typography	t_token-chars	a_sent-tokens	elips	elipstecken eller tre efterföljande punkttecken ska användas. Inte två eller fler än tre punkter vid elips
tnc-16	grammar	m_tree	a_sent-tokens	komma-efter-bindeord	komma efter och, eller, men och utan när de används för att sammanfoga två huvudsatser
tnc-40	formation	o_token-chars	a_sent-tokens	bindestreck-vid-icke-sammansättning	t.ex. icke-kemisk, icke-metaller icke-proteinkväve, ickerökare och ickevåld. Bedömningskriteriet är "tydlighet" hos ordet.

Table 1: Rule examples

utan (Eng. *and, or, but, without*) when they are used to connect two main clauses. This rule was categorized as a *grammar rule* information on main clauses and sub clauses in the sentence and must be able to access the tokens in the sentence in any order.

Several rules need lexical semantic information about the word, e.g., in *SR-TNC paragraph 100* which states that only when a geographical proper name refers to the actual place should it be capitalized (Swedish). For example, *Manchester* should be capitalized when it refers to the city of *Manchester*, not when it refers to the cloth *manchester*. This is hard to deduce or include in texts, but a task for Language Technology research might be to notify the writer of the possible error by e.g. asking the writer *"When you write Manchester, do you mean the city or the cloth?"*.

From the brief analysis of SR-TNC, it is also clear that there is also a need for rules that describe how new words are produced. It is impossible to create a dictionary containing all possible wordforms, so perhaps a more dynamic component than the standard dictionary needs to be created. In languages such as Swedish, word compounding is one kind of productive mechanism. Efforts have been made to cope with compound words when performing spell checking (Domeij et al 1994), other kinds of out of vocabulary words must also be caught, such as inflection of foreign words and new abbreviations.

6 Conclusion

Analysis of rules for writing in handbooks is needed to develop a framework which is capable of incorporating such guidelines. The current state of language technology has not achieved a level where all rules can be implemented in a software language checker due to analysis methods, available semantic metadata and the subjective nature of certain guidelines.

However, the analysis can provide insights into which areas within language technology need further research to provide such a tool.

Regarding the implementation of rules following this categorization scheme, some trials have been done. Here a pragmatic approach was chosen adding stylistically preferred words to the dictionary. This approach is not a general approach, but even so, may be a feasible approach when considering e.g. domain specific technical documentation.

References

Almqvist, I., & Hein, A. (2000). A Language Checker of Controlled Language and its Integration in a Documentation and Translation Workflow. *Proceedings of the Twenty-second International Conference on Translating and the Computer* .

Bustamante, F. R., & León, F. S. (1996). GramCheck: A Grammar and Style Checker. *Proceedings of the 16th International Conference of Computational Linguistics (Coling –96)*, (pp. 175-181).

Domeij, R., Hollman, J., & Kann, V. (1994). Detection of spelling errors in Swedish not using a word list en claire. *Quantitative Linguistics , 1*, 195-201.

Domeij, R., Knutsson, O., Carlberger, J., & Kann, V. (1999). Granska - an efficient hybrid system for Swedish grammar checking. *NODALIDA 1999*.

Naber, D. (2003). *A rule-based style and grammar checker*. Technische Fakultät. Universität Bielefeld.

Sågvall Hein, A. (1998). A Chart-Based Framework for Grammar Checking Initial Studies. *Proceedings of NODALIDA '98, 11.* Center for Sprogteknologi, Denmark.

ISSN 1736-6305 Vol. 11
http://hdl.handle.net/10062/16955

Something Old, Something New – Applying a Pre-trained Parsing Model to Clinical Swedish

Martin Hassel
DSV, Stockholm University
Kista, Sweden
xmartin@dsv.su.se

Aron Henriksson
DSV, Stockholm University
Kista, Sweden
aronhen@dsv.su.se

Sumithra Velupillai
DSV, Stockholm University
Kista, Sweden
sumithra@dsv.su.se

Abstract

Information access from clinical text is a research area which has gained a large amount of interest in recent years. Automatic syntactic analysis for the creation of deeper language models is potentially very useful for such methods. However, syntactic parsers that are tailored to accommodate for the distinctive properties of clinical language are rare and costly to build. We present an initial study on the applicability of an existing parser, pre-trained on general Swedish, to clinical text in Swedish. We manually evaluate twelve documents and obtain a 92.4% part-of-speech tagging accuracy and a 76.6% labeled attachment score for the syntactic dependency parsing.

1 Introduction

The increasing use of electronic patient records has made it possible to explore this rich source of information by means of natural language processing. In order for the many potential applications to be successful, lexical information is often insufficient; syntactic information, such as dependency structures, is also needed.

The *MaltParser* system (Nivre et al., 2007) may be employed to provide such an analysis: it allows a dependency parser to be induced from a treebank, i.e. a syntactically annotated corpus. By building a treebank one can generate a parser for any language or sublanguage. This is, however, a somewhat demanding task.

The purpose of this paper is to evaluate to which degree a pre-trained model is directly transferable to a new domain, in this case clinical text. Given the linguistic differences between clinical and general Swedish (Dalianis et al., 2009), it may prove necessary to create a model tailored specifically to the clinical domain.

2 Background

There are a number of parsers that have been developed for Swedish, two of which are grammar-based dependency parsers (Knutsson et al., 2003). The *MaltParser*, however, is language-independent and data-driven, allowing parsers to be induced for any language or sublanguage. This approach is advantageous when the linguistic data resources are available (Nivre et al., 2007). The system has been successfully applied to an array of languages, yielding an average labeled attachment score[1] of 80.8%[2] across 13 languages (84.6% for Swedish) (Nivre, 2008).

Clinical text differs from general text in terms of both language and content, making it a discourse of its own. It is written by professionals responsible for patient care and is primarily used for record-keeping and transfer of information between healthcare personnel (Allvin et al., 2010).

In addition to the fragmentary style of clinical language and the prevalence of misspellings and abbreviations, there is also a significant difference in the respective vocabularies. This makes the application of natural language processing methods—including syntactic parsing—to clinical text a potential challenge (Dalianis et al., 2009).

Haverinen et al. (2009) have built a treebank for clinical Finnish[3], which was used to induce a domain-specific dependency parser using the *MaltParser* system. They annotated the corpus using the Stanford Dependency scheme, which was adapted to accommodate for properties of the Finnish language in general and clinical Finnish in particular. Using a standard version of Nivre's arc-eager parsing algorithm (Nivre et al., 2007), they report an overall labeled attachment score of 69.9%.

---

[1] The proportion of scoring tokens that are assigned both the correct head and the correct dependency relation label.

[2] Using Nivre's algorithm.

[3] 1,019 intensive care unit nursing documents.

A comparative study of intensive care unit documents written in Swedish and Finnish respectively shows that, despite significant linguistic differences, there are many structural and content-related similarities, such as missing predicates, copulas and subjects (Allvin et al., 2010).

3 Method

We apply the pre-trained model for Swedish, *SweMalt*[4], developed for the *MaltParser* system, on a set of Swedish clinical assessment entries[5], where each entry is treated as a document. These entries are written by physicians from an emergency ward. The model is trained on the *Talbanken* section of the *Swedish Treebank*[6]. As input to the system, we need part-of-speech (PoS) tagged data. We use the *Granska Tagger* (Carlberger and Kann, 1999) in this initial step. No cleaning or other pre-processing is performed on the documents prior to applying the PoS tagger; however, the evaluation is performed only on content tokens, i.e. punctuation and formatting issues are ignored.

As there is no morphologically and syntactically annotated corpus of Swedish clinical text that can be used for evaluation, we manually evaluate twelve randomly extracted documents with regards to the following: (1) PoS tagging accuracy and (2) labeled and unlabeled attachment score (LAS and UAS), as well as labeled accuracy score (LA), of the syntactic parses. For the evaluation of the syntactic parses, we use the visualization tool provided by *MaltEval*[7].

The results are evaluated manually by two researchers, both educated in (Swedish) linguistics, but with no formal training in the specific morphological and syntactic schemas used by *MaltParser*. One document is evaluated jointly, while the remaining eleven documents are evaluated individually, after which differences are resolved through discussion.

---

[4]Available at `http://maltparser.org/mco/swedish_parser/swemalt.html`

[5]This research has been carried out after approval from the Regional Ethical Review Board in Stockholm (Etikprövningsnämnden i Stockholm), permission number 2009/1742-31/5.

[6]For a description of the treebank, see `http://stp.ling.uu.se/~nivre/swedish_treebank/`

[7]Available at `http://w3.msi.vxu.se/~jni/malteval/`

4 Results

In Table 1 we present overall information about the twelve documents used in the experiment. Sentences vary greatly in length, ranging from two to 36 content tokens, but consist of around ten words per sentence on average. The documents are very short (5.6 sentences on average), ranging from only one sentence to ten.

	#	min - max	avg $\pm$ std
Sentences	68	1 - 10 (/d)	5.6$\pm$2.0 (/d)
Tokens	676	2 - 36 (/s)	9.9$\pm$6.4 (/s)
		4 - 128 (/d)	57.6$\pm$30.5 (/d)

Table 1: General statistics for the twelve documents. Minimum, maximum, average and standard deviation for sentences per document and tokens per sentence and document. d = document, s = sentence.

Analysis and measure	# errors	% score
PoS, accuracy	51	92.4
Syntactic parse, LAS	142	76.6
Syntactic parse, UAS	117	80.7
Syntactic parse, LA	133	78.1

Table 2: Results of part-of-speech (PoS) tagging and syntactic parses. LAS = Labeled Attachment Score, UAS = Unlabeled Attachment Score, LA = Label Accuracy Score.

4.1 Part-of-Speech Tagging

In general, the PoS tagging results were very high (see Table 2). However, some mistakes frequently recur. One of the most common words, *pat* ("patient", abbreviated), was consistently assigned the class proper name (PM), which is erroneous. Moreover, other abbreviations such as *ua* (*utan anmärkning*, "without remarks") and *ca* ("approx.") were, in many cases, broken up in the morphological analysis, or split in the original text (with a space or a colon inserted in between), which led to errors in the PoS assignments.

Moreover, the documents contain many clinical terms, such as disease names, medications, wards, etc. These were sometimes tagged as nouns (NN), sometimes as proper names (PM), although not always consistently. These cases are not easy to discriminate, as they, in context, work either way. For instance, the disease *dvt* (*djup ventrombos*, "deep venous thrombosis", abbreviated) is tagged as a proper name (PM), while *myocardit* (*myocarditis*) has been tagged as a noun (NN). These conflicting analyses are not, however, problematic for the syntactic analysis.

4.2 Syntactic Parsing

The overall results of the syntactic parsing are presented in Table 2. The most common errors are related to conjunctions, adverbials and prepositional constructions. These are also among the most common dependency relation types, with PA (*Complement of preposition*) being the most frequent (77 instances).

Many sentences lack a main predicate (32%), which is known to be a problematic issue for syntactic parsers (Haverinen et al., 2009). Moreover, main subjects are often omitted (43%), which further complicates the analysis. This feature is not unique to Swedish in the clinical domain (Allvin et al., 2010). In Figure 1, we see an example of a rather typical sentence, where there is no predicate or subject, with several errors in the syntactic analysis as a result.

In general, shorter sentences such as *således dvt* ("thus dvt") are analyzed correctly (ROOT → *dvt* → CA → *således*), while longer sentences contain several errors, in particular sentences with complicated conjunctional, conditional and prepositional constructions.

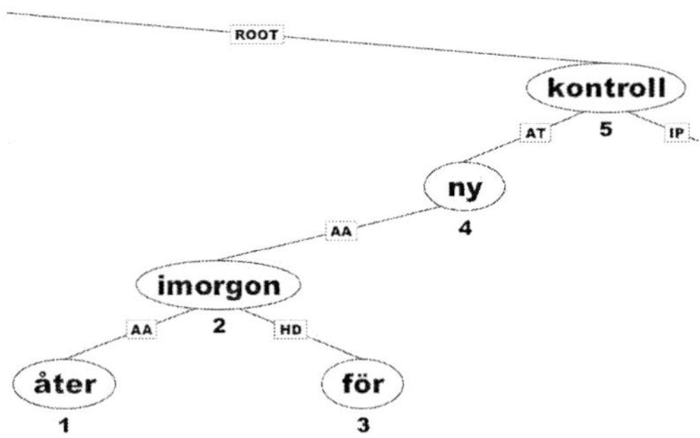

Figure 1: Example parse tree for the sentence *åter imorgon för ny kontroll* ("back tomorrow for new check-up")

5 Discussion

Although this study is performed on a very small set of documents, the general results could be interpreted as indicators. The twelve documents were randomly extracted from a total of 150 parsed documents. A comparison of the general characteristics—the average number of tokens per sentence, common tokens and dependency relations—of the sample set with that of all the parsed documents shows that the evaluation was conducted on a data set that is at least fairly representative of Swedish emergency ward documentation.

5.1 Part-of-Speech Tagging

The pre-trained *SweMalt* model presupposes input text that has been morphosyntactically disambiguated using the Stockholm-Umeå Corpus (SUC) tag set (Ejerhed et al., 1992). It should thus be noted that there has not been any tailoring to resolve differences between morphosyntactic categories in the *Granska Tagger* system compared to the SUC categories. This fact could possibly influence results in the syntactic parses, as the parser might encounter tags that it does not recognize[8] and the lack of information on past participles, for instance, might be harmful for the parser.

We have not evaluated the full morphosyntactic tag, but rather focused on the part-of-speech. The results of the PoS tagging were very high (92.4% accuracy), which is in line with state-of-the-art performance of Swedish PoS taggers. Carlberger and Kann (1999) report an accuracy of 92.0% for unknown words and 96.3% for all words when evaluated on a part of SUC. Since the clinical domain is also new to the tagger, it is in this study exposed to a higher degree of unknown words in the form of medical brands, tests and diseases, as well as ad-hoc abbreviations of much of the aforementioned terminology (Allvin et al., 2010). These prove to be a challenge already in the tokenisation step of the analysis.

5.2 Syntactic Parsing

The syntactic parsing results (see Table 2) are lower than state-of-the-art results of (general) Swedish (LAS: 84.6%, UAS: 89.5%, LA: 87.4% (Nivre, 2008)). However, the results are still within the range of average overall parser performances accross languages (LAS: 80.8%). Compared to other parsing results for clinical language, we observe higher LAS scores than those presented in Haverinen et al. (2009) (LAS: 69.9% for

---

[8]The Granska Tagger has, apart from removing 14 tags/features, introduced 5 new tags.

a statistical parser, LAS: 75.2% for a rule-based parser). Although the results are not directly comparable to the mentioned previous studies (e.g. in both Nivre (2008) and Haverinen et al. (2009), the parsing model is not evaluated on a new domain; there are, of course, language differences; different evaluation methods are used; etc.), we believe the general trends are comparable.

The distribution of the most common dependency relation types can—with such reservations as stated above—be compared to those reported for general Swedish in (Nivre et al., 2007). Despite differences in dependency relation schemes, we observe some similarities in the distribution patterns. For example, prepositional dependency relations (PA, *Complement of preposition*, and PR, *Preposition dependent*) and conjunctional relations (CJ, *Conjunct* and CC, *Coordination*) are among the most common (approx. 10% respectively). One important difference is, however, the number of adverbial dependency relation types in the different schemes. In Nivre et al. (2007) only one adverbial relation is used, while in this setting there are ten. Since there are so many different adverbial types in our setting, and the adverbial relations are one of the larger sources of errors in our evaluation, one possible explanation might be the low frequency per adverbial type.

Other than that, although we have not quantified the amount of errors per dependency relation type, similar tendencies are apparent. For instance, among error types categorized as the "medium-accuracy set" in Nivre et al. (2007), we find error types linked to incorrect attachment, e.g. modifier attachment ambiguities and attachment ambiguities. These are common error types in our experiment as well. The general indications are thus that the error types found in this evaluation are not necessarily domain-dependent; however, modeling syntactic analyses of sentences lacking predicates and/or subjects would probably be needed in order to improve results. This particular characteristic seems to be typical for clinical language (see e.g. Haverinen et al. (2009)).

5.3 Conclusion

The main finding is that the morphological characteristics of Swedish clinical language do not differ greatly from general language and that existing tools can be used successfully when it comes to PoS information. Syntactic parsing also works

well in most cases, but the errors that are produced are relatively severe. One solution to this would be to enrich an existing treebank with only these types of sentences. Along these lines, we plan to use this evaluated set as a small gold standard for further development of parsing Swedish clinical documentation, as well as for studying domain adaptation for other professional languages.

References

Helen Allvin, Elin Carlsson, Hercules Dalianis, Riita Danielsson-Ojala, Vidas Daudaravičius, Martin Hassel, Dimitrios Kokkinakis, Heljä Lundgren-Laine, Gunnar Nilsson, Ø ystein Nytrø, Maria Skeppstedt, Hanna Souminen, and Sumithra Velupillai. 2010. Characteristics and Analysis of Finnish and Swedish Clinical Intensive Care Nursing Narratives. In *Second Louhi Workshop on Text and Data Mining of Health Documents (Louhi-10)*, number 2, pages 53–60, Los Angeles, U.S. Association for Computational Linguistics (ACL).

Johan Carlberger and Viggo Kann. 1999. Implementing an efficient part-of-speech tagger. *Software Practice and Experience*, 29(9):815–832, July.

Hercules Dalianis, Martin Hassel, and Sumithra Velupillai. 2009. The Stockholm EPR corpus: Characteristics and some initial findings. In *Proc. 14th ISHIMR*, volume 219, pages 243–249, Kalmar, Sweden.

Eva Ejerhed, Gunnel Källgren, Ola Wennstedt, and Magnus Åström. 1992. The linguistic annotation system of the The Stockholm-Umeå corpus project. Technical Report DGLUUM-R-33, Department of General Linguistics, University of Umeå.

Katri Haverinen, Filip Ginter, Veronika Laippala, and Tapio Salakoski. 2009. Parsing clinical Finnish: Experiments with rule-based and statistical dependency parsers. In Kristiina Jokinen and Eckhard Bick, editors, *Proc. 17th NODALIDA 2009*, number 1998, pages 65–72.

Ola Knutsson, Johnny Bigert, and Viggo Kann. 2003. A robust shallow parser for Swedish. In *Proc. NODALIDA 2003*, Reykavik, Iceland.

Joakim Nivre, Johan Hall, Jens Nilsson, Atanas Chanev, Gülsen Eryigit, Sandra Kübler, Svetoslav Marinov, and Erwin Marsi. 2007. MaltParser: A language-independent system for data-driven dependency parsing. *Natural Language Engineering*, 13(2):95–135, January.

Joakim Nivre. 2008. Algorithms for deterministic incremental dependency parsing. *Computational Linguistics*, 34(4):513–553, December.

ISSN 1736-6305 Vol. 11
http://hdl.handle.net/10062/16955

Knowledge-free Verb Detection
through Tag Sequence Alignment

Christian Hänig

University of Leipzig

Natural Language Processing Group

Department of Computer Science

04103 Leipzig, Germany

`chaenig@informatik.uni-leipzig.de`

Abstract

We present an algorithm for verb detection of a language in question in a completely unsupervised manner. First, a shallow parser is applied to identify – amongst others – noun and prepositional phrases. Afterwards, a tag alignment algorithm will reveal *fixed points* within the structures which turn out to be verbs.

Results of corresponding experiments are given for English and German corpora employing both supervised and unsupervised algorithms for part-of-speech tagging and syntactic parsing.

1   Introduction

Recently, along with the growing amount of available textual data, interest in unsupervised natural language processing (NLP) boosts, too.

Especially companies gradually discover its value for market research, competitor analysis and quality assurance to name just a few. During the last decades, language resources were created for many languages, but some domains have very specialized terminology or even particular grammars and for those, no proper resources exist. Hence, unsupervised approaches need to evolve into the direction of information extraction, which still needs huge manual and costly effort in most cases.

In this paper, we want to introduce an approach for unsupervised verb detection solely relying on unsupervised POS tagging and unsupervised shallow parsing. This algorithm will facilitate deep unsupervised parsing as it can provide useful information about verbs along with argument assignments and thus, it is a crucial step for information extraction from data sources for which no suitable language models exist. According to our knowledge, there is no algorithm approaching the problem of unsupervised verb detection so far.

2   Verb detection

Verbs represent natural language relations. The arguments of a verb can be nominal phrases, prepositional phrases or other nominal or prepositional expressions. These phrases can be detected in an unsupervised manner. Besides approaches to chunking (see (Skut and Brants, 1998)), several shallow parsers exist (e. g. unsuParse, see (Hänig et al., 2008; Hänig, 2010)) which are applicable to extract the aforementioned phrase types. Since unsupervised parsers do not use any a priori knowledge about language, one drawback exists: phrases are not labeled in a human-readable way (e. g. *NP* or *PP*), not even if they induce labeled parse trees (see (Reichart and Rappoport, 2008))[1].

2.1   Tag Sequence Alignment

In order to detect verbs we employ a tag sequence alignment algorithm (TSA) which is independent from POS and phrase labels. First, we use shallow parsing to detect significant phrases containing, amongst others, *NPs* and *PPs*. Afterwards, we align different sequences of the resulting phrases and POS tags to each other. We assume that verbs dominate the structure of a sentence decisively and mark fixed points within the sequence while their arguments can be exchanged and moved to different positions. In a more formal way:

A sequence s of a sentence with length n is defined as

$$s = (s_0 \ldots s_{n-1}) \qquad (1)$$

where s_i can be a phrase tag or a POS tag. Hence, the sequence of a simple sentence may look like (NP VBD NP PP). Each sentence can be described as a sequence of tag groups representing phrases. Such a sequence may contain only one group (the

---

[1]Although our algorithm does not rely on knowledge derived from labels of phrases and/or POS tags, we use human-readable labels (PennTree tagset) throughout this paper for better readability.

whole sentence) or up to n groups where each group consists of exactly one tag (e. g. three groups: (NP), (VBD) and (NP PP)). To build those groups, the sequence is split at certain indices. So, every grouping is defined by a set of separation indices contained in the power set given in Equ. 2.

$$PI(n) = P(\{0 \ldots n-2\}) \qquad (2)$$

Formally, each of the 2^{n-1} possible groupings is given by

$$g(s, I) =$$
$$((s_0 \ldots s_{i_0})(s_{i_0+1} \ldots s_{i_1}) \ldots (s_{i_{x-1}+1} \ldots s_{n-1}))$$
$$(3)$$

where $I \in PI(n)$ is a sorted set of separation indices between two component groups ($|I| = x$).

The similarity of two groupings is defined as

$$sim_{seq}(g(s, I), g(t, J)) =$$
$$\begin{cases} |I| \neq |J|: & 0 \\ \nexists i: g(s, I)_i = g(t, J)_i: & 0 \\ else: \\ \quad \frac{1}{|I|} \sum_{i=0}^{|I|-1} sim(g(s, I)_i, g(t, J)_i) \end{cases}$$
$$(4)$$

First, the number of groups has to be equal in both groupings, otherwise these groupings are not considered to be a valid alignment. Second, there has to be at least one exact match containing only simple POS tags and no phrases as we want to detect POS tags being fixed points within the sequences. If these two conditions are met, we can calculate the similarity as the average of the context similarities between all corresponding groups of the two groupings[2]. In order to find the alignment between two sequences s and t holding the highest similarity, we match every possible grouping of s with every possible grouping of t.

2.2 Detection of verbs in a corpus

Having the possibility to calculate the best alignments of tag sequences, we apply this algorithm to a whole corpus. After POS tagging and shallow parsing, all sentences are transformed into their corresponding sequences. We only regard sequences with a minimum support of at least 10 occurrences within the corpus.

Iteratively, sequences are aligned to each other starting with the most frequent sequence which is

solely split into its components (e. g. (NP VBZ PP) is split into ((NP) (VBZ) (PP))). Then – in order of frequency – every sequence is either aligned to an existing sequence (e. g. (NP VBZ NP PP) is split into ((NP) (VBZ) (NP PP)) due to high similarity to ((NP) (VBZ) (PP))) or represents a new sequence which is different to the others. A threshold ϑ draws the line between those two possibilities. In the latter case, all subsequences of the sequence are tested for high context similarity to already detected verbs. This is done to cover verbal expressions consisting of more than one component, e. g. for modal auxiliaries like (MD VB). Afterwards the new sequence is split into its compounds like the first tag sequence, except for the subsequence showing high similarity to verbal expressions which is put into one group.

After processing the most frequent sequences, several graph structures containing the aligned sentences are created (e. g. in Figure 1).

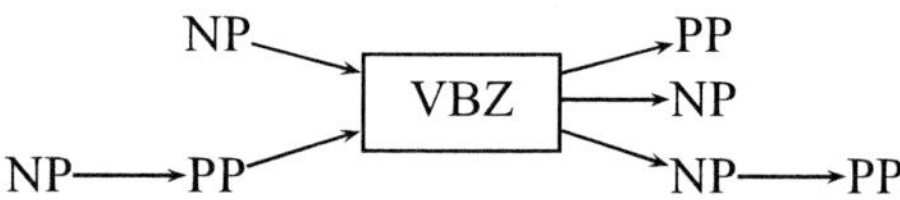

Figure 1: Resulting graph structure of several aligned tag sequences

The part-of-speech building the fixed point in the graph (as VBZ in the example) is considered to occupy a central role within the sequences. Thus, all parts-of-speech (excluding phrases) in all alignments holding this property and which are not contained in the phrases extracted by the shallow parser will be marked as verbs.

2.2.1 Tag list expansion

As we do not use all sequences (only the ones matching a certain minimum support) and not all tag sequences achieve a high similarity to other ones, not all verbs are detected. Hence, we use all extracted tags T to generate a set of words W_T consisting of all words which are annotated by one of those tags. Afterwards, we calculate a relative score for each tag of the tagset expressing the coverage

$$cov(tag) =$$
$$\frac{|words\ annotated\ by\ tag \cap words \in W_T|}{|words\ annotated\ by\ tag|}$$
$$(5)$$

We expand the set of extracted verbs to tags which are well covered by words which already have

---

[2]We apply the cosine measure.

been detected. Every POS tag t with $cov(t) \geq 0.5$ is considered to contain verbs, too.

3   Evaluation

The proposed algorithm is applied to both supervisedly and unsupervisedly annotated corpora to provide comprehensive results. Both configurations were processed for two languages: English and German. We used the corpora *en100k* and *de100k* from *Projekt Deutscher Wortschatz* (see (Quasthoff et al., 2006)), each containing 100k sentences. We want to point out, that the supervised setup's purpose is only to verify our theory on high quality prerequisites.

For supervised preprocessing steps, we used the Stanford POS Tagger (see (Toutanova and Manning, 2000)) and Stanford Parser (see (Klein and Manning, 2003)). Sentence patterns are created by extraction of all kinds of prepositional phrases and noun phrases.

We applied unsuPOS (see (Biemann, 2006)) for unsupervised part-of-speech tagging. Afterwards, we trained a model for unsuParse (see (Hänig, 2010)) on these data sets for unsupervised shallow parsing (using only phrases with a significance of at least 10% of the most significant one). In this case, we annotated all phrases found by unsuParse.

In either configurations we applied a threshold of $\vartheta = 0.8$ and took all sentence patterns having a frequency of at least 10% of the most frequent one into account.

3.1   Part-of-speech tagsets

Each of the four possible setups relies on a different tagset. As it is very important for interpretation of obtained results, we will shortly introduce those tagsets along with the classes containing verbs.

3.1.1   Penn Tree Tagset

The Penn Tree Tagset (see (Santorini, 1990)) is applicable to English data. It contains 45 tags containing 7 tags describing verbs. Table 1 gives a short overview about its tags along with their relative frequencies (amongst all tags containing verbs) in the evaluation data set.

3.1.2   Stuttgart-Tübingen Tagset (STTS)

For German data, the Stuttgart-Tübingen Tagset (see (Thielen et al., 1999)) is well established. It contains 54 tags, 12 of them contain verbs (see Table 1).

Penn Tree Tagset		STTS	
Tag	Relative frequency	Tag	Relative frequency
MD	6.05%	VAFIN	24.74%
VB	18.21%	VAIMP	0.00%
VBD	26.81%	VAINF	2.67%
VBG	10.51%	VAPP	1.17%
VBN	15.99%	VMFIN	7.81%
VBP	9.48%	VMINF	0.18%
VBZ	12.95%	VMPP	0.01%
		VVFIN	34.04%
		VVIMP	0.06%
		VVINF	12.27%
		VVIZU	0.98%
		VVPP	16.07%

Table 1: Verb tags for English and German

3.1.3   unsuPOS word classes

Unsupervised induced word classes are not labeled in a comparable way as other tagsets. Hence, we give a short overview over the most frequent classes containing verbs in a descriptive way (see Tables 2 and 3). For English, we apply the *MEDLINE-model* which has been trained on 34 million sentences, the *German-model* has been trained on 40 million sentences[3].

Tag	Description	Rel. frequency
6	classify, let, sustain	20.82%
15	navigating, expending	8.75%
26	underlined, subdivided	34.85%
478	are	2.90%
479	is	6.26%

Table 2: unsuPOS classes for English verbs

Tag	Description	Rel. frequency
9	fragten, beteten	7.88%
37	erfüllt, verringert,	16.03%
42	zugucken, dauern,	28.37%
334	ist, war, wäre	7.43%
380	sind, waren, seien	2.97%

Table 3: unsuPOS classes for German verbs

4   Results

We calculated precision and recall scores for the extracted verb classes (see Table 4), the corre-

---

[3] unsuPOS and models for some languages can be downloaded here: http://tinyurl.com/unsupos

sponding tag sets are given in Table 5.

	Precision	Recall	F-Measure
English			
supervised	1.000	0.553	0.712
sup. w/ exp.	1.000	0.894	0.944
unsupervised	1.000	0.440	0.611
German			
supervised	1.000	0.789	0.882
sup. w/ exp.	1.000	0.816	0.899
unsupervised	1.000	0.627	0.771

Table 4: Precision, recall and f-measure values

	Verb detection	Expansion
English		
supervised	VBD VBP VBZ MD	VBN VB
unsupervised	26 478 479	112 126 *336 350*
German		
supervised	VVFIN VVINF VAFIN VMFIN	VAINF VVIMP
unsupervised	9 37 42 334 380	135 *142 166 175* 230 ...

Table 5: Extracted POS tags

For both the supervised and unsupervised data sets all extracted parts-of-speech contain verbs only. Regarding the supervised data sets for English and German, TSA detects 55.3% and 78.9% of all verbs, respectively. Tag set expansion yields a significant improvement for English (raising recall to 89.4%), while the improvement for German is marginal. This observation is not very surprising as German is morphologically richer than English.

The results on unsupervised data are perfectly accurate, too. For this setup, tag list expansion does not have a measurable impact on our results (approx. 0.02%) and can be neglected. However, expansion adds some classes including some incorrect ones (the *italic* ones in Table 5). The lower recall results from a much higher number of different word classes (about 500 in our case) induced by an unsupervised POS tagger. The lack of POS tag disambiguation is the reason for the inefficiency of our expansion step, since almost no word form is tagged by different tags.

5 Conclusions and further work

We have shown that alignment of tag sequences containing chunks or shallow parses can detect verbs in a completely unsupervised manner. Although the actual alignment covers the most common verb classes, expansion increases the number of correctly detected verbs.

In the future, we plan to evaluate other approaches to unsupervised POS tagging. We also want to incorporate unsupervised morphological analysis to improve the performance on morphologically rich languages.

References

Chris Biemann. 2006. Unsupervised part-of-speech tagging employing efficient graph clustering. In *Proceedings of the COLING/ACL-06 Student Research Workshop*.

Christian Hänig. 2010. Improvements in Unsupervised Co-Occurrence Based Parsing. In *Proceedings of the Fourteenth Conference on Computational Natural Language Learning*.

Christian Hänig, Stefan Bordag, and Uwe Quasthoff. 2008. Unsuparse: Unsupervised parsing with unsupervised part of speech tagging. In *Proceedings of the Sixth International Language Resources and Evaluation (LREC'08)*.

Dan Klein and Christopher D. Manning. 2003. Fast exact inference with a factored model for natural language parsing. In *In Advances in Neural Information Processing Systems 15 (NIPS)*.

U. Quasthoff, M. Richter, and C. Biemann. 2006. Corpus portal for search in monolingual corpora. In *Proceedings of the LREC 2006*.

Roi Reichart and Ari Rappoport. 2008. Unsupervised induction of labeled parse trees by clustering with syntactic features. In *Proceedings of the 22nd International Conference on Computational Linguistics*.

Beatrice Santorini. 1990. Part-of-speech tagging guidelines for the Penn Treebank Project. Technical report, University of Pennsylvania.

W. Skut and T. Brants. 1998. Chunk tagger-statistical recognition of noun phrases. *Arxiv preprint cmp-lg/9807007*.

C. Thielen, A. Schiller, S. Teufel, and C. Stöckert. 1999. Guidelines für das Tagging deutscher Textkorpora mit STTS. Technical report, University of Stuttgart and University of Tübingen.

Kristina Toutanova and Christopher D. Manning. 2000. Enriching the knowledge sources used in a maximum entropy part-of-speech tagger. In *In EMNLP/VLC 2000*.

ISSN 1736-6305 Vol. 11
http://hdl.handle.net/10062/16955

"Andre ord" – a Wordnet Browser for the Danish Wordnet, DanNet

Anders Johannsen
University of Copenhagen
Copenhagen, Denmark
ajohannsen@hum.ku.dk

Bolette S. Pedersen
University of Copenhagen
Copenhagen, Denmark
bspedersen@hum.ku.dk

Abstract

A publically available wordnet browser will, if it does not remain in obscurity, have to cater to two different audiences: the professional lexicographers and the general public. This demonstration paper describes the wordnet browser "Andre ord" which has been developed for the Danish wordnet, DanNet. The first version was released in autumn 2009, followed by the release of a refined version in late 2010. The browser applies the open source framework Ruby on Rails and the graphing toolkit Protovis, and is itself open source. In the paper we discuss what design compromises might be needed when accommodating professionals and non-specialists alike, although our main concern is giving the general public an intuitive impression of the resource. To this aim we adopt the familiar, dictionary-like word-in-synset as the basic unit of the browser idea, but at the same time try to convey the idea that every piece of information in the wordnet is located somewhere in a larger semantic network structure.

1 Introduction and related work

In a certain sense, wordnet browsers abound. No doubt owing to its generous open source licence, content from the Princeton WordNet crop up in all sorts of dictionary-like applications. We have encountered it such diverse places as iPhone applications, writing assistants, web-based dictionaries, and as stand-alone software. In most of these settings the wordnet structure is disregarded, and the content is couched into an ordinary dictionary format that is familiar to most people. For our present purposes we will not consider these as wordnet browsers, but direct our attention to three of the comparably fewer that offer a full experience.

The official Princeton Wordnet browser[1] (Princeton University) exposes a text-like interface to the wordnet. A query for a word brings up a page that lists the various synsets it is a part of. Each synset can then be expanded by a click, which reveal its relations to other synsets along with additional facts about the synset, such as its allowed sentence frames. Hierarchical relations, which occur in for example "inherited_hypernym", are marked by indentation. All of the data in Wordnet is accessible by this interface and no attempt is made to restrict the output, even when this leads to pages of unwieldy length.

Visuwords[2] conceptualizes Wordnet as a network structure and employs a force-directed graph layout to visualize the connections between synsets. This type of layout algorithm, which progresses by simulating the graph as a physical system, with edges behaving like, for instance, springs, and nodes as charged particles, takes a short while to settle down, making the graph appear very lively at first. When entering a word it constructs a graph centered on a node with that label, linking to all synsets that include the query word. Ambiguity is thus not resolved but purposely kept in the graph illustration. Wordnet relations that originate in the synsets are also drawn, although if there are more than a few of each type they seem to get capped arbitrarily. Visuwords use color coding extensively, both on its own, to distinguish between synsets in various parts-of-speech, and in combination with shapes for telling different relation types apart.

While not a full-fledged wordnet browser, Nodebox[3] does contain an inspirational visualization of a wordnet synset. It uses a radial node-link diagram, which packs nodes along the radius of a circle. Edges are drawn by the use of line segments. Contrasting with Visuwords, the layout is static, and less dense with just one disambiguated synset and a single relation type being

---

[1] http://wordnetweb.princeton.edu/perl/webwn

[2] http://www.visuwords.com/

[3] http://nodebox.net/code/index.php/WordNet

displayed at a time, improving the over-all readability as well as calming the appearance of the graph. Because only one kind of information is visualized the graph does not use any color or shape encoding.

The rest of the paper is organised as follows. We introduce the DanNet resource in Section 2, and Section 3 describes the design considerations made. Technical details of "Andre ord" are given in Section 4. Finally, Section 5 briefly presents some ideas for future implementation.

2 Presentation of the resource: DanNet

DanNet (cf. wordnet.dk) is an open-source, lexical-semantic resource for Danish built in collaboration between The University of Copenhagen and Det Danske Sprog- og Litteraturselskab. The resource is meant for integration in computational systems that include a semantic aspect, such as writing aids and intelligent information navigation systems. Currently, it has been integrated in the Danish version of OpenOffice where it is used as a facility to suggest broader and more narrow terms, and it is integrated in a search module developed for The Municipality of Odense by the Danish company LAT-computing. Furthermore, the resource has been used in several research projects concerned with word sense disambiguation and search.

DanNet is a classical wordnet in the sense that it conforms to the framework of Princeton WordNet (Fellbaum 1998) and EuroWordNet (Vossen (ed.) 1999) with a few exceptions. However, in contrast with most other wordnets, DanNet has been constructed using a merge approach where the wordnet is constructed monolingually (based on Den Danske Ordbog) and thereafter linked to Princeton WordNet. This strategy can be seen in contrast to the more widely adopted expand approach where synsets are translated from Princeton WordNet into the target language.

At the time of writing, DanNet contains 62,000 synsets and is still under development within the DK-CLARIN project, until mid of 2011. DK-CLARIN is the Danish branch of the EU project CLARIN, an acronym which expands to a common language resources and technology infrastructure.

3 Design considerations

A publically available wordnet browser will, if it does not remain in obscurity, have to cater to two different audiences: the professional lexicographers and the general public. Sadly, their expectations and skill sets do not always align. To most people a wordnet will not be something readily familiar, and so the concept of, for instance, a synset will have to be set down before an uninitiated user can make sense of relations between such entities. This is a major challenge since the famously impatient web surfers of today do not like prolonged explanations.

However, as nearly everyone knows their way around a standard dictionary where a headword leads to a definition, emphasizing the similarity between a wordnet and a dictionary, rather than pointing out the differences, might reduce the burden of explanation. This has lead us to adopt the word-in-synset as the basic unit of the browser, that is: a synset pinned down by a particular choice of one of its synonyms. Each word-in-synset is presented on a separate page. Even though such a page in effect shows a synset, the notion itself is never brought to attention of the user. For browsing purposes this eliminates the need to explain the more abstract concept of a synset, but still preserving the relational nature of the wordnet.

Furthermore, we have sought to enhance the ease of use of the browser by shifting the display of important relation information from what would, in some cases, require some very long tables to a single, prominently placed graph. Our particular choice of graph, which is accounted for in the next section, very compactly encodes hundreds of relations. Even so there sometimes is a conflict between completeness and comprehensiveness. If the number of relations exceeds a certain limit they can no longer be displayed in the graph without sacrificing readability. In that case we favor comprehensiveness and drop relations according to a developed scheme. Luckily, we only have to resort to this option in 0,2 % of the cases.

In the wordnet browsers surveyed in the "Related works" section of the paper, pages are generated on the basis of a word, a possibly ambiguous string entered by the user and corresponding to one or more synsets. Thus each page view is often required to serve information about multiple synsets that are unrelated (in the wordnet sense), and perhaps distributed across different parts-of-speech. As such this agglomeration of synsets does not provide insight into the structure of the wordnet. We avoid bewildering the user by having him go through a disambiguation process in case of ambiguity at the end of which a single word-in-synset is chosen for display.

Another important consideration is how to highlight the situatedness of the data. We wanted to convey to the user the idea that every piece of information in the wordnet is located somewhere in a larger semantic network structure. We found no single way of effectively communicating this, but rely instead on the combination of several cues; the shortest path to the top node, which is printed like a breadcrumb, the relations to adjacent synsets being displayed in a manner suggestive of a network structure, and a chart that summarizes the complete hierarchy of hyperonomy relations that terminate in the current synset.

Returning, finally, to the problem of the dual audiences: the professionals who arrive with certain theoretically founded expectations, and the casual visitors with a more fleeting interesting in linguistics. We had the good fortune of not being in charge of developing the only browser for the DanNet project, albeit the only public one, and that allowed us to maintain a focus on the laymen perspective since a custom in-house tool already existed. Our concern with the professional audience was consequently less to indulge their desires for specialist functionality and more to make sure that our depiction of the resource was still valid and sound according to their point of view. For while the resource should be as easily accessible as possible, it should be no more so, to quote a phrase; under no circumstances did we want to distort the content of the wordnet to make it easier to understand.

So even if "Andre ord" was not designed with lexicographers in mind, they have nonetheless derived much utility from it. Perhaps owing to the more visual nature of this browser, it has proven very effective at spotting, for instance, relation type and inheritance errors.

4 Technical description

"Andre ord" is a web application, deployed at http://andreord.dk. It is built using the open source framework Ruby on Rails[4], and is itself open source. Protovis[5] from the Stanford Visualization Group is the foundation on which the graphs are constructed. Here we provide an overview of the elements of the central word-in-synset page as well as what steps are needed to arrive at that page.

Before any data from the wordnet can be displayed the user must type in a query. The query should be a single, uninflected word that exists in the wordnet. Helpful suggestions from the database continuously guide the match.

If the query corresponds to a single word-in-synset, it is displayed. Otherwise the user is redirected to a disambiguation page. Here, a list of matches is displayed along with their glosses. Furthermore, each word-in-synset is assigned a unique heading to make them easier to distinguish from each other. The heading is typically the word itself joined by either a hyperonym, a hyponym, or, in case they are not unique, a counter. A partial listing for the word "dronning" (queen) is "dronning (insekt)", "dronning (dame)", "dronning (kort)", and "dronning (regent)" (the translations for the parenthesized words are: "insect", "lady", "playing cards", and "ruler"). These (particular) headings are obviously very helpful for disambiguation.

On the main page two types of visualizations can be toggled. The first one, depicted below, is preselected ("blæseinstrument" is wind instrument).

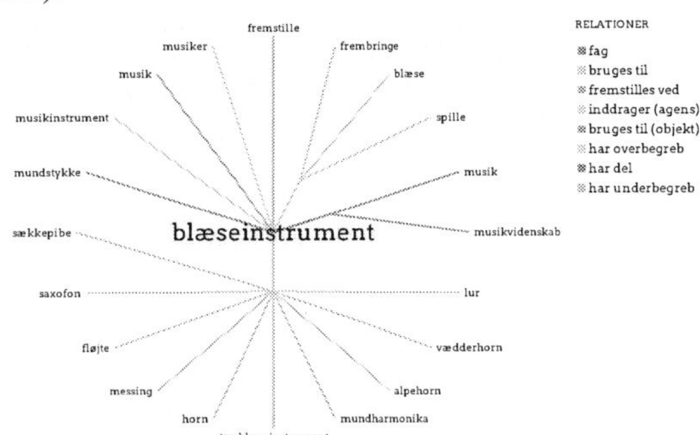

Figure 1: Word-in-synset relations

Here all relations that have the currently displayed synset as a source is shown. The graph is modelled as a two level node-link diagram. Relations connect via an intermediate relation type node, visually clustering nodes that share relation type. Color is used to mark the relation type and can be resolved in the accompanying legend. Graph layout is remarkably simple. Since the number of edge nodes is known in advance, and the level count is fixed, it suffices to group the relations by relation type, plot them as equally spaced points on a circle with a chosen radius, then connect them by line segments to a point on a smaller, inner circle which sits exactly midway between the extremes of the relation type group.

---

⁴ http://rubyonrails.org/
⁵ http://vis.stanford.edu/protovis/

As a final step the points on the inner circle are connected to the centre.

The graph can be navigated by clicking. Mouse-over reveals further information about the word-in-synset below the pointer, such as gloss and associated words.

If the number of relations on a given synset exceeds the capacity of this visualization, a capping policy kicks in. It works by grouping the relations by type, then iteratively picking one relation for display from each group, stopping when the limit has been reached. The idea is that smaller relation groups are shown in their entirety while larger ones get allotted the same share, regardless of their size. Fortunately, capping is rarely necessary as the radial layout, coupled with slanted labels, can fit a rather large number of relations.

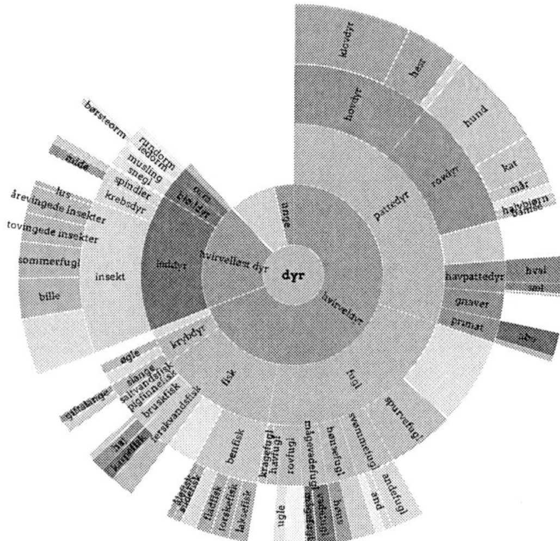

Figure 2: Aggregated hyponyms for "dyr"

The other visualization explores in depth the hyponym relation. In non-technical terms, it answers the question: what is this concept composed of? The answer comes in the form of a sunburst diagram, which is especially well suited for expressing these sorts of nested composed-of relationships. An important thing to notice is that proportionality is preserved so it is possible to visually compare the size (recursively enumerated hyponym count) of each hyponym.

There are synsets, typically situated near the top of the concept hierarchy, for which the number of recursive hyponyms far exceed what can be shown in the diagram. We decide on the most important hyponyms in the following manner. First, the recursive traversal is limited to a depth of four levels, and edge synsets are disregarded. Second, an algorithm is run that collapses synsets

too small to be shown (measured by the angular space available for the label) into a special "rest" category, marked by the use of a translucent color and no label. The reason for keeping synsets in the rest category is to maintain proportionality.

Apart from the visualizations the page contains pragmatic language use examples, a trace of the shortest path to the top synset, a complete list of hyponyms with glosses, and lastly, the ontological type of the synset.

5 Conclusion and future work

The development and release of "Andre ord" has highly increased the interest and knowledge of DanNet in the Danish community, both among linguistic and computational researchers and among commercial developers. We are delighted, and also a bit surprised, of the volume of the feedback. It shows that there is value in designing something not meant for ourselves.

Regarding future extensions, the following issues are under consideration. Currently there is no way to distinguish between an inherited relation (typically shared between sister terms) and a relation defined directly on the synset, even though the latter is considered more important. This extra dimension could be encoded using, for example, shape, such as a dotted line, or by attaching a slight glow to the line representing the relation. Another concern is how to heighten the layman user's appreciation of the subtler details of the wordnet. Though it is our firmly held belief that a public wordnet browser should be intuitive and largely self-explanatory, a little linguistic background information here and there may not be that harmful to the enterprise.

References

Fellbaum, C. (ed). 1998. *WordNet – An Electronic Lexical Database*. The MIT Press, Cambridge, Massachusetts, London, England.

Pedersen, B.S, S. Nimb, J. Asmussen, N. Sørensen, L. Trap-Jensen, H. Lorentzen. 2009. DanNet – the challenge of compiling a WordNet for Danish by reusing a monolingual dictionary. *Language Resources and Evaluation, Computational Linguistics Series*. Volume 43, Issue 3:269-299.

Princeton University "About WordNet." WordNet. Princeton University. 2010. <http://wordnet.princeton.edu>

Vossen, P. (ed). 1999. *EuroWordNet, A Multilingual Database with Lexical Semantic Networks*. Kluwer Academic Publishers, The Netherlands.

ISSN 1736-6305 Vol. 11
http://hdl.handle.net/10062/16955

Modularisation of Finnish Finite-State Language Description—Towards Wide Collaboration in Open Source Development of Morphological Analyser

Tommi A Pirinen
University of Helsinki
Helsinki, Finland
`tommi.pirinen@helsinki.fi`

Abstract

In this paper we present an open source implementation for Finnish morphological parser. We shortly evaluate it against contemporary criticism towards monolithic and unmaintainable finite-state language description. We use it to demonstrate way of writing finite-state language description that is used for varying set of projects, that typically need morphological analyser, such as POS tagging, morphological analysis, hyphenation, spell checking and correction, rule-based machine translation and syntactic analysis. The language description is done using available open source methods for building finite-state descriptions coupled with autotools-style build system, which is de facto standard in open source projects.

1 Introduction

Writing maintainable language descriptions for finite-state systems has traditionally been a laborious task. Even though finite-state technology has been de facto standard for writing computational language descriptions for more than two decades now (Beesley and Karttunen, 2003), it has some recognised flaws and problems both caused by shortcomings of actual implementations and background technology (Wintner, 2008). Commonly language description is performed by a single linguist or language technologist. The descriptions typically wind up being complex enough that modifying them requires a great amount of studying and understanding before one is able to do the smallest of modifications to the system. In the current times that all proper, healthy, scientific projects should be open source and globally developed, this poses a challenge for such project's internal structure. Another source of problem in such collaboration is that background of contributors for language description varies from computer scientists to linguists (Maxwell and David, 2008) to computer-savvy native language speakers, all of whom should be able to contribute to the project. The solutions we propose for this is to embrace proper modularisation in language descriptions to allow multiple specific entry points to contributors.

In this paper we describe a new implementation of the Finnish language description called omorfi[1], made to support large variety of NLP applications and different audiences. While the background theory for implementing finite-state description of Finnish was laid out already in Koskenniemi (1983), and morphophonological system does not have significant changes, the actual system was rewritten from the scratch. The rewriting was originally done by single linguist as usual, in a master's thesis project (Pirinen, 2008), but afterwards it has been extended as full-fledged open source project and used in various contexts. This extended development has necessitated a better modularised framework to allow people of varying level of familiarity with finite-state technology and Finnish to contribute on their prospective parts of the description without causing of modularisation problems for other applications of the finite-state analysers.

The projects that have used and use omorfi as language description include spell checking and correction (Pirinen and Lindén, 2010b), lemmatising for IR applications (e.g. Kurola (2010)), named entity recognition, rule-based machine translation Forcada et al. (2010)[2], and syntactic disambiguation and analysis. The demands for even the basic morphology with all these different applications are very different with regards to productivity; lexical coverage and accuracy as well as depth

---

[1] http://home.gna.org/omorfi
[2] http://www.apertium.org/

"

of tagging, so it has became obvious that no one lexical automaton will work for everyone. For this reason the modularisation has to provide easily configurable options and modifiability for all end-points.

One of the key points in modular structure here is that we ensure that modifying will not typically break already working parts, so contributors adding new words or moving hyphens will not cause problems in other parts of description as much as possible.

2 Modularisation of Finite-State Language Description

The modularisation scheme we ended up with in finite-state description of Finnish has grown organically around rather standard description of finite-state morphology. The further development followed from development of finite-state technology along years from initial implementation of omorfi at publication of Pirinen (2008).

In omorfi we use a hierarchical set of abstract modules implemented to encapsulate the system. As mentioned, the classical modules of morphotactic combinatorics (i.e. Xerox compatible lexc language description) and morphophonology (i.e. Xerox compatible twolc description) is still present. The morphotactic combinatorics has already been split to sub modules for two reasons. First is primarily practical fact that code base for morphotactic combinatorics for words of Finnish is huge. Second and perhaps the more important distinction is the fact that central and integral part of the life force of morphophonological description of the all languages is to keep up with constant influx of new lexical items to the language; neologisms, proper nouns and other coinages. From further new modules, orthographical variations was implemented to create detached support for certain obvious variations of Finnish written data, e.g. the typewriter and SF7-ASCII era digraphs like sh and zh in stead of š and ž respectively. The hyphenation and syllabification of Finnish language is also one obvious service for morphological dictionary to provide; for Finnish the compound boundaries cannot typically be discriminated without a dictionary (Lindén and Pirinen, 2009a). One of the features that has become rather obvious along years for morphological parsers is the fact that all computational linguistic applications must require their own very special version of morphological

analysis, so in omorfi we have chosen to avoid lock-ins for any specific type of *tag sets*, and instead go for one version of analysis to contain certain superset of all needed forms and rewrite as needed. The statistical models is one of recent developments of finite-state technology, and there is a lot to offer for language models here so the whole family of weighted finite-state training and models is also implemented in omorfi as a separate module here, which for most intents and purposes does work independently of any other part of the language description.

3 Implementation

Here we briefly discuss implementation of modules, mainly to discuss about practices that help the cooperation. Naturally full discussion of the modules is found in the documentation of the system[3]. The system implementation is harnessing the autotools framework and unix style tools of HFST to incrementally build the finite-state automata using finite-state algebra, such as composition to extend them, originally noted even in Beesley and Karttunen (2003). The crucial thing for this modular approach is that it can be applied incrementally, each module can be replaced or disabled entirely at needs of end application, and with autotools framework all this can be performed by simple command-line switch to `./configure`.

3.1 Lexical Data—Lexicon and Features of Lexical Items

The initial part of morphotactics deals with lexicographical data. This is the part where most modification and cooperation can be used, the lexical items in language change all the time in introduction of new word forms, and the expertise needed to extend the lexicon does not require significant expertise beyond understanding of the language. For this case we provide different entry formats for new lexical data; csv, XML and so on. The minimal data to enter for new word form is morphological part of speech. Additionally a paradigm classification is typically needed for working inflection and derivation. While this is facilitated as much as possible, further research for easy lexicon management is still required.

The other practical example as to why easy modification of lexical data is crucial is that for example for rule-based machine translation benefits

---

[3] `http://home.gna.org/omorfi/`

from mapping between lexical units of source language and target language. Similarly for forthcoming syntactic constraint grammar work in vein of (Karlsson, 1990). For this reason easy access to lexical units is required for users of morphology.

3.2 Traditional Morphotactics and Phonology—The Lexc and Twolc Model

The various lexical data sources are joined back to traditional lexc format, which is combined with word stem variation definitions and inflectional data to produce lexical automaton. This is compose-intersected with morphophonology descriptions to produce the analyser already; as these parts rarely need changes beyond bug-fixes and are unlikely to benefit from open source cooperation beyond initial linguist work, they are still in same form as traditional finite-state morphology by Beesley and Karttunen (2003), even if it was deemed monolithic and fragile for such collaboration.

3.3 Analysis Formats and Sets

Another thing that is quickly obvious for interoperability is that all projects using morphological analyser, for whatever purpose, require their own analysis format. Instead of converging to standard we have temporarily solved this by making our analyser to contain superset of required features at all times, and providing rules to rewrite the tagsets. The rulesets can be compiled to finite-state networks and composed like usual. Typical rules are of course relatively simple contextless rewriting, for example the annotation for singular nominative is +sg+nom or <sg><nom>, for different applications, so a simple composition in style of NUM=SG:+sg is enough for providing the singular nominatives to that analysis style. Ideally of course this would be solved by using more suitable abstract data type for the annotations than character string (Wintner, 2008), ideally derived from standardized set of features, such as ISOCat as is also suggested by (Maxwell and David, 2008).

3.4 Orthographical variations

When dealing with data from various sources, such as old literature or *spoken* standard language found in instant messaging etc., there are certain variations on spelling rules. These has also been implemented as independent rule set compiled to composable finite-state automaton. Incidentally both mapping of typewriter digraphs sh and zh to š and ž

correspondingly and omission of final component of i-final diphthong of spoken language are both definable as rule working on morphological analyser as an independent unit.

3.5 Hyphenation and syllabification

Hyphenation is in practice also one of the applications of the language. It has been defined as a rule set over half-build morphological analyser, since it can neatly abuse build-time information of the analyser, such as word and morpheme boundaries. The syllables could also conversely be used by other parts of the description if needed.

3.6 Error models

Error model is a crucial part of spell-checking system, for the correction task. This is implemented as finite-state filter that can be applied with on-the-fly composition (Pirinen and Lindén, 2010a) to perform the error correction for spell checking, or for example error-tolerant analysis.

3.7 Statistical models

Statistical models provide for disambiguating language models and spell-checking tasks for example. The statistical models used are simple finite-state automata or training sets combinable to the language description by use of composition (Lindén and Pirinen, 2009a; Lindén and Pirinen, 2009b).

3.8 Filtering the Analyser

The models needed for different task may need widely different dictionaries and allowed wordforms, and not always the statistical models are sufficient to discriminate between good word forms. So we also provide filter rule sets, to limit features, such as derivation and compounding, and lexical units, such as archaic or dialectal words. For example for the spell-checker's error detection lexicon or information retrieval task compounding and derivation can be largely allowed, whereas in the spelling correction the suggestions should be relatively conservative for plausible but non-existing compounds and derivations.

4 Discussion and Future Work

In this article we have showed that finite-state description can be implemented in modularised manner enabling wide cooperation in the open source context for people with varying background. Furthermore we have demonstrated the ease of proper abstraction in finite-state language description using easily available open source tools while still providing open source community with the de facto standard build system of autotoolset for wide distribution, packaging and deployment.

What we did not address here is the easy way of coupling up-to-date documentation with our modularised language description. The next step to research is to see into integrating the notion of literate programming in this framework. This topic has already been widely researched by Maxwell and David (2008), specifically in case of finite-state language descriptions.

Acknowledgements

We thank Donald Killian for pointing us towards the ongoing discussion about shortcomings of finite-state morphologies and the HFST research group, and our colleagues for fruitful discussions.

References

Kenneth R Beesley and Lauri Karttunen. 2003. *Finite State Morphology*. CSLI publications.

Mikel L. Forcada, Mireia Ginestí i Rosell, Jacob Nordfalk, Jim O'Regan, Sergio Ortiz-Rojas, Juan Antonio Pérez-Ortiz, Gema Ramírez-Sánchez, Felipe Sánchez-Martínez, and Francis M. Tyers. 2010. Apertium: a free/open-source platform for rule-based machine translation platform. *Machine Translation. to appear*.

Fred Karlsson. 1990. Constraint grammar as a framework for parsing unrestricted text. In H. Karlgren, editor, *Proceedings of the 13th International Conference of Computational Linguistics*, volume 3, pages 168–173, Helsinki.

Kimmo Koskenniemi. 1983. *Two-level Morphology: A General Computational Model for Word-Form Recognition and Production*. Ph.D. thesis, University of Helsinki.

Joel Kurola. 2010. Työpaikkailmoitusten sisällön ja osaamisvaatimusten käsittely. Bachelor's thesis (in Finnish).

Krister Lindén and Tommi Pirinen. 2009a. Weighted finite-state morphological analysis of finnish compounds. In Kristiina Jokinen and Eckhard Bick, editors, *Nodalida 2009*, volume 4 of *NEALT Proceedings*.

Krister Lindén and Tommi Pirinen. 2009b. Weighting finite-state morphological analyzers using hfst tools. In Bruce Watson, Derrick Courie, Loek Cleophas, and Pierre Rautenbach, editors, *FSMNLP 2009*, 13 July.

Michael Maxwell and Anne David. 2008. Joint grammar development by linguists and computer scientists. In *Workshop on NLP for Less Privileged Languages, Third International Joint Conference on Natural Language Processing*, Hyderabad, India.

Tommi A Pirinen and Krister Lindén. 2010a. Building and using existing hunspell dictionaries and TeX hyphenators as finite-state automata. In *Proccedings of Computational Linguistics - Applications, 2010*, pages 25–32, Wisła, Poland.

Tommi A Pirinen and Krister Lindén. 2010b. Finite-state spell-checking with weighted language and error models. In *Proceedings of the Seventh SaLT-MiL workshop on creation and use of basic lexical resources for less-resourced languagages*, pages 13–18, Valletta, Malta.

Tommi Pirinen. 2008. Suomen kielen äärellistilainen automaattinen morfologinen analyysi avoimen lähdekoodin menetelmin. Master's thesis, Helsingin yliopisto.

Shuly Wintner. 2008. Strengths and weaknesses of finite-state technology: A case study in morphological grammar development. *Nat. Lang. Eng.*, 14:457–469, October.

ISSN 1736-6305 Vol. 11
http://hdl.handle.net/10062/16955

A Prague Markup Language Profile
for the SemTi-Kamols Grammar Model

Lauma Pretkalniņa, Gunta Nešpore, Kristīne Levāne-Petrova, Baiba Saulīte
Institute of Mathematics and Computer Science
University of Latvia
Raiņa bulv. 29, Rīga, LV-1459, Latvia
`{lauma,gunta,kristine,baiba}@ailab.lv`

Abstract

In this paper we demonstrate a hybrid treebank encoding format, derived from the dependency-based format used in Prague Dependency Treebank (PDT). We have specified a Prague Markup Language (PML) profile for the SemTi-Kamols hybrid grammar model that has been developed for languages with relatively free word order (e.g. Latvian). This has allowed us to exploit the tree editor TrEd that has been used in PDT development. As a proof of concept, a small Latvian treebank has been created by annotating 100 sentences from "Sophie's World".

1   Introduction

Two general approaches can be distinguished in the syntactic representation: the phrase structure approach (Chomsky, 1957) and the dependency approach (Tesnière, 1959). Dependency grammars are usually treated and implemented in a simplified way, if compared to Tesnière's original approach, sacrificing the linguistic details for the benefit of efficient parsing algorithms (Jarvinen and Tapanainen, 1998). In the result, each running-word is treated as a separate part of sentence, which is involved in a separate dependency relation. The SemTi-Kamols hybrid dependency grammar for Latvian implements and extends Tesnière's basic concepts (Bārzdiņš et al., 2007; Nešpore et al., 2010).

Manual development of a Latvian treebank (according to the SemTi-Kamols model) would be very laborious and the tool support is crucial. The SemTi-Kamols model is based on the de-pendency approach, therefore we have chosen to adapt the annotation tool TrEd (Hajič et al., 2001) that has been proven itself developing the Prague Dependency Treebank (Hajič et al., 2000). The SemTi-Kamols model is more complex than that of PDT analytical layer, as we use both dependencies and phrase structures in the same tree.

TrEd itself is a rather generic-purpose tree editor that can be customized to specific treebank requirements by providing an appropriate extension module. The main component of such a module is a schema that describes the data format. The module also contains style sheets specifying how the data should be represented visually. It may contain some macros for additional support as well — to automate the common annotation tasks or to detect common annotation errors.

2   SemTi-Kamols model

Apart from dependency links, the SemTi-Kamols model is based on a concept of "x-word": a syntactic unit describing analytical word forms and relations other than subordination (Bārzdiņš et al., 2007; Nešpore et al., 2010). From the phrase structure perspective, x-words can be viewed as non-terminal symbols, and as such substitute (during the parsing process) all entities forming respective constituents. From the dependency perspective, x-words are treated as regular words, i.e., an x-word can act as a head for depending words and/or as a dependent of another head word. The following constructions are treated as x-words:

- analytic forms of a verb, e.g. the perfect tense;

- numerals (e.g. *trīsdesmit trīs* 'thirty three') and other multi-word units;

- prepositional phrases;

- coordination etc.

3   Data format

Our data format is specified in the XML-based Prague Markup Language (PML). PML is the default input format for TrEd; it is also the main data format of PDT (Pajas and Štěpánek, 2006).

We have adapted the multi-layer annotation approach from PDT (Hajič et al., 2000; Pajas and Štěpánek, 2006). PDT has four annotation layers: *w, m, a, t*. At the *w or* word level, text is divided in tokens and paragraphs. The *m* or morphological level adds morphological annotations and spelling error corrections. At the *a* or analytical level syntactic annotations (dependency links) are added. The top level is the tectogrammatical level *t*, which contains semantic annotations. All the levels (their nodes) are connected through unique IDs. In this paper we address only the first three levels.

The first level (*w*) is taken from PDT as is. The second level (*m*) is adapted with minor changes. We use the possibility to annotate spelling mistakes in the source text at this level. We use most of PDT spellchecking categories and we have added one more to indicate that two tokens form one morphological unit.

The third level (*a*) is the most interesting case. In PDT all relations between parts of sentence are represented using dependencies only, while for the SemTi-Kamols model we need more sophisticated means to deal with both dependencies and phrase structure components (x-words). Further we will examine our *a*-level tree structure.

To operate with a PML document in TrEd, it is necessary to specify which elements correspond to the nodes of the parse tree to be drawn on TrEd's pane, as the rest of the elements describe attributes of these nodes. The tree structure itself corresponds to the (tree) structure of the PML/XML document. The possible structure of the document also needs to be described. It is done by providing the corresponding PML schema to TrEd. PML elements are linked with tree nodes by adding the attribute "role" (with values "root", "node", "childlist" etc.) to the definitions of appropriate elements in PML schema.

Here the first issues arise, as TrEd supports nodes with only one child-list. However, we would like to create a scheme, where each node can have two types of children. One type would represent dependants, the other type — constitu-

ents of parent node (this is the case of an x-word). Each node would be able to have any number of children of any of those types. Also, there must be a simple way, how human-annotator can change whether the particular node is parent's dependant or constituent from TrEd. To achieve this, all the children must have the same node type definition in the PML schema. It seems that the only reasonable solution to handle nodes with both types of children is to use artificial nodes.

For each node we introduce one optional child of a special kind — a "container for constituents". If parent node has no container node for constituents as a child, all the children are parent's dependants (see fig. 1). If there is such a container node, its siblings are considered as parent's dependants, but the container node's children — as constituents of the container node's parent. If the node has the container node as a child, there is no token from text, corresponding to this node; in this case, no tokens correspond to the container nodes, too. On the one hand, this makes our PML schema more complicated, but, on the other hand, this significantly improves its usability for a human-annotator.

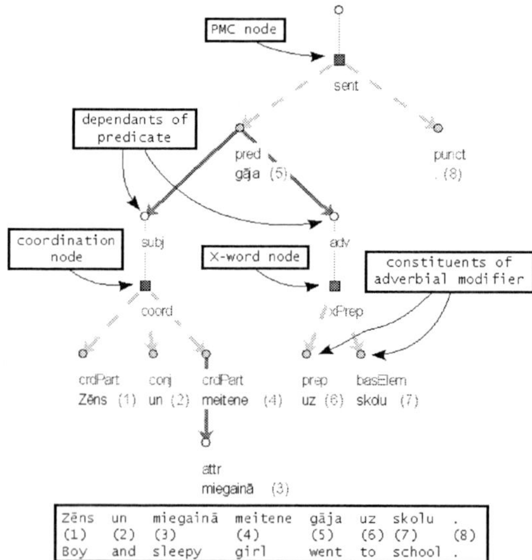

Zēns	un	miegainā	meitene	gāja	uz	skolu	.
(1)	(2)	(3)	(4)	(5)	(6)	(7)	(8)
Boy	and	sleepy	girl	went	to	school	.

Figure 1: Tree for sentence *Zēns un miegainā meitene gāja uz skolu* 'The boy and the sleepy girl went to the school'

The distinction has been made between three types of containers for constituents. One type is coordination (both coordinated parts of sentence and clauses), other type is so-called genuine x-words (x-words mentioned above other than coordination); the last type is PMC nodes. PMC (punctuation mark constructs) are the phrase-like systems which hold together some subtrees with corresponding punctuation marks.

PMC is a novelty in attribution to SemTi-Kamols model. As in Latvian the punctuation represents the grammatical structure of the sentence, showing it in the syntax tree is significant to create comprehensive model for the sentence. Nonetheless, to interpret PMC as fully eligible phrase structure would be inadequate in relation syntax theory of Latvian, as PMC components have far more flexible structure as x-words or coordination. PMC nodes handle punctuation marks for constructions like direct speech, subordinate clauses, insertions and parenthesis etc.

Distinction between coordination and genuine x-words was made to make SemTi-Kamols model closer to the original Tesnière's model.

For the dependent children we denote their syntactic roles. For the constituent children we denote their function in the phrase they constitute. We hope, this will facilitate detection of inconsistent markup avoiding issues mentioned by Boyd et al. (2008). For each container node for constituents we add a tag showing the type of x-word (e.g., x-predicate or x-preposition), coordination or PMC. For x-words and coordinate parts of sentence we provide a tag similar to those used at the morphological level. This tag describes the function carried out in the sentence by the whole unit.

Every token in a sentence (even punctuation marks) corresponds to some node in the tree, but not all the nodes have corresponding tokens. As mentioned above, the container nodes for constituents and their direct parents have no corresponding tokens, but there is one more case with no corresponding token. We handle omitted parts of sentence using nodes with no corresponding tokens, for example, elliptical predicate is displayed as "empty" node with additional tag. In all other ways these nodes act as normal nodes — they can have both dependants and constituents.

4   Additional support

We have developed an extension module for TrEd to enable TrEd to work with the trees described above. This extension contains not just schemas, but also helper macros and style sheets.[1]

---

[1] Module is provided under GPL and can be downloaded here http://eksperimenti.ailab.lv/tred/

We developed two basic ways for visual representation of the trees from Latvian Treebank. One way is the Full view (Fig. 2). It is created to be used for annotators, and it displays every single node as it is, and adds red warnings to the nodes that have probably incorrect roles.

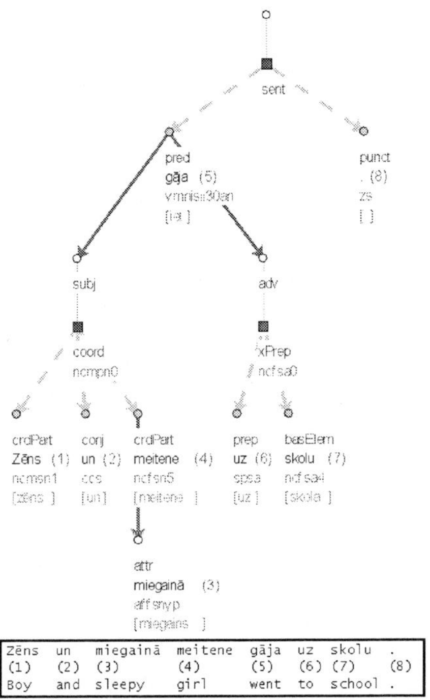


```
Zēns   un     miegainā  meitene  gāja   uz   skolu   .
(1)    (2)    (3)                (4)      (5)    (6)  (7)      (8)
Boy    and    sleepy    girl     went   to   school  .
```

Figure 2: A sentence in the Full view with grammatical information

The other way is the Compact view. It is created to be used for end-users of corpora who don't want to be buried in technical complexities yet need to have full access to all the data. In the Compact view (Fig. 3) container nodes for constituents are displayed as differently colored edges from their parent to their children, thus obtaining the representation we wanted in the beginning of interaction with TrEd. Also there is a possibility to choose, whether to show the grammatical information — lemma and tag. The Compact view can't be used to edit trees.

TrEd implicitly validates data against given PML schema. TrEd does not permit editing, which leads to incompatibility with schema. These features act as a simple error preventing mechanism. As PML schema is not all-powerful we have developed additional macros to check easy-detectable deviations from the intended tree structure. In most cases detected deviations are mistakes made by annotator, but in some cases this was the way to discover incompleteness in our intended structure.

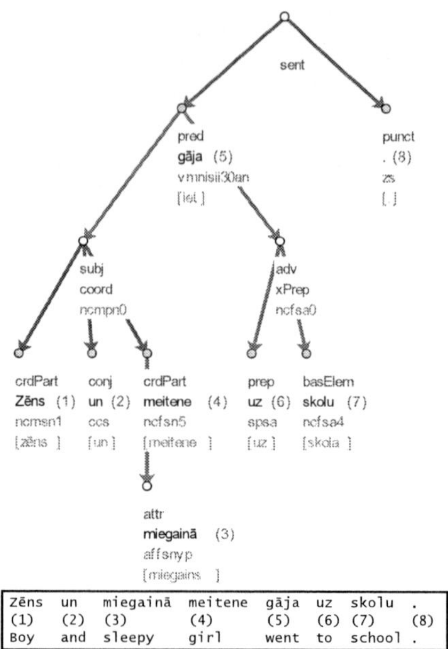

Figure 3: A sentence in the Compact view with grammatical information

5 "Sophie's World"

As a proof of concept, we have annotated first 100 sentences of J. Gaarder's "Sophie's World" using the developed infrastructure.

Annotation was done as follows. First, the morphological markup was added in a semi-automated way. After that, linguist trained in work with TrEd manually created preliminary trees. Finally, trees where discussed and verified by general meeting consisting from 2 or 3 linguists and the architect of PML schema for Latvian Treebank. This multi-step process allowed us to repeatedly verify whether the intended schema and data format is appropriate for the Latvian language, whether it can represent all the encountered phenomena of the language, whether the later added schema additions is consistent with the initial intentions.

6 Conclusion

The integration of PDT tools and SemTi-Kamols' grammar model so far has proved to be successful and should be continued by integrating PDT tools with the rule-based SemTi-Kamols' partial parser (Bārzdiņš et al. 2007). The next step would be to develop a bigger treebank to cover all the syntactic constructs of Latvian and to obtain more precise results and statistical information to build a statistical parser. Though, even the 100 sentences annotated so far

covers most of syntactic constructions typical for standard Latvian.

Acknowledgments

This work is funded by the State Research Programme "National Identity" (project No 3) and the Latvian Council of Sciences project "Application of Factored Methods in English-Latvian Statistical Machine Translation System".

Reference

Guntis Bārzdiņš, Normunds Grūzītis, Gunta Nešpore, Baiba Saulīte. 2007. *Dependency-Based Hybrid Model of Syntactic Analysis for the Languages with a Rather Free Word Order.* Proceedings of the 16th Nordic Conference of Computational Linguistics (NODALIDA), pp. 13–20

Adriane Boyd, Markus Dickinson, Detmar Meurers. 2008. *On Detecting Errors in Dependency Treebanks.* Research on Language and Computation 6(2), pp. 113–137.

Noam Chomsky. 1957. *Syntactic Structures.* The Hague: Mouton

Jan Hajič, Alena Böhmová, Eva Hajičová, Barbora Vidová Hladká. 2000. *The Prague Dependency Treebank: A Three-Level Annotation Scenario.* A. Abeillé (ed.): Treebanks: Building and Using Parsed Corpora, Amsterdam: Kluwer, pp. 103–127.

Jan Hajič, Barbora Vidová Hladká, Petr Pajas. 2001. *The Prague Dependency Treebank: Annotation Structure and Support.* Proceedings of the IRCS Workshop on Linguistic Databases, Proceedings of the IRCS Workshop on Linguistic Databases, Philadelphia, USA, pp. 105–114.

Timo Järvinen, Pasi Tapanainen. 1998. *Towards an implementable dependency grammar.* Proceedings of the Workshop on Processing of Dependency-Based Grammars, pp. 1–10.

Gunta Nešpore, Baiba Saulīte, Guntis Bārzdiņš, Normunds Grūzītis. 2010. *Comparison of the SemTi-Kamols and Tesnière's Dependency Grammars.* Proceedings of the 4th International Conference on Human Language Technologies — the Baltic Perspective, Frontiers in Artificial Intelligence and Applications, Vol. 219, IOS Press, pp. 233–240

Petr Pajas, Jan Štěpánek. 2006. *XML-Based Representation of Multi-Layered Annotation in the PDT 2.0.* Proceedings of the LREC Workshop on Merging and Layering Linguistic Information (LREC 2006), pp. 40–47.

Lucien Tesnière. 1959. *Éléments de syntaxe structurale.* Klincksieck, Paris. (Translation to Russian: Теньер Л. 1988. *Основы структурного синтаксиса.* Ред. В.Г. Гак. Москва, Прогресс.)

ISSN 1736-6305 Vol. 11
http://hdl.handle.net/10062/16955

Dialect Classification in the Himalayas: a Computational Approach

Anju Saxena
Department of Linguistics and Philology
Uppsala University, Sweden
anju.saxena@lingfil.uu.se

Lars Borin
Språkbanken, Department of Swedish
University of Gothenburg, Sweden
lars.borin@svenska.gu.se

Abstract

Linguistic fieldwork data – in the form of basic vocabulary lists – for nine closely related language varieties are compared using an automatic procedure with manual feedback, whose major advantage is its complete consistency. The results of the vocabulary comparison turn out to be in accord with other linguistic features, making this methodology a promising addition to the toolbox of genetic lingusitics.

1 Introduction

The aim of the work presented here is to examine genetic relationships among nine Tibeto-Burman varieties spoken in the Kinnaur region in India, using a semi-automatic computational approach. The focus in this presentation is on lexical items, although grammatical features are also taken into account in our work.

2 Background: Kinnauri varieties and the language data used

The Tibeto-Burman varieties to be discussed here are collectively referred to as Kinnauri and are spoken[1] in the Kinnaur region in the Himachal Pradesh state in India. They belong to the West-Himalayish sub-branch of the Tibeto-Burman language family, which in turn forms one of the two primary subdivisions of the Sino-Tibetan language family. There is brief mention of some Kinnauri varieties in some older works (e.g., Gerard 1842; Cunningham 1844). However, to date there has not been any systematic, comparative linguistic study of the Kinnauri varieties, and consequently no systematic basis for examining how the Tibeto-Burman varieties spoken in Kinnaur relate to one another.

The fieldwork to collect the data used in this investigation was conducted in the following villages in Kinnaur: Nichar (Ni), Sangla (Sa), Chitkul (Ch), Kalpa (Ka), Kuno (Ku), Labrang (La), Poo

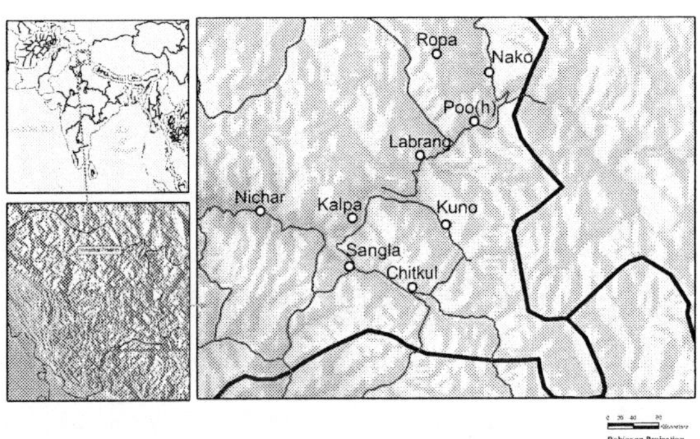

Figure 1: Villages in Kinnaur where data collection was conducted

(Po), Ropa (Ro) and Nako (Na). See figure 1. The main motivation for selecting these villages was to include data from as diverse geographical regions as possible. The data comprise (i) a basic vocabulary list (a revised Swadesh list; Swadesh 1955) for all sites (242 senses); (ii) an extended IDS list for Sangla and Nako (1884 senses);[2] and (iii) selected grammatical constructions.

3 Procedure for word list comparison

The procedure which we have used for comparing the word lists here is similar to recent work in dialectometry (e.g., Nerbonne and Heeringa 2009) and lexicostatistics (e.g., Holman et al. 2008) in relying on a completely automatic comparison of the items in the word lists. However, it differs from most of this work – a notable exception being the work reported on by McMahon et al. (2007) – in its usage of rules tailored to the particular linguistic configuration under investigation, rather than a general method for string comparison. In this respect, it falls somewhere in between traditional glottochronology – where expert statements are required about the cognacy of items – and these modern approaches – which rely entirely on surface form for determining identity of items – although closer to the latter than the former.

---

[1]None of them have a conventional written form.

[2]See <http://lingweb.eva.mpg.de/ids>. For practical reasons, the IDS list could be collected only for two varieties, and we chose two varieties spoken at the extreme ends of the main river valley running through Kinnaur.

"

new/183*	Sa	Ni	Ka	Ro	Ch	La	Po	Ku	Na
new/183*	[1] ɲug	[1] ɲug	[2] ɲuk	[3] ɲukʰ:	[4] nʊɪ	[4] nʊɪ	[5] sɔma	[5] sɔma	[5] sɔma
red/172	[1] ʃʊɪg	[1] ʃʊig	[1] ʃʊig	[1/2] ʃʊig; ʃʊik	[3] məɪ	[3] məi	[4] marpo	[4] marbo	[4] marʋo
small/32	[1/2] dzikts; gaʈo	[2/3] gaʈo; dzɪk	[4] dzɪgits	[4] dzɪgɪts	[5] ats	[6] tsɪgɪts	[7] ɔun:	[7] ɔun:	[7] ɔun
warm/180	[1] bok	[1/1] bok:; bɔk:	[1] bɔk:	[1] bɔk:	[2/3] tatʰra; ta	[4] kocʰra	[5/6] ɖɔnmo; ʈanmo	[6] ʈɔnmo	[7] ʈɔnmo
white/175	[1] tʰog	[1] tʰog	[1] tʰog	[1] tʰog	[2] tʃaɪn	[3] tʃai	[4] karʋo	[4] karbo	[4] karʋo
yellow/174	[1] pɪg	[1] pig	[2] pik	[2/1] pik; pig	[3] lei	[3] lei	[4] sekʰa	[5] sɛrbo	[5] serʋo

(a) Comparison and assignment to equivalence classes of some adjectives

	Ni	Ka	Ro	Ch	La	Po	Ku	Na
Sa	13/19 (68%)	9/19 (47%)	11/19 (57%)	1/18 (5%)	1/18 (5%)	1/17 (5%)	0/19 (0%)	1/19 (5%)
Ni		12/19 (63%)	10/19 (52%)	1/18 (5%)	1/18 (5%)	0/17 (0%)	0/19 (0%)	0/19 (0%)
Ka			11/19 (57%)	1/18 (5%)	1/18 (5%)	0/17 (0%)	0/19 (0%)	0/19 (0%)
Ro				1/18 (5%)	1/18 (5%)	1/17 (5%)	0/19 (0%)	1/19 (5%)
Ch					8/18 (44%)	0/17 (0%)	0/18 (0%)	1/18 (5%)
La						0/17 (0%)	1/18 (5%)	1/18 (5%)
Po							10/17 (58%)	9/17 (52%)
Ku								11/19 (57%)

(b) Comparison of all adjectives

	Ni	Ka	Ro	Ch	La	Po	Ku	Na
Sa	67/94 (71%)	69/94 (73%)	51/94 (54%)	44/94 (46%)	28/93 (30%)	10/93 (10%)	13/95 (13%)	11/94 (11%)
Ni		61/93 (65%)	42/93 (45%)	36/93 (38%)	25/92 (27%)	9/92 (9%)	9/94 (9%)	8/93 (8%)
Ka			51/93 (54%)	41/93 (44%)	27/92 (29%)	10/92 (10%)	11/94 (11%)	9/93 (9%)
Ro				37/93 (39%)	37/92 (40%)	14/92 (15%)	20/94 (21%)	16/93 (17%)
Ch					29/92 (31%)	8/92 (8%)	11/94 (11%)	10/93 (10%)
La						16/91 (17%)	20/93 (21%)	17/92 (18%)
Po							48/93 (51%)	57/92 (61%)
Ku								53/94 (56%)

(c) Comparison of all nouns

	Ni	Ka	Ro	Ch	La	Po	Ku	Na
Sa	107/157 (68%)	106/155 (68%)	85/161 (52%)	60/158 (37%)	36/156 (23%)	13/156 (8%)	16/159 (10%)	14/162 (8%)
Ni		102/153 (66%)	74/156 (47%)	49/154 (31%)	33/152 (21%)	10/151 (6%)	11/155 (7%)	9/156 (5%)
Ka			86/154 (55%)	54/151 (35%)	34/149 (22%)	11/148 (7%)	13/152 (8%)	10/154 (6%)
Ro				53/157 (33%)	45/155 (29%)	16/154 (10%)	22/158 (13%)	18/160 (11%)
Ch					44/155 (28%)	10/154 (6%)	13/157 (8%)	13/157 (8%)
La						20/152 (13%)	24/156 (15%)	21/155 (13%)
Po							76/154 (49%)	87/155 (56%)
Ku								84/158 (53%)

(d) Comparison of all words in the word list

Table 1: Some results of the comparisons

The main methodological advantage of our approach is its consistency, and not as claimed for the work just referred to, that it should be language-independent. Instead, in our case we try to apply a principle sometimes formulated in computational linguistics as "Don't guess if you know" (Tapanainen and Voutilainen, 1994, 47), which leads us to include language-specific knowledge in the form of correspondence rules among dialects.

The following proceedure was used in this investigation, developed in collaboration between a computational linguist (Borin) and the linguist who collected the language data (Saxena):

- After the data collection and initial processing of the data,
- a list of observations of relationships among varieties was made by the linguist.
- This list formed the basis for developing a set of principles for comparing the linguistic correspondences in these Kinnauri varieties. These were formulated by the linguist and computational linguist together and their purpose was to determine which segmental differences to disregard for the purpose of considering items in different varietes as the same.
- The principles were encoded by the computational linguist as context-sensitive phonological segment equivalence rules in a small computer program for comparing items fully automatically in order to achieve consistency.
- The equivalence rules were revised after inspection of the result, and the program run again on the data. This process went through a few iterations until the linguist was satisfied with the result.

The results are indicative and sometimes subject to revision, but interesting. They come in the form of two kinds of tables:

- tables of individual lexical items, where items considered the same in different varieties get the same numerical index (table 1a);
- summary tables, where similarities among all lexical items of a particular grammatical or semantic category (nouns, kinship terms, etc.) are shown as ratios and percentages (see tables 1b–1d).

4 Results

The findings of this survey will be illustrated here by focusing on the following lexical sets: adjectives, nouns, numerals and all words. In table 1a, all Swadesh list items are further identified by their Swadesh list number added to the end of the English word and separated from the word by a slash: *small/32*.

Data on adjectives are shown in tables 1a and 1b. Yellow indicates Kinnauri varieties which show 50% or more similarity, blue indicates 10% or less similarity. Sangla, Nichar, Kalpa and Ropa share a higher degree of similarity with one another. Similarly, there is a higher degree of similarity between Poo, Kuno and Nako. But there is very little similarity between the varieties of the Sangla group and the varieties of the Nako group.

Table 1c gives corresponding figures for nouns.

The numerals 1–10 in the Kinnauri varieties are cognates to a very large extent – consistent with the Tibeto-Burman numeral forms noted by Hodson (1913). For the numerals 1, 4, 7, 8 and 10 these varieties use two distinct cognate forms: Poo, Kuno and Nako use the same forms as noted by Hodson (1913) for Central Tibetan, while Nichar, Sangla, Kalpa, Ropa, Chitkul and Labrang use another set of forms.[3] These data, which lack of space prevents us from showing, thus support the pattern emerging from the comparisons that we show here.

5 Summary and discussion

See table 1d. This comparison suggests that

1. the Kinnauri varieties on the two extremes of this table form two separate sub-groups, referred to here as the "Sangla group" at the left end and the "Nako group" at the right end.
2. The core members of the Sangla group are Sangla, Nichar and Kalpa, with Ropa as a more peripheral member. The core members of the Nako group are Poo, Kuno and Nako. They show a high degree of mutual similarity (mostly more than 50%).
3. These tables also display a consistent sharp distinction between the Sangla group and the Nako group, where the degree of similarity between the two groups is less than 10% in most cases.
4. Concerning the status of the remaining two varieties, Chitkul and Labrang:

   a. The degree of similarity between Chitkul and Labrang is neither very high nor very low. It is 28%
   b. Concerning their relationship to the two groups, Chitkul – much more than Labrang – shows a relatively higher degree of similarity with the Sangla group (31–37%) than with the Nako group (6–8%).

---

[3] A similar subgrouping pattern emerges also concerning the formation of higher numerals in the Kinnauri varieties.

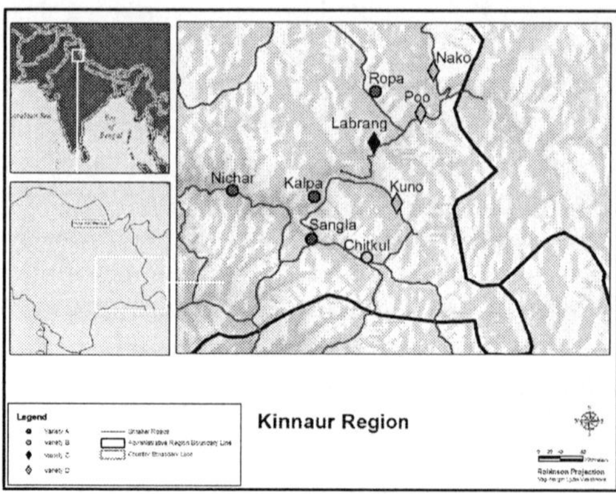

Figure 2: Dialect groups according to our study

c. The status of Labrang is interesting. It shows the highest affinity with Ropa and Chitkul (28–29%) – even though not very high. Labrang does not show much similarity with either group

The systematic comparison of these linguistic features has revealed how the various Kinnauri varieties are similar or dissimilar to one another, thus providing the linguistic basis for examining the relationship among them. The results show that the investigated varieties can be classified into three (or possibly four) groups, where Sangla, Nichar, Ropa and Kalpa form one group; Poo, Kuno and Nako form another group; Chitkul and Labrang fall somewhere in between, being (separately) more to one or the other group concerning some linguistic features, but distinct with regard to other linguistic features. See figure 2.

6 Conclusions and future work

Due to restrictions of space, many details concerning the data collection process, language consultants, geography and demography of Kinnaur, language contact, other investigated linguistic features, etc., have been omitted here. These will be described in future publications from our project.

The automatic vocabulary comparison has yielded good results which are in accord with other linguistic evidence for the genetic linguistic subgrouping of the investigated Kinnauri varieties. A clear methodological advantage is the complete consistency of the comparison. The method will be developed further and its relationship to other similar work investigated, e.g., the work at Groningen on dialectometry (Nerbonne and Heeringa, 2009) as well as work at MPI Leipzig and elsewhere on the theory and methodology of automated large-scale lexicostatistics (Holman et al., 2008; Ringe, 1999; Ringe et al., 2002; Wichmann and Grant, 2010).

Acknowledgements

The research reported on here was supported by the Swedish Research Council (the project *Digital areal linguistics* 2010–2012, VR dnr 2009-1448).

References

Lieutenant J.D Cunningham. 1844. Notes on Moorcroft's travels in Ladakh, and on Gerard's account of Kunáwar, including a general description of the latter district. *Journal of the Asiatic Society of Bengal*, XIII:172–253.

Alexander Gerard. 1842. A vocabulary of the Kunawar languages. *Journal of the Asiatic Society of Bengal (Calcutta*, 11:478–551.

T.C. Hodson. 1913. Note on the numeral systems of the Tibeto-Burman dialects. *Journal of the Royal Asiatic Society of Great Britain and Ireland*, pages 315–336, Apr.

Eric W. Holman, Søren Wichmann, Cecil H. Brown, Viveka Velupillai, André Müller, and Dik Bakker. 2008. Explorations in automated lexicostatistics. *Folia Linguistica*, 42(2):331–354.

April McMahon, Paul Heggarty, Robert McMahon, and Warren Maguire. 2007. The sound patterns of Englishes: Representing phonetic similarity. *English Language and Linguistics*, 11(1):113–142.

John Nerbonne and Wilbert Heeringa. 2009. Measuring dialect differences. In Jürgen Erich Schmidt and Peter Auer, editors, *Language and space: Theories and methods*, pages 550–567. Mouton De Gruyter, Berlin.

Don Ringe, Tandy Warnow, and Ann Taylor. 2002. Indo-European and computational cladistics. *Transactions of the Philological Society*, 100(1):59–129.

Don Ringe. 1999. How hard is it to match CVC-roots? *Transactions of the Philological Society*, 97(2):213–244.

Morris Swadesh. 1955. Towards greater accuracy in lexicostatistic dating. *International Journal of American Linguistics*, 21(2):121–137.

Pasi Tapanainen and Atro Voutilainen. 1994. Tagging accurately – don't guess if you know. In *Proceedings of the Fourth Conference on Applied Natural Language Processing*, pages 47–52, Stuttgart. ACL.

Søren Wichmann and Anthony P. Grant, editors. 2010. *Quantitative approaches to linguistic diversity. Commemorating the centenary of the birth of Morris Swadesh*. Benjamins. Special issue of *Diachronica* 27:2.

ISSN 1736-6305 Vol. 11
http://hdl.handle.net/10062/16955

Extraction of Knowledge-Rich Contexts in Russian – A Study in the Automotive Domain

Anne-Kathrin Schumann
Universität Wien / SIA Tilde
Vienna, Austria / Riga, Latvia
anne.schumann@tilde.lv

Abstract

This paper presents ongoing research aiming at the automated extraction of knowledge-rich contexts (KRCs) from a Russian language corpus. The notion of KRCs was introduced by Meyer (2001) and refers to a term's co-text (Sebeok, 1986) as a reservoir of potentially important information about a concept. From a terminological point of view, it seems that KRCs contain exactly the kind of information that should be included into a terminology database. Accordingly, the question how KRCs can be automatically acquired has been widely studied in recent years. However, many languages including Russian still lack thorough study. This paper presents preliminary experimental results obtained on a specialized corpus in the automotive domain.

1 Shifting paradigms in terminology: dealing with contexts

Terminology studies today are marked by a notable shift of paradigms. The increasing use of corpora has not left the discipline untouched and triggered research mainly in the field of terminology extraction (cf. Ahmad and Rogers, 2001). Work on context extraction is a rather recent development, but the idea that a term's co-text yields not only linguistic, but also semantic information and corpora can be used for conceptual analysis is now widely accepted. Accordingly, Dubuc and Lauriston (1997) describe defining and explanatory contexts for terminology, Pearson (1998) provides a detailed study of defining contexts in English and ISO 12620: 2009 (ISO 2009) describes context types similar to those put forward by Dubuc and Lauriston. However, actual implementations of KRC extraction are still rare and many major languages have not been studied yet. Moreover,

important theoretical and methodological issues remain unresolved. These include questions concerning the epistemological status of automatically extracted information and the notion of "concept" in a corpus-based setting. Aussenac-Gilles *et al.* (2000), for example, define the concept as a "normalized meaning", i. e. the result of corpus-based processes rather than stable, text-independent notions. It still needs to be shown how these developments relate to practical terminology work.

Our research aims at tackling these issues by giving an evaluation of corpus-based techniques in context extraction as well as by contributing to their further development. In the following section, we outline main directions of research in KRC extraction. Section 3 presents preliminary experimental results. Section 4 summarizes the results obtained and outlines further work.

2 Related work

In KRCs, knowledge about a concept's attributes or the relations it forms with other concepts is made explicit by means of cue words or other linguistic patterns (Meyer, 2001, Jacquemin and Bourigault, 2003). These can be referred to as Knowledge Patterns or KPs (Barrière, 2004). The following approaches to context extraction can be differentiated:

- pattern-based approaches: The use of linguistic patterns for context extraction was suggested by Hearst (1992) and consists in defining lexico-syntactic patterns that indicate a semantic relationship. Studies in this tradition are Pearson (1998), Meyer (2001), Barrière (2004), Malaisé *et al.* (2005), Aussenac-Gilles and Jacques (2006), Sierra *et al.* (2008), and others.

- bootstrapping of semantic relations: This method starts from pre-defined patterns or seed relations and derives new relation instances for an iterative process of pattern generalisation. Examples are, again, Hearst (1992), Brin (1998), Condamines and Rebeyrolle (2001), Agichtein and Gravano (2000), Alfonseca *et al.* (2006), Xu (2007), and Auger and Barrière (2008).

Various approaches that combine linguistic information with machine learning have been developed (Maedche, Staab, 2000; Buitelaar *et al.* 2004). A particularly interesting approach is presented by Mustafaraj *et al.* (2006) who map semantic information on frame-semantic representations and use machine learning for automated role annotation.

3 KRCs in Russian: method outline

Although frame-semantic (Fillmore, 1985) methods seem to be linguistically sounder than patterns which give the impression of being *ad hoc* constructions, they exhibit serious drawbacks. Frame representations are not readily available for many languages. In multilingual and multidisciplinary terminology, therefore, the use of robust patterns that can be easily adapted to new domains and languages seems to be more feasible.

In our study, a list of tentative patterns was created by analysing relevant contexts in specialized texts. A specialized corpus was built using the BABOUK crawler (TTC, 2010). The Russian automotive corpus spans roughly 350 000 words in plain text. On this corpus, a series of extraction experiments was carried out. A Perl script was used to extract sentences containing previously defined patterns. Pattern occurrences were counted and relevant occurrences measured against overall occurrences. This method was proposed by Barrière (2004) similarly to traditional precision metrics.

In a first experimental cycle, extraction was based on simple keyword search. Precision for all KPs was between 0,40 and 0,60. For a second cycle, 159 target terms were selected from the corpus and combined with refined patterns. Regular expressions were used for extraction in order to retrieve inflected forms. Consequently, the detected KPs should be regarded as semantic paradigms rather than lexical units. The final list of regular expressions contains 5212 items and is based on 22 KPs with the term in pre- and 11

KPs with the term in postposition. Table 1 visualizes keywords used for KP definition:

Key-word	Transla-tion	Context type	Corpus occurr-ences
obespeči-vaet	provide, make sure	functional	155
sostoit	consist of	Meronymy	260
sluzhit	serve to	functional	117
podraz-delâût	classify	classification	9
pozvol-âet	allow, enable	functional	115
Različaût	differen-tiate	classification	15
vklûčaet v sebâ	contain, com-prise	Meronymy	18
predstav-lâet soboj	is, cons-titutes	definition, explanation	56
ustanav-livaût	fix, mount	position indication, Meronymy	196
prednaz-načen	serve to, is meant to	functional	112
i drugie	and others	enumeration, classification	20

Table 1: Keywords of tentative knowledge patterns

Before the second extraction cycle, stop sentences were filtered out from the corpus, i. e.:

- incomplete sentences

- questions

- sentences beginning with stop words such as determiners and pronouns

These measures are essential for excluding sentences with anaphoric reference or single-case information which are responsible for a big share of noise in KRC extraction (cf. Meyer, 2001), but also for dealing with the particularities of internet text and unwanted pattern occurrences. By these measures, precision could be improved for some of our patterns. Sentences a) and b) are extracted example sentences:

a) Šassi avtomobilâ <u>sostoit</u> iz transmissii i hodovoj časti i mehanizmov upravleniâ.

The chassis of a car <u>comprises</u> the transmission, the frame and control equipment.

b) Sistema ohlaždeniâ <u>služit</u> dlâ otvoda izlišnego tepla ot detalej dvigatelâ, nagrevaûŝihsâ pri ego rabote.

The cooling system <u>serves</u> to remove excess heat from those parts of the motor which heat up during exploitation.

The results in the extraction experiments are still too variable to be considered final. Moreover, relevance decisions are not always straightforward. Questionable cases are erroneous sentences and associative contexts (cf. ISO, 2009). Another yet open problem is the extraction of lists containing classifications following introductory sentences on KPs such as *Različaût*, without which the KRC is worthless. In other cases, the extracted sentence is a KRC, but relates not to the target term, but to a closely related term. This is due to the absence of syntactic information, because of which KPs can be located at any position in the sentence, e. g. within dependency relations. In the experiment reported here these cases have, however, been evaluated as relevant KRCs. Table 2 presents Russian KPs that by now can be considered reliable:

KP	Precision across experimental cycles
sostoit	0,87-0,95
sluzhit	0,80-0,92
prednaz-načen	1,00
Različaût	1,00

Table 2: Reliable KPs

Other patterns such as *predstavlâet soboj* have stable results as well, but their occurrences in the studied corpus are too few to allow for final precision estimates.

4 Interpretation of results and future work

The outlined results shed light on two important shortcomings of pattern-based KRC extraction. The first one is data sparseness. Reliability estimations require large corpora that provide many pattern occurrences. This problem calls for a search strategy that uses the web as a corpus, otherwise dealing with very large local corpora and long lists of regular expressions will become intractable. There also is some hope that the problem of data quality mentioned in the previous section can be overcome by more data.

The second aspect is precision. It is clear that the KRCs described so far have an accidental element. The use of syntactic information in pattern creation may alleviate these shortcomings and provide a sound basis for the automated semantic analysis of extracted sentences by using semantic situation templates (Xu, 2007).

However, the advantage of the work described in this paper consists in its using light-weight methods. Acceptable results can be achieved for at least some of the tested patterns by means of a hand full of simple commands and tasks. In our view, this advantage of pattern-based approaches should not be given up easily. Our further work will therefore be directed at overcoming the difficulties mentioned. Moreover, bootstrapping methods will be tested by using reliable patterns established so far as seeds in order to identify more KPs. The developed method will be evaluated by means of an extraction task in a new domain and transferred to new languages such as German and Latvian.

Acknowledgments

The research described in this paper was funded under the CLARA project (FP7/2007-2013), grant agreement n° 238405.

References

Alain Auger, Caroline Barrière. 2008. Pattern-based approaches to semantic relation extraction. A state-of-the-art. *Terminology*, 14 (1): 1-19.

Alexander Maedche, Steffen Staab. 2000. Mining Ontologies from Text. *Lecture Notes in Computer Science*, 1937: 189-202.

Anne Condamines, Josette Rebeyrolle. 2001. Searching for and identifying conceptual relationships via a corpus-based approach to a Terminological Knowledge Base (CTKB). Didier Bourigault, Christian Jacquemin, Marie-Claude L'Homme (eds.): Recent Advances in Computational Terminology. (Natural Language Processing 2). John Benjamins. Amsterdam, Philadelphia: 127-148.

Caroline Barrière. 2004. Knowledge-rich Contexts Discovery. *Lecture Notes in Computer Science,* 3060: 187-201.

Charles J. Fillmore. 1985. Frames and the Semantics of Understanding. Quaderni di Semantica VI (2): 222-254.

Christian Jacquemin, Didier Bourigault. 2003. Term Extraction and Automatic Indexing. Ruslan Mitkov (ed.). *The Oxford Handbook of Computational Linguistics.* Oxford University Press. Oxford: 599-615.

Eni Mustafaraj, Martin Hoof, Bernd Freisleben. 2006. Mining Diagnostic Text Reports by Learning to Annotate Knowledge Roles. Anne Kao, Steve Poteet (eds.). *Natural Language Processing and Text Mining.* Springer. London: 45-70.

Enrique Alfonseca, Maria Ruiz-Casado, Manabu Okumura, Pablo Castells. 2006. Towards Large-scale Non-taxonomic Relation Extraction: Estimating the Precision of Rote Extractors. 2nd Workshop on Ontology Learning and Population: Bridging the Gap between Text and Knowledge, July 22, Sydney, Australia.

Eugene Agichtein, Luis Gravano. 2000. *Snowball*: Extracting Relations from Large Plain-Text Collections. 5th ACM International Conference on Digital Libraries 2000, June 2-7, San Antonio, USA.

Fei-Yu Xu. 2007. *Bootstrapping Relation Extraction from Semantic Seeds*. PhD Thesis. Saarland University Saarbrücken, Uszkoreit.

Gerardo Sierra, Rodrigo Alarcón, César Aguilar, Carme Bach. 2008. Definitional verbal patterns for semantic relation extraction. *Terminology*, 14 (1): 74-98.

Ingrid Meyer. 2001. Extracting knowledge-rich contexts for terminography. Bourigault, Jacquemin, L'Homme (eds.): 279-302.

International Organization for Standardization. 2009. *International Standard ISO 12620: 2009 – Terminology and Other Language and Content Resources – Specification of Data Categories and Management of a Data Category Registry for Language Resources.* ISO. Geneva.

Jennifer Pearson. 1998. *Terms in Context.* (Studies in Corpus Linguistics 1). John Benjamins. Amsterdam, Philadelphia.

Khurshid Ahmad, Margaret Rogers. 2001. Corpus Linguistics and Terminology Extraction. Sue Ellen Wright, Gerhard Budin (eds.). *Handbook of Terminology Management.Vol 2: Application-Oriented Terminology Management.* John Benjamins. Amsterdam, Philadelphia: 725-760.

Marti A. Hearst. 1992. Automatic Acquisition of Hypernyms from Large Text Corpora. COLING 1992, August 23-28 1992, Nantes, France.

Nathalie Aussenac-Gilles, Brigitte Biébow, Sylvie Szulman. 2000. Revisiting Ontology Design: A Method Based on Corpus Analysis. *Lecture Notes in Computer Science*, 1937: 172-188.

Nathalie Aussenac-Gilles, Marie-Paule Jacques. 2006. Designing and Evaluating Patterns for Ontology Enrichment from Text. *Lecture Notes in Computer Science*, 4248: 158-165.

Paul Buitelaar, Daniel Olejnik, Michael Sintek. 2004. A Protégé Plug-In for Ontology Extraction from Text Based on Linguistic Analysis. 1st European Semantic Web Symposium May 10-12, Heraklion, Greece.

Robert Dubuc, Andy Lauriston. 1997. Terms and Contexts. Sue Ellen Wright, Gerhard Budin (eds.). *Handbook of Terminology Management. Vol. 1: Basic aspects of terminology management.* John Benjamins. Amsterdam, Philadelphia: 80-87.

Sergey Brin. 1998. Extracting Patterns and Relations from the World Wide Web. International Workshop on the Web and Databases, March 27-28 1998, Valencia, Spain.

Thomas Albert Sebeok. 1986. *Encyclopedic Dictionary of Semiotics*. *Vol. 1.* (Approaches to Semiotics 73). de Gruyter. Berlin, New York.

TTC project: Terminology Extraction, Translation Tools, Comparable Corpora. 2010. *Deliverable 2.1: First version of the crawler for comparable corpora.* The project is funded under the European Community's FP7/2007-2013, grant agreement n° 248005.

Véronique Malaisé, Pierre Zweigenbaum, Bruno Bachimont. 2005. Mining defining contexts to help structuring differential ontologies. *Terminology*, 11 (1): 21-53.

ISSN 1736-6305 Vol. 11
http://hdl.handle.net/10062/16955

Iterative Reordering and Word Alignment for Statistical MT

Sara Stymne
Department of Computer and Information Science
Linköpings universitet, Linköping, Sweden
sara.stymne@liu.se

Abstract

Word alignment is necessary for statistical machine translation (SMT), and reordering as a preprocessing step has been shown to improve SMT for many language pairs. In this initial study we investigate if both word alignment and reordering can be improved by iterating these two steps, since they both depend on each other. Overall no consistent improvements were seen on the translation task, but the reordering rules contain different information in the different iterations, leading us to believe that the iterative strategy can be useful.

1 Introduction

Reordering is a problem for translation between languages with different word order, such as English and German, where especially the placement of verbs vary widely. A common strategy for approaches that tackle reordering differences in connection with SMT is to perform reordering of the source language corpus prior to training the system, in order to make the word order more similar to that of the target language. Some of the reordering strategies proposed uses word alignments between texts as their main knowledge source for learning reorderings. Word alignments are also created automatically with methods that perform better when the word order in the two languages is similar. This leads us to the hypothesis that we should be able to improve both reordering rules and word alignments by performing the two tasks iteratively.

2 Previous work

Pre-translation reordering is usually performed by applying rules, that can either be handwritten rules targeting known syntactic differences (Collins et al., 2005), or be learnt automatically (Xia and Mc-Cord, 2004). In these studies the reordering decision was taken deterministically on the source side. This decision can also be delayed to decoding time by presenting several reordering options to the decoder as a lattice (Rottmann and Vogel, 2007). There have also been attempts to integrate reordering rules into a PBSMT decoder (Elming, 2008). A different way to use reordering, was investigated in Holmqvist et al. (2009), who used the reordering only to improve the word alignment, and moved the words back into original order after the alignment phase. For most of the automatically learnt rules, some rule-extraction method is used, that only takes the word alignments into account.

This work is inspired by the approach of Holmqvist et al. (2009), but further develops it both by iterating word alignment and reordering, and by creating rules that can be used on monolingual test data. The machine learning used in this study is similar to that of Elming (2008), who also uses Ripper. A different feature set is used, however. The rules are employed in a single preprocessing step, choosing the one best reordering for each sentence, similar to Xia and McCord (2004).

3 Iterative Alignment and Reordering

The steps performed in the iterative word alignment and reordering are:

1. Word align the training data
2. Learn reordering rules based on the word alignments
3. Reorder the training data with the learnt rules
4. Word align the reordered data
5. Change the order back into original order, and adjust the newly learnt word alignments
6. Learn new reordering rules based on the new word alignments
7. Repeat step 3-6

Type	LC	LS	RS	RC
Word	able	to refuse	new tasks	if
POS	A	INFMARK> V	A N	CS
Dep	comp_V	pm_V mod_A	attr_N obj_V	pm_V
Func	PCOMPL-S	INFMARK> -FMAINV	A> OBJ	CS
Syntax	NH	VG	NP	CS

Table 1: Example of a positive training example

Any automatic method can be used for word alignment. Learning reordering rules should be based on the word alignments as a knowledge source, for the iterations to be useful. In this particular implementation of the main strategy we use the standard IBM models up to model 4, as implemented in GIZA++ (Och and Ney, 2003) for word alignment, and a rule induction learner for the reordering rule learning.

Orig	I(PRON,subj_V) would(+FAUXV) therefore once more ask you to ensure that we(SUBJ) get(V) a Dutch channel as well .(PUNC)
Reo	**I therefore** *would* once more ask you to ensure that we **a Dutch channel as well** *get* .
German	**Deshalb** *möchte* ich sie nochmals ersuchen , dafür sorge zu tragen , daß **auch ein niederländischer Sender** *eingespeist wird* .

Table 2: Sample rule application (Only annotations relevant to rule application are shown)

4 Reordering

We used rule-induction learning, as implemented in Ripper (Cohen, 1995). A rule-induction learner produces rules for the positive class(es), where each rule only contains a subset of all features. Some example rules can be seen in Table 3. The rules are human readable, allowing us to analyse them in a useful manner, and to apply them to unseen source text in a simple way.

The reordering rules were learnt for the English source side of the corpus, which was parsed using a commercial functional dependency parser[1], from which we extracted information on the following levels: words, POS-tags, dependency information, functional tag and surface syntax. The different levels of annotation for each word, allows the learner to learn rules of different generalisation levels, possibly mixing higher-order categories with surface form in the same rule.

The reorderings were considered between two consecutive sequences, left sequence, LS, and right sequence, RS, taking the left and right one word context (LC and RC) into account. LS and RS are limited to maximum 10 tokens, and we only extract the maximum sequences for each possible reordering. Only swaps, i.e. cases where LS and RS are consecutive are considered, following Elming (2008). For each of these four sequences and contexts we stored information for each of the five syntactic levels, resulting in a total of 20 features, as exemplified in Table 1. For rules where

one of LS or RS are at least 3 words long, we also store a wild card version of the example, where the middle words are replaced by an asterisk. A training example was considered positive (Swap) if the rightmost alignment point of RS is directly preceding the leftmost alignment point of LS, and negative (NoSwap) otherwise.

To apply the rules created by Ripper, we did not actually use Ripper, since the examples are created based on word alignments, that are not available at test time. Instead we applied a left-to-right matching directly on parsed text. All rules were applied to each sentence by first finding a matching left context, then in turn a consecutive matching left sequence, right sequence, and right context. Many of the rules, however, did not contain all these sequences, and in those cases we allowed a word sequence of up to seven words to match for LS and RS. To to be able to apply the rules safely, rules that did not either contain either both LS and RS, or one of those and both LC and RC were discarded.

In the first step a lattice was created containing all matching reorderings in a sentence, where each edge was weighted with the Ripper accuracy of the rule for the first application point of a rule, and by a small constant for all other edges. The 1-best path through the lattice was found by normalizing the scores of the outgoing edges of each node, and multiplying the normalized scores for each path, choosing the path with the highest score. Table 2 shows a sentence after application of rules (a,c) from Table 3, resulting in a word order closer to German than the original English sentence.

---

[1]Connexor machinese syntax, http://www.connexor.eu/

ID	Iter	Acc	LC	LS	RS	RC
a	1	0.82	Func:SUBJ	POS:V	–	POS:PUNC
b	1	0.73	Syntax:NH	word:could	–	Syntax:EH
c	1	0.88	POS:PRON Dep:subj_V	Func +FAUXV	word:therefore	–
d	2	0.68	Syntax:>N POS:DET	Syntax:NP POS:N	Syntax:VP	–
e	2	0.86	Func:A> POS:DET	Syntax:NP POS:N	Syntax:'VP * NH'	POS:PUNC

Table 3: Sample rules from both iterations, with Ripper accuracy

Iteration	Training		Test	
	Swap	NoSwap	Swap	NoSwap
1	689200	5974222	172084	1495241
2	648527	5827045	162533	1457786

Table 4: Reordering training/test data per iteration

5 Experiments

The experiments were performed on English-to-German translation using a standard phrase-based SMT system, trained using the Moses toolkit (Koehn et al., 2007), with a 5-gram language model. The SMT system used a distance-based reordering penalty (distortion penalty), which adds a factor δ^n for movements over n words, where phrase movement is also limited to a distance of six words. In addition we applied a monotone model, which prohibits any phrase reorderings, and thus is unlikely to work well for the baseline system, but could work well for the systems where the source language has been reordered to mimic the target language. The translation systems were trained and tested using the Europarl corpus (Koehn, 2005). The training part contained 439513 sentences, where sentences longer than 40 words was filtered out. The test set has 2000 sentences and the development set had 500 sentences.

We performed two iterations of the iterative reordering rules learning and word alignment algorithm. After each iteration we trained a PBSMT system, which will be called Reo1 and Reo2, and which will be compared to baseline without any reorderings. Reo1 is similar to many previous approaches to reordering, since it is based on only one iteration of alignment and reordering.

5.1 Reordering Results

At each iteration, each training example was assigned to the training set with a probability of 0.8, and used for testing otherwise. Table 4 shows the number of examples of each type for the first two iterations. The data is rather skewed, with only around 10% of the examples being positive. Evaluating the rules on this automatically created test data gave a precision of around 55% and a recall of around 8% for the Swap class, in both iterations. Especially the recall is very low, but it can be compared to the recall of Elming (2008) of around 15%, which is also low. Table 3 shows a sample of the rules. Relatively few features are used in each rule, and it was quite common that not all of the four word sequences were used in the rules.

The number of rules was very different between the two iterations, with 77 rules in iteration 1 and only 14 rules in iteration 2. One possible explanation for this could be that the word alignments were improved, and thus that less rules that are due to noisy alignments were created, in iteration 2, but further investigation is needed to draw this conclusion. The function of the rules is also different between the iterations. Nearly all rules in iteration 2 concerns subject-verb inversion (d)[2]. The rules in iteration 1 are more varied, even though many move verbs towards the end of the sentence (a,b). Other examples of rules are those that handle adverb placement (c), but there are also some rules that are hard to explain linguistically, such as (e), which moves a noun to the end of a sentence. All linguitstic levels are used in the rules, and are often mixed. Out of the totally 91 rules, 28 are lexicalized (b,c). It is encouraging that new types of rules are learnt in iteration 2, but at the same time many of the useful rule types from iteration 1 unfortunately are missing.

5.2 Translation Results

Translation results are reported on the standard MT metrics Bleu (Papineni et al., 2002), Meteor (Lavie and Agarwal, 2007), and PER, position independent word error rate. PER does not take word order into account, which the other two metrics do.

The results with distortion penalty are presented in Table 5, and for monotone decoding in Table 6. As expected the results are overall higher with the distance-based reordering model in the decoder. On the systems with a distortion penalty there

---

[2]letters refer to rule ID in Table 3

System	Bleu	Meteor	1-PER
Base	20.15	26.87	0.712
Reo1	19.76	26.49	0.731
Reo2	20.13	26.99	0.736

Table 5: Results with distortion penalty

System	Bleu	Meteor	1-PER
Base	19.32	26.25	0.742
Reo1	19.40	26.39	0.737
Reo2	19.59	26.30	0.703

Table 6: Results with monotonous decoding

are very small differences between the systems on Bleu and Meteor, except for Reo1, which has the lowest score, whereas there is a small tendency of improvement for the systems with reordering on PER, which indicates that these systems are somewhat better with regard to lexical choice, which might be the result of better word alignment. For the monotone system there is a small tendency of improvement for the systems with reordering on Bleu and Meteor. The Reo2 system has a bad score on PER, however, indicating that this system likely has better word order than the other systems, since it has the highest Bleu score.

6 Conclusion

We have presentend a novel approach to reordering for SMT that could potentially improve both reordering rule learning and word alignment, by applying them iteratively. Initial experiments show that the rules we learn change with each iteration, to a large extent targeting different phenomena. The results on the SMT task, however, do not show any overall improvements; the systems with reordering largely perform on par with the baseline system without external reorderings. We still believe that the novel iterative approach can be useful, especially since we have shown that we learn different linguistically motivated rules in each iteration. Besides, there are plenty of room for improvements to the application of the main algorithm, such as using a different rule learning algorithm, preferably with a better accuracy of its rules, and by using a reordering lattice as translation input instead of 1-best input, which has been successful in previous research. We also want to investigate using a higher number of iterations, and of combining rules phrase tables and/or with high accuracy from different iterations.

References

William W. Cohen. 1995. Fast effective rule induction. In *Proceedings of the 12th International Conference on Machine Learning*, pages 115–123, Tahoe City, CA, USA.

Michael Collins, Philipp Koehn, and Ivona Kučerová. 2005. Clause restructuring for statistical machine translation. In *Proceedings of the 43rd Annual Meeting of the ACL*, pages 531–540, Ann Arbor, Michigan, USA.

Jakob Elming. 2008. *Syntactic Reordering in Statistical Machine Translation*. Ph.D. thesis, Copenhagen Business School, Denmark.

Maria Holmqvist, Sara Stymne, Jody Foo, and Lars Ahrenberg. 2009. Improving alignment for SMT by reordering and augmenting the training corpus. In *Proceedings of the Fourth Workshop on Statistical Machine Translation*, pages 120–124, Athens, Greece.

Philipp Koehn, Hieu Hoang, Alexandra Birch, Chris Callison-Burch, Marcello Federico, Nicola Bertoldi, Brooke Cowan, Wade Shen, Christine Moran, Richard Zens, Chris Dyer, Ondrej Bojar, Alexandra Constantin, and Evan Herbst. 2007. Moses: Open source toolkit for statistical machine translation. In *Proceedings of the 45th Annual Meeting of the ACL, demonstration session*, pages 177–180, Prague, Czech Republic.

Philipp Koehn. 2005. Europarl: A parallel corpus for statistical machine translation. In *Proceedings of MT Summit X*, pages 79–86, Phuket, Thailand.

Alon Lavie and Abhaya Agarwal. 2007. METEOR: An automatic metric for MT evaluation with high levels of correlation with human judgments. In *Proceedings of the Second Workshop on Statistical Machine Translation*, pages 228–231, Prague, Czech Republic.

Franz Josef Och and Hermann Ney. 2003. A systematic comparison of various statistical alignment models. *Computational Linguistics*, 29(1):19–51.

Kishore Papineni, Salim Roukos, Todd Ward, and Wei-Jing Zhu. 2002. BLEU: A method for automatic evaluation of machine translation. In *Proceedings of the 40th Annual Meeting of the ACL*, pages 311–318, Philadelphia, Pennsylvania, USA.

Kay Rottmann and Stephan Vogel. 2007. Word reordering in statistical machine translation with a POS-based distortion model. In *Proceedings of the 11th International Conference on Theoretical and Methodological Issues in Machine Translation*, pages 171–180, Skövde, Sweden.

Fei Xia and Michael McCord. 2004. Improving a statistical MT system with automatically learned rewrite patterns. In *Proceedings of the 20th International Conference on Computational Linguistics*, pages 508–514, Geneva, Switzerland.

ISSN 1736-6305 Vol. 11
http://hdl.handle.net/10062/16955

A Double-Blind Experiment On Interannotator Agreement: The Case Of Dependency Syntax And Finnish

Atro Voutilainen and Tanja Purtonen
Department of Modern Languages
University of Helsinki
`atro.voutilainen@helsinki.fi tanja.purtonen@helsinki.fi`

Abstract

Manually performed treebanking is an expensive effort compared with automatic annotation. In return, manual treebanking is generally believed to provide higher-quality/value syntactic annotation than automatic methods. Unfortunately, there is little or no empirical evidence for or against this belief, though arguments have been voiced for the high degree of subjectivity in other levels of linguistic analysis (e.g. morphological annotation). We report a double-blind annotation experiment at the level of dependency syntax, using a small Finnish corpus as the analysis data. The results suggest that an interannotator agreement can be reached as a result of reviews and negotiations that is much higher than the corresponding labelled attachment scores (LAS) reported for state-of-the-art dependency parsers.

1 Introduction

There is ongoing effort in many countries on treebank annotation to support linguistic research, statistical language modelling and other tasks (Haverinen et al., 2009; Kromann, 2003; Marcus et al., 1993; Mikulova et al., 2006; Nivre et al., 2006). Treebanks are usually text collections with (tens of) thousands of sentences annotated according to a dependency syntactic or phrase structure representation documented as an annotator's manual.

Annotation can be made automatically or manually. Treebanks created with a parser can be very large, because automatic parsing is a fast and inexpensive operation. Manual annotation is slower: the creation of manually annotated treebanks tends to take many years, as reported by several presenters at a recent CLARA Treecourse in Prague

(Dec. 2010). Still, treebanks annotated by hand are considered more valuable, because manual annotation is believed to result in higher accuracy.

Unfortunately, it is difficult to find empirical evidence to support or question this belief in annotation accuracy benefits. At other levels of linguistic analysis, the so-called "double blind experiment" has been used for measuring interannotator agreement (Kilgarriff, 1999; Voutilainen, 1999). At the syntactic level, we are not aware of such experiments.

Without relevant empirical data, one can question the investment needed for manually annotating a treebank, e.g. by using the following conjecture: if human annotators can after negotiations disagree about the correct analysis even in 5% of words at the POS level (Church, 1992), annotator disagreement in the (assumedly) more complex task of syntactic annotation is likely to be so much higher, that there might be no actual advantage in annotation quality, when comparing a manually annotated treebank with an automatically annotated one.

In this paper, we report a small-scale double-blind experiment on dependency syntactic annotation using Finnish-language text as empirical data. We provide interannotator agreement figures before and after the negotiation phase, as well as more observations on types and apparent reasons for annotation differences.

Our experiment suggests that with a carefully documented linguistic representation, human annotators can agree on a syntactic analysis to a much higher degree (jointly achieving labelled attachment scores of close to 99%) than what even the best syntactic analysers are reported to reach (80-90% LAS scores). – How much of the high agreement rate can be generalised to other dependency syntactic annotation models and practices remains a topic for future research.

Next, we outline the key characteristics of

the syntactic representation and its specification. Then we describe the double-blind experiment and empirical data. This is followed by quantitative results and general observations.

2 Syntactic Representation And Its Specification

The syntactic representation used in this experiment can be characterised as follows:

- each word has a unique syntactic head;

- the representation is surface-syntactic (no empty categories postulated);

- dependency structures can be non-projective (Finnish as a free word-order language has unbounded dependencies);

- grammatical markers or attributes (e.g. articles, quantifiers, other modifiers, prepositions, postpositions, conjunctions, auxiliaries) are treated as dependents; semantically "heavy" words are preferred as heads;

- to each dependency relation, a syntactic function is attached;

- the syntactic function palette contains 15 basic functions (e.g. auxiliary, phrasal particle, subject, object, vocative).

Here is a sample syntactic analysis where what is normally called formal subject "se" (english "it") is analysed as a phrase marker for the actual subject clause; note also phrase marker analysis of the postposition "kannalta".

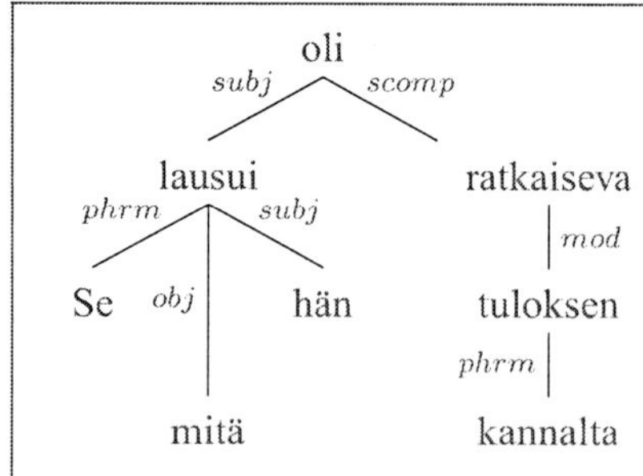

Se [it] mitä [what] hän [s/he] lausui [said] oli [was] tuloksen [result.Gen] kannalta [prom-the-point-of.Postp] ratkaiseva [decisive]. ("What s/he said was decisive for the result")

The syntactic specification is based on an initial draft completed when annotating some 19,000 hand-picked corpus-based sentences used as examples in a descriptive grammar of Finnish (Hakulinen et al., 2004). Specifying the grammatical representation as an annotator's manual was expected to be more successful because the inventory of grammatical constructions is readily available in the form of such a "grammar definition corpus". The manual will be published online at `http://www. ling.helsinki.fi/kieliteknologia/ tutkimus/treebank`.

3 Test Arrangements

The double-blind experiment was conducted as follows. Firstly, two trained annotators independently marked the function and the dependency of every word in their own corpus version, presented in spreadsheet form similar to CONLL-X (`http://nextens.uvt.nl/ ~conll/#dataformat`). The text was automatically tokenised and morphologically analysed, and the annotators were aware that there can be errors in morphological analysis (but no corrections to morphology were made). The annotators were encouraged to consult the annotator's manual, the syntactically annotated grammar definition corpus and the descriptive Finnish grammar (`http://kaino.kotus. fi/visk/etusivu.php`) from which the example sentences were extracted.

Secondly, these manually annotated versions of the text were automatically compared with each other. Words with a different analysis were marked with a symbol "LOOK", which was added also to some random words to minimize the risk of only guessing the other annotator's analysis. At this point (round 1), the annotators were not aware of each other's answers, and independently made the corrections to their own corpus versions.

Thirdly, the reanalysed texts were automatically compared with each other, and words with a different analysis were re-marked. At this point (round 2), the annotators saw each other's answers, and they negotiated about the disagreements, and documented their negotiations. On the basis of the negotiations, the differences between analyses appear to result from five main reasons ("D:a–e" in tables 2 and 3):

- (D:a) Lack of attention.

- (D:b) Incomplete specification in the manual. After negotiating, the annotators could find a common solution (to be added to the manual).

- (D:c) Incomplete specification of the manual, but after negotiations the annotators agreed that a separate study is needed to cover the phenomenon. So, at this stage category could not be analysed consensually and unambiguously.

- (D:d) Real ambiguity.

- (D:e) Domino effect.

The routine was successively applied to each text in the test corpus.

The test corpus consisted of three texts from three genres, totalling 2039 words and 176 sentences:

- fiction: 561 words of a novel by Jostein Gardner ("Sophie's world");

- news: 694 words from online editions of "Helsingin Sanomat" and "Tietoviikko" (11.1.2011);

- Wikipedia: 784 words from three Wikipedia articles on geography and history.

4   Results

The results from the double-blind experiment are presented in Tables 1–3.

Corpus and stage	Agreement rate
fiction (1)	89.7% (503/561)
fiction (2)	92.6% (519/561)
fiction (3)	98.6% (553/561)
news (1)	90.8% (630/694)
news (2)	96.3% (668/694)
news (3)	98.7% (685/694)
wikipedia (1)	88.9% (697/784)
wikipedia (2)	94.8% (743/784)
wikipedia (3)	99.2% (778/784)

Table 1: Word-level interannotator agreement rates for dependency relation+function analysis before review (1), before negotiation (2), after negotiation (3).

Data	D:a	D:b	D:c	D:d	D:e	Total
Fiction (2)	8	2	4	4	14	32
News (2)	4	2	6	3	7	22
Wiki (2)	9	9	2	2	16	38
Total (2)	21	13	12	9	37	92

Table 2: Classification of differences in dependency relation analysis.

Data	D:a	D:b	D:c	D:d	D:e	Total
Fiction (2)	6	8	4	3	14	35
News (2)	5	4	6	1	7	23
Wiki (2)	2	10	4	-	16	32
Total (2)	13	22	14	4	37	90

Table 3: Classification of differences in dependency function analysis.

The following two tables show the different analyses classified to the differences in the dependency relation analysis (table 2) and in dependency function analysis (table 3).

The disagreement rate diminished clearly between rounds 1 and 2 and 3. Still, many clerical errors (due to inattention) persisted even at stage 2. Syntactic annotation with a spreadsheet may be more error-prone than with a tree editor.

5   Discussion

Some general points are in order. Firstly, the grammar corpus is created from the example sentences in (Hakulinen et al., 2004). The descriptive grammar appears to focus on traditional (theoretically interesting) types of syntactic phenomena, like common vs special clause types. Much less attention seems to be given e.g. to different types of names and titles and their combinations, to quantitative expressions, and to expressions with numerals or other fixed-form material. In this experiment, the annotators were able to analyse even syntactically complex and long sentences (e.g. many embedded sentences) remarkably consistently, but the annotations repeatedly differed in the case of "local" expressions such as temporal or areal expressions, which were not covered in the annotator's manual.

The annotation differences between genres were remarkable. It may result from the fact that the news articles are mostly written using standard language, but in the fiction text, there are many elliptical sentences. A difference between analyses, especially in the elliptical cases, often causes the domino effect, and in the test corpus, 41% of all differences in annotation are caused by the domino effect at word level.

The test corpus consisted of continuous text, but the annotated 19,000-sentence grammar definition corpus contains mostly isolated sentences. To account for elliptical constructions (and other super-sentential phenomena), the grammar/manual definition phase should benefit from continuous corpus texts, in addition to systematic grammar corpus sentences, to enable a more informed analysis.

In this experiment, the double-blind-method was used for estimating, to what extent interannotator agreement can be reached; and the aim was not to avoid differences in annotation. Still, many of the (initial) differences in syntactic annotation can probably be avoided by providing also a visual interface to the annotators, who in this experiment worked with tabular spreadsheet format only. Also, the annotator's manual needs a fair supply of annotated example sentences to concretise the more abstract descriptive statements on some particular category.

To conclude: in this paper, we have documented a double-blind experiment on syntactic annotation to provide an initial understanding (based on limited empirical data) on what level of annotation consistency can be reached by human annotators at the level of syntactic analysis. Our experiment shows that a much higher agreement rate (around 99%) on the correct syntactic annotation can be reached than is reported as the corresponding word-level labelled attachment score (LAS) for state-of-the-art dependency parsers (close to 90% LAS for English; 70–80% LAS for other languages with richer morphology and less rigid word order).

Acknowledgments

We wish to thank members of the FIN-CLARIN HFST team for their support of this work, in particular Sam Hardwick for programming support. We also gratefully acknowledge constructive reviews of the three anonymous NODALIDA referees.

References

Kenneth W. Church. 1992. Current Practice in Part of Speech Tagging and Suggestions for the Future. In Simmons (ed.), *Sbornik praci: In Honor of Henry Kucera*. Michigan Slavic Studies. Michigan. 13–48.

Auli Hakulinen, Maria Vilkuna, Riitta Korhonen, Vesa Koivisto, Tarja Riitta Heinonen and Irja Alho. 2004. *Iso suomen kielioppi* [Large Finnish Grammar]. Helsinki: Suomalaisen Kirjallisuuden Seura. Online version: http://scripta.kotus.fi/visk URN:ISBN:978-952-5446-35-7.

Katri Haverinen, Filip Ginter, Veronica Laippala, Tapio Viljanen and Tapio Salakoski. 2009. Dependency Annotation of Wikipedia: First Steps towards a Finnish Treebank. *Proceedings of The Eighth International Workshop on Treebanks and Linguistic Theories (TLT8)*, pp. 95–105.

Adam Kilgarriff. 1999. 95% Replicability for Manual Word Sense Tagging. *Proceedings of the Ninth Conference of the European Chapter of the Association for Computational Linguistics.*

Matthias Kromann. 2003. The Danish Dependency Treebank and the underlying linguistic theory. *Proc. of the TLT 2003.*

Mitchell Marcus, Beatrice Santorini and Mary Marcinkiewicz. 1993. Building a large annotated corpus of English: the Penn Treebank. *Computational Linguistics*, 19(2).

Marie Mikulova, Alevtina Bemova, Jan Hajic, Eva Hajicova, Jiri Havelka, Veronika Kolarova, Lucie Kucova, Marketa Lopatkova, Petr Pajas, Jarmila Panevova, Magda Razimova, Petr Sgall, Jan Stepanek, Zdenka Uresova, Katerina Vesela, and Zdenek Zabokrtsky. 2006. Annotation on the Tectogrammatical Level in the Prague Dependency Treebank. Annotation Manual. Technical Report 30, UFAL MFF UK, Prague, Czech Rep.

Joakim Nivre, Jens Nilsson and Johan Hall. 2006. Talbanken05: A Swedish Treebank with Phrase Structure and Dependency Annotation. *Proceedings of the fifth international conference on Language Resources and Evaluation (LREC2006).*

Atro Voutilainen. 1999. An experiment on the upper bound of interjudge agreement: the case of tagging. *Proceedings of the Ninth Conference of the European Chapter of the Association for Computational Linguistics.*

Automatic Question Generation from Swedish Documents as a Tool for Information Extraction

Kenneth Wilhelmsson
Swedish School of Library and Information Science
University of Borås
kenneth.wilhelmsson@hb.se

Abstract

An implementation of automatic question generation (QG) from raw Swedish text is presented. QG is here chosen as an alternative to natural query systems where any query can be posed and no indication is given of whether the current text database includes the information sought for. The program builds on parsing with grammatical functions from which corresponding questions are generated and it incorporates the article database of Swedish Wikipedia. The pilot system is meant to work with a text shown in the GUI and auto-completes user input to help find available questions. The act of question generation is here described together with early test results regarding the current produced questions.

1 Introduction

Question generation has been the focus of several recent international workshops where the field has been defined as including sub-fields like tutorial dialogue and FAQ generation. In this paper, the focus is on the *Text-to-Question* subtask. Rus and Graesser (2009) define the task as follows: "given a text, the goal of a QG system performing the Text-to-Question Question Generation task would be to exhaustively create a set of Text-Question pairs, such that every possible question that could be generated would be included in the set", see Table 1.

The formulation thus includes the notion of *all* possible questions to which a text can be said to provide answers. This can for example mean all the questions from the explicit propositions but also facts deduced using various algorithms for inference, anaphora resolution etc. This is a complicating factor as this set is hard to estimate and will make it impossible to compute the relative coverage of the set of questions produced.

It is not clear what counts as one unique question, and whether producing various formulations of the same question is advantageous. In a prac-tical user scenario, there can be benefits to generating variations of the same question (using e.g. substitution of synonymous words) to help the user find at least one way of expressing the query in a large question set produced by a natural query system.

Given:
- Text T

Create:
- Text-Questions pairs $\{P_1...P_n\}$ each represented as a (K_i, Q_i) pair, where K_i, the target text, indicates which text segment from T represents the answer and the Q_i represents a question that would elicit K_i

Table 1: The Text-to-Question task as characterized by Rus and Graesser (2009)

The situation described in this paper is the use of a natural language query system which explicitly generates a set of questions per text as an alternative to the functionality of several systems which permits a user to pose queries in question form freely, but which never guarantee that these are answered by the current database. If the system uses a black-box algorithm for finding the answers and/or uses a database that is unknown or vast (like the entire Internet), this can be particularly striking. An example is *PowerSet* (Converse et al 2008) which will rank text segments of all of English *Wikipedia* using a collection of different techniques, when a question is formulated in natural language. The proposed answers (text segments) will be presented to the user according to best match ranking given the question. That approach, like that of Harabagiu et al (2000), mixes the task of information retrieval (search for documents) with that of information extraction. From the user perspective, it may be unknown whether a (formulation of a) question is in fact answered at all by the data-base in these types of systems where any question string can be formulated.

This paper deals with an implementation of automated question generation from raw text in Swedish. The focus here is on the actual question generation task by syntactic means, the user interface and some preliminary tests of the current state of the implementation. The system incorporates the Swedish *Wikipedia* article data-base and generates questions for one text article, or other input text, at a time. This means that the current text subject (the available information) is somewhat known to the user. In fact, the text source is visible in the user interface, shown in Figure 1, and the questions produced will mark and scroll the corresponding answer into view when a question is selected.

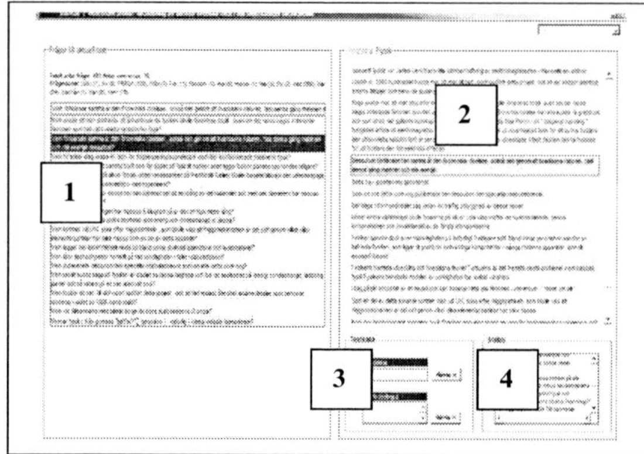

Figure 1: The GUI of the program

1) Autocompleting input form for choice of question
2) The text source in which the suggested questions will mark and scroll to the corresponding section with answers
3) Forms for choice of *Wikipedia* article or arbitrary text input
4) Statusbox displaying various information during a run

2 The Initial Steps: Text Pre-processing and Syntactic Parsing

The first steps of the text-to-question task includes sentence splitting, tokenization, POS tagging and syntactic parsing with mark-up of grammatical functions on the main clause level. In the process, the text is tagged, whereafter it is parsed and questions are finally extracted.

A trigram-based Hidden Markov Model POS tagger is used to provide input for the syntactic parsing. The parsing of Swedish free text is carried out using a heuristic algorithm based on the sentence schema for Nordic languages, originally introduced for Danish by Diderichsen (1946). The parser, which is described by Wilhelmsson (2010), makes use of the sentence schema by avoiding identification of multi-word constituents (unbounded constituents) by explicit matching, resulting in a format shown in Example 1.

```
<subjekt>Ni som frågar</subjekt>
<pfv>hade</pfv>
<adverbial>nog</adverbial>
<adverbial>ändå</adverbial>
<piv>kunnat</piv>
<piv>köpa</piv>
<objekt>en vän</objekt>
<objekt>en present</objekt>
<tom>.</tom>
```

Example 1: The XML output format from the parser for the Swedish sentence '*You, who ask, would anyway probably have been able to buy a friend a present*' includes labels *pfv* (primary finite verb), *piv* (primary non-finite verb) and *tom* (empty).

3 Swedish Question Generation from Parses with Grammatical Functions

The question generation of this project primarily involves questions corresponding to the unbounded constituents which fall into two main groups. The *nominal* ones are subjects, objects/predicatives and the rest are the various types of *adverbials*, of which certain kinds like sentence adverbials, are not considered here. The approach here particularly aims at a high precision value, i.e. the share of correct answers for the generated questions. On the other hand, the system presented does not attempt to make an exhaustive coverage of all questions (recall). The input to the question generation is a separate main clause. A construction with coordinated finite VPs on the main clause level similarly will produce a main clause of the second VP by inheriting the most recent main clause level subject in the sentence (*Halley's Comet is the best-known of the short-period comets, and is visible from Earth every 75 to 76 years. → Halley's Comet is the best-known of the short-period comets, Halley's Comet is visible from Earth every 75 to 76 years*).

3.1   The Process of Question Generation

The question types considered are similar in that all these questions are built up using a three-step procedure of syntactic fronting of the unbounded constituents and substitution of suitable question elements with *wh*-words or similar. The procedure is shown in Figure 2. First, the currently fronted element is placed in the canonical (non-fronted) position. This V1 form will in general be the corresponding *yes/no*-question. V1 questions are considered to be of slightly less interest than the others since they generally just confirm facts (the existence of such a question – *'Is Halley's Comet the best-known of the short-period comets?'* – just indicates the validity of that fact). The second step is fronting of each unbounded constituent from this arrangement, producing that number of paraphrases which are grammatical in Swedish. Finally, each fronted element is replaced by e.g. the corresponding *wh*-word to form a question which is collected.

[-] Kartlade Rutherford atomen på institutet?

Basic V1 form *(Was the atom surveyed at the institute by Rutherford?)* is the first step

Rutherford kartlade [-] atomen på institutet.

⇓

Vem kartlade atomen på institutet?
Who surveyed the atom at the institute?

Atomen kartlade Rutherford [-] på institutet.

⇓

Vad kartlade Rutherford på insitutet?
(Lit:) *What surveyed Rutherford at the institute?*

På institutet kartlade Rutherford atomen [-].

⇓

Var kartlade Rutherford atomen?
(Lit:) *Where surveyed Rutherford the atom?*

Figure 2: The basic procedure for question generation from declarative sentences

The number of questions produced can be lower than the number of unbounded constituents present in the sentence due to incomplete parses, as a general result of the method's focus on producing correct questions safely and rule-based with this transformation-like technique.

3.2   Questions Regarding Nominal Grammatical Categories

The nominal constituents correspond to a small set of Swedish *wh*-words corresponding to *what, which* and *who/whom*. The system currently works by determining the head word if it is an NP. If this is a personal pronoun or otherwise corresponds to an animate reference, e.g. a personal name or animate noun, *who* is used, whereas *vad/what* is the default. *What*-questions are currently the most common type of question and typically constitute half of the generated questions to a text.

3.3   Questions Regarding Adverbials

Question generation for adverbials is interesting as the choice of corresponding fronted initial part is more complicated than for nominals. Adverbials are structurally prepositional phrases, adverb phrases, noun phrases with a head from a particular group of nouns *(denna gång/this time)* and a subset of sub clauses. Whereas many of the members of the groups have clearly corresponding question words, the major PP type is particularly large in Swedish (133 different prepositions are currently covered) and have correspondences that often are determined by the head of the prepositional complement, rather than the preposition. This is particularly the case, as in English, for some of the most common prepositions: *i/in på/on* etc. Current adverbial questions considered are:

- NP adverbials *(denna gång/this time)*, which predominantly refer to time and are replaced by *när/when*.
- PP adverbials. Swedish is particularly rich in prepositions since adverb + preposition compounds *(inifrån/"from-within")* are frequent.
- The subset of sub clause types which corresponds to adverbials *(eftersom/since)*.

Particularly in the case of prepositional objects a pied piping question (*Till vad/To what*) is mostly preferred as a question form.

4 Results and Possible Improvements

Aspects examined in evaluation of QG systems have e.g. been represented by the following categories of errors from Heilman and Smith (2009), which can be overlapping: "Ungrammatical", "Does not make sense", "Vague", "Obvious answer", "Missing answer", "Wrong *wh*-word", "Formatting" and "Other". The lack of formal definitions of these terms has not encouraged such evaluations at this early point.

4.1 Preliminary Tests

In a minor test with the current system, ten random Wikipedia articles were used, including 78 sentences. The system produced 309 questions (in average about 4.0 per sentence) in 6.3 seconds. Grammatical correctness of the questions is currently not very high according to manual tests. Higher correctness is however likely to be achieved after further work with rules for choice of question words. Since the approach is essentially manual and few sentences are deemed as impossible to analyze, or to generate questions from, the potential correctness of the approach is seen as high. At present, no similar system seems to exist for Swedish text that could be used for comparisons.

The idea of producing all possible questions for an input text is far from realized here. Future work may concern other "safe" conclusions, yielding new questions, such as propositions of on sub-clause levels in constructions with factual

verbs (*She knows it will work* → *it will work*) or questions regarding grammatical modifiers *(They sold the new boat → Which boat did they sell?)*.

4.2 Expanding the Set of Formulations of Questions

Ideally, the question set produced consists entirely of questions that are correctly answered by the text. The user of this type of system however faces a different task: finding a formulation of a question she has in mind that corresponds to the text. To help the user find information, it has been assumed that creating additional alternative formulations of questions will generally be helpful. The main difficulty with expanding the question set using synonym substitution (*What automobile/What car*) is that few word pairs qualify as true substitutes. Earlier tests have been carried out testing substituting present base form words with synonyms according to the Swedish *WordNet* (Viberg et al 2002) and *Folkets synonymordlista* (Kann and Rosell 2005). The proportion of truly substitutable word pairs in Wikipedia texts was about 50-60 percent for these sources, considering all suggestions without any word sense disambiguation. In *Folkets Synonymordlista*, there is however a great potential advantage in the fact that each pair of suggested synonyms are judged with a numerical scale up to 5.0. Setting a high threshold score, like 4.5, will leave a smaller number of synonym pairs but increase the appropriateness of the substitution.

References

Converse, Tim, Ronald M Kaplan, Barney Pell, Scott Prevost, Lorenzo Thione, and Chad Walters. "Powerset's Natural Language Wikipedia Search Engine." *Wikipedia and Artificial Intelligence: An Evolving Synergy. Papers from the 2008 AAAI Workshop.* Chicago, USA: AAAI Press, 2008. 67.

Diderichsen, Paul. *Elementær Dansk Grammatik.* Köpenhamn: Gyldendahl, 1946.

Ejerhed, Eva, Gunnel Källgren, and Benny Brodda. *Stockholm-Umeå corpus version 2.0.* Institutionen för Lingvistik, Stockholms universitet, Institutionen för Lingvistik, Umeå universitet, 2006.

Harabagiu, Sanda M, Marius A Paşca, and Steven J Maiorano. "Experiments with Open-Domain Textual Question Answering." *Proceedings of the 18th conference on Computational linguistics - Volume 1.* Saarbrücken: International Conference On Computational Linguistics, 2000. 292 - 298.

Heilman, Michael, and Noah A Smith. "Ranking Automatically Generated Questions as a Shared Task." *Proceedings of the AIED Workshop on Question Generation.* Brighton, UK, 2009. 30-37.

Kann, Viggo, and Magnus Rosell. "Free Construction of a Free Swedish Dictionary of Synonyms." *Proceedings of 15th Nordic Conference on Computational Linguistics – (NODALIDA 05).* Joensuu, 2005.

Rus, Vasile, and Arthur C Graesser. *The Question Generation Shared Task and Evaluation Challenge.* Workshop Report, Memphis, USA: The University of Memphis, 2009.

Viberg, Åke, Kerstin Lindmark, Ann Lindvall, and Ingmarie Mellenius. "The Swedish WordNet Project." *Proceedings of Euralex 2002.* Köpenhamn, 2002. 407-412.

Wilhelmsson, Kenneth. *Heuristisk analys med Diderichsens satsschema - tillämpningar för svensk text.* Gothenburg, Sweden: Department of Philosophy, Linguistics and Theory of Science, 2010.

ISSN 1736-6305 Vol. 11
http://hdl.handle.net/10062/16955

IV Student Papers

Linguistic Motivation in Automatic Sentence Alignment of Parallel Corpora: the Case of Danish-Bulgarian and English-Bulgarian

Angel Genov and Georgi Iliev
Department of Computational Linguistics, Institute for Bulgarian
Bulgarian Academy of Sciences
52 Shipchenski prohod, bl. 17, Sofia 1113, Bulgaria
`{angel,georgi}@dcl.bas.bg`

Abstract

We report the results from a sentence-alignment experiment on Danish-Bulgarian and English-Bulgarian parallel texts applying a method based in part on linguistic motivations as implemented in the TCA2 aligner. Since the presence of cognates has a bearing on the alignment score of candidate sentences we attempt to bridge the gap between source and target languages by transliteration of the Bulgarian text, written originally in Cyrillic. An improvement in F_1-measure is achieved in both cases.

1 Background

Parallel language resources are fundamental to some of the leading empirical methods in natural language processing today, and machine translation in particular. Due to economic and political considerations until now little attention has been paid to the availability and quality of parallel texts when it comes to so-called medium density languages, as defined in (Varga et al., 2005). A major development in this regard has been the release of the JRC-Acquis Multilingual Parallel Corpus (Steinberger et al., 2006) but a brief investigation of the aligned versions of the JRC-Acquis for the language pairs at hand fails to convince us of the quality of alignment in the corpus in its current state. However, due to the lack of a reference parallel text to perform evaluation, this intuition can neither be confirmed nor rejected at present.

In an attempt to achieve better clarity and provide a basis for further evaluation and comparison, we performed a sentence-alignment experiment on a Danish-Bulgarian and an English-Bulgarian parallel corpus, where translation has taken place in the indicated direction.

2 Alignment Method

Unlike the alignment methods adopted for the purposes of the JRC-Acquis, where a language-independent approach was needed to achieve coverage of most official EU languages, we chose to apply a partially linguistically motivated method to sentence alignment, as implemented in the Translation Corpus Aligner (TCA) 2 (Hofland and Johansson, 2006). The TCA2 is a GUI sentence alignment tool which calculates alignments on the basis of sentence length, a bilingual dictionary of anchor words, and the presence of (near) identical proper names and numbers and cognates in alignment candidates. It is a new implementation of a program which was used, among other things, for the alignment of the English-Norwegian Parallel Corpus (Johansson et al., 1996).

3 Corpora

For English-Bulgarian alignment we used the "1984" parallel corpus developed as part of the MULTEXT-East project (Erjavec, 2010), and provided by the MULTEXT-East Consortium under a research license. It contains a richly annotated hand-aligned parallel text. For our purposes we stripped the English-Bulgarian parallel text of George Orwell's "1984" of all annotation which was not relevant to sentence alignment. Thus the version of the "1984" corpus we used contains only XML tags marking sentence boundaries. The English text contains 6737 sentence units, and the Bulgarian text contains 6707 sentence units.

For Danish-Bulgarian alignment we used the original text of Thomas Rathsack's "Jæger – i krig med eliten" (*Commando – Fighting With the Elite*) published by Politiken's Internet edition on 16 September 2009 (Rathsack, 2009). The Bulgarian translation was provided for research purposes by the respective Bulgarian publisher. The sentence boundaries in the two texts were initially determined automatically. The resulting sentence boundaries were post edited and sentences were aligned by hand. The parallel corpus thus created contains XML tags marking sentence boundaries only. The Danish text contains 4483 sentence units, and the Bulgarian text contains 4565 sentence units.

We are not aware of previous work in the evaluation of sentence alignment as regards the Danish-Bulgarian language pair.

4 Language-Dependent Input

The TCA2 uses a bilingual dictionary of anchor words whose presence improves the alignment score of candidate sentences. TCA results reported in previous work (Santos and Oksefjell, 2000) have been based on anchor lists of approximately 1000 entries. In the experiment at hand we followed a resource-light strategy, which means we tried to keep the manual input at minimum, while preserving language-dependency.

The heuristics applied in compiling the bilingual dictionaries involved counting the number of occurrences of individual lemmas in the respective Bulgarian texts, disregarding any stop words, and selecting some of the most frequent nominals (that is nouns, adjectives, numerals and pronouns). To them we added some "polar" adverbs (such as "always" and "never"), some time words and the names of the twelve months of the year. The respective anchor lists contain 116 entries each.

One special feature of the TCA2 is the use of multiple variants in one and the same anchor entry, as well as the Kleene star, allowing us to cover a number of morphological and orthographic variations, as otherwise the number of anchor entries would have exploded, in particular in the Danish and the Bulgarian anchor lists.

DA-BG	2*,to*,begge,både/2*,два*,две*,дву*
EN-BG	woman,women/жена*,жени*

Table 1: Sample anchor word entries

It is possible that defining dictionary entries by means of the Kleene star could increase the number of false positives disproportionately, but that is not confirmed by the reported results.

5 Transliteration

An important element of the TCA2 tool is the assignment of a score to alignment candidates based on the presence of cognates (Simard et al., 1992) in them – words that are spelled identically or similarly in the source and target language. Both source languages use the Latin alphabet, whereas Bulgarian is written in Cyrillic. That fact effectively prevents any attempt at basing an alignment score on cognates, which we found to be suboptimal in the case of the TCA2 aligner.

A clear solution lies in the fact that Bulgarian spelling is mostly phonetic. Thus we were able to apply a straightforward transliteration method to convert the entire target text into Latin characters to explore the ability to use cognates in order to improve sentence alignment of the two parallel corpora. The transliteration method so adopted preserves the original length of the Bulgarian text as far as possible and does not take into account the specifics of the source language.

English original:

How often, or on what system, the Thought <u>Police</u> plugged in on any <u>individual</u> wire was guesswork.

Bulgarian original:

Можеше само да се правят предположения колко често и по какъв принцип <u>Полицията</u> на мисълта се включва в <u>индивидуалните</u> системи.

Bulgarian transliterated:

Mojeshe samo da se praviat predpolojeniia kolko chesto i po kakav princip <u>Policiiata</u> na misalta se vkliuchva v <u>individualnite</u> sistemi.

Example 1: Cognates identified upon transliteration of the target text

It can be seen from Example 1 above that cognates become evident by applying even a crude transliteration approach.

6 Evaluation Method

In order to evaluate the performance of the TCA2 we apply the standard metrics of recall, precision and F_1-measure (Jurafsky and Martin, 2008) to the output of the automatic aligner against the hand-aligned "gold standards", calculated as shown in Example 2 below:

Precision = number of correct alignments / number of proposed alignments

Recall = number of correct alignments / number of reference alignments

F_1-measure = 2 * Recall * Precision / (Recall + Precision)

Example 2: Calculation of precision, recall and F_1-measure

It should be noted that the manually aligned corpora do not contain any 0-1 or 1-0 alignments, whereas TCA2 allows 0-1 and 1-0 alignments and such alignments are present in the TCA2 automatic output. Other possible alignments are 1-1, 1-2, 2-1.

7 Results

We performed a total of 3 runs of the TCA2 aligner on each language pair, gradually enhancing the linguistic input in the system, as follows:

1st run: sentence-delimited source and target texts, no anchor words, no transliteration of the target text.

2nd run: sentence-delimited source and target texts, anchor words, no transliteration of the target text.

3rd run: sentence-delimited source and target texts, anchor words, transliteration of the target text.

The results are summarized in Table 2 below:

DA-BG, "Jæger – i krig med eliten"			
	Precision	Recall	F_1-measure
1st run	93.96	93.83	**93.9**
2nd run	97.23	97.12	**97.17**
3rd run	98.39	98.12	**98.26**
EN-BG, "1984"			
	Precision	Recall	F_1-measure
1st run	61.52	63.41	**62.45**
2nd run	87.77	89.17	**88.46**
3rd run	91.52	92.33	**91.92**

Table 2: Evaluation results

8 Discussion of Results

As expected, there was an improvement in all three metrics on each of the first three stages. It must be noted that the weights of different alignment criteria have not been optimized for the specific language pairs at hand, which means that further improvement may be expected. Most notable at present is the 26% improvement in F_1-measure of the English-Bulgarian alignment caused by the enhancement of the TCA2 system with an anchor list, irrespective of the limited size of the list (116 entries in total). It could be argued that the Danish-Bulgarian improvement on the 2nd run is as significant because the higher F_1-measure on the 1st run could be accounted for by the presence of many military terms and English words and expressions which were preserved in the Bulgarian translation of "Jæger – i krig med eliten", which in turn were treated as cognates / proper names by the TCA2 aligner already on the first run.

Most interesting is probably the improvement caused by the transliteration of the Bulgarian text. One disadvantage of phonetic spelling in Bulgarian is that it fails to preserve the original spelling of loan words, thus reducing the number of actual cognates in the text. We expect that by fine-tuning the transliteration rules dependent on the language pair in order to "anglicize" or "danify" the target language, respectively, following the philosophy of (Hana and Feldman, 2004), as applied to Russian and Czech, we could achieve further improvement in sentence alignment based on cognates. However, this will be the subject of a separate detailed study.

9 Conclusion and Future Work

We have shown that by investing a minimum amount of effort we can achieve significant improvement in the partially linguistically motivated approach to sentence alignment of the TCA2 aligner, bringing its performance, as expressed by the F_1-measure, well above 90 per cent in the case of Danish-Bulgarian, and above 90 per cent in the case of English-Bulgarian alignment. By applying a simple transliteration approach to the Bulgarian target we were able to achieve additional improvement of TCA2's performance.

Unlike the evaluation described in (Santos and Oksefjell, 2000), our main purpose was to explore the feasibility of applying a language-dependent method in sentence alignment to parallel texts where Bulgarian is the target language, not so much as to evaluate the performance of the TCA2 program itself. One difficulty which is not an issue in other alignment tasks, and which we addressed successfully, was the need to bridge the gap between the Cyrillic and the Latin alphabets. Furthermore, while the English-Portuguese evaluation was based on proofreading the results (and only those that were not 1-to-1 correspondencies), the Danish-Bulgarian and the English-Bulgarian alignments were evaluated on the basis of a gold standard which allowed us to calculate the improvement in a traditional manner, by way of the F_1-measure.

Driven by those preliminary results we intend to investigate the systematic differences occurring in the spelling of some loan words in Bulgarian from a morphological perspective. The results of the investigation could then be encoded in the form of language-specific transliteration rules to achieve further improvement in the performance of linguistically motivated sentence-alignment methods.

Acknowledgements

We are grateful to Knut Hofland and the team at the University of Bergen for making the TCA2 program available to us.

This work was supported by the Mathematical Logic and Computational Linguistics: Development and Permeation (2009-2011) Project. The financial support is granted under Contract No. BG051PO001-3.3.04/27 of 28 August 2009.

References

Tomaz Erjavec. 2010. MULTEXT-East Version 4: Multilingual Morphosyntactic Specifications, Lexicons and Corpora. In Nicoletta Calzolari (Conference Chair), Khalid Choukri, Bente Maegaard, Joseph Mariani, Jan Odijk, Stelios Piperidis, Mike Rosner, and Daniel Tapias, editors, *Proceedings of the Seventh conference on International Language Resources and Evaluation (LREC'10)*, Valletta, Malta, May, 19-21. European Language Resources Association (ELRA).

Jiri Hana and Anna Feldman. 2004. Portable Language Technology: Russian via Czech. In *Proceedings from the Midwest Computational Linguistics Colloquium, June 25-26, 2004*, Bloomington, Indiana.

Knut Hofland and Stig Johansson. 2006. The Translation Corpus Aligner: A program for alignment of paralell texts. In Stig Johansson and Signe Oksefjell, editors, *Corpora and Cross-linguistic Research. Theory, Method, and Case Studies*, number 24 in Language and Computers: Studies in practical Linguistics, pages 87–100. Rodopi, Amsterdam – Atlanta.

Stig Johansson, Jarle Ebeling, and Humanities Bergen. 1996. Coding and Aligning the English-Norwegian Parallel Corpus. In B. Altenberg K. Aijmer and M. Johansson, editors, *Languages in Contrast: Papers from a Symposium on Text-based Cross-linguistic Studies (Lund, 4-5 March 1994)*, pages 87–112, Lund. Lund University Press.

Daniel Jurafsky and James H. Martin. 2008. *Speech and Language Processing (2nd Edition) (Prentice Hall Series in Artificial Intelligence)*. Prentice Hall, 2 edition.

Thomas Rathsack. 2009. Jæger – i krig med eliten. http://www.politiken.dk, September, 16.

Diana Santos and Signe Oksefjell. 2000. An evaluation of the translation corpus aligner, with special reference to the language pair English-Portuguese. In *Proceedings of the 12th Nordisk datalingvistikkdager, Trondheim, Department of Linguistics, NTNU*.

Michel Simard, George F. Foster, and Pierre Isabelle. 1992. Using Cognates to Align Sentences in Bilingual Corpora. In *Proceedings of the Fourth International Conference on Theoretical and Methodological Issues in Machine Translation*, pages 67–81.

Ralf Steinberger, Bruno Pouliquen, Anna Widiger, Camelia Ignat, Tomaz Erjavec, Dan Tufis, and Daniel Varga. 2006. The JRC-Acquis: A multilingual aligned parallel corpus with 20+ languages. *CoRR*, abs/cs/0609058.

Dániel Varga, László Németh, Péter Halácsy, András Kornai, Viktor Trón, and Viktor Nagy. 2005. Parallel corpora for medium density languages. In *Proceedings of the Recent Advances in Natural Language Processing 2005 Conference. RANLP, Borovets.*, pages 590–596, Bulgaria.

ISSN 1736-6305 Vol. 11
http://hdl.handle.net/10062/16955

Finding Statistically Motivated Features Influencing Subtree Alignment Performance

Gideon Kotzé
University of Groningen
Groningen, The Netherlands
g.j.kotze@rug.nl

Abstract

In this paper, we present results of an on-going investigation of a manually aligned parallel treebank and an automatic tree aligner. We establish the features that show a significant correlation with alignment performance. We present those features with the biggest correlation scores and discuss their significance, with mention of future applications of these findings.

1 Introduction

A greater emphasis towards syntax-based approaches in machine translation has contributed towards a greater need for the use of subsententially aligned parallel treebanks for training data or example databases (Tinsley et al., 2007a; Vandeghinste and Martens, 2010; Sun et al., 2010). Several methods exist to induce alignments on a phrasal level, for example Wang et al. (2002), Tinsley et al. (2007b), Gildea (2003), Groves et al. (2004), Zhechev and Way (2008) and Tiedemann and Kotzé (2009, 2009b). The latter two papers describe a tree-to-tree based approach to alignment, requiring both sides of the parallel corpus to be syntactically annotated.

We apply this latter implementation to word aligned and parsed parallel sentences to produce links between the nonterminal nodes of phrase-structure parse trees that denote phrasal equivalence. For example, the English noun phrase "yesterday's sitting" is linked to its Dutch equivalent, "de vergadering van gisteren" (NP/NP link).

By evaluating and generating statistics from these links, we hope to find specific features that significantly impact the alignment performance. In this paper, we focus on lexical, structural and link features, all of which may play a statistical role in performance. Additionally, lexical and structural features could be used to help predict an expected score given a syntactically annotated sentence pair, and may help point out more specific linguistic and annotation issues. Our findings may help us to improve future alignment models and may provide us with more insight into the alignment process and the linguistics of the two languages involved.

In section 2, we introduce the software and techniques in our research methodology, and explain how we get our data and statistics. After that, in section 3, we present and discuss our statistical data. Finally, in section 4, we present our conclusion.

2 Approach

In (Tiedemann and Kotzé, 2009) and (Tiedemann and Kotzé, 2009b), a discriminative method of automatic tree alignment is presented using a maximum entropy classifier, classifying any given source/target node pair as either linked or unlinked. The software has been developed into a freely available and flexible toolkit called Lingua-Align (Tiedemann, 2010). Features extracted from the training data are used to classify the node pairs of new trees and include structural, lexical, alignment, contextual and history features.

Testing the tree aligner requires a data set consisting of syntactically parsed and translationally equivalent sentence pairs that are also word aligned. We opted for a selection of 140 Dutch/English sentence pairs from the Europarl 3 corpus (Koehn, 2005). The sentences have been aligned with the sentence aligner that is distributed with Europarl. The Dutch sentences were parsed using the Alpino parser (Van Noord, 2006) and the English sentences using the Stanford parser ((Klein and Manning, 2003a), (Klein and Manning, 2003b)). Although the output formats of the parsers differ from each other, it poses no problem as Lingua-Align can process them and is not dependent on any specific tagset.

Since Lingua-Align does not produce its own word alignments, we used the Viterbi alignments of GIZA++ (Och and Ney, 2003). These alignments, as well as the symmetric alignments that are produced by Moses (Koehn et al., 2007) are among the many features used to build the Lingua-Align model. The word alignment model is trained on all sentence aligned text in the Europarl corpus, consisting of 1,080,417 sentence pairs. The resulting word alignments are used when Lingua-Align encounters a new sentence pair to process. To produce our manual training data, we use the Stockholm TreeAligner (Lundborg et al., 2007), which currently requires the Tiger-XML representation format for viewing, to which we converted our trees. A distinction is made between good and fuzzy links, reflecting the level of confidence of the link. This is used by default in Lingua-Align.

We pre-processed the manually produced data set by applying ten-fold cross validation, yielding a balanced F-score of 72.95 when comparing the accuracy of the automatically produced terminal and nonterminal node links with the gold standard.

For every automatically aligned tree pair, we first extract a set of basic statistics. They are:

- based on all links with reference to the gold standard, the alignment precision, recall and balanced F-score

- node counts (terminals and nonterminals)

- link counts (good and fuzzy, terminals and nonterminals)

- sentence lengths and normalized ratios

- tree level/height and normalized ratios

- averages of normalized tree level and sentence length ratios

- average path of terminal nodes to the root node

- standard deviation of these paths

For each tree, we further assign a score based on its parse quality using manual inspection. The scores are on a scale of 1 to 3, where 1 is a good parse, 2 is not so good but reasonable, and 3 is a bad parse.

Ratios were normalized by taking the length of the longer unit into account. For example, if a

Dutch tree sentence has a length of 10 tokens and the English tree a length of 12, the sentence length ratio would be 0.83 according to the following formula:

$$1 - ((abs(x - y))/max(x, y)$$

Eventually, we have for each tree pair, and in some cases for each tree, a set of data values that we can investigate for possibly significant correlations with alignment evaluation scores. After extracting these statistics, we can produce distributions of the different variables over the whole set of sentence pairs.

Evaluation scores are based on all links, including those between terminal nodes. Because word alignment links are not produced by Lingua-Align but by GIZA++, the scores also indicate a measure of difference between the word alignments in the training data and those of GIZA++. We would like to study the nonterminal node linking performance of Lingua-Align itself more explicitly by keeping the word alignments fixed. We therefore proceeded to replace the manual word alignment links by those in the GIZA++ output. Naturally, since the word alignment training and testing sets are now similar, this resulted in a significant increase in accuracy, with an F-score of 82.05 when taking all links into account.

Because of the fact that Lingua-Align removes some terminal node links in the output to conform to well-formedness, the word alignment output is still slightly different from the input. However, we now consider training and testing conditions similar enough in order to measure more clearly the performance of the tree aligner itself. Because the evaluation scores take all links into account, we proceeded to calculate the precision, recall and F-scores for the nonterminal node links only. Links between terminal and nonterminal nodes are considered nonterminal node links, since they are produced by Lingua-Align. We obtain a new average F-score of 73.43.

In the next section, we present the distribution of the scores and the most important correlations, with a discussion of our findings.

3 Presentation and discussion of statistical data

Figure 1 presents a diagram representing the distribution of F-scores for all sentence pairs as produced by Lingua-Align. We use the F-scores pertaining to precision and recall for all nonterminal node links (including between terminal and nonterminal nodes) involved as a measure, and also present those measures in the diagram. It is clear that alignment accuracy can vary quite extensively, with the line tending towards a logarithmic curve. It is also interesting to note that recall correlates much more with the F-scores than precision does, while it is clear that precision regularly outperforms recall.

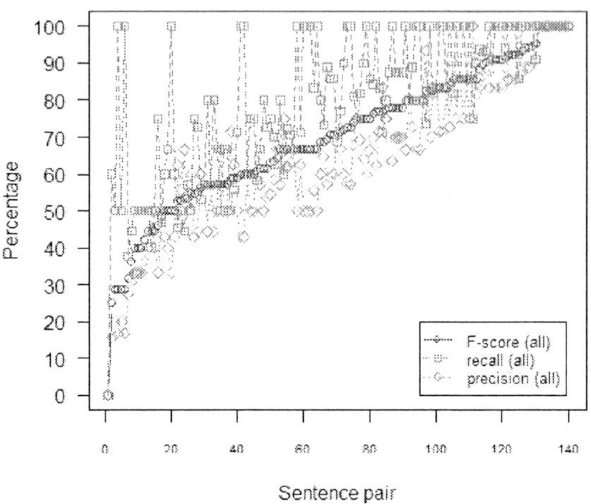

Figure 1: Distribution of F-score, precision and recall of nonterminal link node evaluation scores

We would like to determine which features correlate most strongly with these F-scores. For every feature set, we calculate the Pearson's correlation coefficient when compared to the set of F-scores. We present the correlations with values above 0.5 in figure 2.

Feature	Correlation coefficient
Normalized ratio: Number of linked terminal nodes and all terminal nodes	0.65
Normalized ratio: Number of linked Dutch nodes and all Dutch nodes	0.62
Normalized ratio: Number of nonterminal nodes and linked nonterminal nodes	0.59
Normalized ratio: Number of linked English nodes and all English nodes	0.57
Normalized ratio: Number of linked Dutch nonterminal nodes and all Dutch nonterminal nodes	0.56
Normalized ratio: Number of linked English nonterminal nodes and all English nonterminal nodes	0.54
Normalized ratio: Number of linked terminal nodes and all linked nodes:	0.51

Figure 2: List of strongest correlations

All the top correlations show a clear link between the ratio of linked nodes and F-score. In fact, the top 20 correlations are all link-based, while differences between sentence lengths has only a mild influence at 0.25. The strongest correlation indicates that a sentence pair with relatively many terminal node links is more likely to achieve a good score. One of the features in the tree alignment model specifies calculating a level of link confidence based on the ratio of the number of leaves in the two subtrees. The more leaves that are linked, the more likely the currently considered nonterminal node links are to be linked as well. Since recall is relatively low in comparison with precision, more linked terminal nodes will probably lead to better F-scores.

In general, trees that have relatively more links have generally high scores. This suggests that the alignment model could be improved by lowering the threshold at which to make links, increasing recall.

We also calculated correlations with tree features, such as tree height ratios and average distances to the root node. However, these correlations are mild to low (+-0.25 and lower) and this emphasizes the relative importance of terminal node and link features in comparison with other types of features.

The manual scores given to Dutch and English parse tree quality also show very poor correlations to the F-scores (-0.04 and -0.1 respectively).

4 Conclusion and future work

We have presented a statistical study of some features affecting the performance of an automatic tree aligner, given a reasonably good alignment model and reasonably good automatic word alignments. Although the data set is rather small, most of the strongest correlations suggest that more links need to be made, with word alignment links as the most important. We will apply these findings with the hope that accuracy will improve.

It also seems that there is no single dominant linear correlation with any of the extracted features with the presented F-scores. Rather, differences between correlations are gradual, and therefore, many of the features probably have an influence on each other. More sophisticated statistical tests could be employed to clearly outline these dependencies.

Many more features can be extracted. In this study, we have mostly focused on counts and ratios at sentence level, but link-centered features describing the typical contexts of good and bad links may provide more insight.

As always, more data is always better, and using a second data set from a different domain may help strengthen or disprove any findings that resulted from the first data set. Additionally, using different alignment models and even different tree aligners may provide more robustness to any future conclusions that we may draw.

Finally, in the future we hope to gain insight into linguistic issues and be able to apply our findings not only to tree alignment, but also to other domains such as parallel sentence filtering or sentence alignment.

Acknowledgements

The research presented in this paper was done in the context of the PaCo-MT project, sponsored by the STEVIN programme of the Dutch Language Union.

References

Daniel Gildea. Loosely Tree-based alignment for Machine Translation. In *Proceedings of the 41st Annual Meeting of the Association of Computational Linguistics (ACL-03)*, pp. 80-87, Sapporo, Japan, 2003.

Declan Groves, Mary Hearne and Andy Way. Robust Sub-Sentential Alignment of Phrase-Structure Trees. In *Proceedings of the 20th International Conference on Computational Linguistics (CoLing 2004)*, pp. 1072-1078, Geneva, Switzerland, 2004.

Dan Klein and Christopher D. Manning. 2003. Fast Exact Inference with a Factored Model for Natural Language Parsing. In *Advances in Neural Information Processing Systems 15 (NIPS 2002)*, Cambridge, MA: MIT Press, pp. 3-10.

Dan Klein and Christopher D. Manning. 2003b. Accurate Unlexicalized Parsing. In *Proceedings of the 41st Meeting of the Association for Computational Linguistics*, pp. 423-430.

Philipp Koehn. A Parallel Corpus for Statistical Machine Translation. In *Proceedings of MT-Summit*, 2005.

Philipp Koehn, Hieu Hoang, Alexandra Birch, Chris Callison-Burch, Marcello Federico, Nicola Bertoldi, Brooke Cowan, Wade Shen, Christine Moran, Richard Zens, Chris Dyer, Ondrej Bojar, Alexandra Constantin, Evan Herbst. Moses: Open Source Toolkit for Statistical Machine Translation. In *Proceedings of the ACL 2007 Demo and Poster Sessions*, pp. 177-180, Prague, June 2007.

Joakim Lundborg, Torsten Marek, Maël Mettler and Martin Volk. Using the Stockholm TreeAligner. In *Proceedings of the 6th Workshop on Treebanks and Linguistic Theories*, pp. 73-78, Bergen, Norway, 2007.

Franz Josef Och and Hermann Ney. A Systematic Comparison of Various Statistical Alignment Models. In *Computational Linguistics*, volume 29, number 1, pp. 19-51, March 2003.

Jun Sun, Min Zhang and Chew Lim Tan. 2010. Exploring Syntactic Structural Features for Sub-Tree Alignment using Bilingual Tree Kernels. In *Proceedings of the 48th Annual Meeting of the Association for Computational Linguistics*, pages 306-315, Uppsala, Sweden, 11-16 July 2010.

Jörg Tiedemann. Lingua-Align: An Experimental Toolbox for Automatic Tree-to-Tree Alignment. In *Proceedings of the Seventh Conference on International Language Resources and Evaluation (LREC'10)*. Valletta, Malta. 2010.

Jörg Tiedemann and Gideon Kotzé. A Discriminative Approach to Tree Alignment. In *Proceedings of Recent Advances in Natural Language Processing (RANLP 2009)*. Borovets, Bulgaria. 2009.

Jörg Tiedemann and Gideon Kotzé. Building a Large Machine-Aligned Parallel Treebank. In *Proceedings of Treebanks and Linguistic Theories (TLT-8)*. Milan, Italy. 2009b.

John Tinsley, Mary Hearne, and Andy Way. 2007a. Exploiting Parallel Treebanks to Improve Phrase-Based Statistical Machine Translation. In *Proceedings of the Sixth International Workshop on Treebanks and Linguistic Theories (TLT-07)*, pages 175-187, Bergen, Norway.

John Tinsley, Ventsislav Zhechev, Mary Hearne and Andy Way. Robust Language Pair-Independent Sub-Tree Alignment. In *Proceedings of Machine Translation Summit XI*, pp. 467-474. Copenhagen, Denmark. 2007b.

Gertjan van Noord. At Last Parsing Is Now Operational. In *Piet Mertens, Cedrick Fairon, Anne Dister, Patrick Watrin (editors): TALN'06. Verbum Ex Machina. Actes de la 13e conference sur le traitement automatique des langues naturelles.* pp. 20-42.

Wei Wang, Jin-Xia Huang, Ming Zhou and Chang-Ning Huang. Structure Alignment Using Bilingual Chunking. In *Proceedings of the 19th Conference on Computational Linguistics*, pp. 1-7. Taipei, Taiwan. 2002.

Vincent Vandeghinste and Scott Martens. (2010). Bottom-up transfer in Example-based Machine Translation. In *Proceedings of EAMT 2010*. European Association for Machine Translation. Saint-Raphael.

Ventsislav Zhechev and Andy Way. Automatic Generation of Parallel Treebanks. In *Proceedings of the 22nd International Conference on Computational Linguistics (CoLing)*, pp. 1105-1112, 2008.

ISSN 1736-6305 Vol. 11
http://hdl.handle.net/10062/16955

Evaluating the speech quality of the Norwegian synthetic voice Brage

Marius Olaussen
Norwegian Library of Talking Books and Braille
Oslo, Norway
`marius.olaussen@nlb.no`

Abstract

This document describes the method, results and conclusions from my master's thesis in Nordic studies. My aim was to assess the speech quality of the Norwegian Filibuster text-to-speech system with the synthetic voice Brage. The assessment was carried out with a survey and an intelligibility test at phoneme, word and sentence level. The evaluation criteria used in the study were intelligibility, naturalness, likeability, acceptance and suitability.

1 Introduction

1.1 Background

Visually impaired and print disabled students in higher education have a need for adapted literature. In Norway the Norwegian Library of Talking Books and Braille (NLB) is responsible for such adaptation. Over half of the academic literature is produced with TTS. All audio books are produced as DAISY books. To strengthen the services given to students, NLB appropriated a million Norwegian kroner by the Ministry of Education and Research. The library signed collaboration with the Swedish Library of Talking Books and Braille (TPB) to adjust their TTS system Filibuster to Norwegian Bokmål. Bokmål is one of the two written varieties of Norwegian. The second variety is Nynorsk. In late 2009, the Norwegian synthetic voice *Brage* was launched.

1.2 The present study

The aim of this study was to evaluate the speech quality of Brage with respect to the suitability to impart academic literature. No similar studies regarding evaluation of synthetic speech quality have previously been carried out in Norway. Four research questions were formulated:

1. How do visually impaired and print disabled students experience the speech quality of Brage assessed by key criteria given in evaluation methodology?
2. How intelligible is Brage compared to other Norwegian synthetic voices?
3. How suitable does Brage seem to be as an imparter of academic literature?
4. How should Filibuster with Brage further develop?

2 Brief description of Filibuster TTS

TPB needed a TTS system especially trained for processing textual challenges distinctive of academic texts. In 2007, the Filibuster TTS system was implemented in production with the first Swedish voice *Folke*. The system is based on concatenation with unit selection.

The Norwegian Filibuster system uses a pronunciation dictionary of somewhat 780,000 entries from The Norwegian language resource collection. All entries are transcribed in SAMPA (Wells, 2005). The speech database was recorded at NLB with a manuscript of 15,604 Norwegian utterances created from a text corpus consisting of 10.8 million words from academic literature, newspapers, magazines and official Norwegian reports (Sjölander and Tånnander, 2009). In addition, an English manuscript of approximately 1,150 English utterances from the CMU ARCTIC database was used (Kominek and Black, 2003). 15 xenophones were applied.

3 Methodology

3.1 A survey

A survey was carried out with a questionnaire designed with the recommendations of the ITU-T evaluation method (Jekosch, 2005). This is a useful method to operationalise key evaluation criteria such as intelligibility, naturalness, likeability, acceptance and suitability.

3.2 An intelligibility test

The SUS test (*Semantically Unpredictable Sentences*) was adopted to perform an intelligibility test supplementary to the survey. The SUS test is primarily a sentence level intelligibility test (Benoît, Grice and Hazan, 1995), but has also been applied at word level (Boula de Mareüil et al., 2006). In this study the SUS test was applied at phoneme, word and sentence level to compare Brage to two other Norwegian synthetic voices, which respondents in the survey stated as their favourites: *Kari* (Acapela Group) and *Stine* (Nuance). Like Brage, both of these voices are based on concatenation with unit selection. One of the reasons for choosing the SUS test over other intelligibility tests is the removal of semantic information. Thus the informants cannot use contextual cues to guess the right words.

The SUS sentences are generated with five syntactic structures (*intransitive, transitive, imperative, interrogative and relative*) limited by a set of syntactic and lexical constraints. The test material mainly consists of high frequent monosyllabic words. The test designers developed SUS generator software, but since the software wasn't supported by later OSs, I decided to develop a new one, in addition to a frequency and part of speech list generator. The monosyllabic frequency lists were based upon all books produced with Brage in the course of one year. All software and both audio and textual test material used in this study are available for download at www.teksttiltale.no.

3.3 Informants

19 visually impaired and 34 other print disabled Norwegian students in higher education participated in the survey. Most of the students had little experience with TTS (57 % stated they had used TTS for less than a year). In the SUS test, 18 informants participated. To avoid biased results that might not correlate to the actual intelligibility, none of the informants were registered as patrons at NLB nor were print disabled.

4 Account of results and discussion

4.1 The SUS test

In the SUS test, Brage received on the average higher scores than Kari and Stine. The sentences were distributed in such a way that six informants heard the same sentence with the same TTS. Of a total of 60 sentences all six informants reiterated 26 sentences correctly with Brage,

compared to 10 sentences with Kari and 7 sentences with Stine. At word level Stine scored 330 of a total of 408 possible points (8 % less than Kari and 14 % less than Brage). Table 1 shows the distribution of scores at phoneme level.

Phonemes	Brage	Kari	Stine
All vowels	0.9926	0.9558	0.8949
- Front	0.9912	0.9561	0.8972
- Central	0.9947	0.9520	0.9173
- Back	0.9938	0.9604	0.8521
All diphthongs	0.9872	0.9872	0.8077
All consonants	0.9777	0.9578	0.9225
- Bilabials	0.9841	0.9722	0.8948
- Labiodentals	0.9773	0.9621	0.9343
- Dentals, alveolars, postalveolars	0.9761	0.9558	0.9279
- Retroflexes	0.9889	0.9889	0.9333
- Palatals	0.9849	0.9697	0.9242
- Velars	0.9762	0.9544	0.9028
- Glottals	1.0000	0.9028	0.9306

Table 1: The SUS test results at phoneme level

A unique feature of the voice quality of Brage, distinguishing this voice from other Norwegian synthetic voices, is the reading speed. To demonstrate this, I carried out a comparison test with eight other Norwegian voices. The test results showed that Brage reads 27 % slower than the average. Kari reads 5 % faster than the average and Stine reads 13 % faster. Since Brage on average scored higher than Kari and Stine in the SUS test, there seems to be a correlation between reading speed and the ability to define word boundaries. Findings indicated that determiners and conjunctions play a role in the intelligibility at sentence level. For instance, there were fewer incorrect reiterations of articles recorded with Brage (3 %), compared to Kari (8 %) and Stine (13 %). Such a possible correlation has also been pointed out in previous studies (Neovius and Raghavendra, 1993).

4.2 The survey

4.2.1 Intelligibility

The findings in the SUS test are to be understood as an indication of the overall intelligibility. The user experienced intelligibility seemed, however, to correlate to the findings of the SUS test; 81 % of the respondents in the survey stated Brage generally had either an intelligible or quite intelligible articulation. The user experienced intelligibility appeared to be closely related to how well the respondents thought Brage handled academic terminology within their branch of study. Respondents who studied law, political sciences, economic sciences and business and management found that Brage did not impart terminology in their curriculum in any acceptable manner.

When it comes to Norwegian Nynorsk, 75 % of the students stated their curriculum didn't contain elements of Nynorsk. However, despite a low coverage of Nynorsk entries in the pronunciation dictionary (0.2 %), 21 % of the students found that Brage handled Nynorsk either well or quite well. To some extent this also applied to English; about half of the respondents (54 %) considered the English pronunciation to be good.

Furthermore, a correlation between experience and speech perception was observed. Among the respondents who considered the overall articulation of Brage to be either unintelligible or quite unintelligible (20 %), 82 % stated that they had been using a Norwegian TTS for less than three years or not at all. Similar observations have also been made in previous studies (Francis, Nusbaum and Fenn, 2007).

Addressing particular textual challenges, the students stated that Brage did not process digits and numeral phrases, homographs and foreign proper names in a satisfactory manner.

4.2.2 Naturalness

57 % of the respondents liked the voice of Brage either well or quite well. Respondents who liked it less or not at all also report they had less experience with speech synthesis. Although many liked the voice itself, 45 % of the respondents thought Brage was unnatural or quite unnatural. None of these students, however, had used speech synthesis for more than six years. In comparison, none of the respondents who had used a Norwegian speech synthesis for seven years or more believed Brage to be unnatural.

86 % of the students stated it was important or quite important that synthetic speech resembles human speech to a technologically possible extent. Nonetheless, 6 % reported that it didn't matter at all. Interestingly, 8 % preferred synthetic speech to human, particularly justifying this with the shorter production time, the potential of larger quantum of academic literature and the direct access to the book content electronically.

Furthermore, 22 % of the respondents found the prosody of Brage to be good, while 26 % had no remarks at all. Prosodic weaknesses specially pointed out concerned stress (15 %), rhythm and intonation (24 %) and incorrect reproduction of syllables (4 %). 60 % of the respondents who thought Brage sounded either unnatural or quite unnatural, had remarks concerning prosodic characteristics. This indicates the importance of prosodic characteristics for the user experienced naturalness of a synthetic voice.

4.2.3 Likeability

34 % of the students thought it was either pleasant or quite pleasant listing to Brage over time, while 30 % stated it was ok, and 36 % found it either unpleasant or quite unpleasant. This may be due to a number of things. Firstly, the individual preferences seemed to vary, particularly regarding reading speed. Similar observations were done in other evaluation studies (Furui, 2007). But still there doesn't seem to have been carried out any studies addressing the cause of such variation.

The practise of speech synthesis seemed to play a key role in the assessment of user experienced likeability; all the students who did not prefer synthetic adaptation (71 %) had been using Norwegian TTS for less than a year. This corroborates the importance of encouraging the use of TTS to a larger extent, in order to get positive user experience (Francis, Nusbaum and Fenn, 2007).

Regarding concentration problems, 83 % stated they would strive more to retain focus when reading texts adapted with synthetic speech, compared to texts adapted with human speech. More experienced students seemed to exert less than those with less experience.

4.2.4 Acceptance

About half of the students (45 %) preferred human to synthetic speech. Students who reported they had more experience, however, showed a greater acceptance for such adaptation.

45 % stated they had good confidence in Brage as imparter of academic literature, while 28 % had some confidence and 26 % little or no confidence whatsoever. The lack of confidence was justified in particular by user experienced intelligibility together with naturalness and likeability. It is therefore crucial to improve the intelligibility, for instance by finding an effective way to ensure that frequent terms in academic literature of various branches of study is pronounced correctly.

5 Conclusions

5.1 Summary

Assessment of the suitability to impart academic literature should be carried out as a sum of the other key evaluation criteria (Jekosch, 2005; King, 2007). In this regard, Brage seemed to impart academic literature in an overall acceptable manner. 15 respondents preferred Brage over other synthetic voices. This is five times as many compared to the other voices. It is interesting that 9 of the 15 respondents preferring Brage, also reported that they had only made use of a Norwegian TTS for less than a year. However, only 4 of these 9 students stated they had knowledge of other Norwegian synthesizers. Thus, this shouldn't necessarily be understood as an acceptance for Brage, but rather for TTS in general.

When it comes to characteristics, a unique feature with Brage is the slow reading pace, which would result in distinct word boundaries, but also frustration among users preferring to read faster.

Academic literature spans a wide range of disciplines. Findings in the study indicate that Brage seemed to be less suited to impart texts within certain disciplines. Prior to a documented acceptable degree of coverage of academic terminology, it is recommended to adapt less suited academic literature with human speech rather than synthetic, until the system has been improved. In the wake of this recommendation, tools for mapping out the coverage of the most frequent academic terminology within different branches of study have recently been developed, providing statistical overview of new and missing entries. A coverage test was carried out with a test material of 70 academic books, divided between seven different branches of study. Results from this test showed that the coverage of terminology within law (42 %), economic sciences, business and management (38 %), and political sciences, was somewhat higher compared to the coverage in academic literature within the branches of study which the respondents in the user survey believed Brage imparted well or in an acceptable manner. This finding seems to indicate that the terminological coverage has less impact on how suitable students find Brage to be imparting their syllabus than previously presumed. These tools are presently being expanded with automatic phonetic transcription and morphological annotation suggestions.

5.2 Further work

Any given academic text will almost invariably contain words not yet listed in the pronunciation dictionary. An intermediate solution to this challenge could be to develop a spelling feature in the DAISY player ensuring the reader access to the text. Furthermore, since 45 % of the informants stated Brage was either unnatural or quite unnatural, initiatives to increase the prosody should be prioritised. One possible solution is phrase splicing (Donovan et al., 1999).

References

Benoît, C., Grice, M. and Hazan, V. 1995. *The SUS test: A method for the assessment of text-to-speech synthesis intelligibility using Semantically Unpredictable Sentences.* Speech Communication, Vol. 18, 1996:381-392.

Boula de Mareüil, P., d'Alessandro, C., Raake, A., Bailly, G., Garcia, M-N. and Morel, M. 2006. *A joint intelligibility evaluation of French text-to-speech synthesis systems: the EvaSy SUS/ACR campaign.* Proc. of LREC2006, Genoa, Italy.

Donovan, R. E., Franz, M., Sorensen, J. S. and Roukos, S. 1999. *Phrase Splicing and Variable Substitution using the IBM Trainable Speech Synthesis System.* Proc. of ICASSP'99, Phoenix, AZ.

Francis, A. L., Nusbaum, H. C. and Fenn, K. 2007. *Effects of Training on the Acoustic-Phonetic Representation of Synthetic Speech.* Journal of Speech, Language and Hearing Research, Vol. 50, Nr. 6:1445-1465.

Furui, S. 2007. *Speech and Speaker Recognition Evaluation.* In Dybkjær, L., Hemsen, H. and Minker, W. 2008. Evaluation of Text and Speech Systems. Text, Speech and Language Technology, Vo. 37. Springer, New York.

King, M. 2007. *General Principles of User-Oriented Evaluation.* In Dybkjær, L., Hemsen, H. and Minker, W. (ed.). Evaluation of Text and Speech Systems. Text, Speech and Language Technology, Vol. 37:125-161. Springer, New York.

Kominek, J. and Black, A. 2003. *CMU ARCTIC databases for speech synthesis.* Report CMU-LTI-03-177. Language Technologies Institute. Carnegie Mellon University, Pittsburgh. http://festvox.org/cmu_arctic/cmu_arctic_report.pdf.

Jekosch, U. 2005. *Voice and Speech Quality Perception. Assessment and Evaluation.* Springer. Heidelberg, Germany.

Neovius, L. And Raghavendra, P. 1993, *Evaluation of comprehension of KTH text-to-speech with 'listening speed' paradigm,* STL-QPSR, Vol. 34:21-30.

Sjölander, K. and Tånnander, C. 2009. *Adapting the Filibuster text-to-speech system for Norwegian Bokmål.* Proc. of FONETIK 2009. Available at http://www.ling.su.se/fon/fonetik_2009/036%20sjolander_tannander_fonetik2009.pdf.

Wells, J. 2005. *SAMPA computer readable phonetic alphabet.* Department of Speech, Hearing and Phonetic Sciences, University College London. http://www.phon.ucl.ac.uk/home/sampa/.

ISSN 1736-6305 Vol. 11
http://hdl.handle.net/10062/16955

A Statistical Part-of-Speech Tagger for Persian

Mojgan Seraji
Department of Linguistics and Philology
Uppsala University, Sweden
`mojgan.seraji@lingfil.uu.se`

Abstract

This paper presents the statistical part-of-speech tagger HunPoS trained on a Persian corpus. The result of the experiments shows that HunPoS provides an overall accuracy of 96.9%, which is the best result reported for Persian part-of-speech tagging.

1 Introduction

Data driven (machine learning) techniques for word sense disambiguation have always been a very active field and have attracted great attention from many researchers in the computational linguistics community. One of the usages of these methods is in the task of automatic part-of-speech tagging and that has resulted in some successful data driven part-of-speech taggers such as MX-POST (Ratnaparkhi, 1996) based on the maximum entropy framework, the memory-based tagger (MBT) (Daelemans et al., 1997), Brill's tagger based on transformation-based learning (TBL) (Brill, 1995) and Trigram 'n' Tags (TnT) based on Hidden Markov models (Brants, 2000). More recent work on data-driven taggers include conditional random fields and support vector machines (Kumar and Gurpreet Singh, 2010) (Gimenez and Marquez, 2004).

HunPoS (Halacsy et al., 2007) is an open source part-of-speech tagger that was released as a reimplementation of TnT. The user can tune the tagger by using different feature settings depending on the language type. Hitherto, a lot of models and implementations have been designed and are already available for the task of tagging and most of them have been tested for English and other languages but not many have been tested on Persian texts. However, some statistical tagging methods; namely a memory-based tagging (MBT) approach and Maximum Likelihood Estimation (MLE), as well as TnT have been tried out, but comparing to other languages like English it is not sufficient. Therefore, the evaluation of other part-of-speech taggers like HunPoS would be of great interest to discover how the tagger performs when applied to Persian compared to other data-driven taggers. This paper describes an evaluation of the performance of the part-of-speech tagger HunPoS on Persian. We apply the tagger on BijanKhan corpus (Bijankhan, 2004) and vary the features used for tagging seen and unseen tokens. This paper contains the following sections. Section 2 presents the open source tagger HunPoS. Section 3 describes briefly the classification, the properties and the script of Persian, prior studies of some statistical tagging methods and also introduces BijanKhan's corpus. In section 4 the design of this experiment follows and it introduces the experimental set-up. Section 5 describes the results of the evaluation. Finally, section 6 concludes this study.

2 HunPoS

HunPoS is an open source reimplementation of TnT that is based on Hidden Markov Models (HMM) with trigram language models, allowing the user to tune the tagger by using different feature settings. The tagger is similar to TnT with the difference that it estimates emission/lexical probabilities based on current and previous tags. One additional difference compared to TnT stands in the fact that the tagger is open source whereas TnT is not. The strong side of TnT, namely its suffix-based guessing algorithm that is used for handling unseen words is also implemented in HunPoS. Moreover, HunPoS inserts a morphological analyzer to narrow down the list of alternatives (possible tags) that the algorithm needs to deal with, which not only speeds up search but also very significantly improves precision. In other words, the morphological analyzer generates the possible tags, to which the weights are assigned by suffix-based gussing algorithm (Halacsy et al., 2007).

3 Persian

3.1 The Persian Language

Persian, also known as Parsi or Farsi belongs to the Indo-Iranian languages, a subfamily of the Indo-European languages. Persian is spoken in Iran (Farsi), Afghanistan (referred to as Dari) and Tajikistan (referred to as Tajiki). The language has been greatly influenced by Arabic vocabulary and has the same alphabet including four additional letters; پ ' چ ' ژ ' گ, which are the sounds of [p], [tʃ], [ʒ], [g], and texts are written from right to left. Although Persian is classified as a SOV language, colloquial speech does not usually follow this order. Assi and Abdolhosseini (2000) notes that the existence of a direct object marker enables the speakers of Persian to use subjects and objects in a free word order. In addition, there are no gender distinctions in Persian as there are for example in English (she/he). Possessiveness is indicated by the genitive morpheme -e (ezafeh) in a conversation but it is invisible in writing. Adverbs can appear virtually everywhere in a sentence and adjectives can follow or precede nouns. In Persian there are several plural markers; "-hâ" and "-ân", Arabic plural suffixes such as "-ât", "-in" and "un" (used only for words of Arabic origin). There is also a plural form in Persian that follows the Arabic template morphology and is called "broken plural".

3.2 Prior Studies of Some Statistical Tagging Methods

The lack of a perspicuous morphology in Persian for marking boundaries in an SOV system makes it difficult to determine where the subject ends and where the object begins. With respect to all the factors existing in Persian such as the complex verbal paradigm as well as the highly ambiguous structure of the noun phrase and so forth, quite good results have been reported on the performance of several part-of-speech tagging methods such as TnT, memory-based tagger (MBT) and Maximum Likelihood Estimation (MLE) (Raja et al., 2007). The utilized corpus in these experiments is the BijanKhan corpus, consisting of nearly 2.6 million words. Training and test set were created by randomly dividing the corpus into two parts with an 85% to 15% ratio and each experiment repeated five times in order to avoid accidental results. The overall accuracies reported for the three taggers in due order are 96.6%, 96.6%, and 95.9% (Raja et al., 2007).

3.3 Corpus

BijanKhan corpus was introduced in 2004 as the first manually tagged Persian (Farsi) corpus in Iran. The corpus is basically gathered from daily news and common texts, and consists of syntactic and semantic annotation of nearly 2.6 million words, done by Prof. M. BijanKhan (and several linguistics students following a particular instruction) prepared at the Research Center of Intelligent Signal Processing (RCISP) in Tehran. The corpus comes with statistical software for the calculation and extraction of language features such as: conditional distribution probability, word frequency, and recognition of homonyms, synonyms, concordances and lexical order with report functionality. In addition, the corpus original tag set contains 550 tags and are organized in a tree structure. The tag name starts with the name of the most general tag and continues with the names of the subcategories until it reaches the name of the leaf tag. An example of a hierarchical tag in third level of depth can be "N_PL_LOC"; where "N" represents noun, "PL" shows the tag plurality, and "LOC" defines the tag as location. This enormous number of tags are used to attain a fine grained part-of-speech tagging that discriminates the subcategories in a general category but since this vast amount of tags makes any machine learning process impracticable Oroumchian et al. (Oroumchian et al., 2006), decided to reduce the number of tags to 40. All tags with three or more levels in hierarchy were accordingly reduced to two-level tags; in other words, the above example reduced to "N_PL". Some two-level tags that were unnecessarily too specific were also reduced to one-level tags. More specifically, these tags are conjunctiones, morphemes, prepositions, pronouns, prepositional phrase, noun phrase, conditional prepositions, objective adjectives and wishes, quantifiers and mathematical signatures (Oroumchian et al., 2006). The corpus was processed in 2007 in order to be more suitable for NLP tasks. This version of BijanKhans corpus is in Unicode text format.

4 Experimental Set-up

This experiment has two phases, model selection and model assessment. The goal of choosing these two phases was to use model selection for estimating the performance of different models in order to choose the best one, and model assessment for having chosen a final model and estimating its generalization error on new data. The corpus was split into a training set for learning or fitting the models, a validation set (development test set) for validating and estimating prediction error for model selection, and a test set preserved for testing and evaluating the generalization error for the final chosen model. The size of each set was 80%, 10% and 10%, respectively, while in the model assessment the sample data was divided into 90% for training and 10% for testing. Prior to tagging we need to train the tagger on a suitable tagged corpus (the Bijankhan corpus) in order to build a model. The tagging process requires two files containing the model built by the training process and an untagged (raw) corpus. The untagged corpus, as its name indicates, contains no part-of-speech tags and it has only one column consisting of one token per line. Since the tagger has several training options we tried to make use of this flexibility by setting several parameters for training. Therefore, we ran several experiments to train the tagger with different feature settings and combining these as well. We experimented with the order of the tag transition probability by setting the option -t to either bigram tagging or the default trigram tagging in order to estimate the probability of a tag based on the previous tags. We also examined the order of the emission probability -e for estimating the probability of a token based on the tag of the token itself as well as the previous tags. For tag distributions of unseen words based on tag distributions of rare words (words seen less than N times in the training corpus) we used the option -f with the default value 10. Finally, we tested the -s parameter that sets the length of the longest suffix to be considered by the algorithm when it estimates an unseen words tag distribution with the default value 10. It is noteworthy that the most desirable possible value of this parameter (-s) may depend on the morphology and orthography of the language involved (Halacsy et al., 2007). Thus, we tested suffixes of length 10 (the default value), 8 and 4.

Tag Transitions	Word Emissions	Accuracy
bigram	unigram	95.8%
bigram	bigram	95.8%
trigram	unigram	96.0%
trigram	bigram	96.0%

Table 1: Comparison of different models for tag transitions and word emissions.

Max Suffix Length	Max Frequency	Accuracy
10	10	96.0%
8	10	96.0%
4	10	95.9%

Table 2: Comparison of different models for unseen words.

5 Results of the Evaluation

5.1 Model Selection

For the purpose of evaluating the results, the tagged file by HunPoS was compared to the gold standard (the original manually tagged validated file) and the differences were registered. We have evaluated the performance of HunPoS from different aspects: the accuracy of the assigned tags, precision, recall and F score (harmonic mean of the precision and recall) for different part-of-speech tags, training the tagger with different feature settings for the tagging lexical probabilities as well as for the treatment of unseen words. The results of training the tagger with a combination of different feature settings showed that by applying the trigram models, as could be predicted, we achieved a higher accuracy than with the bigram models (Table 1). In order to examine the tagger performance for unseen words we had the possibility to vary the length of the suffixes. Therefore, since the optimal value of this parameter can be dependent on the morphology and orthography of the language, we tested suffixes of length 10 (the default value), 8, and 4. Looking at the results appearing in Table 2, we can infer a decrease in accuracy when reducing the length of the suffixes. Thus, for Persian, suffix length set to 10 yields the best results. The accuracy of the model selection as it is depicted in Table 3 is 96.0%.

5.2 Model Assessment

Finally, in the model assessment, we augmented the size of the training data from 80% to 90% by adding the validation set (the development test set)

Total Tokens	268424
Tokens Correctly Tagged	257794
Tokens Incorrectly Tagged	10630
Accuracy	96.0%

Table 3: Tagger performance in the model selection

to the training set and using the 10% test set that we had preserved from the beginning of this study for evaluation. In order to evaluate the results of the model assessment, the file tagged by HunPoS was compared to the gold standard (the original manually tagged test file) and the differences were recorded. Results in Table 4 shows the accuracy achieved in the model assessment. However, we can also conclude that the tagger performance was probably influenced by the size of the training set, since the accuracy increased with the extension of the training data.

Total Tokens	268008
Tokens Correctly Tagged	259618
Tokens Incorrectly Tagged	8390
Accuracy	96.9%

Table 4: Tagger performance in the model Assessment

6 Conclusion

An evaluation of the open source part-of-speech tagger HunPoS on Persian was presented here. We applied the tagger to a Persian corpus and trained it with different feature settings. The experimental results revealed an overall accuracy of 96.9% for the Persian language. By training the tagger with different feature settings in this study we can deduce that applying the default settings of the tagger can yield the best results for Persian. Moreover, the size increment of the training data in the model assessment (90%) led the system to achieve higher accuracy. Finally, to conclude this paper, we can state that with respect to the performance of other data-driven part-of-speech taggers, such as TnT, memory-based tagger, and Maximum Likelihood Estimation, HunPoS is a good alternative for part-of-speech tagging of Persian. The results reported in this paper are the best published results so far, although the scores may not be directly comparable to those of Raja et al. (2007) because we do not know whether the two studies used the same training-test split.

References

Mostafa S. Assi and Haji M. Abdolhosseini. 2000. *Grammatical Tagging of a Persian Corpus.* International Jouranal of Corpus Linguistics 5(1):69-82.

Mahmood Bijankhan. 2004. *The Role of the Corpus in writing a Grammar: An Introduction to a Software.* Iranian Journal of Linguistics, 19.

Thorsten Brants. 2000. *TnT a Statistical Part-of-Speech Tagger.* In Proceedings of the 6th Applied Natural Language Processing Conference (ANLP-00), Seattle, Washington, USA.

Erik Brill. 1995. *Transformation-based error-driven learning and natural language processing: A case study in part-of-speech tagging.* Computational Linguistics, 21:543-566.

Walter Daelemans, Jakob Zavrel, Peter Berck, and Steven Gillis. 1997. *A memory-based part-of-speech tagger generator.* In Eva Ejerhed and Ido Dagan, editors, Proceedings of the Fourth Workshop on Very Large Corpora.

Jesus Gimenez and Lluis Marquez. 2004. *SVMTool: A general POS tagger generator based on Support Vector Machines.* In LREC, Lisbon, Portugal.

Peter Halacsy, Andras Kornai, and Csaba Oravecz. 2007. *Hunpos an open source trigram tagger.* In Proceedings of the 45th Annual Meeting of the Association for Computational Linguistics, Companion Volume Proceedings of the Demo and Poster Sessions. Association for Computational Linguistics, Prague, Czech Republic, pages 209-212.

Dinesh Kumar and Josan Gurpreet Singh. 2010. *Part of Speech Tagger for Morphologically Rich Indian Languages: A Survey.*

Farhad Oroumchian, Samira Tasharofi, Hadi Amiri, Hossein Hojjat, and Fahimeh Raja. 2006. *Creating a Feasible Corpus for Persian POS Tagging.* Technical report, no.TR3/06, University of Wollongong in Dubai.

Fahimeh Raja, Hadi Amiri, Samira Tasharofi, Hossein Hojjat, and Farhad Oroumchian. 2007. *Evaluation of part-of-speech tagging on Persian text.* The Second Workshop on Computational approaches to Arabic Script-based Languages, Linguistic Institute Stanford University.

Adwait Ratnaparkhi. 1996. *A maximum entropy model for part-of-speech tagging.* In Proceedings of the Conference on Empirical Methods in Natural Language Processing (EMNLP).

ISSN 1736-6305 Vol. 11
http://hdl.handle.net/10062/16955

Identification of Context Markers for Russian Nouns

Anastasia Shimorina
St. Petersburg State University
St. Petersburg, Russia
shinas@yandex.ru

Maria Grachkova
St. Petersburg State University
St. Petersburg, Russia
maaag86@mail.ru

Abstract

The research project presented in this paper aims at identification of context markers for Russian nouns and their use in construction identification. The body of contexts has been extracted from the Russian National Corpus (RNC). The context processing procedure takes into account the lexical and semantic information represented in the corpus annotation. Merged meaning of words are taken into consideration. The reported results contribute to task of building a comprehensive lexicographic resource — the Index of Russian lexical constructions.[1]

1   Introduction

The importance of corpus data is now widely recognised. The corpus shows functioning of language units in their natural domain of occurrence and it serves for various linguistic tasks (e.g., (Rakhilina et al., 2006)). This research project uses the Russian National Corpus (RNC, http://www.ruscorpora.ru/) as a resource providing context markers of word meanings. Context marker of a target word is a linguistic unit occurring in one context with this word and specifying its particular meaning. RNC has a multilevel annotation, it includes lexical (lemma) tags (*lex*), morphological (grammatical) tags (*gr*), and semantic (taxonomy) tags (*sem*). These tags should be taken into account when operating with context markers. Context markers find an application in construction identification and word sense disambiguation (WSD) (e.g., (Agirre and Edmonds, 2007; Navigli, 2009; Mihalcea and Pedersen, 2009; Proceedings of the NAACL

HLT Workshop... 2010; Sahlgren and Knutsson, 2009), etc.). Corpus-based WSD implies extraction and statistical processing of word collocations, which makes it possible to distinguish separate meanings of lexical items in context (e.g., (Kobricov et al., 2005; Lashevskaja and Mitrofanova, 2009; Pedersen, 2002; Schütze, 1998), etc.).

2   Linguistic data and experiments

Four Russian polysemous words were subjected to analysis: *organ* 'institution, part of the body, musical instrument, etc.', *luk* 'onion, bow', *glava* 'head, chief, cupola, chapter, etc.', and *dom* 'building, private space, family, etc.'. Sets of contexts were extracted from the RNC, the largest annotated corpus of Russian texts containing about 400 M tokens. We deal with the disambiguated portion of the RNC where morphological and semantic ambiguity is resolved. The size of context set for each noun ranges from 1000 to 3500. The texts are supplied with three core types of annotation: (1) lemmas — lexical markers (canonical, dictionary forms of inflected words); (2) grammatical markers (morphosyntactic tagsets referring to POS and other inflectional grammatical features like case, gender, tense, etc.); (3) taxonomy markers (semantic tagsets referring to lexical-semantic classes). Taxonomy markers are available for the most frequent nouns, pronouns, adjectives, verbs and adverbs and represent a rather coarse-grained cross-classification of the lexicon (e.g. 'concrete', 'human', 'animal', 'space', 'construction', 'tool', 'container', 'substance', 'movement', 'part', 'diminutive', 'causative', 'verbal noun', and other lexical-semantic classes, cf. http://www.ruscorpora.ru/en/corpora-sem.html). Each word sense is formalized with a set of taxonomy markers, cf. *dom* 'house': 'concrete' + 'construction' + 'container'. A list of contexts is made for each meaning of considered words.

---

[1] This work was funded by the Russian Foundation for Basic Research (grant No 10-06-00586-a).

Further, we extract automatically from these contexts the lexical-semantic and statistical information about words that are to the left (right) of the analyzed noun. This information is presented as a set of semantic tags. The semantic tagsets are arranged by their frequency of occurrence, then we consider only the statistically significant sets. The frequency tagsets are analyzed in terms of what lexical units are behind the semantic tagsets. These lexemes are most probably the context markers of the considered words.

A Python-based WSD and Construction Identification toolkit (Lyashevskaya et al., in press) was used in order to extract and analyze context markers. The toolkit makes it possible to carry out linguistic and statistical analysis of contexts for polysemous words in various modes. It performs (1) generation of context classes corresponding to particular meanings of a target word; and (2) generation of lists of the most frequent constructions where a particular meaning of a target word occurs.

3 Identification of context markers

Context markers were determined for each meaning of the words listed above. The markers can be of various nature, e.g. they may represent different parts of speech. Much attention was paid to lexical-semantic tags of context markers. For example, the target word *glava* 'chief' frequently co-occurs with the following lexemes forming its right context: *gosudarstvo* ('state' <r:concr t:space>), *federacija* ('federation' <r:concr t:space>), *region* ('region' <r:concr t:space pt:part pc:space>), *gorod* ('city' <r:concr t:space sc:constr>), *fond* ('fund' <r:concr t:space pt:set sc:money>). These context markers can be combined to form a group of concrete nouns identifying space and place (<r:concr t:space>). To take another example, the target word *luk* 'onion' regularly co-occurs with such nouns as *ogurec* ('cucumber' <r:concr t:fruit t:food>), *orekh* ('nut' <r:concr t:fruit t:food pt:part pc:plant>), and *kartoška* ('potato' <r:concr t:fruit t:food pt:aggr sc:fruit>). These nouns may be referred to as a group of concrete nouns denoting food. These examples show that the identification of context markers can be carried out not in terms of particular lexemes, but in terms of the lexical-semantic classes they belong to.

Context markers may differ not only in type, but also in the position they occupy with respect to a target word. Therefore, the right and left contexts of target words were examined separately. For instance, semantic tags indicating abstract nouns of perception (<r:abstr t:perc>) regularly occur in the right context of the target word *organ* ('part of a body'). This fact allows us to consider them as context markers for the word in question. But when we explored the left context of the same word in the same meaning, we found out that other lexemes often serve as its context markers: e.g., adjectives, such as *čelovečeskij* 'human', *donorskij* 'donor' (<dt:hum>), nouns *zabolevanije*, *bolezn'* 'disease' (<t:disease>), etc. The context markers mentioned above are not to be found in any occurrences of the word *organ* in other meanings. The combinations of target words and identified context markers are considered as constructions. The characteristic features of construction are stability and frequency of occurrence.

In order to prove the stability of obtained constructions we adopt a statistical approach. A lexeme under consideration and its context marker act as a bigram. Bigram search service (http://www.aot.ru/) provides the necessary information about the stability of bigrams. These statistical data show that the collocations have a high Mutual Information (MI), cf. Table 1.

Left context	MI	Right context	MI
pravoohranitelnyj 'law-enforcement'	13.61	*gosbezopasnost* 'a state security'	11.23
ispolnitelnyj 'executive'	10.79	*pravoporyadok* 'law and order'	10.68
zakonodatelnyj 'legislative'	10.39	*samoupravlenie* 'self-government'	9.19
predstavitelnyj 'representative'	9.33	*zdravoohranenie* 'public health'	8.76

Table 1: Statistical results for the word *organ* 'institution'.

4 Problem of merged meanings

In automatic text processing, dictionary compiling, WSD procedure etc. linguists often have to deal with polysemous words with merged meanings. These meanings represent combinations of two or more independent meanings which are almost indistinguishable in certain contexts. In NLP tasks mentioned above such polysemous words which reveal both independent and merged meanings represent a special problem. It is hardly possible to provide unambiguous analysis of such words.

A few attempts were made in computational linguistics to solve the problem of merged meanings. For instance, the so-called "Shishkebab" approach (Philpot et al., 2003) is used in formal ontology Omega (http://omega.isi.edu/). This method implies simultaneous attribution of two or more meanings combined in particular context to the same lexeme (e.g., *Library* IS_A Building&Institution&Location). About 400 patterns for merged meanings (e.g., *X* IS_A Country&Nation&Government; *X* IS_A Company&Product&Stock; etc.) were described in (Hovy, 2005).

This section presents the results of context markers identification experiments carried out for a noun *dom* ('house'). In the semantic structure of this polysemous noun besides six independent meanings ('building', 'private space', 'family', 'common space', 'institution', 'dynasty') there are five merged meanings formed by pairs ('building & private space', 'building & institution', 'private space & family') and triples ('building & private space & institution', 'building & private space & family') of independent ones. In the experiments we analyzed 3000 contexts for the considered noun, which were extracted from the RNC. Of the total number of contexts there are 842 contexts where the noun in question reveals merged meanings (cf. Table 2).

All occurrences of the target word found in RNC were analyzed with the exception of contexts for rare meanings found in less than 10 contexts (such as *dom* 'common place' or *dom* 'dynasty').

In the experiments we extracted lexical markers of the noun *dom* on the basis of the most frequent semantic annotation of the words adjacent to *dom*. The lexical markers of merged meanings were compared with the ones of independent meanings to decide whether additional statistical patterns should be introduced in further experiments. As the consequence of such comparison we managed to find out certain regularities in occurrence of context markers.

Some context markers allow to predict the occurrence of merged meaning with high precision. For example, context markers of merged meaning 'building & institution' are found in such pairs as *destkij dom* ('orphan's home'), *invalidnyj dom* ('home for disabled people'), *rodil'nyj dom* ('maternity hospital'), *dom otdyha* ('holiday center'), *dom kino* ('film theatre'), etc. The context marker which obviously indicates the meaning 'building & private space & family' can be found in such phrase as *hozjain doma* ('host'). However, there are context markers which indicate purely independent meanings. For example, noun *žitel'* ('tenant') in *žiteli doma* points out to mean-

ing 'building'. In many cases such as *rodnoj dom* ('home'), *roditel'skij dom* ('one's parent's home') the merged meaning 'building & private space' is more frequent than independent. It should be noted that in the most cases we observe tendency of intersection between context markers for merged and independent meanings. For example, such adjectives as *derevjannyj* ('wooden'), *kirpičnyj* ('made of brick'), *novyj* ('new'), *sosednij* ('neighbouring'), etc. may indicate both independent meaning 'building' and merged meaning 'building & institution'.

Word meanings	Semantic annotation	Number of contexts in RNC
dom		3,000 (total)
dom 'building'	<r:concr t:constr top:contain>	1,694
dom 'private space'	<r:concr t:space>	95
dom 'family'	<r:concr t:group pt:set sc:hum>	72
dom 'common space'	<r:concr t:space der:shift der:metaph>	4
dom 'institution'	<r:concr t:org>	292
dom 'dynasty'	<r:concr pt:set sc:hum>	1
dom (merged meanings)		842
dom 'building & private space'	<r:concr t:constr top:contain | r:concr t:space>	501
dom 'building & institution'	<r:concr t:constr top:contain | r:concr t:org>	250
dom 'private space & family'	r:concr t:space | r:concr t:group pt:set sc:hum	10
dom 'building & private space & institution'	<r:concr t:constr top:contain | r:concr t:space | r:concr t:org>	36
dom 'building & private space & family'	<r:concr t:constr top:contain | r:concr t:space | r:concr t:group pt:set sc:hum>	45

Table 2: Russian noun *dom*: semantic annotation and frequencies of meanings (number of contexts in RNC).

5 Conclusion

A set of experiments on context markers identification were successfully carried out for contexts of polysemous Russian nouns which had been extracted from RNC. Different types of context markers were described.

The work demonstrates application of the obtained context markers in construction identification task. The results of experiments also reveal the necessity of special treatment of words with merged meanings and introduction of additional statistical patterns corresponding to these meaning in different construction identification systems. Further work implies the application of the data as filters for context preprocessing and for statistical WSD.

References

Agirre E., Edmonds Ph. (eds.). 2007. *Word Sense Disambiguation: Algorithms and Applications.* Text, Speech and Language Technology, vol. 33. Springer-Verlag, Berlin, Heidelberg, New York.

Hovy E. 2005. *Ontologies (Series of Lectures).* Vilem Mathesius Lecture Series. Prague.

Kobricov B., Lashevskaja O., and Shemanajeva O. 2005. *Sn'atije leksiko-semanticheskoj omonimii v novostnyh i gazteno-zhurnal'nyh tekstah: poverhnostnyje fil'try i statisticheskaja ocenka.* Internet–matematika 2005: Avtomaticeskaja obrabotka webdannyh. Moscow. pp. 38–57.

Lashevskaja O., Mitrofanova O. 2009. *Disambiguation of Taxonomy Markers in Context: Russian Nouns.* Jokinen, K., Bick, E. (eds.) NODALIDA 2009. NEALT Proceedings Series, volume 4, pp. 111–117.

Lyashevskaya O., Mitrofanova O., Grachkova M., Romanov S., Shimorina A., and Shurygina A. *Automatic Word Sense Disambiguation and Construction Identification Based on Corpus Multilevel Annotation.* [in press].

Mihalcea R., Pedersen T. 2009. *Word Sense Disambiguation Tutorial.* URL: http://www.d.umn.edu/~tpederse/WSDTutorial.html

Navigli R. 2009. *Word Sense Disambiguation: a Survey.* ACM Computing Surveys, 41(2), pp. 1–69.

Pedersen T. 2002. *A Baseline Methodology for Word Sense Disambiguation.* Proceedings of the Third International Conference on Intelligent Text Processing and Computational Linguistics, February 17–23, 2002, Mexico City. pp. 126–135.

Philpot A., Fleischman M., Hovy E. 2003. *Semi-Automatic Construction of a General Purpose Ontology.* Proceedings of the International Lisp Conference. New York, NY.

Proceedings of the NAACL HLT Workshop on Extracting and Using Constructions in Computational Linguistics, pp. 25–31. Los Angeles, CA. 2010.

Rahilina E., Kobricov B., Kustova G., Lashevskaja O., and Shemanajeva O. 2006. *Mnogoznachnost' kak prikladnaja problema: leksiko-semanticheskaja razmetka v Nacional'nom korpuse russkogo jazyka.* Kompjuternaja lingvistika i intellektual'nyje tehnologii: Trudy mezhdunarodnoj konferencii Dialog 2006. Moscow. pp. 445–450.

Sahlgren M., Knutsson O. 2009. *Workshop on Extracting and Using Constructions in NLP.* NODALIDA 2009. SICS Technical Report T2009:10.

Schütze H. 1998. *Automatic Word Sense Discrimination.* Computational Linguistics, 24(1), pp. 97–123.

Association for Computational Linguistics
209 N. Eighth Street
Stroudsburg, Pennsylvania 18360

ISBN 978-1-5108-3464-4

9 781510 834644